Philip Schaff

Literature and Poetry

Studies on the english Language; the Poetry of the Bible; the Dies irae; etc.

Philip Schaff

Literature and Poetry
Studies on the english Language; the Poetry of the Bible; the Dies irae; etc.

ISBN/EAN: 9783337081256

Printed in Europe, USA, Canada, Australia, Japan

Cover: Foto ©ninafisch / pixelio.de

More available books at **www.hansebooks.com**

AND

POETRY

STUDIES ON THE ENGLISH LANGUAGE; THE POETRY OF THE BIBLE;
THE DIES IRÆ; THE STABAT MATER; THE HYMNS OF ST. BERNARD;
THE UNIVERSITY, ANCIENT AND MODERN;
DANTE ALIGHIERI; THE DIVINA COMMEDIA

BY

PHILIP SCHAFF D.D. LL.D

PROFESSOR OF CHURCH HISTORY IN THE UNION THEOLOGICAL SEMINARY,
NEW YORK

NEW YORK
CHARLES SCRIBNER'S SONS
1890

COPYRIGHT, 1890, BY
CHARLES SCRIBNER'S SONS.

WM. F. FELL & CO.,
PRINTERS,
PHILADELPHIA.

DEDICATED

TO

MY FAMILY

CONTENTS.

                                                                                              PAGE

I. THE ENGLISH LANGUAGE: HETEROGENEOUS IN FORMATION, HOMOGENEOUS IN CHARACTER, UNIVERSAL IN DESTINATION FOR THE SPREAD OF CIVILIZATION, ... 1-62

Language and Reason, 1.—Origin of Language, 2.—Diversity of Language, 3-4.—The English Language—Grimm's Judgment, 5.—The Composite Character of the English Race and Language, 6.—The Proportion of Saxon, Latin, and other Elements in English, 7-8.—The Anglo-Saxon Stock, 9-14.—The Saxon Element in the English Bible, 14.—Illustrations from Shakespeare, 15.—The Latin Element, 16.—Original Latinisms, 16-19.—French Latinisms, 19-21.—The Gradual Mingling of the Saxon and Norman, 21-23.—The Relation of the Norman and Saxon Elements, 23-25.—Illustrations from Milton, 26.—Illustrations from Daniel Webster, 26-29.—The Other Elements of the English Language, 29.—The Celtic Element, 29.—The Danish, or Norse Element, 30.—Hebrew Words, 31.—Greek Words, 31.—Dutch Words, 32.—Italian Words, 33.—Spanish Words, 33. Arabic Words, 33.—Persian Words, 33.—Turkish Words, 34.—Slavonic Words, 34.—Indian Words and Names, 34.—Americanisms, 34.—Hybrid Words, 35.—The Organic Union of these Elements, 36.—Results of this Mixture. Spelling, 37.—New Middle Sounds, 38.—Musical English—Illustrations from Byron, Tennyson, and Poe, 37-38.—Simplicity of the Grammar, 40-41.—Brevity, 42-45.—Monosyllabic Character, 45.—Illustrations from Shakespeare, Wordsworth, Byron, Tennyson, 46-50.—Large Number of Synonyms, 51-54.—Perfectibility, 54-55.—Cosmopolitan Destination, 55.—Spread of the English Language, 56-59.—Providential Design, 59-60.—The English Language and the Bible, 60-62.—Conclusion, 62.

II. THE POETRY OF THE BIBLE, ... 63-133

Origin of Poetry and Music, 64.—Poetry and Inspiration, 65.—Poetry and Religion, 65.—The Poetry of the Bible, 66.—The Spirit of Bible Poetry, 70.—Poetic Merit, 74.—Tributes of Poets and Scholars to Hebrew Poetry, 77. Classification of Bible Poetry, 79.—Lyric Poetry, 80.—The Song of Lamech, 82.—The Song of Moses, 83.—Lyrics in the Later Historical Books, 86.—David's Lament of Jonathan, 88.—The Psalter, 91.—The Lamentations,

93.—Lyrics in the New Testament, 95.—Didactic Poetry, 97.—
The Proverbs, 99.—Ecclesiastes, 104.—Fable and Parable, 105.—
Prophetic Poetry, 106.—Dramatic Poetry, 112.—The Song of
Songs, 113.—The Book of Job, 116.—The Form of Bible Poetry:
Poetic Diction, 120.—Versification, 122.—Parallelism of Members, 125.—Literature on Bible Poetry, 130.

III. THE DIES IRÆ, ... 134–186
The Received Latin Text, 134.—The Name and Use of the
Poem, 134.—Contents, 134.—Character and Value, 138.—Opinions of Critics, 141.—Origin and History, 145.—Thomas of Celano, 146.—The Text of Mantua, 149.—The Text of Hämmerlin of Zürich, 150.—A Political Perversion, 151.—Translation of
the Dies Iræ, 152.—English Translations, 155.—German Translations, 173.—Literature, 182.—Chronological List of English
Versions, 183.

IV. THE STABAT MATER DOLOROSA, ... 187–217
The Two Stabat Maters, 187.—The Mater Dolorosa, 188.—
Character and History of the Hymn. 190.—Francis of Assisi,
195.—Jacobus de Benedictis, 196.—English Translations, 198.
—German Translations, 210.—Literature, 216.

V. THE STABAT MATER SPECIOSA, ... 218–231
The Latin Text, 218.—The Discovery of the Mater Speciosa,
220.—Authorship, 222.—Merits, 222.—English Translations,
223.—German Translations, 229.

VI. ST. BERNARD AS A HYMNIST, ... 232–255
Sketch of St. Bernard of Clairvaux, 232.—"Jesu dulcis Memoria," 233.—The Benedictine Text, 234.—Mone's Text, 237.—
English Translations, by Caswall, 239.—By J. W. Alexander,
241.—By Ray Palmer, 242.—By A. Coles, 242.—German Translation by Count Zinzendorf, 243.—St. Bernard's Passion
Hymns, 245.—Ad Cor Christi: "Summi Regis Cor, Aveto,"
245.—Translation of Edward A. Washburn, 246.—Ad Faciem
Christi: "Salve Caput Cruentatum," 248.—Translation by Mrs.
E. R. Charles, 249.—By A. Coles, 250.—Modern Reproductions of Ancient Hymns, 252.—Gerhardt's "O Haupt voll Blut
und Wunden." 253.—J. W. Alexander's "O Sacred Head now
Wounded," 253.

VII. THE UNIVERSITY: PAST, PRESENT, AND FUTURE, ... 256–278
The Mediæval University, 256. The University of Bologna,
262. The Eighth Centenary of the University of Bologna,
265.—The American University, 273.—Appendix, 278.

CONTENTS.

	PAGE
VIII. DANTE ALIGHIERI,	279–337

Dante, Shakespeare, Goethe, 279.—Life of Dante, 284.—Dante and Beatrice, 286.—The Donna Pietosa, 292.—Dante's Education, 298.—His Learning, 299.—His Marriage, 299.—Dante in Public Life, 300.—His Banishment. Dante and Boniface VIII., 303.—Dante in Exile, 304.—Can Grande, the Veltro, and the Dux, 308.—Dante in Ravenna, 312.—Death and Burial, 313.—Posthumous Fame, 314.—The Sixth Centenary of Dante's Birth, 315.—Character and Habits of Dante, 316.—Portraits of Dante, 317.—The Works of Dante, 319.—The New Life, 319.—The Banquet, 319.—On the Empire, 320.—The Canzoniere, 322.—On Popular Eloquence, 323.—On Water and Earth, 323.—Letters, 324.—The Creed, 324.—The Comedy, 325.—Note on Giotto's Portrait of Dante, 325.

Dante Chronicle,	326
Dante Literature,	338

IX. POETIC TRIBUTES TO DANTE 338–344

Michael Angelo Buonarotti, 338.—Ludwig Uhland, 339.—W. W. Skeat, 340.—Henry Wadsworth Longfellow, 343.—Alfred Tennyson, 343.—Emanuel Geibel, 344.

X. THE DIVINA COMMEDIA 345–429

General Estimate, 345.—The Sources of the Commedia, 348.—Name of the Poem, 352.—Time of Composition, 354.—Duration of the Vision, 356.—Dante's Cosmology, 357.—Explanation of the Commedia, 360.—Design of the Commedia, 365.—The Way to Paradise, 367.—The Poetic Form of the Commedia, 370.—The Dark Forest, 372.—The Inscription to Hell, 373.—Eternal Punishment, 375.—Vestibule or Fore-Hell, 378.—The Structure of the Inferno, 380.—Sin and Punishment, 382.—Impartiality of Dante, 383.—The Nine Circles of the Inferno, 384.—The Purgatorio, 392.—The Paradiso, 395.—The Beatific Vision, 403.—Dante's Theology, 405.—Dante's Relation to the Papacy and the Reformation, 410.—Dante and the Joachimites, 416.—Dante and Schelling. The Three Ages of Christianity, 424.

ALPHABETICAL INDEX, ... 431–436

ILLUSTRATIONS.

Dante's Universe,	357
Dante's Inferno,	380
Dante's Purgatorio,	392
The Rose of the Blessed, in Dante's Paradiso,	403

THE ENGLISH LANGUAGE:

ITS COSMOPOLITAN CHARACTER AND MISSION FOR THE SPREAD OF CIVILIZATION.

LANGUAGE AND REASON.

Language, next to reason, is the greatest gift of God to man. It raises him above the brute creation and makes him the prophet and king of nature. It is the inseparable companion of reason, its utterance and embodiment, the interpreter of thought and feeling, the medium of intercourse, the bond of society, and the source of all that happiness which springs from contact between heart and heart. It is the "armory of the human mind, and at once contains the trophies of its past and the weapons of its future conquests."

So close is the connection between intelligence and speech, between thought and word, that the one may be called the inward speech, or speech concealed, and the other the outward thought, or thought revealed. Hence, also, the intimate relation between grammar, which treats of the laws of language, and logic, which teaches the laws of thought; the one is the logic of speech, the other the grammar of reason. The second person of the holy Trinity is called by St. John the "Logos," or the personal Word; for in him God is revealed to himself, and through him he reveals himself to the world.

A distinguished writer on comparative philology denies this connection between reason and language. He maintains that language belongs not to man as an individual, but as a member of society, and that a solitary child would never frame a language, but remain a mute all his life. Granted, but such a child would also remain ignorant and would never become a man intellectually or morally. All his mental faculties would lie dormant or be extinguished altogether. It is idle to reason from a sheer possibility which God never intended, and which would destroy the very nature and destiny of man. For man is essentially and constitutionally a social as he is a rational being. In the same degree in which the mind produces thoughts it also clothes them in words of some kind, although they may not be expressed or uttered. If a man thinks he knows a thing, but cannot say it, his knowledge is to the same extent defective; the idea may be begotten, but it is not born until it assumes shape and form in some word or words, or some symbolic signs, however imperfectly they may convey the meaning. And it must be admitted that language even in its most perfect state is only a partial revelation of reason which has hidden depths transcending the resources of grammar and dictionary. All human knowledge "ends in mystery."[1]

ORIGIN OF LANGUAGE.

The origin of language must be divine, like that of reason itself. In creating Adam a rational being or with the faculty of knowledge, God endowed him at the same time not, indeed, with a full-formed grammar and diction, as little as with a minute positive knowledge of all surrounding objects, but with the power or capacity and with the organ of articulate speech, and taught him also the actual use of words as signs of ideas. This capacity grew and developed itself with the expansion of reason and observation, knowledge and experience, by an inherent law and impulse or instinct under the direction of the Creator. Adam himself named his female companion and the objects of

---

[1] The *science* of language as such is of recent growth, but has made astonishing progress in connection with comparative philology. It was nurtured by Wilhelm von Humboldt, the brothers Schlegel, Bopp, Grimm, Pott, in Germany; by Rask, in Denmark; Burnouf and Renan, in France; Max Müller, in England; Marsh, Brown, Dwight, Schele de Vere, White, Whitney, in America. See Müller's *Lectures on the Science of Language*, 8th ed. 1875, 2 vols.; and Whitney's *Language and the Study of Language*, 1867. For the chief authorities on the English language I refer to the long list of Skeat in his *Etym. Dict.*, pp. xxiii.-xxviii., and to the list at the head of Goold Brown's *Grammar of English Grammars*, 10th ed., by Berrian (New York, 1875, pp. xi.-xx.).

nature as they passed before him, but he did it at the suggestion of God and with the faculty imparted to him.[1]

Every language commenced, as it does now in children, with a scanty list of root-words, mostly onomatopoëtic and exclamatory or interjectional, expressing the most obvious objects of sense and sensations of the heart, and reached its relative perfection by a slow and gradual historical growth corresponding to the growth of civilization and literature.

Professor Skeat closes the preface to his *Etymol. Dictionary* (Oxford, 1882) with the truthful remark, "The speech of man is influenced by physical laws, in other words, by the working of Divine power. It is therefore possible to pursue the study of language in a spirit of reverence similar to that in which we study what are called the works of nature; and by the aid of that spirit we may gladly perceive a new meaning in the sublime line of our poet Coleridge, that

"'Earth, with her thousand voices, praises God.'"

DIVERSITY OF LANGUAGE.

The diversity of language is traced by the Bible to the pride and confusion of Babel. But it was nevertheless decreed and is controlled by divine Providence like the diversity of nations. God made of one blood all nations of the earth, says Paul, and determined the bounds of their habitation. He raises up nations for particular purposes and assigns them a peculiar work.

Every language reflects the genius of the nation which uses it as the organ of its inner life, and serves the special mission which it is called to fulfill in the great family of nations and in the drama of history. The knowledge of the language, therefore, is the key to the knowledge of the people with which it is identified.

The Hebrew language, by its simplicity and sublimity, was admirably adapted to be the organ of the earliest revelations of

---

[1] Comp. Gen. i. 19. Webster makes language itself, as well as the faculty of speech, the immediate gift of God, but supposes it to have been very limited in vocabulary. See Introd. to his *Dictionary*.

God, of primitive history, poetry, and prophecy, which prepared men for Christianity. Its literature remains to this day an ever fresh fountain of popular instruction and devotion.

The Greek abounds in wealth, vitality, elasticity, and beauty; and hence it became the organ not only of every branch of ancient classical science and art, but also of the eternal truths of Christianity.

The Latin embodies the commanding power, dignity and majesty of the old Roman people which conquered the world by the sword and organized it by law. It ruled the literature of Europe long after the downfall of the Western empire and became the fruitful mother of all Romanic languages. It is still and will remain the official organ of the Roman Church.

Of the Romanic languages again, each has its peculiar merit and beauty.

The Italian, spoken by an imaginative, excitable, art-loving people, in a warm climate, under serene skies, sounds like music itself, and glows with all the fire of passion. "It melts like kisses from a woman's mouth."[1]

The Spanish, by its pathos and *grandezza*, reminds us of the days of Castilian chivalry.

The French is the medium of travel, fashion, and diplomacy on the Continent of Europe, and expresses the clearness, directness, and precision, the polished ease and elegance, the sprightly vigor, the mercurial vivacity, and martial fire, but also the lightness and fickleness of the French, whom one of their most philosophic writers, M. de Tocqueville, characterizes as at once "the most brilliant and the most dangerous nation of Europe."

The German language, in native strength, fullness, depth, and flexibility, as also in the leavening influence of its literature upon the progress of knowledge, strongly resembles the ancient Greek, and is best adapted for the mining operations of thought, for every kind of speculative and scientific research and every form of poetry, but far less for business, commerce, political life, forensic and parliamentary eloquence, than either the French or the English.

[1] "*Lingua Toscana in bocca Romana e la bellissima lingua del mondo.*"

THE ENGLISH LANGUAGE—GRIMM'S JUDGMENT.

The character of the English language cannot be better expressed than in the words of Professor Jacob Grimm, the author of the most learned German grammar and, jointly with his brother, of the best German dictionary.

"Among all the modern languages," he says, "none has, by giving up and confounding all the laws of sound, and by cutting off nearly all the inflexions, acquired greater strength and vigor than the English. Its fullness of free middle sounds which cannot be taught, but only learned, is the cause of an essential force of expression such as perhaps never stood at the command of any other language of men. Its entire highly intellectual and wonderfully happy structure and development are the result of a surprisingly intimate marriage of the two noblest languages in modern Europe, the Germanic and the Romance; the former (as is well known) supplying in far larger proportion the material groundwork, the latter the intellectual conceptions. As to wealth, intellectuality, and closeness of structure, none of all the living languages can be compared with it. In truth, the English language, which by no mere accident has produced and upborne the greatest and most commanding poet of modern times as distinguished from the ancient classics—I can, of course, only mean Shakespeare—may with full propriety be called a world-language; and like the English people it seems destined hereafter to prevail even more extensively than at present in all the ends of the earth."[1]

[1] *Ueber den Ursprung der Sprache*, Berlin, 1852, p. 50 : "Keine unter allen neueren Sprachen hat gerade durch das Aufgeben und Zerrütten aller Lautgesetze, durch den Wegfall beinahe sämmtlicher Flexionen eine grössere Kraft und Stärke empfangen, als die englische, und von ihrer nicht einmal lehrbaren, nur lernbaren Fülle freier Mitteltöne ist eine wesentliche Gewalt des Ausdruckes abhängig geworden, wie sie vielleicht noch nie einer menschlichen Zunge zu Gebote stand. Ihre ganze, überaus geistige, wunderbar geglückte Anlage und Durchbildung war hervorgegangen aus einer überraschenden Vermählung der beiden edelsten Sprachen des späteren Europas, der germanischen und romanischen, und bekannt ist, wie im Englischen sich beide zu einander verhalten, indem jene bei weitem die sinnliche Grundlage hergab, diese die geistigen Begriffe zuführte. An Reichthum, Vernunft und gedrängter Fuge lässt sich keine aller noch lebenden Sprachen ihr an die Seite setzen. Ja die englische Sprache, von der nicht umsonst der grösste und

This remarkable eulogy on the language of Great Britain and North America has the more weight as it comes from a foreign scholar who is not blinded by national prejudice and vanity, and is universally acknowledged to be one of the first masters of the entire field of Teutonic philology and literature.

I shall choose it as the text of my dissertation.

THE COMPOSITE CHARACTER OF THE ENGLISH RACE AND LANGUAGE.

The origin, growth and material of the English language clearly indicate its comprehensive destiny. The character and history of the nation and of the language singularly correspond in this case. Every stage in the progress of the one forms an epoch for the other. Every invasion of England left its permanent trace in the language and enriched its power and capacity. The English language contains the fossil poetry, philosophy, and history of the English people. The changes and enrichments of the language have been brought about by the irresistible force of time and custom, and by the multiform pursuits, the migratory habits, and universal trade of the English race, but most of all by the successive immigrations of foreigners.

It is well known that the English people are not a homogeneous race, but an organic mixture of different national elements. So also their language derived its material from many sources, like a mighty river in its majestic flow through fertile valleys to the boundless sea. Almost every language of Europe, besides some of Asia, Africa and America, has furnished its contribution.

Professor Skeat distributes the English words under the following heads: English (*i e.*, Anglo-Saxon and Middle English of the earlier period), Old Low German, Low German, Dutch, Scandinavian, German, French from German, Teutonic (in a general sense), Celtic, Romanic Languages (including Italian,

---

überlegenste Dichter der neuen Zeit, im Gegensatz zur classischen alten Poesie — ich kann natürlich nur Shakespeare meinen — gezeugt und getragen worden ist, sie darf mit vollem Rechte eine Weltsprache heissen und scheint gleich dem englischen Volke ausersehen, künftig noch in höherem Masse an allen Enden der Erd... zu walten."

French, Spanish and Portuguese), Latin, French from Latin, French from Low Latin, Provençal from Latin, Italian from Latin, Spanish from Latin, Portuguese from Latin, Low Latin, Greek, French from Latin from Greek, Slavonic, Lithuanian, Asiatic Aryan Languages (Persian, Sanskrit), European non-Aryan Languages, Semitic Languages (Hebrew, Arabic), Hindustani, Malay, African Languages, American Languages, and Hybrid Words (made up from two different languages).[1]

The two principal sources are the German, or Anglo-Saxon, and the Latin, or Norman-French; the other elements are small side-currents which have enriched to a greater or less extent almost every other civilized language of modern Europe.

THE PROPORTION OF SAXON, LATIN, AND OTHER ELEMENTS IN THE ENGLISH LANGUAGE.

The authorities which I have consulted differ in their estimates of the proportion of these various elements which enter into the English language. Dr. R. G. Latham, the late distinguished professor of the English language and literature in the University College of London, supposes that of forty thousand English words thirty thousand are Anglo-Saxon, five thousand Anglo-Norman, one hundred Celtic, sixty Latin, fifty Scandinavian, and the rest miscellaneous.[2] The number of words of direct Latin origin seems here considerably understated.

Archbishop Richard Chenevix Trench estimates that of a hundred parts of the English language sixty are Saxon, thirty Latin and French, five Greek, and the remaining five from all other sources which have contributed to its stock.[3]

This is probably correct as an average estimate. But we must make a material distinction between the language of the dictionary or the language at rest and the language in actual use or the language in motion. The latter is more predominantly Saxon than the former.

The entire vocabulary of the English language as found in the

---

[1] *Etymol. Dict.*, pp. 747-771.
[2] *A Handbook of the English Grammar* (American ed., New York, 1852), pp. 62, 63. Comp. Preface to his enlarged ed. of Johnson's *Dictionary*.
[3] *English Past and Present* (New York ed., 1855), p. 19.

dictionaries exceeds the number of one hundred thousand words. But of these only about ten thousand are used for ordinary written composition, and perhaps not more than five thousand for common intercourse.[1]

Now, we may safely say that the living English is more predominantly Saxon than the dictionary English, and the spoken English even more than the written. Sharon Turner and Noah Webster assert that more than four-fifths of modern English words in actual use are of Saxon descent.[2]

This is no doubt true of the daily conversational language. But we doubt its general applicability to book language, where the proportion of native Saxon to foreign words depends very much upon the education and taste of the author and the nature of his subject, and can therefore not be absolutely determined. It is stated that in the Authorized Version of the Bible and in Shakespeare 60 per cent. of the vocabulary are of Saxon origin (which would very nearly correspond to the Saxon proportion in the language itself); that in Milton's poetical works about two-thirds of the vocabulary are foreign, but that in the sixth book of *Paradise Lost* four-fifths of all the words are Saxon. The style of Johnson abounds in Latinisms, but in the preface to his *Dictionary* there are "72 per cent. of Saxon words."[3]

---

[1] C. P. Marsh says (*Lectures on the English Language*, New York, 1860, p. 183): "Few writers or speakers use as many as ten thousand words, ordinary persons of fair intelligence not above three or four thousand. If a scholar were to be required to name, without examination, the authors whose English vocabulary was the largest, he would probably specify the all-embracing Shakespeare and the all-knowing Milton. And yet in all the works of the great dramatist, there occur not more than fifteen thousand words, in the poems of Milton not above eight thousand."

[2] See Webster's *Dict.*, ed. of 1850, Introd., p. li. Note. In the ed. of Goodrich & Porter, 1864, p. xxviii., it is stated that the preponderance of Saxon words varies from 60 to more than 90 per cent.

[3] A. H. Welsh, in *Development of English Literature and Language*, Chicago, 1886 (7th ed.), vol. I., 53, allows a much higher percentage to Anglo-Saxon in the various departments of literature. His estimate of the relative proportion of Anglo-Saxon is as follows: Bible, 93; Poetry, 88; Prayer-Book, 87; Fiction, 87; Essay, 78; Oratory, 76; History, 72; Newspaper, 72; Rhetoric, 69.

THE ANGLO-SAXON STOCK.

The various languages of the earth, amounting to about nine hundred, are now divided by comparative philologists into three great families, called the ARYAN (formerly called INDO-GERMANIC), the SEMITIC, and the TURANIAN (a doubtful nomenclature for an indefinite number of languages with the agglutinative structure). The Aryan family again embraces the tongues of India and Persia, the Greek and Latin, the Romanic, the Celtic, the Teutonic, and the Slavonic languages and dialects.

The English, like the Dutch, Frisian, Gothic, Icelandic, Swedish, Danish, and High German, belongs to the Teutonic or Germanic branch, and shares all its main characteristics. The grammar, the bone and sinew, the heart and soul of the English language, are thoroughly Germanic, whatever be the number of its foreign ingredients.

It partakes of the main characteristics of the family to which it belongs. The Germanic language, with its various dialects, is a free, independent, original language. It is neither obtruded by a foreign conqueror, nor learned by slaves, as the Spanish, English, and French were learned by the Indians and African negroes, nor derived from an older language, like the idioms of southern Europe, which are descended from the Latin. It preceded the Christianization of the nations of central and northern Europe and accompanied them through all their phases of development to the present time. It embraces the two great periods of mediæval and modern civilization. It has a primitive vigor, exuberant wealth, and is adapted to all the manifestations of the human mind. It is equal to the deepest researches of thought and the highest flights of fancy. Most of its words have their meaning, not by agreement and conventional usage, but by nature. It rolls with the thunder and flashes with the lightning; it roars with the storm and blusters with the sea; it whispers with the breeze and lisps with the leaf; it rushes with the mountain torrent and murmurs with the brook; it shouts with heaven and bellows with hell.

The Germanic dialect which underlies the present English is called ANGLO-SAXON, from the tribes which imported it from

Germany to England. It goes back to the origin of the English race in the middle of the fifth, if not the fourth, century, when, according to the "Saxon Chronicle," various German tribes, especially the Angles and Saxons[1] under the leadership of Hengist and his brother Horsa[2]—the Romulus and Remus of English history—migrated in successive invasions from the regions between the Elbe and the Rhine into Britain, wresting the larger part from its original inhabitants of the Celtic stock, changing it from Britain to England and laying the foundation for that remarkable people which from that rock-bound island extends the sceptre of its dominion to the extremities of the globe. They were then heathen savages, but endowed with all the physical, intellectual, and moral requisites for a great nation.

The Anglo-Saxon language belongs to the Low German branch of the Teutonic family, and is therefore allied with the various dialects, called *Platt-Deutsch*, with the Friesic, and the Netherlandish, or Dutch. But it also differs from them all. It was probably a mixture of the dialects of the different German tribes, who met in England, and is so far indigenous, like the later English itself. There is no proof that it was spoken anywhere but in Great Britain. It never attained to its full development, like the Continental German. Its progress was arrested by the Norman conquest.

The most considerable monument of the original Anglo-Saxon tongue is the *Beowulf*, an essentially pagan epic, revised by some Christian writer. Caedmon, first a swine-herd, then a monk at Whitby (about 680), sung, as by inspiration, the wonders of creation and redemption, and became the father of Christian Saxon poetry. The works of King Alfred, the best of British rulers, may be taken as the best specimens of Saxon prose.

Of the Continental or German Saxon we have but fragmentary remains, of a later period, especially in *Heliand* (from *heal*, *Heil*-

---

[1] Hence the combination Anglo-Saxon. Gildas, the oldest British author, who wrote in the sixth century, more than one hundred and fifty years before Bede, mentions only the Saxons, with genuine Celtic hatred—"*ferocissimi illi nefandi nominis Saxones.*" Latham doubts the immigration of Jutes or Danes from Jutland, as attested by the Saxon historian Bede.

[2] Both these terms are common to the Teutonic and Scandinavian dialects, and signify the genus *horse* (comp. the German *Hengst* and *Ross*).

and, *i.e.*, Saviour), a life of Christ in alliterative meter, of the ninth or tenth century. But several hundred years before, in the fourth century, the Arian bishop Ulphilas, or Wulfila (Wölflein, *i.e.*, Little Wolf) had translated the Bible into the cognate Gothic, of which considerable fragments have been published by Angelo Mai, Massmann, Bernhardt, Stamm, and in fac-simile by Uppström.[1]

In many words and grammatical forms the present English is nearer the original Saxon and Gothic than the present German, and reveals more clearly its kinship with the Sanscrit, the oldest sister of the Indo-Germanic or Aryan languages.[2]

Some hold that spoken English is as old as spoken Sanscrit. Skeat says (*Etym. Dict.*, p. xiii.): "Sometimes Sanscrit is said to be an 'elder sister' to English; the word 'elder' would be better omitted. Sanscrit has doubtless suffered less change, but even twin-sisters are not always alike, and, in the course of many years, one may come to look younger than the other."

The Anglo-Saxon is not simply the prevailing element in the present English, but it is its proper basis and main structure. It supplies the essential parts of speech, the article, the pronouns

---

[1] See also specimens in the first volume of Wilhelm Wackernagel's *Altdeutsches Lesebuch*, pp. 6–26, with a dictionary, and in Braune's *Gothic Grammar*, with specimens and glossary, translated by G. H. Balg. New York, Westermann & Co., 1883.

[2] Compare, for illustration, the following table which I borrow from an article on comparative philology by B. W. Dwight, in the *Bibliotheca Sacra* for 1858, p. 119:—

SANSCRIT.	GREEK.	LATIN.	GERMAN.	ENGLISH.
bhu, *to be*,	φύω,	fui,	bin,	be.
bhratar, *a brother*,	φράτηρ,	frater,	Bruder,	brother.
bhar, *to bear*,	φέρω,	fero,	bären,	bear.
gâ, *to go*,	βαίνω,	venio,	gehen,	go.
go, *a cow*,	βοῦς,	bos,	Kuh,	cow.
hard, *the heart*,	καρδία,	cor,	Herz,	heart.
lubh, *to desire*,	λίπτομαι,	libet,	lieben,	love.
naman, *a name*,	ὄνομα,	nomen,	Name,	name.
path, *a way*,	πάτος,	passus,	Pfad,	path.
su, *to scatter about*,	σπείρω,	serere,	säen,	sow.
stri, *to strew*,	στόρνυμαι,	sternere,	streuen,	strew.
svadus, *sweet*,	ἡδύς,	suavis,	süss,	sweet.
yayam, *you*,	ὑμεῖς,	vos,	euch,	you.

—personal, demonstrative, relative, and interrogative—the prepositions, the numerals, the auxiliary verbs, the conjunctions, and all those little particles which bind words into sentences and form the joints, sinews, and ligaments of the language. It controls the grammatical inflections, the terminations of the noun and verb, and of the comparative (-*er*) and superlative (-*est*), and the entire syntactic structure. It makes all foreign words bend to its laws of declension and conjugation, although both have been considerably simplified and abridged in consequence of the friction with other elements. "The Latin," says Trench, "may contribute its tale of bricks, yea, of goodly and polished hewn stones, to the spiritual building; but the mortar, with all that holds and binds these together and constitutes them into a house, is Saxon throughout." Selden, in his "Table Talk," compares the Saxon to the substance of a cloak, and the other elements to the pieces of red, blue, green, and orange-tawny afterward put upon it.

As to the vocabulary, the Saxon portion is not only by far the largest, but furnishes those words which are most indispensable and most frequently used in all the ordinary concerns of life and which express the essential, intellectual, and moral conditions, and relations of man. Thus for the family we have the purely Saxon words: house, home, kindred (husband,[1] wife[2]), father, mother, child, son, daughter, brother, sister, friend, neighbor, boy, girl, maid, youth, man, woman, bride, lord, and lady;[3] for

---

[1] Anglo-Saxon: *husbonda*, i. e., master of the house or family. The explanation *house-band*, the bond of the house, as beautifully expressed in the couplet,

"The name of the *husband* what is it to say?
Of wife and of *household* the *band* and the stay,"

must be given up. The word is of Scandinavian origin, and corresponds to the Icelandic *húsbóndi*, a contracted form of *húsbúandi* or *búandi*, from *hús*, house, and pres. part. *búandi*, from *búa*, to dwell, inhabit. Comp. the German *bauen*, *Bauer*; Dutch, *Boer*.

[2] The Anglo-Saxon *wif* and the German *Weib* are usually derived from *wearing*, *woof*, *web* (*weban*), one of the earliest and most ordinary branches of female industry and in-door employments. Kluge connects it, less probably, with the Sanscrit *WIP*, inspired, inwardly moved (of priests) because the Germans originally honored in woman "*sanctum aliquid et providum*."

[3] The last two words occur in no other Teutonic language, and although undoubtedly Saxon, are of somewhat doubtful etymology. The common

the members of the human body: head, eye, ear, nose, hair, mouth, tongue, breast, bosom, heart, arm, hand, finger, foot, bone, flesh, and blood; for the faculties and actions of the mind: soul, feeling, will, understanding, wit, word, speech, deed (although here we meet with a number of Latin words, as mind, reason, intellect, memory, sense, conscience, imagination, action); for the necessities and actions of daily life: food, bread, water, milk, eat, drink, sit, stand, walk, go, come, rest, sleep, dream, wake, live, and die; for the essential affections and conditions: love, hatred, health, sickness, happiness, woe, mirth, sorrow, life, death, grave; for the elements and common objects of nature: earth, land, sea, fire, sun, moon, stars, heaven, wind, storm, thunder, light, heat, cold; for the changes in the day and season: day, night, morning, noon, evening, spring, summer, fall, winter; for the domestic animals: horse, mare, colt, cow, ox, steer, calf, sheep, pig, boar, swine, cat, dog, mouse, deer; for the chief products of the earth and the main instruments of cultivating it: wheat, rye, oats, barley, plow, spade, sickle, flail.

Most of the onomatopoëtic or sound-imitating words are Saxon, as bang, buzz, bellow, break, crash, creak, gurgle, hiss, hum, howl, hollow, murmur, roar, shriek, snap, snarl, storm, thunder, whistle, whine, tick-tick, pee-wee, bow-wow, chit-chat, sing-song. So also most of the compound words, as god-man, house-wife, key-stone, north-east, top-knot, elm-tree, pine-wood, foot-fall, horse-shoe, shoe-maker, snuff-box, morning-cloud, water-fall. A large proportion of the language of humor and colloquial pleasantry point to the same source.

Finally, the Saxon furnishes some of the fundamental terms in morals and religion, as God, good, bad, evil, sin, belief, love, hope, fear, heaven,[1] hell, gospel (*i. e.*, God's spell, or good

---

derivation of *lord* (A. S. *hláford*) from *hláf* or *loaf, bread,* and *ford* or *afford*—*bread-giver,* does not explain *lady,* which in Saxon is written *hlæfdige*. Tooke and Richardson derive *lord* from *hlif-ian, to raise,* and *ord*—*ortus, origin,* so as to mean *high-born. Lady* would then mean *lifted, elevated*. But the A. S. *hláford* most likely stands for *hláf-weard, loaf-keeper,* i. e., the master of the house, father of the family, and is equivalent in meaning to *husband.* So Skeat.

[1] Some derive *heofon, heaven,* from A. S. *hebban,* German *heben*—*elevated, arched*. Kluge, however, connects *heaven* and *Himmel* and derives both from an old Germanic stem *hem, him*: probably connected with the stem *ham, to cover, conceal*.

news),[1] righteousness, holiness, godliness. On the other hand, it can be abused for the hardest swearing.

The Saxon would be sufficient for all the ordinary purposes of life. We can live and die, love and hate, work and play, laugh and cry, tell tales and sing songs, in Saxon; but the foreign elements greatly enrich and embellish our intellectual, emotional and spiritual existence and enjoyments.

THE SAXON ELEMENT IN THE ENGLISH BIBLE.

One of the chief excellencies of our Protestant version of the Bible, as compared with the Roman Catholic or Douay version, is the predominance of the Saxon element, while the latter, being based upon the Latin Vulgate, employs too many Latin terms. The idiom of the Authorized Version of 1611 is chiefly due to the previous labors of William Tyndale, who first translated the New Testament from the original Greek into English, and died a martyr of his immortal work.

Let us give a few specimens. In the Lord's Prayer fifty-four words are Saxon, and the remaining six, which are of Latin origin (trespasses, trespass, temptation, deliver, power, glory), could easily be replaced by Saxon (sins, sin, trial, free, might, brightness) without materially altering the sense. The Douay Bible has for *daily* bread *supersubstantial* bread (from the Vulgate), which the common reader cannot understand.

In the sublime beginning of the Gospel of John, from verse 1 to 14, out of more than two hundred words only four or five are not of Saxon descent.

The most exquisite passages of the Old Testament are likewise almost exclusively Saxon.

Take the first verses in Genesis:—

"In the beginning God *created*" (for which might be substituted the Saxon *made*) "the heavens and the earth. . . . . And God said, Let there be light: and there was light."

---

[1] The exact English equivalent for the Greek εὐαγγέλιον. For this reason some prefer the derivation of the first syllable from the adjective *good*, to the derivation from *God* (*God's word*, *God's story*, i. e., the life of Christ), but the latter is supported by the analogy of the Icelandic, and the Old High German *gotspell*, (*God-story*, not *good-spell*. *God* and *good*, however, are closely connected.

The twenty-third Psalm would lose nothing of its beauty if the few Latin terms were exchanged for Saxon, as follows:—

"The Lord is my shepherd: I shall not want. He maketh me to lie down in green *pastures* (*meadows*): he leadeth me beside the still waters. He *restoreth* (*quickeneth*) my soul: he leadeth me in the paths of righteousness for his name's sake. Yea, though I walk through the *valley* (*dale*) of the shadow of death, I will fear no evil: for thou art with me; thy rod and thy staff they *comfort* (*strengthen*) me. Thou *preparest* (*spreadest*) a *table*[1] (*board*) before me in the *presence* (*sight*) of mine *enemies* (my *foes*): thou *anointest*[2] my head with oil; my cup runneth over (is overflowing). *Surely* (*Truly*, or more literally, according to the Hebrew, *Only*) goodness and mercy (*love*) shall follow me all the days of my life: and I will dwell in the house of the Lord forever."

The attempt to turn the whole into Latin or French English would utterly fail.

Nor could you improve such truly Saxon passages as these:—

"My heart is smitten and withered like grass."

"Thou hast *delivered* (*freed*) my eyes from tears, my soul from death, and my feet from falling."

"Under the shadow of thy wings will I *rejoice* (be happy)."

"If heart and flesh fail, thou art the strength of my heart and my *portion* (*lot*) for ever."

ILLUSTRATIONS FROM SHAKESPEARE.

It is the Saxon element which gives the chief strength to English poetry. We select a few passages from the greatest of all dramatic poets.

In the following quotation from the Merchant of Venice there are only three French words in fifty-five, the rest all Saxon:—

"All that glitters is not gold
Often have you heard that told:
Many a man his life hath sold,
But my outside to behold:
Guilded *tombs* do worms infold.

[1] This corresponds to the German *Tafel* as well as the Latin *tabula*; else the Saxon *board* might be substituted for it.

[2] Literally *fatten*, in allusion to the richness and abundance of the unction; but the term used in the common version from the French *oindre* and the Latin *unguere* could not well be improved. The Saxon *smear*, would here be tasteless and vulgar, and *salve* (A. G. *sealf*, Goth. *salbon*, Ger. *salben*) would mean to heal by ointment.

> Had you been as wise as bold,
> Young in limbs, in *judgment* old,
> Your answer had not been inscrolled :
> Fare you well ; your *suit* is cold."

The lines put into the mouth of Hamlet's father, unsurpassed for terrific beauty, with the exception of Dante's inscription on the gate of hell, have one hundred and eight Saxon and only fifteen Latin words :—

> " I am thy father's *spirit*
> Doomed for a *certain term* to walk at night ;
> And for the day, *confined* in flaming fire,
> Till the foul *crimes*, done in my days of *nature*,
> Are burned and *purged* away. But that I am forbid
> To tell the *secrets* of my *prison* house,
> I could a tale unfold, whose lightest word
> Would harrow up thy soul ; freeze thy young blood ;
> Make thy two eyes, like stars, start from their *spheres* ;
> Thy knotted and *combined* locks to *part*,
> And each *particular* hair to stand on end,
> Like quills upon the fretful *porcupine*.
> But this *eternal* blazon must not be
> To ears of flesh and blood. List, list, O list !
> If thou didst ever thy dear father love."

THE LATIN ELEMENT.

The LATIN is the second constituent element of the present English language.

We must carefully distinguish two classes of Latin words, those which are directly derived from the old Roman language, and those which are indirectly derived from it through the medium of the French. The latter can generally be recognized at once by the traces of a double process of transformation through which they have passed before they became anglicized.

ORIGINAL LATINISMS.

I. The first class or the pure Latin embraces again at least three distinct subdivisions corresponding to as many periods in the history of the language.

(*a*) The oldest Latin terms were engrafted upon the original

Saxon long before the Norman invasion, through the influence mainly of the Christian Church, which was established among the Anglo-Saxons toward the close of the sixth century.¹

They relate chiefly to ecclesiastical affairs and have found their way also into other Germanic dialects with the introduction of Christianity. They are to a large part of Greek origin, but came to the Saxons through the medium of the Latin Vulgate and church books. Most of them are so thoroughly nationalized as to sound like native words.

To the Saxon period belong saint from *sanctus*, religion from *religio*, bishop and archbishop from *episcopus* (from the Greek ἐπίσκοπος) and *archiepiscopus*, priest from *presbyter*² (πρεσβύτερος), deacon from *diaconus* (διάκονος), apostle, angel (likewise originally Greek), preach (Saxon *prædician*, German *predigen*) from *prædicare*, prove (*profian*) from *probare*, minster from *monasterium*, cloister from *claustrum*, master from *magister*, monk (*munuc*) from *monachus* (μόνος, μοναχός), porch from *porticus*, provost from *præpositus*, pall from *pallium*, candle from *candela*, chalice from *calix*, mint from *moneta*, psalter from *psalterium* (ψαλτήριον), mass from *missa* (*dismissa est ecclesia*), palsy from *paralysis* (παράλυσις), alms from *eleemosyna* (from ἔλεος), abyss, anathema, anthem, antiphon, cathedral, character, canon, canonical, catholic, ecclesiastic, laic, school, system, Testament, trinity, unity; perhaps also the stem verbs bib from *bibere*, carp from *carpere*, cede from *cedere* (or the French *ceder*), urge from *urgere*.

(*b*) The second class of Latinisms are theological and philosophical terms, not found in classical nor patristic Latin, and introduced during the reign of scholasticism in the middle ages, as real, virtual, entity, nonentity, equivocation, beatitude,³ soliloquy (the last two being first used by St. Augustin).

---

¹ A few Latin terms relating mostly to military affairs, as *street* from *strata*, the endings—*coln* (as in *Lincoln*) from *colonia*,—*cester* (as in *Gloucester*—*gloria castra*) from *castra*, were already introduced in the Celtic period under Caesar and the heathen Romans, but they are too insignificant to be regarded as a separate class.

² Rather than from *præstes*, which would not account for the second *e* in the German *Priester* and the French *prêtre*. Milton says, "Presbyter is priest writ large."

³ Cicero coined both *beatitas* and *beatitudo* (*Nat. Deor. I, 34, 95*), but they

Dunce and duncery are likewise from the scholastic period, according to Trench and Skeat. Duns Scotus, the standard divine of the Franciscans, was anything but a blockhead; but his name may have been used reproachfully by the rival school of Thomists (the Dominicans), or by the enemies of scholasticism. Most of the sectarian terms, as Arians, Apollinarians, Eutychians, Nestorians, Pelagians, Lutherans, Zwinglians, Puritans, Methodists, etc., were originally terms of reproach invented by enemies.

(c) The third stratum of English Latin of direct derivation is modern, and comprises a considerable number of scientific and technical terms, which can easily be distinguished from the older importations by their unaltered condition, the language having now lost to a great extent its former power of assimilation. In these cases even the Latin plural is generally retained, as in *axis* and *axes*, *crisis* and *crises*, *basis* and *bases*, *formula* and *formulæ*, *calculus* and *calculi*, *magus* and *magi*, *colossus* and *colossi*, *fundamentum* and *fundamenta*, *medium* and *media*, *datum* and *data*, *momentum* and *momenta*, *erratum* and *errata*, *stratum* and *strata*, *index* and *indices*, *radix* and *radices*, also *appendix*, *ratio*, *stimulus*, *emporium*, *apparatus*, *species*, *series*.

In the same class we may embrace Latin phrases which have become naturalized, as *ab ante*, *ab ovo*, *ad libitum*, *ad nauseam*, *a posteriori*, *a priori*, *cui bono*, *de facto*, *de jure*, *ex-officio*, *ex-parte*, *brutum fulmen*, *in medias res*, *in memoriam*, *ipsissima verba*, *jure divino*, *nil admirari*, *non multa sed multum*, *non sequitur*, *obiter dictum*, *obsta principiis*, *otium cum dignitate*, *tabula rasa*, *terra firma*, *via media*, *vox populi vox Dei*.

There are some Latin words of comparatively recent introduction which have undergone a considerable change and are transformed into the English idiom, as mob from *mobile* (*vulgus*), which was introduced in the reign of Charles I.

(d) A number of words which Latham calls di-morphic, exist in a double form, the original Latin and the French Latin, the latter being generally cut a syllable or two shorter, and often

did not pass into usage among classical writers until Augustin naturalized *beatitudo* (*De Civ. Dei*, xxi. 17, where he uses the plural *beatitudines*). *Soliloquia* is the title of one of his devotional tracts.

representing a different shade of meaning, as pauper and poor (from *pauper* and *pauvre*), probe and prove (from *probare* and *eprouver*), secure and sure (from *securus* and *sur*), also fidelity and fealty, species and spice, blaspheme and blame, granary and garner, hospital and hotel, persecute and pursue, faction and fashion, particle and parcel, potion and poison, redemption and ransom, tradition and treason. We may add presbyter and priest, monastery and minster; but priest (Saxon *preost*) and minster (Saxon *mynster*) are older than presbyter and monastery.

In a few cases the substantive was borrowed from the French, as people from *peuple* (*populus*), parish from *paroisse* (*parochia*); while at a later period the corresponding adjective was taken directly from the Latin, as popular and parochial. Bishop and episcopal or episcopalian (for *bishoply*, German *bischöflich*) are an instance of a double formation from the Latin.

FRENCH LATINISMS.

II. The second and by far the largest class of Latin words have come to us through the medium of the Norman French or Romance, which itself was a daughter of the Latin, with a number of Celtic and Teutonic elements incorporated into its vocabulary.

The French English can easily be distinguished from the Latin English by the spelling. Thus Saviour comes from the Latin *Salvator*, but through the French *Sauveur*; honour from *honor*, through *honeur*; favour from *favor*, through *faveur*; judgment from *judicium*, through *jugement*; people from *populus*, through *peuple*; crown from *corona*, through *couronne*; treasure from *thesaurus*, through *trésor*; emperor from *imperator*, through *empereur*.

Through the same medium we have received arms, armour, army, navigation, navy, bachelor, barber, battery, battle (*bataille*, from *batere*, to beat), beverage, bullet, calamity, channel, chant, chapel, charity, charm, dainty, dame (*domina*), fable, fabric, language, madam, mademoiselle, magistrate, mansion, merit, prime, etc., etc.

The Normans adopted, with the Christian religion, the language, laws, and arts of the Romanized Gauls and Romanized

Franks, or rather they developed, in their new home, a national character and language of their own, which differed both from that of their rude Scandinavian kinsmen on the shores of the North Sea and the Baltic, and from that of the original Romanesque provincials on the banks of the Seine.

In this modified shape as semi-civilized, Romanized, Frenchified Normans, after a residence in France of more than a century and a half, they successfully invaded England in 1066 under Duke William the Conqueror, who had a slight pretext of right to the English crown by his relationship to Edward the Confessor and the alleged bequest of the sovereignty to him by that king. They defeated the Saxons in the battle of Hastings, took possession of the country, gave kings to the throne, knights and nobles to the estates, judges to the tribunals, bishops to the church, teachers to the schools, but also tyrants to the peasantry, oppressors to the burghers, and brought untold misery upon the people of England for several generations.

To get a proper view of the extent of this conquest and its effect, we must dismiss all idea of the present England, when no such thorough transformation could take place by any foreign invasion, owing to the numerical strength and high grade of civilization to which it has long since attained.

It is estimated that the Saxon population at the time of the conquest amounted to about a million and a half or two millions, of whom more than a hundred thousand were destroyed during the cruel and despotic reign of William the Conqueror. The number of Normans who emigrated with him or followed during his reign and that of the next successors, can hardly be less than from two to three hundred thousand souls. For at the battle of Hastings alone he had sixty thousand fighting men.[1]

The Normans had the advantage in point of education and position. The influence of their language was favored by the use of the Latin in worship and among the learned, and more directly by the English possessions in France and the frequent wars and intercourse between the two nations.

---

[1] See the particulars in Thierry's "Norman Conquest," Hallam's "Middle Ages," Creasy's "Rise and Progress of the English Constitution" (ch. v. and vi.), and Freeman's "History of the Norman Conquest."

Yet they could not internally conquer the stubborn Saxon element, but were even more influenced by it in the course of time than the Saxons were by them. They never made a Normanland or a New France out of England. Instead of converting the Saxons into Frenchmen, they became Englishmen themselves, just as the Normans had become Frenchmen in France, and the Goths Spaniards in Spain. Fortunately for the future destiny of England both nationalities were yet in a crude and semi-barbarous condition, and hence they could be so molded and assimilated as to constitute at last a new nationality which is neither Saxon nor Norman, but combines the excellencies of both.

THE GRADUAL MINGLING OF THE SAXON AND NORMAN.

This was a very slow process. For nearly three hundred years the two languages stood in hostile antagonism, or rather in neutral indifference, side by side as two distinct currents, like the waters of the Monongahela and Alleghany in the Ohio river, or the Missouri and Mississippi after their junction above St. Louis. The Norman was spoken by the lords and barons in their feudal castles, in parliament, in the courts of justice, in the schools, and on the chase; the Saxon by the people in their rural homes, fields, and workshops. There was an English proverb in the middle ages: "Jack would be a gentleman if he could speak French."

Some traces of the distinct existence of the Norman are still preserved in those technical phrases which give the royal assent to the different laws of parliament, as " *La reine le veut ;* " " *Soit fait comme il est désiré ;* " " *La reine remercie ses bons sujets, accepte leur bénévolence et ainsi le veut.* " Cromwell signed the bills in plain English, but the Romanizing Stuarts characteristically restored these vestiges of the Norman conquest.

During the long intellectual winter which followed the Norman conquest the germ of a new and nobler nationality and language was gradually maturing under the snow-covered soil for a vigorous and prolific growth in the approaching spring. The profound truth of the Word, "That which is sown is not quickened except it die," is applicable also in this case. The Saxon and Norman, together with the remaining Celtic and Danish elements, slowly melted and coalesced into a harmonious whole, and came out of the process a new and better race than any that preceded it. The Saxon gave up a part of his vocabulary, the Norman a part of his together with all his grammar, and the result was the English language with its meagre but simple system of grammatical inflection and its rich vocabulary.

This process was completed in the fourteenth century. The commencement of the English (that is, Normanized Saxon) language and literature coincides with a reformatory national movement which, although suppressed for several generations, triumphed at last under a modified form in the sixteenth century. Wycliffe, by his translation of the Latin Bible in 1380, is the father of English prose, as his sympathizing contemporary, Chaucer, by his "Canterbury Tales," is the father of English poetry.[1]

In the same age Edward III. ordered, in 1362, the pleadings of the court to be carried on in English instead of French. But the first bill of the lower house of Parliament in the English language dates from 1425. Since that time the language has, of course, undergone considerable changes, so that the writings before the Reformation cannot be fully understood now without the help of a glossary. Yet in all the essential features it is the same. The groundwork of the new language remained Saxon. But the Norman disturbed its inflections, articulation, and pronunciation, simplified its syntax and enriched its vocabulary, although the gain in this respect was partly neutralized by the loss of corresponding terms.

The change introduced into the vocabulary may be illustrated by the following two paragraphs which exhibit successively the Norman and Saxon elements:[2]

---

[1] Coleridge calls Chaucer the "myriad-minded," and Marsh places him as to original power and all the highest qualities of poetry above all contemporary writers with the single exception of Dante. "He is eminently," (says he, *Lectures*, p. 22), "the creator of our literary dialect, the introducer, if not the inventor, of some of our poetical forms." The more it is to be regretted that many of his works are disfigured, stained, and polluted by a grossness of thought and of language which strangely and painfully contrasts with the delicacy, refinement, and moral elevation of his other productions.

[2] This illustration is borrowed mainly from Prof. Schele de Vere's "*Outlines of Comparative Philology.*" New York, 1853.

"With the Norman *conquest* the French was *introduced* in the higher *circles*; the King alone *retained* his *name*, but the *state* and the *court* became French; the *administration* was *carried* on *according* to the *constitution*; *treaties* were *concluded* by the *ministers* in their *cabinet* and *submitted* for *approval* to the *sovereign*; the *privy council* was *consulted* on the *affairs* of the *empire*, and *loyal subjects* sent *representatives* to *parliament*. Here the *members debated* on *matters* of *grave importance*, on *peace* and *war*, *ordered* the *army* and the *navy*, *disposed* of the *national treasury*, *contracted debts*, and had their *sessions* and their *parties*. Brilliant *feasts* and *splendid tournaments collected* the *flower* of *chivalry*; *magnificent balls* where *beauty* and *delicious music enchanted* the *assembled nobles*, gave new *splendor* to *society*, *polished* the *manners* and *excited* the *admiration* of the *ancient inhabitants*, who, *charmed* by such *elegance*, *recognized* in their *conquerors persons* of *superior intelligence*, *admired* them, and *endeavored to imitate* their *fashions*."

"But—to continue this illustration in Saxon—the dominion of the Norman *did* not extend to the *home* of the Saxon; it *stopped* at the *threshold* of his *house*; there, around the *fireside* in his *kitchen* and the *hearth* in his *room*, he *met* his *beloved kindred*; the *bride*, the *wife*, and the *husband*, *sons* and *daughters*, *brothers* and *sisters*, *tied* to each *other* by *love*, *friendship*, and *kind feelings*, knew *nothing dearer* than their own *sweet home*. The Saxon's *flock*, still *grazing* in his *fields* and meadows, *gave* him *milk* and *butter*, *meat* and *wool*; the *herdsman watched* them in *spring* and *summer*, the *ploughman drew* his *furrows*, and used his *harrows*, and in *harvest*, the *cart* and the *flail*; the *reaper plied* his *scythe*, *piled* up *sheaves* and *hauled* his *wheat*, *oats*, and *rye* to the *barn*. In his *trade* by *land* and *sea*, he still *sold* and *bought*, in the *store* or the *shop*, the *market* or the *street*; he *lent* or *borrowed*, *trusted* his *neighbor*, and with *skill throve* and *grew wealthy*. He continued to *love freedom*, to *eat* and to *drink*, to *sleep* and to *awake*, to *walk* and to *ride*, to *fish* and to *hunt*, to *sing* and to *play*, to *read* and to *write*, to *think* and to *feel*, to *speak* and to *do*, to *live* and to *die*."

THE RELATION OF THE NORMAN AND SAXON ELEMENTS.

The Norman French imparted to the English nearly all the terms connected with the feudal system, as sovereign, prince, duke, marquis, count, viscount, baron, chancellor, treasurer, tournament, challenge, throne, sceptre, empire, realm, royalty, chivalry, domain, homage, villain, palace, castle; with the exception, however, of king and queen, lord and lady, which are Saxon, and earl, which is Scandinavian. The reason of this exception lies in the historical fact that the Norman conqueror claimed the throne of England not by a new title but by the regular line of succession.

The French furnished also the terms of government and law, as state, government, honor, dignity, office, parliament, constitution, administration, privy council, treaty, court, warrant, esquire. But the word law itself is derived neither from *lex* nor *loi*, but from the Saxon verb *lecgan*, to lie down, or more directly from its passive participle *lagu*, pronounced laugu, laid down, fixed, like statute from *statuere*, and Gesetz from *setzen*.

Several important military terms, as army, navy, peace, war, and names for the articles of luxury and ornament are likewise Norman. But the instruments of agriculture are called in true Saxon, plough, share, rake, scythe, sickle, spade; so are also the chief products of the earth, as wheat, rye, corn, oats, grass, hay, flax.

It is characteristic that the truly Saxon names of living animals, as ox, steer, cow, calf, sheep, hog, deer, when killed and prepared for the table are changed into French, as beef, veal, mutton, pork, and venison. Even to this day French cookery retains the ascendency in fashionable hotels and restaurants all over the world.

The names of common and indispensable articles of dress are Saxon, as shirt, breeches, hose, shoes, hat, cloak; but articles of a later form of civilization and subject to the changes of fashion are Norman, as gown, coat, boots, mantle, cap, bonnet.

The common residence for all men is signified by the Saxon terms, house, and home; while the aristocratic residences of the few are named with the French terms, palace, castle, manor, mansion. From the Saxon we have "room" and "kitchen," with the necessary articles of furniture, as stool, bench, bed, board; but the French gave us chambers, parlors, galleries, pantries, laundries, with tables, chairs, and couches.

The Latin gives us often the general term, as color, while the Saxon furnishes the concrete or particular terms, as white, black, green, red, blue. The one gives the more elegant and dignified, the other the more homely, but stronger expression, as sweat for perspiration, stench for bad odor, smear for anoint.

It may be said, therefore, that the Norman represents the aristocratic, the Saxon the democratic element in the English language. The former supplied, as Grimm says, "the spiritual conceptions;" while the latter forms the material groundwork, and also the top (remember the words king and queen). The reason of this is not the incapacity of the Saxon, but the higher education and acquired dominion of the Normans. The French infused into the English a higher degree of intellectuality, vivacity, gravity and dignity, and enriched its vocabulary of chivalry, courtesy and fashion.

Archbishop Whateley, in his "Elements of Rhetoric," makes the true remark "that a style composed chiefly of words of French origin, while it is less intelligible to the lowest classes, is characteristic of those who in cultivation of taste are below the highest. As in dress, furniture, deportment, etc., so also in language, the dread of vulgarity constantly besetting those who are half conscious that they are in danger of it drives them into the extreme of affected finery."

The English is a happy medium between the French and German, more grave and forcible than the French, less harsh and cumbersome than the German, and simpler in grammar, more easily acquired and handled than either.

ILLUSTRATIONS FROM MILTON AND WEBSTER.

Milton is generally considered as the greatest master of the Latin element among the English poets (as Shakespeare certainly is the prince of the Saxon element); yet in his speech for a free press he severely reproves authors who are "apishly Romanizing, and whose learned pens can cast no ink without Latin." Charles James Fox, the great English orator, goes too far when he says: "Give me an elegant Latin and a homely Saxon word, and I will always choose the latter." The preference given to the one or the other should depend upon the nature of the subject and proper regard to the beauty, harmony and euphony of speech. The Saxon has always the advantage of force and expressiveness, but the Latin supplies the element of dignity and melody. We may say with Coleridge that Milton's

Latin gives "a stately march and majestic, organ-like harmony" to his diction.

Take for illustration his impressive sonnet on the persecution of the Waldenses in Piedmont:—

> "Avenge, O Lord, thy slaughtered saints, whose bones
> Lie scattered on the Alpine mountains cold,
> Even them who kept thy truth so pure of old,
> When all our fathers worshipped stocks and stones."

Or his sublime Nativity Hymn:—

> "This is the month and this the happy morn,
> Wherein the Son of heaven's eternal King,
> Of wedded maid and Virgin Mother born,
> Our great redemption from above did bring."

Gibbon is the most Latinizing of English historians. The stately march of his artfully constructed and well-rounded sentences suits his grand subject, the decline and fall of the Roman Empire, but it becomes as monotonous as a military procession.

Daniel Webster, the most majestic orator that America has produced, was a close student of the English Bible and John Milton. The prose of the American Demosthenes blends Saxon strength and Latin dignity in beautiful harmony. Take the following classic passages from three of his most celebrated speeches. The proportion of Latin words to Saxon in these specimens is fully one-third.

The first is his definition of true patriotic eloquence, from his eulogy on Adams and Jefferson, delivered in Faneuil Hall, Boston, August 2d, 1826:—

"When public bodies are to be addressed on momentous occasions, when great interests are at stake, and strong passions excited, nothing is valuable in speech farther than it is connected with high intellectual and moral endowments. Clearness, force, and earnestness are the qualities which produce conviction. True eloquence, indeed, does not consist in speech. It cannot be brought from far. Labor and learning may toil for it, but they will toil in vain. Words and phrases may be marshaled in every way, but they cannot compass it. It must exist in the man, in the subject, in the occasion. Affected passion, intense expression, the pomp of declamation, all may aspire to it; they cannot reach it. It comes, if it come at all, like the outbreaking of a fountain from the earth, or the bursting forth of volcanic fires, with spontaneous, original, native force. The graces taught in the schools, the costly ornaments and studied contrivances of speech shock and disgust men, when their own lives, and the fate of their wives, their children, and their country hang on the decision of the hour. Then words have lost their power, rhetoric is in vain, and all elaborate oratory contemptible. Even genius itself then feels rebuked and subdued, as in the presence of higher qualities. Then patriotism is eloquent; then self-devotion is eloquent. The clear conception, outrunning the deductions of logic, the high purpose, the firm resolve, the dauntless spirit, speaking on the tongue, beaming from the eye, informing every feature, and urging the whole man onward, right onward to his subject,—this, this is eloquence; or rather it is something greater and higher than all eloquence, it is action, noble, sublime, godlike action."

The second specimen is the peroration of his national and patriotic anti-nullification speech against Colonel Robert Y. Hayne, delivered in the United States Senate, January 26th, 1830. Edward Everett pronounced it the most celebrated speech ever delivered in Congress, and I doubt whether any of the grand effusions of the elder or the younger Pitt, of Burke, Fox, or Brougham in the British Parliament are superior to it.

"While the Union lasts, we have high, exciting, gratifying prospects spread out before us, for us and our children. Beyond that I seek not to penetrate the veil. God grant that in my day, at least, that curtain may not rise! God grant that on my vision never may be opened what lies behind! When my eyes shall be turned to behold, for the last time, the sun in heaven, may I not see him shining on the broken and dishonored fragments of a once glorious Union; on States dissevered, discordant, belligerent; on a land rent with civil feuds, or drenched, it may be, in fraternal blood! Let their last feeble and lingering glance rather behold the gorgeous ensign of the Republic, now known and honored throughout the earth, still full high advanced, its arms and trophies streaming in their original lustre,[1] not a stripe erased or polluted, not a single star obscured,

---

[1] An evident reminiscence from his favorite author, Milton, in his description of the imperial banner of hell, *Paradise Lost*, Book I., v. 535, s. 99 :—

"Who forthwith from the glittering staff unfurl'd
Th' imperial ensign, which, *full high advanc'd*,
Shone like a meteor, *streaming* to the wind,
With gems and golden *lustre* rich emblaz'd,
Seraphic *arms* and *trophies*: all the while
Sonorous metal blowing martial sounds;
At which the universal host up sent
A shout that tore hell's concave, and beyond
Frighted the reign of Chaos and Old Night."

In Bk. V., 598, Milton speaks of "ten thousand thousand ensigns *high advanc'd . . . stream* in the air."

This description again was probably suggested by Tasso's description of the banner of the Crusaders, when first unfolded in Palestine.

bearing for its motto no such miserable interrogatory as, 'What is all this worth?' nor those other words of delusion and folly, '*Liberty first and Union afterward;*' but everywhere, spread all over in characters of living light, blazing on all its ample folds, as they float over the sea and over the land, and in every wind under the whole heavens, that other sentiment, dear to every true American heart, *Liberty and Union, now and forever, one and inseparable.*"

This passage uttered thirty years before the civil war, sounds like a prophecy of that event, which Webster would gladly have prevented as the direst calamity, but we have lived to see it over-ruled by divine Providence for stronger union and larger liberty built upon the ruins of secession and slavery.

In the same speech occurs that magnificent eulogy on Massachusetts, which is unsurpassed in its kind:—

"Mr. President, I shall enter on no encomium upon Massachusetts—she needs none. There she is—behold her, and judge for yourselves. There is her history: the world knows it by heart. The past, at least, is secure. There is Boston, and Concord, and Lexington, and Bunker Hill—and there they will remain forever. The bones of her sons, falling in the great struggle for independence, now lie mingled with the soil of every State; and there they will lie forever. And, Sir, where American liberty raised its first voice, and where its youth was nurtured and sustained, there it still lives, in the strength of its manhood and full of its original spirit. If discord and disunion shall wound it . . . it will stand, in the end, by the side of that cradle in which its infancy was rocked . . . ; and it will fall at last, if fall it must, amidst the proudest monuments of its own glory, and on the very spot of its origin."

The third example is the conclusion of Webster's second great anti-nullification speech, delivered in the United States Senate, February 16, 1833, against John C. Calhoun, the able and honest arch-nullifier, and in favor of the Force-Bill authorizing President Jackson to employ the United States military power, if necessary, for the collection of duties on imports in South Carolina, then in an attitude of open rebellion against the federal government. It is only inferior in eloquence to the peroration in the anti-Hayne speech, and equally patriotic:—

"Mr. President, if the friends of nullification should be able to propagate their opinions, and give them practical effect, they would, in my judgment, prove themselves the most skillful architects of ruin, the most effectual extinguishers of high-raised expectation, the greatest blasters of human hopes, which any age has produced. They would stand up to proclaim, in tones which would pierce the ears of half the human race, that the last great experiment of representative government had failed. They would send forth sounds, at the hearing of which the doctrine of the divine right of kings would feel, even in its grave, a returning sensation of vitality and resuscitation. Millions of eyes of those who now feed their inherent love of liberty on the success of the American example, would turn away from beholding our dismemberment, and find no place on earth whereon to rest their gratified sight. Amidst the incantations and orgies of nullification, secession, disunion, and revolution, would be celebrated the funeral rites of constitutional and republican liberty."

THE OTHER ELEMENTS OF THE ENGLISH LANGUAGE.

Besides the Germanic and Romanic which constitute the body of the present English tongue, several other languages have furnished contributions. These are, however, far less numerous and important, and enter more or less into the composition of other modern languages of Europe. Each language has contributed such terms as express the leading ideas and principal strength of the respective nations. From the Hebrew we have religious; from the Greek, scientific, philosophical and artistic; from the Italian, musical terms.

Among these additional contributory streams we mention first—

THE CELTIC ELEMENT.

This is properly the oldest, since the Britons, a branch of the Celtic nationality, were the original inhabitants of England at the time of Cæsar's invasion. Their memory is continued in the name of Great Britain. The Celtic idiom is still spoken in two dialects, the Welsh in Wales, and the Gaelic in Ireland and the Highlands of Scotland (Irish Gaelic and Scotch Gaelic). But owing to the complete subjection of the Britons by the Anglo-Saxons and the irreconcilable national antagonism of the two races, as well as owing to the fact that the Celtic has less vitality and power of resistance than any other European language, there are comparatively very few Celtic words in the English, and those few belong mostly to servile life.

Take the following characteristic specimens: basket (Welsh *basged, bascaid*), button (*botwm*), bran, cobble, crockery, crook, flaw, funnel, grid, gruel, mattock, wicket, wire, rail, rug, tackle; also babe, cradle, bad, bald, bump, bugbear, cart, char, dock, drudge, druid, bard, clan, plaid, gown, griddle, lad, lass, pat, pet, pretty, prop, puddle.

A number of proper names are Celtic, as Thames, Kent, and probably also London—*i. e.*, "city of ships." The last sounds like a prophecy from pre-Roman times of the future importance of the commercial metropolis of the world, where—

> "*Tausend Schiffe landen an und gehen;*
> *Da ist alles Herrliche zu sehen,*
> *Und es herrscht der Erde Gott, das Gold.*"

The Celtic element may be compared to the Indian in our American English.

THE DANISH OR NORSE (ICELANDIC) ELEMENT.

This dates from the Danish piratical invasions in the ninth and tenth centuries. But as the Scandinavian dialects belong to the Germanic stock, many words supposed to be from that source are Germanic, and probably belonged to the original Anglo-Saxon.

We mention as specimens: aloft (compare the German *Luft, luftig*), already, anger, askew, awe, awn, aye, baffle, bang, bark, bawl, beach, blunder, blunt, boulder, box, bulk, bulwark, cast, club, crash (German, *krachen*), dairy, dastard, dazzle, fellow, gabble, gain, glade, ill, jabber, jam, kidnap, kidney, kill, kneel, limber, litter, loft, log, lug, lull, lumber, lump, lunch, lurch, lurk, mast, mistake, mistrust, nab, nag, nasty, niggard, horse, plough (*Pflug*), raft, ransack, rug, rump, saga, sale, scald, shriek, shrill, skin, skull, sledge, sleigh, sled, tackle, tangle, tipple, tipsy, trust, Valhalla, viking, window, wing.

The ending -*by*, which signifies town, is Norse, and occurs in many proper names of towns and villages, as Hornby, Naseby, Whitby, Derby, Appleby, Netherby. In Lincolnshire, one of the chief resorts of Danish immigration, nearly one-fourth of the towns and villages have this ending, while in Hampshire it is unknown. The names of the Islands in the English Channel, Jersey, Guernsey and Alderney, by their ending *ey*, which means island (as in Orkney), betray likewise Scandinavian descent, although probably through the medium of the Normans who imported a number of other Norse terms to the banks of the Seine. Most of the Danish words are provincial and confined to the northern and north-eastern counties, which were exposed most to Danish invasion.

HEBREW WORDS.

From the Hebrew we have, besides a large number of significant proper names from Adam and Eve down to Jesus, John and Mary, several religious terms which passed into the Septuagint and Greek Testament, then into the Latin Vulgate, and were properly retained by the English translators of the Bible, as Jehovah Zebaoth (plural: hosts), Messiah, rabbi, hallelujah, hosannah, cherub, seraph (with the Hebrew plurals cherubim and seraphim), ephod, Gehenna (Hell, the place of torment), Sheol (Hades, the unseen spirit-world), jubilee, manna, maranatha, pascha, sabbath, sanhedrin, Satan, shekinah, shibboleth, Amen.

GREEK WORDS.

The noble and rich Greek language has supplied the English as well as other European languages with nearly all the technical names for the various branches of learning and art, from the alphabet up to the highest regions of metaphysical and theological speculation, as theology, with its subdivisions of exegesis, archaeology, hermeneutics, apologetics, polemics, symbolics, dogmatics, ethics, homiletics, catechetics, etc.; philosophy, with logic, anthropology, psychology, aesthetics, metaphysics, etc.; grammar, rhetoric, philology, history, mathematics, arithmetic, astronomy, anatomy, calligraphy, geography, orthography, stenography, physiology, pathology; architecture, music and poetry; also with a considerable number of indispensable political terms, as monarchy, oligarchy, theocracy, aristocracy, democracy, anarchy, policy.

Of miscellaneous words which point to the same source we may mention: architect, poet, pedagogue, cosmopolite, hero, sophist, apocalypse, analogy, anomaly, antagonism, apathy, antipathy, sympathy, anthem, euphony, harmony, melody, psalmody, hymn and hymnology, catastrophe, crisis, diagnosis, diæresis, diadem, diagram, dropsy (ὕδρωψ from ὕδωρ, water), dynasty, dogma, epitome, hypocrisy, megrim (corrupted from the Latin and Greek *hemicrania*, half the head), program, palsy (from παράλυσις), tansy (derived by some from ἀθανασία, through the Latin *athanasia* and the old French *athanasie*—more than doubtful); the adjectives, graphic (from the verb γράφειν), plastic, exegetical, critical, hypercritical, skeptical, and the verbs, platonize, romanize, judaize, evangelize.[1]

Most of the Greek terms, especially the theological, philosophical, and political, have come to us through the medium of the Latin Bible and Latin literature, as Christianity (with the Latin ending for Christianism), Bible, canon, apocrypha, angel, apostle, evangelist, prophet, bishop, priest, deacon, baptism, eucharist, scepter, ascetic, ocean (hence, the Latin c for the Greek κ); a few through the Gothic, as is most probably the case with church, which like all the similar words in the Teutonic and Slavonic languages, points to κυριακόν—*i. e.*, belonging to the Lord, the Lord's house, the Lord's people, and was used as the equivalent in sense, though not in etymology, to the Greek ἐκκλησία and the Latin *ecclesia*—(*i. e.*, assembly, congregation). Still others are taken directly from the Greek with their proper ending, as phenomenon, criterion (phænomena and criteria), diapason, demon, pandemonium.

Not a few words for modern inventions are, as in other languages, by tacit consent and for international convenience, newly formed from the Greek, as electrotype, lithography, melanotype, phonography, photograph, photography, stereoscope, stereotype, telescope, telegraph, telegram, telephone.

DUTCH WORDS.

Of Dutch origin are the modern sea terms sloop, schooner, yacht; also a number of other words, as ballast, bluff, blunderbuss, boom, boor, brandy, bush, drill, duck, fop, frolic, gruff, hatchel, hackle, moor, mump, reef, skate, swab, switch, trigg, uproar, wagon.

---

[1] The last seems to have been first used by Wycliffe in his translation of Luke i. 19.

The Dutch settlers in New York introduced some words which were unknown, at least till recently, in England, as cold slaa, or slaw (*kool salade*), made of cabbage, and boss (*baas*) for master-workman, together with a number of geographical terms, which will perpetuate the history of the first settlement of Manhattan Island, or New Amsterdam, and of the Knickerbockers.

ITALIAN WORDS.

The beautiful Italian language has furnished us musical terms, as virtuoso, prima donna, piano forte, violin (violino), orchestra (properly from the Greek ὀρχήστρα and ὀρχέομαι, to dance), soprano, alto, allegro; also stanza, canto, piazza, gazette (from *gazetta*, originally a Venetian coin for the reward of the first newspaper), umbrella (from the Latin *umbra*, shade), pantaloon (*pantaleone*, French *pantalon*), charlatan (from *ciarlatano* through the medium of the French), gondola, and bandit (*bandito*, outlawed).

SPANISH WORDS.

The Spanish has presented us with the alligator, alpaca, bigot, cambist, cannibal, cargo, cortes, don, filibuster (freebooter), gala, guano, hurricane, mosquito, negro, punctilio, stampede, potato, tobacco, tomato, tariff.[1] From the same language is probably also the verb capsize (*capuzar*), to sink a ship by the head.

ARABIC WORDS.

From the time of the ascendency of the Moors in Spain and the period of the crusades we have several mathematical, astronomical, medical and chemical terms, as alchemy, alcohol, alcove, alembic, algebra, alkali, almanac, amber, assassin, azure, cipher, elixir, harem, hegira, nadir, rajah, sheik, sofa, talisman (originally from the Greek τέλεσμα), vizier, zenith, zero.

PERSIAN WORDS.

Bazaar, dervish, lilac, pagoda, caravan, scarlet, shawl, tartar, tiara, peach, scimetar.

---

[1] From the Spanish promontory and fortress, *Tarifa*, which commands the entrance to the Mediterranean, where the Moors watched all merchant ships. Hence, the proper spelling would be tarif.

TURKISH WORDS.

Turban, tulip, dragoman, divan, firman, effendi, and that indispensable article, coffee (which is also Arabic).

SLAVONIC WORDS.

These are few and mostly Russian, as drosky, knout, rouble, steppe, verst, ukase.

INDIAN WORDS AND NAMES.

The Indian aborigines of our country have given us terms of savage life, as wigwam, squaw, hammock, tomahawk, canoe, moccasin, hominy (parched corn), and a large number of geographical names which are generally more musical and expressive than the imported foreign names repeated *ad nauseam*.

It is to be regretted that not more of the native and beautiful names of rivers and mountains were retained, as Mississippi (*i.e.*, the father of waters), Missouri (muddy river,) Ohio (probably the beautiful river, la belle rivière, as the French called it), Minnehaha (laughing water, introduced in Longfellow's Hiawatha), Potomac, Susquehanna, Monongahela, Niagara, Allegheny, Massachusetts, Connecticut, Iowa, Kansas, Nebraska, Dakota, Idaho, Wyoming, Alaska, etc.

AMERICANISMS.

Americanisms of recent native growth are mostly of a political character, as caucus, a term of uncertain origin, for a secret political meeting; doughface, a term invented by the sarcastic John Randolph to denote a pliable politician, or a nose of wax. The political party terms: Democrats, Republicans, Know-Nothings, Abolitionists, Secessionists, Federals, Confederates, have a peculiar historical meaning in the United States which is hardly warranted by the etymology, or at least is new in its application. The Democratic party received for many years before and after the civil war its chief support from the slave-holding aristocracy of the South; and the Republicans monopolized the general conception of republicanism at first in the interest of a Northern party which opposed the further extension of negro-slavery, but afterwards overleaped the sectional boundaries. In the proper sense of the word all Americans are Republicans, as distinct from Monarchists and Imperialists; and all are Democrats or advocates of popular self-government, in opposition to class-aristocracy or oligarchy.

The civil war gave currency to a number of terms, as bushwhacker for guerrilla, secesh (a vulgarism for secessionist), and skedaddle for running away in a panic or fight (probably of Scandinavian origin, and possibly connected with the Greek σκεδάννυμι, to scatter), which have found their way from the newspapers into the latest editions of Webster and Worcester. "Contraband" was, during the war, employed of runaway negro slaves, and was so first used by Gen. Butler, when in Maryland, in 1861. "Mugwump" is an ugly nickname given to those Republicans who, during the Presidential campaign in 1884, partly in the interest of civil service reform, partly from opposition to a high tariff, voted the Democratic ticket and elected Cleveland. It ought to drop out of use. "Blizzard," a fierce whirlwind and blinding snow-drift, is an onomatopoetic word of North-Western origin (connected with blow, blast, bluster), dating from about 1880. The blizzard of March 12, 1888, has become historic: it broke up all communication for several days, and New York had to learn by cablegram *via* London that Boston was snowed up.

The following words are also of American origin: accountability (for accountableness), bigbugs (people of consequence), blatherskite, bogus, bore (an unwelcome or troublesome visitor), bottom-land, bottom-facts (a word first used, I believe, by Henry Ward Beecher during his trial), breadstuff, brush up, buffalo-robe, bunkum or buncombe (a speech made for the gratification of constituents, or for mere show, from Buncombe County, North Carolina), cat's-paw, Christianization, denominationalism, churchliness, dilly-dally (to loiter), lager-beer (imported from Germany), loafer, tramp, constructive mileage, dead-head, wire-pullers, sockdolager, to wind up, to have a good time.

HYBRID WORDS.

These are made up of two different languages, often in strange conjunction. Examples: across (from the Saxon *a* or *an*, *on*, and the Latin *crux*), bailiwick (from the French *baillie*, government, and the Saxon *wic*, a village), interloper (half Latin, half Dutch), Christmas (Greek and Latin), disarm (from the Latin *dis* and Saxon *arm*, French *désarmer*), disapprove, disappear, develop (from the Latin *dis* and the French *veloper*, *développer*), disfranchise, disregard, embark (from the prefex *em* or *en* and *barque*, French *embarquer*, Italian *imbarcare*), embarrass, forearm, forecast, forecastle, hobby-horse, life-guard, loggerhead, (half Danish, half Saxon), mishap (from the Saxon and German *mis* or *miss*, and the Icelandic *happ*), outcast, outcry, outfit, refresh (from the Latin prefix *re* and the Saxon *fresh*, German *frisch*, Old French *refraishir*), regain, relish, remark, reward, seamstress, undertake (from the Saxon *under* and the Scandinavian *taka*, allied to the Latin *tangere*), unruly (from the Saxon negative prefix and the Latin *regula*, *regulare*, Old French *reuler*, Modern French *régler*), until (unto and *Ziel*, i. e. end). A curious combination of Latin and Saxon is the term nonesuch for unequaled (as in the title of William Secker's book, "The Nonesuch Professor in His Meridian Splendor," 1660).

THE ORGANIC UNION OF THESE ELEMENTS.

We now proceed to consider the mixture of these different elements, and the advantages resulting from it.

The various elements of which the English language is composed are not outwardly and mechanically related to each other, but they have inwardly and organically coalesced by a long historical process. They are not like the primary, secondary, tertiary, and other strata and deposits in geology, but they form a living unit. All foreign elements are thoroughly anglicized, and have been so assimilated and engrafted upon the original trunk as to constitute a distinct idiom with a character of its own, like the English nation itself.

The English tongue is the child of a Saxon queen and a Norman king, inheriting some of their best qualities, and endowed at the same time with an original genius, thus representing at once the flower of an old, and the promise of a new dynasty.

" Wo sich das Strenge mit dem Zarten.
Wo Starkes sich und Mildes paarten;
Da gibt es einen guten Klang."

RESULTS OF THIS MIXTURE. SPELLING.

The first and most obvious result of this mixture was the confusion of the laws of spelling and sound. This is a most serious inconvenience to learners. The pronunciation of the English cannot be learned from books, but only from living intercourse and long practice. Every vowel, instead of signifying one definite sound, has several, some even four and five or more different sounds,[1] as the *a* in father, fall, fat, what; the *o* in dove, move, wolf, note, and not; the *i* in bite, bit, and bird; the *u* in duck, tune, and bull; the *ou* in dough, cough, tough, tour, plough; or certain letters represent different articulations of the organs, as *th* in thin, and thine; and a number of words, though spelled very differently, cannot be distinguished in pronunciation, as is the case with to, too, and two, or with write, right, rite, and (wheel-)wright.

The orthography and pronunciation of the English defies all laws, is most perplexing to a foreigner, and hinders the progress of the language. It becomes intolerable, at least to continental ears, if applied to other languages, as the Greek and Latin, and only tends to confusion among classical scholars. Max Müller denounces the present system of spelling as "corrupt, effete, and utterly irrational." W. D. Whitney says that every theoretical and practical consideration is in favor of reform.

The English alphabet being borrowed from the Roman, is altogether insufficient both in respect to vowels and consonants. We have only twenty-six letters wherewith to write at least thirty-two sounds. It is to be hoped that sooner or later this difficulty will be removed by the substitution of a phonetic for the traditional orthography, although such a change would have the serious inconvenience of obliterating the etymological origin of words.

The accent also has changed, and in words derived from the French it has receded from the last to the second last syllable.

---

[1] Dr. Worcester has here gone beyond Dr. Webster, and unnecessarily, we think, multiplied the sounds. In his "key" he marks seven different sounds of *a* (three more than Webster), five sounds of *e* (three more than Webster), five of *i* (two more than Webster), six of *o* (one more than Webster), six of *u* (three more than Webster), and four of *y*. This seems to be more nice than wise.

NEW MIDDLE SOUNDS.

But this disadvantage of the English as an object for the learner is more than compensated by an advantage in the increased number of sounds and a consequent addition to the efficiency of speech and poetic composition. Besides the eighteen articulations of the ancient Romans we have at least fourteen other vowel and semi-vowel sounds. The mingling of Saxon, Norman, and Celtic vowels has given rise to a number of middle sounds between a, i, o, and u, which impart to the spoken English a greater force, fullness and variety of sound. Generally speaking the various Germanic dialects (including the Platt-Deutsch, the Dutch, the Danish and the Swedish), owing to the preponderance of consonants over the vowels, are by no means musical and cannot be compared in this respect with the ancient Greek and Latin, and the Romanic languages of Southern Europe. The English, too, is vigorous and effective rather than harmonious and pleasing. But a skilful use of those peculiar middle sounds imparts to the English the charm of a deep, rich, and solemn melody. The Germans, as a people, are more musical than the English, and have produced the greatest composers; but the English language is more musical than the German.

No British poets, perhaps, understood the music of words better than Byron and Tennyson. Take the following examples from "Childe Harold's Pilgrimage:"—

> "I stood in Venice, on the Bridge of Sighs,
>   A palace and a prison at each hand :
> I saw from out the wave her structures rise
>   As from the stroke of the enchanter's wand :
>   A thousand years their cloudy wings expand
> Around me, and a dying glory smiles
>   O'er the far times, when many a subject land
> Look'd to the wingéd Lion's marble piles,
> Where Venice sate in state, throned on her hundred isles!"
> . . . .
> "In Venice Tasso's echoes are no more,
>   And silent rows the songless gondolier ;
> Her palaces are crumbling to the shore,
>   And music meets not always now the ear :

> Those days are gone—but Beauty still is here.
> States fall, arts fade—but Nature doth not die,
>   Nor yet forget how Venice once was dear,
> The pleasant place of all festivity,
> The revel of the earth, the masque of Italy!"
>
> . . . .
>
> "Roll on, thou deep and dark blue Ocean—roll!
>   Ten thousand fleets sweep over thee in vain;
> Man marks the earth with ruin—his control
>   Stops with the shore; upon the watery plain
> The wrecks are all thy deed, nor doth remain
> A shadow of man's ravage, save his own,
>   When for a moment, like a drop of rain,
> He sinks into thy depths with bubbling groan,
> Without a grave, unknell'd, uncoffin'd and unknown.
>
> . . . .
>
> "Thou glorious mirror, where the Almighty's form
>   Glasses itself in tempests; in all time,
> Calm or convulsed—in breeze, or gale, or storm,
>   Icing the pole, or in the torrid clime
>   Dark-heaving;—boundless, endless, and sublime—
> The image of Eternity—the throne
>   Of the Invisible; even from out thy slime
> The monsters of the deep are made; each zone
> Obeys thee; thou goest forth, dread, fathomless, alone."

Among Tennyson's poems, the "Charge of the Light Brigade," to which we shall refer for another purpose, is unsurpassed for its military music.

Of American poets, Edgar Poe's "Song of the Bell," and especially his "Raven," will at once suggest themselves as striking specimens for illustration. The "Raven" owes its celebrity certainly not to its thoughts, but almost exclusively to the strange, melancholy music of versification sounding from a dark midnight scenery to the ear and filling the soul with ghostly visions of terror and despair. The whole is too long for quotation. We select the first and the last stanzas:—

> "Once, upon a midnight dreary, while I pondered, weak and weary,
>   Over many a quaint and curious volume of forgotten lore,
> While I nodded, nearly napping, suddenly there came a tapping,
>   As of some one, gently rapping, rapping at my chamber door;
> 'Tis some visitor,' I muttered, 'tapping at my chamber door—
>   Only this, and nothing more.'"
>
> . . . .

> "And the raven, never flitting, still is sitting, still is sitting
>   On the pallid bust of Pallas just above my chamber door:
> And his eyes have all the seeming of a demon that is dreaming,
>   And the lamp-light, o'er him streaming, throws his shadow on the floor;
>   And my soul from out that shadow that lies floating on the floor
>   Shall be lifted—nevermore!"

Longfellow's "Hiawatha" is full of melody, though it becomes somewhat monotonous and tedious. His "Psalm of Life," too, is very musical, especially this stanza:—

> "Art is long, and Time is fleeting,
>   And our hearts, though stout and brave,
> Still, like muffled drums, are beating
>   Funeral marches to the grave."

Of less-known poems we may refer to Francis Mahony's (Father Prout's) "Bells of Shandon," beginning—

> "With deep affection
> And recollection
> I often think of
>   Those Shandon bells,
> Whose sounds so wild would,
> In the days of childhood,
> Fling round my cradle
>   Their magic spells.
>
> "On this I ponder
> Where'er I wander,
> And thus grow fonder,
>   Sweet Cork, of thee,
> With thy bells of Shandon,
> That sound so grand on
> The pleasant waters
>   Of the river Lee."

SIMPLICITY OF THE GRAMMAR.

While in point of pronunciation the English language is one of the most difficult to acquire for a foreigner, it is easiest and simplest as to its grammatical structure. It is a general fact that languages are richer in their youth and become poorer in grammatical forms as they progress in age and culture. A savage language spoken on the Gaboon river, in Africa, is said to possess an unbounded flexibility, copiousness and melody.

Most of the Indian dialects, too, are very complex in organization and structure. But the perfection of a language does not consist in the number of words, the variety of forms, and mechanical regularity of grammatical inflection. The inflectional element of language is its most accidental, and hence its least permanent and least important element. The decay in material exuberance is a growth in intellectuality and freedom from useless incumbrances. What is lost in variety is gained in clearness and precision. A tree thrives and bears better for being trimmed of all useless branches. It is a principle in mechanics to produce with the smallest possible means the greatest possible effect.

In this respect the English stands without a rival among the various languages of Christendom. It is the simplest, most direct, and practical language, most easily acquired and most easily used. As compared with the ancient languages, or with the German, it is very poor in ground-forms, inflections and the details of syntax. Its words appear to the etymologist bruised and broken. But this very poverty and mutilation is a source of greater strength and efficacy. The English lost the liberty of the ancient Saxon and modern German in the syntactical arrangement of words; but what it thus lost in rhetorical and poetical convenience, it gained in simplicity, clearness and logical order of construction. Good English, like good French, requires short, concise, direct and easily intelligible sentences. Long, involved, and complicated periods may be allowed only as exceptions.

This, too, is to be attributed in part to its composite character. The collision and commingling of so many different elements facilitated and hastened the natural progress of language from materialism to intellectualism, from exuberance to simplicity. The Saxons expressed their meaning as briefly as possible to their Norman masters and dropped all unessential letters. The Normans learned just enough of the Saxon to make themselves understood without regard to grammatical inflections and terminations.

BREVITY.

It is in this way that the English acquired that remarkable brevity which makes it the best business language. Voltaire once playfully remarked that an Englishman gained half an hour in speaking with a Frenchman. The Latin words had already lost in syllables or sound by becoming French. They were still more abridged, bruised, and broken by being engrafted upon the Saxon. Take the following illustrations.

Words originally of four or more syllables become trisyllables or dissyllables :—

Latin.	French.	English.
abbreviare	abréger	abridge
cadentia	chance	chance
creatura	creature	creature
concupiscere	convoiter	covet
consuetudo	costume and coutume	custom
decipere	décevoir	deceive
dependere	dependre	depend
desiderium	desir	desire
diabolus	diable	devil
episcopus	(evêque)	bishop
flagitare	flatter	flatter
gratificari	gratifier	gratify
gubernare	gouverner	govern
innocencia	innocence	innocence
judicium	jugement	judgment
(re)memorare	remembre	remember
obedire	obeir	obey
occurrere	(occurrent)	occur
peregrinus	pélerin	pilgrim
periculum	peril	peril
praedicare	prêcher	preach
praevalere	prevaloir	prevail
producere	produire	produce
redemptio	rançon	ransom
remanere	(remaindre)	remain
respondere	répondre	respond

Latin.	French.	English.
scandalum	scandale and esclandre	scandal and slander
sententia	sentence	sentence
silvaticus	sauvage	savage
viaticum	voyage[1]	voyage[1]

Trisyllables changed into dissyllables or monosyllables:—

Latin.	French.	English.
bibere	boire	bib
carpere	(cueillir)	carp
cedere	ceder	cede
cantare	chanter	chant
catena	chaîne	chain
cerasus	cerise	cherry
chirurgus	chirurgien	surgeon
civitas	cité	city
clamare	(clameur)	claim
congressus	congrès	congress
corona	couronne	crown
crudelis	cruel	cruel
debitor	débiteur	debtor
debitum	dette (débet)	debt
decretum	decret	decree
digestum	digeste	digest
dignari	daigner	deign
flagellum	fleau	flail
fragilis	frêle	frail
frigère	frire	fry
gaudium	joie	joy
jungere	joindre	join
lectio	leçon	lesson
legalis	loyal	loyal
mensura	mesure	measure
natura	nature	nature
numerus	nombre	number
persicum	pêche	peach
placere	plaire	please

[1] This may be from *roie*, *ria*, *Weg*.

Latin.	French.	English.
pretium	prix	price and praise
rabies	rage	rage
regalis	royal	royal
salvare	sauver	save
Salvator	Sauveur	Saviour
Scriptura	écriture	Scripture
securus	sûr	sure and secure
sigillum	scellé and sceau	seal
spolium	(spolier)	spoil
tractare	traiter	treat
urgere	(urgent)	urge
videre	voir (vue)	view

Dissyllabic words shortened to monosyllables:

Latin.	French.	English.
caput (κεφαλή)	chef	chief
chorus (χορός)	chœur	choir
clarus	clair	clear
costa	côte (coste)	coast
crassus	gros	gross (cross, course)
fides	foi	faith
fructus	fruit	fruit
judex	juge	judge
nomen (ὄνομα)	nom	noun and name
pisum (πίσον)	pois	pea
praeda	proie	prey
poena	peine	pain
quartus	quart	quart
salvus	sauf (sauve)	safe
sensus	sens	sense
sonus	son	sound

The Saxon element has likewise undergone a process of curtailment. All letters and grammatical inflections which are not absolutely necessary were gradually dropped. Thus we lost the h before l (as in loaf for hlaf, lot for hlot), the case-ending in the noun (except the s of the genitive for the Saxon es), the plural termination en (except in some irregular nouns, as oxen), the verbal prefix ge or ga, as in deal for gedælan (German theilen, getheilt), deem for gedeman (ziemen, geziemt), and the verbal termination an in the infinitive still retained in the modern German (en), as come for cuman (German kommen), cook for gecoenian (kochen), deal for dælan or gedælan (theilen), dip for dippan (tupfen, tauchen, taufen), drill for thirlian (drillen), drive for drifan (treiben), give for gifan (geben), love for lufian (lieben), mean for menan (meinen), pluck for pluccian (pflücken), shoot for sceotan (shiessen, schossen), shall for sceolan (sollen), wed for weddian, weep for wepan (weinen), write for writan or gewritan (schreiben).

Even in our age the English in their zeal to gain time, express themselves as briefly as possible, and have a tendency to abridge still further. Thus they say broke for broken, bus for omnibus, cab for cabriolet, pro tem for pro tempore. Also the double forms, sung and sang, drunk and drank, the distinction between the past tense and the passive participle, and the use of the subjunctive, in connection with if (as, if it is, for if it be), are likely to pass away under the force of the law of convenience and time-saving economy.

MONOSYLLABIC CHARACTER.

From this process of abridgment results the fact that the English language, especially the Saxon portion of it, has an unusual number of monosyllables. Nearly all the monosyllables are relics of earlier polysyllables. In this monosyllabic character and poverty of inflections and formative elements the English resembles the Chinese. The monosyllabic character gives it a very decided advantage for commerce, business, and all the practical concerns of life. It reduces the expense of correspondence by telegraph and telephone.[1] In poetry it limits the number of double rhymes, which is quite an inconvenience in doing full justice to the Italian terza rima in Dante's *Divina Comedia*, or the famous Latin *Dies irae, dies illa*. But this defect is amply

[1] Orton, late President of the Western Union Telegraph Company, New York, said that English was twenty-five per cent. cheaper for telegraphic purposes than any other. Notices posted up in, say four languages, prove the same, generally, in the relation of four English, six French, eight German, and nine or ten Spanish words, to express the same idea.

compensated by the peculiar force which the monosyllabic character imparts to English poetry.

Dr. Jos. Addison Alexander, of Princeton, wrote the following two sonnets consisting exclusively of monosyllables, which appeared under the title "Monosyllables" in the *Princeton Magazine*, May 18th, 1850, and which we may quote here as curiosities of literature.

I.

"Think not that strength lies in the big round word,
　Or that the brief and plain must needs be weak;
To whom can this seem true that once has heard
　The cry for help, the tongue that all men speak
When want, or woe, or fear is in the throat,
　So that each word gasped out is like a shriek
Pressed from the sore heart, or a strange wild note
　Sung by some fay or fiend. There is a strength
Which dies if stretched too far, or spun too fine,
　Which has more height than breadth, more depth than length:
Let but this force of thought and speech be mine,
　And he that will may take the sleek, fat phrase,
Which glows and burns not, though it gleam and shine—
　Light, but no heat—a flash, but not a blaze!"

II.

'Nor is it mere strength that the short word boasts;
　It serves of more than fight or storm to tell,
The roar of waves that clash on rock-bound coasts,
　The crash of tall trees when the wild winds swell,
The roar of guns, the groans of men that die
　On blood-stained fields. It has a voice as well
For them that far off on their sick beds lie;
　For them that weep, for them that mourn the dead;
For them that laugh, and dance, and clap the hand;
　To joy's quick step, as well as grief's slow tread,
The sweet, plain words we learnt at first keep time,
　And though the theme be sad, or gay, or grand,
With each, with all, these may be made to chime,
　In thought, or speech, or song, in prose or rhyme."

Illustrations of monosyllabic poetry from Shakespeare are abundant. Some of the most familiar passages are monosyllabic. Take the following:—

From Hamlet:—

"To be or not to be: that is the question."

The words of Macbeth to Banquo's ghost:—

"Thou canst not say I did it:
Ne'er shake thy gory locks at me."

The despairing exclamation of Richard III:—

"A horse! a horse! My kingdom for a horse!"

William Wordsworth introduces his poems referring to the period of childhood with Saxon monosyllables (except three dyosyllables and two Latin words):—

"My heart leaps up when I behold
A rainbow in the sky:
So was it when my life began;
So it is now I am a man;
So be it when I shall grow old,
Or let me die!
The Child is father of the Man;
And I could wish my days to be
Bound each to each by natural piety."

The following lines on the departure of a friend are not found in Byron's works, but were published under his name in Lady Blessington's "Memoirs:"—

"I heard thy fate without a tear,
Thy loss with scarce a sigh;
And yet thou wert surpassing dear—
Too loved of all to die.

I know not what hath seared mine eye,
The tears refuse to start;
But every drop its lids deny,
Falls dreary on my heart.

Yes—deep and heavy one by one
They sink and turn to care;
As caverned waters wear the stone,
Yet dropping harden there.

They cannot petrify more fast,
Than feelings sunk remain
Which, coldly fixed, regard the past,
But never melt again."

Hood's "Song of the Shirt" consists largely of monosyllables, and its ever returning

> "Stitch! Stitch! Stitch!"
> "Work! Work! Work!"

has a singular effect upon the imagination.

The beautiful evening hymn of Keble, which has passed into most modern hymn-books, begins:—

> "Sun of my soul, thou Saviour dear,
> It is not night, if Thou be near."

Tennyson, like Shakespeare, is full of Saxon monosyllables. Take the following specimens:—

> "And on her lover's arm she leant,
> And round her waist she felt it fold,
> And far across the hills they went,
> In that new world which now is old."

The poem on the Foolish Virgins (Matt. 25: 11, 12), in "Guinevere," is almost wholly monosyllabic:—

> "Late, late, so late! and dark the night and chill!
> Late, late, so late! but we can enter still.
> 'Too late, too late! ye cannot enter now.'"

The same is true of most part of his "In Memoriam." Take the beautiful lines:—

> "Our little systems have their day;
> They have their day and cease to be:
> They are but broken lights of Thee,
> And Thou, O Lord, art more than they."

Or the New Year's poem:—

> "Ring out the old, ring in the new."

Or the oft quoted lines:—

> "There lives more faith in honest doubt,
> Believe me, than in half the creeds."

I cannot refrain from quoting in full his Crimean battle song, "The Charge of the Light Brigade," which has no rival in any language. He wrote it after reading the first report of that memorable charge of 607 sabres upon a whole army, at Balaklava, in obedience to orders. It appeared first in the London *Times*, in autumn, 1854, but has undergone several revisions. I quote it from the authorized Boston edition (Houghton, Osgood & Co., 1878, p. 183), and add some variations, taken in part from a manuscript copy of Tennyson in possession of my friend, John E. Parsons, Esq., of New York.

1.

Half a league, half a league,
   Half a league onward,
All in the valley of Death
   Rode the six hundred.
" Forward, the Light Brigade !
Charge for the guns ! " he said ;
Into the valley of Death
   Rode the six hundred.

2.

" Forward, the Light Brigade ! "
Was there a man dismay'd ?
Not though the soldier knew
   Some one had blundered :[1]
" Charge," was the captain's cry,[2]
Theirs not to make reply,
Theirs not to reason why,
Theirs but to do and die,
Into the valley of Death
   Rode the six hundred.

3.

Cannon to right of them,
Cannon to left of them,
Cannon in front of them,
   Volley'd and thunder'd ;
Storm'd at with shot and shell,
Boldly they rode and well
Into the jaws of Death,
Into the mouth of Hell
   Rode the six hundred.

---

[1] Originally (in the MS. referred to)—
   " For up came an order which
     Some one had blundered :
   ' Forward, the Light Brigade !
    Take the guns !' Nolan said."

[2] This line is omitted in the Boston edition and in the MS., but I found it in one of the recensions.

4.

Flash'd all their sabres bare,
Flash'd as they turn'd in air,[1]
Sabring the gunners there,
Charging an army, while
    All the world wonder'd:
Plunged in the battery-smoke
Right through[2] the line they broke;
Cossack and Russian
Reel'd from the sabre-stroke.[3]
Strong was the sabre-stroke,
Making an army reel,
    Shatter'd and sunder'd.
Then they rode back, but not—
    Not the six hundred.

5.

Cannon to right of them,
Cannon to left of them,
Cannon behind them
    Volley'd and thunder'd,
Storm'd at with shot and shell,
While horse and hero fell,
They that had fought so well
Rode thro' the jaws of Death,
Half a league back again,[4]
Back from the mouth of Hell,
All that was left of them—
    Left of six hundred.

When can their glory fade?
O the wild charge they made!
    All the world wonder'd.
Honor the charge they made!
Honor the Light Brigade,
    Noble six hundred.![5]

---

[1] The MS. reads, "Flashed *all at once* in air."   [2] Or, "Fiercely."

[3] The MS. has a better reading:—
    "With many a desperate stroke
    The Russian line they broke."

[4] Omitted in the Boston edition and in the MS.

[5] This agrees with the MS., but in my memorandum book I find the following beautiful conclusion from another recension:—
    "Honor the brave and bold!
    Long shall the tale be told,
    Yea, when our babes are old,
        How they rode onward."

LARGE NUMBER OF SYNONYMS.

The union of the Saxon with the Norman was bought at a great sacrifice of Saxon words which were retained in the pure German. Thus the Anglo-Saxon has several words for language, most of which are lost in modern English, as gereord, getheode, leden, reord, spell (retained in gospel), spæc, spræc, (speech, German, Sprache), tunge (tongue, German, Zunge).

But this loss is more than made up by corresponding French and Latin terms, and by the advantage of a large number of synonyms or duplicates, and even triplicates and quintuplicates, for expressing the same idea with a different shade of meaning.[1]

This is a great convenience, especially to the philosopher, the orator, and the poet.

I will select some examples of synonymous nouns, adjectives, and verbs.

The Saxon *freedom* and the Latin *liberty* are often used indiscriminately as rhetorical or metrical considerations may suggest, yet the former is the general, the latter the specific term; the one expresses the state and power of self-determination and self-government as an inherent and inalienable right, the other implies deliverance from a previous state of servitude or restraint.

---

[1] I found the following characteristic passage in a newspaper, without the name of the author, under the title " Wonders of the English Language :"—

"The construction of the English Language must appear most formidable to a foreigner. One of them, looking at a picture of a number of vessels, said: 'See, what a flock of ships!' He was told that a flock of ships was called a fleet, and that a fleet of sheep was called a flock. And it was added, for his guidance in mastering the intricacies of our language, that a flock of girls is called a bevy, that a bevy of wolves is called a pack, and a pack of thieves is called a gang, and a gang of angels is called a host, and a host of porpoises is called a shoal, and a shoal of buffalo is called a herd, and a herd of children is called a troop, and a troop of partridges is called a covey, and a covey of beauties is called a galaxy, and a galaxy of ruffians is called a horde, and a horde of rubbish is called a heap, and a heap of oxen is called a drove, and a drove of blackguards is called a mob, and a mob of whales is called a school, and a school of worshipers is called a congregation, and a congregation of engineers is called a corps, and a corps of robbers is called a band, and a band of locusts is called a swarm, and a swarm of people is called a crowd, and a crowd of gentlefolks is called *élite*, and the *élite* of the city's thieves and rascals are called the roughs."

Hence, we say a slave is set at liberty (not at freedom), if he was a born slave, while he is restored to freedom, if he was originally free. The liberty of the press is the best guarantee for the freedom of thought and speech. The Saxon *love* is the affection of the heart, the Latin *charity*, although originally as comprehensive as the former, is love in active exercise; the former applies to God as well as man, and to man in his relation both to his Maker and his fellow-creatures; while the latter, according to more recent usage, means only love of man to man, or active benevolence. *Shepherd* may be used both figuratively (as in Psalm xxiii. and John x.) and literally, while *pastor* is only employed figuratively. *Ship* signifies the sailing vessel, whether for commerce or war, whether propelled by wind or steam, while *nave*, from *navis* (ναῦς), is used as an architectural term in speaking of the main divisions of a church from the entrance to the altar. *Murder* is the unlawful killing of a man with malicious intention, *manslaughter* is killing without such intention; while the Latin *homicide* is the general term for both. Then we have **righteousness** and **justice**, **might** and **power**, **strength** and **force**, **need** and **necessity**, **gift** and **donation**, **heathen** and **pagan** (both applied to idolaters as villagers or dwellers on heaths after the triumph of Christianity in the cities), **calling** and **vocation**, **wood** and **forest**, **stream** and **river**, **dale** and **valley**, **waterfall** and **cascade**, **land** and **country**, **storm** and **tempest**, **grief** and **dolor**, **woe** and **misery**, **handbook** and **manual**, **answer** and **response**, **forerunner** and **precursor**, **feather** and **plume**, **lie** and **falsehood**, **godliness** and **piety**, **creator** and **maker**, **behavior** and **conduct**, **friendship** and **amity**, **happiness** and **beatitude**, **mistake**, **error** and **blunder**, **feeling**, **sentiment**, **emotion** and **affection**, **wedlock**, **marriage** and **matrimony**, **betterment** (now almost obsolete except as a technical term in jurisprudence, but of frequent occurrence among the best writers of the seventeenth century) and **improvement**, **bent** and **inclination**, **body** and **corpse**, **diet** and **food**, **track** and **vestige**, **hint** and **suggestion**, **building**, **edifice** and **structure**.

Of adjectives I mention **lovely** (worthy of love) and **amiable** (of sweet disposition), **readable** (of the contents of a book) and **legible** (of handwriting), **everlasting** (without end) and **eternal** (without beginning and without end, if applied to God), almighty and omnipotent, priestly and sacerdotal, kingly and royal, early and timely, handsome and beautiful (stronger), ripe and mature, twofold (threefold, fourfold, etc.) and double (triple, quadruple, etc.), bodily and corporeal, burdensome and onerous, bloody and sanguine, boyish and puerile, womanly and feminine, fearful and timid, yearly and annual, laughable, ludicrous and ridiculous (the last with the additional idea of contempt mixed with merriment), inside and interior, outside and exterior, still, tranquil and quiet, bold and brave, mild, meek and gentle, holy (*halig, heilig*), pious (*pius*), devout (*dévot, devotus*), religious (*religiosus*).

Of verbs we have answer and respond, bewail and lament, get and obtain, heap and accumulate, heal and cure, forbid and prohibit, forsake and abandon (the latter much stronger, like giving up hopelessly), handle and manage, hide and conceal, happen and occur, hallow and sanctify, make up and constitute, soften and mollify, rot and putrefy, try and attempt, whiten and blanch, unfold and develop, wish and desire, christen (Greek Saxon) and baptize (Greek Latin), hinder and prevent, hold and contain, stick, cleave and adhere, waste and dissipate, watch and observe, reckon and calculate, die and expire, outlive and survive.

Sometimes we have the choice between a Greek and Latin word, as between apocalypse and revelation, epitome and extract or abridgment, hypothesis and supposition, sympathy and compassion, theism and deism. The last two etymologically are synonyms, but in modern usage theism has assumed a peculiar philosophical sense implying transcendent personality in opposition to pantheism; while deism is more particularly, though arbitrarily, applied to that notion of the Deity which puts him outside of the world and denies a special revelation.

The careful reader of the Anglican Common Prayer Book must be aware of the frequent use of the Saxon together with its corresponding Latin synonyms in those portions which are not translations from the Latin, but original, as in the exhortation to the confession of sin: acknowledge and confess, dissemble and cloak, humble and lowly, goodness and mercy, assemble and meet together. This may be attributed to the desire of the compilers of that admirable Liturgy to reach the heart of all classes of the people at a time when the language was yet in a comparatively unsettled condition.

PERFECTIBILITY.

Finally, the composite character of the English language imparts to it a pliability, expansiveness, and perfectibility which no other language possesses. Considering its age, it has still a considerable power of assimilation and digestion. Already one of the most copious of modern languages, with a vocabulary of over one hundred thousand words, it is still increasing, if not by organic growth, at least by accretion. It has a craving appetite and is as rapacious of words and as tolerant of forms as is the Saxon race of territory and religion. It imports new words from all languages, as the English and Americans import merchandise from all portions of the globe. It seizes upon foreign terms as they are needed, subjects them at once to all the rules of the vernacular, and naturalizes them. Or it coins new words from the German, Latin, and French, according to the etymological laws of these various languages, without doing violence to its own laws.

Thus the Germanizing words fatherland for native land, handbook for manual, standpoint (*Standpunkt*) for point of view, churchly and churchliness (not to be confounded with the Anglican party terms high-churchman and high-churchism, but corresponding to *kirchlich* and *Kirchlichkeit*), church history (*Kirchengeschichte*) for ecclesiastical history, doctrine history (*Dogmengeschichte*), symbolics (*i. e.*, comparative dogmatics), apologetics, world-historical (*weltgeschichtlich*), church-historical (*kirchengeschichtlich*), epoch-making (*epochemachend*)), neological, rationalistic, separatistic, dogmatical, christological,[1] were formed within the present century, mostly in America, by admirers of

---

[1] *Christology*, however, is old English, as Trench proves by a passage from Dr. Jackson, of the seventeenth century. R. Fleming wrote a "Christology" in 1705, in 3 vols. Webster has it in his dictionary, but limits the sense by defining it: "A discourse or treatise concerning Christ." The term *rationalist*, although now conveying a definite historical sense, was similarly used already in Cromwell's time, of a sect which made reason the test of belief. "What their reason dictates to them in Church and State stands for good until they be convinced with better."

modern German literature and have already passed into general use.[1]

Then we have a number of Latin formations, unknown to the ancient classics, as nonconformist, nonconformity, nonjuror, nonresidence, nonsuit, nondescript, nonentity, which are of older date, mostly from the seventeenth century; while a number of similarly coined words, omitted by Johnson, Walker, and Richardson, but embodied in Webster, are probably of American origin, as nonconductor, nonexistence, nonessential, nonepiscopal, nonelect (a Calvinistic term), nonelection (a political term used by Jefferson and others for failure of an election).

COSMOPOLITAN DESTINATION.

All these peculiarities of the English point out its cosmopolitan destination. We use this word, of course, only in a relative sense. The English can never absorb the thousand tongues now spoken on earth. Our many-sided humanity will never be contented with one speech. The difference of languages and dialects will last as long as the difference of nations and races. The German, the French, the Spanish, the Russian, will expand with the nations that use them.

But the progress of humanity and of Christianity require the *preponderance* of one language as a common medium of international intercourse and a connecting link between the various members of the civilized world.

Such a sway the Greek attained in the countries around the Mediterranean after the conquest of Alexander the Great, and then the Latin in the Western Roman empire and in the Catholic Church during the Middle Ages down to the Reformation. Since the time of Louis XIV. the French gained the ascendancy at the courts and in all the higher circles of Europe; it is still the language of diplomacy, and its acquisition is a necessity for every well-educated gentleman; as a knowledge of the German is indispensable to a scholar on account of its invaluable and ever-growing literature.

---

[1] Not so honorable are some other German contributions, as *sauerkraut, smierkäs, prezel,* and *lager-bier,* which are *too tonic* for the Anglo-American stomach.

But in our age the English is rapidly becoming the world-language and extends over a larger territory than any of its predecessors, with every prospect of a steady advance for the next generations.

It is spoken by a greater number of civilized men and Christians than any other speech, and establishes its peaceful empire on the ruins of decaying dialects and races. Already it holds the balance of power among the tongues, and with its literature and science is perpetually circumnavigating the globe. It is emphatically the language of the modern age and of the coming age, of progressive intelligence and civilization. It is the prevailing language of Christian missions in heathen lands. It is the westernmost branch of the Aryan family of languages, and

"Westward the course of empire takes its way."

SPREAD OF THE ENGLISH LANGUAGE.

The English is now spoken in England, Scotland and Ireland, and all the British dependencies in Europe, as Heligoland, Gibraltar, Malta and Cyprus. It is taught as a regular branch of higher education in the best Colleges and Universities on the continent of Europe, and in all commercial cities, and is rapidly gaining on the French. In Egypt it has acquired new strength through the construction of the Suez canal, the increasing travel on the Nile, and the suppression of Arabi Pasha's rebellion by the short, sharp and decisive English campaign of 1882.[1] In Asia it follows the British sway and the highways of commerce to the vast empire of East India with its two hundred millions of heathen and Mohammedan inhabitants, who exhibit a growing desire to learn the language of their rulers, as a means of promotion and medium of a new Anglo-Indian literature. I have heard converted Brahmins speak and preach in the purest

[1] When I landed at Alexandria some years ago, a Bedouin recommended me his donkey, called "Yankee Doodle," because "he speak English." When I ascended the great pyramid of Gheezeh, another of those sons of the desert amused me with the broken fragments of half a dozen languages, the English prevailing, such as: "*Va piano ;*" "*Allez doucement ;*" "Go ahead;" "Half way up;" and arriving on the top he exclaimed: "All serene," "Well done," "I good guide," "You good man," "Dear doctor," "Baksheesh."

Anglo-Saxon. It is largely used in the islands and seaports of China even by native Chinese, in a corrupt form. It is firmly established in Southern Africa and extends every day with the widening British settlements of the Cape and the Western coast, including Sierra Leone and Liberia, where American influence co-operates with the English in making it the harbinger of Christian civilization among the colored races of that mysterious continent, which, thanks to English-speaking missionaries like Livingstone and explorers like Stanley, is now open to foreign immigration and development. It accompanies the British navy and merchant ships to the South Sea, and must ultimately replace the barbarous native dialects of Australia, New South Wales, Van Diemen's Land, New Zealand and the Polynesian group of islands, as the natives become Christianized and civilized. The empire of Japan is fast getting Anglicized and Christianized. The English has become the court language. A New York publisher is shipping every year 50,000 American school-books for the schools of Japan. The English classics are daily read in countries of which Shakespeare and Milton never heard, and by millions who but recently were ignorant of the very existence of England.

If we look to the American hemisphere, the same language prevails in all the British possessions of North America from the Atlantic to the Pacific, including a territory of over three millions and four hundred thousand square miles and a population of about five millions, and increasing very rapidly by immigration. It prevails in the British West Indies and the Bermuda Islands.

But what is still more important, the English is now and must ever remain the speech of the great Anglo-Saxon Republic, from Maine to California, from the Northern lakes to the Gulf of Mexico. Every other language, the Indian dialects, the Spanish, the Dutch, the Danish, the Swedish, the French, and even the German, are being swept away by the irresistible current of the English tongue. The German and Scandinavian languages are gaining in the first generation by constant immigration, but in the second or third generation they are losing; while the English, without an act of tyranny or injustice to its neighbors, without any effort even, but by the mere silent power of its presence, is daily gaining upon them. In less than a century our nation has grown from three to fifty millions (in 1880), and in another century it may number two hundred millions; for the overflow of all European nations is flowing to our hospitable shores and adopting our tongue.

No intelligent immigrant should complain of this course of things which is evidently the design of Providence. The unity of language tends strongly to unite and consolidate our nationality, and to increase our power and influence. And as no other language can possibly compete with this rival on the soil of North America, the Dutchmen, Frenchmen, Germans, and Scandinavians should rejoice that the English rather than any other language, that is, the very language which comes nearest to their own, is destined ultimately to take the place of their beloved mother tongue. The Frenchman will naturally prefer his native tongue as the more elegant and graceful, but he may derive comfort from the fact that almost one-fourth of his own vocabulary is perpetuated in the English. The German, the Hollander, the Swede, the Norwegian and the Dane can emphatically say to their English neighbor, as to his character and speech: You are flesh of my flesh and bone of my bone; we are children of the same Teutonic mother, and we will thank an all-wise Providence which has reunited our energies on the virgin soil of a new world to work out his designs.

Nor should we overlook the fact that the English is generally spoken with more uniformity and purity by the people of the United States than even in England, which presents a variety of dialects, widely differing from one another, like the Scottish and the Yorkshire dialects. We have hardly any traces of different dialects and provincialisms. Neither France, nor Germany, nor Great Britain presents such a unity of language as our own country as far as it uses the Saxon tongue.[1] And as

---

[1] "There was never a case," says W. D. Whitney (*Language and the Study of Language*, N. Y., 1867, p. 172), "in which so nearly the same language was spoken throughout the whole mass of so vast a population as is the English now in America." The differences in the English of New England, the Southern States, the Northwest and the Pacific coast, are confined to a limited number of provincialisms, and affect also the pronunciation, but they are not sufficiently marked to constitute separate dialects. The English his-

the power and influence of our institutions, commerce, literature and art grows and extends with the rapidity of the railroad and telegraph, our national language follows this progress step by step, even to the soil of Liberia, to spread thence into the unexplored interior, to turn the haunts of the slaver into Christian homes, and the curse of American slavery, now happily extinguished by the blood of our civil war, into a blessing for Africa.

The English is also the language of the ocean. It is better understood and more widely spoken than any other tongue on the ships which cross the Atlantic, or Pacific, the Mediterranean, the Suez Canal, the Indian and Chinese Seas. Even on the Fjords of Norway and in the Gulf of Finland, you will scarcely meet a captain that cannot fluently converse in English.

The Samoan Conference, held this year (1889) at Berlin, between Germany, Great Britain and the United States, marks a new departure in the preference given to English for diplomacy. Formerly the Latin was used in international conferences and treaties, and is still used by the papal court. Then the French took its place and kept it in all international conferences till 1878. But in the Samoan conference, for the first time on the continent of Europe, the English was exclusively used in the discussions and in the treaty.[1] A significant fact for the future. The English race surpasses all others in successful colonization and commercial enterprise, and hence its language must inevitably become the chief organ of international communication.

torian, Edward A. Freeman, after a visit to the United States in 1882, wrote in the *Fortnightly Review:* "I never found any difficulty in understanding an American speaker, but I have often found it difficult to understand a Scotch or even a northern English speaker. The American speaks my own language; he speaks my own dialect of that language, but he speaks it with certain local differences."

[1] The conference was opened in French, but by a vote of six to three English was substituted in the preliminary negotiations and discussions. The American and British Commissioners naturally preferred their own tongue, and as Count Herbert Bismarck, who, as Minister of Foreign Affairs of Germany, presided over the conference, speaks English as fluently as he does German and French, there was no objection to the wishes of the majority.

PROVIDENTIAL DESIGN.

Who could have dreamed of such a result fourteen hundred years ago, when the savage heathen Angles and Saxons under the lead of Hengist and Horsa sailed from northern Germany to England, or eight hundred years ago, when William the Bastard, a semi-civilized robber and pirate, following the instincts of his Norman ancestors, subdued the island?

Truly, the history of the English people and language is a wonderful commentary on the truth, that "God's ways are not our ways." Those very events which to other nations would have brought ruin, proved a blessing to England. The very absence of great monarchs (with few exceptions, as Alfred, Elizabeth, Cromwell, William III., and Victoria) has secured to her a higher degree of national liberty and strength. The frequent changes of her language have increased its wealth and enlarged its destiny. The very isolation in an inhospitable home has promoted the cultivation of domestic virtues, the development of national resources, and brought out that power of self-government which fitted her to become the mistress of empires in distant parts of the globe. The very loss of the American colonies has proved a gain to England at home, and still more to her genius and language under a new and independent form in this new world of freedom and of the future.

THE ENGLISH LANGUAGE AND THE BIBLE.

Never was a nobler mission intrusted to any language. The crowning glory of this mission is its intimate connection with the triumph of the Christian religion over the nations of the earth.

We hold in the highest esteem the Greek language as the vehicle of ancient classical culture and the original organ of the everlasting truths of the gospel. But the actual use of the Greek Testament and the Latin Vulgate dwindles almost into insignificance before the circulation of the common English Bible, which is scattered by hundreds of millions of copies over the face of the earth.[1] For general accuracy, popularity, and thorough natural-

---

[1] It is estimated that in England alone between two and three millions of English Bibles are printed annually, and probably as many in the United

ization it stands unsurpassed and unequaled among all the ancient and modern translations of the oracles of the living God, and as to purity and beauty of diction it is the noblest monument of English literature. And though it may be superseded ultimately by the Anglo-American Revision of 1881 in its present or in some improved shape, we must remember that this is not a new version, but only an improvement of the old, and retains the idiom of the version of 1611 with its strong hold upon the memory and affections of the people. Yea, we may say, that the Revision will renew the youth of the venerable mother, and make her even a greater blessing for generations to come than she has been in generations past. The extraordinary interest with which the Revision was first received is certainly a most hopeful sign of the times, and proves beyond controversy that the Bible is more deeply imbedded in the affections of the English-speaking race and more inseparably connected with its progress and prosperity than with any other nation of the world. Of the Revised New Testament of 1881 about three millions of copies were sold in less than a year, and over thirty American reprints appeared; yea, the greater part of the text was telegraphed from New York to two daily papers of Chicago in advance of the arrival of the book. A fact without a parallel in the history of literature.

The Revision is sometimes charged with sacrificing idiomatic English to idiomatic Greek, and rhythm to accuracy. If so, it deserves commendation, for truth is more important than rhythm. But the objection is not well founded. In many cases the rhythm has been improved. Take the following examples:—

States, where, besides the Bible House in New York, many publishing and printing houses are exclusively engaged in the multiplication of Bibles. In the Bible House of New York three thousand to four thousand Bibles are daily manufactured. In 1886 the British and Foreign Bible Society sold and gave away 568,610 whole English Bibles and 1,123,903 English New Testaments, the American Bible Society 295,769 English Bibles and 326,918 English New Testaments (all of the authorized version), besides a large number of parts (as the Psalter and the Gospels). The works which come next in the English book market are Bunyan's Pilgrim's Progress, Robinson Crusoe, and Shakespeare. Of Shakespeare about twenty thousand copies are said to be annually sold in England.

AUTHORIZED VERSION.   *Luke* VI. 49.   REVISED VERSION.

"But he that heareth and doeth not, is like a man that without a foundation built an house upon the earth: against which the stream did beat vehemently, and immediately it fell, and the ruin of that house was great."

"But he that heareth and doeth not, is like a man that built a house upon the earth without a foundation; against which the stream brake, and straightway it fell in; and the ruin of that house was great."

AUTHORIZED VERSION.   *Matt.* VIII. 32.   REVISED VERSION.

"And behold, the whole herd of swine ran violently down a steep place into the sea, and perished in the waters."

"And behold, the whole herd rushed down the steep into the sea, and perished in the waters."

2 Thess. I. 11.

"Fulfil all the good pleasure of his goodness, and the work of faith with power."

"Fulfil every desire of goodness and every work of faith, with power."

Col. IV. 10.

"Marcus, sister's son to Barnabas."

"Mark, the cousin of Barnabas."

Rev. VII. 17.

"Unto living fountains of water."

"Unto fountains of waters of life."

But the Authorized Version has the great advantage of venerable age and sacred associations, which in the minds of many conservative Bible readers far outweigh its imperfections, and will long keep it in private and public use. It fully deserves the eulogy of the ardent hymnist, Frederick W. Faber, who after his secession to Rome could not forget "the uncommon beauty and marvelous English of the Protestant Bible," and who said of it with as much beauty as truth: "It lives on the ear like a music that can never be forgotten, like the sound of church bells, which the convert hardly knows how he can forego. Its felicities often seem to be almost things rather than mere words. The memory of the dead passes into it. The potent traditions of childhood are stereotyped in its verses. The power of all the griefs and trials of man is hidden beneath its words.

It is the representative of his best moments, and all that there has been about him of soft, and gentle, and pure, and penitent, and good, speaks to him forever out of his English Bible."

CONCLUSION.

The progress of the language of Great Britain and America is the progress of commerce and industry, of a rich and healthy literature, of the arts and sciences, of the highest form of civilization known in history, of the power of self-government, of civil and religious freedom, of domestic virtue, of happy homes, of active philanthropy, of national prosperity, and of the truths of Christianity, bearing on its banner the angelic inscription :—

"Glory to God in the highest,
Peace on earth among men of his good pleasure."

Well may we bid Godspeed to the progress of the Anglo-Norman and Anglo-American tongue, as the chief organ for the spread of Christian civilization.

"Go forth, then, noble Saxon tongue,
And speed the happy time
When truth and righteousness shall reign
In every zone and clime ;
When earth's oppressed and savage tribes
Shall cease to pine and roam,
All taught to prize the English words:
Faith, Freedom, Heaven, and Home."

THE POETRY OF THE BIBLE.

ORIGIN OF POETRY AND MUSIC.

Poetry and music are the highest and most spiritual of the fine arts. They are twin sisters. They hail from a prehistoric age. The Bible traces their origin to the celestial world. When man was created in God's image, "the morning stars sang together, and all the sons of God shouted for joy." Christianity was sung into the world by an anthem of the angelic host.

Raphael paints St. Cecilia, the patroness of church music, as standing between St. Paul and St. John, St. Augustin and Mary Magdalene, as holding an organ in her hands, and listening with rapture to a higher and sweeter chorus of six angels in heaven. The master-compositions of Händel, Mozart, and Beethoven make the impression of supernatural inspiration, and sound like voices from a higher and purer world. We may call the creations of music, to use the language of a great English divine[1]—"the outpourings of eternal harmony in the medium of created sound; they are echoes from our Home; they are the voice of Angels, or the Magnificat of Saints, or the living laws of Divine governance, or the Divine attributes; something are they beside themselves, which we cannot compass, which we cannot utter—though mortal man, and he perhaps not otherwise distinguished above his fellows, has the gift of eliciting them."

As poetry and music began in heaven, so they will end, without end, in heaven and constitute an unfailing fountain of joy and bliss to the innumerable army of the redeemed.

In these arts the power of creation is continued. Every true poet, as the word indicates,[2] is a maker or creator. To create anything out of nothing is indeed the sole prerogative of the Almighty. But the poet recreates out of existing material. He has at his command the starry heavens and flowery fields, the

---

[1] Cardinal Newman, in the last of his sermons preached in the University of Oxford (1843).   [2] ποιητής, from ποιεω, to make, to create.

snow-capped mountains and fertile valleys, the boundless ocean and the murmuring brook, the beauties of nature and the experiences of history, the feelings and passions of individuals and the rise and fall of nations; out of these exhaustless stores he constructs an ideal world of beauty for the delight of man.

This creative power of poetry has found classic expression in the passage of Shakespeare, who himself possessed it in a most eminent degree:—

> "The poet's eye, in a fine frenzy rolling,
> Doth glance from heaven to earth, from earth to heaven,
> And as imagination bodies forth
> The forms of things unknown, the poet's pen
> Turns them to shapes, and gives to airy nothing
> A local habitation and a name."

POETRY AND INSPIRATION.

In a wider sense all true poetry is inspired by a higher power. The poet and the prophet are akin. They were regarded by the Greeks as friends of the gods; and all ceremonies, oracles and mysteries of religion were clothed in poetic dress. They often give utterance to ideas which they do not fully understand. Their genius is carried beyond the ordinary consciousness and self-possession; it soars above the clouds; it moves in an ecstatic condition of mind, bordering on madness.

> "Great wits to madness, sure, are near allied,
> And thin partitions do their walls divide."[1]

Goethe makes the remark that "the unconscious" is the deepest element in poetry, and that his tragedy of Faust proceeded from a "dark state" of his mind.

There is, however, a twofold inspiration, Divine and Satanic. The poetry which administers to the sensual passions, which idolizes the creature, which ridicules virtue and makes vice lovely and attractive, is the product of the evil spirit.

POETRY AND RELIGION.

Poetry and music came from the same God as religion, and are intended for the same holy end. They are the handmaids

[1] Dryden.

of religion, and the wings of devotion. Nothing can be more preposterous than to assume an antagonism between them. The abuse can never set aside the right use. The best gifts of God are liable to the worst abuse.

Some have the false notion that poetry is necessarily fictitious and antagonistic to truth. But poetry is the fittest expression of truth; it is the truth in festal dress, the silver picture of the golden apple, the ideal embodied in and shining through the real.

"Let those," says Lowth, "who affect to despise the Muses, cease to attempt, for the vices of a few who may abuse the best of things, to bring into disrepute a most laudable talent. Let them cease to speak of that art as light and trifling in itself, to accuse it as profane or impious; that art which has been conceded to man by the favor of his Creator, and for the most sacred purposes; that art, consecrated by the authority of God Himself, and by His example in His most august ministrations."[1] Dean Stanley says:[2] "There has always been, in certain minds, a repugnance to poetry, as inconsistent with the gravity of religious feeling. It has been sometimes thought that to speak of a book of the Bible as poetical, is a disparagement of it. It has been in many churches thought that the more scholastic, dry and prosaic the forms in which religious doctrine is thrown, the more faithfully is its substance represented. To such sentiments the towering greatness of David, the acknowledged preëminence of the Psalter, are constant rebukes. David, beyond king, soldier or prophet, was the sweet singer of Israel. Had Raphael painted a picture of Hebrew as of European Poetry, David would have sat aloft at the summit of the Hebrew Parnassus, the Homer of Jewish song."

THE POETRY OF THE BIBLE.

The Jews paid little attention to the arts of design; sculpture and painting were forbidden in the second commandment, on account of the danger of idolatry. For the same reason they are forbidden among the Moslems. As to architecture, the only

---

[1] *Lectures on Hebrew Poetry*, Stowe's ed., p. 28.
[2] *History of the Jewish Church*, Vol. II., p. 164, Am. ed.

great and beautiful work of this art was the temple of Jerusalem. Nothing can be more striking to a traveller than the contrast between Egypt covered all over with ruins of temples, statues and pictures of the gods, and Palestine which has no such ruins. The remains of the few synagogues are of the plainest kind and destitute of all ornament.

But in poetry the case is reversed. Of all ancient nations, except the Greeks, the Hebrews have by far the richest poetry, and in *religious* poetry they greatly excel the Hindoos, Persians, Egyptians, Greeks and Romans.

More than one-third of the Old Testament is poetry. This fact is concealed and much of the beauty of the Bible lost to English readers by the absence of quantity, metre and rhyme, and by the uniform printing of poetry and prose in our popular Bibles. The current versicular division is mechanical and does not correspond to the metrical structure of Hebrew poetry. The Revised Version corrects the defect, at least in part, namely in the book of Job and in the Psalter, in the poems scattered through the historical books, as Gen. iv. 23–24; xlix. 2–27; Ex. xv. 1–21; Deut. xxxii. 1–43; xxxiii. 2–29; Judges v. 2–31, etc., and in a few lyric sections of the Prophets (Jonah iv. 2–10; Habakkuk iii. 2–19). The same method ought to have been carried through the Prophets, all of whom, except Daniel, delivered the prophetic messages in poetry.

The older commentators and divines paid little or no attention to the literary and æsthetic features of the Bible. The study of Hebrew poetry as poetry is comparatively recent and dates from the middle of the eighteenth century, although its power and beauty were felt long before. Lowth, Herder and Ewald are the first masters in this department of Biblical literature.

The poetry of the Old Testament is contained in the Poetical Books, which in the Jewish Canon are included among the *Hagiographa* or *Holy Writings*. They embrace the Book of Job, the Psalter, the Proverbs, Ecclesiastes, and the Song of Solomon. Besides these the Lamentations of Jeremiah and most of the Prophets are likewise poetic in sentiment and form, or they vibrate between poetry and prose. A number of lyric songs, odes, and prophecies are scattered through the historical books.

The poetic sections of the New Testament are the *Magnificat* of the blessed Virgin, the *Benedictus* of Zachariah, the *Gloria in Excelsis* of the Angels, the *Nunc Dimittis* of Simeon, the Parables of our Lord, the Anthems of the Apocalypse, and several poetic quotations in the Epistles.

But we may say that the whole Bible is cast in a poetic mould. The Hebrews were a highly imaginative people. The Hebrew language, as Herder says, is itself a poem. Some of the prose of the Bible is equal to the best poetry, and blends truth and beauty in harmony. It approaches also, in touching the highest themes, the rhythmical form of Hebrew poetry, and may be arranged according to the parallelism of members. Moses was a poet as well as an historian. Every prophet or seer is a poet, though not every poet is a prophet.[1]

The prose of the New Testament is no less poetic than that of the Old. What can be at once more truthful, more eloquent, and more beautiful than the Beatitudes and the whole Sermon on the Mount, the Parables of our Lord, the Prologue of St. John, the seraphic description of love by St. Paul, and his triumphant pæan at the close of the eighth chapter of the Epistle to the Romans? In the opinion of Erasmus, an excellent judge of literary merit, Paul was more eloquent than Cicero.[2]

In this wider sense the Bible begins and ends with poetry, and clothes the first and last facts of Divine revelation in the garb of beauty. The retrospective vision of the first creation and the prospective vision of the new heavens and the new earth are presented in language which rises to the summit of poetic sublimity and power. There is nothing more pregnant and sublime in thought, and at the same time more terse and classical in expression, than the sentence of the Creator:—

"Let there be light! And there was light."

There can be no nobler and higher conception of man than

---

[1] Isaac Taylor says (*The Spirit of Hebrew Poetry*, page 68): "Biblical utterances of the first truths in theology possess the grandeur of the loftiest poetry, as well as a rhythmical or artificial structure."

[2] "*Quid unquam Cicero dixit grandiloquentius?*" says Erasmus, in reference to the eighth chapter of Romans. The heathen Longinus placed Paul among the greatest orators.

that with which the Bible introduces him into the world as the very image and likeness of the infinite God. And the idea of a paradise of innocence, love and peace at the threshold of history is poetry as well as reality, casting its sunshine over the gloom of the fall, and opening the prospect of a future paradise regained. Then, passing from the first chapter of Genesis to the last of the Apocalypse, how lovely and comforting is St. John's description of the New Jerusalem. It has inspired those hymns of heavenly homesickness, from "*Ad perennis vitæ fontem*" to "Jerusalem the Golden," which cheer the weary pilgrim on his home-bound journey through the wilderness of life.

The poetry of the Old Testament has always been an essential part of Jewish and Christian worship. The Psalter was the first, and for many centuries the only hymn-book of the Church. It is the most fruitful source of Christian hymnody. Many of the finest English and German hymns are free reproductions of Hebrew psalms; the 23d Psalm alone has furnished the keynote to a large number of Christian hymns, and the 46th Psalm to Luther's masterpiece:—

"*Ein' feste Burg ist unser Gott.*"

As among other nations, so among the Jews, poetry was the oldest form of composition. It precedes prose, as youth precedes manhood, and as feeling and imagination are active before sober reflection and logical reasoning.

Much of the Hebrew poetry is lost. Solomon composed a thousand and five songs (1 Kings iv. 32). "The Books of the Wars of Jehovah" (Num. xxi. 14) and "The Book of Jashar," or the Upright (Josh. x. 13; 2 Sam. i. 18) were at least partly poetic. Jeremiah composed an elegy for Josiah (2 Chron. xxxv. 25).

Poetry and music were closely connected, and accompanied domestic and social life in seasons of joy and sorrow. They cheered the wedding, the harvest and other feasts (Jos. ix. 3; Judg. xxi. 19; Amos vi. 5; Ps. iv. 8). They celebrated victory after a battle, as the song of Moses, Ex. xv., and the song of Deborah, Judg. v.; they greeted the victor on his return, 1 Sam. xviii. 8. The shepherd sung while watching his flock, the hunter in the pursuit of his prey. Maidens deplored the death of Jephthah's daughter in songs (Judg. xi. 40), and David, the death of Saul and Jonathan (2 Sam. i. 18), and afterward of Abner (2 Sam. iii. 33). Love was the theme of a nobler inspiration than among the sensual Greeks, and the Song celebrates the Hebrew ideal of pure bridal love, as reflecting the love of Jehovah to His people, and prefiguring the union of Christ with His church.

THE SPIRIT OF BIBLE POETRY.

The poetry of the Bible is in the highest and best sense the poetry of revelation and inspiration. It is animated by the genius of the true religion, by the Spirit of Jehovah; and hence rises far above the religious poetry of the Hindoos, Parsees and Greeks, as the religion of revelation is above the religion of nature, and the God of the Bible above the idols of the heathen. It is the poetry of truth and holiness. It never administers to trifling vanities and lower passions; it is the chaste and spotless priestess at the altar. It reveals the mysteries of the Divine will to man, and offers up man's prayers and thanks to his Maker. It is consecrated to the glory of Jehovah and the moral perfection of man.

The most obvious feature of Bible poetry is its intense Theism. The question of the existence of God is never raised, and an atheist is simply set down as a fool (Ps. xiv.). The Hebrew poet lives and moves in the idea of a living God, as a self-revealing, personal, almighty, holy, omniscient, all-pervading and merciful Being, and overflows with his adoration and praise. He sees and hears God in the works of creation and in the events of history. Jehovah is to him the Maker and Preserver of all things. He shines in the firmament; He rides on the thunder-storm; He clothes the lilies; He feeds the ravens and young lions, and the cattle on a thousand hills; He gives rain and fruitful seasons. He is the God of Abraham, Isaac and Jacob, of Moses, David, and the Prophets. He is the ever-present help and shield, the comfort and joy of Israel. He is just and holy in His judgments, good, merciful and true in all His dealings. He rules and overrules even the wrath of man for His own glory and the good of His people.

To this all-prevailing Theism corresponds the anthropology and ethics of the Bible. Man is always represented under his most important moral and religious relations, in the state of innocence, in the terrible slavery of sin, and in the process of redemption and restoration to more than his original glory and dominion over the creation. Hebrew poetry reflects in fresh and life-like colors the working of God's law and promise on the heart of the pious, and every state of his experience, the deep emotions of repentance and grief, faith and trust, gratitude and praise, hope and aspiration, love and peace.

Another characteristic of Bible poetry is the combination of childlike simplicity and sublimity. The grandest ideas are set forth and brought home to the heart of every reader who has a lively organ for religious truth. The Psalms and the Parables are alike suited to the capacity of the young and the old, the cultured and the uncultured. They are popular and yet elevated, luminous and yet profound, easily comprehended and yet inexhaustibly deep. We never get tired of them, and every reading reveals new treasures.

More than this, the Bible poetry has a cosmopolitan character and a universal interest. It is as well adapted to Christians in America in this nineteenth century as it was to the Jews in Palestine centuries before Christ.

The scenery and style are thoroughly oriental and Hebrew, and yet they can be translated into every language without losing by the process—which cannot be said of any other poetry. Greek and Roman poetry have more art and variety, more elegance and finish, but no such popularity, catholicity and adaptability. The heart of humanity beats in the Hebrew poet. It is true, his experience falls far short of that of the Christian. Yet nearly every phase of Old Testament piety strikes a corresponding chord in the soul of the Christian; and such are the depths of the Divine Spirit who guided the genius of the sacred singers that their words convey far more than they themselves were conscious of, and reach prophetically forward into the most distant future.

All this applies with special force to the Psalter, the holy of holies in Hebrew poetry, and in the Psalter to the psalms which bear the name of David, "the singer of Israel." He was placed by Providence in the different situations of shepherd, courtier, outlaw, warrior, conqueror, king, that he might the more vividly set forth Jehovah as the Good Shepherd, the ever-present Helper, the mighty Conqueror, the just and merciful Sovereign. He was open to all the emotions of friendship and love, generosity and mercy; he enjoyed the highest joys and honors; he suffered poverty, persecution and exile, the loss of his dearest friend, treason and rebellion from his own son. Even his changing moods and passions, his sins and crimes, which with their swift and fearful punishments form a domestic tragedy of rare terror and pathos, were overruled and turned into lessons of humility, comfort and gratitude. All this rich spiritual biography from his early youth to his old age, together with God's merciful dealings with him, are written in his hymns, though with reference to his inward states of mind rather than his outward condition, so that readers of very different situation or position in life might yet be able to sympathize with the feelings and emotions expressed. His hymns give us a deeper glance into his inmost heart and his secret communion with God than the narrative of his life in the historical books. They are remarkable for simplicity, freshness, vivacity, warmth, depth and vigor of feeling, childlike tenderness and heroic faith, and the all-pervading fear and love of God. "In all his works," says the author of Ecclesiasticus (xlvii. 8–12), "he praised the Holy One; to the Most High he sang with all his heart in words of glory, and loved Him that made him. He set singers also before the altar, that by their voices they might make sweet melody and daily sing praises in their songs. He beautified their feasts and set in order the solemn times until the end, that they might praise His holy name, and make the temple resound from the morning. The Lord took away his sins and exalted his horn forever; He gave him a covenant of kings and a throne of glory in Israel."[1]

---

[1] Comp. Ewald's admirable portrait of David as a poet, in the first volume of *Die Dichter des A. B.*, p. 25. Dean Perowne, in his Commentary on the *Psalms*, Vol. I., pp. 8, 9, third ed. (1873), gives this truthful description of him: "As David's life shines in his poetry, so also does his character. That

This inseparable union with religion, with truth and holiness, gives to Hebrew poetry an enduring charm and undying power for good in all ages and countries. It never gets out of date, and never grows old. The dew of youth is upon it. It brings us into the immediate presence of the great Jehovah, it raises us above the miseries of earth, it dispels the clouds of darkness; it inspires, ennobles, purifies and imparts peace and joy; it gives us a foretaste of heaven itself. Ewald truly says of Hebrew poetry: "It is the interpreter of the sublimest religious ideas for all times, and herein lies its most important and imperishable value."[1]

In this respect the poetry of the Bible is as far above classic poetry as the Bible itself is above all other books. Homer and Virgil dwindle into insignificance as compared with David and Asaph, if we look to the moral effect upon the heart and the life

character was no common one. It was strong with all the strength of man, tender with all the tenderness of woman. Naturally brave, his courage was heightened and confirmed by that faith in God which never, in the worst extremity, forsook him. Naturally warm-hearted, his affections struck their roots deep into the innermost centre of his being. In his love for his parents, for whom he provided in his own extreme peril—in his love for his wife Michal—for his friend Jonathan, whom he loved as his own soul—for his darling Absalom, whose death almost broke his heart—even for the infant whose loss he dreaded—we see the same man, the same depth and truth, the same tenderness of personal affection. On the other hand, when stung with a sense of wrong or injustice, his sense of which was peculiarly keen, he could flash out into strong words and strong deeds. He could hate with the same fervor that he loved. Evil men and evil things, all that was at war with goodness and with God—for these he found no abhorrence too deep, scarcely any imprecations too strong. Yet he was, withal, placable and ready to forgive. He could exercise a prudent self-control, if he was occasionally impetuous. His true courtesy, his chivalrous generosity to his foes, his rare delicacy, his rare self-denial, are all traits which present themselves most forcibly as we read his history. He is the truest of heroes in the genuine elevation of his character, no less than in the extraordinary incidents of his life. Such a man cannot wear a mask in his writings. Depth, tenderness, fervor, mark all his poems."

[1] Winer, too, derives from the religious character of Hebrew poetry its "sublime flight and never-dying beauty." Angus says: "The peculiar excellence of the Hebrew poetry is to be ascribed to the employment of it in the noblest service, that of religion. It presents the loftiest and most precious truths, expressed in the most appropriate language."

of the reader. The classic poets reach only a small and cultured class; but the singers of the Bible come home to men of every grade of education, every race and color, every condition of life, and every creed and sect. The Psalter is, as Luther calls it, "a manual of all the saints," where each one finds the most truthful description of his own situation, especially in seasons of affliction. It has retained its hold upon the veneration and affections of pious Jews and Christians for these three thousand years, and is even now and will ever be more extensively used as a guide of private devotion and public worship than any other book. "When Christian martyrs, and Scottish Covenanters in dens and caves of the earth, when French exiles and English fugitives in their hiding-places during the panic of revolution or of mutiny, received a special comfort from the Psalms, it was because they found themselves literally side by side with the author in the cavern of Adullam, or on the cliffs of Engedi, or beyond the Jordan, escaping from Saul or from Absalom, from the Philistines or from the Assyrians. When Burleigh or Locke seemed to find an echo in the Psalms to their own calm philosophy, it was because they were listening to the strains which had proceeded from the mouth or charmed the ear of the sagacious king or the thoughtful statesman of Judah. It has often been observed that the older we grow, the more interest the Psalms possess for us as individuals; and it may at most be said that by these multiplied associations, the older the human race grows, the more interest do they possess for mankind."[1]

POETIC MERIT.

In its religious character, as just described, lies the crowning excellence of the poetry of the Bible. The spiritual ideas are the main thing, and they rise in richness, purity, sublimity and universal importance immeasurably beyond the literature of all other nations of antiquity.

But as to the artistic and æsthetic form, it is altogether subordinate to the contents, and held in subserviency to the lofty aim. Moses, David, Solomon, Isaiah, and the author of the Book of

---

[1] Stanley: *Hist. of the Jewish Church*, II. 167.

Job, possessed evidently the highest gifts of poetry, but they restrained them, lest human genius should outshine the Divine grace, or the silver picture be estimated above the golden apple. The poetry of the Bible, like the whole Bible, wears the garb of humility and condescends to men of low degree, in order to raise them up. It gives no encouragement to the idolatry of genius, and glorifies God alone. "Not unto us, O Lord, not unto us, but unto Thy name give glory" (Ps. cxv. 1).

Hence an irreligious or immoral man is apt to be repelled by the Bible; he feels himself in an uncongenial atmosphere, and is made uneasy and uncomfortable by the rebukes of sin and the praise of a holy God. He will not have this book rule over him or disturb him in his worldly modes of thought and habits of life.

Others are unable to divest themselves of early prejudices for classical models; they esteem external polish more highly than ideas, and can enjoy no poetry which is not cast in the ancient Greek or modern mould, and moves on in the regular flow of uniform metre, stanza, and rhyme. And yet these are not essential to true poetry. The rhyme was unknown to Homer, Pindar, Sophocles, Virgil and Horace; it was even despised by Milton as "the invention of a barbarous age to set off wretched matter and lame metre, as the jingling sound of like endings trivial to all judicious ears and of no true musical delight." This is indeed going to the opposite extreme; for although rhyme and even metre are by no means necessary in the epos and drama, they yet belong to the *perfection* of some forms of *lyric* poetry, which is the twin sister of music.

If we study the Bible poetry on its own ground, and with unclouded eyes, we may find in it forms of beauty as high and enduring as in that of any nation ancient or modern. Even its artless simplicity and naturalness are the highest triumph of art. Simplicity always enters into good taste. Those poems and songs which are the outgushings of the heart, without any show of artificial labor, are the most popular, and never lose their hold on the heart. We feel that we could make them ourselves, and yet only a high order of genius could produce them.

Where is there a nobler ode of liberty, of national deliverance and independence, than the Song of Moses on the overthrow of Pharaoh in the Red Sea (Ex. xv.)? Where a grander panorama of creation than in the one hundred and fourth Psalm? Where a more charming and loving pastoral than the twenty-third Psalm? Where such a high view of the dignity and destiny of man as in the eighth Psalm? Where a profounder sense of sin and Divine forgiveness than in the thirty-second and fifty-first Psalms? Where such a truthful and overpowering description of the vanity of human life and the never-changing character of the holy and just, yet merciful God, as in the ninetieth Psalm? Where have the infinite greatness and goodness of God, his holiness, righteousness, long-suffering and mercy, the wonders of His government, and the feeling of dependence on Him, of joy and peace in Him, of gratitude for His blessings, of praise of His glory, found truer and fitter embodiment than in the Psalter and the Prophets? Where will you find more sweet, tender, and delicate expression of innocent love than in the Song of Songs, which sounds like the singing of birds in sunny May from the flowery fields and the tree of life in Paradise? The Prayer of Moses (Psalm xc.) has been styled "the most sublime of human compositions, the deepest in feeling, loftiest in theologic conception, the most magnificent in its imagery." Isaiah is, in the judgment of the ablest critics, one of the greatest of poets as well as of prophets, of an elevation, a richness, a compass, a power and comfort that are unequalled. No human genius ever soared so high as this evangelist of the old dispensation. Jeremiah, the prophet of sorrow and affliction, has furnished the richest supply of the language of holy grief in seasons of public calamity and distress, from the destruction of Jerusalem down to the latest siege of Paris; and few works have done this work more effectively than his *Lamentations*. And what shall we say of the Book of Job, the Shakespeare in the Bible? Where are such bold and vivid descriptions of the wonders of nature, of the behemoth, the leviathan, and of the war-horse? What can be finer than Job's picture of wisdom, whose price is far above rubies? And what a wealth of comfort is in that wonderful passage, which inspired the sublimest solo in the sublimest musical composition, those words graven in the rock forever, where this patriarchal sage and saint of the order of Melchisedec expresses his faith and hope that his "Redeemer liveth," and that the righteous shall see Him face to face.

TRIBUTES OF POETS AND SCHOLARS TO HEBREW POETRY.

The times for the depreciation of Bible poetry have passed. Many of the greatest scholars and poets, some of whom by no means in sympathy with its religious ideas, have done it full justice. I quote a few of them who represent different standpoints and nationalities.

Henry Stephens, the greatest philologist of the sixteenth century, thought that there was nothing more poetic (ποιητικώτερον), nothing more musical (μουσικώτερον), nothing more thrilling (γοργώτερον), nothing more full of lofty inspiration (διθυραμβικώτερον) than the Psalms of David.

John Milton, notwithstanding his severe classic taste, judges: "There are no songs comparable to the songs of Zion, no orations equal to those of the Prophets, and no politics like those which the Scriptures teach." And as to the Psalms, he says: "Not in their divine arguments alone, but in the very critical art of composition, the Psalms may be easily made to appear over all the kinds of lyric poesy incomparable."

Sir William Jones: "I have regularly and attentively read the Holy Scriptures, and am of the opinion that this volume, independently of its divine origin, contains more true sublimity, more exquisite beauty, more important history and finer strains both of poetry and eloquence, than could be collected from all other books."

Sir D. K. Sandford: "In lyric flow and fire, in crushing force and majesty, the poetry of the ancient Scriptures is the most superb that ever burnt within the breast of man."

John von Müller, the German Tacitus: "There is nothing in Greece, nothing in Rome, nothing in all the West, like David, who selected the God of Israel to sing Him in higher strains than ever praised the gods of the Gentiles."

Herder, who was at home in the literature of all ages and countries, is full of enthusiastic admiration for the pure and sublime beauties of Hebrew poetry, as may be seen on almost every page of his celebrated work on the subject. He regards it as "the oldest, simplest, sublimest" of all poetry, and in the form of a dialogue between Alciphron and Eutyphron, after the Platonic fashion, he triumphantly vindicates its merits against all objections, and illustrates it with admirable translations of choice passages.

Goethe pronounced the book of Ruth "the loveliest thing in the shape of an epic or idyl which has come down to us."

Alexander von Humboldt, in his "Cosmos" (where the name of God scarcely occurs, except in an extract from the heathen Aristotle), praises the Hebrew description of nature as unrivalled, especially the 104th Psalm, as "presenting in itself a picture of the whole world." "Nature," he says, "is to the Hebrew poet not a self-dependent object, but a work of creation and order, the living expression of the omnipresence of the Divinity in the visible world."

Thomas Carlyle calls the Book of Job, "apart from all theories about it, one of the grandest things ever written by man. A noble book! All men's book! Such living likenesses were never since drawn. Sublime sorrow, sublime reconciliation; oldest choral melody, as of the heart of manhood; so soft and great as the summer midnight; as the world with its seas and stars. There is nothing written, I think, of equal literary merit."

Isaac Taylor: "The Hebrew writers as poets were masters of all the means and the resources, the powers and the stores, of the loftiest poetry, but subservient to a far loftier purpose than that which ever animates human genius."

Heinrich Ewald calls the old Hebrew poetry "unique in its kind and in many respects unsurpassed, because as to its contents it is the interpreter of those sublime religious thoughts which lived in Israel, and are found nowhere else in antiquity in such purity, vigor and durability, and as to its form it has a wonderful simplicity and naivete flowing from that sublimity of thought."

Dean Stanley: "The Psalms are beyond question poetical from first to last, and he will be a bold man who shall say that a book is less inspired, or less true, or less orthodox, or less

Divine, because it is like the Psalms. The Prophet, in order to take root in the common life of the people, must become a Psalmist."

J. J. Stewart Perowne: "The very excellence of the Psalms is their universality. They spring from the deep fountains of the human heart, and God, in His providence, and by His Spirit, has so ordered it, that they should be for His Church an everlasting heritage. Hence they express the sorrows, the joys, the aspirations, the struggles, the victories, not of one man, but of all. And if we ask, How comes this to pass? the answer is not far to seek. One object is ever before the eyes and the heart of the Psalmist. All enemies, all distresses, all persecutions, all sins, are seen in the light of God. It is to Him that the cry goes up; it is to Him that the heart is laid bare; it is to Him that the thanksgiving is uttered. This it is which makes them so true, so precious, so universal. No surer proof of their inspiration can be given than this, that they are 'not of an age, but for all time,' that the ripest Christian can use them in the fulness of his Christian manhood, though the words are the words of one who lived centuries before the coming of Christ in the flesh."

CLASSIFICATION OF BIBLE POETRY.

Strictly speaking, there are only three classes of pure poetry in which imagination and feeling are controlling factors. These are LYRIC, EPIC, and DRAMATIC.

Lyric poetry is the poetry of subjective emotions; epic poetry, the poetry of objective narration; dramatic poetry, the poetry of living action.[1]

But there is a mixed kind, called DIDACTIC poetry. It is the product of reflection as well as of imagination. It runs into philosophy and ethics. The first three kinds have their aim in themselves. Didactic poetry has its aim beyond itself, in instruction or improvement, and uses the poetic form as a means to an end.

Bible poetry is chiefly lyric and didactic. Many writers

---

[1] Goethe says: "*Es gibt nur drei echte Naturformen der Poesie: die klar erzählende, die enthusiastisch aufgeregte und die persönlich handelnde: Epos, Lyrik und Drama.*"

admit only these two kinds.[1] But we must add to them as subordinate forms, PROPHETIC and DRAMATIC poetry.

Prophetic poetry may be regarded as a branch of didactic, or, perhaps better, as a substitute for epic poetry. The revealed religion excludes mythology and hero-worship, which control the epic poetry of the heathen. It substitutes for them monotheism, which is inconsistent with any kind of idolatry. The real hero, so to speak, of the history of revelation is Jehovah Himself, the only true and living God, to whom all glory is due. And so He appears in the prophetic writings. He is the one object of worship, praise and thanksgiving, but not the object of a narrative poem. He is the one sovereign actor, who in heaven originates and controls all events on earth, but not one among other actors, coöperating or conflicting with finite beings.

There are epic elements in several lyric poems which celebrate certain great events in Jewish history, as the Song of Moses, Exod. xv., and the Song of Deborah, Judg. v.; yet even here the lyric element preponderates, and the subjectivity of the poet is not lost in the objective event as in the genuine epos. The Book of Ruth has been called an epos. The Prologue and Epilogue of Job are epic, and have a truly narrative and objective character; but they are only the framework of the poem itself, which is essentially didactic in dramatic form. In the apocryphal books the epic element appears in the book of Tobit and the book of Judith, which stand between narrative and fiction, and correspond to what we call romance or novel.

Dramatic poetry occurs in close connection with lyric and didactic poetry, but is subordinate to them, and is not so fully developed as in Greek literature.

I. LYRIC POETRY.

Lyric poetry, or the poetry of feeling, is the oldest and predominant form of poetry among the Hebrew as all other Semitic

---

[1] So Perowne (*The Book of Psalms*, Vol. I., p. 1, third ed.) : "The poetry of the Hebrews is mainly of two kinds, lyrical and didactic. They have no epic and no drama. Dramatic elements are to be found in many of their odes, and the Book of Job and the Song of Songs have sometimes been called Divine dramas ; but dramatic poetry, in the proper sense of that term, was altogether unknown to the Israelites."

nations. It is the easiest, the most natural, and best adapted for devotion both private and public. It wells up from the human heart, and gives utterance to its many strong and tender emotions of love and friendship, of joy and gladness, of grief and sorrow, of hope and desire, of gratitude and praise. Ewald happily describes it as "the daughter of the moment, of swift, rising, powerful feelings, of deep stirrings and fiery emotions of the soul."[1]

Lyric poetry, as the name indicates,[2] is closely connected with music, its twin sister. The song of Lamech and the song of Moses were accompanied by musical instruments. David was a poet and a musician and sang his hymns to the sound of the harp or guitar. The minstrel and gleeman of the middle ages represent the same union.

Among the Greeks the epos appears first; but older lyric effusions may have been lost. Among the Hindoos they are preserved in the Vedas. Lyric poetry is found among all nations which have a poetic literature; but epic poetry, at least in its fuller development, is not so general, and hence cannot be the primitive form.

Lyric poetry contains the fruitful germs of all other kinds of poetry. When the poetic feeling is kindled by a great event in history, it expresses itself more or less epically, as in the battle and victory hymns of Moses and Deborah. When the poet desires to teach a great truth or practical lesson, he becomes didactic. When he exhibits his emotions in the form of action and real life, he approaches the drama. In like manner the

---

[1] Ewald, *Dichter des A. B. L.*, p. 17: "*Die lyrische Dichtung oder das Lied ist überall die nächste Art von Dichtung, welche bei irgend einem Volke entsteht. Sie ist es deren Wesen nach: denn sie ist die Tochter des Augenblicks, schnell emporkommender gewaltiger Empfindungen, tiefer Rührungen und feuriger Bewegungen des Gemüthes, von welchen der Dichter so ganz hingerissen ist, dass er in sich wie verloren, nichts als sie, so gewaltig wie sie in ihm leben, aussprechen will. Sie ist es ebenso der Zeit nach: das kurze Lied ist die beständigste, unverwüstlichste Theil von Poesie, die erste und letzte Regung dichterischer Stimmung, wie eine unversiegbare Quelle, welche zu jeder Zeit sich wieder frisch ergiessen kann. Sie ist also auch bei allen Völkern nothwendig die älteste, die, welche zuerst eine dichterische Gestaltung und Kunst gründet und allen übrigen Arten von Dichtung die Wege bahnt.*" On p. 91 Ewald says: "*Und so bleibt das Lied in seinem ganzen reinen und vollen Wesen wie der Anfang so das Ende aller Dichtung.*"

[2] From λύρα, a stringed instrument.

lyric poetry may give rise to mixed forms which appear in the later stages of literature.[1]

THE SONG OF LAMECH.

The oldest known specimen of lyric poetry and of all poetry (excepting the Divine poem of creation) is the song of Lamech to his two wives (Gen. iv. 23). It has already the measured arrangement, alliteration and musical correspondence of Hebrew parallelism. It is a proud, fierce, defiant "sword-song," commemorating in broken, fragmentary utterances the invention of weapons of brass and iron by Lamech's son, Tubal-Cain (*i. e.*, lance-maker), and threatening vengeance:—

> "Adah and Zillah! hear my voice;
> Ye wives of Lamech, listen to my speech:
> For I have slain[2] a man for wounding me,
> Even a young man for bruising me.
> Lo! Cain shall be avenged seven-fold,
> But Lamech seventy and seven-fold." [3]

---

[1] Ewald, *l. c.*, p. 1 sq.: "*Der besondere Zweck, welchen der Dichter verfolgen mag, kann im Allgemeinen nur ein dreifacher sein: er will entweder mit seinen geflügelten Worten wie mit einer Lehre andre treffen, oder er will erzählend beschreiben, oder endlich er will das volle Leben selbst ebenso lebendig wiedergeben: und so werden* LEHRDICHTUNG, SAGENDICHTUNG (*Epos*, *und* LEBENSDICHTUNG (*Drama*) *die drei Arten höherer Dichtung sein, welche sich überall wie von selbst ausbilden wollen. Erst wenn sie sich vollkommen ausgebildet haben, entstehen auch wohl neue* ZWITTERARTEN, *indem das Lied als die Urart aller Dichtung seine eigenthümliche Weise mit einer derselben neu verschmilzt und diese stets nächste und allgegenwärtigste Urdichtung sich so in neuer Schöpfung mannichfach verjüngt.*"

[2] The perfect, *I have slain* (הָרַגְתִּי, Sept. ἀπέκτεινα, Vulg. *occidi*), is probably used in the spirit of arrogant boasting, to express the future with all the certainty of an accomplished fact. Chrysostom, Theodoret, Jerome, Jarchi and others set Lamech down as a murderer (of Cain), who here confesses his deed to ease his conscience; but Aben-Ezra, Calvin, Herder, Ewald, Delitzsch, take the verb as a threat: "I will slay any man who wounds me." Dillmann combines the past and the future: "*Das Perfectum kann nicht den Vorsatz ausdrücken, auch nicht die blosse Gewissheit, sondern nur die vollzogene That, die er aber in ähnlichem Falle zu wiederholen nicht zögern wird.*" The R. V. puts the future into the margin: *I will slay.*

[3] The law of blood for blood is strongly expressed also in the tragic poetry

Here we have the origin of *secular* poetry, and also of music (for the other son of Lamech, Jubal, *i. e.*, Harper, invented musical instruments), in connection with the progressive material civilization of the descendants of Cain.

The other poetic remains of the ante-Mosaic age are the Prediction of Noah concerning his three sons (Gen. ix. 25–27), and the death-chant of Jacob (Gen. xlix. 1-27); but these belong rather to prophetic poetry.

THE SONG OF MOSES.

In the Mosaic age we meet first with the song of deliverance which Moses sang with the children of Israel unto the Lord after the overthrow of Pharaoh's host in the Red Sea (Ex. xv. 1-18). It is the oldest specimen of a patriotic ode,[1] and may be called the national anthem, or the *Te Deum* of the Hebrews. It sounds through all the thanksgiving hymns of Israel, and is associated by the Apocalyptic Seer with the final triumph of the Church, when the saints shall sing "the song of Moses, and the song of the Lamb" (Rev. xv. 3). Its style is archaic, simple, and grand. It is arranged for antiphonal singing, chorus answering to chorus, and voice to voice; the maidens playing upon the timbrels. It is full of alliterations and rhymes which cannot be rendered, and hence it necessarily loses in any translation.[2]

of Greece, especially in the *Eumenides* of Æschylus, also the *Chœphoræ*, 398 (quoted by Prof. T. Lewis, in Lange's Com. on *Gen. in loc.*):—

> "There is a law that blood once poured on earth
> By murderous hands demands that other blood
> Be shed in retribution. From the slain
> Erynnys calls aloud for vengeance still,
> Till death in justice must be paid for death."

[1] From שִׁיר, to sing.

[2] Dr. Ley (p. 210 *sqq.*) arranges the Hebrew text octametrically and says: "*Dieser alte Festgesang ist durchaus octametrisch, hat lauter regelmässige Strophen mit Ausnahme der ersten.*" Herder says of this poem, of which he gives a free German translation: "*Der Durchgang durchs Meer hat das älteste und klingendste Siegeslied hervorgebracht, das wir in dieser Sprache haben. Es ist Chorgesang: eine einzelne Stimme malte vielleicht die Thaten selbst, die der Chor auffing und gleichsam verhallte. Sein Bau ist einfach, voll Assonanzen und Reime, die ich in unsrer Sprache ohne Wortzwang nicht zu geben wüsste; denn die ebrä-*

"I will sing unto Jehovah,
  For He hath triumphed gloriously:
The horse and his rider
  Hath He thrown into the sea.
Jehovah is my strength and song,
  And He is become my salvation.
This is my God, and I will praise Him;[1]
  My father's God, and I will exalt Him.

Jehovah is a man of war;
  Jehovah is His name.
Pharaoh's chariots and his host
  Hath He cast into the sea:
And his chosen captains
  Are sunk in the Red Sea.
The depths cover them;
  They went down to the bottom like a stone.

Thy right hand, O Jehovah, is glorious in power,
  Thy right hand, O Jehovah, dasheth in pieces the enemy.
And in the greatness of Thy majesty
  Thou overturnest them that rise up against Thee.
Thou sendest forth Thy wrath,
  It consumeth them like stubble.
And with the blast of Thy nostrils the waters were piled up,
  The floods stood upright as an heap,
  The depths were congealed in the heart of the sea.

ische Sprache ist wegen ihres einförmigen Baues solcher klingenden Assonanzen voll. Leichte, lange, aber wenige Worte verschwehen in der Luft, und meistens endigt ein dunkler, einsylbiger Schall, der vielleicht den Bardict des Chors machte." Lange thus happily characterizes this ode (Comm. on Ex.): "Wie der Durchgang durch das Rothe Meer als eine fundamentale Thatsache des typischen Reiches Gottes seine Beziehung durch die ganze Heilige Schrift ausbreitet, wie er sich rückwärts auf die Sündfluth bezieht, weiter vorwärts auf die christliche Taufe, und schliesslich auf das Endgericht, so gehen auch die Reflexe von diesem Liede Moses durch die ganze Heilige Schrift. Rückwärts ist es vorbereitet durch die poetischen Laute der Genesis und durch den Segen Jakobs, vorwärts geht es durch kleine epische Laute über auf das Abschiedslied des Moses und seinen Segen, 5 Mos. 32, 33. Zwei grossartige Seitenstücke, welche folgen, das Siegslied der Debora und das Rettungslied des David, 2 Sam. 22 (Ps. 18), leiten dann die Psalmenpoesie ein, in welcher vielfach der Grundton unseres Liedes wieder mit anklingt, Ps. 77, 78, 105, 106, 114. Noch einmal ist am Schlusse des N. T. von dem Liede Mosis die Rede: es tönt fort als das typische Triumphlied des Volkes Gottes bis in die andere Welt hinein, Offenb. xv. 3."

[1] The Auth. V.: "I will prepare him an habitation" (sanctuary), would

The enemy said, I will pursue, I will overtake,
    I will divide the spoil,
My lust shall be satisfied upon them :
    I will draw my sword,
    My hand shall destroy them.

Thou didst blow with Thy wind,
    The sea covered them :
    They sank as lead in the mighty waters.

Who is like unto Thee, O Jehovah, among the gods?
    Who is like Thee, glorious in holiness,
    Fearful in praises, doing wonders?
Thou didst stretch out Thy right hand,
    The earth swallowed them.

Thou in Thy mercy hast led the people
    Which Thou hast redeemed,
Thou hast guided them in Thy strength
    To Thy holy habitation.

The people have heard, they tremble :[1]
    Pangs have taken hold on the inhabitants of Philistia.
Then were the chiefs of Edom dismayed ;
    The mighty men of Moab, trembling taketh hold upon them.
All the inhabitants of Canaan are melted away :
    Terror and dread fall upon them.

By the greatness of Thine arm they are as still as a stone ;
    Till Thy people pass over, O Jehovah,
Till the people pass over,
    Which Thou hast purchased.

Thou shalt bring them in,
    And plant them in the mountain of Thine inheritance,
The place, O Jehovah, which Thou hast made for Thee to dwell in,
    The sanctuary, O Jehovah, which Thy hands have established.
Jehovah shall reign for ever and ever."

anticipate the building of the tabernacle, but is not justified by the Hebrew. The Revision renders as above.

[1] The poet, after giving thanks for the past, looks to the future and describes the certain consequences of this mighty deliverance, which struck terror into the hearts of all enemies of Israel, and must end in the conquest of Canaan, as promised by Jehovah.

Here the song ends, and what follows (ver. 19) is probably a brief recapitulation to fix the event in the memory :—

> "For the horses of Pharaoh went in with his chariots
>   And with his horsemen into the sea,
> And Jehovah brought again the waters of the sea upon them ;
>   But the children of Israel walked on dry land
>   In the midst of the sea."

Moses wrote also that sublime farewell song which celebrates Jehovah's merciful dealings with Israel (Deut. xxxii.), the parting blessing of the twelve tribes (Deut. xxxiii.), and the ninetieth Psalm, called "A Prayer of Moses, the man of God," which sums up the spiritual experience of his long pilgrimage in the wilderness, and which proves its undying force at every sick bed and funeral service. What can be more sublime than the contrast this Psalm draws between the eternal, unchangeable Jehovah and the fleeting life of mortal man.

> "Lord, Thou hast been our dwelling place
>   In all generations.
> Before the mountains were brought forth,
>   Or ever Thou hadst formed the earth and the world,
> Even from everlasting to everlasting
>   Thou art God.
>
> Thou turnest man to destruction ;
>   And sayest, Return, ye children of men.
> For a thousand years in Thy sight
>   Are but as yesterday when it is past,
> And as a watch in the night.
> . . . .
> The days of our years are threescore years and ten,
>   Or even by reason of strength fourscore years ;
>   Yet is their pride but labor and sorrow ;
>   For it is soon gone, and we fly away.
> . . . .
> So teach us to number our days,
>   That we may turn our hearts unto wisdom."

LYRICS IN THE LATER HISTORICAL BOOKS.

The Book of Joshua (x. 12, 13) contains a poetic quotation from the book of Jashar (the Upright), which was probably a collection of patriotic songs in commemoration of providential deliverances and heroic deeds. In describing the victory of Joshua over the Amorites at Gibeon, the poet says:—

> "Sun, stand still upon Gibeon,
>   And thou, moon, upon the valley of Ajalon!
> And the sun stood still, and the moon stayed her course,
>   Until the nation were avenged of their enemies."

This passage has the rhythm, parallelism and alliteration of Hebrew poetry, and expresses in a bold, oriental figure the idea that all the powers of nature are made subservient to the interests of the theocracy. The Song of Deborah (Judges v. 20) expresses the same idea:—

> "The stars in their courses fought against Sisera,
>   The river of Kishon swept them away."

The period of the Judges was, like the Middle Ages, a period of striking contrasts, wild disorder, heroic virtue and romantic poetry. Then might was right, and every man did what seemed good in his sight. The people were constantly exposed to invasion from without and civil war from within, but Providence raised deliverers who were both captains and judges, and restored peace and order. The spirit of that age found utterance in the Song of Deborah (Judges v. 2–31), eight hundred years before Pindar. It is a stirring battle-song, full of fire and dithyrambic swing, and all the more remarkable as the product of a woman, the Jeanne d'Arc of Israel:—

> "Hear, O ye kings;
>   Give ear, O ye princes:
> I, even I, will sing to Jehovah;
>   I will sing praise to Jehovah, the God of Israel.
> When Thou didst go forth out of Seir,
>   When Thou didst march out of the field of Edom,
> The earth trembled, the heavens also dropped,
>   Yea, the clouds dropped water.
> The mountains quaked at the presence of Jehovah,
>   Even yon Sinai at the presence of Jehovah, the God of Israel."[1]

[1] For an English translation of the whole song, see Dean Stanley, *Jewish Church*, II. 332. An admirable German translation by Herder, and another by Cassel in Lange's *Bibelwerk*.

Another but very different specimen of female poetry is Hannah's hymn of joy and gratitude when she dedicated her son Samuel, the last of the Judges, to the service of Jehovah (1 Sam. ii. 1–10). It furnished the key-note to the *Magnificat* of the Virgin Mary after the miraculous conception.

The Book of Ruth is an idyllic poem in prose, and exhibits in contrast to the wild commotion of the period of the Judges, a picture of domestic peace and happiness and the beauty of filial devotion.

DAVID'S LAMENT OF JONATHAN.

The reign of David was the golden age of lyric poetry. He was himself the prince of singers in Israel. "His harp was full-stringed, and every angel of joy and sorrow swept over the cords as he passed." His religious poetry is collected in the Psalter. The beautiful 18th Psalm is also incorporated in 2 Sam. xxii. Of his secular poetry the author of the Books of Samuel has preserved us two specimens, a brief stanza on the death of Abner, and his lament for the death of Saul and Jonathan (2 Sam. i. 19–27). The latter is a pathetic and touching elegy full of the strength and tenderness of the love of friendship. His generosity in lamenting the death of his persecutor who stood in his way to the throne, enhances the beauty and effect of the elegy.

"Thy Glory, O Israel,[1] is slain upon thy heights.
(CHORUS)   *How are the heroes fallen!*

[1] Or, "The Glory (the Beauty) of Israel." Ewald, Bunsen, Keil, take ישראל as vocative, "O Israel;" the A. V. ("the beauty of Israel"), De Wette, Erdmann (*Die Zierde Israels*), and others, as genitive. צבי means *splendor, glory* (Isa. iv. 2; xiii. 19; xxiv. 16, and is often used of the land of Israel, and of Mount Zion, which is called "the mountain of holy beauty," הר צבי קדשי, Dan. xi. 45); also a *gazelle*, from the beauty of its form (1 Kings v. 3; Isa. xiii. 14). The gazelles were so much admired by the Hebrews and Arabs that they even swore by them (Cant. ii. 7; iii. 5). Herder (*Israel's Reh*), and Ewald (*Der Steinbock, Israel*—to avoid the feminine *die Gazelle*) take it in the latter sense, and refer it to Jonathan alone. Ewald conjectures that Jonathan was familiarly known among the soldiers of Israel as *the Gazelle* on account of his beauty and swiftness. Jonathan was, of course, much nearer to the heart of the poet, but in this national song David had to identify him with Saul, so that both are included in the Glory of Israel. The Revised Version has "Thy Glory, O Israel," in the text, and "The Gazelle" in the margin.

Tell it not in Gath,
   Publish it not in the streets of Ashkelon;
Lest the daughters of the Philistines rejoice,
   Lest the daughters of the uncircumcised triumph.

Ye mountains of Gilboa, no dew nor rains
   Come upon you, and ye fields of offerings,[1]
For there the shield of the hero lies rusting,[2]
   The shield of Saul not anointed with oil.[3]

From the blood of the slain, from the fat of the heroes,
   The bow of Jonathan turned not back,
And the sword of Saul
   Returned not empty.

Saul and Jonathan, lovely and pleasant in their lives,
   And in their death they are not divided.
They were swifter than eagles,
   They were stronger than lions.

Ye daughters of Israel, weep over Saul,
   Who clothed you in scarlet with delight,
Who put ornaments of gold
   Upon your apparel.[4]

---

[1] שדי הרומות, Sept. ἀγροὶ ἀπαρχῶν. Vulg. *neque sint agri primitiarum*, fertile fields from which the first-fruits are gathered and sent to the sanctuary. The A. V. renders with Jerome: "*nor (let there be)* fields of offerings," the R. V.: "neither fields of offerings." On the different interpretations and conjectures see Erdmann in Lange's *Com.* It is a poetical malediction or imprecation of such complete barrenness that not even enough may grow on that bloody field for an offering of first-fruits.

[2] Or *polluted* by blood and dust. A great indignity to a soldier. Homer says that the helmet of Patroclus was rolled under the horses' feet, and soiled with blood and dust (Il. xvi. 794). The E. V., following the Vulgate (*abjectus*), translates נגעל *vilely cast away*.

[3] *But with blood.* By oil the shield of the warrior is kept bright. The A. V., following again the Vulgate (*quasi non esset*), supplies "*as though he had* not *been* anointed," i. e., as if he had not been a king (1 Sam. x. 1). So also Herder: "*Königs Schild, als wär er nimmer mit Oel geheiligt.*" But the more natural interpretation is: "the shield of Saul *was not* anointed with oil," as was usual in preparation for battle, and after it had been polluted by blood or corrupted by rust (Isa. xxi. 5). The unanointed shield here is an emblem of utter defeat and helplessness. The R. V. has in the text "not anointed with oil," and puts on the margin: "Or, *as of one not anointed.*"

[4] Lowth: "This passage is most exquisite composition. The women of Israel are most happily introduced, and the subject of the encomium is most admirably adapted to the female characters."

(CHORUS) *How are the heroes fallen in the midst of the battle!*
O Jonathan, slain upon thy heights!

I am distressed for thee, my brother Jonathan,
Very pleasant hast thou been unto me:
Thy love to me was wonderful,
Passing the love of women.[1]

(CHORUS) *How are the heroes fallen,*[2]
And the weapons of war[3] *perished."*

Lyric poetry continued to flourish during the reigns of David and Solomon, then declined with the decline of the nation, and revived for a short period with the restoration of the temple and the theocracy, when the harps were taken from the willows to accompany again the songs of Zion. It is a matter of dispute among commentators whether the Psalter contains hymns of the Maccabæan age.[4]

---

[1] The sweet, tender, devoted, enduring love with which woman loves. A picture of the ideal of friendship sanctified by the consecration of their hearts to Jehovah. The Vulgate inserts here the clause: *Sicut mater unicum amat filium suum, ita ego te amabam,* which has no foundation either in the Hebrew or the Septuagint.

[2] The repetition of this lament, probably by the chorus, is entirely in keeping with the nature of an elegy, which likes to dwell upon the grief, and finds relief by its repeated utterance.

[3] The כְּלֵי מִלְחָמָה are the heroes themselves, as the living weapons of war. So Ewald and Erdmann (*die Rüstzeuge des Streits*). Comp. Isa. xiii. 15; Acts ix. 15, where St. Paul is called "a chosen vessel" (σκεῦος). It is less lively and poetic to understand it literally of the material of war, as the Vulgate does (*arma bellica*), and Herder who renders:—

"*Ach wie fielen die Helden, und ihre Waffen des Krieges
Liegen zerschlagen umher.*"

[4] Hitzig and other radical critics assign several Psalms to the heroic age of the Maccabees, when the Hebrew canon was in all probability already closed. But Hengstenberg, Hävernick, Keil, among the orthodox divines, Gesenius, Ewald, Thenius, Dillmann, among the liberal critics, deny the possibility of Maccabæan Psalms. Ewald says (Preface to third ed. of his *Com. on the Ps.*) against Hitzig: "Nothing can be more false and perverse than to suppose that there can be Maccabæan poems in the Psalter." Delitzsch (*Com. über den Psalter*, new ed., 1-67, p. 9), admits the possibility, but denies the existence of such late Psalms.

THE PSALTER.

The Psalter is the great depository of the lyric poetry of the Jewish church and the inexhaustible fountain of devotion for all ages. Of its poetic merit and enduring spiritual value we have already spoken.[1]

All the Psalms are religious lyrics, but of different kinds, which are designated by different terms in the titles:[2]

Shir (Sept. ᾠδή), song for the voice alone.

Mizmôr (Sept. ψαλμός), psalm, song of praise, with instrumental accompaniment (ψαλμός).

Maschil (σύνεσις, εἰς σύνεσιν), a skillfully constructed ode, a reflective, contemplative, didactic song.

Michtham (στηλογραφία or εἰς στηλογραφίαν, lit., song of inscription), a golden poem, or a song of mysterious, deep import. (Delitzsch: catch-word poem.)

Shiggaion, an excited, irregular, dithyrambic ode.

Thehillah, a hymn of praise. The plural *thehillîm* is the Hebrew title of the Psalter.

Thephillah, a prayer in song. (Pss. xvii., lxxxvi., xc., cxlii., Hab. iii.)

Shir jedidoth, song of loves, erotic poem (Ps. xlv.).

Shir hamma'aloth (Sept. ᾠδὴ τῶν ἀναβαθμῶν, Vulg. *canticum graduum*, A. V. "song of degrees"), most probably a song of the goings up, *i.e.*, a pilgrim song for the journeys to the yearly festivals of Jerusalem. So, also, the R. V., which renders the title "song of ascents." These pilgrim songs are among the most beautiful in the whole collection.

Kinah (θρῆνος), a lament, dirge, elegy.[3] Here belong the laments of David for Saul and Jonathan, 2 Sam. i. 19–27, for Abner (2 Sam. iii. 33, 34), and for Absalom (2 Sam. xviii. 33), the psalms of mourning over the disasters of Judah (Pss. xlix., lx., lxxiii., cxxxvii.), and the Lamentations of Jeremiah.

---

[1] See above, pp. 71, 72, 74, 76, 77, 78, 79.

[2] For particulars on the names and musical titles in the inscriptions of the Psalms, some of which are very obscure and variously interpreted, we must refer to the commentaries of Ewald, Hitzig, Delitzsch, Moll (in Lange), Hupfeld (Riehm's edition), Perowne, and Cheyne.

[3] From קִינָה, to cry woe, woe! Comp. the German, *Klaglied*, *Trauerlied*, *Tadtenlied*, *Grablied*.

The titles of the Psalms are not original, but contain the ancient Jewish traditions, more or less valuable, concerning the authorship, historical occasion, musical character and liturgical use of the Psalms. Seventy-three poems are ascribed to David (לדוד);[1] twelve to Asaph (לאסף), one of David's musicians (Pss. l., lxxiii–lxxxiii.); eleven or twelve to the sons of Korah, a family of priests and singers of the age of David (Pss. xlii.– xlix., lxxxiv., lxxxv., lxxxvii., lxxxviii.); one to Heman the Ezrahite (lxxxviii.);[2] one to Ethan the Ezrahite (lxxxix); two to Solomon (lxxii., cxxvii.); one to Moses (xc.); while fifty are anonymous and hence called *Orphan* Psalms in the Talmud. The Septuagint assigns some of them to Jeremiah (cxxxvii.), Haggai, and Zechariah (cxlvi., cxlvii.).

The Psalter is divided into five books, and the close of each is indicated by a doxology and a double *Amen*. In this division several considerations seem to have been combined—authorship and chronology, liturgical use, the distinction of the divine names (Elohistic and Jehovistic Psalms), perhaps also the five-fold division of the Thorah (the Psalter being, as Delitzsch says, the subjective response or echo from the heart of Israel to the law of God). We have an analogy in Christian hymn- and tune-books, which combine the order of subjects and the order of the ecclesiastical year, modifying both by considerations of

---

[1] Thirty-seven in the first Book, Ps. iii.–xli., 18 in the second, 1 in the third, 2 in the fourth, 15 in the fifth Book. The Septuagint ascribes to David 85 Psalms (including xcix. and civ., which are probably his). The N. T. quotes as his also the anonymous Pss. ii. and xcv. (Acts iv. 25, 26; Heb. iv. 7). Ps. ii. certainly has the impress of his style and age (as Ewald admits). But some of the Psalms ascribed to him, either in the Hebrew or Greek Bible, betray by their Chaldaisms a later age. Hengstenberg and Alexander mostly follow the Jewish tradition; Delitzsch (*Commentar über die Psalmen*, p. 7) thinks that at least fifty may be defended as Davidic; while Hupfeld, Ewald, and especially Hitzig, considerably reduce the number. Ewald regards Pss. iii., iv., vii., viii., xi., xv., xviii., xix., xxiv., xxix., xxxii., ci., as undoubtedly Davidic; Ps. ii., xviii., xxvii., lxii., lxiv., cx., cxxxviii., as coming very near to David.

[2] This Psalm is called *shir mizmor* and *maschil*, and is ascribed both to the sons of Korah and to Heman the Ezrahite, of the age of Solomon (1 Kings v. 11). The older commentators generally regard the former as the singers of the *shir*, the latter as the author of the *maschil*. Hupfeld thinks that the title combines two conflicting traditions.

convenience, and often adding one or more appendixes. The five books represent the gradual growth of the collection till its completion after the exile, about the time of Ezra. The collection of the first book, consisting chiefly of Psalms of David, may be traced to Solomon, who would naturally provide for the preservation of his father's poetry, or, at all events, to King Hezekiah, who "commanded the Levites to sing praise unto the Lord with the words of David and of Asaph, the Seer" (2 Chron. xxi. 30; Prov. xxxv. 1).

The Revised Version has restored the Hebrew division, which is ignored in King James' Version.

If we regard chiefly the contents, we may divide the Psalms into Psalms of praise and adoration, Psalms of thanksgiving, Psalms of faith and hope under affliction,[1] penitential Psalms, didactic Psalms, historic Psalms, Pilgrim Songs (cxx.–cxxxvi.), and prophetic or Messianic Psalms.

THE LAMENTATIONS.

The Lamentations (קינות, θρῆνοι, elegia) of Jeremiah likewise belong to lyric poetry. They are the most extensive elegy in the Bible. They are a funeral dirge of the theocracy and the holy city after its destruction by Nebuchadnezzar and the Chaldees, and give most pathetic utterance to the most intense grief. The first lines strike the key-note. Jerusalem is personified and bewailed as a solitary widow:—

(ALEPH) "How sitteth solitary
    The city once full of people!
    She has become as a widow!
    She that was great among the nations,
    A princess over the provinces,
    Has become subject to tribute.

(BETH) She weepeth bitterly in the night,
    And her tears are upon her cheeks;
    She hath no comforter
    From among all her lovers:
    All her friends have turned traitors to her,
    They have become her enemies.

---

[1] What the Germans would call *Kreuz- und Trost-Psalmen*.

(LAMED)　Is it nothing to you, all ye that pass by?
　　　　　　Behold and see,
　　　　　If there be any sorrow like unto my sorrow,
　　　　　　Which is inflicted on me,
　　　　　Wherewith Jehovah hath afflicted me
　　　　　　In the day of his fierce anger."

The ruin and desolation, the carnage and famine, the pollution of the temple, the desecration of the Sabbath, the massacre of the priests, the dragging of the chiefs into exile, and all the horrors and miseries of a long siege, contrasted with the remembrance of former glories and glad festivities, and intensified by the awful sense of Divine wrath, are drawn with life-like colors and form a picture of overwhelming calamity and sadness. "Every letter is written with a tear, every word is the sob of a broken heart!"

Yet Jeremiah does not forget that the covenant of Jehovah with his people still stands. In the stormy sunset of the theocracy he beheld the dawn of a brighter day, and a new covenant written, not on tables of stone, but on the heart. The utterance of his grief, like the shedding of tears, was also a relief, and left his mind in a calmer and serener frame. Beginning with wailing and weeping, he ends with a question of hope, and with the prayer:—

　　　　　"Turn us unto Thee, O Jehovah.
　　　　　　And we shall be turned;
　　　　　Renew our days as of old!"

These Lamentations have done their work very effectually, and are doing it still. They have soothed the weary years of the Babylonian Exile, and after the return they have kept up the lively remembrance of the deepest humiliation and the judgments of a righteous God. On the ninth day of the month of Ab (July) they are read year after year with fasting and weeping by that remarkable people who are still wandering in exile over the face of the earth, finding a grave in many lands, a home in none. Among Christians the poem is best appreciated in times of private affliction and public calamity; a companion in mourning, it serves also as a book of comfort and consolation.

The poetic structure of the Lamentations is the most artificial in the Bible. The first four chapters are alphabetically arranged, like the 119th and six other Psalms, and Proverbs xxxi. 10–31. Every stanza begins with a letter of the Hebrew alphabet in regular order; all the stanzas are nearly of the same length; each stanza has three nearly balanced clauses or members which together constitute one meaning; chaps. i., ii. and iv. contain twenty-two stanzas each, according to the number of Hebrew letters; the third chapter has three alphabetic series, making sixty-six stanzas in all. Dante chose the terza rima for his sublime vision of Hell, Purgatory, and Paradise; Petrarca the complicated sonnet for the tender and passionate language of love. The author of Lamentations may have chosen his structure as a discipline and check upon the intensity of his sorrow — perhaps also as a help to the memory. Poems of this kind once learnt, are not easily forgotten. "In the scatterings and wanderings of families," says Isaac Taylor, "and in lonely journeyings, in deserts and cities, where no synagogue-service could be enjoyed, the metrical Scriptures—infixed as they were in the memory, by the very means of these artificial devices of verses and of alphabetic order, and of alliteration—became food to the soul. Thus was the religious constancy of the people and its brave endurance of injury and insult sustained and animated."

LYRICS IN THE NEW TESTAMENT.

The Christian dispensation opens with a series of lyrical poems of thanksgiving and praise for the fulfilment of the hopes of Israel and the salvation of mankind from the curse of sin and death by the coming of the Messiah. These poems are the last of Hebrew psalms and the first of Christian hymns. They connect the Old and New Testaments. They can be translated word for word into Hebrew, and were probably composed in that language. They are contained in the first two chapters of Luke, which have all the charms of poetry and innocent childhood, and may be called the Gospel of Paradise Regained.[1]

---

[1] Renan calls Luke the most literary among the Evangelists, and his Gospel the most beautiful book in existence ("*c'est le plus beau livre qu'il y ait*"). *Les Évangiles*, p. 282 sq.

These poems resound from Sunday to Sunday throughout the churches of Christendom, and will never grow old. They strike the key-note of Christian hymnody. They are called after the first words in the Latin version, the "Magnificat" of the Virgin Mary (i. 46), which is divided into four stanzas of four lines each, and begins:—

> "My soul doth magnify the Lord,
> And my spirit has rejoiced in God my Saviour;"

the "Benedictus" of Zachariah (i. 68), who, being filled with the Holy Spirit, prophesied, saying,

> "Blessed be the Lord, the God of Israel;
> For he hath visited and wrought redemption for his people;"

the "Gloria in Excelsis" of the heavenly host announcing the birth of the Saviour (ii. 14):—

> "Glory to God in the highest,
> And on earth peace among men of his good pleasure;"[1]

and the "Nunc Dimittis" of the aged Simeon (ii. 29), who was permitted to hold the Christ-child in his arms and sang:—

> "Now lettest Thou Thy servant depart, O Lord,
> According to Thy word, in peace."

The "Ave Maria," the favorite prayer of Roman Catholics, is an amplified combination of the salutation of the angel (i. 28):—

---

[1] Or, "of his good will." The Revised Version: "in whom He is well pleased." This translation is supported by the best ancient authorities, which read the genitive (εὐδοκίας, bonae voluntatis, of good will or pleasure), instead of the nominative (εὐδοκία, voluntas). It gives a double parallelism with three corresponding ideas: "glory" and "peace;" "God" and "men;" "in the highest" (in heaven) and "on earth." The textus receptus (εὐδοκία), suggests a triple parallelism, the third being a substantial repetition of the second. The Authorized Version follows this text but ignores the preposition ἐν by translating "towards men," instead of "among men." The Revised Version adopts the older reading in the text and gives the other in the margin ("good pleasure among men"). Dr. Hort (*Notes and Select Readings*, ii. 56) suggests a more equal division of the lines by connecting "and on earth" with the first clause, thus:—

> "Glory to God in the highest and upon earth;
> Peace among men of his good pleasure."

> "Hail, thou art highly favored,
> The Lord is with thee;"

and of the salutation of Elizabeth (i. 42):—

> "Blessed art thou among women,
> And blessed is the fruit of thy womb."

There are fragments or reminiscences of primitive Christian hymns scattered throughout the Epistles, and the Apocalypse. Paul exhorts his readers to "teach and admonish one another with psalms and hymns and spiritual songs, singing with grace in your hearts unto God" (Col. iii. 16). The passage, 1 Tim. iii. 16, is best explained as a quotation from a hymn in praise of Christ, especially if we adopt (with the Revised Version) the better attested reading "Who" ($ὅς$, referring to a preceding "Christus" or "Logos"), instead of "God" ($θεός$):—

> "He who was manifested in the flesh,
> Justified in the spirit,
> Seen of angels,
>
> Preached among the nations,
> Believed on in the world,
> Received up in glory."[1]

Another quotation from an unknown source is introduced by "*he* saith," Eph. v. 14:—

> "Awake, thou that sleepest,
> And arise from the dead,
> And Christ shall shine upon thee."

The passage 1 Pet. iii. 10–12 reads like a psalm and is metrically arranged in the Test. of Westcott and Hort.

II. DIDACTIC POETRY.

Didactic poetry is the combined product of imagination and reflection. It seeks to instruct as well as to please. It is not simply the outpouring of subjective feeling which carries along its own end and reward, but aims at an object beyond itself. It is

---

[1] Westcott and Hort in their Greek Test. divide the passage into two stanzas of three lines each.

the connecting link between pure poetry and philosophy. It supplies among the Shemitic nations the place of ethics, with this difference, that it omits the reasoning and argumentative process, and gives only the results of observation and reflection in a pleasing, mostly proverbial, sententious style, which sticks to the memory. It is laid down in the Proverbs and Ecclesiastes. Many Psalms also are didactic (i., xxxvii., cxix., etc.), and the Book of Job is a didactic drama.

The palmy period of didactic or gnomic poetry was the peaceful and brilliant reign of Solomon, which lasted forty years (B. C. 1015–975). He was a favorite child of nature and grace. He occupies the same relation to the Proverbs as David does to the Psalter, being the chief author and model for imitation. He was the philosopher, as David was the warrior and singer, of Israel. The fame of his wisdom was so great that no less than three thousand proverbs were ascribed to him. "God gave Solomon wisdom and understanding exceeding much, and largeness of heart, even as the sand that is on the sea-shore. And Solomon's wisdom excelled the wisdom of all the children of the east, and all the wisdom of Egypt. For he was wiser than all men; than Ethan the Ezrahite, and Heman, and Chalcol, and Darda, the sons of Mahol: and his fame was in all the nations round about. And he spake three thousand proverbs: and his songs were a thousand and five. And he spake of trees, from the cedar that is in Lebanon even unto the hyssop that springeth out of the wall: he spake also of beasts, and of fowl, and of creeping things, and of fishes. And there came of all peoples to hear the wisdom of Solomon, from all kings of the earth, who had heard of his wisdom." (1 Kings iv. 29–34.) According to a rabbinical tradition, Aristotle derived his philosophy from the Solomonic writings which Alexander the Great sent him from Jerusalem.[1]

[1] Comp. on the wisdom of Solomon, Ewald's *Geschichte des Volkes Israel*, Vol. III. pp. 374 sqq.; and Stanley's *Lectures on the History of the Jewish Church*, Vol. II. pp. 252 sqq. Ewald exclaims with reference to the visit of the Queen of Sheba (p. 379): "*O glückliche Zeit, wo mächtige Fürsten mitten in ihren von heiligen Gottesruhe angrüssigten Ländern so zu einander wallfahrten, so in Weisheit, und was noch mehr ist, im regen Suchen derselben wetteifern können!*"

THE PROVERBS.

The usual word for a didactic poem is *mâshâl* (מָשָׁל‎ παροιμία, παραβολή), a likeness, similitude, comparison; then, in a wider sense, a short, sharp, pithy maxim, sententious saying, gnome, proverb. It is couched in figurative, striking, pointed language. Brevity is the soul of a proverb as well as of wit. A proverb contains *multum in parvo*. It condenses the result of long observation and experience in a few words which strike the nail on the head and are easily remembered. It is the philosophy for the people, the wisdom of the street. The Orientals, especially the Arabs, are very fond of this kind of teaching. It suited their wants and limits of knowledge much better than an elaborate system of philosophy. And even now a witty or pithy proverb has more practical effect upon the common people than whole sermons and tracts.[1]

The Proverbs of the Bible are far superior to any collection of the kind, such as the sayings of the Seven Wise Men of Greece, the Aurea Carmina attributed to Pythagoras, the Remains of the Poetæ Gnomici, the collection of Arabic proverbs. They bear the stamp of Divine inspiration. They abound in polished and sparkling gems. They contain the practical wisdom (chokma) of Israel, and have furnished the richest contributions to the dictionary of proverbs among Christian nations. They trace wisdom to its true source, the fear of Jehovah (chap. i. 7).

Nothing can be finer than the description of Wisdom in the eighth chapter, where she is personified as the eternal companion and delight of God, and commended beyond all earthly treasures :—

> "Wisdom is better than rubies,
> And no precious things compare with her.
>
> I, wisdom, dwell with prudence,
> And find out knowledge and discretion.
>
> The fear of Jehovah is to hate evil;
> Pride, haughtiness, and the evil way,
> And the perverse mouth, do I hate.

---

[1] Cicero says: "*Gravissimae sunt ad beate vivendum breviter enunciatae sententiae.*"

Counsel is mine, and sound knowledge;
　I am understanding; I have strength.

By me kings reign,
　And princes decree justice.
By me princes rule,
　And nobles, even all the judges of the earth.

I love them that love me;
　And they that seek me early shall find me.

Riches and honor are with me,
　Yea, enduring riches and righteousness.
My fruit is better than gold, yea, than refined gold;
　And my increase than choice silver.

I walk in the way of righteousness,
　In the midst of the paths of judgment;
To ensure abundance to those that love me,
　And to fill their storehouse.

* * * * * * * *

Blessed is the man that heareth me,
　Watching daily at my gates,
　Waiting at the posts of my doors!
For whosoever findeth me findeth life;
　And shall obtain favor from Jehovah."

The description of the model Hebrew woman in her domestic and social relations (chap. xxxi. 10–31, in the acrostic form) has no parallel for truthfulness and beauty in ancient literature, and forms the appropriate close of this book of practical wisdom; for from the family, of which woman is the presiding genius, springs private and public virtue and national prosperity.

"The Book of Proverbs," says a distinguished Anglican divine, "is not on a level with the Prophets or the Psalms. It approaches human things and things divine from quite another side. It has even something of a worldly, prudential look, unlike the rest of the Bible. But this is the very reason why its recognition as a Sacred Book is so useful. It is the philosophy of practical life. It is the sign to us that the Bible does not despise common sense and discretion. It impresses upon us, in the most forcible manner, the value of intelligence and prudence, and of a good education. The whole strength of the Hebrew language, and of the sacred authority of the book is thrown upon these homely truths. It deals, too, in that refined, discriminating, careful view of the finer shades of human character, so often overlooked by theologians, but so necessary to any true estimate of human life. 'The heart knoweth its own bitterness, and the stranger does not intermeddle with its joy.' How much is there, in that single sentence, of consolation, of love, of forethought! And, above all, it insists, over and over again, upon the doctrine that goodness is '*wisdom*,' and that wickedness and vice are '*folly*.' There may be many other views of virtue and vice, of holiness and sin, better and higher than this. But there will always be some in the world who will need to remember that a good man is not only religious and just, but wise; and that a bad man is not only wicked and sinful, but a miserable, contemptible fool."[1]

The poetic structure of the Proverbs is that of Hebrew parallelism in its various forms. They consist of single, double, triple, or more couplets; the members corresponding to each other in sense and diction, either synonymously or antithetically. Delitzsch calls them two-liners, four-liners, six-liners, eight-liners.[2] The first section, x.–xxii. 16, contains exclusively two-liners. Besides these there are a few three-liners, five-liners and seven-liners, where the odd line is either a repetition or a reason for the idea expressed in the first lines. A few specimens will make this clear.

1. Single synonymous couplets :—

CHAP. III. 1. "My son, forget not my law:
And let thy heart keep my commandments."

12. "Whom Jehovah loveth He correcteth:
Even as a father the son in whom he delighteth."

---

[1] Dean Stanley, Vol. II., p. 269. A different view is presented and elaborately defended in the commentary of Rev. John Miller, of Princeton (New York, 1872), who maintains that the Proverbs, being an inspired book, can have no secular, but must have throughout a spiritual, meaning. He charges King James' version with making the book "hopelessly secular in many places" (p. 12). This view is paradox rather than orthodox.

[2] *Zweizeiler, Vierzeiler, Sechszeiler, Achtzeiler. Commentary on Proverbs*, Leipz., 1873. pp. 8 sqq.

13. "Blessed is the man who finds wisdom :
　　　And the man who obtains understanding."

XI. 25. "The liberal soul shall be made fat :
　　　And he that watereth shall himself be watered."

XVI. 32. "He that is slow to anger is better than the mighty :
　　　And he that ruleth his own spirit than he who taketh a city."

2. Single antithetic couplets :—

CHAP. X. 1. "A wise son maketh a glad father :
　　　But a foolish son is the grief of his mother."

12. "Hatred stirreth up strifes :
　　　But love covereth all sins."

16. "The wages of the righteous is life :
　　　The gain of the wicked is sin."

XIII. 9. "The light of the righteous shall be joyous :
　　　But the lamp of the wicked shall go out."

24. "He that spareth his rod hateth his son :
　　　But he that loveth him giveth him timely chastisement."

XVIII. 17. "He that is first in his own cause seemeth right :
　　　But his neighbor cometh and searcheth him."

3. Single couplets which merely express a comparison —

CHAP. XXVII. 8. "As a bird that wandereth from her nest,
　　　So is a man that wandereth from his place."

15. "A continual dropping in a very rainy day,
　　　And a contentious woman are alike."

16. "As in water face answereth to face,
　　　So the heart of man to man."

4. Single couplets where the second member completes the idea of the first or assigns a reason or a qualification :—

CHAP. XVI. 24. "Pleasant words are as a honey-comb,
　　　Sweet to the soul and health to the bones."

31. "The hoary head is a crown of glory,
　　　If it be found in the way of righteousness."

5. Three-liners:—

    CHAP. III. 3. "Let not mercy and truth forsake thee:
                  Bind them about thy neck;
   (*Synonymous*)   Write them upon the table of thine heart."

    XXVIII. 10. "Whoso causeth the righteous to go astray in an evil
                  way:
                 He shall fall himself into his own pit,
   (*Antithetic*)   But the upright shall inherit good things."

    XXVII. 10. "Thine own friend and thy father's friend forsake not:
                 Neither go into thy brother's house in the day of
                    thy calamity;
   (*Reason*)   For better is a neighbor near than a brother afar off."

6. Double couplets or four-liners: xxiii. 15 sq.; xxiv. 3 sq.; 28 sq.; xxx. 5 sq., 17 sq.; xxii. 22 sq., 24 sq. These are all synonymous, or synthetic, or corroboratory, but there seems to be no example of an antithetic four-liner.

7. Five-liners; the last three usually explaining and confirming the idea of the first two lines: xxxiii. 4 sq.; xxv. 6 sq.; xxx. 32 sq.

8. Triple couplets or six-liners, which spin out an idea with more or less repetition or confirmations and illustrations: xxiii. 1–3, 12–14, 19–21; xxiv. 11 sq.; xxx. 29–31.

9. Seven-liners: xxiii. 6–8. The only specimen in the Proverbs.

10. Quadruple couplets or eight-liners: xxiii. 22–25.

But these four, six and eight-liners, so-called, may be easily resolved into two, three or four single couplets. Take, *e.g.*, chap. xxiii. 12–14, which Delitzsch quotes as a six-liner, and we have there simply three couplets which carry out and unfold one idea, or expand the mashal sentence into a mashal poem:

        "Apply thy heart to instruction:
           And thine ears to the words of knowledge.
        Withhold not correction from the child:
           For if thou beat him with a rod, he shall not die.
        Thou shalt beat him with the rod,
           And shalt deliver his soul from Sheol."

ECCLESIASTES.

Ecclesiastes or Koheleth is a philosophic poem, not in broken, disconnected maxims of wisdom, like the Proverbs, but in a series of soliloquies of a soul perplexed and bewildered by doubt, yet holding fast to fundamental truth, and looking from the vanities beneath the sun to the eternal realities above the sun. It is a remarkable specimen of Hebrew scepticism subdued and moderated by Hebrew faith in God and his commandments, in the immortality of the soul, the judgment to come, the paramount value of true piety. It corresponds to the old age of Solomon, as the Song of Songs reflects the flowery spring of his youth, and the Proverbs the ripe wisdom of his manhood.[1] Whether written by the great monarch, or more probably by a much later author, it personates him (i. 12) and gives the last sad results of his experience after a long life of unrivalled wisdom and unrivalled folly, namely, the overwhelming impression of the vanity of all things earthly, with the concluding lesson of the fear of God, which checks the tendency to despair, and is the star of hope in the midnight darkness of doubt.

The key-note is struck in the opening lines, repeated at the close (xii. 8):—

> "O vanity of vanities! Koheleth saith;
> O vanity of vanities! all—vanity!"

This is the negative side. But the leading positive idea and aim, or "the end of the matter," is expressed in the concluding words:—

> "Fear God and keep His commandments,
> For this is all of man.[2]
> For God shall bring everything into judgment,
> Whether it be good or whether it be evil."

Some regard Koheleth as an ethical treatise in prose, with regular logical divisions. But it is full of poetic inspiration,

---

[1] This comparison was made by Rabbi Jonathan on the assumption of the Solomonic authorship of the three works.

[2] The Authorized Version inserts "the whole *duty* of man." The Revised Version puts on the margin as an alternate rendering: "This is *the duty* of all men."

and in part at least also poetic in form, with enough of rhythmical parallelism to awaken an emotional interest in these sad soliloquies and questionings of the poet. Prof. Tayler Lewis (in his additions to Zöckler's Commentary in Lange's Biblework), has translated the poetic portions in Iambic measure, with occasional use of the Choriambus. We transcribe two specimens from chap. vii. and chap. xi. :—

> "Better the honored name than precious oil ;
> Better the day of death than that of being born.
> Better to visit sorrow's house than seek the banquet hall ;
> Since that (reveals) the end of every man,
> And he who lives should lay it well to heart.
>   Better is grief than mirth :
> For in the sadness of the face the heart becometh fair.
> The wise man's heart is in the house of mourning,
> The fool's heart in the house of mirth.
> Better to hear the chiding of the wise
>   Than hear the song of fools.
> For like the sound of thorns beneath the pot,
> So is the railing laughter of the fool.
>   This, too, is vanity.
>
> . . . .
>
> "Rejoice, O youth, in childhood ; let thy heart
> Still cheer thee in the day when thou art strong.
> Go on in every way thy will shall choose,
> And after every form thine eyes behold ;
> But know that for all this thy God will thee to judgment bring.
> O, then, turn sorrow from thy soul, keep evil from thy flesh ;
> For childhood and the morn of life, they, too, are vanity.
> Remember thy Creator, then, in days when thou art young ;
> Before the evil days are come, before the years draw nigh
> When thou shalt say—delight in them is gone."

FABLE AND PARABLE.

To didactic poetry belong also the fable and the parable. They are usually composed in narrative prose, but the matter is all fiction and imagination. Both are allegories in the style of history ; both are conscious fictions for the purpose of instruction, and differ from the myth, which is the unconscious product of the religious imagination and identifies fiction with fact. But they differ in regard to the reality of the imagery and the nature of the aim. The fable rests on admitted impossibilities and introduces irrational creatures, animals or plants, to teach maxims of secular prudence and a lower, selfish morality; while the parable takes its illustrations from real life, human or animal, with its natural characteristics, and has a higher moral aim. "The fable seizes on that which man has in common with the creatures below him; the parable rests on the truth that man is made in the image of God." The former is fitted for the instruction of youth, which does not raise the question of veracity and revels in the marvellous; the latter is suited for a riper age, and is much better fitted as a medium of religious instruction.

There are no fables in the New Testament, and only two in the Old, viz., the fable of Jotham: the trees choosing their king, Judges ix. 8–15, and the fable of Jehoash: the cedars of Lebanon and the thistle, 2 Kings xiv. 9, and 2 Chr. xxv. 18. The riddle (parable) of Ezekiel xxii. 1–10 introduces two eagles as representatives of human characters, but without ascribing to them human attributes.

The parable occurs in 2 Sam. xii. 1 (the poor man's ewe lamb), Isa. v. 1 (the vineyard yielding wild grapes), also 1 Kings xx. 39; xxii. 19. It was cultivated by Hillel, Shammai and other Jewish rabbis, and appears frequently in the Gemara and Midrash. It is found in its perfection in the Gospels.

The parables of our Lord illustrate the various aspects of the kingdom of heaven (as those in the Synoptical Gospels), or the personal relation of Christ to His disciples (as the parable of the Good Shepherd, and that of the Vine and the Branches, in the Gospel of John). They reveal the profoundest ideas in the simplest and most lucid language. But what they reveal to the susceptible mind, they conceal to the profane, which sees only the outer shell, and not the inner kernel of the truth. They are at once pure truth and pure poetry. Every trait is intrinsically possible and borrowed from nature and human life; and yet the composition of the whole is the product of the imagination. The art of illustrative teaching in parables never rose so high before or since, nor can it ever rise higher.[1]

---

[1] Ewald (p. 51) says of the parables of Christ: "*Was hier aus der Menschenwelt erzählt wird, ist vollkommen wahr, d. i. den menschlichen Verhältnissen*

III. PROPHETIC POETRY.

This is peculiar to the Bible and to the religion of revelation. Heathen nations had their divinations and oracles, but no divinely inspired prophecy. Man may have forebodings of the future, and may conjecture what may come to pass under certain conditions; but God only knows the future, and he to whom He chooses to reveal it.

Prophecy is closely allied to poetry. The prophet sees the future as a picture with the spiritual eye enlightened by the Divine mind, and describes it mostly in more or less poetic form. Prophetic poetry combines a didactic and an epic element.[1] It rouses the conscience, enforces the law of God, and holds up the history of the future, the approaching judgments and mercies of God, for instruction, reproof, comfort and encouragement. Prophecy is too elevated to descend to ordinary prose, and yet too practical to bind itself to strict rules. Daniel, like St. John in the Apocalypse, uses prose, but a prose that has all the effect of poetry. Jonah and Haggai likewise wrote in prose, Malachi in a sort of middle style. The other prophets employ prose in the narrative and introductory sections, but a rhythmical flow of diction in the prophecies proper, with divisions of clauses and stanzas, and rise often to the highest majesty and power. The sublime prayer of Habakkuk (ch. iii.) is a lyric poem and might as well have a place in the Psalter.

The earliest specimens of prophetic poetry are the prediction

---

vollkommen entsprechend, so dass keiner, der es hört, an seinem Dasein zweifeln kann, und ist dennoch nur Bild, nur Lehre, und nicht anders gemeint. Aber mit der höchsten Wahrheit der Schilderung dieses menschlichen Lebens verbindet sich hier ihre höchste Einfalt, Lieblichkeit und Vollendung, um ihr den unwiderstehlichsten Zauber zu geben."

Ewald treats prophecy as a part of didactic poetry. "Ein reiner Dichter," he says (p. 51), "im ursprünglichsten Sinne des Wortes ist der Prophet nicht: was er ausspricht, soll von vorne an bestimmend, vorschreibend, belehrend auf Andere wirken. Aber sein Wort will von der Begeisterung Flügeln getragen von oben herab treffen, und muss so von vorn an erhaben in gleicher Höhe sich bis zum Ende halten. . . . So drängt sich denn dem Propheten die längst gepflegte Dichterweise unwillkührlich auf, ähnlich hebt und senkt sich bei ihm der Strom der Rede, nur der Gesang fällt vor der ungewöhnlichen Höhe und dem Ernste seiner Worte leicht von selbst weg."

of Noah, Gen. ix. 25–27, the blessing of Jacob, Gen. xlix., the prophecies of Balaam, Numb. xxiv., and the farewell blessing of the twelve tribes by Moses, Deut. xxxiii. They are prophetical lyrics or lyrical prophecies, and hence may also be classed with lyrical poetry like the Messianic Psalms.

The golden age of prophetic poetry began eight centuries before Christ, and continued till the return from the exile, warning the people of the approaching judgments of Jehovah, and comforting them in the midst of their calamities with his promise of a brighter future when the Messiah shall come to redeem His people and to bless all the nations of the earth.

The poetry of the Prophets varies according to their temperament and subject. Amos, a herdsman of Tekoa, in the tribe of Judah, who prophesied in the eighth century before Christ, abounds in illustrations from pastoral and rustic life, and contains some rare specimens of sublime thought beautifully expressed. Hosea, his contemporary (between 790 and 725 B.C.), is bold, vigorous, terse, pregnant, but abrupt and obscure. Jeremiah is the melancholy poet of the downfall of the theocracy, full of tender pathos, and fills the heart with holy grief, but also with hope of a new and better covenant. Ezekiel, a younger contemporary of Jeremiah, is dark and enigmatic, but elevated and forcible. He presents a variety of visions, symbolical actions, parables, proverbs, allegories, " wheels within wheels, with living creatures welded." He draws illustrations from architecture, from Solomon's temple, and the winged and human-headed lions which were dug up in our age from the dust of long-lost Nineveh. Habakkuk belongs to the later Babylonian period. Ewald thus describes him in his book on the Hebrew Prophets: " Great as Habakkuk is in thought, he is no less so in language and literary skill; he is the last prophet belonging to the age preceding the destruction of Jerusalem who is master of a beautiful style, of forcible description, and an artistic power that enlivens and orders everything with charming effect. We are still able to admire in him the genuine type and full beauty of ancient Hebrew prophecy; he is its last pure light, and although he already reproduces much from older books, he still maintains complete independence."

The greatest poet among the prophets is Isaiah, who lived in the Assyrian period (between 760 and 698). He at the same time comes nearest to the gospel, and is called the Evangelist of the Old Covenant. He gathers up all past prophecies and sends them enriched into the future. He excels in the grandeur and variety of images and in sudden contrasts. Ewald admirably describes him. "In Isaiah," he says, "we see the prophetic authorship reaching its culminating point. Everything conspired to raise him to an elevation to which no prophet, either before or after, could as writer attain. Among the other prophets each of the more important ones is distinguished by some one particular excellence and some one peculiar talent; in Isaiah all kinds of talent and all beauties of prophetic discourse meet together, so as mutually to temper and qualify each other; it is not so much any single feature that distinguishes him, as the symmetry and perfection as a whole. . . . In the sentiment he expresses, in the topics of his discourses, and in the manner, Isaiah uniformly reveals himself as the kingly prophet."

A few selections must suffice, one from the first and one from the second Part. We have nothing to do here with the critical question of the authorship of the collection which bears his name and which refers partly to the Assyrian, partly to the Babylonian period, but which nevertheless has a unity of spirit with minor differences of style.

The following is a beautiful description of the happy Messianic age (ch. xxxv.):—

> "The wilderness and the solitary place shall be glad;
>   And the desert shall rejoice, and blossom as a rose.
> It shall blossom abundantly,
>   And rejoice even with joy and singing.
> The glory of Lebanon shall be given unto it,
>   The excellency of Carmel and Sharon:
> They shall see the glory of Jehovah,
>   The excellency of our God.

---

[1] And yet he was numbered among the prose writers till the time of Lowth. It is strange that even so able a scholar as Dr. Jos. Addison Alexander, in his commentary on Isaiah, should protest (from early habit) against what he calls "the fantastic and injurious mode of printing most translations of Isaiah, since the days of Lowth, in lines analogous to those of classical and modern verse."

Strengthen ye the weak hands,
    And confirm the feeble knees.
Say to them that are of a fearful heart,
    Be strong, fear not ;
Behold, your God will come with vengeance,
    With the recompense of God ;
He will come and save you.

Then the eyes of the blind shall be opened,
    And the ears of the deaf shall be un-stopped.
Then shall the lame man leap as an hart,
    And the tongue of the dumb shall sing ;
For in the wilderness shall waters break out,
    And streams in the desert.

And the glowing sand shall become a pool,
    And the thirsty ground springs of water ;
In the habitation of jackals, where they lay,
    Shall be grass with reeds and rushes.
And an highway shall be there, and a way,
    And it shall be called the way of holiness.

The unclean shall not pass over it ;
    For it shall be for those :
The wayfaring men, yea fools, shall not err therein.
    No lion shall be there,
Nor shall any ravenous beast go up thereon,
    They shall not be found there.

But the redeemed shall walk there ;
    And the ransomed of the Lord shall return,
And come with singing unto Zion ;
    And everlasting joy shall be upon their heads :
They shall obtain gladness and joy,
    And sorrow and sighing shall flee away."

In the second part, from ch. xl. to the close, called Deutero-Isaiah, the prophet—whether it be Isaiah, or " the great Unknown," at the close of the exile—describes the approach of the Messianic salvation, and draws, lineament for lineament, the physiognomy of the suffering and triumphant Saviour, for the comfort of all ages. The fifty-second and fifty-third chapters are the holy of holies of Hebrew prophecy, the gospel of the Old Testament.

" How beautiful upon the mountains are the feet of him
    That bringeth good tidings,
That publisheth peace,
    That bringeth good tidings of good,
That   ablisheth salvation ;
    That saith unto Zion, Thy God reigneth !
The voice of thy watchman ! they lift up the voice,
    Together do they sing ;
For they shall see, eye to eye,
    When Jehovah returneth to Zion.

Break forth into joy,
    Sing together, ye waste places of Jerusalem ;
For Jehovah hath comforted His people,
    He hath redeemed Jerusalem.
Jehovah hath made bare His holy arm
    In the eyes of all the nations ;
And all the ends of the earth
    Shall see the salvation of our God.
    . . . .

Behold, My Servant shall prosper,
    He shall be exalted and lifted up and be very high.
Like as many were astonished at thee
    (His visage was so marred, more than any man,
And His form more than the sons of men),
    So shall He sprinkle many nations ;
Kings shall shut their mouths at Him :
    For that which had not been told them they shall see ;
And that which they had not heard
    They shall attentively consider.

Who hath believed our report ?
    And to whom is the arm of the Lord revealed ?
For He grew up before Him as a tender plant,
    And as a root out of a dry ground :
He hath no form nor comeliness ; and when we see Him,
    There is no beauty that we should desire Him.
He was despised, and rejected by men ;
    A Man of sorrows, and acquainted with grief :
And as one from whom men are hiding their face,
    He was despised, and we esteemed Him not.

Verily He hath borne our griefs,
    And carried our sorrows :
Yet we did esteem Him stricken,
    Smitten of God and afflicted.

But He was pierced for our transgressions,
    He was bruised for our iniquities:
The chastisement of our peace was upon Him;
    And with His stripes we are healed.
All we like sheep went astray;
    We turned every one to his own way;
And Jehovah laid on Him the iniquity of us all.

He was oppressed, yet He humbled himself,
    And opened not His mouth:
As a Lamb that is brought to the slaughter,
    And as a sheep that before her shearers is dumb;
Yea, He opened not His mouth.
He was taken away by oppression and judgment;
    And His life who shall recount?
    For He was cut off from the land of the living:
    For the transgression of my people was He stricken.

And they made His grave with the wicked,
    And with the rich in His death;
Although He had done no violence,
    Neither was any deceit in His mouth:
Yet it pleased Jehovah to bruise Him;
    He hath put Him to grief.

When He shall offer Himself a sacrifice for sin,
    He will see His seed, He will prolong His days,
And the pleasure of Jehovah will prosper in His hands.
He will see of the travail of His soul, and will be satisfied:
By His knowledge will My righteous Servant justify many;
    For He will bear their iniquities.

Therefore I shall give Him a portion among the great,
    And He will divide the spoil with the strong:
Because He hath poured out His soul unto death,
    And was numbered with the transgressors:
And He bare the sin of many,
    And made intercession for the transgressors."

IV. DRAMATIC POETRY.

If we start with the Greek conception of the drama, there is none in the Bible. But if we take the word in a wider sense, and apply it to lengthy poetic compositions, unfolding an action and introducing a number of speakers and actors, we have two dramas in the Old Testament. The Song of Solomon is a lyric drama or melo-drama; the Book of Job is a didactic drama.

The best judges of different ages and churches, as Gregory of Nazianzen, Bossuet, Lowth, Ewald, Renan, Stanley, recognize the dramatic element in these two poems, and some have even gone so far as to suppose that both, or at least the Canticles, were really intended for the stage.[1] But there is not the slightest trace of a theatre in the history of Israel before the age of Herod, who introduced foreign customs; as there is none at the present day in the Holy Land, and scarcely among the Mohammedan Arabs, unless we regard the single reciters of romances (always men or boys) with their changing voice and gestures as dramatic actors. The ruins of large theatres east of the Jordan are of post-Christian date and were erected by the Romans. The modern attempts to introduce theatres in Beirut and Cairo have signally failed, or are patronized almost exclusively by foreigners.

THE SONG OF SONGS.

The Canticles, or Song of Songs, presents the Hebrew ideal of pure bridal and conjugal love in a series of monologues and dialogues by different persons: a lover, king Solomon (Shelomoh, the Peaceful), a maiden named Shulamith, and a chorus of virgins, daughters of Jerusalem. There are no breaks or titles to indicate the change of scene or speakers, and they can be recognized only by the sense and the change of gender and number in the personal pronoun. The English version is much obscured by a neglect of the distinction of feminine and masculine pro-

---

[1] Ewald (*Die Dichter des A. B.*, I. 72 sqq.) asserts very positively, but without proof, that dramas were enacted on the great festivals, and at the courts of David and Solomon. He calls the Canticles "the purest model of a comedy (*Lustspiel*)"; Job, "a genuine tragedy (*Trauerspiel*)." He admits, however, that in no case could God (who is one of the actors in Job) have been introduced on a Jewish stage, like the gods in the Greek dramas. Renan (*Le Cantique des Cantiques*) denies the existence of public theatres among the Hebrews, owing to the absence of a complicated mythology which stimulated the development of the drama among the Hindoos and Greeks, but maintains that the Song of Songs, being a dramatic poem, must have been represented in private families at marriage feasts.

nouns in the Hebrew. These defects have been mended in the Revised Version.

The poem is full of the fragrance of spring, the beauty of flowers, and the loveliness of love. How sweet and charming is the lover's description of spring, ch. ii. 10–14:

> "Rise up, my love, my fair one, and come away!
>   For, lo, the winter is past,
> The rain is over and gone;
>   The flowers appear on the earth;
> The time for the singing of birds is come,
>   And the voice of the turtle is heard in our land.
> The fig-tree ripeneth her green figs,
>   And the vines are in blossom,
> They give forth their fragrance.
>
> Arise, my love, my fair one, and come away!
> My dove, in the clefts of the rock,
> In the recess of the cliffs,
> Let me see thy countenance,
> Let me hear thy voice;
> For sweet is thy voice,
> And thy countenance is comely."[1]

The Song of Solomon canonizes the love of nature, and the love of sex, as the Book of Esther canonizes patriotism or the love of country. It gives a place in the Book of inspiration to the noblest and strongest passion which the Creator has planted in man, before the fall, and which reflects His own infinite love to His creatures, and the love of Christ to His Church. *Procul abeste profani!* The very depth of perversion to which the passion of love can be degraded, only reveals the height of its origin and destiny. Love is divine. Love in its primal purity is a "blaze" or "lightning flash from Jehovah" (Shalhebeth-Jah, ch. viii. 6), and stronger than death. As it proceeds from

---

[1] Logau calls the month of May "a kiss which heaven gives to earth."

> " *Dieser Monat ist ein Kuss,*
>   *Den der Himmel gibt der Erde,*
> *Dass sie jetzo seine Braut,*
>   *Künftig eine Mutter werde.*"

God so it returns to Him; for "God is love; and he that dwelleth in love, dwelleth in God, and God in him" (1 John iv. 16). Tersteegen, one of the purest and deepest German hymnists, in his sweet hymn: "*Ich bete an die Macht der Liebe*," traces all true earthly love and friendship to Christ as the fountain-head, in these beautiful lines:—

> "Ehr' sei dem hohen Jesusnamen,
> In dem der Liebe Quell entspringt,
> Von dem hier alle Bächlein kamen,
> Aus dem der Sel'gen Schaar dort trinkt."

As to the artistic arrangement or the number of acts and cantos in each act of this melodrama of Love there is considerable difference among commentators. Some divide it into five acts, according to the usual arrangement of dramas (Ewald, Böttcher, Zöckler, Moody, Stuart, Davidson, Ginsburg), some into six (Delitzsch, Hahn), some into seven, corresponding to the seven days of the Jewish marriage festival for which the successive portions of the poem are supposed to have been intended to be sung (Bossuet, Percy, Williams). Ewald subdivides the five acts into thirteen, Renan into sixteen, others into more or less cantos. On the other hand, Thrupp and Green give up the idea of a formal artistic construction, such as the Indo-European conception of a drama would require, and substitute for it a looser method of arrangement or aggregation, with abrupt transitions and sudden changes of scene. All the parts are variations of the same theme, of pure bridal love as the image of a divine and spiritual love. Those who regard the poem as an idyl rather than a drama (Sir William Jones, Good, Fry, Noyes, Herbst, Heiligstedt) divide it into a series of songs, but likewise differ as to the number and the pauses.

This is not the place to enter into the wilderness of interpretations of this wonderful and much-abused poem, except to protest against those profane rationalistic expositions which can find in it no more than a sensuous, erotic meaning, and make its position in the sacred canon inexplicable, as well as against those arbitrary allegorical impositions which, in violation of all the laws of hermeneutics, force upon the words a meaning which the author never dreamed of. Dr. Angus makes some judicious remarks on the subject.[1] "Much of the language of this poem," he says, "has been misunderstood by early expositors. Some have erred by adopting a fanciful method of explanation, and attempting to give a mystical meaning to every minute circumstance of the allegory. In all figurative representations there is always much that is mere costume. It is the general truth only that is to be examined and explained. Others, not understanding the spirit and luxuriancy of eastern poetry, have considered particular passages as defective in delicacy, an impression which the English version has needlessly confirmed, and so have objected to the whole, though the objection does not apply with greater force to this book than to Hesiod or Homer, or even to some of the purest of our own authors. If it be remembered, that the figure employed in this allegory is one of the most frequent in Scripture, that in extant oriental poems it is constantly employed to express religious feeling, that many expressions which are applied in our translation to the person, belong properly to the dress, that every generation has its own notions of delicacy (the most delicate in this sense being by no means the most virtuous), that nothing is described but chaste affection, that Shulamith speaks and is spoken of collectively, and that it is the general truth only which is to be allegorized, the whole will appear to be no unfit representation of the union between Christ and true believers in every age. Properly understood, this portion of Scripture will minister to our holiness. It may be added, however, that it was the practice of the Jews to withhold the book from their children till their judgments were matured."

THE BOOK OF JOB.

The Book of Job is a didactic drama, with an epic introduction and close. The prologue (chs. i. and ii.) and the epilogue (ch. xlii. 7–17) are written in plain prose, the body of the poem in poetry. It has been called the Hebrew tragedy, but it differs from other tragedies by its happy termination. We better call it a dramatic theodicy. It wrestles with the perplexing problem

---

[1] *Bible Handbook*, Lond. Ed., p. 149.

of ages, *viz.*, the true meaning and object of evil and suffering in the world under the government of a holy, wise and merciful God. The dramatic form shows itself in the symmetrical arrangement, the introduction of several speakers, the action, or rather the suffering of the hero, the growing passion and conflict, the secret crime supposed to underlie his misfortune, and the awful mystery in the background. But there is little external action (δρᾶμα) in it, and this is almost confined to the prologue and epilogue. Instead of it we have here an intellectual battle of the deepest moral import, mind grappling with mind on the most serious questions which can challenge our attention. The outward drapery only is dramatic, the soul of the poem is didactic. It is inspired by the Hebrew idea of Divine Providence, which differs from the Greek notion of blind Fate, as the light of day differs from midnight, or as a loving father differs from a heartless tyrant. It is intended for the study, not for the stage.[1]

The book opens, like a Greek drama, with a prologue, which introduces the reader into the situation, and makes him acquainted with the character, the prosperous condition, the terrible misfortunes, and the exemplary patience of the hero. Even God, and His great antagonist, Satan, who appears, however, in heaven as a servant of God, are drawn into the scenery, and a previous arrangement in the Divine council precedes and determines the subsequent transaction. History on earth is thus viewed as an execution of the decrees of heaven, and as controlled throughout by supernatural forces. But we have here the unsearchable wisdom of the Almighty Maker and Ruler of men, not the dark impersonal Fate of the heathen tragedy.

---

[1] W. A. Wright (in W. Smith's *Dictionary of the Bible*, III., 2553) says of the Book of Job: "Inasmuch as it represents an action and a progress, it is a drama as truly and really as any poem can be which develops the working of passion and the alternations of faith, hope, distrust, triumphant confidence and black despair, in the struggle which it depicts the human mind as engaged in, while attempting to solve one of the most intricate problems it can be called upon to regard. It is a drama as life is a drama, the most powerful of all tragedies; but that it is a dramatic poem intended to be represented upon the stage, or capable of being so represented, may be confidently denied."

This grand feature of Job has been admirably imitated by Goethe in the prologue of Faust.

The action itself commences after seven days and seven nights of eloquent silence. The grief over the misfortunes which, like a swift succession of cyclones, had suddenly hurled the patriarchal prince from the summit of prosperity to the lowest depths of misery, culminating in the most loathsome disease, and intensified by the heartless sneers of his wife, at last bursts forth in a passionate monologue of Job, cursing the day of his birth (ch. iii.).

> "Let the day perish wherein I was born,
> And the night which said:
> There is a man-child conceived.
>
> . . . .
>
> Why did I not die in the womb?
> Why did I not give up the ghost,
> When I came out of the belly?
>
> . . . .
>
> As a hidden untimely birth;
> As infants who never saw light.
>
> There the wicked cease from troubling;
> And there the weary are at rest."

Then follows the metaphysical conflict with his friends, Eliphaz, Bildad and Zophar, who now turn to enemies, and "miserable comforters," "forgers of lies, and botchers of vanities." The debate has three acts, with an increasing entanglement, and every act consists of three assaults of the false friends, and as many defences of Job (with the exception that, in the third and last battle, Zophar retires and Job alone speaks).[1] The poem reaches its height in Job's triumphant assertion of faith in his Redeemer (ch. xix. 23–27), by which "the patriarch of Uz rises to a level with the patriarch of Ur as a pattern of faith."

---

[1] The significance of the ruling number three reminds one of the trilogies in Dante's *Divina Commedia*.

> "Oh, that my words were now written!
>   Oh, that they were inscribed in a book!
> That with an iron pen and lead
>   They were graven in the rock forever!
> For I know that my Redeemer liveth,
>   And that He shall stand up at the last upon the earth;
> And after my skin hath been thus destroyed,
>   Yet without my flesh[1] shall I see God;
> Whom I shall see for myself
>   And mine eyes shall behold, and not another."

After a closing monologue of Job, expressing fully his feelings and thoughts in view of the past controversy, the youthful Elihu, who had silently listened, comes forward, and in three speeches administered deserved rebuke to both parties, with as little mercy for Job as for his friends, but with a better philosophy of suffering, whose object he represents to be correction and reformation, the reproof of arrogance and the exercise of humility and faith. He begins the disentanglement of the problem and makes the transition to the final decision.

At last God Himself, to whom Job had appealed, appears as the Judge of the contest, and humbles him by unfolding before his eyes a magnificent panorama of creation and showing him the boundaries of his knowledge. He points him to the mysteries of the stars in heaven, as "the cluster of the Pleiades," and "the bands of Orion," and in the animal world on earth, as the lion, the wild ox, the behemoth (hippopotamus), "who eateth grass as an ox, who moveth his tail like a cedar," the leviathan (the crocodile), "in whose neck abideth strength, and terror danceth before him," and of the war-horse (xxxix. 21–25):—

> "He paweth in the valley,
>   And rejoiceth in his strength;
>   He goeth forth to meet the armed men.

---

[1] According to the Hebrew text (*mibbesari*, *i. e.*, with my naked spirit or by direct spiritual intuition. The passage teaches the immortality of the soul, but not the resurrection of the body which comes out in the last books of the Old Testament). The A. V. and Luther wrongly translate "*in my flesh*," "*in meinem Fleische*," following the text of the Vulgate: "*et rursum circumdabor pelle mea, et in carne mea videbo Deum meum.*" The R. V. reads in the text "*from* my flesh," and in the margin "*without* my flesh."

> He mocketh at fear, and is not dismayed;
>   Neither turneth he back from the sword.
> The quiver rattleth against him,
>   The flashing spear and the javelin.
> He swalloweth the ground with fierceness and rage;
>   Neither believeth he that it is the voice of the trumpet.
> As oft as the trumpet soundeth he saith, Aha!
>   And he smelleth the battle afar off,
>   The thunder of the captains and the shouting."

Job is overwhelmed with a sense of the infinite power and wisdom of the Almighty, and of his own impotence and ignorance, and penitently confesses his sin and folly (xlii. 2–6):—

> "I know that Thou canst do all things,
>   And that no purpose of thine can be restrained.
> Who is this that hideth counsel without knowledge?
>   I have then uttered what I understood not,
>   Things too wonderful for me, which I knew not.
> But hear me now, and let me speak;
>   Thee will I ask, and do Thou teach me.
> I had heard of Thee by the hearing of the ear;
>   But now mine eyes behold Thee.
> Therefore I abhor it[1] (I recant),
>   And repent in dust and ashes."

This repentance and humble submission is the moral solution of the mighty problem, if solution it can be called.

A brief epilogue relates the temporal or historical solution, the restoration and increased prosperity of Job after this severest trial of his faith.

To the external order corresponds the internal dialectic development in the warlike motion of conflicting sentiments and growing passions. The first act of the debate shows yet a tolerable amount of friendly feeling on both sides. In the second the passion is much increased, and the charges of the opponents against Job are made severer. In the last debate Eliphaz, the

---

[1] The Hebrew verb has no pronominal object; this is either the person of Job (Sept. *ἐμαυτόν*; Vulg. *me*; A. and R. V. *myself*; Luther, *mich*), or his argument, his foolish wisdom (Aben Ezra: *quicquid antea in te sum temere locutus et imperite*). Ewald translates indefinitely: "*Drum widerrufe ich und übe Reue.*" Similarly Zöckler: "*Darum widerrufe ich und thue Busse.*"

leader of the rest, proceeds to the open accusation of heavy crimes against the sufferer, with an admonition to repent and turn to God. Job, after repeated declarations of his innocence and vain attempts at convincing his opponents, appeals at last to God as his Judge. God appears, convinces him of his ignorance, and brings him to complete submission.

This is as far as the Hebrew religion could go. In the Christian dispensation we know God not only as a God of power and wisdom, whose paths are past finding out, but also as a God of love and mercy, who maketh all things to work together for good to those that love him. Yet there are many dark problems of Providence which we cannot understand until we shall see face to face and know even as we are known.

The Book of Job, considering it as a mere poem, stands on a par with the Iliad, the Æneid, the Divina Commedia, Macbeth, Hamlet, and Faust, and considering its antiquity and moral bearing, it is superior to all. The dark mystery of suffering has never been more profoundly debated, and never been brought nearer to solution, except by the teaching and example of Christ and the sacrifice on the Cross.

The poem is also remarkable for its universal import. Whether written in the patriarchal, or Mosaic, or Solomonic, or a still later age, Job is represented as a man who lived before or independent of the Mosaic economy, and outside, yet near the Holy Land; ignorant of the written law and the temple, and yet a worshiper of Jehovah; a mysterious stranger of the type of Melchisedek, "without father, without mother, without genealogy," yet a true prophet and priest of the Most High, and a comforter of the children of affliction in all ages.

THE FORM OF BIBLE POETRY. POETIC DICTION.

We must now consider the artistic form of the poetry of the Bible, and the questions of versification, metre and rhyme.

The language of Hebrew, as well as of all other poetry, is in one respect more free, in other respects more bound, than the language of prose. It is the language of imagination and feeling, as distinct from the language of sober reflection and judgment. It is controlled by the idea of beauty and harmony. It is the speech of the Sabbath-day. It soars above what is ordinary and common. It is vivid, copious, elevated, sonorous, striking, impressive. Hence the poet has more license than the prose-writer; while, on the other hand, he submits to certain restraints of versification to secure greater æsthetic effect. He is permitted to use words which are uncommon or obsolete, but which, for this very reason, strike the attention and excite the emotion. He may also use ordinary words in an extraordinary sense.

The licenses of the Hebrew poets are found in the following particulars:—

1. Archaic forms and peculiar words, some of Aramaic or even a prior Shemitic dialect: *Eloah* for *Elohim* (God), *enosh* for *adam* (man), *orach* for *derech* (path), *havah* for *haiah* (to be), *millah* for *dabar* (word), *paal* for *asah* (to do), *katal* for *razah* (to kill). Sometimes they are accumulated for poetic effect.[1] The modern knowledge of Assyrian and Babylonian literature sheds light upon these poetic archaisms.

2. Common words in an uncommon sense: *Joseph* for the nation of Israel; adjectives for substantive objects, as *the hot* for the sun, *the white* for the moon (Cant. vi. 10), *the strong* for a bull (Ps. l. 13), *the flowing* for stream (Isa. xliv. 3).

3. Peculiar grammatical forms, or additional syllables, which give the word more sound and harmony, or an air of antiquity; as the paragogic *ah* (ה ָ) affixed to nouns in the absolute state, *o* (וֹ), and *i* (יִ) affixed to nouns in the construct state; the feminine termination *ath*, *atha* (for the ordinary *ah*); the plural ending *in* and *ai* (for *im*); the verbal suffixes *mo*, *amo* and *emo*; the pronominal suffixes to nouns and prepositions—*amo* (for *am*), and *chu* (for *an*); also lengthened vowel forms of pronouns and prepositions—*lamo* (for *lo* or *lahem*), *minai* (for *min*), *lemo* (for לְ), *bemo* (for בְּ), *kemo* (for כְּ), *eleh* (for אֶל), *adai* (for עַד).

---

[1] So in the highly poetic Ps. viii. 8 we have *zoneh* (sheep) for the prosaic *zon*; *alaphim* (oxen) for *bakar*; *sadai* (field) for *sadeh*; and *bahamoth sadai* (beasts of the field) instead of *haiath haarez*.

VERSIFICATION.

Hebrew poetry has a certain rhythmical flow, a rise and fall (*arsis* and *thesis*), versicular and strophic divisions, also occasional alliterations and rhymes, and especially a correspondence of clauses called "parallelism," but no regular system of versification, as we understand it. It is not fettered by mechanical and uniform laws; it does not rest on quantity or syllabic measure; there is no equal number of syllables in each line or verse, nor of lines in each stanza or strophe. It is poetry of sense rather than sound. The thought is lord over the outward form. It differs in this respect from classical, modern, and also from later Hebrew poetry. "Compared with the poetry of other ancient nations," says Ewald, "Hebrew poetry represents a more simple and childlike age of mankind, and overflows with an internal fullness and grace that cares very little for external ornament and nice artistic law."[1]

This freedom and elasticity of Hebrew poetry gives it, for purposes of translation, a great advantage above ancient and modern poetry, and subserves the universal mission of the Bible, as the book of faith and spiritual life for all nations and in all languages. A more artificial and symmetrical structure would make the translation a difficult task, and either render it dull and prosy, by a faithful adherence to the sense, or too free and loose, by an imitation of the artistic form. Besides it would introduce confusion among the translations of different Christian nations. The Iliad of Homer, the Odes of Horace, Dante's Divina Commedia, Petrarca's Sonnets, Milton's Paradise Lost, Goethe's Faust, cannot be translated in prose without losing their poetic

---

[1] Ewald (*l. c.*, p. 104) denies the existence of rhyme in Hebrew poetry; yet the occasional rhymes and alliterations in the song of Lamech, the song of Moses, the song of Deborah, *etc.*, can hardly be merely accidental. Delitzsch (in his *Com. on the Psalms*, Leipz., 1867, p. 17) says: "*Die althebräische Poesie hat weder Reim noch Metrum, welche beide erst im 7. Jahr n. Chr. von der jüdischen Poesie angeeignet wurden.*" But afterwards he qualifies this remark and admits that the beginnings of rhyme and metre are found in the poetry of the O. T., so that there is an element of truth in the assertion of Philo, Josephus, Eusebius and Jerome, who find there the Greek and Roman metres.

charm, yea, their very soul. They must be freely reproduced in poetic form, and this can only be done by a poetic genius, and with more or less departure from the original. But the Psalms, the Book of Job, and Isaiah can be transferred by a good and devout scholar, in form as well as in substance, into any language, without sacrificing their beauty, sublimity, force, and rhythm. The Latin, English and German Psalters are as poetic as the Hebrew, and yet agree with it and among themselves. It is impossible not to see here the hand of Providence, which made the word of truth accessible to all.

The few acrostic or alphabetical poems can hardly be called an exception, viz., Pss. xxv., xxxiv., xxxvii., cxi., cxii., cxix. and cxlv., the Lamentations, and the last chapter of Proverbs (xxxi. 10 sqq.). For the alphabetical order is purely external and mechanical, and at best only an aid to the memory. Pss. cxi. and cxii. are the simplest examples of this class; each contains twenty-two lines, according to the number of the Hebrew alphabet, and the successive lines begin with the letters in their regular order. Ps. cxix. consists of twenty-two strophes, corresponding to the number of Hebrew letters; each strophe begins with the letter of the alphabet, and has eight parallelisms of two lines each, and the first line of each parallelism begins with the initial letter of the strophe. The remaining four acrostic Psalms are not so perfect in arrangement.

Many attempts have been made by Jewish and Christian scholars to reduce the form of Hebrew poetry to a regular system, but they have failed. Josephus says that the Song of Moses at the Red Sea (Ex. xv.) and the farewell Song of Moses (Deut. xxxii.), are composed in the hexameter measure, and the Psalms in trimeters, pentameters and other metres. But he and Philo were anxious to show that the poets of their nation anticipated the Greek poets even in the art of versification. Eusebius says that Deut. xxxii. and Psalm xviii. have the heroic metre of sixteen syllables, and that other metres were employed by the Hebrews. Jerome, the most learned among the Christian fathers (appealing to Philo, Josephus, Origen and Eusebius for proof), asserts that the Psalter, the Lamentations, the Book of Job and almost all the poems of the Bible are composed in hexameters and pentameters, with dactyls and spondees, or in other regular metres, like the classic poems of Pindar, Alcæus and Sappho; he points also to the alphabetical arrangement of Pss. cxi., cxii., cxix., cxlv., and the Lamentations. But the Jews, the custodians of the Hebrew text, ignored such system and arranged the poetic accentuation simply for cantillation in the synagogue.

Among later scholars some deny all metrical laws in Hebrew poetry (Joseph Scaliger, Richard Simon); others maintain the rhythm without metre[1] (Gerhard Vossius); others both rhythm and metre (Gomarus, Buxtorf, Hottinger); others a full system of versification, though differing much in detail (Meibom, Hare, Anton, Lautwein, Bellermann, Saalschütz, E. Meier, Ley, Bickell, Cheyne, Briggs); while still others, believing in the existence of such a system, in whole or in part, think it impossible to recover it (Carpzov, Lowth, Jahn, to some extent also Herder, De Wette, Winer and Wright). Ewald discusses at great length the Hebrew rhythm, metre and strophes, also Hebrew song and music, but without making the matter very clear. Professor Merx, of Heidelberg, finds in the Book of Job a regular syllabic and strophic structure, eight syllables in each stich or line, and an equal number of stichs in each strophe, but he is obliged to resort to arbitrary conjectures of lacunæ or interpolations in the masoretic text. Dr. Julius Ley, in two elaborate treatises (1875, 1887), constructs a minute system of Hebrew versification which is very ingenious but very artificial. He bases it on accentuation, and lays down the principle that the Hebrew metre is not regulated by syllables but by risings (*Hebungen*), and the risings by the accent which generally falls on the last syllable. He distinguishes hexametric, octametric, decametric strophes, disticha, tristicha, tetrasticha, pentasticha, hexasticha, octasticha, enneasticha. Professor Bickell, a distinguished Orientalist in the Roman Catholic University of Innsbruck, defends similar views and furnished specimens of Hebrew poems in metrical arrangement in conformity with Syriac poetry,[2] but in

---

[1] All metre is rhythm, but not all rhythm is metre, as Augustin says (*De Musica*).

[2] *Carmina Veteris Testamenti Metrice*, and *Dichtungen der Hebräer*, 1882.

violation of the traditional accentuation and vocalization. Gietman agrees with him in principle, but Ecker raised energetic protest.

The great objection to those elaborate systems of Hebrew versification is that they are too artificial and cannot be carried out except by violent and arbitrary construction. They must resort to substitution and compensation to account for irregularities, and violate more or less the masoretic system. In most cases they give us no more than a rhythm. The stanzas are of unusual length, and usually no more than periods in prose. The rhyme seldom extends beyond two or three verses, and has no such fixed rules, as it has in modern and also in Arabic poetry. The same is the case with the alliteration and assonance; they do occur, but only occasionally and irregularly. The spirit always controls the letter, and the thought determines the expression.

PARALLELISM OF MEMBERS.

But while the theories of a uniform and fully developed system of versification are at least doubtful, it is generally admitted that Hebrew poetry is marked throughout by what is called the *parallelismus membrorum*.[1] It is not confined to Hebrew poetry, but is found also in Assyrian, Babylonian and Akkadian hymns.[1] This parallelism consists of a certain rhyth-

---

He had previously published *S. Ephræmi Syri Carmina Nisibena*, 1866. Bickell is a convert from Lutheranism.

[1] The term was introduced by Bishop Lowth, who first developed the system of parallelism in its various forms. But the thing itself was known before under different names. Aben Ezra calls it *duplicatio* (*caphul*), Kimchi, *duplicatio sententiæ verbis variatis*. See Delitzsch, *l. c.* p. 18. Rabbi Azariah, and especially Schöttgen (*Horæ Hebraicæ*, Vol. I. 1249-1263), seem to have anticipated the main features of Lowth's system. The theory of Lowth was further developed by Bishop Jebb (died at Limerick, 1833): *Sacred Literature, comprising a review of the principles of composition laid down by Bishop Lowth*, London, 1831. Jebb has shown that parallelism pervades a great portion of the New Testament. The same was done to excess by Dr. John Forbes: *The Symmetrical Structure of Scripture, or the Principles of Hebrew Parallelism*, Edinburgh, 1854.

[2] It is also found in didactic poetry among the Chinese, although only in antithetic form. So I was told by the late missionary bishop, Dr. Schereschrewsky, of Peking.

mical and musical correspondence of two or more sentences of similar, or opposite meaning; so that idea answers to idea in somewhat different words. It serves, by a felicitous variation, to give full expression and harmony to the thought. The parallel members complete or illustrate each other, and produce a music of vowels and consonants. Parallelism reflects the play of human feeling, and supplies the place of regular metre and rhyme in a way that is easily understood and remembered, and can be easily reproduced in every language. It is like the ebbing and flowing of the tide, or like the sound and its echo. Ewald happily compares it to " the rapid stroke as of alternate wings," and to "the heaving and sinking as of the troubled heart." It is found even in the earliest specimen of Hebrew poetry, the Song of Lamech (Gen. iv. 23). It must, therefore, answer to a natural and primitive impulse of poetic sentiment. "*Amant alterna camœnæ*," says Virgil. The classic hexameter and pentameter are a continual parallelism, where, as Herder describes it, "the poetic flowers which, in Hebrew verse, grow on separate stems, are woven into an unbroken wreath."[1]

There are different forms of parallelism, according to the nature of the internal relation of the members. The correspondence may be either one of harmony, or one of contrast, or one of progressive thought, or one simply of comparison, or of symmetrical structure. Since Lowth, it has become customary to distinguish three classes of parallelisms: *synonymous, antithetic,* and *synthetic* or *constructive.* The majority belong to the third class, and even those which are usually counted as synonymous, show more or less progress of thought, and might as well be assigned to the third class. A large number of parallelisms cannot be classified.

1. SYNONYMOUS (also called gradational) parallelism expresses

---

[1] Compare Schiller's distich :

"*Im Hexameter steigt des Springquells flüssige Säule;
Im Pentameter drauf fällt sie melodisch herab.*"

And the happy rendering of Coleridge :

"In the hexameter rises the fountain's silvery column;
In the pentameter aye falling in melody back."

the same idea in different but equivalent words, as in the following examples:—

    Ps. ii. 4. "He that sitteth in the heavens shall laugh:
        The Lord shall have them in derision."
    Ps. viii. 4. "What is man that Thou art mindful of him?
        And the son of man that Thou visitest him?"
    Ps. xix. 1, 2. "The heavens declare the glory of God:
        And the firmament showeth his handiwork."
        "Day unto day uttereth speech:
        And night unto night proclaimeth knowledge."
    Ps. ciii. 1. "Bless the Lord, O my soul:
        And all that is within me, bless His holy name."
Judg. xiv. 14. (Samson's riddle).
        "Out of the eater came forth meat,
        And out of the strong came forth sweetness."

These are parallel couplets; but there are also parallel triplets, as in Ps. i. 1:—

        "Blessed is the man
    That walketh not in the counsel of the ungodly,
      Nor standeth in the way of sinners,
      Nor sitteth in the seat of the scornful."

The priestly blessing, Numbers vi. 24–26, is a synonymous tristich:—

"Jehovah bless thee and keep thee:
  Jehovah make His face shine upon thee and be gracious unto thee:
  Jehovah lift up His countenance upon thee, and give thee peace."

Similar triplets occur in Job iii. 4, 6, 9; Isa. ix. 20.

Parallel quatrains or tetrastichs are less frequent, as in the oracle of Jehovah to Rebekah predicting the future of Jacob and Esau, Gen. xxv. 23:—

"Two nations are in thy womb,
  And two peoples will separate themselves from thy bowels;
  And people will prevail over people,
  And the elder will serve the younger."

In Ps. ciii. 11, 12, the first member corresponds to the third, and the second to the fourth:—

    "For as the heavens are high above the earth,
      So great is His mercy toward them that fear Him.
    So far as the East is from the West,
      So far has He removed our transgressions from Him."

When the two members are precisely the same in word and sense, they are called *identic* parallelism: but there are no cases of mere repetition, unless it be for the sake of emphasis, as in Isa. xv. 1; Ps. xciv. 1, 3.

Occasionally this parallelism is completed by a closing rhyme, as Gen. iv. 23; 1 Sam. xviii. 7; Prov. xxii. 10; xxiii. 22.

2. ANTITHETIC parallelism expresses a contrast or antithesis in sentiment:—

  Ps. I. 6. "For the Lord knoweth the way of the righteous:
      But the way of the ungodly shall perish."

Ps. xxxviii. 9. "Evil-doers shall be cut off:
      But those that wait upon the Lord, they shall inherit
       the earth."

  Prov. x. 1. "A wise son rejoiceth his father:
      But a foolish son is the grief of his mother."

  Prov. x. 7. "The memory of the just is a blessing:
      But the name of the wicked shall rot."

 Prov. xii. 10. "A righteous man regardeth the life of his beast:
      But the tender mercies of the wicked are cruel."

  Hos. xiv. 9. "The ways of the Lord are right, and the just shall walk
      in them;
      But the transgressors shall fall therein."

3. SYNTHETIC or CONSTRUCTIVE parallelism. Here the construction is similar in form, without a precise correspondence in sentiment and word as equivalent or opposite, but with a gradation or progress of thought, as in Ps. xix. 7–11; cxlviii. 7–13; Isa. xiv. 4–9. We quote the first:—

"The law of Jehovah | is perfect, | restoring the soul:
 The testimony of Jehovah | is sure, | making wise the simple.
The precepts of Jehovah | are right, | rejoicing the heart:
 The commandment of Jehovah | is pure, | enlightening the eyes.
The fear of Jehovah | is clean, | enduring forever:
 The judgments of Jehovah | are true, | and righteous altogether.
More to be desired are they | than gold, | yea, than much fine gold:
 Sweeter also | than honey | and the honeycomb,
Moreover, by them | is Thy servant warned:
 In keeping of them | there is great reward."

> 1 Sam. xviii. 7. "Saul smote his thousands:
> And David his myriads."

To these three kinds of parallelism Jebb (*Sacred Literature*) adds a fourth, which he calls *introverted* parallelism, where the first line corresponds to the last (fourth), and the second to the penultimate (third), as in Prov. xxiii. 15, 16:—

> "My son, if thy heart be wise,
> My heart also shall rejoice;
> Yea, my reins shall rejoice,
> When thy lips speak right things."

De Wette distinguishes four, slightly differing from Lowth, Delitzsch six or eight forms of parallelism.

The pause in the progress of thought determines the division of lines and verses. Hebrew poetry always adapts the poetic structure to the sense. Hence there is no monotony, but a beautiful variety and alternation of different forms. Sometimes the parallelism consists simply in the *rhythmical correspondence* of sentences or clauses, without repetition or contrast, or in carrying forward a line of thought in sentences of nearly equal length, as in Psalm cxv. 1–11:—

> "Not unto us, Jehovah, not unto us,
> But unto Thy name give glory,
> For thy mercy,
> For Thy truth's sake.
> Wherefore should the nations say,
> 'Where is now their God?'
> But our God is in the heavens;
> He has done whatsoever He pleased.
> Their idols are silver and gold,
> The work of the hands of men.
> A mouth have they, but they speak not;
> Eyes have they, but they see not;
> Ears have they, but they hear not;
> Noses have they, but they smell not;
> Hands have they, but they handle not;
> Feet have they, but they walk not;
> Neither speak they through their throat.
> They that make them shall be like unto them;
> Yea, every one that trusteth in them.

> O Israel, trust thou in Jehovah:
> He is their help and their shield.
> O house of Aaron, trust ye in Jehovah:
> He is their help and their shield.
> Ye that fear Jehovah, trust in Jehovah:
> He is their help and their shield."

This looser kind of parallelism or rhythmical correspondence and symmetrical construction of sentences, characterizes also much of the Hebrew prose, *e. g.*, the Decalogue, and is continued in the New Testament, *e. g.*, in the Sermon on the Mount (especially the Beatitudes), in the Lord's Prayer, in the Prologue of John, in Rom. v. 12 sqq.; viii. 28 sqq.; 1 Cor. xiii. 1 sqq.; 2 Tim. ii. 11, and other passages which we are accustomed to read as prose, but which even in form are equal to the best poetry—gems in beautiful setting, apples of gold in pictures of silver.

LITERATURE ON BIBLE POETRY.

In conclusion, I present a classified list of the principal works on the Poetry of the Bible:—

I. SPECIAL WORKS ON HEBREW POETRY.

* **Robert Lowth** (son of William Lowth, who wrote a Commentary on the Prophets, born at Winchester, 1710, Prof. of Poetry, Oxford, since 1741, Bishop of London, since 1777, died 1787): *De Sacra Poesi Hebraeorum Prælectiones Academicæ*, Oxford, 1753; with copious notes by *John David Michaelis* (Prof. in Göttingen, d. 1791), Gött., 1770; another ed. with additional notes by *Rosenmüller*, Leipz., 1815; best Latin edition, with the additions of Michaelis, Rosenmüller, Richter, and Weiss, Oxon., 1828. English translation ("*Lectures on the Sacred Poetry of the Hebrews, with the principal notes of Michaelis*") by *G. Gregory*, 1787; reëdited, with improvements, by *Calvin E. Stowe*, Andover, 1829. Comp. also Lowth's preliminary dissertation to his translation of Isaiah (1778; 13th ed., Lond., 1842). Lowth's work is the first scholarly attempt at a learned and critical discussion of Hebrew poetry. Its chief merit is the discovery of parallelism.

* **J. Gottfried Herder** (an almost universal genius and scholar, poet, historian, philosopher and theologian, born 1744, at Mohrungen, in East Prussia, died as court chaplain at Weimar, 1803): *Geist der Hebräischen Poesie* (*Spirit of Hebr. Poetry*), Dessau, 1782; 3d ed. by *Justi*, Leipz., 1825; reprinted in Herder's collected works. Full of enthusiasm for the purity and sublimity of Hebrew poetry. English translation by President

James Marsh, Burlington, Vt., 1833, 2 vols. Comp. also the first twelve *Letters* of Herder *on the Study of Theology*. While Lowth discussed chiefly the *form* of Hebrew poetry, Herder eloquently and enthusiastically expounded its *spirit*.

Leutwein: *Versuch einer richtigen Theorie von der biblischen Verskunst.* Tübingen, 1775.

L. T. Kosegarten: *Ueber den Dichtergeist der heil. Schriftsteller und Jesu Chr.* Greifswald, 1794.

Bellermann: *Versuch über die Metrik der Hebräer.* Berlin, 1813.

A. Gügler: *Die heil. Kunst der Hebräer.* Landshut, 1814.

J. L. Saalschütz: *Von der Form der hebräischen Poesie.* Königsberg, 1825.

M. Nicolas: *Forme de la poesie hébraique.* Paris, 1833.

Fr. Delitzsch: *Zur Geschichte der jüdischen Poesie vom Abschluss der heil. Schriften des A. Bundes bis auf die neueste Zeit.* Leipz., 1836.

J. G. Wenrich: *Commentatio de poesos Hebraicae atque Arabicae origine, indole, mutuoque consensu atque discrimine.* Lips., 1843 (276 pp.).

J. G. Sommer: *Vom Reime in der hebr. Volkspoesie*, in his *Bibl. Abhandlungen.* Bonn, 1846, pp. 85-92.

* **H. Hupfeld**: *Rhythm and Accentuation in Hebrew Poetry*, transl. by Prof. Charles M. Mead in the Andover "*Bibliotheca Sacra*" for 1867. Hupfeld was the successor of Gesenius in Halle, and one of the ablest Hebrew scholars and commentators on the Psalms (d. 1866).

* **Isaac Taylor** (Independent, a learned layman, d. 1865): *The Spirit of the Hebrew Poetry*, repub., New York, 1862 (with a biographical introduction by Dr. Wm. Adams). The work of an able and ingenious amateur in full sympathy with the spirit of Hebrew Poetry.

Ernst Meier: *Geschichte der poetischen National-Literatur der Hebräer.* Leipz., 1856. The same: *Die Form der Hebräischen Poesie.* Tübingen, 1853.

H. Steiner: *Ueber hebräische Poesie.* Basel, 1873.

Albert Werfer: *Die Poesie der Bibel.* Tübingen, 1875.

Julius Ley (Prof. in Marburg): *Grundzüge des Rhythmus, des Vers- und Strophenbaus in der hebräischen Poesie.* Halle, 1875. By the same: *Leitfaden der Metrik der hebräischen Poesie nebst dem ersten Buche der Psalmen nach rhythmischer Vers- und Strophenabtheilung mit metrischer Analyse.* Halle, 1887.

B. Meteler. *Grundzüge der hebräischen Metrik der Psalmen.* Münster, 1879.

G. Bickell (R. Cath. Prof. in Innsbruck): *Metrices biblicae regulae exemplis illustratae*, and *Supplementum metrices biblicae*. Innsbruck, 1879; *Die hebr. Metrik*, 1881; *Carmina Veteris Testamenti metrice*, 1882.

G. Gietmann: *De re metrica Hebraeorum.* Freiburg i. B., 1880.

J. Ecker: *Prof. Bickell's Carmina V. T. metrice; der neuste Versuch einer hebr. Metrik.* Münster, 1883.

Older essays on Hebrew poetry and music by Ebert, Gomarus, Schramm, Fleury, Dannhauer, Pfeiffer, Leyser, Le Clerc, Hare, and others may be found in the XXXI-st and XXXIId vols. of **Ugolino's** *Thesaurus Antiquitatum Sacrarum* (Venet. 1744–'69, 34 vols.).

II. ESSAYS AND ARTICLES IN BOOKS, CYCLOPÆDIAS, AND REVIEWS.

G. B. Winer: *Poesie, hebräische*, in his *Bibl. Realwörterbuch*, Vol. II., 264–268 (3d ed., 1849).

Ed. Reuss: *Hebräische Poesie*, in Herzog's *Real-Encyclopædie*, Vol. V., 598–608; revised ed., V., 671–684. Abridged translation with bibliographical additions in Schaff-Herzog, II. 953 sqq.

W. A. Wright: *Hebrew Poetry*, in Smith's *Dictionary of the Bible* (enlarged Am. ed.), Vol. III., pp. 2549–2561.

Ludwig von Diestel (d. 1879): *Dichtkunst der Hebräer*, in Schenkel's *Bibellexicon*, I., 607–615.

Gust. Baur: *Dichtkunst*, in Riehm's *Handwörterbuch des bibl. Alterthums*, 274–280.

A. S. Aglen: *The Poetry of the Bible*. Several Art. in *The Bible Educator*. Ed. by E. H. Plumptre. Vols. I.–IV. Lond., 1875.

Wm. Robertson Smith: *The Poetry of the Old Testament*, in "*The British Quarterly Review*" for Jan., 1877, pp. 26–70.

Richard Holt Hutton: *The Poetry of the Old Testament*, in his "*Lit. Essays*." London, 1880. Pp. 204–237.

C. A. Briggs (Prof. in the Union Theol. Seminary, New York): *Hebrew Poetry*, in the "Homiletical Quarterly," ed. by Caldwell and Excell. London, 1881. By the same: *Biblical Study*. New York and Edinb., 1883. Ch. IX., pp. 248–295.

III. COMMENTARIES AND ISAGOGICAL WORKS.

* **H. Ewald:** *Die Dichter des Alten Bundes*, in 3 Parts. Göttingen, 1835–'37; 2d ed., 1865 sqq.; 3d ed., 1868. English translation, London, 1880 sqq. Full of genius and independent research. Engl. translation, London, 1880 sqq. See also his *Propheten des Alten Bundes*, 1840; 3d ed. 1868, 3 vols. Engl. translation, Lond., 1876–81, 5 vols.

R. Weber: *Die poet. Bücher des A. Bundes*. Stuttg., 1853–'60.

Ph. Schaff: *Introduction to the Poetical Books of the O. T.* In Lange's Com. on Job, Am. ed. New York, 1874.

E. Meier: *Die poet. Bücher des A. T.* Stuttgart, 1864.

Tayler Lewis: *Metrical Version of Koheleth*, with an introduction (in an Appendix to his translation of Zöckler on *Koheleth* in Lange's Commentary). New York, 1870.

The relevant sections in the Critical Introductions to the Old Testament by DE WETTE, HAEVERNICK, KEIL, BLEEK, REUSS (§§ 122–129, p. 141 sqq.), and the numerous Commentaries on the Psalms, the Book of Job, the Proverbs, and the Song of Songs.

THE DIES IRÆ.

1. "Dies iræ, dies illa,
   Solvet sæclum in favilla,
   Teste David cum Sibylla.

2. Quantus tremor est futurus,
   Quando judex est venturus,
   Cuncta stricte discussurus!

3. Tuba, mirum spargens sonum,
   Per sepulchra regionum,
   Coget omnes ante thronum.

4. Mors stupebit et natura,
   Quum resurget creatura,
   Judicanti responsura.

5. Liber scriptus proferetur,
   In quo totum continetur,
   Unde mundus judicetur.

6. Judex ergo quum sedebit
   Quidquid latet apparebit,
   Nil inultum remanebit.

7. Quid sum miser tunc dicturus,
   Quem patronum rogaturus,
   Quum vix justus sit securus?

8. Rex tremendae majestatis,
   Qui salvandos salvas gratis,
   Salva me, fons pietatis.

9. Recordare, Jesu pie,
   Quod sum causa tuae viæ;
   Ne me perdas illa die.

10. Quærens me sedisti lassus,
    Redemisti crucem passus,
    Tantus labor non sit cassus.

11. Justæ judex ultionis,
    Donum fac remissionis
    Ante diem rationis.

12. Ingemisco tamquam reus,
    Culpâ rubet vultus meus:
    Supplicanti parce, Deus.

13. Qui Mariam absolvisti,
    Et latronem exaudisti,
    Mihi quoque spem dedisti.

14. Preces meae non sunt dignae,
    Sed Tu, bone, fac benigne,
    Ne perenni cremer igne.

15. Inter oves locum præsta,
    Et ab hædis me sequestra,
    Statuens in parte dextra.

16. Confutatis maledictis,
    Flammis acribus addictis;
    Voca me cum benedictis.

17. Oro supplex et acclinis,
    Cor contritum, quasi cinis:
    Gere curam mei finis."

---

18. [Lacrymosa dies illa,
    Qua resurget ex favilla,
    Judicandus homo reus,
    Huic ergo parce, Deus!

19. Pie Jesu, Domine,
    Dona eis requiem. Amen.]

This is the famous DIES IRÆ after the received text of the Roman Missal. Mohnike and Daniel give also the various readings and the text of Hämmerlin, which differs considerably and has six additional stanzas. Of this and the text from the marble slab at Mantua I shall speak below. I have put the last six lines in brackets because they depart from the triplet and triple rhyme, and are no part of the original poem, but were added for liturgical purposes.

THE NAME AND USE OF THE POEM.

The poem is variously called "*Prosa de Mortuis;*" "*De Die Judicii;*" "*In Commemoratione Defunctorum;*" but usually, from its opening words, "*Dies Iræ.*" It is used in the Latin Church, regularly, on the Day of All Souls (November 2), and, at the discretion of the priest, in masses for the dead and on other funeral solemnities. It is frequently accompanied with music, which doubles the effect of the poem, especially Mozart's *Requiem*, his last masterpiece, which is itself like a wondrous trumpet spreading wondrous sounds.

CONTENTS.

The DIES IRÆ is a judgment hymn written for private devotion. It is an act of humiliation and prayer in contemplation of the impending day of retribution, when all secrets shall be revealed and all men be judged according to their deeds done in this life. It is a soliloquy cast in the mould of Augustinian theology. It vibrates between a profound sense of man's guilt and a humble trust in Christ's mercy. The poet is the single actor, and prays for himself. Without a prelude he brings before us the awful theme with a few startling words from the Holy Scriptures. He first describes the general judgment as a future fact, with its accompanying terrors; then he gives expression to the sense of guilt and dismay, and ends with a prayer for the mercy of the Saviour, which prompted Him to die for poor sinners, to forgive Mary Magdalene, and to promise the penitent robber, in his dying hour, a seat in Paradise.

The poem is based upon the prophetic description of the great Day of Jehovah as described in Zephaniah i. 15, 16 :—

"That day is the day of wrath,
A day of trouble and distress,
A day of wasteness and desolation,
A day of darkness and gloom,

> A day of clouds and thick darkness,
> A day of the trumpet and alarm
> Against the fenced cities,
> And against high battlements."[1]

The first words of this prophecy, according to the Latin translation, "*Dies iræ, dies illa,*" furnished the beginning and the key-note of the poem. In like manner the STABAT MATER derived its theme and inspiration from a few words of the Bible in the Vulgate (John xix. 25). The author of DIES IRÆ had also in view the Lord's description of His coming and of the general judgment, Matt. xxiv. and xxv., and several passages of the New Testament, especially 2 Pet. iii. 7–12: "The day of the Lord will come as a thief, in which the heavens shall pass away with a great noise, and the elements shall be dissolved with fervent heat, and the earth and the works that are therein shall be burned up." The "*tuba mirum spargens sonum,*" in verse 3, is an allusion to 1 Cor. xv. 52: "The trumpet shall sound, and the dead shall be raised," and 1 Thess. iv. 16: "The Lord Himself shall descend from heaven with a shout, with the voice of the archangel, and with the trump of God." The "*liber scriptus,*" in verse 5, is the record of all human actions, which will be opened on the judgment day, Dan. vii. 10; Rev. xx. 12. The reference to it calls to mind the sinful deeds and deepens the sense of guilt and awe.[2] In verse 7 the writer had undoubtedly in mind Job iv. 18; xv. 15, and especially 1 Pet. iv. 18: "If the righteous is scarcely saved (*si justus vix salvabitur*), where shall the ungodly and sinner appear?" The second line in verse 8 expresses the idea of salvation by free grace as taught in Rom. iii. 24 ("being justified freely by his grace," *justificati gratis per gratiam ipsius*); Eph. ii. 8; 2 Tim. i. 9, etc. The first line in verse 10: "*Quærens me sedisti* (not, *venisti*) *lassus,*" is a touching allusion to the incident related John iv. 6: "*Jesus* FATIGATUS *ex itinere,* SEDEBAT *sic supra fontem,*" unless it be

---

[1] According to the translation of the Vulgate, "DIES IRÆ, DIES ILLA, *dies tribulationis et angustiæ, dies calamitatis et miseriæ, dies tenebrarum et caliginis, dies nebulæ et turbinis, dies tubæ et clangoris super civitates munitas et super angulos excelsos.*"

[2] A writer in the London "Spectator" for March 7, 1868, mistakes this book for the Bible.

referred to the whole state of humiliation. Mary, in verse 13, is Mary Magdalene, or the sinful woman to whom Christ said: "Thy faith hath saved thee; go in peace," Luke vii. 50. Verses 15 and 16 are suggested by the description of the judgment, Matt. xxv. 33 sqq.

David is mentioned in the first stanza as the representative of the Old Testament prophets, with reference probably to several Psalms in which the judgment of the world is foretold, as Ps. xcvi. 13 ("He cometh, He cometh to judge the earth; He shall judge the world with righteousness"); cii. 26 ("The heavens shall perish"). In some copies and translations, however, *Peter* is substituted for *David*, on account of 2 Pet. iii. 7–12.

With David is joined the *Sibyl* as the representative of the unconscious prophecies of heathenism, with allusion to the Sibylline Oracles of the destruction of the world. The writer no doubt had in view chiefly those lines of Sibylla Erythræa, which form an acrostic on the words ΙΗΣΟΥΣ ΧΡΙΣΤΟΣ ΘΕΟΥ ΥΙΟΣ ΣΩΤΗΡ, i. e. "Jesus Christ, Son of God, Saviour," and which are quoted by Eusebius in Greek, and by St. Augustin in a Latin metrical version, retaining the acrostic form.[1] This apocryphal feature is somewhat repugnant to modern taste, and hence omitted or altered in many Protestant versions of the poem.[2] But it is in perfect keeping with the patristic and scholastic use of the Sibylline Oracles, the 4th Eclogue of Virgil, and other heathen testimonies of the same kind, for apologetic purposes. It gives to the idea of the judgment of the world a universal character, as being founded in the expectations of Gentiles, Jews, and Christians, and indicated by the light of reason as well as by the voice of revelation. The mediæval painters and Michael Angelo likewise placed the Sibyl alongside of the prophets of Israel.

---

[1] Augustin, *De Civitate Dei*, lib. xviii., cap. 23 (translated in Schaff's ed. of "The City of God," p. 572 sq.). The oracle consists of 27 lines, and commences:—

"*Judicii signum tellus sudore madescet;*
E cœlo Rex adveniet per sæcla futurus:
Scilicet in carne præsens ut judicet orbem."

[2] Some Roman Catholic Missals, as those of Paris and Metz (1778), substitute from Matt. xxiv. 30, for *David cum Sibylla*:—

"*Crucis expandens vexilla.*"

The original poem appropriately closes with the words: "*Gere curam mei finis.*" The last six lines break the unity and symmetry of the poem, they differ from the rest in rhyme and measure, and turn the attention from the writer to the departed faithful as the subject of his prayer (*huic, eis*). They are, therefore, an addition by another hand, probably from a funeral service already in public use.

CHARACTER AND VALUE.

The DIES IRÆ is the acknowledged masterpiece of Latin church poetry, and the greatest judgment hymn of all ages. No single poem of any nation or language has acquired such a celebrity, and been the subject of so much praise and comment. It has no rival. It stands solitary and alone in its glory, and will probably never be surpassed.

"It would be difficult," says Coles, "to find, in the whole range of literature, a production to which a profounder interest attaches than to that magnificent canticle of the middle ages, the DIES IRÆ. Among poetic gems it is the diamond." The Germans call it, with reference to its majesty and antique massiveness, the gigantic hymn (*Gigantenhymnus*). In simplicity and faith it fully equals an older anonymous judgment hymn of the seventh or eighth century, commencing: "*Apparebit repentina magna dies Domini;*"[1] while in lyric fervor and effect, as well as in majesty and terror, it far surpasses it and all the numerous imitations of later times. The STABAT MATER DOLOROSA bears many points of resemblance, being likewise the product of the Franciscan order, a regular part of the Catholic worship, the theme of glorious musical compositions, and multiplied by a large number of translations. It is equal, or even superior, to the DIES IRÆ in pathos, but does not reach its power and grandeur, and offends Protestant ears by addressing the Virgin Mary rather than Christ.

The DIES IRÆ breathes, it is true, the mediæval spirit of legal-

---

[1] See the Latin text in Daniel, *Thes. Hymnol.* 1. 194, and the English version of John M. Neale in Schaff's *Christ in Song*, p. 287 sqq. (London edition).

istic and ascetic piety, and looks forward to the solemn winding-up of the world's history with feelings of trembling and fear rather than of hope.[1] The concluding prayer for the dead, which, however, is a later addition, implies that the souls of the departed (in Purgatory) may be benefited by the prayers of the living. But with this exception the poem is free from the objectionable features of Romanism; while it is positively evangelical in representing salvation as an act of the free grace of Christ, "*qui salvandos salvat gratis.*" And in the lines, "*Quem patronum rogaturus, Quum vix justus sit securus,*" it virtually renounces the doctrine of the advocacy of the Virgin and the Saints, and takes refuge only in Christ. Beneath the drifting mass of mediaeval traditions there was an undercurrent of simple faith in Christ, which meets us in the writings of St. Anselm, St. Bernard, the sermons of Tauler, and in the inimitable *Imitation of Christ* by Thomas à Kempis. When Christians come to die, they ask nothing but mercy and rely solely on the merits of the Redeemer. The nearer they approach Christ and eternity the nearer they approach each other. Copernicus composed the following epitaph for himself:

> "Not the grace bestowed upon Paul do I pray for;
> Not the mercy by which Thou pardonedst Peter:
> That alone which Thou grantedst the crucified robber,—
> That alone do I pray for."

The DIES IRÆ is as much admired by Protestants as by Roman Catholics. Protestant writers have done most for its illustration and translation, and Goethe has best described its effect upon the guilty conscience (in the cathedral scene of *Faust*):

> "Horror seizes thee!
> The trump sounds!
> The grave trembles!
> And thy heart
> From the repose of its ashes,
> For fiery torment
> Brought to life again,
> Trembles up."

---

[1] The bright aspect of the judgment as the day of complete redemption is set forth in the mediaeval companion hymn, "*Dies iræ, dies vitæ.*" See Schaff's *Christ in Song*, p. 296.

The secret of the power of the Dies Iræ lies first in the intensity of pious feeling with which its great theme is handled. The poet realizes the impending judgment of the world as an awful and overpowering event that is as certain as the approach of night. He hears the trumpet of the archangel sounding through the open sepulchres. He sees the dead rising from the dust of ages, and stands aghast before the final conflagration and collapse of the universe. He sees the Son of Man seated in terrific majesty on the judgment throne, with the open book of the deeds of ages, dividing the good from the bad and pronouncing the irrevocable sentence of everlasting weal and everlasting woe. And with the spirit of an humble penitent he pleads for mercy, mercy at the hands of Him who left his throne of glory and died on the cross for the salvation of sinners. The poem is a cry from the depth of personal experience, and irresistibly draws every reader into sympathetic excitement. That man is indeed to be pitied who can read it without shaking and quivering with emotion.

The second element of its power lies in the inimitable form which commands the admiration of every man of taste for poetry or music. The poem is divided into stanzas; each stanza is a triplet with a triple double rhyme, which strikes the ear like solemn music and excites deep emotion. Dante may have caught from it the inspiration of the spirit and form of his Divina Commedia with its triplets and terza rima. Each word is the right word in the right place, and could not be spared. And what a combination of simplicity and majesty in the diction as well as the thought! Whatever there is of power, dignity and melody in the old Roman tongue is here combined with unadorned simplicity, as in no other poem, heathen or Christian, and is made subservient to the one grand idea of the poem. The Dies Iræ is onomato-poetic. It echoes, as well as human language can do, the collapse and wreck of the universe, the trembling and wailing of sinners before the judgment seat of an infinitely holy and righteous God, and the humble pleading for mercy from the All-Merciful. Every word sounds like the peal of an organ, yea, like the trumpet of the archangel summoning the dead to endless bliss or to endless woe. The stately metre, the triple rhyme, the selection of the vowels in full harmony with the thought and feeling, heighten and complete the effect upon the ear and the heart of the hearer. The music of the vowel assonances and consonances, *e. g.*, the double u in the 2d and 7th stanzas (*futurus, venturus, discussurus; dicturus, rogaturus, securus*), the o and u in the 3d stanza (*sonum, regionum, thronum*), the i and e in the 9th stanza (*pie, viae, die*), defy the skill of the best translators in any language.[1]

OPINIONS OF CRITICS.

We add the judgments of eminent writers.

Frederick von Meyer, a senator of Frankfort-on-the-Main, and author of a revision of Luther's German Bible, in introducing two original translations of the DIES IRÆ, calls it "an awful poem, poor in imagery, all feeling. Like a hammer it beats the human breast with three mysterious rhyme-strokes. With the unfeeling person who can read it without terror, or hear it without awe, I would not live under one roof. I wish it could be sounded into the ears of the impenitent and hypocrites every Ash Wednesday, or Good Friday, or any other day of humiliation and prayer in all the churches."[2]

Daniel, the learned hymnologist, justly styles the DIES IRÆ "*uno omnium consensu sacrae poeseos summum decus et ecclesiae*

---

[1] In another place (*Christ in Song*, London ed., 1870, p. 290) I have thus characterized this poem: "The secret of the irresistible power of the DIES IRÆ lies in the awful grandeur of the theme, the intense earnestness and pathos of the poet, the simple majesty and solemn music of its language, the stately metre, the triple rhyme, and the vowel assonances chosen in striking adaptation to the sense,—all combining to produce an overwhelming effect, as if we heard the final crash of the universe, the commotion of the opening graves, the trumpet of the archangel that summons the quick and the dead, and as if we saw 'the King of tremendous majesty,' seated on the throne of justice and mercy, and ready to dispense eternal life and eternal woe."

[2] "*Der Lichtbote*" (Frankfort-on-the-Main, 1806): "*Wie ein Hammer schlägt es mit drei geheimnissvollen Reimklängen an die Menschenbrust. Mit dem Unempfindlichen, der es ohne Schrecken lesen und ohne Grauen hören kann, möchte ich nicht unter einem Dache wohnen.*" Daniel, ii. 112, erroneously ascribes this admirable description to Guericke (1849), who must have borrowed it from Meyer (1806).

latinæ κειμήλιον pretiosissimum," and adds: "*Quot sunt verba tot pondera, immo tonitrua.*"[1]

Albert Knapp, one of the most gifted religious poets of Germany, compares the Latin original to a blast from the trump of the resurrection, and declares it inimitable in any translation.[2]

Dean Milman places it next to the *Te Deum*, and remarks: "There is nothing, in my judgment, to be compared with the monkish *Dies iræ, dies illa*, or even the *Stabat Mater.*"

Dr. William R. Williams, an American Baptist divine, and a scholar of cultivated literary taste, has appended to his essay on the "Conservative Principle of our Literature," a fine note on DIES IRÆ, in which he characterizes it thus: "Combining somewhat of the rhythm of classical Latin with the rhymes of the mediæval Latin, treating of a theme full of awful sublimity, and grouping together the most startling imagery of Scripture as to the last judgment, and throwing this into yet stronger relief by the barbaric(?) simplicity of the style in which it is set, and adding to all these its full and trumpet-like cadences, and uniting with the impassioned feelings of the South, whence it emanated, the gravity of the North, whose severer style it adopted, it is well fitted to arouse the hearer."[3]

Archbishop Trench, who among other useful works has prepared an admirable collection of Latin Church poetry, and written one of the best translations of DIES IRÆ, remarks: "The metre so grandly devised, of which I remember no other example,[4] fitted though it has here shown itself for bringing out some of

---

[1] *Thes. Hymnol.*, ii., p. 112.

[2] *Evangelischer Liederschatz*, 3d ed., p. 1347.

[3] *Miscellanies*, N. Y., 1850, p. 78.

[4] This is an error. There are verses of striking resemblance attributed by some to St. Bernard, but probably of much later date (see Mohnike, *l. c.*, p. 9):

"*Quum recordor moriturus
Quid post mortem sim futurus,
Terror terret me venturus,
Quem exspecto non securus.
Terret dies me terroris,
Dies iræ ac furoris,
Dies luctus ac mæroris,
Dies ultrix peccatoris,
Dies iræ, dies illa.*"

the noblest powers of the Latin language—the solemn effect of the triple rhyme, which has been likened [by Fred. von Meyer] to blow following blow of the hammer on the anvil—the confidence of the poet in the universal interest of his theme, a confidence which has made him set out his matter with so majestic and unadorned a plainness as at once to be intelligible to all—these merits, with many more, have combined to give the DIES IRÆ a foremost place among the masterpieces of sacred song.[1]

Abraham Coles, the author of seventeen distinct translations of DIES IRÆ, says of it among other things: "Every line weeps. Underneath every word and syllable a living heart throbs and pulsates. The very rhythm, or that alternate elevation and depression of the voice which prosodists call the *arsis* and the *thesis*, one might almost fancy were synchronous with the contraction and the dilatation of the heart. It is more than dramatic. The horror and the dread are real, are actual, not acted!"

"The DIES IRÆ," to quote from the celebrated French philosopher Victor Cousin, "recited only, produces the most terrible effect. In those fearful words, every blow tells, so to speak; each word contains a distinct sentiment, an idea at once profound and determinate. The intellect advances at each step, and the heart rushes on in its turn."[2]

Mrs. Charles, the accomplished authoress of the "Schönberg-Cotta Family" and other popular works, thus speaks of the DIES IRÆ: "That hymn rose alone in a comparative pause, as if Christendom had been hushed to listen to its deep music, ranging as it does through so many tones of human feeling, from the trembling awe and the low murmurs of confession, to tender, pathetic pleading with One who, though the 'just, avenging Judge, yet sate weary on the well of Samaria, seeking the lost, trod the mournful way, and died the bitterest death for sinful men.' Its supposed author, Thomas of Celano, in the Abruzzo, lived during the fourteenth [thirteenth] century, was a Franciscan monk, and a personal friend of St. Francis himself, whose life he wrote. But so much doubt has hung about the authorship, and if Thomas of Celano was the author, so

---

[1] *Sacred Latin Poetry*, 2d ed., p. 296.

[2] *Lectures on the True, the Beautiful, and the Good*, p. 177.

little is known of him—even the date of his birth and death not being ascertained—that we may best think of the DIES IRÆ as a solemn strain sung by an invisible singer. There is a hush in the great choral service of the universal Church, when suddenly, we scarcely know whence, a single voice, low and trembling, breaks the silence; so low and grave that it seems to deepen the stillness, yet so clear and deep that its softest tones and words are heard throughout Christendom, and vibrate throughout every heart—grand and echoing as an organ, yet homely and human as if the words were spoken rather than sung. And through the listening multitudes solemnly that melody flows on, sung not to the multitudes, but 'to the Lord,' and therefore carrying with it the hearts of men, till the singer is no more solitary, but the selfsame tearful, solemn strain pours from the lips of the whole Church as if from one voice, and yet each one sings it as if alone, to God."[1]

Edwards and Park, in their *Selections from German Literature*,[2] quote a remark of Tholuck, as to the deep sensation produced by the singing of this hymn in the University church at Halle: "The impression, especially that which was made by the last words, as sung by the University choir alone, will be forgotten by no one." An American clergyman, present on the occasion, said: "It was impossible to refrain from tears, when, at the seventh stanza, all the trumpets ceased, and the choir, accompanied by a softened tone of the organ, sung those touching lines—

'*Quid sum miser tunc dicturus.*'"

Literary men and secular poets have been captivated by the DIES IRÆ as well as men in full religious sympathy with its solemn thoughts and feelings.

Goethe introduced several stanzas with thrilling effect in the cathedral scene of *Faust* to stir up the conscience of poor Margaret, who is seized with horror at the thought of the sounding trump, the trembling graves, and the fiery torment.

Justinus Kerner, a Suabian poet and a friend of Uhland and Schwab, made good use of it in his poem *Die Wahnsinnigen*

---

[1] *The Voice of Christian Life in Song*, N. York ed., 1859, p. 170.

[2] Andover, Mass., 1839, p. 185.

Brüder, where four impious brothers enter a church to ridicule religion, but are suddenly brought to pause and repent, by hearing this judgment hymn.

Dr. Johnson, with his coarse, yet noble and manful nature, could never repeat, without bursting into a flood of tears, the stanza ending—

"*Tantus labor non sit cassus.*"

The Earl of Roscommon, "not more learned than good," in the moment in which he expired, uttered with the most fervent devotion two lines of his own version:—

"My God, my Father, and my Friend,
Do not forsake me in my end!"

Sir Walter Scott happily reproduced some stanzas of the DIES IRÆ in English, and, following the example of Goethe, inserted them in the sixth canto of his "Lay of the Last Minstrel." On his dying bed, when the strength of his body and mind was failing, he was distinctly overheard repeating portions of the Latin original. In a letter to Crabbe, he remarks: "To my Gothic ear, the STABAT MATER, the DIES IRÆ, and some of the other hymns of the Catholic Church, are more solemn and affecting than the fine classical poetry of Buchanan; the one has the gloomy dignity of a Gothic church, and reminds us constantly of the worship to which it is dedicated; the other is more like a pagan temple, recalling to our memory the classical and fabulous deities."

The DIES IRÆ has also given rise to some of the greatest musical compositions of Palestrina, Durante, Pergolese, Haydn, Vogler, Winter, Cherubini, Gottfried Weber, Neukomm, and of Mozart, in his famous *Requiem*, during the composition of which he died (1791).

ORIGIN AND HISTORY

The author of the DIES IRÆ was unconcerned about his fame, and probably unconscious of the merits of the poem, as he certainly was of its unparalleled success. Like the cathedral builders, he wished to be unknown, feeling that God alone is great, and that man is nothing. He wrote the poem from a sort of inward necessity and under the power of an inspiration which prompts every great work of genius. His object was to excite himself to repentance and faith by a description of the terrors of the judgment day. The poem emanated from a subjective state of mind, probably without any regard to public use, but was soon found to be admirably adapted for divine worship on solemn occasions, especially the day for the commemoration of the departed. The deepest subjectivity in lyric poetry often proves to be the highest order of objectivity. The same may be said of the hymns of Paul Gerhardt and of many Moravian hymns.

The authorship of DIES IRÆ cannot be determined with absolute certainty. It became early a subject of dispute between rival monastic orders. There is no positive evidence to decide the question, but the probability is in favor of THOMAS A CELANO, so called from his native little town Celano, in Abruzzo Ulteriore, in Italy, on the Adriatic. He was an intimate friend and the first biographer of St. Francis of Assisi,[1] Superior of the Franciscan Convents at Cologne, Mayence, Worms and Speier, and died, after his return to Italy, about A. D. 1255.

The very first notice of the poem, which, however, is one hundred and thirty years later than the age of the supposed author, ascribes it to Thomas. This notice is found in a superstitious book entitled, *Liber Conformitatum*, written in 1385 by a Franciscan monk, Bartholomæus Albizzi, of Pisa (died 1401), in which he tries to show, by forty points of comparison, that St. Francis of Assisi became completely conformed to our Saviour, especially by the impression of the five stigmata on his body.[2]

Here he speaks incidentally of brother Thomas of Celano in this way: "*Locum habet Celani de quo fuit frater Thomas, qui*

---

[1] His biography of St. Francis, known under the name of *Legenda Antiqua*, is published in the *Acta Sanctorum* for October, tom. ii. Mohnike (*l. c.* p. 30) is in error on this point, when he says that it was never printed. It is called *Legenda Antiqua*, to distinguish it from the *Legenda Major* of Bonaventura, a later and fuller biography of St. Francis.

[2] On this book and the stigmatization miracle, compare an interesting essay of Tholuck on the Miracles of the Catholic Church, in his *Miscellanies*, vol. i., p. 97 *sqq.*; also the biographies of St. Francis by Hase (1856), Mrs. Oliphant (1870), Cherance (1879), and Bernardin (1880).

mandato Apostolico [*i.e.*, by order of Pope Gregory IX.] *scripsit sermone polito legendam primum beati Francisci, et* PROSAM DE MORTUIS QUÆ CANTATUR IN MISSA ' DIES IRÆ,' ETC., DICITUR FECISSE." This passage proves only the existence of a tradition in favor of the authorship of Thomas and the use of the DIES IRÆ in the mass toward the close of the fourteenth century.

The learned and laborious Irish historian of the Franciscans, Lucas Wadding (born 1580, died 1657), in his two works, *Annales Minorum* (1625–1654), and *Scriptores Ordinis Minorum* (1650), defends the tradition, though without positive proof, and ascribes to Thomas two other hymns, both in honor of St. Francis.[1] He was followed by Rambach, Mohnike, Finke, Lisco, Daniel, Mone, Koch, Palmer, Trench, W. R. Williams, Coles, and nearly all the modern writers on the subject. Mohnike, after a careful examination of the question of authorship, arrives at the conclusion (*l. c.*, p. 31): "Thomas of Celano must be regarded as the author of the DIES IRÆ until—which can scarcely be expected—it can be irrefragably proven that another composed it."

There is no doubt that his claims are much stronger than those of any other to whom the rivalry of monastic orders or the conjecture of critics has ascribed the authorship—viz., Gregory the Great (died 604), St. Bernard (died 1153), St. Bonaventura (died 1274), Latinus Frangipani, also called Malabranca, a Dominican (died 1296), Thurston, Archbishop of York (died 1140), Felix Hämmerlin, or Malleolus, of Zurich (1389 to 1457).

The extraordinary religious fervor and devotion which characterize the early history of the Franciscan order, may be considered as an argument of internal probability for the authorship of Thomas of Celano. The other two hymns ascribed to him, though far inferior in merit, are by no means destitute of poetic talent. Many a poet has risen once, under the power

---

[1] The one commencing "*Fregit victor victualis*," the other, "*Sanctitatis nova signa.*" Wadding supposed that these poems were lost; but the first was printed in one of the earlier Paris Missals, the other in the *Acta Sanctorum* for Oct. 2, p. 301. See both in Daniel's *Thes. Hymnol.*, tom. v., p. 314, 317. Comp. Trench's *Sacred Latin Poetry*, p. 295 (2d ed.).

of inspiration, far above the level of his ordinary works. St. Francis himself had a poetic nature. Another Franciscan monk, Jacopone, who died half a century after Thomas, is the reputed author of the STABAT MATER, which stands next to the DIES IRÆ in the whole range of Latin hymnology. Thus we are indebted, in all probability, to the Franciscan order for the most sublime, as well as for the most pathetic hymn of the middle ages.

Mone[1] has suggested the idea that the DIES IRÆ arose not, as heretofore supposed, from the individual contemplation of a monk in his lonely cell, but was intended for the funeral service of the Church, and inspired by older judgment hymns in public use. In one of these, which he found in a MS. at Reichenau from the twelfth or thirteenth century, the passage occurs:—

"*Lacrymosa dies illa,
Qua resurgens ex favilla
Homo reus judicandus.*"

The closing suspirium and prayer for the departed,

"*Pie Jesu, Domine,
Dona eis requiem,*"

is likewise found in older hymns and missals. Mone conjectures that the author of DIES IRÆ himself appended these closing lines to his poem. Daniel[2] and Philip Wackernagel[3] are disposed to adopt his view. But it seems to me much more probable, as already remarked, that the original poem closed with "*Gere curam mei finis,*" and that the remaining six lines, with their different versification and the change from the first person to the third ("*huic*" and "*eis*"), were added from older sources by the compilers of mediæval missals. Then we have a perfectly uniform production, free from any allusion to Purgatory.

The poem cannot be traced beyond the thirteenth century.[4] In the second half of the fourteenth it was in public use in Italy.

---

[1] *Lateinische Hymnen des Mittelalters,* 1853, vol. i., p. 408.

[2] Tom. v., p. 110.

[3] *Das Deutsche Kirchenlied von der ältesten Zeit,* etc., vol. i., p. 138.

[4] Daniel (ii., p. 113): "*Ipsius nimirum carminis natura indicat, illud multo magis post quam ante Thomæ Celanensis ætatem in lucem prodiisse.*"

From the land of its birth it gradually passed into the church service of other countries, scattering along its track "the luminous footprints of its victorious progress as the subduer of hearts."

DIFFERENT TEXTS.

The question as to the best text of the DIES IRAE must be decided in favor of the received text which is found in the Missals. But it has probably undergone several slight modifications before it assumed its present authorized shape. We have besides two texts which differ from the received, not only by a number of verbal variations, but also in length.

One of these texts is said to be inscribed on a marble slab of the Church of St. Francis of Assisi at Mantua, and opens with the following four stanzas, which serve as an introduction and give the poem the aspect of a solitary devotional meditation:—

1. "Cogita (Quaeso), anima fidelis, Ad quid respondere velis Christo venturo de cœlis,	1. "Weigh with solemn thought and tender, What response, thou, soul, wilt render Then, when Christ shall come in splendor,
2. Quum deposcet rationem Ob boni omissionem, Ob mali commissionem.	2. And thy life shall be inspected, All its hidden guilt detected, Evil done and good neglected.
3. Dies illa, dies iræ, Quem eumemur prævenire, Obviumque Deo ira,	3. For that day of vengeance neareth: Ready be each one that heareth, God to meet when He appeareth,
4. Seria contritione, Gratiæ apprehensione, Vitæ emendatione."	4. By repenting, by believing, By God's offered grace receiving, By all evil courses leaving."

Then follows the "Dies iræ, dies illa," as we now have it from the first to the sixteenth stanza, ending with,

"*Voca me cum benedictis.*"

Instead of the eighteenth stanza and the last six lines, the Mantua text offers this concluding stanza:—

"Consors ut beatitatis Vivam cum justificatis In ævum æternitatis. Amen!"	"That in fellowship fraternal With inhabitants supernal I may live the life eternal. Amen!"

Dr. Mohnike, of Stralsund, who published this text (*l. c.*, p. 45–47) in 1824, as he supposed, for the first time, from a manuscript copy made in the seventeenth century by Charisius, burgomaster of Stralsund (1676), regards it as the original form of the hymn, or at least as coming nearest to it.[1] This conjecture derives some support from the fact that other hymns were abridged or altered for the Missal and the Breviary (*e. g.*, St. Bernard's "*Jesu dulcis memoria*").[2] But this consideration is overruled by the questionable date of the Mantua inscription, as compared with the present text, which was already mentioned in 1385, and by the evident inferiority of the introductory stanzas, which are flat and prosy compared with the rest. There could be no more startling and majestic opening than the ancient Scripture words, "*Dies iræ, dies illa.*" The STABAT MATER, likewise, opens with a Scripture sentence.

The second rival of the received text is found among the poems of Felix Hämmerlin (Malleolus) of Zurich, a distinguished ecclesiastic of his age, a member of the Councils of Constance and Basel, and a reformer of various abuses, who ended his life (A.D. 1457) in the prison of the Franciscan convent at Lucerne. Among several poems which he composed in prison was found a *Dies Iræ*, which was published from the manuscripts of the public library of Zurich, by Leonhard Meister, also by Mohnike (p. 39–42), and Lisco (ii. 103–105). It opens like the received text, which it presents with some verbal variations till stanza 17th (inclusive), and then adds the following seven stanzas, which we give with the translation of Dr. Coles (p. xviii.):—

18. "*Lacrymosa die illa,*
    Quum resurget ex favilla,
    Tamquam ignis ex scintilla,
	18. "On that day of woe and weeping
	    When, like fire from spark upleaping,
	    Starts, from ashes where he's sleeping,

[1] Charisius, however, copied his text not directly from the original at Mantua, but, as Daniel shows (ii. 11*), from the *Florilegium Magnum*, published at Frankfort-on-the-Main, 1621, p. 1862, without any allusion to the Mantua inscription. This work reads in the first line *Quarso* for *Cogita*. Lisco (t. 80), Williams (*Miscellanies*, p. 80), and Coles (*l. c.*, p. xiv.) adopt the conjecture of Mohnike.

[2] The Roman Breviary deals very freely with original texts. Protestant hymnology likewise furnishes some examples of appropriating a part only of a longer poem and omitting the first stanzas, *e. g.* Keble's evening hymn: "Sun of my soul, my Saviour dear," and Meta Heusser's Easter hymn: "*Lamm das gelitten, und Löwe der siegreich gerungen,*"—both great favorites, though not intended for hymns by the authors.

19.	Judicandus homo reus; Huic ergo parce, Deus, Esto semper adjutor meus!	19.	Man, account to Thee to render; Spare the miserable offender, Be my Helper and Defender!
20.	Quando cœli sunt movendi, Dies adsunt tunc tremendi, Nullum tempus pœnitendi.	20.	When the heavens away are flying, Days of trembling then and crying, For repentance time denying;
21.	Sed salvatis lœta dies, Et damnatis nulla quies, Sed dæmonum effigies.	21.	To the saved a day of gladness, To the damned a day of sadness, Demon forms and shapes of madness.
22.	O tu Deus majestatis, Almæ candor Trinitatis, Nunc conjunge cum beatis.	22.	God of infinite perfection, Trinity's serene reflection, Give me part with the election!
23.	Vitam meam fac felicem, Propter tuam genetricem, Jesse florem et radicem.	23.	Happiness upon me shower, For Thy Mother's sake, with power, Who is Jesse's root and flower.
24.	Præsta nobis tunc levamen, Dulce nostrum fac certamen, Ut clamemus omnes Amen."	24.	From Thy fulness comfort pour us, Fight Thou with us or fight for us, So we'll shout, Amen, in chorus."

Every reader must feel at once that these additions are but weak repetitions of the former verses. They are disfigured, moreover (ver. 23), by Mariolatry, of which the original is entirely free.

A POLITICAL PERVERSION.

The DIES IRAE did not escape profanation. Some Roman priest, about the year 1700, gratified his hatred of Protestantism by perverting this judgment hymn into a false prophecy of the downfall of the Reformed religion in Holland and England, which he hoped from the restoration of the Stuarts and the union of the French and Spanish crowns in the Bourbon family. Here are a few specimens of this wretched parody as quoted by Guhrauer, Lisco and Daniel:[1]

> "Dies irae, dies illa,
> Solvet fœdus in favilla,
> Teste Tago, Scaldi, Scylla.

[1] Lisco (p. 111 sqq.) gives also Guhrauer's German translation, which begins:—

> "Jener Tag, der Tag der Wehen,
> Lässt den Bund in Nichts vergehen,
> Tajo, Schelde werden's sehen."

Quantus tremor est futurus,
Dum Philippus est venturus,
Has Paludes aggressurus!

. . .

Hic Rex ergo cum sedebit,
Vera fides refulgebit,
Nil Calvino remanebit.

Quid sum miser tunc dicturus,
Quem Patronum rogaturus,
Quum nec Anglus sit securus?

Magne Rector liliorum,[1]
Amor, timor populorum,
Parce terris Batavorum.

. . .

Preces meæ non sunt dignæ,
Sed, Rex magne, fac benigne,
Ne bombarum cremer igne.

. . .

Confutatis Calvi boutis,
Patre, nato, restitutis,[2]
Redde mihi spem salutis!

Ora supplex et acclinis
Calvinismus fiat cinis,
Lacrymarum ut sit finis!"

TRANSLATIONS OF THE DIES IRÆ.

No poem has so often challenged and defied the skill of translators and imitators as the DIES IRÆ. A collection of the English and German translations alone would fill a respectable volume. The dictionary of rhyme has been nearly exhausted upon it, and every new attempt must of necessity present points of resemblance to former versions.

But the very fact that it is untranslatable will ever call forth new attempts. The large number of translations proves that none comes fully up to the original. Its music, majesty and grandeur can be only imperfectly rendered. "Its apparent

---

[1] Louis XIV., of France, in allusion to the lilies on his armorial shield.

[2] James II., of England, and his son, the Prince of Wales, expelled in 1688 by Parliament and the Protestant William of Orange.

artlessness and simplicity indicate that it can be turned readily into another language, but its secret power refuses to be thus transferred." "The song of Thomas," says Daniel,[1] "is not only in words but in spirit intensely Latin and uncongenial to any other language." He finds the chief difficulty in reproducing the vowel assonances which constitute the musical power and effect of the original.

By far the greatest number of translations are German and English.

Mohnike gives, in full or in part, 24 German versions made prior to 1824, and added 21 more in 1832. Lisco, in his monograph on the *Dies Iræ*, 1840, increased the number to 54, exclusive of incomplete versions. In a subsequent monograph on the *Stabat Mater*, 1843, he republished in full, in three parallel columns, 53 German versions of the *Stabat Mater Dolorosa*, and, in an appendix, 17 additional versions of the DIES IRÆ. This would make in all 71 German translations before the year 1843. But this list has since considerably increased, so that the whole number of German translations now existing cannot fall short of eighty, if not a hundred. Some eminent poets, as Herder, A. W. von Schlegel, and Albert Knapp, are among the German translators of the DIES IRÆ.

Larger in number, and equal or superior in merit, are the English versions. I counted over a hundred and fifty.[2] They are mostly of recent date. The English language, by its solemnity, music and force, is admirably adapted for the DIES IRÆ, notwithstanding its comparative poverty in double rhymes. The oldest translation was made in 1621 by Joshua Sylvester, in 10 stanzas of 6 lines each. Then followed, in 1646, the free and vigorous reproduction of Crashaw, an Anglican clergyman of poetic genius, who from the school of Archbishop Laud went over to the Roman Church. The Earl of Roscommon (1633–1684), a nephew of the famous Earl of Strafford, and the only virtuous popular poet in the licentious age of the Restoration, a poet,

 "To whom the wit of Greece and Rome was known,
 And every author's merit but his own,"

---

[1] *Thes. Hymnol.*, ii., 121.   [2] See the list at the close of the essay.

made a more faithful version, in iambic triplets. In the present century Sir Walter Scott, by his partial, but most happy reproduction, awakened a new literary interest in the poem, to which we owe the easy and elegant version of Lord Macaulay from the year 1826. High dignitaries and eminent divines of the Church of England, as Archbishop Trench and Dean Alford, adhered more closely to the original. Several members of the Anglo-Catholic school of Oxford, Isaac Williams, W. J. Irons, and E. Caswall (the last seceded to Rome) furnished excellent translations.

In America, ministers and laymen of various denominations have taken part in this rivalry and nearly or fully doubled the number of English translations. Among them are Dr. W. R. Williams (Baptist), Dr. H. Mills (Presbyterian), Dr. Robert Davidson (Presbyterian), Charles Rockwell, Edward Slosson, Epes Sargent, Erastus C. Benedict (Dutch Reformed), General John A. Dix (Episcopalian), Thomas C. Porter (German Reformed), Dr. Ch. P. Krauth (Lutheran), Samuel W. Duffield (Presbyterian), Dr. Franklin Johnson (Baptist), Dr. W. S. McKenzie (Baptist), Rev. A. H. Fahnestock (Presbyterian).

The palm among American translators must be awarded to a physician, Abraham Coles, of Scotch Plains, New Jersey. He prepared, between 1847 and 1859, thirteen versions, six of which are in the trochaic measure and double rhyme of the original, five in the same rhythm, but in single rhyme, one in iambic triplets, like Roscommon's, the last in quatrains, like Crashaw's version. The first two appeared anonymously in the Newark *Daily Advertiser*, 1847, and a part of one found its way into Mrs. Stowe's *Uncle Tom's Cabin*, the other into H. W. Beecher's *Plymouth Collection of Hymns and Tunes*. The thirteen versions were published together with an introduction in a beautiful volume, in antique type, on tinted paper, New York (Appletons), 1866. He has since published three additional versions in double rhyme, New York, 1881 ("*The Microcosm and other Poems*"). In August, 1889, he made one more version in single rhyme and four lines. These seventeen versions show a rare fertility and versatility, and illustrate the possibilities of variation without altering the sense.

THE DIES IRÆ.

ENGLISH VERSIONS.

Of these translations I select some of the best in double and in single rhyme. Of others I can only give one or more stanzas.

WILLIAM JOSIAH IRONS, D.D. (died 1883).
First published on a fly sheet, 1848.

1. Day of Wrath! O Day of mourning!
   See! once more the Cross returning—[1]
   Heav'n and earth in ashes burning!

2. O what fear man's bosom rendeth,
   When from heav'n the Judge descendeth,
   On whose sentence all dependeth!

3. Wondrous sound the Trumpet flingeth,
   Through earth's sepulchres it ringeth,
   All before the throne it bringeth!

4. Death is struck, and Nature quaking—
   All creation is awaking,
   To its Judge an answer making!

5. Lo, the Book, exactly worded,
   Wherein all hath been recorded;—
   Thence shall judgment be awarded.

6. When the Judge His seat attaineth,
   And each hidden deed arraigneth,
   Nothing unaveng'd remaineth.

7. What shall I, frail man, be pleading?
   Who for me be interceding?—
   When the just are mercy needing.

8. King of majesty tremendous,
   Who dost free salvation send us,
   Fount of pity! then befriend us!

ABRAHAM COLES, M.D. (No. 1.)
First published 1847.

1. Day of wrath, that day of burning,
   Seer and Sibyl speak concerning,
   All the world to ashes turning.[2]

2. Oh, what fear shall it engender,
   When the Judge shall come in splendor,
   Strict to mark and just to render!

3. Trumpet, scattering sounds of wonder,
   Rending sepulchres asunder,
   Shall resistless summons thunder.

4. All aghast then Death shall shiver,
   And great Nature's frame shall quiver,
   When the graves their dead deliver.

5. Book, where actions are recorded
   All the ages have afforded,
   Shall be brought and dooms awarded.

6. When shall sit the Judge unerring,
   He'll unfold all here occurring,
   No just vengeance then deferring.

7. What shall I say, that time pending,
   Ask what advocate's befriending,
   When the just man needs defending?

8. Dreadful King, all power possessing,
   Saving freely those confessing,
   Save Thou me, O Fount of Blessing!

[1] Dr. Irons, like Dean Alford, follows the reading of the Parisian Missal,
    "*Dies iræ, dies illa,
    Crucis expandens vexilla,
    Solvet sæclum in favilla.*"

[2] I prefer the original form of this stanza as it appeared in the Newark *Daily Advertiser* for March 17, 1847:—
    "Day of wrath, that day of burning,
    All shall melt, to ashes turning,
    As foretold by seers discerning."

9. Think, kind Jesu'—my salvation
Caus'd Thy wondrous Incarnation;
Leave me not to reprobation!

10. Faint and weary Thou hast sought me,
On the Cross of suffering bought me:—
Shall such grace be vainly brought me?

11. Righteous Judge of retribution,
Grant Thy gift of absolution,
Ere that reckoning-day's conclusion!

12. Guilty, now I pour my moaning,
All my shame with anguish owning;
Spare, O God, Thy suppliant groaning!

13. Thou the sinful woman savest;
Thou the dying thief forgavest,
And to me a hope vouchsafest.

14. Worthless are my prayers and sighing,
Yet, good Lord, in grace complying,
Rescue me from fires undying!

15. With Thy favor'd sheep, O place me!
Nor among the goats abase me;
But to Thy right hand upraise me.

16. While the wicked are confounded,
Doom'd to flames of woe unbounded,
Call me, with Thy saints surrounded.

17. Low I kneel, with heart-submission;
See, like ashes, my contrition —
Help me in my last condition!

18. Ah! that Day of tears and mourning!
From the dust of earth returning,
Man for judgment must prepare him;—
Spare! O God, in mercy spare him!
Lord, Who didst our souls redeem,
Grant a blessed requiem! Amen."

9. Think, O Jesus, for what reason
Thou didst bear earth's spite and treason,
Nor me lose in that dread season!

10. Seeking me Thy worn feet hasted,
On the cross Thy soul death tasted;
Let such travail not be wasted!

11. Righteous Judge of retribution!
Make me gift of absolution
Ere that day of execution!

12. Culprit-like, I plead, heart-broken,
On my cheek shame's crimson token:
Let the pardoning word be spoken!

13. Thou, who Mary gav'st remission,
Heard'st the dying Thief's petition,
Cheer'st with hope my lost condition.

14. Though my prayers be void of merit,
What is needful, Thou confer it,
Lest I endless fire inherit!

15. Be there, Lord, my place decided,
With Thy sheep, from goats divided
Kindly to Thy right hand guided!

16. When th' accursed away are driven,
To eternal burnings given,
Call me with the blessed to heaven!

17. I beseech Thee, prostrate lying,
Heart as ashes, contrite, sighing,
Care for me when I am dying!

18. Day of tears and late repentance,
Man shall rise to hear his sentence:
Him, the child of guilt and error,
Spare, Lord, in that hour of terror!"

RICHARD C. TRENCH.
Archbishop of Dublin (d. 1886).

1. O that day, that day of ire,
Told of Prophet, when in fire,
Shall a world dissolved expire!

2. O what terror shall be then,
When the Judge shall come again,
Strictly searching deeds of men:

HENRY ALFORD.
Dean of Canterbury (d. 1871).

1. Day of anger, that dread Day
Shall the Sign in Heaven display,
And the Earth in ashes lay.

2. O what trembling shall appear,
When His coming shall be near,
Who shall all things strictly clear;

THE DIES IRÆ.

3. When a trump of awful tone,
   Thro' the caves sepulchral blown,
   Summons all before the throne.

4. What amazement shall o'ertake,
   Nature, when the dead shall wake,
   Answer to the Judge to make.

5. Open then the book shall lie,
   All o'erwrit for every eye,
   With a world's iniquity.

6. When the Judge His place has ta'en,
   All things hid shall be made plain,
   Nothing unavenged remain.

7. What then, wretched! shall I speak,
   Or what intercession seek,
   When the just man's cause is weak?

8. King of awful majesty,
   Who the saved dost freely free;
   Fount of mercy, pity me!

9. Jesus, Lord, remember, pray,
   I the cause was of Thy way;
   Do not lose me on that day.

10. Tired Thou satest, seeking me—
    Crucified, to set me free;
    Let such pain not fruitless be!

11. Terrible Avenger, make
    Of Thy mercy me partake,
    Ere that day of vengeance wake.

12. As a criminal I groan,
    Blushing deep my faults I own;
    Grace be to a suppliant shown.

13. Thou who Mary didst forgive,
    And who bad'st the robber live,
    Hope to me dost also give.

14. Though my prayer unworthy be,
    Yet, O set me graciously
    From the fire eternal free.

15. 'Mid Thy sheep my place command,
    From the goats far off to stand;
    Set me, Lord, at Thy right hand.

16. And when them who scorned Thee here
    Thou hast judged to doom severe,
    Bid me with Thy saved draw near!

17. Lying low before Thy throne,
    Crushed my heart in dust, I groan;
    Grace be to a suppliant shown!

3. When the Trumpet shall command
   Through the tombs of every land
   All before the Throne to stand.

4. Death shall shrink and Nature quake.
   When all creatures shall awake,
   Answer to their God to make.

5. See the Book divinely penned,
   In which all is found contained,
   Whence the world shall be arraigned!

6. When the Judge is on His Throne,
   All that's hidden shall be shown,
   Naught unfinished or unknown.

7. What shall I before Him say?
   How shall I be safe that day,
   When the righteous scarcely may?

8. King of awful majesty,
   Saving sinners graciously,
   Fount of mercy, save Thou me!

9. Leave me not, my Saviour, one
   For whose soul Thy course was run,
   Lest I be that day undone.

10. Thou didst toil my soul to gain;
    Didst redeem me with Thy pain;
    Be such labor not in vain!

11. Thou just Judge of wrath severe,
    Grant my sins remission here,
    Ere Thy reckoning day appear.

12. My transgressions grievous are,
    Scarce look up for shame I dare:
    Lord, Thy guilty suppliant spare!

13. Thou didst heal the sinner's grief,
    And didst hear the dying thief;
    Even I may hope relief.

14. All unworthy is my prayer;
    Make my soul Thy mercy's care,
    And from fire eternal spare!

15. Place me with Thy sheep, that band
    Who shall separated stand
    From the goats, at Thy right hand!

16. When Thy voice in wrath shall say,
    Cursèd ones, depart away!
    Call me with the blest, I pray!

17. Lord, Thine ear in mercy bow!
    Broken is my heart and low;
    Guard of my last end be Thou!

THE DIES IRÆ.

W. R. WILLIAMS, D. D.
(Died in New York, 1885.)[1]

1. Day of wrath! that day dismaying;
As the seers of old were saying,
All the world in ashes laying.

2. What the fear! and what the quaking!
When the Judge his way is taking,
Strictest search in all things making.

3. When the trump, with blast astounding,
Through the tombs of earth resounding,
Bids all stand, the throne surrounding.

4. Death and Nature all aghast are,
While the dead rise fast and faster,
Answering to their Judge and Master.

5. Forth is brought the record solemn;
See, o'erwrit in each dread column,
With man's deeds, the Doomsday volume.

6. Now the Sovreign Judge is seated;
All, long hid, is loud repeated;
Naught escapes the judgment meted.

7. Ah! what plea shall I be pleading?
Who for me be interceding,
When the just man help is needing?

8. Oh, thou King of awful splendor,
Of salvation free the Sender,
Grace to me, all gracious, render.

9. Jesus, Lord, my plea let this be,
Mine the woe that brought from bliss Thee;
On that day, Lord, wilt Thou miss me?

10. Wearily for me Thou soughtest;
On the cross my soul Thou boughtest;
Lose not all for which Thou wroughtest!

11. Vengeance, Lord, then be Thy mission:
Now, of sin grant free remission
Ere that day of inquisition.

---

18. In that day, that mournful day,
When to judgment wakes our clay,
Show me mercy, Lord, I pray!

SAMUEL W. DUFFIELD.
(Died in Bloomfield, N. J., 1887.)

1. Day of wrath, thine awful morning
Burns to ashes earth's adorning,
As the saint and seer give warning.

2. Then what terror of each nation
When the Judge shall take His station,
Strictly trying His creation.

3. When the trumpet tone of thunder,
Bursting bands of tombs asunder,
Bids men face that throne of wonder.

4. Death and Nature He surprises,
Who, a creature, yet arises
Unto those most dread assizes.

5. There that written book remaineth
Whose sure registry containeth
That which all the world arraigneth.

6. Therefore when He judgeth rightly
We shall view each act unsightly:
Nothing shall be pardoned lightly.

7. With what answer shall I meet Him,
By what advocate entreat Him,
When the just may scarcely greet Him?

8. King of mightiest coronation,
Some through grace gain approbation—
Save me, source of all salvation!

9. Hear me, O Thou Holy Saviour,
Brought to earth through my behaviour—
Take not then away Thy favour.

10. Seeking me Thy love outwore Thee,
And the cross, my ransom, bore Thee:
Let this not seem light before Thee.

11. Righteous Judge of my condition,
Grant me, for my sins, remission,
Ere the day which ends contrition.

---

[1] Published in his *Miscellanies*, second ed., New York, 1850, p. 88–9. The author kindly submitted it to me (in 1868), with a few improvements (in verses 17 and 19), and the modest remark: " The imperfections of the translation are excusable only from its having preceded the more finished rendering of my friend, Dr. Coles."

THE DIES IRÆ.

12. Low in shame before Thee groaning;
    Blushes deep my sin are owning;
    Hear, O Lord, my suppliant moaning!

13. Her of old that sinned forgiving,
    And the dying thief receiving,
    Thou, to me too, hope art giving.

14. In my prayer though sin discerning,
    Yet, good Lord, in goodness turning,
    Save me from the endless burning!

15. 'Mid Thy sheep be my place given;
    Far the goats from me be driven;
    Lift, at Thy right hand, to heaven.

16. When the cursed are confounded,
    With devouring flame surrounded,
    With the blest be my name sounded.

17. Low, I beg, as suppliant bending;
    With crushed heart, my life forth spending;
    Lord, be nigh me in my ending!¹

18. Ah that day! that day of weeping!
    When in dust no longer sleeping,
    Man to God in guilt is going—
    Lord, be then Thy mercy showing!

THOMAS C. PORTER, D.D. (1882).²

1. Day of Wrath! that awful day
   Shall the world in ashes lay,
   David and the Sibyl say.⁴

---

12. In my guilt, for pity yearning,
    With my shame my face is burning;
    Spare me, Lord, to Thee returning!

13. Thou, once touched by Mary's crying,
    Who didst save the thief, though dying,
    Gavest hope to me when sighing.

14. Poorly are my prayers ascending,
    But do Thou in mercy bending,
    Leave me not to flames unending.

15. Give me with Thy sheep a station,
    Far from goats in separation—
    On Thy right my habitation.

16. When the wicked meet conviction,
    Doomed to fires of sharp affliction,
    Call me forth with benediction.

17. Now I pray Thee, naught commending,
    Flames of pride to ashes tending;
    Guard me then when earth is ending.

18. O that day so full of weeping,
    When, in dust no longer sleeping,
    Man must face his worst behaviour;
    Therefore, spare me, God and Saviour!

PHILIP SCHAFF, D.D. (1868).³

1. Day of Wrath! that woful day
   Shall the world in ashes lay;
   David and Sibylla say.⁴

---

¹ This stanza was substituted for the one in 1850:—

"Bowed and prostrate, hear me crying;
Heart in dust before Thee lying,
Lord, my end, O be Thou nigh in!"

² Professor of Biology in Lafayette College, Easton, Pa. He kindly wrote to me July 16th, 1889: "You are at full liberty to make what use you see fit of my translation of the *Dies Iræ*, published in *The Guardian*, by the Reformed Church Board of Publication, at Philadelphia, October, 1882."

³ First published in *Hours at Home*, New York, 1868, May, p. 39. Suggested in part by Alford and Caswall, but more literal.

⁴ This is an undesigned coincidence of two independent translations. In order to avoid it, I would substitute a less literal version:—

Day of Wrath! that day foretold
By the saints and seers of old,
Shall the world in flames infold.

THE DIES IRÆ.

2. Oh! the trembling there will be!—
Every eye the Judge shall see,
Come for strictest scrutiny.

3. Loud shall peal the trumpet's tone,
Through the graves of every zone,
Forcing all before the throne.

4. Death and Nature, in surprise,
Shall behold the creature rise,
Summoned to the grand assize.

5. Now, the books[1] shall be unrolled,
In whose volumes manifold
All the deeds of time are told.

6. When His seat the Judge has ta'en,
Hidden things will hide in vain—
Nothing unavenged remain.

7. What shall I, a wretch, then say?
Unto what kind patron pray,
When the righteous feel dismay?

8. King of dreadful majesty,
Whose salvation is so free,
Fount of pity, save Thou me!

9. Jesu, Lord, remember, I
Caused Thy coming down to die:
Lest I perish, hear my cry!

10. By Thee weary I was sought,
By Thy bitter passion bought:
Can such labor go for naught?

11. Just Avenger, let me win
Full remission of my sin
Ere the day of doom begin.

12. Like a criminal I groan;
Blushing, all my guilt I own:
Hear, O God! a suppliant's moan!

13. Mary's pardon came from Thee,
And the robber's on the tree,
Giving also hope for me.

14. Though my prayers no merit earn,
Let Thy favor on me turn,
Lest in quenchless fire I burn.

15. From the goats my lot divide;
'Midst the sheep, a place provide,
On Thy right hand justified.

---

2. What a trembling, what a fear,
When the dread Judge shall appear,
Strictly searching far and near!

3. Hark! the trumpet's wondrous tone,
Through sepulchral regions blown,
Summons all before the throne.

4. Death shall shiver, Nature quake,
When the creatures shall awake,
Answer to their Judge to make.

5. Lo, the Book of ages spread,
From which all the deeds are read
Of the living and the dead.

6. Now before the Judge severe
All things hidden must appear,
Nought shall pass unpunished here.

7. Wretched man, what shall I plead,
Who for me will intercede,
When the righteous mercy need?

8. King of awful majesty,
Author of salvation free,
Fount of pity, save Thou me!

9. Recollect, good Lord, I pray,
I have caused Thy bitter way,
Me forget not on that day!

10. Weary did'st Thou seek for me,
Did'st redeem me on the tree:
Let such toil not fruitless be!

11. Judge of righteousness severe,
Grant me full remission here
Ere the reckoning day appear.

12. Sighs and tears my sorrow speak,
Shame and grief are on my cheek:
Mercy, mercy, Lord, I seek.

13. Thou didst Mary's guilt forgive,
And absolve the dying thief:
Even I may hope relief.

14. Worthless are my prayers, I know;
Yet, O Lord, thy mercy show,
Save me from eternal woe!

15. Make me with Thy sheep to stand,
Far from the convicted band,
Placing me at Thy right hand.

---

[1] Changed to the plural. See Rev. xx. 12.

THE DIES IRÆ. 161

16. As the wicked, clothed in shame,
Pass to fierce tormenting flame,
With the blessed call my name.

17. Broken-hearted, low I bend;
From the dust my prayer I send:
Let Thy mercy crown my end!

---

18. When, on that most tearful day,
Man, to judgment waked from clay,
Quails at Thine uplifted rod,
Spare the guilty one, O God!

19. Jesu, Lord, their trials o'er,
Grant them rest for evermore!
Amen."

16. When the damn'd are put to shame,
Cast into devouring flame,
With the blest then call my name.

17. Suppliant at Thy feet I lie,
Contrite in the dust I cry,
Care Thou for me when I die!"

---

18. [Day of tears and day of dread,
When, arising from the dead,
Guilty man awaits his doom;
God, have mercy on his soul!

19. Gentle Jesus, Lord of grace,
Grant to them eternal rest!
Amen.]

REV. W. S. McKENZIE, D. D. (1889).

Dr. McKenzie, of Boston, is the author of the following two translations, one in double, the other in single rhyme, which were first published in *The Beacon*, and *The Watchman*, Boston, 1887, and were kindly placed at my disposal in this final shape by the author, August 12, 1889.

I.

1. Day of wrath and consternation!
World-wide sweeps that conflagration,
Long foretold by inspiration.

2. Sudden fear on men is falling!
For the Judge, to judgment calling,
Searcheth all with gaze appalling.

3. Peals the trumpet's blast of wonder;
Bursting every tomb asunder;
Citing all with voice of thunder.

4. Death and Nature, awestruck, quaking,
See the sleeping dead awaking
At the call the Judge is making.

5. God's own Book of registration
Bears impartial attestation
In the great adjudication.

6. On His throne the Judge is dealing
With each hidden deed and feeling;
Wrath against all wrong revealing.

II.

1. The day of wrath! That day draws near,
Far back foretold by Saint and Seer,
That earth in flames would disappear.

2. What dread will seize the human race!
The Judge will come with frowning face,
And search out every hiding place.

3. The trumpet's peal, the world around,
Will through sepulchral vaults resound,
And wake the millions under ground.

4. Then Death and Nature with surprise
Will watch the sleeping dead arise,
To answer in the grand assize.

5. The Book of God's recording pen,
Containing deeds and thoughts of men,
For Judgment will be opened then.

6. And when the Judge ascends His throne,
All secret things will He make known,
And nought of wrong will He condone.

11

7. What defence shall I be making?
Who my part will then be taking,
When the just with fear are quaking?

8. O thou King of awful splendor—
Yet a Saviour, loving, tender,
Source of love! be my defender.

9. Blessèd Jesus! my salvation
Brought Thee down from exaltation:
Rescue me from condemnation.

10. Worn and wasted Thou hast sought me;
With Thy death-pangs Thou hast bought me;
Shield the hope such anguish brought me.

11. Stay, just Judge, Thine indignation;
Grant me pardon and salvation
Ere the Judgment proclamation.

12. Bowed with guilt, my soul is groaning;
Guilt my crimsoned face is owning—
Spare, O God, a suppliant moaning.

13. Mary found in Thee remission;
Thou did'st heed the thief's petition:
Grant me grace in my contrition.

14. Never can my prayers commend me;
Graciously do Thou befriend me,
And from quenchless flames defend me.

15. When the sheep shall be selected,
Severed from the goats rejected,
Raise me to Thy right perfected.

16. When Thy foes in flames are wailing,
Where all cries are unavailing,
Summon me to joys unfailing.

17. Low before Thee I am bending;
Sharp remorse my soul is rending:
Succor me when life is ending.

18. On that day of woe and weeping,
When from dust where he is sleeping,
Man shall wake and rise to meet Thee,
Spare him, Jesus, I entreat Thee.

---

7. Ah, wretched me! what will I say,
What advocate for me will pray,
When saints will scarce escape that day?

8. Thou King majestic, pity me!
Thou savest all redeemed by Thee:
Thou Fount of love! my Saviour be.

9. Remember, holy Christ, I pray,
When thou didst tread the doleful way:
And spare me in the Judgment day.

10. With weary steps Thou soughtest me!
What pangs my pardon wrung from Thee!
Shall such keen anguish wasted be?

11. O righteous Judge of future woe,
Forgiving grace on me bestow
Before to judgment I must go.

12. My groans cannot my guilt erase;
My crimes I own with crimsoned face;
My God! I plead for pardoning grace.

13. By Magdalen was pardon found;
The dying thief by Thee was crowned;
To me, e'en me, let grace abound.

14. My tears and pleas may worthless be;
But Thou, good Lord, hast wrought for me;
From quenchless flames then set me free.

15. Among Thy sheep appoint my place;
Do not with goats my name embrace;
But welcome me before Thy face.

16. And when the wicked stand aghast,
To bitter flames are hurled at last,
O let my lot with saints be cast.

17. Now prostrate in the dust I lie;
In ashes of repentance sigh:
Be Thou near me when death draws nigh.

18. In that last day of bitter cries,
When from the dust the dead shall rise,
And man to Judgment must repair,
Then spare him, Lord, in mercy spare.

THE DIES IRÆ.

Specimens of other English Versions.

RICHARD CRASHAW (1646).

"Heard'st thou, my soul, what serious things
  Both the Psalm and Sibyl sings
  Of a sure Judge, from whose sharp ray
  The world in flames shall fly away?"

EARL OF ROSCOMMON (died 1684).

"The day of wrath, that dreadful day,
  Shall the whole world in ashes lay,
  As David and the Sibyls say."

SIR WALTER SCOTT (died 1832).
A Condensed Reproduction (1805).

"That day of wrath, that dreadful day!
When heaven and earth shall pass away,
What power shall be the sinner's stay?
How shall he meet that dreadful day?

When, shriv'lling like a parched scroll,
The flaming heavens together roll,
And louder yet, and yet more dread,
Swells the high trump that wakes the dead.

Oh! on that day, that wrathful day,
When man to judgment wakes from clay,
Be Thou, O Christ! the sinner's stay,
Though heaven and earth shall pass away."

This partial version, or free reproduction rather, has found its way into every good English and American hymn book, and thus has become much more popular than any other translation.

LORD MACAULAY.
From the *Christian Observer*, 1826.

"On that great, that awful day,
This vain world shall pass away.
Thus the Sibyl sang of old;
Thus hath holy David told.

There shall be a deadly fear
When the Avenger shall appear,
And unveiled before His eye
All the works of men shall lie."

Canon F. C. Husenbeth.
Missal for the Laity (1831).

"The dreadful day, the day of ire
  Shall kindle the avenging fire
    Around the expiring world;
And earth, as Sibyls said of old,
And as the prophet king foretold,
    Shall be in ruin hurled."

Lord A. W. C. Lindsay (1847).

"Day of wrath and doom of fire—
Hark the Seer's, the Sibyl's lyre—
Earth and heaven shall expire."

Rev. E. Caswall. *Lyra Catholica* (1849).

"Nigher still, and still more nigh
Draws the Day of Prophecy,
Doomed to melt the earth and sky."

William John Blew (1851).

"Day of vengeance, day of sorrow,
Fiery morn that knows no morrow—
Seer's and Sibyl's word to borrow."

Mrs. Charles (1858).
From *The Voice of Christian Life in Song*.

"Lo, the Day of Wrath, the Day
Earth and heaven melt away,
David and the Sibyl say.

Stoutest hearts with fear shall quiver,
When to Him who erreth never,
All must strict account deliver.

Lo, the trumpet's wondrous pealing,
Flung through each sepulchral dwelling,
All before the throne compelling."

THE DIES IRÆ.

ABRAHAM COLES, M. D., LL. D.

Dr. ABRAHAM COLES, of Scotch Plains, N. J., prepared in all seventeen versions, including one of 1889, not yet published (see p. 154). These are the first stanzas :—

No. 1. "Day of wrath, that day of burning,
Seer and Sibyl speak concerning,
All the world to ashes turning."

No. 2. "Day shall dawn that has no morrow,
Day of vengeance, day of sorrow,
As from Prophecy we borrow."

No. 3. "Day of Vengeance and of Wages,
Fiery goal of all the ages,
Burden of prophetic pages!"

No. 4. "Day of Prophecy! it flashes,
Falling spheres together dashes,
And the world consumes to ashes."

No. 5. "Day of vengeance, and of scorning,
World in ashes, world in mourning,
Whereof Prophets utter warning!"

No. 6. "Day of wrath and consternation,
Day of fiery consummation,
Prophesied in Revelation!"

No. 7. "Day of wrath, that day of days,
Present to my thought always,
When the world shall burn and blaze!"

No. 8. "O, that dreadful day, my soul!
Which the ages shall unroll,
When the knell of Time shall toll!"

No. 9. "Day foretold, that day of ire,
Burden erst of David's lyre,
When the world shall sink in fire!"

No. 10. "Lo! it comes, with stealthy feet,
Day, the ages shall complete,
When the world shall melt with heat!"

No. 11. "Day of wrath, that day of dole,
When a fire shall wrap the whole,
And the earth be burnt to coal!"

No. 12. "O Day of wrath! O day of fate!
　　　　Day foreordained and ultimate,
　　　　When all things here shall terminate!"

No. 13. "That day, that awful Day, the last,
　　　　Result and sum of all the Past,
　　　　Great necessary day of doom,
　　　　When wrecking fires shall all consume!"

No. 14. "Day of audit and decision,
　　　　Fiery wreck and world collision,
　　　　Witnessed in prophetic vision!"

No. 15. "Day of fiery wrath unsparing!
　　　　End of all things here declaring!
　　　　David thus and Sibyl swearing!"

No. 16. "Day of wrath! that day dismaying,
　　　　All the world in ashes laying,
　　　　David thus and Sibyl saying!"

No. 17. "Day of wrath that day of doom,
　　　　All to ashes shall consume;
　　　　Whereof David witness bears;
　　　　As the Sibyl too declares."

HENRY MILLS, D.D., of Auburn, N. Y. (1856).

"Day of wrath—the sinner dooming,
　Earth with all its work consuming,—
　Scripture warns—that day is coming!"

WILLIAM G. DIX (1852).

"That day of wrath—upon that day
　To ashes earth shall pass away,
　Both David and the Sibyl say.

3.　The trump shall spread its startling sound
　　Through sepulchres beneath the ground,
　　And gather all the throng around.

17.　Thou gav'st to sinful Mary peace;
　　Thou to the thief didst grant release:
　　Let not my hope of pardon cease."

Epes Sargent, Esq., New York (1852).

"Day of ire, that day impending,
Earth shall melt, in ashes ending—
Seer and Sibyl so portending.

2. Ah! what trembling then, what quailing,
When shall come the Judge unfailing,
Every human life unveiling."

Rev. C. Z. Weiser, Pennsburg, Pa. (1859).

"O Day of wrath! that Day of days
To ashes shall the earth emblaze—
Say David's hymns and Sibyl lays."

Robert Davidson, D.D., New York (1860).

"Day of wrath! that day is hasting,
All the world in ashes wasting,
David with the Sibyl testing."

Rev. Charles Rockwell (1860).

"Day of wrath! Oh! direful day!
Earth in flames shall pass away,
Virgil [?] and the Sibyl say."

From Poems by *Somniator*.
Philadelphia *Bulletin*, 1860.

"The Sibyl's leaf, the Psalmist's lay
Alike portend a wrathful day,
When heaven and earth shall melt away."

Anonymous.

1. "Day of wrath! that day appalling!
Words of ancient seers recalling:
Earth on fire, in ashes falling.

2. Oh, in hearts of men what trembling,
At that Judge's bar assembling,
Where of sins is no dissembling.

3. Louder and yet louder breaking
From the sky, the caverns shaking,
Angel trumps the dead awaking."

GENERAL JOHN ADAMS DIX (1863).
"Day of vengeance, without morrow!
Earth shall end in flame and sorrow,
As from Saint and Seer we borrow."

This version, which has been highly praised and widely circulated, was made at Fortress Monroe, Va., during the civil war, in which the brave and patriotic name of General Dix occupies a distinguished place. But it does not stand close examination. In the first stanza the rhymes ("morrow, sorrow, borrow") are borrowed from Coles (No. 2), but the "Day of Wrath" (which is the key-note of the whole poem) is changed into a "Day of vengeance," and "Saint and Seer" are substituted for "David and Sibylla." The author was himself dissatisfied and changed it in a revised edition, 1875, as follows:—

"Day of vengeance, lo! that morning,
On the earth in ashes dawning.
David with the Sibyl warning."

Most of the other stanzas present striking coincidences with older renderings, especially of Irons and Coles; but some rhymes will naturally occur to different translators. Take the following specimens:—

A. COLES, No. 1 (1847).
13. "Thou to Mary gav'st remission,
Heard'st the dying thief's petition,
Cheer'st with hope my lost condition."

JOHN A. DIX (1863).
13. "Thou to Mary gav'st remission,
Heard'st the dying thief's petition,
Bad'st me hope in my contrition."

W. J. IRONS (1848).
10. "Faint and weary Thou hast sought me,
On the cross of suffering bought me;
Shall such grace be vainly brought me?

11. Righteous Judge of retribution,
Grant Thy gift of absolution,
Ere that reckoning day's conclusion."

ADOLPHE PÉRIÈS, of Philadelphia (1861).
"Righteous Judge of retribution,
Grant us sinners absolution
Ere the day of dissolution."

JOHN A. DIX (1863).

10. "Worn and weary, Thou hast sought me,
By Thy cross and passion bought me—
Spare the hope Thy labors brought me.

11. Righteous Judge of retribution,
Give, O give me absolution,
Ere the day of dissolution."

Dr. COLES, in the eleventh stanza of his first translation of 1847, had anticipated Irons, Périès, and Dix:—

"Righteous Judge of retribution,
Make me gift of absolution
Ere that day of execution."

Compare also Dr. H. MILLS (1856):—

"Righteous Judge of retribution,
Bless my soul with absolution
Ere that day of execution."

EDWARD SLOSSON, of the bar of New York.
From the New York *Journal of Commerce*, March 10, 1866.

"Day of Wrath! of days that Day!
Earth in flames shall melt away,
Heathen seers with Prophets say."

ERASTUS C. BENEDICT, ESQ.

Mr. Benedict, a lawyer of New York, prepared three translations, first published in the *Christian Intelligencer*, 1864, and then in his *Hymn of Hildebert, and other Mediæval Hymns*, N. Y., 1867, pp. 103-120:—

No. 1. "Day of Wrath! that final day,
Shall the world in ashes lay!
David and the Sibyl say."

No. 2. "Day of threatened Wrath from heaven,
To the sinful, unforgiven!
Earth on fire, to ashes driven!"

No. 3. "Day of Wrath, with vengeance glowing!
Seer and Sibyl long foreknowing!
Earth and time to ruin going!

2. How the guilty world will tremble,
When the Judge shall all assemble,
And not one will dare dissemble!

3. When the trumpet's summons, swelling
Through Death's dark and dusty dwelling,
To the throne is all compelling!"

ANONYMOUS.
From the N. York *Evening Post*, July 20, 1866.

1. "A day of wrath and woe that day
The world in ashes melts away;
So David and the Sibyl say."

PROF. C. M. DODD, Indiana State University (1867).

"Day of wrath! that day foretold!
Which in ashes earth shall fold;
Witness Seer and Sibyl old."

J. HOSKYNS ABRAHALL.
From the *Christian Remembrancer*, Jan., 1868.

"Day of wrath and tribulation,
Day in vasty conflagration
Heaven and earth together blending,
And the world's long cycle ending—
Know, it cometh; be thou heeding
Hebrew seers and heathen's reading."

ANONYMOUS. (R. H. HUTTON?)
From the London *Spectator* for March 7, 1868.

1. "The day of wrath, that haunting day
Shall the whole age in ashes lay,
Thus David and the Sibyl say.

2. What terror then shall seize the breast,
When the great Judge is manifest
To institute the awful quest."

ARTHUR P. STANLEY, Dean of Westminster (d. 1881).
From *Macmillan's Magazine*, December, 1868.

"Day of wrath, O dreadful day,
When this world shall pass away,
And the heavens together roll,
Shrivelling like a parchèd scroll,
Long foretold by saint and sage,
David's harp and Sibyl's page."

John D. Van Buren.

From *The Stabat Mater and other Versions*, Albany (Joel Munsell), 1872.

"Day of wrath! terrific morning!
Earth in ashes at its dawning
David, Sibyl, both give warning."

John O'Hagan. Dublin, 1874.

"Day of wrath, that day whose knelling
Gives to flame this earthly dwelling;
Psalm and Sibyl thus foretelling."

Anonymous.

From *The Catholic World*, New York, 1882 (p. 42).

"The judgment day, that day of dread,
Shall see the world in ashes laid,
As David and the Sibyl said."

W. J. Copeland, Rector of Farnham.

From *The Dublin Review*, 1883 (p. 382).

"Day of doom, that day of ire,
Earth shall sink in crumbling fire;
Seer's and Sibyl's burden dire."

Prior James D. Aylward.

From *The Dublin Review*, 1883 (p. 383).

"Day of wrath and grief and shame,
Shall fold the world in sheeted flame
As psalm and Sibyl's songs proclaim."

Franklin Johnson, D. D. (1883).

1. "Day of wrath, that day of burning!
Earth shall end, to ashes turning:
Thus sing Saint and Seer discerning.

2. How shall quake both high and lowly
When the judge shall come, most holy,
Strict to search all sin and folly.[1]

---

[1] The author, a Baptist clergyman of Old Cambridge, Mass., who published this version in 1883, speaks of the tantalizing effort to reproduce "the

3. There is heard a sound of wonder!
   Mighty blasts of trumpet thunder,
   Rend the sepulchres asunder!"

JOHN MASON BROWN.
From *The Catholic World*, N. York, Nov., 1884 (p. 177).

"That day of wrath, of God's dread ire,
Shall wrap the Universe in fire,
Foretold by Seer and Psalmist's lyre."

HON. JOHN L. HAYES, LL.D. (Cambridge, Mass.).
From *The Independent*, New York, Dec. 30, 1886.

"That day of doom and dread amaze,
The earth dissolved, the heavens ablaze,
Foreseen by seers' and Sibyl's gaze."

JOHN S. HAGER (U. S. Senator 1874–'75).
From *The Overland Monthly*, Vol. VII, San Francisco, 1886 (p. 530).

"Day of wrath, that day when burning
Earth dissolves, to ashes turning;
Witness Psalm and Sibyl's warning."

REV. ALFRED H. FAHNESTOCK.
From the *Presbyterian Journal*, Philadelphia, July 22, 1889.

1. "Day of wrath, that day of dooming,
   All the worlds in flames consuming,
   Seers behold with aspect glooming.

2. Lo! how great the trepidation,
   When the Judge of all creation
   Maketh close investigation!

3. Loud the awful trumpet sounding,
   Calls, with voice through tombs rebounding,
   All before the throne astounding.

burden of thought, the sublime pictures, the throbs of emotion, the weird measure, and delicate associations" of the original, and suggests, in a letter to me, August 28, 1889, the following substitute for the second stanza (to get rid of "folly"):—

"How man's heart with terror quaketh
Earthward when His way Christ taketh,
And strict search in all things maketh."

4. Death and Nature, awed and quaking,
   See the human creature waking,
   And in judgment answer making.

5. Then the book is shown containing
   All men's deeds, all guilt explaining,
   Not a soul unjudged remaining."

GERMAN VERSIONS.

The following specimens will give an idea of the German translations. The first stanza is selected, as it is generally characteristic of the whole.

CATHOLIC HYMN BOOK, Munich (1613).

"An jenem Tag, nach David's Sag,
Soll Gottes Zorn erbrinnen:
Durch Feuers Flamm, muss allesamm,
Gleichwie das Wachs zerrinnen."

ANDREAS GRYPHIUS (1659).

"Zorntag! Tag, der, was wir ehren,
Wird durch schnelle Glut zerstören,
Wie Sibyll und Petrus lehren."

These seem to be the two oldest German translations, but inferior to the English translations of the seventeenth century.

FRANZ XAVIER RIEDEL (1773).

"Am Tag' des Zorns, an jenem Tage
Nach Davids und Sibyllens Sage
Versinkt in Asche diese Welt."

CHR. D. EBELING (1800).

"Erden wanken, Welten beben,
Wenn du, Herr, dich wirst erheben,
Richtend über Tod und Leben."

J. G. VON HERDER (1802).

1. "Tag des Schreckens! Tag voll Beben!
   Wenn die Grüfte sich erheben
   Und die Todten wiedergeben!

2. Welch ein Zittern, welch ein Zagen!
   Wenn im Donner jetzt der Richter
   Kommt und ruft, die uns verklagen!

  3. Furchtbar schallet die Drommete,
   Aus den Grüften aller Erde
   Zwingt sie alles in's Gericht."

Herder's version, though superior to its predecessors, is incomplete (only eight stanzas), unequal, and unworthy of his great genius.

    A. W. VON SCHLEGEL (1802).

  1. "Jenen Tag, den Tag des Zoren,
   Geht die Welt in Brand verloren,
   Wie Propheten hoch beschworen.

  2. Welch ein Graun wird sein und Zagen,
   Wenn der Richter kommt, mit Fragen
   Streng zu prüfen alle Klagen!

  3. Die Posaun' im Wundertone,
   Wo auch wer im Grabe wohne,
   Rufet alle her zum Throne.

  4. Tod, Natur mit Staunen sehen
   Dann die Creatur erstehen,
   Zur Verantwortung zu gehen."

This is the first really good German version, and betrays the skill of a master. Yet Schlegel himself (in a letter to Königsfeld) admitted the failure of the first stanza; *Zoren* for *Zorn* is antiquated, and the Sibyl should not be omitted in a faithful version, unless it be intended for public worship.

    FR. VON MEYER (1806).

  "Tag des Zorns, mit wildem Raube
   Wandelst du die Welt zu Staube,
   So bezeugt's der heil'ge Glaube."

The whole version, as modified in 1824, is given by Lisco.

    CATHOLIC HYMN BOOK OF MUNICH (1810).

  1. "Erden wanken, Welten beben,
   Wenn du, Herr! dich wirst erheben,
   Richtend über Tod und Leben.

  2. Ach vor jenen Ungewittern,
   Die der Welten Bau erschüttern,
   Werden alle Frevler zittern."

This version was made use of in several editions of Mozart's *Requiem*.

J. G. FICHTE, the celebrated philosopher (1813).

1. "Jenen Tag, den Tag der Fülle,
   Fällt die Welt in Graus und Stille.
   David zeugt's und die Sibylle.

2. Angst ergreift die Creaturen,
   Wie sie in azurnen Fluren
   Sehn des nah'nden Richters Spuren."

M. F. JÄCK (1815).

"Welche bange Trauerstunde,
Wenn, nach der Propheten Munde,
Glüht die Erd' im Feuerschlunde."

Lisco quotes another from Jäck:—

"Tag, prophetisch uns verkündet,
Wenn du kömmst, wie Staub verschwindet
Dann, was sich auf Erden findet."

FR. KIND (1817).

"Tag des Zorns, du wirst erfüllen
Davids Wort und der Sibyllen,
Wirst die Welt in Asche hüllen."

SCHMEDDING (1817).

"Jener Tag, den Zorn entzündet,
Da die Welt in Asche schwindet,
Ward prophetisch uns verkündet."

AD. L. FOLLEN (1819).

"Tag des Zornes, wann er taget,
Feuerloh die Zeit zernaget,
Wie Sibyll mit David saget."

J. P. SILBERT (1820).

1. "Tag des Zornes, furchtbar stille!
   Du verglühst des Erdballs Fülle,
   Zeugt mit David die Sibylle.

2. Welch ein Zittern und Erbeben,
   Wird im Glanz der Richter schweben,
   Streng zu richten Aller Leben!

3. Hehr wird die Posaune klingen,
   Wird durch ferne Grüfte dringen,
   Alle vor den Thron zum zwingen.

4. Die Natur, der Tod sicht bebend
   Das Geschöpf der Gruft entschwebend,
   Und dem Richter Antwort gebend.

5. Und ein Buch erscheint zur Stunde;
   Dies, entfaltend jede Kunde,
   Liegt dem Weltgericht zum Grunde."

This excellent version rivals with that of Schlegel.

A. C. DÖRING (1821).

"Tag des Zorns, wo Gott einst richtet,
Und die Welt in Glut vernichtet,
Wie Propheten uns berichtet."

J. H. VON WESSENBERG, Bishop of Constance (1820).

"Furchtbar wird der Tag sich röthen,
Kundgethan von den Propheten,
Der die Welt in Staub wird treten"

W. A. SWOBODA (Prag, 1826).

"Tag des Zornes, Tag der Klagen!
Zeit und Welt wirst du zerschlagen,
Wie uns die Propheten sagen."

CHRISTIAN MEUSCH (1827).

"Jener Tag der Zornesfülle
Löst die Welt zu Aschenhülle;
David zeugt's und die Sibylle."

J. A. SCHOLTZ (1828).

"Jener Tag in Zornes Fülle
Löst in Brand der Zeiten Hülle,
David zeugt's und die Sibylle."

Claus Harms (1828).

"Zorntag, grösster aller Tage,
 Aller Bibeln ernste Sage,
 Mit dem Feuer, mit der Waage."

J. Em. Veith (1829).

"Tag des Zornes, Tag der Zähren
 Wird die Welt in Asche kehren,
 Wie Sibyll' und David lehren."

J. C. W. Niemeyer (Halle, 1833).

"Jener Rachetag der Sünden
 Wird die Welt zu Asche zünden,
 Wie Sibyll' und David künden."

Chevalier Bunsen (1833).

"Tag des Zorns, O Tag voll Grauen,
 Da die Welt den Herrn soll schauen,
 Nach dem Wort, dem wir vertrauen."

Carl Simrock (1834).

"Tag des Zornes, des Gerichtes!
 Was von Staub in Flammen bricht es:
 David und Sibylle spricht es."

Mohnike (1834).

"Tag des Zorns! in Flammenwehen
 Wird die Welt zu Staub vergehen,
 Wie Propheten längst gesehen."

Franke (1839).

"Einst am Richttag wird verschwinden
 Zeit und Welt in Feuerschlünden,
 Wie uns heil'ge Sänger künden."

Dr. H. A. Erhard, of Münster.

"Tag des Grimmes, Tag voll Schelten,
 Der in Asche legt die Welten,
 Wie uns heil'ge Seher melden."

F. v. Pechlin (Lisco, p. 152).

"Ja, ein Tag wird Zorn enthüllen,
 Durch den Brand der Welt erfüllen
 David's Wort und der Sibyllen."

F. G. Lisco, D.D. (1840).

"Tag des Zorns, Tag zu vergelten!
Feuers Glut verzehrt die Welten,
Denn der Seher Wort muss gelten."

Chr. L. Couard, D.D. (1840).

"Tag des Zorns, in Aschenhülle
Kleid'st du einst der Welten Hülle,
David zeugt's und die Sibylle."

From another version by the same, quoted by Lisco, his fellow-pastor in Berlin (1840):—

"Tag des Zorns, in Flammenmeeren
Wirst du einst die Welt verzehren,
Wie Sibyll' und David lehren."

Anonymous (1840).

"Schreckenstag der Zornesfülle!
Weltenpracht wird Aschenhülle!
David zeugt's und die Sibylle."

Anonymous (1840.)

"Tag des Zorns, der wird erfüllen
David's Spruch und der Sibyllen,
Und die Welt in Asche hüllen."

Dr. L. Steckling (1840).

"Tag der Zorngewalt, der hohen,
Du zerstörst die Welt in Lohen,
Wie Sibyll' und David drohen."

Robert Lecke (1842).

"Jener Tag, wo Gott wird richten,
Soll die Welt zu Staub vernichten,
Wie Propheten uns berichten."

Lecke made and published at his own expense, at Munich, 1842, no less than twelve translations, which, however, do not rise above mediocrity.

Karl Fortlage (1844).

"Jener Tag voll Zorn und Ringen
Wird die Welt in Glut verschlingen,
Wie Sibyll' und David singen."

ALBERT KNAPP (1850).
"An dem Zorntag, an dem hohen,
Stürzt die Welt in Feuerlohen,
Wie Prophetenschwüre drohen."

Knapp made an earlier version in 1829, which is the basis of the one in the Würtemberg Hymn Book, 1849:—

"Jenen Tag, den Tag der Wehen,
Wird die Welt im Staub vergehen,
Wie Prophetenspruch geschehen."

LEBRECHT DREVES (1846).
"Tag des Zorns, bei deinem Tagen
Wird die Welt zu Staub zerschlagen,
Wie Sibyll' und David sagen."

G. A. KÖNIGSFELD (1847).
"An dem Zorntag, jenem hehren,
Wird die Glut das All verzehren,
Wie Sibyll' und David lehren."

In his second collection of Latin hymns with translations, published in Bonn, 1865, Königsfeld gives a revised version, changing the first line thus:—

"Jenen Zorntag, jenen schweren."

FRIEDRICH HEINRICH SCHLOSSER (1851).
"Tag des Zorns, der Tag der Fülle,
Deckt die Welt mit Aschenhülle,
David zeugt es und Sibylle."

VON SELD. In Daniel's *Thes. Hymnol.*, ii, p. 110.
"Zorn und Zittern bange Klag ist,
Wenn der letzte aller Tag ist,
Wie die alte heil'ge Sag ist."

H. A. DANIEL (1855). Two versions.
No. 1. "Tag des Zorns, du Tag der Fülle,
Kehrst die Welt in Staubgerülle—
So zeugt David und Sibylle."

No. 2. "David und Sibylla spricht:
Erd und Himmel bleiben nicht,
Wenn der jüngste Tag anbricht."

KARL RÖLKER (1858).

1. "Jener Zorntag, Tag der Klagen
Wird die Welt zu Asche schlagen,
Wie Sibyll' und David sagen.

2. Welche Angst entsteht, welch Bangen,
Wenn der Richter kommt gegangen,
Streng zu prüfen, was begangen.

10. Suchtest mich mit müden Schritten,
Hast am Kreuz mir Heil erstritten,
Nicht umsonst sei dies erlitten!"

The best among these German versions are those of Schlegel, Silbert, Bunsen, Knapp and Daniel. But none of them has become so popular as the free reproduction in the old German hymn: "*Es ist gewisslich an der Zeit*," by Bartholomäus Ringwaldt, 1582.

FRENCH VERSIONS.

The French language is bright, brilliant, and rhetorical, but less adapted for poetry, especially of this solemn kind. I have seen but one French translation, by an anonymous author, in Lisco's "*Stabat Mater*," from an older print of 1702. It begins:—

"*O jour du Dieu vengeur, où pour punir les crimes
Un déluge brûlant sortira des abîmes,
Et le ciel s'armera de foudres et d'éclairs;
Quel trouble en tous les cœurs, quand ce juge sévère,
Lançant de toute part les traits de sa colère,
Sur un trône de feu paraîtra dans les airs!*"

There are several good translations into Dutch. A translation into modern Greek, by the Rev. Mr. Hildner, a missionary of the Church of England at Syra, was first published in Tholuck's *Literary Advertiser* for 1842, and then by Daniel, *Thesaurus Hymnol.*, tom. ii., p. 105. Daniel (ii. 387) gives also a Hebrew version by L. Splieth.

THE DIES IRÆ.

TWO VERSIONS IN GERMAN.

I add in conclusion two German translations which I made in 1858, together with an English version[1], when I was preparing a German hymn book for the German Reformed Church in America. They claim no poetic merit, but one of them, with some alterations, has found a place in several German hymn books.

I.

1. An dem Tag der Zornesflammen
   Stürzt die Welt in Staub zusammen,
   Nach dem Wort, das Ja und Amen.

2. Welch' ein Grauen bei der Kunde,
   Dass der Richter naht zur Stunde,
   Mit dem Flammenschwert im Munde!

3. Die Posaune wird erschallen
   Durch der Gräber dumpfe Hallen.
   "Auf zum Throne!" rufend Allen.

4. Tod und Leben seh'n mit Beben
   Die Geschöpfe sich erheben,
   Antwort vor Gericht zu geben.

5. Jetzt wird sich ein Buch entfalten,
   Drinnen Alles ist enthalten,
   Darnach wird der Richter schalten.

6. Also wird der Richter sitzen,
   Das Verborgenste durchblitzen
   Nichts vor seiner Rache schützen.

7. Wie wird dann mir sein zu Muthe,
   Wer lenkt ab des Zornes Ruthe,
   Wenn kaum sicher ist der Gute?

8. König schrecklicher Gewalten,
   Frei ist deiner Gnade Schalten,
   Heiland, lass mich Gnad' erhalten!

9. Jesu! mir zum Heil erkoren,
   Denk', auch mir wardst Du geboren,
   Dass ich einst nicht geh' verloren.

10. Ich war Ziel ja deines Strebens;
    Kreuzestod der Preis des Lebens;
    So viel Müh' sei nicht vergebens!

11. Richter mit der heil'gen Wage,
    Hilf mir, dass ich nicht verzage
    An dem grossen Rachetage.

II.

1. An dem Tag der Zornesfülle
   Sinkt die Welt in Aschenhülle:
   So zeugt Gottes Wort und Wille.[2]

2. Welch' ein Zittern, welch' ein Zagen
   Wenn der Richter kommt, mit Fragen,
   Alle Sünder anzuklagen.

3. Die Posaun' im Wundertone
   Schallt durch Gräber jeder Zone
   Fordernd alle zu dem Throne.

4. Erd' und Hölle werden zittern
   In des Weltgerichts Gewittern,
   Die das Todtenreich erschüttern.

5. Und ein Buch wird aufgeschlagen,
   Drinnen Alles eingetragen,
   Dess die Sünder anzuklagen.

6. Als dann wird der Richter thronen,
   Alles Gute zu belohnen,
   Keine Sünde zu verschonen.

7. Was soll dann ich Armer sagen,
   Wen um Schutz zu bitten wagen,
   Wenn Gerechte fast verzagen?

8. König, furchtbar hoch erhaben,
   Brunnquell aller Gnadengaben,
   Dein Erbarmen lass mich laben!

9. Milder Jesu! wollst bedenken,
   Dass Du kamst den Zorn zu lenken;
   Ew'ges Heil auch mir zu schenken.

10. Du hast ja für mich gerungen,
    Sünd' und Tod für mich bezwungen;
    Solch' ein Sieg ist Dir gelungen!

11. Richter der gerechten Rache,
    Aller Schuld mich ledig mache,
    Eh' zum Zorntag ich erwache.

[1] See above, p. 159 sq.

[2] Literally: "David zeugt's und die Sibylle;" but the Sibyl is out of place in a Protestant hymn book.

12. Ach ich muss vor Schaam erröthen,
    Sich' mich reuig vor Dich treten;
    Hör' mein brünstig Fleh'n und Beten.

13. Der Marien Du erhöret,
    Und dem Schächer Huld gewähret,
    Hast auch hoffen mich gelehret.

14. Zwar mein Fleh'n ist zu geringe;
    Nur um freie Gnad' ich ringe,
    Dass die Glut mich nicht verschlinge.

15. Zu den Schaafen lass mich kommen,
    Fern den Böcken, angenommen
    Dir zur Rechten bei den Frommen.

16. Wenn Du zu den Feuerflammen
    Die Verworfnen wirst verdammen,
    Ruf' mit Sel'gen mich zusammen.

17. Herr, zerknirscht im tiefsten Grunde,
    Bet' ich, dass ich noch gesunde,
    Sorge für die letzte Stunde!

    Jesu, treuster Heiland Du,
    Schenke uns die ew'ge Ruh!
        Amen.

12. Sieh' ich seufze schuldbeladen,
    Schaamroth über schweren Schaden,
    Hör' mein Fleh'n, o Gott, in Gnaden.

13. Der Du lossprachst einst Marien.
    Und dem Schächer selbst verziehen,
    Hast auch Hoffnung mir verliehen.

14. Zwar unwürdig ist mein Flehen
    Doch lass Gnad' für Recht ergehen,
    Mich die ew'ge Glut nicht sehen.

15. Wollst mich von den Böcken trennen,
    Deinen Schaafen zuerkennen,
    Platz zu Deiner Rechten gönnen.

16. Wenn die Bösen in's Vorderben
    Stürzen zu dem ew'gen Sterben,
    Ruf' mich mit den Himmelserben.

17. Tief im Staub ring' ich die Hände,
    Und den Seufzer zu Dir sende;
    Gieb mir, Herr, ein selig Ende!

    Jesu, Allerbarmer Du,
    Schenk' uns all'n die ew'ge Ruh!
        Amen.

LITERATURE.

G. C. F. MOHNIKE: *Kirchen-und literarhistorische Studien und Mittheilungen.* Stralsund, 1824, Bd. I., Heft 1 (*Beiträge zur alten kirchlichen Hymnologie*), pp. 1-111; and *Hymnol. Forschungen*, 1832, Theil II., 149-160. (My copy has the autograph of Gieseler, the church historian.)

G. W. FINK: *Thomas von Celano*, in Ersch und Gruber's "Encyclop." Sect. 1, Bd. XVI. 7-10.

F. G. LISCO (Pastor in Berlin): *Dies Iræ, Hymnus auf das Weltgericht.* Berlin, 1840 (152 pp., 4to). Contains fifty-four German translations, besides a number of fragments, and adds historical remarks, mostly from Mohnike. In an Appendix to a similar monograph on the *Stabat Mater* (Berlin, 1843), Lisco notices seventeen additional translations of the *Dies Iræ*, and gives a chronological list of 78 German versions complete or incomplete, and 4 Dutch versions.

W. R. WILLIAMS: *Miscellanies.* New York, second ed., 1850, pp. 78-90.

H. A. DANIEL: *Thesaurus Hymnologicus.* Lips., Tom. II. (1855), pp. 103-131; and Tom. V. (1856), pp. 110-116. (The Preface to Vol. I. is dated May 21, 1841.)

RICHARD CHENEVIX TRENCH (Archbishop of Dublin, d. 1886): *Sacred Latin Poetry.* London and Cambridge, 1849; second ed., 1864; third ed., 1874, revised, pp. 302-307. He is mistaken if he says (p. 307) that the German versions of the *Dies Iræ* are more numerous than the English.

ABRAHAM COLES (M.D., PH. D., LL.D.) : *Dies Iræ in thirteen original versions, with photographic illustrations.* New York (Appletons), 1859; fifth ed., 1868 (p. 65). Comp. his *Microcosm and other Poems*, New York, 1881, pp. 277-285, which contains three additional translations (see above, pp. 154 and 165).

An anonymous publication [by Mrs. A. E. NOTT], entitled *The Seven Great Hymns of the Mediæval Church*, New York (Anson D. F. Randolph & Co.), third ed., 1867, pp. 11-97, gives seven English versions of the *Dies Iræ*, by Gen. Dix, Roscommon, Crashaw, Irons, Slosson, and Coles (2 versions). The 5th ed., 1868 (pp. 153), has some additions.

PHILIP SCHAFF: *Dies Iræ.* Two articles in "*Hours at Home,*" New York (Ch. Scribner), 1868, May and July Nos., pp. 39-48, and 261-268. They form the basis of this essay.

ORBY SHIPLEY: *Fifty Versions of "Dies Iræ."* Two articles in "The Dublin Review," London, 1883, Vol. IX, 48-77, and 399-396. The writer gives (p. 56 sq.) a list of 50 English versions, with names of authors, date, religion, metre and rhyme. He omits the American versions, but charges Dr. Coles, without naming him (p. 51), with "an unpardonable offense" (!) for publishing thirteen different versions of his own.

FRANKLIN JOHNSON: *The Dies Iræ.* Privately printed, Cambridge, Mass., 1883 (pp. 38). The Latin text with an English version in double rhyme, and notes. (A copy in the Library of Harvard College, Cambridge, Mass.) See above, p. 171.

K. R. ROELKER: *Die altkirchliche Hymnenpoesie.* Osnabrück, 1888. A posthumous fragment of 94 pages, with German translations of *Dies Iræ.*

Compare also the hymnological works of MONE, KOCH, and WACKERNAGEL. To these will soon be added a comprehensive *Cyclopædia of Hymnology*, edited by Julian, and to be published in 1890 by J. Murray, in London, and Charles Scribner's Sons, in New York.

JOHN EDMANDS (Librarian of the Mercantile Library in Philadelphia) : *Bibliography of the Dies Iræ of Thomas de Celano.* In the "Bulletin of the Mercantile Library of Philadelphia," Vol. I., No. 9 (Oct. 1, 1884), pp. 160-166, and No. 10 (Jan. 1, 1885), pp. 179-188. A very full and accurate list of English versions down to 1884, to which I am chiefly indebted for the following

CHRONOLOGICAL LIST OF ENGLISH TRANSLATIONS OF THE DIES IRÆ
FROM 1621-1889.

The translations marked by an asterisk are the best, as far as I can judge, either from personal examination or from the name of the translator and his other works.

Joshua Sylvester: London, 1621. 10 stanzas of 6 lines each.

***Richard Crashaw:** London, 1646, often reprinted. 17 stanzas of 4 lines each. A reproduction. See pp. 153 and 163.

W. Drummond, of Hawthornden: London, 1656.

A. C. Crowther and **T. V. Sadler:** 1657.

James Dymock: London, 1687.

Anonymous: 1694.

*W. Dillon, Earl of Roscommon: London, 1696, 1717, and often.
Andrew Dickinson: 1768.
*Sir Walter Scott: 1805, often republished in his works and in many hymn books. An abridged reproduction, in 3 stanzas of 4 lines each. See p. 163.
Anonymous: In "Christian Observer," London, May, 1819.
Anonymous: 1825.
*Lord Th. B. Macaulay: London, 1826, and often. See p. 163.
F. C. Husenbeth: London, 1831.
William Hay: 1831.
*Isaac Williams: London, 1831, and often.
Richard Parkinson: London, 1832.
Anonymous: 1833.
John Chandler: 1837.
Anonymous: In "Christian Observer," London, Jan., 1837.
J. R. Beste London, 1839.
Daniel French: 1839.
Anonymous: "N. Y. Evangelist," Oct. 16, 1841.
William Young: 1842.
*Henry Alford (D. D., Dean of Canterbury): London, 1844, and often. See p. 156.
*Richard C. Trench (Archbishop of Canterbury): London, 1844, and since. See p. 156.
Henry Mills: Auburn, 1845. "Horæ Germanicæ," 2d ed., 1856, Appendix (p. 363 sq.). See pp. 166 and 169.
Edw. V. Hyde Kenealy: 1845.
John Williams: Hartford, 1845.
W. F. Wingfield: 1845 ("Prayers for the Dead").
James D. Aylward: Dublin, 1846.
H. H. Brownell: New York, 1847.
*Abraham Coles (M.D. and LL.D.): New York, 1847 sqq. Seventeen translations between 1847 and Aug., 1889. Two of them often reprinted. See pp. 154, 155, 165.
Lord A. W. C. Lindsay: London, 1847. See p. 164.
*William J. Irons: London, 1848. First printed on a fly-leaf and very often republished in hymn books and other collections. See p. 155.

Matthew Bridges: London, 1848.
J. Newton Brown: New York, 1848.
Richard Dalton Williams: 1848.
*Edward Caswall: "Lyra Catholica," London, 1849. Many reprints. See pp. 154, 164.
Brabazon William Disney: Dublin, 1849. (See Brit. Mus. Catal.)
Arthur B. Rowan: Dublin, 1849.
Robert Campbell: Edinburgh, 1850.
Howel W. Lloyd: London (?), 1850.
*William R. Williams (D. D., Baptist minister in New York): New York, 1850. See p. 158.
William John Blew: London, 1851.
Charles Porterfield Krauth: Baltimore, 1851. ("Literal, without rhyme," Edmands.)
*Arthur Tozer Russell: 2 versions. London, 1851.
Epes Sargent: New York, 1852 and 1867. See p. 167.
*William G. Dix: New York, "Literary World," Dec. 11, 1852. See p. 166.
Anonymous: "Z.," in "Lit. World," New York, Dec. 11, 1852.
R. G. Loraine: 1854. "Libretto to Mozart's Requiem."
S. Dryden Phelps: New York, 1855.
James Aitken Johnstone: 1856.
H. Jas. Buckoll: "Rugby School Collection," 1857.
W. Bright (D. D., Professor of Church History in Oxford): London, 1858.
*Mrs. Elizabeth Charles: London, 1858. See pp. 143 and 164.
Richard Furman: Charleston, 1859.
John William Hewett: London, 1859.
W. Snyden (Methodist New Connection): 1859.
Anonymous: "Somniator," Philadelphia, 1859 and 1860. P. 166.
C. Z. Weiser: Philadelphia, 1859. P. 167.
Mrs. F. J. Partridge: London, 1860. Repeated.
Robert Davidson: New York, 1860. P. 167.
Dr. Noris: 1860.
Charles Rockwell: New York, 1860. P. 167.

P. S. Worsley: In "Blackwood's Magazine," May, 1860.

Adolphe Périès (a merchant of Philadelphia): Philadelphia, 1864. P. 169.

Herbert Kynaston: London, 1862.

George Alex. Crooke: Philadelphia, 1863.

John Adams Dix: Cambridge, 1863 (priv. print., often reprinted. A second version, containing the author's reasons for feeling dissatisfied with the first, Cambridge, 1875 (priv. print.), and in "Scribner's Monthly," New York, 1876. The variations of the two versions are printed in parallel columns in General Dix's *Memoirs* by his son, Dr. Morgan Dix, of Trinity Church, New York, 1883, II., 371; with several letters containing critical estimates of the first version, II., 234–9. P. 168.

Crammond Kennedy: In "American Baptist," New York, April, 1863.

Anonymous: 1864.

James Ross: In "New York Observer," 1864.

Anonymous: London, 1864.

C. B. Cayley: London, 1864.

Francis Trappes: London, 1865.

Marshall H. Bright: New York, 1866 (priv. print.).

Anonymous: Boston. In "Littell's Living Age," Aug. 11, 1866.

W. H. Robinson: London, 1866.

J. W. Slater: 3 versions, unrhymed, 1866.

Edward Slosson: New York, 1866. See p. 169.

Anonymous: In "New York Evening Post," July 20, 1866. See p. 169.

Erastus C. Benedict: 3 versions, 1864–'67. P. 169.

C. M. Dodd: 1867. P. 170.

Benjamin Johnson: Atlanta, Ga., 1867.

Anonymous: "Round Table," New York, Feb. 23, 1867. ("Contains two cantos, made by D. A. C. from the versions of Coles, Irons, Dix, Slosson, and Caswall." Edmands.)

Anonymous: Boston. In "Littell's Living Age," Jan. 26, 1867.

John Wesley Thomas: 1867.

Roger S. Tracy: In "New York Evening Post," Jan., 1868.

Arthur P. Stanley (Dean of Westminster, d. 1881): In Macmillan's "Magazine," for December, 1868, pp. 167–'69, with an introductory note by the Dean, in which he states that he freely used the versions of Walter Scott, Trench and Irons. 10 stanzas of 6 lines each. (Mr. Edmands dates this version from 1864, but was unable to give me his authority. It may have been first privately printed.) See p. 170.

J. Hoskyns Abrahall: In "Christian Remembrancer," London, Jan., 1868. A paraphrastic translation in 17 stanzas of 6 lines each. See p. 170.

Mrs. Margaret Junkin Preston: In the "Presbyterian," Philadelphia, Jan. 18, 1868 (but the version was made in 1851).

R. Holt Hutton: In the London "Spectator" for March 7, 1868. See p. 170.

Philip Schaff: New York, 1868. See p. 159.

Robert Corbet Singleton: London, 1868.

Horace Castle: 1869.

Anonymous: In "Lippincott's Magazine," Philadelphia, 1869.

Samuel W. Duffield: 1870. Five versions. See p. 158.

Asahel C. Kendrick: New York, 1870.

W. Cooke: In the "Hymnary," 1871.

John D. van Buren: Albany, 1872.

Anonymous: Signed "Trinity," in "The Churchman," March 9, 1872, New York.

John Anketell: "Am. Church Review," New York, 1873.

C. A. Walworth: "Catholic World," New York, 1873.

Charles H. A. Esling: "Catholic Record," Philadelphia, March, 1874.

Charles Kent: London, 1874.

John O'Hagan: Dublin, 1874. P. 171.

John Wallace: London, 1874.

Anonymous: Messenger of the Sacred Heart, 1875.

Hamilton M. Macgill: London, 1876.
Mrs. Emily Righton: 1876.
William McIlvaine: Belfast, 1878.
Samuel J. Watson: 1878.
William W. Nevin: In "The Press," Philadelphia, Jan. 18, 1878.
Osmund Seager: London, 1878.
J. Howard West: Gettysburg, Pa., 1878.
Oliver Crane: Hartford, 1879.
Nathaniel B. Smithers: 1879.
Joel Swartz: In "Lutheran Observer," Philadelphia, Aug. 22, 1879.
Orlando Dobbin: 1879.
William B. Robertson: "Presbyterian Hymnal," Philadelphia, 1879.
D. T. Morgan: London, 1880.
D. Y. Heisler: In "Reformed Quarterly Review," 1880.
Randolph W. Lowrie: In "The Churchman," New York, April 3, 1880.
Anonymous: 1880.
Charles Elliot: In "The Standard," Chicago, Feb. 24, 1881.
Anatole Police: London, 1881.
Matthias Sheeleigh: In "Lutheran Observer," Philadelphia, May 20, 1881.
James A. Whitney: "New York Observer," May 19, 1881.
°**Henry C. Lea:** Philadelphia, 1882. "Translations and other rhymes" (priv. print.).
Joseph J. Marrin: "Catholic World," New York, 1882.
Emily Clemens Pearson: Hartford, 1882.

°**Thomas C. Porter:** Philadelphia, 1882. See p. 159.
Miss Elizabeth Cleveland: New York "Independent," April 12, 1883.
William John Copeland: "Dublin Review," Jan., 1883. P. 173.
W. Hilton: "Dublin Review," 1883.
°**Franklin Johnson:** Cambridge, Mass., 1883. See p. 171.
M. Woolsey Stryker: New York "Evangelist," Nov., 1883. Another version, April 3, 1864.
°**Thomas MacKellar:** Philadelphia, 1883.
James D. Aylward: "Dublin Review," April, 1883. Two versions in single rhymes. P. 171.
John Mason Brown: "Catholic World," New York, Nov., 1884.
George M. Davie: "Catholic World," New York, Nov., 1884. P. 172.
Henry Rawes: 1884 (fly-sheet; unrhymed).
°**Hon. John Hayes** (LL. D., Cambridge, Mass.): In "The Independent," New York, Dec. 30, 1886. P. 172.
°**John S. Hager:** In "The Overland Monthly," San Francisco, 1886 (Vol. VII., 530). P. 172.
°**W. G. McKenzie:** Boston, 1887 and 1889. Two versions. See p. 161.
Alfred H. Fahnestock: "Presbyterian Journal," Philadelphia, July 22, 1889. See p. 172.

This list gives us over one hundred and fifty translations (counting Coles 17, Benedict 3, Duffield 5, Dix 2, McKenzie 2, and omitting the anonymous) from ministers and laymen of various denominations—Roman Catholic, Episcopalian, Presbyterian, Baptist, etc. No hymn has such a history. Next to it comes, perhaps, Luther's EIN FESTE BURG, of which Rev. Dr. B. Pick, of Allegheny (as he informed me), has collected 131 versions in all languages.

One good translation is worth a hundred poor ones and will outlive them. Many were stillborn, or not born at all. But the ever-increasing number is a proof of the popularity and untranslatableness of the DIES IRÆ, the greatest religious lyric of all ages.

THE STABAT MATER DOLOROSA.

There are two mediæval hymns which begin with the words *Stabat Mater*. They resemble each other like twin sisters, or rather like mother and daughter. Both are dedicated to the Virgin Mary, one to Mary at the Cross, the other to Mary at the Cradle, of the Saviour. One is a Good-Friday hymn, the other is a Christmas hymn. Both breathe the same burning love to Christ and his Mother and the desire to become identified with her by sympathy in the intensity of her grief and her joy. They are the same in structure, and excel alike in the touching music of language and the soft cadence that echoes the sentiment. Both describe first the situation, then identify the author with the situation, and address the Virgin as an object of that worship which the Roman Church claims for her as the Mother of the Saviour and the Queen of Saints. Both bear the impress of mediæval piety and of the monastic order which gave them birth.

The Good-Friday hymn has long been known under the name of *Stabat Mater*, and admired as the most pathetic poem of Latin church poetry, inferior only to the more sublime and impressive DIES IRÆ; the Christmas hymn has recently been brought to light, and is a worthy companion, though of inferior merit. We may hereafter distinguish the two as the MATER DOLOROSA and the MATER SPECIOSA.

THE MATER DOLOROSA.

The Latin original from the Roman Missal, with textual variations.

1. Stabat Mater dolorosa
   Juxta crucem lacrymosa,
      Dum[1] pendebat Filius,
   Cujus animam gementem
   Contristatam[2] ac dolentem
      Pertransivit gladius.

2. O quam tristis et afflicta
   Fuit illa benedicta
      Mater Unigeniti!
   Quae moerebat et dolebat
   Et tremebat, cum[3] videbat
      Nati poenas inclyti.

3. Quis est homo, qui non fleret,
   Matrem Christi[4] si videret
      In tanto supplicio?
   Quis non posset contristari,
   Piam Matrem contemplari
      Dolentem cum Filio.

4. Pro peccatis suae gentis
   Vidit Jesum in tormentis
      Et flagellis subditum,
   Vidit suum dulcem natum
   Morientem,[5] desolatum,
      Dum emisit spiritum.

5. Eia[6] Mater, fons amoris!
   Me sentire vim doloris
      Fac, ut tecum lugeam.
   Fac, ut ardeat cor meum
   In amando Christum Deum
      Ut sibi complaceam.

6. Sancta Mater, istud agas
   Crucifixi fige plagas
      Cordi meo valide.[7]
   Tui nati vulnerati
   Tam dignati pro me pati
      Poenas mecum divide.

7. Fac me tecum vere flere[8]
   Crucifixo condolere,
      Donec ego vixero.
   Juxta crucem tecum stare
   Te libenter sociare,[9]
      In planctu desidero.

8. Virgo virginum praeclara
   Mihi tam[10] non sis amara,
      Fac me tecum plangere.
   Fac ut portem Christi mortem
   Passionis fac consortem[11]
      Et plagas[12] recolere.[13]

9. Fac me plagis vulnerari
   Cruce hac inebriari[14]
      Ob amorem Filii.
   Inflammatus et accensus
   Per te, Virgo,[15] sim defensus
      In die judicii.

10. Fac me cruce custodiri,
    Morte Christi praemuniri,
       Confoveri gratia.[16]
    Quando corpus morietur
    Fac ut animae donetur
       Paradisi gloria.[17]

THE STABAT MATER DOLOROSA.   189

TEXTUAL VARIATIONS.

[1] Alii: *qua, sc. cruce.* So also Mone. [2] Mone et al.: *contristantem.*
[3] Mone: *dum.*   [4] Mone: *Christi Matrem.*
[5] Mone: *Moriendo.*
[6] So the Missal, Stella, Daniel. Other MSS. read *pia.*
[7] Al.: *vicide.*
[8] Stella and Mone better: *vere tecum flere.*
[9] Mone et al. better: *Meque* (or *et me*) *tibi sociare.*
[10] Mone: *jam.*
[11] Stella: *passionis ejus sortem.* Al.: *suæ sortem*
[12] Al.: *parnam.*   [13] Al.: *plagis te colere.*
[14] Mone and others: *Cruceque* (or *Cruce fac*) *me fac beari.* An attempt to weaken the force and audacity of the author's metaphor—the drunkenness of love.
[15] Al.: *pia.*   [16] Mone and others:—

"*Christe, cum sit hinc transire,
   Da per Matrem me venire
   Ad palmam victoriæ.*"

[17] Wackernagel adds from mediæval MSS. the first half of an eleventh stanza where the author, as in the variation of the tenth stanza just quoted from Mone (II., 147), addresses himself to Christ directly:—

"*Christe, cum sit hinc exire,
   Da per Matrem me venire
   Ad palmam victoriæ.*"

The text of Georgius Stella (chancellor and historian of Genoa, d. about 1420), which is given by Daniel (*Thes. Hymnol.* II, 131 sq.), inserts three additional stanzas of inferior merit, as follows:—

3. *Quis non potest contristari,
   Matrem Christi contemplari
       Dolentem cum Filio.
   In me sistat dolor tui,
   Crucifixo fac me frui
       Dum sum in exilio.*

4. *Hunc dolorem fac me moestum,
   Nec me facias alienum
       Ab hoc desiderio.
   Illum corde, illum ore,
   Semper feram cum dolore
       Et mentis martyrio.*

9. *Alma salus, advocata
   Morte Christi desolata,
       Miserere populi;
   Virgo dulcis, virgo pia,
   Virgo clemens, o Maria,
       Audi preces servuli.*

CHARACTER AND HISTORY OF THE HYMN.

The MATER DOLOROSA—usually called the *Stabat Mater*, also the *Lament of the Blessed Virgin*[1]—is a passion hymn which describes the intense suffering of Mary at the cross of her Divine-human Son as He offered himself a sacrifice for the sins of the world. It expresses in words what Carlo Dolce and other painters of the Mater Dolorosa express in color. It is based on the prophecy of the aged Simeon, who said to Mary in the Temple: "A sword shall pierce through thine own soul" (Luke ii., 35), and on the last interview of our Lord with his earthly mother, when she stood with her sister (Salome, the mother of St. John) and two other women (Mary wife of Cleophas, and Mary Magdalene) by the cross, and when He commended her to the beloved disciple and the beloved disciple to her (John, xix., 25). From the former passage the poet borrowed the last line of the first stanza (*pertransivit gladius*); from the latter he took the opening sentence, according to the Latin version ("*Stabat mater juxta crucem ejus*"). The first two words of this version furnished the key-note and gave the name to the poem; as the prophetic words of Zephania: "*Dies Iræ*," gave theme and title to the judgment hymn of Thomas a Celano.

This touching incident in the history of the Passion—that most amazing spectacle ever presented to the gaze of heaven and earth—has never found a more impressive expression than in this hymn. It describes first the agony of the mother of the dying Saviour, and then prays to be identified with her suffering and with his crucifixion, that dying to sin, he may stand in the day of judgment and partake of Christ's glory in heaven.

The MATER DOLOROSA is by common consent the most tender and pathetic of Latin hymns. Daniel calls it "the queen of sequences."[2] It is inferior to the DIES IRÆ in force and majesty, but equal in melody, and superior in tenderness. The difference

---

[1] *Planctus Beatæ Virginis*, or *Sequentia de Septem Doloribus B. Virginis*, or *De Compassione B. V.*

[2] *Thes. Hymnol.*, V. 59. The term *sequentia* or *prosa* was first applied to hymns in rhythmical *prose* which *followed* the Alleluia after the reading of the Epistle, and afterwards to *rhymed* hymns as well. See Schaff, *Church History*, vol. iv., 430.

corresponds to the theme: one is a judgment hymn, and hence solemn, awful, overpowering, like "The Day of Wrath"; the other is a passion hymn, and hence tender, touching and sympathetic, like Mary standing at the cross. Both breathe the same spirit of profound repentance and glowing love to Christ.

The secret of the power of the MATER DOLOROSA lies in the intensity of feeling with which the poet identifies himself with his theme, and in the soft, plaintive melody of its Latin rhythm and rhyme, which cannot be transferred to any other language. It draws the reader irresistibly into sympathy with the agony described, and makes him a fellow-sufferer with Mary. It fills him with grief for his own sins which have cost such a sacrifice, and with gratitude for the love of the Son of God, who spared not his own life for our redemption.[1]

The only objectionable feature in this incomparable poem is a touch of what Protestants call Mariolatry, which excludes it from evangelical hymn books unless the prayer to Mary be changed into a prayer to Christ.[2] It fixes the pious contemplation on the human mother rather than her Divine Son, and ascribes to her the functions of the Holy Spirit. There breathes also through the ninth stanza a morbid passion for the miracle of stigmatization which the legend reports of St. Francis of Assisi. But we must judge the poet from the standpoint of mediæval piety, and not forget that some truth underlies every error of the

---

[1] Dr. Coles (*Stabat Mater*, p. 6) thus characterizes the author: "He has clairvoyance and second sight. The distant and the past are made to him a virtual here and now. He is in Italy, but he is also in Judæa. He lives in the thirteenth century, but is an eye witness of the crucifixion in the beginning of the first. He has immediate vision. All that is transpiring on Golgotha is distinctly pictured on the retina of his mind's eye. And by the light which is in him he photographs what he sees for the use of others. His *eccе !* is no pointless indication, but an actual showing. The wail he utters is a veritable echo of that which goes up from the cross. Everything is true to nature and to life." . . . "He prays that he may be permitted to bear a part, not in the way of sympathy merely, but of suffering also, and this too, the same both in kind and degree; that enduring stripe for stripe, wound for wound, there might be to him in every stage of the Redeemer's passion, groan answering to groan."

[2] This is done by Monsell, Knapp and other Protestant translators. See Schaff's *Deutsches Gesangbuch*, No. 117.

Roman Church and gives it such a hold on the pious feelings of her members. It is, after all, Christ's sufferings which were reflected in Mary's agony; as it is the heavenly beauty of the Christ-child which shines on the face of the Madonnas of Raphael. We must also give to Roman Catholics credit for their distinction between different kinds of worship; adoration (*latria*), which belongs to God alone; veneration (*dulia*), which is due to Saints in the presence of God; and a special degree of veneration or semi-adoration which is claimed for the Virgin Mary, as the Mother of the Saviour and the Queen of Saints in heaven. They do not pray to Mary as the giver of the mercies desired, but only as the interceder, thinking that she is more likely to prevail with her Son than any poor unaided sinner on earth.

The poem soon became popular. It was spread all over Europe by the Flagellants or Brethren of the Cross (*Crucifcatres, Cruciferi*) in their penitential processions. It gradually found a place in almost every breviary and missal, and, with slight changes, in many evangelical hymn books. Its charm is felt by every man of religious feeling and poetic taste, and even by persons who have little religious sympathy with the theme.

"The loveliness of sorrow," says the German poet Tieck,[1] speaking of the Stabat Mater and Pergolesi's composition, "in the depth of pain, the smiling in tears, the childlike simplicity, which touches on the highest heaven, had to me never before risen so bright in the soul. I had to turn away to hide my tears, especially at the place,

'*Videt suum dulcem natum.*'"

Goethe had this poem in mind when he put this prayer into the mouth of Margaret as she looked with a guilty conscience at a picture of the Mater Dolorosa:—

> "Ach neige,
> Du Schmerzenreiche
> Dein Antlitz gnädig meiner Noth!
>
> Das Schwert im Herzen,
> Mit tausend Schmerzen
> Blickst auf zu deines Sohnes Tod.

[1] Tieck's *Phantasus*, quoted by Lisco and Daniel (II., 139 sq.).

"Zum Vater blickst du,
Und Seufzer schickst du
Hinauf um sein' und deine Noth."

The MATER DOLOROSA has furnished the text to some of the noblest musical compositions by Palestrina, Pergolesi, Astorga, Haydn, Bellini, Rossini, Neukomm. That of Palestrina is still annually performed in the Sistine chapel during Passion week, and draws thousands of eager listeners of all creeds. That of Pergolesi, the last and most celebrated of his works, has never been surpassed, if equaled, in the estimation of critics. Of these melodies it has been said:—

"Es hören, wenn du das Schwert im tief zerrissenen Busen
Der göttlichen Mutter beweinst, mitweinende Engel die zu."

FRANCIS OF ASSISI. JACOBUS DE BENEDICTIS.

The reputed author of the MATER DOLOROSA is GIACOMO DA TODI, better known as GIACOPÓNE or JACOPONE. His proper name was JACOBUS DE BENEDICTIS, or GIACOMA DE BENEDETTI, being a descendant of the noble family of the Benedetti at Todi, in Umbria, in Italy. He was an older contemporary of Dante, and lived in the latter part of the thirteenth and beginning of the fourteenth century.

He successfully studied and practiced law, but was converted in consequence of the sudden death of his wife in a theatre which broke down during the performance of a popular play. He withdrew from the world, sold his goods for the benefit of the poor, and joined the order of the Franciscans, remaining, however, merely a lay brother. This Order, founded by St. Francis of Assisi (1182-1226), was then still in the fervor of the first love, and carried away many of the noblest and most enthusiastic youths.

The ruling idea and aim of the order was the literal imitation of the poor and humble life of Christ. St. Francis died of the wounds of Christ, which are said to have impressed themselves on his hands and side by a miracle, or, perhaps, through the plastic power of an imagination intoxicated with the contemplation and love of the crucified Redeemer. He was himself a poet, loved all creatures of God, and preached to the sun and moon, to birds and fishes as his brothers and sisters. He may be called the father of Italian hymnology. He was the first to use the vulgar Italian speech for religious poetry in place of the Latin. His "Song of the Sun" (*Cantico del Sole*) or "Song of the Creatures" (*Cantico delle Creature*), although not mentioned as his before 1385, was probably written about 1224, two years before his death, and nearly a century before Dante finished his *Divina Commedia*, which created a national Italian literature. I give a translation of this unique hymn with its irregular cadence, broken rhymes and faltering measures, which was sung in his convent every day. It faithfully expresses the childlike simplicity, naiveté and all-embracing love of the piety of St. Francis, that "seraphic stranger on earth."[1]

[1] Ozanam, *Les Poëtes Franciscains en Italie au treizième siècle* (Paris, third ed. 1859), p. 73, says: " Le Cantique du Soleil est cité pour la première fois par Barthélemy de Pise, dans un livre écrit en 1385, cent soixante ans après la mort du saint, et cependant on ne peut en contester l'authenticité. . . . Le poëme de saint François est bien court, et cependant on y trouve toute son âme : sa fraternelle amitié pour les créatures; la charité qui poussait cet homme humble et timide à travers les querelles publiques; cet amour infini, qui après avoir cherché Dieu dans la nature e l'avoir servi dans l'humanité souffrante, n'aspirait plus qu'à le trouver dans la mort. . . . Ce n'est qu'un cri; mais c'est le premier cri d'une poésie naissante, qui grandira et qui saura se faire entendre de toute la terre." An admirable description. Ozanam gives a French prose translation of the poem, p. 71–73. Mrs. Oliphant an English version quoted above, in Ch. XV of her charming monograph on *Francis of Assisi*, published by Macmillan & Co., London. These are the first three stanzas of the original (from Ozanam, p. 339):—

 1. "*Altissimo omnipotente bon Signore,*
  Tue son le laude, la gloria, e l'onore,
   Et ogni benedictione :
   A te solo se confanno,
  Et nullo homo è degno di nominare te."

 2. *Laudato sia Dio mio Signore*
  Cum tutte le tue creature,
  Specialmente messer lo frate Sole :
  Lo quale giorna et illumina nui per lui,
  Et ello è bello et radiante cum grande splendore :
  De te Signore porta significatione."

  "*Laudato sia mio Signore per sor Luna et per le Stelle;*
  In celo le hai formate clare è belle."

"Highest omnipotent good Lord,
  Glory and honor to Thy name adored,
    And praise and every blessing:
      Of everything Thou art the source,
No man is worthy to pronounce Thy name.

"Praised by His creatures all,
  Praised be the Lord my God.
By Messer Sun, my brother above all,
  Who by his rays lights us and lights the day
Radiant is he, with his great splendor,
  Thy glory, Lord, confessing.

"By Sister Moon and Stars my Lord is praised,
  Where clear and fair they in the heavens are raised.

"By Brother Wind, my Lord, Thy praise is said,
By air and clouds and the blue sky o'erhead,
By which Thy creatures all are kept and fed.

"By one most humble, useful, precious, chaste,
By Sister Water, O my Lord, Thou art praised.

  "And praised is my Lord
By Brother Fire—he who lights up the night
Jocund, robust is he, and strong and bright.

"Praised art Thou, my Lord, by Mother Earth—
Thou who sustainest her, and governest,
And to her flowers, fruit, herbs, dost color give and birth."

This is the original hymn. St. Francis afterward on a special occasion added the following verse:—

  "And praised is my Lord
By those who, for Thy love, can pardon give,
And bear the weakness and the wrongs of men.
Blessed are those who suffer thus in peace,
By Thee, the Highest, to be crowned in heaven."

A little later, when weak and worn out by bodily sufferings and his labors for humanity, on being warned in a vision that in two years he would enter into his eternal rest, he greeted death in this concluding stanza:—

> "Praised by our Sister Death, my Lord, art Thou,
> From whom no living man escapes.
> Who die in mortal sin have mortal woe;
> But blessed they who die doing Thy will.—
> The second death can strike at them no blow.
>
> "Praises, and thanks, and blessing to my Master be:
> Serve ye Him all, with great humility."

Animated by the spirit of St. Francis, Jacopone went to fanatical extremes in his zeal for ascetic holiness and spiritual martyrdom. He endeavored by self-sought tortures to atone for his own sins, and to "fill up that which is behind in the afflictions of Christ," for the good of others. He was subject to fits of insanity. The world called him a crank, or a fool, or a genius run mad. To grow in the grace of humility he exposed himself to the ridicule of contemporaries by the oddity of his appearance and conduct. He literally became a fool for Christ. At one time during public plays at Todi, he is said to have suddenly appeared among the crowd almost *in puris naturalibus*, with a saddle on his back and a bridle in his mouth, walking on all fours like a horse. Perhaps he wished to imitate the Hebrew Prophets in their symbolic actions to arouse attention and to impress more deeply his lessons of wisdom. Among the early Quakers we find similar excesses of abnormal piety. He was called GIACOPÓNE, or the GREAT JACOB, at first in derision, perhaps also to distinguish him from the many Jacobs among the Franciscans. For the syllabic suffix *óne* in Italian indicates greatness or elevation; as *alberone*, great tree, from *albero*; *cappellone*, from *capello*, hat; *portone*, from *porta*, door; *salone*, from *sala*, saloon.

For ten years he carried on his ascetic excesses, but then he withdrew into a life of solitary mystic contemplation of God's infinite love, and had no higher desire than to suffer for Him who had died for his sins. He was frequently seen sighing, sometimes weeping, sometimes embracing a tree and exclaiming, "O sweet Jesus! O gracious Jesus! O beloved Jesus!" Once when weeping loudly, on being asked the cause, he answered: "Because Love is not loved." A sentiment worthy of the author of the MATER DOLOROSA.

In his poems he fearlessly exposed the vices of all classes of society, and censured the grasping, avaricious Pope Boniface VIII., who punished him by excommunication and hard imprisonment. When Boniface once passing by his prison asked him when he expected to get out, Jacopone foretold his future fate by the prompt reply, "When you will get in."

After the imprisonment and death of this pope, in 1303, Jacopone was set free, and closed his earthly pilgrimage at an advanced age, December 25th, 1306, and was buried at Todi. "He died," says Lucas Wadding, the historian of the Franciscan order, "like a swan, having composed several hymns just before his death." The inscription on his grave tells the story of his life: "*Ossa B. Jacoponi de Benedictis, Tudertini, Fratris Ordinis Minorum, qui stultus propter Christum nova mundum arte delusit et calum rapuit. Obdormivit in Domino die xxv. Martii, anno Domini MCCXCVI.*" This date is a gross error, since he survived Boniface VIII., who died 1303. Wadding corrects the date by omitting X and substituting December 25th, 1306.[1]

The *Poesie* or *Cantaci spirituali* of Jacopone are full of mystic fervor and mark the dawn of the Italian language and literature at a time when the immortal author of the *Divina Commedia* was still a youth, and Petrarca was just born. They were first printed at Florence in 1490, nearly two hundred years after the death of the author, under the title *Laude di frate Jacopone da Todi*, and repeatedly since.

In the second edition of these poems, which appeared at Brescia, 1495, there is an appendix of several Latin poems, among which is one *De Contemptu Mundi*, and also the famous *Stabat Mater Dolorosa*.[2] On this ground, as well as on account

---

[1] The fullest account of his life is found in Lucas Wadding's learned *Annales Minorum seu trium Ordinum a S. Francisco institutorum.* Rome, 2d. ed. 1731 sqq. (21 vols. in all), vol. IV., p. 407 sqq.; vol. V., p. 606 sqq., and vol. VI., p. 76 sqq. (A copy of this work is in the Astor Library, New York). And in Ch. IV. and V. of Ozanam's *Poëtes Franciscains* (p. 131–217).

[2] The same edition, according to Brunet, contains also the *Mater Speciosa*.

of the general agreement of the hymn with what we know of Jacopone and with the spirit of the early Franciscan poetry, Lucas Wadding vindicated the *Stabat Mater* as Jacopone's, who has ever since been commonly regarded as the author.[1]

In the absence of authentic or cotemporary evidence, this opinion is no more than a probable conjecture; but it is preferable to other conjectures. The MATER DOLOROSA has also been ascribed, without proof, to St. Bernard of Clairvaux (died 1151), in whose works it has found a place. Pope Benedict XIV.,[2] Mone, and Phil. Wackernagel[3] ascribe it to the great Pope Innocent III. (who died 1216), at least in its original form (six stanzas), and to Jacopone in its revised and enlarged form (stanzas 2, 6, 7, 8). But neither Mone nor Wackernagel furnishes the least evidence for the conjecture. George Stella, of Genoa, ascribes it to Pope John XXII., the second of the Popes of Avignon (1316–1334), and gives an enlarged text of 13 stanzas.[4]

Whoever was the author, he wrote, like Thomas a Celano and Thomas a Kempis, not for fame, but for the glory of Christ and the good of mankind. The two greatest hymns of the Middle Ages, and the best book of devotion are unselfishly anonymous.

ENGLISH TRANSLATIONS.

Like the DIES IRÆ, only in a less degree, the STABAT MATER has again and again tried the skill of translators with the same result of disappointment. The sentiment can be reproduced, but the music of the Latin rhythm and double rhyme is inimitable.

---

[1] See Wadding's *Scriptores Ord. Minorum*, etc., Romæ 1650, fols. 180, 181, quoted by Daniel, *Thes. Hymnol.*, II., p. 141. This work of Wadding I could not find in New York. In his voluminous *Annals* of the Franciscan Order, which I have examined, Wadding says nothing of the *Stabat Mater*, but ascribes to Jacopone the poem *De Contemptu Mundi*, commencing, "Cur mundus militat sub vana gloria." (Vol. VI., p. 79 sq.) This poem is translated by Dr. Coles in his *Old Gems in New Settings* (New York, 1868, p. 72 sqq.:
"Why toileth the world in the service of glory."

[2] "*De Festis Jesu Christi*," II., c. 4, § 5, as quoted by Mone in his collection of *Latin Hymns* vol. II., p. 149.

[3] *Das Deutsche Kirchenlied*, etc., 1864, sqq., vol. I., pp. 136 and 161.

[4] Daniel II., 131 sq. See above p. 189.

The English and German translations are the most numerous and successful. Lisco, in a special monograph, gives fifty-three German and several Dutch versions. The English versions are less numerous and mostly of recent date. As in the case of the DIES IRAE, the Americans have equaled their English brethren in zeal, and the best American translators (A. Coles, E. C. Benedict, John A. Dix, Franklin Johnson, and W. S. McKenzie) are Protestants. I select the principal versions (with permission of the authors, as far as I could obtain it).

REV. EDWARD CASWALL, M. A. (ROM. CATH.), 1849.

From "*Lyra Catholica, containing all the Breviary and Missal Hymns,*" etc., London, 1849, p. 138 (Am. ed., N. York, 1851, p. 184.) Caswall, following the Breviaries, divides the hymn into three parts for Vespers, Matins and Lauds.

(VESPERS.)

1. At the Cross her station keeping,
   Stood the mournful Mother weeping,
      Close to Jesus to the last:
   Through her heart, His sorrow sharing,
   All His bitter anguish bearing,
      Now at length the sword had pass'd.

2. Oh, how sad and sore distress'd
   Was that Mother highly blest
      Of the sole-begotten One!
   Christ above in torment hangs;
   She beneath beholds the pangs
      Of her dying glorious Son.

3. Is there one who would not weep,
   Whelm'd in miseries so deep
      Christ's dear Mother to behold?
   Can the human heart refrain
   From partaking in her pain,
      In that Mother's pain untold?

4. Bruis'd, derided, curs'd, defil'd,
   She beheld her tender Child
      All with bloody scourges rent;
   For the sins of His own nation,
   Saw Him hang in desolation,
      Till His spirit forth He sent.

5. O thou Mother! fount of love!
   Touch my spirit from above,
      Make my heart with thine accord:
   Make me feel as thou hast felt;
   Make my soul to glow and melt
      With the love of Christ my Lord.

(MATINS.)

6. Holy Mother! pierce me through;
   In my heart each wound renew
      Of my Saviour crucified:
   Let me share with thee His pain,
   Who for all my sins was slain,
      Who for me in torments died.

7. Let me mingle tears with thee,
   Mourning Him who mourn'd for me,
      All the days that I may live:
   By the Cross with thee to stay;
   There with thee to weep and pray;
      Is all I ask of thee to give.

(LAUDS.)

8. Virgin of all virgins best!
   Listen to my fond request:
      Let me share thy grief divine;
   Let me, to my latest breath,
   In my body bear the death
      Of that dying Son of thine.

9. Wounded with His every wound,
   Steep my soul till it hath swoon'd
     In His very blood away;
   Be to me, O Virgin, nigh,
   Lest in flames I burn and die,
     In His awful Judgment day.

10. Christ, when Thou shalt call me hence,
    Be Thy Mother my defence,
      Be Thy Cross my victory;
    While my body here decays,
    May my soul Thy goodness praise,
      Safe in Paradise with Thee.

REV. J. S. B. MONSELL (1811–1875).

In the following version, by a slight change, Christ is addressed instead of Mary:—

1. Stood the mournful Mother weeping,
   By the cross her vigil keeping,
     While her Jesus hung thereon:
   Through her heart, in sorrow moaning,
   With Him grieving, for Him groaning,
     Through that heart the sword hath gone.

2. Oh, how sad and sore distressed
   Was she, the forever blessed,
     Mother of the undefiled!
   She who wept, and mourned, and trembled,
   When she saw such pains assembled
     Round about the Holy Child.

3. Who that sees Christ's Mother bending
   'Neath His load of sorrow, rending
     Her sad soul in woe so deep;
   Who that sees that pious Mother
   With Him weeping, could do other
     Than, himself afflicted, weep?

4. For the sins of each offender,
   Sinless soul, and body tender,
     Sees she 'neath the cruel rod:
   Sees her own sweet Son, her only,
   Dying, desolate, and lonely,
     Pouring out His soul to God.

5. Jesu! fount of love! Thee loving,
   And my soul Thy sorrow moving,
     Make me watch and keep with Thee:
   As my God and Christ Thee knowing,
   Let my loving heart be glowing
     With a holy sympathy.

6. Holy Father! let affliction
   For Thy dear Son's crucifixion
     Pierce my heart; and grant this prayer,—
   That while He for me was wounded,
   With indignities surrounded,
     I His cup of grief may share.

7. Make me truly weep and never
   From the Crucified me sever,
     Long as I on earth shall live:
   By the cross of Jesus weeping,
   Vigil with His mother keeping,
     To my prayer this answer give.

8. God of saints! thou King most holy!
   Comforter of spirits only!
     Fill me with my Saviour's grief;
   That, His death devoutly bearing,
   And His bitter passion sharing,
     I may bring Him some relief.

9. Make me with His stripes be stricken,
   With the cross my spirit quicken,
     For the love of Christ I pray:
   That with love inflamed, attended,
   I by love may be defended
     In the awful Judgment Day.

10. By the cross forever guarded,
    And, through Christ's dear dying, warded
      By the grace that never dies;
    When my mortal body, dying,
    In the quiet grave is lying,
      Take my soul to paradise,
      To adore
    Thee, my God, forevermore!

THE STABAT MATER DOLOROSA.

ABRAHAM COLES, M.D., Scotch Plains, New Jersey, 1867.

1. Stood th' afflicted mother weeping,
   Near the cross her station keeping,
   Whereon hung her Son and Lord;
   Through whose spirit sympathizing,
   Sorrowing and agonizing,
      Also passed the cruel sword.

2. Oh! how mournful and distressed
   Was that favored and most blessed
      Mother of the Only Son!
   Trembling, grieving, bosom-heaving,
   While perceiving, scarce believing,[1]
      Pains of that Illustrious One.

3. Who the man, who, called a brother,
   Would not weep, saw he Christ's Mother
      In such deep distress and wild?
   Who could not sad tribute render
   Witnessing that Mother tender
      Agonizing with her child?

4. For His people's sins atoning,
   Him she saw in torments groaning,
      Given to the scourger's rod;
   Saw her darling offspring, dying
   Desolate, forsaken, crying,
      Yield His spirit up to God.

5. Make me feel thy sorrow's power,
   That with thee I tears may shower,
      Tender Mother, fount of love!
   Make my heart with love unceasing
   Burn towards Christ the Lord, that pleasing
      I may be to Him above.

6. Holy Mother, this be granted,
   That the slain one's wounds be planted
      Firmly in my heart to bide.
   Of Him wounded, all astounded—
   Depths unbounded for me sounded,[2]
      All the pangs with me divide.

7. Make me weep with thee in union;
   With the Crucified, communion
      In His grief and suffering give;
   Near the cross with tears unfailing
   I would join thee in thy wailing
      Here as long as I shall live.

8. Maid of maidens, all excelling!
   Be not bitter, me repelling,
      Make thou me a mourner too:
   Make me bear about Christ's dying,
   Share His passion, shame defying,
      All His wounds in me renew.

9. Wound for wound be there created;
   With the cross intoxicated
      For thy Son's dear sake, I pray—
   May I, fired with pure affection,
   Virgin, have through thee protection
      In the solemn judgment day.

10. Let me by the cross be warded,
    By the death of Christ be guarded,
       Nourished by divine supplies.
    When the body death hath riven,
    Grant that to the soul be given
       Glories bright of paradise.

The esteemed and venerable author sent me (Sept. 17, 1889) the following new version of the first three stanzas as an alternative for the corresponding stanzas of his first version; the last seven remaining the same:—

[1] This is a happy reproduction of the musical quadruplication of the double rhymes in the original:—

    "Quæ mœrebat et dolebat
     Et tremebat, cum videbat."

[2] "Tui nati vulnerati
   Tam dignati pro me pati."

THE STABAT MATER DOLOROSA.

1. Stood the Mother, O how tearful,
   Near the Cross, the gibbet fearful,
     Whereon hung her Son and Lord;—
   Through whose spirit, sympathizing,
   Sorrowing and agonizing,
     Also passed the cruel sword.

2. O how mournful! how distressed!
   How distraught that Mother blessèd
     Of the sole-begotten One!
   By that sight of horror shaken,
   What dire griefs did they awaken—
     Woes of that Illustrious One!

3. Who could his emotions smother,
   If he saw Christ's dearest Mother
     In such deep distress and wild?
   Who could tears refuse to render,
   Witnessing that Mother tender,
     Agonizing with her Child?

Another Version of Dr. Abraham Coles.

This new version, in single rhyme, was prepared on September 17, 1859, and is here published for the first time by kind permission of the author:—

1. Bathed in tears the Mother stood,
   Close beside the fatal wood,
     Where her Son extended hung:
   Through whose soul the sword then passed,
   Wakening groans that followed fast,
     Pangs foreseen, by Simeon sung.

2. O what anguish tore her breast,—
   Mother, singularly blest,
     Of the God-begotten One!
   How rang out her piteous wail,
   As they drove each cruel nail
     In the flesh of her great Son!

3. Who loud weeping could forbear,
   If he saw Christ's Mother there
     In such boundless grief and pain?
   Who could a spectator be,
   And not share her agony
     Witness of her Offspring slain?

4. For transgressors of the law,
   She in torments Jesus saw—
     Saw Him writhe beneath the rod;—
   Saw her dear Son, desolate,
   Dying, victim of man's hate,
     Breathe His spirit out to God.

5. Tender Mother, love's sweet Source!
   Let me feel thy sorrow's force,
     So that I may mourn with thee!
   May my heart with worship glow
   Loving Christ as God, that so
     I to Him may pleasing be!

6. Holy Mother, this impart—
   Strongly fix there in my heart
     Wound-prints of the Crucified!—
   Pains thy own Son wounded bore,
   Aching heart and sufferings sore,
     Faithfully with me divide!

7. Let me share thy grief of soul,
   With the Crucified condole,
     All the while I live below!
   Near the Cross, thee close beside,
   I would gladly stand and bide
     In companionship of woe.

8. Virgin of all virgins first,
   Lest I be for fault amerced,
     Be not bitter, be thou kind!
   Let me marks of Christ's death bear,
   Wound-prints of His passion wear,
     Stamped upon my heart and mind!

9. Wounded with His wounds let me
   With the Cross enamoured be,
     On account of love so vast;
   Fired and kindled I depend
   On thee, Virgin, to defend
     In the Judgment at the last.

10. By the Cross me make secure,
    By Christ's death make my life sure,
      Nourish me with needed grace!
    When on earth I cease to live,
    To my soul immortal give
      There in Paradise a place!

ERASTUS C. BENEDICT, of New York, 1867.

First published in the "Christian Intelligencer," N. York (the organ of the Reformed Dutch Church), then somewhat changed in his "*The Hymn of Hildebert and other Mediæval Hymns with Translations,*" New York (Anson D. F. Randolph), 1867, pp. 65–69.

1. Weeping stood His mother, sighing
   By the cross where Jesus, dying,
      Hung aloft on Calvary;
   Through her soul, in sorrow moaning,
   Bowed in grief, in spirit groaning,
      Pierced the sword in misery.

2. Filled with grief beyond all others,
   Mother—blessed among mothers—
      Of the God-begotten one!
   How she sorroweth and grieveth,
   Trembling as she thus perceiveth
      Dying her unspotted one!

3. Who could there refrain from weeping,
   Seeing Christ's dear mother keeping
      In her grief, so bitterly?
   Who could fail to share her anguish,
   Seeing thus the mother languish,
      Lost in woe so utterly?

4. For the trespass of his nation
   She beheld his laceration,
      By their scourges suffering.
   She beheld her dearest taken,
   Crucified, and God forsaken,
      Dying by their torturing.

5. Mother, fountain of affection,
   Let me share thy deep dejection,
      Let me share thy tenderness;
   Let my heart, thy sorrow feeling,
   Love of Christ, the Lord, revealing,
      Be like thine in holiness!

6. All His stripes, oh! let me feel them,
   On my heart for ever seal them,
      Printed there enduringly.
   All His woes, beyond comparing,
   For my sake in anguish bearing,
      Let me share them willingly.

7. By thy side let me be weeping,
   True condolence with Him keeping,
      Weeping all my life with thee;
   Near the cross with thee abiding,
   Freely all thy woes dividing,
      In thy sorrow joined with thee.

8. Virgin, of all virgins fairest,
   Let me feel the love thou bearest,
      Sharing all thy suffering;
   Let me feel the death they gave Him,
   Crucified in shame to save them,
      Dying without murmuring.

9. Let me feel their blows so crushing,
   Let me drink the current gushing
      From His wounds when crucified.
   By a heavenly zeal excited,
   When the judgment fires are lighted,
      Then may I be justified.

10. On the Cross of Christ relying,
    Through His death redeemed from dying,
       By His favor fortified;
    When my mortal frame is perished,
    Let my spirit then be cherished,
       And in heaven be glorified.

GENERAL JOHN ADAMS DIX, 1868.

General Dix prepared this version, as he says, "more leisurely" than his earlier version of the DIES IRÆ, while he was American Minister Plenipotentiary in Paris, sitting in a gilded saloon under the shadow of the Triumphal Arch,—in striking contrast to the lonely cell of an ascetic Franciscan friar in which the original was born. He printed it privately at Cambridge, Mass., 1868. It is reprinted in *The Memoirs of John Adams Dix, compiled by* his son, *Morgan Dix*, N. York (Harper & Brothers), 1883, Vol. II., 240 sq. Comp. his remarks on p. 233. This version is superior to either of his two versions of the *Dies Irae*:—

1. Near the Cross the Saviour bearing
    Stood the Mother lone, despairing,
        Bitter tears down falling fast.
    Wearied was her heart with grieving,
    Worn her breast with sorrow heaving:
        Through her soul the sword had
            passed.

2. Ah! how sad and broken-hearted
    Was that blessed Mother, parted
        From the God-begotten One!
    How her loving heart did languish
    When she saw the mortal anguish
        Which o'erwhelmed her peerless Son!

3. Who could witness without weeping
    Such a flood of sorrow sweeping
        O'er the stricken Mother's breast?
    Who contemplate without being
    Moved to kindred grief by seeing
        Son and Mother thus oppressed?

4. For our sins she saw Him bending
    And the cruel lash descending
        On His body stripped and bare;
    Saw her own dear Jesus dying,
    Heard His spirit's last outcrying
        Sharp with anguish and despair.

5. Gentle Mother, love's pure fountain!
    Cast, O cast on me the mountain
        Of thy grief that I may weep;
    Let my heart with ardor burning,
    Christ's unbounded love returning,
        His rich favor win and keep.

6. Holy Mother, be thy study
    Christ's dear image scarred and bloody
        To enshrine within my heart!
    Martyred Son! whose grace has set me
    Free from endless death, O let me
        Of Thy sufferings bear a part.

7. Mother, let our tears commingle,
    Be the crucifix my single
        Sign of sorrow while I live;
    Let me by the Cross stand near thee,
    There to see thee, there to hear thee—
        For each sigh a sigh to give.

8. Purest of the Virgins! turn not
    Thy displeasure on me—spurn not
        My desire to weep with thee.
    Let me live Christ's passion sharing,
    All His wounds and sorrows bearing
        In my tearful memory.

9. Be, ye wounds, my tribulation!
    Be, thou Cross, my inspiration!
        Mark, O blood, my Heavenward
            way.
    Thus to fervor rapt, O tender
    Virgin, be thou my defender
        In the dreadful Judgment day.

10. With the Cross my faith I'll cherish;
    By Christ's death sustained I'll perish,
        Through His grace again to rise.
    Come then, Death, this body sealing,
    To my ransomed soul revealing
        Glorious days in Paradise.

REV. DR. FRANKLIN JOHNSON, of Cambridge, Mass., 1885.

Dr. Johnson gives also a second version "adapted to the devotional use of Protestants," in which he changes the address from Mary to Jesus, ver. 6-10.

1. Stood the mournful mother weeping,
    Near the cross her vigil keeping,
        Where He hung, her Son adored.
    Through her soul, of hope forsaken,
    And of mighty sorrows shaken,
        Pierced the sharp relentless sword.

2. Of all women has none other
    Suffered like the blessed mother
        Of God's sole begotten Son,
    Who with fervent love unfailing
    And with anguish unavailing
        Gazed upon that dying One.

3. Who is hard, yet being human,
   That bereaved and weeping woman
      To behold with tearless eyes?
   Who, his bosom sternly steeling,
   Would not feel with all her feeling
      Of her Son's keen agonies?

4. Long she saw that loved One languish
   For His people's sins in anguish,
      Saw His meekness 'neath the rod,
   Saw her Son, of all deserted—
   Earth and Heaven from Him averted—
      Yield His spirit up to God.

5. Mother, fount of love's devotion,
   I, beholding thine emotion,
      Would thy burden with thee bear;
   Let me thine affection borrow
   For thy Son in all His sorrow,
      That thy mourning I may share.

6. Holy Mother, with affliction
   Of His saving crucifixion
      Fill and thrill mine inmost heart;
   With thy Son, His wounds receiving
   That have caused thy soul its grieving,
      May I ever have a part.

7. I would weep with all thy weeping,
   Vigil with thy vigil keeping,
      Till my mortal life shall fail;
   Near the cross and near beside thee,
   Where these agonies betide thee,
      I would stand and with thee wail.

8. Virgin, virgins all excelling,[1]
   For thy love and grief a dwelling
      Pure and holy make in me;
   Let me bear Christ's crucifying;
   Let me know the pains of dying
      That He suffered on the tree.

9. Let my heart with His be riven;[2]
   Let His cup to me be given;
      Let me of its depths partake;
   And, still flaming thus with fervor,
   Let me find thee my preserver
      When the Judgment day shall break.

10. Through the cross thy blessing send
       me;[3]
    Let Christ's death from sin defend me;
       Care for me in tender love;
    When this mortal flesh shall perish,
    Let thy Son my spirit cherish
       In His Paradise above.[4]

HON. JOHN L. HAYES (Cambridge, Mass.).
From "The Independent." New York, Dec. 30, 1886.

1. Stood the grief-struck Mother weeping,
   At the Cross her vigil keeping,
      Where her suffering Son was bound;
   And her heart with anguish groaning
   And His agony bemoaning,
      Bleeds with every bleeding wound.

2. Oh! What sorrow and affliction,
   She the font of benediction,
      Bore for her beloved Son!
   With what grief and what bewailing,
   And what trembling and heart-failing,
      Looked she on the martyred One!

3. Who could hold his tears from flowing
   For Christ's stricken Mother, knowing
      All her misery and pain?
   Who withhold his lamentation,
   In the mournful contemplation
      Of her grieving for the slain?

4. She, for sinners' sure salvation,
   Saw her Son in condemnation
      Whipped with scourges, led to death;
   Saw Him, without consolation,
   In despair and desolation
      Utter His expiring breath.

[1] In the second version: "Jesus, all our thoughts excelling."
[2] "Let my heart with Thine be riven."
[3] "Through Thy cross Thy blessing send me,
    Let Thy death from sin defend me."
[4] "Evermore my spirit cherish,
    In Thy Paradise above."

5. Thou, O Mother! love-bestowing!
   Make me, with thy grief o'erflowing,
   Make me mourn and weep with thee!
   Fill my heart with love all burning,
   Unto Christ His love returning,
   That thy blessing fall on me.

6. Holy Mother! by thy favor
   May the wounds of Christ forever
   Be engraven on my heart;
   Of His suffering and wounding
   May I, through thy grace abounding,
   Though unworthy, bear a part.

7. With thy tears let mine fall duly;
   At the cross lamenting truly
   May I weep till life shall end;
   Near His cross give me my station,
   And with thee association,
   That my griefs with thine may blend.

8. Virgin, than all virgins fairer!
   In thy pain let me be sharer;
   Let me always with thee mourn.
   Give me part in Christ's affliction;
   Let His stripes and crucifixion
   In my heart of hearts be borne.

9. With His wounds may I be sinking;
   Of His cup may I be drinking,
   With His blood inebriate be!
   Lest by flames I be consumed,
   And in day of judgment doomed,
   Virgin blest, I call on thee!

10. By the Cross may I be guarded;
    By Christ's death from dangers warded,
    Through His grace that open lies!
    When my dust to dust is given,
    And my soul its bonds hath riven,
    Give me place in Paradise!

Two Versions of REV. W. S. MCKENZIE, D.D., Boston, Mass., 1887.
First published in "The Beacon," Boston, Mass., May 7, 1887.

IN DOUBLE RHYME.

1. Stood the Virgin Mother weeping
   Near the cross, sad vigils keeping
   O'er her son there crucified:
   Through her soul in sorrow moaning,
   Racked with grief, with anguish groaning,
   Pierced the sword as prophesied.

2. Ah! how doleful and dejected
   Was that woman, the elected
   Mother of the Holy One;
   Who, with weeping and with grieving,
   Stood there trembling, while perceiving
   How they smote her peerless Son.

3. Who could see without emotion
   Christ's dear mother, all devotion,
   Crushed beneath such misery?
   Could one see her desolation,
   Would he hush her lamentation
   For her Son in agony?

SINGLE RHYME.

1. The Virgin Mother sighed and wept,
   As near the cross she steadfast kept,
   Where her Son in torture hung:
   Her stricken heart with anguish groaned,
   With grief o'erwhelmed she cried and moaned,
   For the sword her bosom wrung.

2. How sad was she, and sore distressed!—
   That Woman once supremely blessed,
   Called to bear the Holy One!
   What tears were hers! what bitter woes!
   Ah! how she quivered as the blows
   Fell upon her peerless Son.

3. And who would not with her have grieved,
   Had he Christ's Mother there perceived,
   Crushed beneath such misery?
   What mortal would from tears refrain,
   Could he but hear her cries of pain
   O'er her Son's sharp agony?

THE STABAT MATER DOLOROSA.

4. For His wicked nation pleading,
   She saw Jesus scourged, and bleeding
     'Neath the smitings of the rod;
   Saw her Son's meek resignation,
   As He died in desolation,
     Yielding up His soul to God.

5. Mother, fount of love's deep yearning,
   I, thy weight of woe discerning,
     Partner in thy tears would be;
   May my heart with ardor glowing,
   And with love to Christ outflowing,
     Sympathize with Him and thee.

6. Make me know thy sore affliction,
   Print the wounds of crucifixion
     Deeply on my inmost heart.
   With thy Son, the wounded, bleeding,
   For me stooping, interceding,
     Let me feel the scourge and smart.

7. Let me join thy lamentation,
   Share thy sweet commiseration,
     And through life a mourner be;
   Near the cross, with thee abiding,
   I would stand, with thee dividing
     All the woes afflicting thee.

8. Virgin, virgins all excelling,
   Make my heart, like thine, love's dwelling,
     Let thy tortures rend my soul;
   Let me share Christ's crucifying,
   Let me feel His pangs of dying,
     Let His sorrows o'er me roll.

9. May I suffer all His bruising;
   Quaff the crimson liquid oozing
     From the wounds of that dear Son.
   Rapt with fervor and affection,
   Grant me, Virgin, thy protection,
     When the Judgment is begun.

10. Let me by the cross be guarded;
    By Christ's death from dangers warded;
      By His grace through life supplied.
    Death the ties of earth may sever;
    I shall live in Christ forever,
      One of Eden's glorified.

1. For His own nation's sinfulness
   She saw her Jesus in distress
     'Neath the smitings of the rod;
   Saw on the cross her own sweet Son,
   Deserted, dying, and undone,
     Breathing forth His plaints to God.

5. Mother, fount whence love doth flow,
   I would that I thy pangs might know,
     Sharing them in sympathy.
   Inspire my soul with love like thine,
   That I may cleave to Christ Divine
     With thy fervent loyalty.

6. O sacred Mother, heed my plea,
   Lay thou the cross of Christ on me,
     Grave it on my inmost heart;
   With Him on whom my sins were laid,
   Who stooped to me, my ransom paid,
     I would bear an equal part.

7. Such tears as thine make me to weep;
   With thee thy vigils let me keep,
     Till my life on earth is past;
   I near the cross with thee would stand,
   With heart to heart and hand to hand,
     Fellow-mourner to the last.

8. Thou purest Virgin! matchless Maid!
   Do not repel my proffered aid;
     Let thy sorrows o'er me roll;
   Christ's dying I would daily bear;
   His crucifixion I would dare;
     Let its tortures rend my soul.

9. Ay, wound me with the wounds He bore!
   And let me quaff the sacred gore
     Gushing from thy mangled Son!
   My soul aglow with love's pure flame,
   O Virgin, shield me with thy name
     When the judgment is begun.

10. May the cross my guardian be;
    May Christ's atonement guerdon me;
      May He keep me in His love.
    When death shall end my earthly strife,
    May I attain to endless life
      In the Paradise above.

THE STABAT MATER DOLOROSA.

ANONYMOUS.

1. There she stood, the Mother weeping!
Nigh the Cross sad watches keeping,
While her Son did hang and bleed!
Bitter were her tears and grieving;
Through that bosom, wildly heaving,
There had passed a sword indeed!

2. There she stood in deep affliction,
She who heard the benediction
"Hail of Heaven, Thou blessed one!"
And, with breast o'erflowed with anguish,
Saw beneath dire tortures languish
Him who was the promised Son!

3. Who, with eye no moisture showing,
Could see Mary's overflowing?
Stricken by so sharp a blow!
Who the generous sigh could smother
As he watched sweet Jesus' mother
Sunk in sympathetic woe?

4. Well she knew 'twas for her nation,
For that sinful generation
That the shameful stripes He bore!
That, beneath men's eyes averted,
Saddened, desolate, deserted,
Breathed He, on the Cross, no more!

5. Mother, full of tendernesses!
I would know of thy distresses!
By community of pain.
Let the love of Christ within me
Burn and flame, until it win me,
Answering love from Him again!

6. Holy mother, by thy favor,
Let the nails which pierced my Saviour,
Pierce and fix my wandering heart!
In His sorrows, which abounded,
In His woundings, Who was wounded,
All for me, oh give me part.

7. Be it mine through life, sincerely
Aye to weep with thee! and nearly
Follow still my Lord divine!
Near the Cross be still my station,
By thy side! Each lamentation
Of thy lips be swelled with mine!

8. Virgin queen of heavenly splendor,
Let me share, oh bosom tender!
Ev'n thy Sorrows' secresies!
Let me bear my Jesus' dying
In my flesh! And to Him flying,
Cherish every wound of His!

9. With His love, oh re-create me!
With His cross inebriate me!
Wound me with love's wounds, I pray!
That secure in thy protection,
Bound to Him with strong affection,
I may meet the judgment day!

10. Be His Cross my tower abiding,
And His death my place of hiding!
Feed me with His grace and love
That, when worms my flesh inherit,
I may rise, a ransomed spirit,
To the Paradise above!

A PROTESTANT TRANSFUSION.

From Dr. HENRY MILLS, of Auburn (1786–1867), *Horæ Germanicæ*, second ed., New York, 1856, Appendix, p. 365, 7 stanzas, of which I give 1, 4, 5, 6, 7. Dr. R. D. Hitchcock, in *Carmina Sanctorum*, No. 195, erroneously ascribes Vers. 1 to Rev. Dr. JAMES WADDELL ALEXANDER (1804–1859). Neither the Rev. Dr. S. D. Alexander of N. York (the brother of J. W. A.), nor Mr. A. D. Randolph (his publisher) could give me any information about a translation of the *Stabat Mater* by Dr. J. W. Alexander.

THE STABAT MATER DOLOROSA.

1. Near the cross was Mary weeping,
   There her mournful station keeping,
   Gazing on her dying Son:
   There in speechless anguish groaning,
   Yearning, trembling, sighing, moaning,—
   Through her soul the sword had gone.

2. What He for His people suffered,
   Stripes, and scoffs, and insults offered,
   His fond Mother saw the whole;—
   Never from the scene retiring,
   Till He bowed His head, expiring,
   And to God breathed out His soul.

3. But we have no need to borrow
   Motives from the Mother's sorrow,
   At our Saviour's cross to mourn.
   'Twas our sins brought Him from heaven,
   These the cruel nails had driven:—
   All His griefs for us were borne.

4. When no eye its pity gave us,
   When there was no arm to save us,
   He His love and power displayed:
   By His stripes He wrought our healing,
   By His death, our life revealing,
   He for us the ransom paid.

5. Jesus, may Thy love constrain us,
   That from sin we may refrain us,
   In Thy griefs may deeply grieve:
   Thee our best affections giving,
   To Thy glory ever living,
   May we in Thy glory live!

ANONYMOUS.

From Schaff's "*Christ in Song*," 1868.

1. At the cross her station keeping,
   Stood the mournful Mother weeping,
   Where He hung, her Son and Lord.
   For her soul, of joy bereavèd,
   Bowed with anguish, deeply grievèd,
   Felt the sharp and piercing sword.

2. Oh, how sad and sore distressèd
   Now was she, that Mother blessèd
   Of the sole-begotten One:
   Deep the woe of her affliction
   When she saw the crucifixion
   Of her ever-glorious Son.

3. Who, on Christ's dear Mother gazing,
   Piercèd by anguish so amazing,
   Born of woman, would not weep?
   Who, on Christ's dear Mother thinking,
   Such a cup of sorrow drinking,
   Would not share her sorrows deep?

4. For His people's sins chastisèd
   She beheld her Son despisèd,
   Scourged, and crowned with thorns entwinèd;
   Saw Him then from judgment taken,
   And in death by all forsaken,
   Till His spirit He resigned.

. . . . . .

5. Jesu, may such deep devotion
   Stir in me the same emotion,
   Fount of love, Redeemer kind!
   That my heart, fresh ardor gaining,
   And a purer love attaining,
   May with Thee acceptance find.

LORD LINDSAY, 1817.

The stanzas of this version are irregular in merit and in form, which varies between the double and single rhyme. I give three stanzas. The whole is printed in full in [Nott's] *Seven Great Hymns of the Mediæval Church* (N. York, 5th ed., 1868, p. 103).

1. By the Cross, sad vigil keeping,
    Stood the mournful mother weeping,
      While on it the Saviour hung;
   In that hour of deep distress,
   Pierced the sword of bitterness
      Through her heart with sorrow
        wrung.

2. Oh! how sad, how woe-begone
   Was that ever-blessed one,
      Mother of the Son of God!

Oh! what bitter tears she shed
   Whilst before her Jesus bled
      'Neath the Father's penal rod!

5. Mary mother, fount of love,
   Make me share thy sorrow, move
   All my soul to sympathy!
   Make my heart within me glow
   With the love of Jesus—so
      Shall I find acceptancy.

JOHN D. VAN BUREN.

From The Stabat Mater, translated by John D. Van Buren, Albany, 1872.

1. Stands, in tears, with bosom heaving,
   By the Cross the Mother, grieving,
      While her Son upon it hung;

Sharpest sword of pain is darting
Thro' her soul, in anguish smarting,
   By the sorest torture wrung.

GERMAN TRANSLATIONS.

Dr. Lisco, in his monograph on the *Stabat Mater*, published in 1843, gives in three parallel columns the text of fifty-three German translations of the MATER DOLOROSA, the oldest by Hermann of Salzburg (d. 1396), the latest of the year 1842, besides some fragments. He makes out a chronological list of 78 full or partial German, and 4 Dutch translations, but ignores the English versions. Among the translators are Klopstock (1771, very free), Riedel (1773), Hiller (1781), Lavater (1785), Ludwig Tieck (1812, very free), Baron De la Motte Fouqué (1817), A. L. Follen (1819), Baron von Wessenberg (1825), Thiersch (1825), Simrock (1834), Friedrich von Meyer (1836), Knapp (1837), Freiberg (1839), Daniel (1840), Lisco (1842), von Seld (1842), Löschke (1842), Baltzer (1842), Graul (1842), Schlosser (1863), Königsfeld (1865).

I give the full text of three, and one or two stanzas of the best of the others. They are all found in Lisco's monograph, except those of Schlosser and Königsfeld.

HERM. ADALB. DANIEL (1840).
From his *Thesaurus Hymnologicus*, II, 135, and Lisco's *Stabat Mater*, p. 15.

1. Voller Thränen, voller Schmerzen,
   Stand die Mutter, wund im Herzen
     An dem Kreuz, da Jesus hing;
   Durch die Seele grammumhüllet
   Seufzerschwer und Qualerfüllet
     Eines Schwertes Schärfe ging.

2. Ach, wie elend, wie gebeuget
   War, die Gottes Kind gesäuget,
     Einst vom Engel benedeit:
   Nun voll Beben sieht sie schweben
   Dort ihr Leben, hingegeben
     In des bittern Todes Leid.

3. Wer ist Mensch, der nicht beweinet
   Christi Mutter, die erscheinet
     So voll Schmerzen, Schmach und
       Hohn?
   Ohne Lied, wer könnte sehen,
   Diese fromme Mutter stehen
     Die da leidet mit dem Sohn?

4. Für die Sünden seiner Brüder
   Sieht sie ihres Jesu Glieder
     Wie die Geissel sie zerreisst:
   Sieht ihr süsses Kind erblassen,
   Sieht den Sohn von Gott verlassen,
     Und verhauchen ihn den Geist.

5. Fromme Mutter! Quell der Liebe,
   Gieb dass innigst mich betrübe
     All dein Leid und deine Pein.
   Christo lass mein Herz entbrennen,
   Lass mich Herr und Gott ihn nennen,
     Mich ihm wohlgefällig sein.

6. Heil'ge Mutter! alle Wunden,
   So dein Sohn am Kreuz empfunden,
     Drücke tief sie in mein Herz.
   Wundgeschlagen hat voll Zagen
   Für mich Plagen Christ getragen—
     Gieb mir Theil an seinem Schmerz.

7. Lass im Weinen uns vereinen,
   Den Gekreuzigten beweinen
     Will auch ich mein Leben lang.
   An dem Kreuz mit dir zu stehen,
   Mich im Leid dir Eins zu sehen
     Sehnt der Seele Liebesdrang.

8. Aller Jungfrau'n Krone! brünstig
   Fleh ich: lass mich hold und gün-
     stig
   Mit dir klagen um den Sohn;
   Lass mich erben Christi Sterben,
   Seine Marter mich erwerben,
     Schmecken seine Passion.

9. Wundenmale lass mir fliessen,
   Mich in Liebesrausch ergiessen
     Zu dem Kreuz mit deinem Sohn:
   Und um solchen Eifers Flammen
   Lass mich, Jungfrau, nicht verdam-
     men
     Vor des Weltenrichters Thron.

10. Christi Kreuz lass mich beschützen
    Christi Tod als Schild mir nützen,
      Schirmen seine Gnädigkeit:
    Und zerfällt der Leib hienieden,
    Lass der Seele sein beschieden
      Paradieses Herrlichkeit.

ALBERT KNAPP (1837).
From his *Liederschatz*, and the new Württemberg Hymn-book of 1842.
An evangelical transformation.

1. Schaut die Mutter voller Schmerzen,
   Wie sie mit zerriss'nem Herzen
     Bei dem Kreuz des Sohnes steht!
   Schauet ihre Trübsalshitze,
   Wie des Schwertes blut'ge Spitze
     Tief durch ihre Seele geht!

[2. Welches tiefen Jammers Beute
    Wurde die gebenedeite
      Mutter dieses Einzigen!
    Welch ein Trauern, welch ein Zagen,
    Welch ein Ringen, welch ein Nagen,
      Bei der Schmach des Göttlichen!][1]

---

[1] This stanza is omitted by Knapp and inserted from the version of Fr. von Meyer, who likewise removed the elements of Roman Mariolatry.

3. Wessen Auge kann der Zähren
   Bei dem Jammer sich erwehren,
   Der des Höchsten Sohn umfängt?
   Wie Er mit gelass'nem Muthe
   Todesmatt in seinem Blute
   An dem Holz des Fluches hängt!

4. Für die Sünden seiner Brüder
   Leidet Er, dass seine Glieder
   Unnennbare Qual zerreisst.
   Für uns ruft Er im Erblassen:
   Gott, mein Gott, ich bin verlassen!
   Und verathmet Seinen Geist.

5. Lass, o Jesu, Quell der Liebe,
   Deines Herzens heil'ge Triebe
   Strömen in mein Herz hinab!
   Lass mich Dich mein Alles nennen,
   Ganz für Dich in Liebe brennen,
   Der für mich Sein Leben gab!

6. Drück, mein König, Deine Wunden,
   Die Du auch für mich empfunden,
   Tief in meine Seel' hinein.
   Lass in Reue mich zerfliessen,
   Mit Dir leiden, mit Dir büssen,
   Mit Dir tragen jede Pein.

7. Lass mich herzlich mit Dir weinen,
   Mich durch's Kreuz mit Dir vereinen;
   Aller Weltsinn sei verflucht!
   Unter'm Kreuze will ich stehen,
   Und Dich zittern, bluten sehen,
   Wenn die Sünde mich versucht.

8. Gieb mir Theil an Deinem Leiden,
   Lass von aller Lust mich scheiden,
   Die Dir solche Wunden schlug!
   Ich will auch mir Wunden schlagen,
   Will das Kreuz des Lammes tragen,
   Welches meine Sünden trug.

9. Lass, wenn meine Thränen fliessen,
   Mich den Gnadenglanz geniessen
   Deines milden Angesichts;
   Decke mich durch Deine Plagen
   Vor den Aengsten und den Klagen
   Einst am Tage des Gerichts.

10. Gegen aller Feinde Stürmen
    Lass mich, Herr, Dein Kreuz beschirmen,
    Deine Gnade leuchte mir!
    Deckt des Grabes finstre Höhle
    Meinen Leib, so nimm die Seele
    Hin in's Paradies zu Dir.

DR. G. A. KÖNIGSFELD (1865).

From his *Lateinische Hymnen und Gesänge aus dem Mittelalter. Neue Sammlung.* Bonn, 1865. The author made two translations, the first of which appeared in 1847, and begins:—

"*Weinend stand die schmerzgebeugte
Mutter an dem Kreuz, das feuchte
Auge an dem Sohne hing.*"

1. Thränenvoll, in Gram zerflossen,
   Stand am Kreuz des göttlich Grossen
   Mutter, wo Er sterbend hing;
   Durch das Herz, das Gram durchwühlte,
   Das ganz mit Ihm litt und fühlte,
   Ihr des Schwertes Schneide ging.

2. Wie war traurig, voller Schmerzen,
   Die begnadet trug am Herzen
   Ihn, den eingebornen Sohn!
   Wie sie jammerte und klagte,
   Wie sie zitterte und zagte,
   Bei des Hohen Qual und Hohn.

3. Welch ein Mensch sollt' da nicht weinen,
   Sieht die Mutter er erscheinen,
   In so tiefen Jammers Noth?
   Wer nicht mit ihr trauernd stehen,
   Wenn die Mutter er gesehen
   Duldend mit dem Sohn den Tod.

4. Für der ganzen Menschheit Sünden
   Sah sie Jesum martern, binden,
   Wilder Geisselhiebe Ziel;
   Sah den Holden sie erblassen,
   In dem Todeskampf verlassen,
   Als des Geistes Hülle fiel.

5. Darum Mutter, Quell der Hulden,
   Lass mich mit dir fühlen, dulden,
   Theilen diese Schmerzen all;
   Lehr' mein Herz mit Glutentrieben
   Christum, Gottes Sohn, zu lieben,
   Dass ich Ihm nur wohlgefall'.

6. Heil'ge Mutter, hilf vollbringen,
   Dass des Kreuzes Male dringen
   Tief mir in das Herz hinein;
   Und der Wunden, werthbefunden,
   Deines Sohn's, mich zu gesunden,
   Lass auch mich theilhaftig sein.

7. Lass mich trauernd mit dir klagen,
   Mit Ihm, der an's Kreuz geschlagen,
   Durch mein ganzes Leben lang;
   Zu dir an das Kreuz mich stellen,
   Gern mich, Mutter, dir gesellen,
   In der tiefsten Sehnsucht Drang.

8. Jungfrau, aller Jungfrau'n Krone,
   Sei mir hold auf deinem Throne,
   Lass mich mit dir traurig sein;
   Lass mich tragen ohne Zagen,
   Mit Ihm theilend Christi Plagen,
   Seiner Wunden Schmerz erneun.

9. Ja, in diesen Schmerz versunken,
   Mach' durch dieses Kreuz mich trunken,
   Durch das Blut von deinem Sohn;
   Mich vom Feuerpfuhl zu retten,
   Mögest du mich einst vertreten,
   Jungfrau! an des Richters Thron!

10. Lass dies Kreuz mich vor Verderben
    Wahren, und durch Christi Sterben
    Schenk' mir Gnade allezeit;
    Und wenn dieser Leib zergangen,
    Lass die Seele dort erlangen
    Paradieses Herrlichkeit!

HERRMANN. Monk of Salzburg, 1366-96.

1. Maria stuend in swinden smerczen
   pey dem krewcz und waint von herczen
   da ir werder sun an hieng.
   Jr geadelte czartte sele
   ser betruebt in jamers quele
   scharff ein sneyduntz swert durchgieng.

J. C. LAVATER, 1785.

1. Jesu Mutter!—Ach, wie schmerzlich!
   Stand am Kreuz und weinte herzlich,
   Weil ihr Sohn da blutend hing!
   Durch die tiefbeklemmte, reine
   Seel', und Mark und die Gebeine
   Drang ein scharf zweischneidend
   Schwert!

FR. JOS. WEINZIERL,
In Cath. Hymn-book, Sulzbach, 1816.

1. Jesu Mutter stand betrübet
   Bey dem Sohn, den sie geliebet,
   Als Er an dem Kreuze hing,
   Wie war sie voll tiefer Trauer,
   Als das Schwert mit Todesschauer
   Ihr empfindsam Herz durchging.

CATHOLIC HYMN-BOOK, Erfurt, 1816.

1. Seht die Mutter voller Schmerzen,
   Wie sie mit betrübtem Herzen
   Bei dem Sohn am Kreuze steht!
   Wie sie weinet, wie sie leidet,
   Wie ein Schwert ihr Herz durchschneidet,
   Und durch ihre Seele geht.

VON BÜLOW, 1817.

1. Weinend stand in Schmerz verloren
   Die den Heiland uns geboren,
   Unter ihm am Kreuzes-Fuss;
   Jammervoll zu ihm gewendet,
   Seufzer bang ihr Herz entsendet,
   Das ein Schwert durchbohren
   muss.

2. Ach, wohl keine Mutter drückte
   Schwerer Leid, als die beglückte
   Dieses Eingebornen hier,
   Die in Klagen und Verzagen
   Ganz zerschlagen sah die Plagen
   Solchen Sohn's vor Augen ihr.

Baron DE LA MOTTE FOUQUÉ, 1817.

1. Als die Schmerzensmutter sehnend
Stand am Kreuz, ihr Auge thränend,
Weil der Sohn erblich in Schmach,
Da geschah's der Allerbängsten,
Dass ein Schwert in tausend Aengsten
Durch die Seel' ihr schneidend
brach.

2. O wie viel des Jammers reihte
Sich um die Gebenedeite,
Die gebar des Heiles Stern,
Die voll Zagen, kaum zu tragen,
Bang' in Klagen sah geschlagen
An das Kreuz den Sohn und Herrn!

ADOLF LUDW. FOLLEN, 1819.

1. An dem Kreuz die schmerzenreiche,
Thränenvolle, kummerbleiche
Mutter bei dem Sohne steht.
Schwerbetrübet, Marter leidend,
Tiefauf stöhnend; ihr ein schneidend
Messer durch die Seele geht.

2. O wie traurig, grambeladen,
Hochgesegnet Weib in Gnaden,
Das den Eingebornen trug!—
Wie sie klagte! wie sie zagte!
Schmerz zernagte die Geplagte,
Als Gott-Sohn die Pein ertrug.

G. CHR. FR. MOHNIKE, 1825.

1. An dem Kreuze voller Schmerzen,
Stand die Mutter, Gram im Herzen,
Sah des lieben Sohnes Pein!
In die Seel' ihr voll Verzagen,
Voller Beben, voller Klagen,
Drang nunmehr das Schwert hinein.

2. O der Trauer, o der Leiden
Jener Hochgebene leiten,
Die den Gottessohn gebar!
Konnt der Zähren sich nicht wehren,
Sah den hehren Sohn entehren,
Seine Schmach ward sie gewahr.

FREIHERR J. H. VON WESSENBERG.
Constanz, 1828.

1. Weinend, mit zerrissnem Herzen
Stand die Mutter, voll der Schmerzen,
Bei dem Kreuz, zum Sohn gekehrt.
Durch die bang' umwölkte Seele
Dunkel, wie des Grabes Höhle,
Drang das Leiden, wie ein Schwert.

MICHAEL KOSMELI, M.D., 1831.

1. Weinend mit betrübtem Herzen,
Stand die Mutter voller Schmerzen,
Als der Sohn am Kreuze hing,
Und den Kelch des Leidens leerte;
Ihr das Weh gleich einem Schwerte
Durch die bange Seele ging.

BARON FRANZ VON MALTITZ, 1834.

1. Weinend stand die schmerzenreiche
Bei dem Kreuz, an dem der bleiche
Sohn im Todeskampfe rang;
Seufzer im zerrissnen Herzen,
Ihre Brust der bittern Schmerzen
Siebenfaches Schwert durchdrang.

2. Welche Worte könnten malen
Um den Einz'gen deine Qualen
Mutter hochgebenedeit?
Wer uns sagen, wer uns klagen,
Was voll Zagen du getragen
Bei dem Opfer Gott geweiht?

K. JOS. SIMROCK, 1834.

1. Stand die Mutter voller Schmerzen,
Weinte bei dem Kreuz von Herzen,
Wo der Sohn herniederhing;
Der die Seele voll Verzagens,
Voll der Seufzer, voll des Klagens,
Ein zerschneidend Schwert durch-
ging.

2. O wie traurig ihm zur Seite
Musste die gebenedeite
Ein'gen Sohnes Mutter sein!
Klag erhebend, sich ergebend
Angsterbebend, nun erlebend
Des erhab'nen Sohnes Pein.

JOH. FR. VON MEYER, 1836.

1. Bei dem Kreuz die schmerzenreiche
Mutter stand, die thränenreiche,
Da ihr Sohn im Sterben hing.
Ach, ein Schwert ihr durch die warme,
Seufzende, so trostesarme,
Schwergebeugte Seele ging.

THE STABAT MATER DOLOROSA.

Fr. von Pechlin, 1840.

1. Weinend stand auf Golgatha,
   Schmerzenreich die Mutter da,
     Als ihr Sohn am Kreuze hing:
   Deren seufzervolle Brust,
   Bebend sich des Weh's bewusst,
     Jetzt des Schwertes Stoss empfing.

2. O wie traurig ihm zur Seite
   Stand die Hochgebenedeite,
     Die gebahr den Gottessohn!
   Welche klagte, sich zernagte,
   Und verzagte, da man wagte
     An dem Heiland grausen Hohn.

Robert Lecke, 1842.

1. Bei dem Kreuz in Thränengüssen,
   Stand die Mutter schmerzzerrissen,
     Als der Sohn in Qualen hing.
   Deren Busen tief aufsichzend,
   Kummervoll nach Tröstung lechzend,
     Ein scharf schneidend Schwert durchfing.

2. O wie traurig die betrübte
   Mutter war, die allgeliebte
     Gottessohn-Gebährerin!
   Die da klagte, sich zernagte,
   Und verzagte, als sie wagte
     Blicke auf den Dulder hin.

Friedrich Gustav Lisco, 1842.

1. An dem Kreuz, in Schmerz verloren,
   Wo Er hing, den sie geboren,
     Stand die Mutter leidbewusst;
   Ihre Seele war voll Beben,
   Hin in Angst und Weh gegeben,
     Und ein Schwert ging durch die Brust.

2. Ach, welch schwerer Kummer drückte
   Sie, des ein'gen Sohns beglückte
     Mutter, wie gebeugt war sie!
   Jetzt muss Wehen, Schmerzergehen,
   Leidenshöhen sie bestehen
     Ob des Sohnes Leidensmüh.

Anonymous, 1842.

1. An dem Kreuze voller Schmerzen,
   Thränenblickend, Qual im Herzen,
     Stand Maria, leidbeschwert.
   Seufzen musste sie und weinen
   Bei dem Tod des Heil'gen, Reinen,
     Und ihr Herz durchdrang das Schwert.

Baron von Seld, 1842.

1. An dem Kreuze schmerzversunken
   Stand die Mutter thränentrunken,
     Als der Sohn, der theure, litt;
   Ihre Seele voller Trauer,
   Ihre Seufzer Todesschauer,
     Und ein Schwert durch's Herz ihr schnitt.

A. Merget, 1842.

1. An dem Kreuze stand die bleiche,
   Thränenvolle, schmerzenreiche
     Mutter, da der Heiland litt;
   Deren bange, gramumhüllte,
   Seufzerschwere, qualerfüllte
     Seele jetzt das Schwert durchschnitt.

2. O wie tief gebeugt vom Leide
   War die hochgebenedeite
     Mutter des Erlösers da;
   Welches Zagen, welche Klagen,
   Als des heil'gen Sohnes Plagen
     Die getreue Mutter sah!

Carl Grau, 1843.

1. Stand am Kreuz die schmerzenreiche
   Mutter, die von Thränen bleiche,
     Als der Sohn gemartert hing;
   Durch die Seele, die verzagte,
   Die zernagte, die geplagte,
     Eines Schwertes Schneide ging.

J. F. H. Schlosser.

From his *Die Kirche in ihren Liedern.*
Freiburg i. B., 2d ed., 1863, vol. I., 205.

1. Stand die Mutter qualentragend
   An dem Kreuze, und erklagend,
     Wo der Vielgeliebte hing:
   Deren Seele bangerstrebend,
   Angstbeladen und erbebend,
     Tief ein scharfes Schwert durchging.

KARL FORTLAGE, 1844.

Thränenvoll mit schwerem Herzen
Stand die Mutter voller Schmerzen,
  Als der Sohn am Kreuze hing;
Und durch ihre Brust voll Trauer,
Krampfgepresst im Todesschauer
  Eines Schwertes Schneide ging.

KARL RÖLKER, 1882.

Christi Mutter stand voll Schmerzen
Bei dem Kreuz mit schwerem Herzen,
  Wo ihr Sohn im Sterben hing.
Durch die Seele ihr voll Trauer
Seufzend unter bangem Schauer,
  Tief das Schwert der Leiden ging.

LITERATURE.

LUCAS WADDING (the learned Irish historian of the Franciscan Order): *Scriptores Ord. Minorum*, Rom., 1650 (fols. 180, 181); *Annales Minorum seu trium a S. Francisco institutorum* (21 vols. in all), Rom. 2d ed., 1731, sqq., vol. IV., 407 sqq.; V., 606, sqq.; VI., 76 sqq. (A copy of this work is in the Astor Library, New York.)

G. C. F. MOHNIKE: *Kirchen- und literarhistorische Studien und Mittheilungen*. Stralsund, 1824, vol. I., Heft II., pp. 335–435. (Two essays on Jacobus de Benedictis and on the *Stabat Mater Dolorosa*.)

FR. GUSTAV LISCO (D.D., pastor in Berlin): *Stabat Mater. Hymnus auf die Schmerzen der Maria. Nebst einem Nachtrage zu den Uebersetzungen des Hymnus Dies Iræ*. Berlin, 1843, 4to, pp. 56. (Contains in 3 parallel columns the text of 53 German translations, with a history of the hymn, and a chronological list of 78 German and four Dutch versions complete and incomplete, of the *Mater Dolorosa* from 1396 to 1842.)

A. F. OZANAM: *Les Poëtes Franciscains en Italie au XIIIe siècle, avec un choix des petites fleurs de Saint-François, traduites de l'Italien*. Paris, 1852; troisième ed. 1859 (pp. 472). There is a German translation of this important work by N. H. JULIUS, Münster, 1853.

T. J. MONE: *Lateinische Hymnen des Mittelalters* (Freiburg, i. B., 1853 sqq.), Vol. II., 147–153; III., 425.

H. A. DANIEL: *Thesaurus Hymnol*. Lipsiæ, Vol. II. (1855), 131–154; and Vol. V. (1856), 59 (the text of Mone).

J. M. N.[EALE]: *Stabat Mater Speciosa*. London, 1867.

PHILIP SCHAFF: *A New Stabat Mater*, in "Hours at Home," N. York, May, 1866; *Christ in Song*, N. Y. and London, 1869, p. 136 sqq.

ERASTUS C. BENEDICT (lawyer in New York, d. 1880): *The Hymn of Hildebert and other Mediæval Hymns with Translations*, New York, 1867 (pp. 128). Contains a translation of the *Mater Dolorosa*, p. 65.

The Seven Great Hymns of the Mediæval Church (by Mrs. A. E. Nott), New York, 5th ed., 1868. The 5th ed. contains 3 versions of the *Mater Dolorosa* (by Lord Lindsay, Gen. Dix and Coles), and Neale's version of the *Mater Speciosa*.

ABRAHAM COLES (M.D., LL.D., of Scotch Plains, N. Jersey): *Stabat Mater, Hymn of the Sorrows of Mary, translated, with photograph*. New York (D. Appleton & Co.), 1867; second ed., 1868, pp. 37. By the same: *Stabat Mater Speciosa. Hymn of the Joys of Mary. With Photograph* (Madonna di Sisto). New York, 1868, pp. 25.

JOHN D. VAN BUREN: *The Stabat Mater and other Versions.* Albany, N. Y. (Joel Munsell), 1872.

R. LAUXMANN: *Jacopone da Todi,* in Herzog's "Encykl.," revised ed., VI., 432-436. Condensed and supplemented in Schaff-Herzog, II., 1138.

W. STORCK: *Ausgewählte Gedichte Jacopone's da Todi. Deutsch von C. Schlüter und W. Storck.* Münster, 1864.

KARL RÖLKER: *Gedichte nebst geschichtlichen Anhang: Jacopone's Leben und Ueber das Stabat Mater* (pp. 125-160). Osnabrück, 1882.

FRANKLIN JOHNSON: *The Stabat Mater Speciosa and the Stabat Mater Dolorosa. With illustrations from the Old Masters.* Boston (D. Lothrop & Co.), 1886 (pp. 36). The original, with translations and photogravure reproductions of six paintings, namely, the Sistine Madonna of Raphael, the Ecce Homo of Guido, the Madonna della Scala of Corregio, the Madonna del Granducca of Raphael, the Mater Dolorosa of Guido, and St. John and Mary by Plockhurst.

Comp. also the list of works on Latin Hymnology, most of which have some notice of the *Stabat Mater,* in Schaff's *Church History,* Vol. IV., 416-420.

THE STABAT MATER SPECIOSA.

See the Literature in the preceding essay, p. 216, especially Ozanam.

THE LATIN TEXT.

To facilitate the comparison we put the corresponding stanzas of the MATER DOLOROSA and MATER SPECIOSA in parallel columns. The latter has twelve stanzas, as given by Ozanam (*l. c.* p. 170 sq.).

MATER SPECIOSA.	MATER DOLOROSA.

1. Stabat Mater speciosa,
   Juxta fœnum gaudiosa,
     Dum jacebat parvulus;
   Cujus animam gaudentem
   Lactabundam ac ferventem
     Pertransivit jubilus.
	1. Stabat Mater dolorosa,
	   Juxta crucem lacrymosa,
	     Dum pendebat Filius;
	   Cujus animam gementem
	   Contristatam ac dolentem
	     Pertransivit gladius.

2. O quam læta et beata
   Fuit illa immaculata
     Mater Unigeniti!
   Quæ gaudebat et ridebat,
   Exultabat, cum videbat
     Nati partum inclyti.
	2. O quam tristis et afflicta
	   Fuit illa benedicta
	     Mater Unigeniti!
	   Quae mœrebat et dolebat
	   Et tremebat, cum videbat
	     Nati poenas inclyti.

3. Quis [jam] est, qui non gauderet,
   Christi Matrem si videret
     In tanto solatio?
   Quis non posset collætari,
   Christi Matrem contemplari
     Ludentem cum Filio?
	3. Quis est homo, qui non fleret,
	   Matrem Christi si videret
	     In tanto supplicio?
	   Quis non posset contristari,
	   Piam Matrem contemplari
	     Dolentem cum Filio.

4. Pro peccatis suæ gentis
   Christum vidit cum jumentis
     Et algori subditum;
   Vidit suum dulcem natum
   Vagientem, adoratum,
     Vili diversorio.
	4. Pro peccatis suae gentis
	   Vidit Jesum in tormentis
	     Et flagellis subditum;
	   Vidit suum dulcem natum
	   Morientem, desolatum,
	     Dum emisit spiritum.

[5. Nato Christo in præsepe,
  Cœli cives canunt læte
    Cum immenso gaudio;
  Stabat senex cum puella
  Non cum verbo nec loquela,
    Stupescentes cordibus.]

6. Eia Mater, fons amoris!
  Me sentire vim ardoris,
    Fac ut tecum sentiam!
  Fac, ut ardeat cor meum
  In amando Christum Deum,
    Ut sibi complaceam.

7. Sancta Mater, istud agas:
  Prone introducas plagas,
    Cordi fixas valide.
  Tui nati cœlo lapsi,
  Jam dignati fœno nasci
    Pœnas mecum divide.

8. Fac me vere congaudere,
  Jesulino cohærere,
    Donec ego vixero.
  In me sistat ardor tui;
  Puerino fac me frui
    Dum sum in exilio.
  Hunc ardorem fac communem,
  Ne me facias immunem
    Ab hoc desiderio.

9. Virgo virginum præclara,
  Mihi jam non sis amara;
    Fac, me parvum rapere.
  Fac, ut pulchrum fantem por-
        tem,[1]
  Qui nascendo vicit mortem,
    Volens vitam tradere.

10. Fac me tecum satiari,
  Nato tuo inebriari,
    Stantem in tripudio.[2]

5. Eia Mater, fons amoris!
  Me sentire vim doloris,
    Fac, ut tecum lugeam!
  Fac, ut ardeat cor meum
  In amando Christum Deum
    Ut sibi complaceam.

6. Sancta Mater, istud agas:
  Crucifixi fige plagas
    Cordi meo valide.
  Tui nati vulnerati
  Tam dignati pro me pati
    Poenas mecum divide.

7. Fac me tecum vere flere
  Crucifixo condolere,
    Donec ego vixero.
  Juxta crucem tecum stare
  Te libenter sociare
    In planctu desidero.

8. Virgo virginum praeclara,
  Mihi tam non sis amara;
    Fac me tecum plangere.
  Fac ut portem Christi mortem
  Passionis fac consortem
    Et plagas recolere.

9. Fac me plagis vulnerari
  Cruce hac inebriari
    Ob amorem Filii.

[1] Ozanam reads: "Fac ut portem pulchrum fantem." But "fantem" does not rhyme with "mortem."

[2] I suggest this as an emendation for the obvious mistake of the original, as given by Ozanam—
    "*Stans inter tripudia.*"

Inflammatus et accensus
Obstupescit omnis sensus
Tali de commercio.

Inflammatus et accensus
Per te, Virgo, sim defensus
In die judicii.

11. Fac me nato custodiri,
Verbo Dei præmuniri,
Conservari gratiâ.
Quando corpus morietur,
Fac, ut animæ donetur
Tui nati visio.[1]

10. Fac me cruce custodiri,
Morte Christi praemuniri,
Confoveri gratia.
Quando corpus morietur,
Fac ut animæ donetur
Paradisi gloria.

[12. Omnes stabulum amantes,
Et pastores vigilantes
Pernoctantes sociant.
Per virtutem nati tui
Ora ut electi sui
Ad patriam veniant.
Amen.]

THE DISCOVERY OF THE MATER SPECIOSA.

The discovery of a companion hymn to the MATER DOLOROSA from the same age, if not by the same author, created not a little sensation among hymnologists and lovers of poetry.

The MATER SPECIOSA is contained in the same edition of the Italian poems of Jacopone, published at Brescia in 1495, which contains the MATER DOLOROSA,[2] but it was buried in obscurity until 1852, when a French scholar, A. F. Ozanam, brought it to light in a work on the Franciscan poets.[3] An improved German edition of this work, by Julius, 1853, contained an admi-

---

[1] Ozanam and Diepenbrock give this as the concluding stanza, and regard the twelfth as an addition by another hand. Ozanam, *Les poëtes Franciscains*, p. 170 sq., gives the Latin text in 23 (25) stanzas of three lines each.

[2] *Le laude del Beato frate Jacopon del sacro ordine de' frati minori de observantia. Stampate in la magnifica cita de Brescia, 1495.* I copy the title from Brunet's *Manuel du Libraire*, Tom. III., 481 (5th ed., Paris, 1862), who describes the contents, and says:—"*Le n° 107 contient le* STABAT MATER, *que Wadding a restitué à Jacopone, et le n° 123 une sorte de parodie du* STABAT, *qui commence ainsi:* STABAT MATER SPECIOSA—JUXTA FENUM GAUDIOSA." Mohnike (*l. c.* p. 375), and Lisco (p. 24) mention the existence of the MATER SPECIOSA, but they never saw it.

[3] *Les poëtes Franciscains en Italie au XIIIᵉ siècle, avec un choix de petites Fleurs de Saint-François, trad. de l' Italien.* Paris, 1852, third ed. 1859. Ozanam gives a good account of St. Francis and Jacopone, and thus characterizes

rable German translation of the newly-discovered poem, by Cardinal Melchior Diepenbrock, then prince-bishop (*Fürstbischof*) of Breslau, a very pious and accomplished prelate of the evangelical school of Sailer.[1]

Dr. John Mason Neale, the distinguished Anglican divine of the Anglo-Catholic school, and reproducer of the choicest Greek and Latin hymns, introduced the MATER SPECIOSA, with a translation, to the English public a few days before his death (August 6, 1866), and thus closed his brilliant and useful hymnological labors.[2] The poem is now as well known as the MATER DOLOROSA, and will always be mentioned as its companion.

the two STABAT MATERS (p. 169): "*Jacopone fit gémir la Vierge désolée, et composa le* STABAT MATER DOLOROSA. *La liturgie catholique n'a rien de plus touchant que cette complainte si triste, dont les strophes monotones tombent comme des larmes; si douce, qu'on y reconnaît bien une douleur toute divine et consolée par les anges; si simple enfin dans son latin populaire, que les femmes et les enfants en comprennent la moitié par les mots, l'autre moitié par le chant et par le cœur. Cette œuvre incomparable suffirait à la gloire de Jacopone: mais en même temps que le* STABAT *du Calvaire, il avait voulu composer le* STABAT *de la crèche, où paraissait la Vierge mère dans toute la joie de l'enfantement. Il l'écrivit sur les mêmes mesures et sur les mêmes rimes; tellement qu'on pourrait douter un moment lequel fut le premier, du chant de douleur ou du chant d'allégresse. Cependant, la postérité a fait un choix entre ces deux perles semblables; et tandis qu'elle conserverait l'une avec amour, elle laissait l'autre enfouie. Je crois le* STABAT MATER SPECIOSA *encore inédit.*" He then gives a prose translation of a part of the MATER SPECIOSA, and the Latin text from MS. nº 7785, f. 109, of the National Library of Paris.

[1] He published the Life of Suso, the poetic mystic (1829), an Anthology of German and Spanish mystic poetry (4th ed., 1862), sermons, pastoral charges, etc. He was born 1798, and died 1853. See his correspondence with Sailer and Passavant, 1860. His life was written by his successor, Bishop Förster, Breslau, 1859, 3d ed., Regensburg, 1878.

[2] *Stabat Mater Speciosa: Full of beauty stood the Mother.* (By J. M. N.) London, 1867. I first directed the attention of the American public to this little book, by an article in "Hours at Home," published by Charles Scribner, New York, May 1867, p. 50–58, but expressed dissent from his view of the authorship; and this article suggested several American translations by Dr. Coles, Mr. Benedict, Dr. Johnson, Dr. McKenzie. Dr. Neale was an eccentric genius, who in the Middle Ages might have been another Jacopone. See an interesting biographical sketch by Bird, in the Schaff-Herzog "Encyclopædia," II., 1610–12.

AUTHORSHIP.

The authorship is uncertain. Ozanam and Neale ascribe both poems to Jacopone. This is improbable. A poet would hardly write a parody on a poem of his own. That man must be exceedingly vain who would make himself a model for imitation; and Jacopone was so humble that he forgot himself and went to the extreme of ascetic self-abnegation. Ozanam seems to assign the priority of composition to the passion hymn.

But Dr. Neale infers, from the want of finish and the number of imperfect rhymes, that Jacopone wrote the MATER SPECIOSA first. In this case the MATER DOLOROSA would be an imitation or parody; but this is absolutely impossible. The MATER DOLOROSA is far superior, and served as a model for the other. The opening of the STABAT MATER was borrowed from the Latin Bible (John xix., 25), with reference to Mary at the Cross, but not at the Cradle. The sixth line, "*pertransibit gladius*," may have suggested "*pertransibit jubilus*," but not *vice versa*. The former was prophesied by Simeon (Luke ii. 35); the latter has no Scripture foundation. The passion hymn soon became popular and passed into public worship; but the Christmas hymn had no such good luck. It is the fame of an original which invites imitation.

We conclude then that the author of the MATER SPECIOSA belonged probably to the Franciscan Order, but lived and wrote after Jacopone, when the MATER DOLOROSA was already well known and widely used. This fact best explains also the enlargement and the supernumerary lines of the eighth stanza. The MATER SPECIOSA wants the last finish, while the MATER DOLOROSA is perfect. The very reason which Dr. Neale urges for the priority of the former, proves its posteriority.

MERITS.

Admitting the inferiority of the imitation, it is very well done. The correspondence runs through the two poems, except the fifth and eleventh stanzas of the MATER SPECIOSA, which are an expansion. They breathe the same love to Christ and his Mother, and the same burning desire to become identified with her by sympathy. They are the same in poetic structure, and excel alike in the touching music of language and soft cadence that echoes the sentiment. Both address the Virgin Mary as the mediatrix between Christ and the poet. Both bear the impress of mediæval piety and of the Franciscan Order in the period of its enthusiastic devotion. The MATER SPECIOSA expresses in words what Raphael's, Corregio's, and Murillo's Madonnas express in color; as the MATER DOLOROSA corresponds to the pictorial representations of Mary at the cross. The birth of the Saviour opens an abyss of joy, as the crucifixion opens an abyss of grief. The writer of the Christmas hymn felt the intense happiness of Mary at the cradle of her divine Son; as the writer of the Good Friday hymn felt the intensity of her agony at the cross. He had the same poetic faculty of expressing, as from intuition and sympathy, the deep meaning of the situation in stanzas of beauty and melody that melt the heart and start the tear. In both situations of joy and grief, Mary stood not only as an individual, but as the representative of the whole Christian Church, which from year to year worships, at Christmas, the Divine Child in Bethlehem; and on Good Friday, the suffering Saviour on Calvary.

TRANSLATIONS.

As in the essay on the MATER DOLOROSA, I add the best English and German versions of the MATER SPECIOSA.

DR. JOHN MASON NEALE, 1867.

He omits the twelfth stanza, which he regards as a later addition.

1. Full of beauty stood the Mother
    By the Manger, blest o'er other,
    Where the Little One she lays;
    For her inmost soul's elation,
    In its fervid jubilation,
    Thrills with ecstasy of praise.

2. O what glad, what rapturous feeling
    Filled that blessed Mother, kneeling
    By the Sole-Begotten One!
    How, her heart with laughter bounding,
    She beheld the work astounding,
    Saw His Birth, the glorious Son.

3. Who is he, that sight who beareth,
    Nor Christ's Mother's solace shareth
    In her bosom as He lay:
    Who is he, that would not render
    Tend'rest love for love so tender,
    Love, with that dear Babe at play?

4. For the trespass of her nation
    She with oxen saw His station
    Subjected to cold and woe:
    Saw her sweetest Offspring's wailing,
    Wise men Him with worship hailing,
    In the stable, mean and low.

5. Jesus lying in the manger,
   Heavenly armies sang the Stranger,
   In the great joy bearing part;
   Stood the Old Man with the Maiden,
   No words speaking, only laden
   With this wonder in their heart.

6. Mother, fount of love still flowing,
   Let me, with thy rapture glowing,
   Learn to sympathize with thee:
   Let me raise my heart's devotion,
   Up to Christ with pure emotion,
   That accepted I may be.

7. Mother, let me win this blessing,
   Let His sorrow's deep impressing
   In my heart engraved remain:
   Since thy Son, from heaven descending,
   Deigned to bear the manger's tending,
   O divide with me His pain.

8. Keep my heart its gladness bringing,
   To my Jesus ever clinging
   Long as this my life shall last;
   Love like that thine own love, give it,
   On my little Child to rivet,
   Till this exile shall be past.
   Let me share thine own affliction;
   Let me suffer no rejection
   Of my purpose fixed and fast.

9. Virgin, peerless of condition,
   Be not wroth with my petition,
   Let me clasp thy little Son:
   Let me bear that Child so glorious,
   Him, whose Birth, o'er Death victorious,
   Will'd that Life for man was won.

10. Let me, satiate with my pleasure,
    Feel the rapture of thy Treasure
    Leaping for that joy intense:
    That, inflam'd by such communion,
    Through the marvel of that union
    I may thrill in every sense.

11. All that love this stable truly,
    And the shepherds watching duly,
    Tarry there the live-long night:
    Pray, that by thy Son's dear merit,
    His elected may inherit
    Their own country's endless light.

ERASTUS C. BENEDICT, ESQ., New York.

From "*The Hymns of Hildebert and other Mediæval Hymns with translations*,"
N. York, 1867.

1. Beautiful, his Mother, standing
   Near the stall—her soul expanding
   Saw her new-born lying there—
   In her soul, new joy created,
   And with holy love elated,
   Rapture glorifying her.

2. She, her God-begotten greeting,
   Felt her spotless bosom beating,
   With a new festivity—
   Holy joy, her bosom warming—
   Radiant smiles her face conforming
   At her Son's nativity.

3. Who could fail to see with pleasure,
   Christ's dear Mother, without measure
   Such a joy expressing there—
   Thus a mother's care beguiling,
   Thus beside the manger smiling,
   Her dear Son caressing there?

4. For the trespass of his nation,
   Suffering now humiliation,
   Chilling with the cattle there—
   Wise men knelt where He was lying,
   Still she saw her dear one crying,
   In a cheerless tavern there.

5. Saviour, cradled in a manger!
   Angels hail the heavenly stranger,
     In their great felicity;
   Virgin and her husband gazing
   Speechless, saw the sight, amazing,
     Of so great a mystery.

6. Fount of love, beyond concealing!
   May the love which thou art feeling,
     Fill my heart, unceasingly—
   Let my heart like thine be glowing—
   Holy love of Jesus knowing,
     And with thee, in sympathy.

7. Holy Mother, for him caring,
   Let the ills thy Son is bearing,
     Touch my heart, indelibly—
   Of thy Son, from Heaven descended,
   In a stable, born and tended,
     Share with me the penalty.

8. With thee, all thy love dividing,
   Be my soul in Christ abiding,
     While this life enchaineth me.
   May thy love, my bosom warming,
   Make my soul to his conforming,
     While exile detaineth me.
   Let my love with thine still blending,
   Be for Jesus never ending,
     Nothing e'er restraining me.

9. Virgin, first in virgin beauty!
   Let me share thy love and duty—
     Clasping with fidelity
   That dear child, who for us liveth,
   By his birth, for death, who giveth
     Life and immortality.

10. With thee, let me, thrilled with pleasure,
    Feel his love, beyond all measure,
      In a sacred dance with thee—
    With a holy zeal excited,
    Every ravished sense delighted
      In a holy trance with thee.

11. All who love this sacred manger,
    Every watching shepherd stranger,
      All, at night, who come with him—
    By thy Son's dear intercession,
    May his chosen take possession
      Of his heavenly home with him.

12. By thy holy Son attended—
    By the word of God defended—
      By his grace forgiving me—
    When my mortal frame is perished,
    May my soul above be cherished—
      Thy dear Son receiving me.

ABRAHAM COLES, M.D., LL.D.

From "*Stabat Mater Speciosa. Hymn of the Joys of Mary.*" New York, 1868.

1. Stood the fair delighted Mother
   By the hay, where like no other,
     Lay her little Infant Boy;—
   Through whose soul-rejoicing, yearning
   And with love maternal burning;—
     Thrilling passed the lyric joy.

2. O, what grace to her allotted,
   Blessed Mother and unspotted,
     Of the Sole-Begotten One!
   Who rejoiced, and laughed sweet laughter
   As she gazed exulting, after
     Birth of her Illustrious Son.

3. Who is he would joy not greatly
   If he saw Christ's Mother, lately
     With such solace happy made?
   Who could not be glad in common
   Contemplating that dear woman
     Playing with her smiling Babe?

4. For his people's sins providing,
   Christ she saw with cattle biding,
     And exposed to winter keen.
   Saw her darling offspring, crying
   As an infant, worshipped, lying
     In a lodging vile and mean.

5. O'er that scene surpassing fable,
   Sing they Christ born in a stable,
      Heavenly hosts, with joy immense;
   Old men stood with maidens gazing
   Speechless at that sight amazing,
      In astonishment intense.

6. Make me, Mother, fount of loving,
   Feel like force of ardor moving,
      That I thus may feel with thee!
   Let my heart with love be burning,
   That in Christ my God discerning
      I to Him may pleasing be!

7. Do this, Mother, be entreated!
   Fix His after wounds, repeated
      Well in my heart crucified!
   Of thy Son the Heavenly Stranger,
   Deigning birth now in a manger,
      Sufferings with me divide.

8. Make me truly share thy pleasure
   Cleave to Jesus and Him treasure,
      While I live, and all the while
   Work in me thy love's completeness,
   Treat me with thy Sweet One's sweet-
      ness
      To the end of my exile!

9. Maid all other maids exceeding,
   Be not bitter to my pleading,
      Let me take the Little One,
   Bear the Babe, His sweet smile wooing,
   Who, in birth wrought death undoing,
      Giving life when His begun!

10. Fill me with thy child's caresses,
    Make me drunk with joy's excesses,
       In thy leaping transport share;
    Fired and kindled, struck with won-
       der,
    Let each sense the power be under
       Of such commerce sweet and rare.

11. All the stable loving, blending
    With the watching shepherds, spend-
       ing
    All the night, compose one band.
    Pray, through strength of His deserv-
       ing
    His elect, with course unswerving
    May attain the heavenly land.

12. Let me by thy Son be warded,
    By the word of God be guarded,
       Kept by grace, refused to none.
    When my body death hath riven,
    Grant that to my soul be given
       Joyful vision of thy Son!

REV. FRANKLIN JOHNSON, D.D., Cambridge, Mass.

From "*The Stabat Mater Speciosa and the Stabat Mater Dolorosa; translated by Franklin Johnson.*" Boston, 1886.

1. Stood the Mother in her beauty,
   Rapt with thoughts of love and duty,
      Near the stall where lay her child;
   And her soul, forgetting sadness,
   Glowed with light of new-born glad-
      ness,
      Filled and thrilled with transport
      mild.

2. Of all women has none other
   Joyed with her, the sinless mother
      Of God's sole begotten Son,
   As with laughter and elation
   She beheld the incarnation
      Of the High and Holy One.

3. Who his heart's delight could smother,
   And regard unmoved Christ's mother
      Playing with her baby boy?
   Who could all her peerless treasure
   Of celestial solace measure,
      Void of sympathetic joy?

4. Then, again, she saw with sighing
   Christ for our offences lying
      Cold among the beasts of earth,
   Worshipped, yet to man a stranger,
   Weeping in that meanest manger
      Where she laid Him at His birth.

5. On that babe thus cradled lowly
    Gazed all heavenly spirits holy,
        Singing loud His worthy praise,
    While, with rapture overladen,
    Joseph and the mother-maiden
        Could not speak for sweet amaze.

6. Mother, fount of love's devotion,
    Let me feel thy deep emotion,
        Let me with thy passion glow,
    Let me thine affection borrow
    For thy Son in joy and sorrow,
        That His blessing I may know.

7. Holy maid, the benediction
    Of His birth to sore affliction
        Paint upon mine inmost heart;
    With thy Son, from heaven descended
    To the manger, poor, unfriended
        May I ever have a part.

8. Grant as well thy joy o'erflowing,
    While I cleave to Christ with growing
        Ardor till my life is spent;
    With thy fervor stir and cheer me;
    Let thy little child be near me
        Through this world of banishment.

9. Virgin, virgins all excelling,
    Pardon words from love outwelling:
        I would seize thy babe from thee,
    And would bear, O sweet abduction!
    Him whose birth was death's destruction,
        Him whose death brought life to me.

10. O for Christ to satiation
    Pure and high intoxication!
        O to dance with joy divine!
    O for fire my soul possessing
    And my flesh and sense repressing,
        Since such fellowship is mine!

11. Ye who love this lowly stable,
    With the shepherds through the sable
        Night keep watch, a sleepless band.
    Mother, by thy Son's dear merit
    Pray that His elect inherit
        Of his grace their fatherland.

12. Let thy Son His blessing send me;
    Let that Word of God defend me;
        Keep me in thy tender love;
    When this mortal flesh shall perish,
    Evermore my spirit cherish
        In thy Paradise above.

REV. W. S. MCKENZIE, D.D., Boston.

The esteemed author prepared two versions, one in double rhyme, first published in "*The Beacon*," Boston, May 14th, 1887, and another in single rhyme, published in the same paper, June, 1887. He placed both, with some corrections, at my disposal.

1. Stood the mother, decked with beauty,
    Joying in maternal duty,
        At the crib where lay her Boy;
    Gladness all her heart was filling!
    Rapture was her bosom thrilling!
        Her whole being throbbed with joy!

2. O what beatific feeling
    Stirred that spotless mother, kneeling
        Near her sole begotten One!
    With what sweet exhilaration,
    With what joy and jubilation,
        Did she greet that high-born Son!

3. Who would curb his own emotion,
    Could he see the fond devotion
        Gushing from Christ's mother's breast?
    Who would check her exultations,
    Or would hush her exclamations
        O'er the Babe she there caressed?

4. Yet for his degraded nation
    She saw Christ's humiliation
        In a stable bare and cold;
    Saw her Child with cattle lying,
    Worshipped, yet an Infant crying
        In a chill and cheerless fold.

THE STABAT MATER SPECIOSA.

5. Angels hailed the new-born Stranger,
    Cradled in the narrow manger,
        With loud anthems from the skies:
    Joseph and the maiden mother,
    Speechless, gazed each at the other,
        Overwhelmed with their surprise.

6. Mother, fount of love's pure yearning,
    With thy passion in me burning,
        Let me share thy bliss with thee:
    May I glow with thy emotion,
    Love thy Christ with thy devotion,
        Serve Him with thy loyalty.

7. Holy Mother, let me languish,
    Feeling all thy Baby's anguish
        Graven on my inmost heart:
    With thy Child, who condescended
    In a stable to be tended,
        Meekly I would bear a part.

8. Nought on earth my heart shall sever
    From thy Jesus; to Him ever
        I will cleave till life is past:
    May the ardor thou art showing,
    As in thee in me be glowing,
        Holding me forever fast.
    If thy fervor shall but bind me
    To the Boy, then thou shalt find me
        Ever—faithful to the last.

9. Virgin, O thou Virgin peerless,
    Scorn me not, if rash and fearless,
        I would wrest thy Babe from thee:
    O in my arms let him repose,
    Whose birth the tyrant did depose,
        And who vanquished death for me.

10. I would revel in thy pleasure!
    Drink it with no stinted measure!
        I would feast and dance with thee!
    Thus excited and elated,
    My whole soul intoxicated,
        Firm our fellowship will be!

11. Let all those who love the manger,
    And like shepherds greet the Stranger,
        Watching through the silent night,
    By thy Son's own intercessions
    Gain the pledged and pure possessions
        In the land of life and light.

12. May his loving care be o'er me;
    May the Son of God restore me;
        May his grace my guerdon be:
    And when earthly bonds are riven,
    May it then to me be given
        That thine Infant I may see.

Rev. W. S. McKenzie.

1. How comely in her motherhood
    The virgin near the manger stood,
        Where was laid her infant boy;
    Seraphic bliss her bosom filled,
    Her heart with sweetest rapture thrilled,
        Her whole being throbbed with joy.

2. There, all enraptured and amazed,
    The sinless mother stood, and gazed
        At her sole begotten One!
    With gladness and with holy mirth
    Her soul exulted o'er the birth
        Of her first-born, peerless Son!

3. And who would not her rapture share,
    Could he but see Christ's mother there;
        Honored with a Babe so blest?
    Who from rejoicing could refrain,
    Or would that mother's joy restrain
        O'er the Infant she caressed?

4. 'Twas in His sinful nation's stead
    Her Christ was laid where beasts are fed,
        In a manger bare and cold:
    She saw her Child, that Holy Son,
    Whom Magi blessed, a weeping One
        In a cheerless cattle-fold.

THE STABAT MATER SPECIOSA.

5. When Christ, their King, was born on earth,
    Angelic hosts proclaimed His birth
    With loud anthems in the skies;
    While Joseph and the Maiden mused
    In silence, speechless, and confused,
        Stupefied with their surprise.

6. Mother, fount whence love doth flow,
    With thy sweet passion may I glow,
        Sharing all thy joy with thee:
    My heart would burn with zeal like thine,
    With love to Christ, thy Son Divine,
        And with thy true loyalty.

7. O holy virgin, hear my plea,
    Thine Infant's sorrows lay on me,
        Grave them on my inmost heart:
    With Him who laid His glory by,
    And in a stable deigned to lie,
        I would bear some humble part.

8. And may my soul with thine rejoice;
    Thy little Jesus be my choice;
        Long as life on earth shall last;
    With thy pure ardor I would burn;
    To thy dear Child my heart would turn,
        Till my exile shall be past:
    If that deep fervor thou hast shown
    To thy sweet Babe, by me be known,
        It will bind me firm and fast.

9. Thou spotless, noblest virgin born!
    Do not, I beg, my boldness scorn,
        If I would seize thy Babe from thee:
    Let me breathe thine Infant's breath
    Who by His birth did vanquish death,
        And whose death brought life to me.

10. O may my soul like thine be thrilled!
    With fervor for thy Child be filled!
        Let me throb with love divine!
    If thus inflamed with love's pure fire,
    Then will my heart henceforth aspire
        To a fellowship with thine.

11. For all who love thy manger Boy,
    And like the shepherds in their joy,
        Keep a watch through all the night,
    O mother, by Christ's merits plead,
    That they may be His chosen seed,
        In the land of life and light.

12. And may thy Child be my defense;
    Thy Son Divine my recompense;
        And through life my guerdon be.
    When death my fleshly frame shall smite,
    May I in heaven's purer light
        Him with clearer vision see.

GERMAN TRANSLATIONS.

1. An der Krippe stand die hohe
    Mutter, die so selig frohe,
        Wo das Kindlein lag auf Streu.
    Und durch ihre freudetrunk'ne
    Ganz in Andachtsglut versunk'ne
        Seele, drang ein Jubelschrei.

2. Welches freud'ge, sel'ge Scherzen
    Spielt im unbefleckten Herzen
        Dieser Jungfrau—Mutter froh'n!
    Seel und Sinne jubelnd lachten
    Und frohlockten im Betrachten,
        Dies ihr Kind sei Gottes Sohn.

3. Wessen Herz nicht freudig glühet
    Wenn er Christi Mutter siehet
        In so hohem Wonnetrost?
    Wer wohl könnte ohn' Entzücken
    Christi Mutter hier erblicken,
        Wie ihr Kindlein sie liebkost?

4. Wegen seines Volkes Sünden
    Muss sie zwischen Thränen finden
        Christum frosterstarrt auf Stroh;
    Sehen ihren süssen Knaben
    Winseln und Anbetung haben
        In dem Stalle kalt und roh.

5. Und dem Kindlein in der Krippe
    Singt der Himmelschaaren Sippe
        Ein unendlich Jubellied.
    Und der Jungfrau und dem Greisen
    Fehlen Worte, um zu weisen,
        Was ihr trauernd Herz hier sieht.

6. Eja Mutter, Quell der Liebe,
    Dass auch ich der Inbrust Triebe
        Mit dir fühle, fleh ich, mach!
    Lass mein Herz in Liebesgluten
    Gegen meinen Gott hinfluten,
        Dass ich Ihm gefallen mag!

7. Heil'ge Mutter, das bewirke;
    Präge in mein Herz, und wirke
        Tief ihm Liebeswunden ein;
    Mit dem Kind, dem Himmelssohne,
    Der auf Stroh liegt mir zum Lohne,
        Lass mich theilen alle Pein.

8. Lass mich seine Freud' auch theilen,
    Bei dem Jesulein verweilen
        Meines Lebens Tage all!
    Lass mich dich stets brünstig grüssen,
    Lass des Kindleins mich geniessen
        Hier in diesem Jammerthal.
    O mach' allgemein dies Sehnen,
    Und lass niemals mich entwöhnen
        Von so heil'gem Sehnsuchtsstrahl.

9. Jungfrau aller Jungfrau'n, hehre,
    Nicht dein Kindlein mir verwehre,
        Lass mich's an mich ziehn mit Macht;
    Lass das schöne Kind mich wiegen,
    Das den Tod kam zu besiegen,
        Und das Leben wiederbracht'.

10. Lass an ihm mit dir mich letzen,
    Mich berauschen im Ergötzen,
        Jubeln in der Wonne Tanz!
    Glutentflammet von der Minne
    Schwinden staunend mir die Sinne
        Ob solches Verkehres Glanz!

11. Lass vom Kindlein mich bewachen,
    Gottes Wort mich rüstig machen,
        Fest mich in der Gnade stehn.
    Und wenn einst der Leib verweset,
    Lass die Seele dann, erlöset,
        Deines Sohnes Antlitz sehn!

DR. G. A. KÖNIGSFELD (1865).

From the second series of his "*Latein. Hymnen und Gesänge aus dem Mittelalter.*" Bonn, 1865.

1. An der Krippe stand die hohe
    Gottesmutter, seelenfrohe,
        Wo Er lag, der kleine Sohn;
    Durch das Herz, von Lust durchglühet
    Und durchbebet wonnig ziehet
        Ihr ein heller Jubelton.

2. Wie war hochbeglückt die Eine,
    Die uns makellos und reine
        Gab den Eingeborenen;
    Wie sie jauchzte, wie sie scherzte,
    Ihn betrachtend kosend herzte
        Ihren Auserkorenen.

3. Wer sollt' da nicht freudvoll stehen,
    Wenn die Mutter er gesehen
        In so hohen Trostes Lust?
    Wer nicht mit ihr Wonne fühlen,
    Sieht er Christi Mutter spielen
        Mit dem Sohne an der Brust?

4. Für der Menschheit Sünden alle
    Sieht sie Jesum in dem Stalle
        Zwischen Thieren, frosterstarrt;
    Sieht sie ihren holden Kleinen
    Angebetet winselnd weinen,
        Eingebettet rauh und hart.

5. Doch dem Kind im Stalle tönen
　Hell und laut von Edens Söhnen
　　Jubellieder ohne Zahl;
　Und der Jungfrau und dem Greise
　Fehlen Worte, fehlt die Weise
　　Für ihr Staunen allzumal.

6. Darum Mutter, Quell der Liebe,
　Gib, dass mit dir ich die Triebe
　　Fühle deiner inn'gen Brunst;
　Dass in meinem Herzen wohne
　Heisse Lieb' zu deinem Sohne,
　　Mich erfreue seine Gunst.

7. Heil'ge Mutter, das erwäge,
　Deine Liebeswunden präge
　　Tief in meinem Herzen ein;
　Dass mit deinem Himmelssprossen,
　Jetzt von nacktem Stroh umschlossen,
　　Auch ich theile jede Pein.

8. Lass mich inn'ge Lust empfinden,
　Hängend an dem Jesukinde,
　　Durch mein ganzes Leben lang;
　In mir deine Liebe fliessen
　Und des Kindleins ich geniessen
　　Hier auf meinem Erdengang.

9. Jungfrau, allen vorgezogen,
　Bleibe stets auch mir gewogen,
　　Lass mir dieses Knäblein lieb;
　Lass das liebliche mich wiegen,
　Das den Tod kam zu besiegen,
　　Dass mir nur das Leben blieb.

10. Wonne lass mich mit dir tauschen,
　In dem Sohne mich berauschen,
　　Hüpfen auf in Wonn' und Lust;
　Glutentflammet, liebestrunken
　Schweigt, im Anblick ganz versunken,
　　All' mein Sinnen in der Brust.

11. Gib, durch deinen Sohn mich schützend
　Und auf Gottes Wort mich stützend,
　　Dass stets seine Gunst mich freut;
　Und wenn Staub der Leib geworden,
　Oeffne du der Seele dorten
　　Deines Sohnes Herrlichkeit!

ST. BERNARD AS A HYMNIST.

St. Bernard, abbot of Clairvaux (1091–1153), was one of the greatest and best men in the Middle Ages, and the central figure in the history of Europe during the second quarter of the twelfth century. He belongs to those rare personalities who influenced the Church and the world in every important sphere of life. He is prominent in the history of monasticism, of theology, of the hierarchy, of the Crusades, of pulpit eloquence and public worship. He was the founder of the Cistercian convent in the wild and barren gorge of Clairvaux (*Clara Vallis*), and a model saint, almost worshiped by his contemporaries and canonized by Alexander III. in 1173, in less than twenty years after his death. He healed the papal schism which broke out after the death of Honorius II., secured by his eloquence and moral weight the recognition of Innocent II., and was the spiritual counselor of kings and popes. He defended orthodox mysticism and the theology of the heart against speculative rationalism and the theology of the intellect in the contest with Peter Abelard. He stirred up the second Crusade (in 1146) by rousing the people of France and Germany to the pitch of enthusiasm for the conquest of the Holy Land, but was doomed to bitter disappointment by the disastrous failure of the expedition. His last work was to make peace between the citizens of Metz and the surrounding nobility.

He was endowed with rare faculties of mind and heart, a sympathetic temper, a lively imagination, and the power of personal magnetism. Love and humility were the crowning traits of his character. He is called the honey-flowing doctor (*Doctor mellifluus*). He converted thousands by his persuasive eloquence and pious example, and cured many by his prayers. There is no spotless saint in this world, but Bernard came near the ideal of Christian holiness, and claimed no merit, but gave all the glory to the free grace of God in Christ. His contemporaries regarded him as a worker of miracles, and ascribed a healing power to his dead bones. One of his miracles reported by tradition has a touch of humor, and teaches a lesson how we may utilize even the evil spirit, and turn an obstacle into a vehicle. When crossing the Alps for a third time in 1137 in the interest of the unity and peace of the Church, the devil broke the wheel of his carriage and tried to pitch him over a precipice; but the saint quietly ordered the enemy to become a wheel himself and to carry him to Italy.

St. Bernard occupies an honorable place among the hymnists of the Church. Several religious poems bear his name and are printed among his works.[1] The best are, a Jesus hymn (*Jubilus rhythmicus de Nomine Jesu*), and seven Passion hymns (*Rhythmica Oratio ad unum quodlibet membrorum Christi patientis et a Cruce pendentis*).[2]

I select the Jesus hymn and two of his Passion hymns.

JESU DULCIS MEMORIA.

This may well be called the sweetest and most evangelical hymn of the Middle Ages; as the DIES IRAE is the grandest, and the STABAT MATER the tenderest. It breathes the deepest love to Christ, as the fountain of all peace and comfort, and the sum of all that is pure and lovely. It is eminently characteristic of the glowing piety and "subjective loveliness" of St. Bernard. It has inspired a number of the best Jesus hymns in other languages.

The poem has no less than 48 quatrains or 192 lines in the Benedictine edition of Bernard's Works. Fabricius and Wackernagel give from other MSS. even 50 quatrains or 200 lines.[3]

---

[1] In the Benedictine edition of Mabillon, 1719, vol. II., and in Migne's reprint, *Patrologia*, Tom. CLXXXIV. (Paris, 1854), fol. 1307-1330. I quote from Migne. Comp. also Mone, *Lat. Hymnen des Mittelalters*, I., pp. 119, 162 sqq., 172 sqq.; 298, 330. Trench gives the Jesus hymn, and the first and the last of the Passion hymns.

[2] The best monographs on St. Bernard are Neander's *Der heil. Bernhard und sein Zeitalter* (Berlin, 1813; 3d. ed. 1865; English translation by Matilda Wrench, London, 1868), and J. C. Morison's *The Life and Times of Saint Bernard* (new ed., London, 1868), but both ignore his poetry.

[3] Phil. Wackernagel. *Das Deutsche Kirchenlied* (Leipzig. 1864 sqq., vol. I., 117-120). He adds from Fabricius two additional quatrains of inferior merit.

It was probably enlarged by transcribers, to serve as a rosary hymn. In this form it is repetitious, monotonous, and wanting in progress. It gains decidedly by abridgment. The MSS. give it in several sections according to the hours of daily devotion. The Roman Breviary retains only 15 quatrains and divides them into three distinct hymns (as Caswall does in his translation). Archbishop Trench likewise selects 15 quatrains of the original.[1] All the German and English versions and reproductions are abridgments.[2]

From the Benedictine Edition of St. Bernard's Works.

1. Jesu dulcis memoria,
   Dans vera cordi gaudia:
   Sed super mel et omnia
   Ejus dulcis praesentia.

2. Nil canitur suavius,
   Nil auditur jucundius,
   Nil cogitatur dulcius,
   Quam Jesus Dei Filius.

3. Jesus, spes poenitentibus,
   Quam pius es petentibus,
   Quam bonus te quaerentibus!
   Sed quid invenientibus!

4. Jesu, dulcedo cordium!
   Fons veri, lumen mentium,
   Excedens omne gaudium,
   Et omne desiderium.

5. Nec lingua valet dicere,
   Nec littera exprimere;
   Expertus potest credere,
   Quid sit Jesum diligere.

6. Jesum quaeram in lectulo,
   Clauso cordis cubiculo:
   Privatim et in publico
   Quaeram amore sedulo.

7. Cum Maria diluculo
   Jesum quaeram in tumulo,
   Clamore cordis querulo,
   Mente quaeram, non oculo.

8. Tumbam perfundam fletibus,
   Locum replens gemitibus:
   Jesu provolvar pedibus,
   Strictis haerens amplexibus.

9. Jesu, rex admirabilis,
   Et triumphator nobilis,
   Dulcedo ineffabilis,
   Totus desirabilis.

10. Mane nobiscum, Domine,
    Et nos illustra lumine,
    Pulsa mentis caligine,
    Mundum replens dulcedine.

---

[1] *Sacred Latin Poetry*, 3d. ed., London, 1874, pp. 251-253. He selects vers. 1-5, 20-23, 27, 44, 45, 47 and 48, and says in a note: "Where all was beautiful, the task of selection was a hard one: but only so could the poem have found place in this volume; while there is gain as well as loss in presenting it in this briefer form."

[2] There are German translations or free reproductions by Möller, Fr. von Meyer, Zinzendorf, Sailer, Königsfeld, etc. See Schaff's *Deutsches Gesangbuch*, No. 160; and *Christ in Song*, pp. 318-322 (London ed.).

11. Quando cor nostrum visitas,
    Tunc lucet ei veritas,
    Mundi vilescit vanitas,
    Et intus fervet charitas.

12. Amor Jesu dulcissimus
    Et vere suavissimus,
    Plus millies gratissimus,
    Quam dicere sufficimus.

13. Hoc probat ejus passio,
    Hoc sanguinis effusio,
    Per quam nobis redemptio
    Datur, et Dei visio.

14. Jesum omnes agnoscite,
    Jesum ardenter quærite,
    Amorem ejus poscite;
    Quærendo inardescite.

15. Sic amantem diligite,
    Amoris vicem reddite,
    In hunc odorem currite,
    Et vota votis reddite.

16. Jesus, auctor clementiæ,
    Totius spes lætitiæ,
    Dulcoris fons et gratiæ,
    Veræ cordis deliciæ.

17. Jesu mi bone, sentiam,
    Amoris tui copiam,
    Da mihi per præsentiam
    Tuam videre gloriam.

18. Cum digne loqui nequeam
    De te, tamen ne sileam:
    Amor facit ut audeam,
    Cum de te solum gaudeam.

19. Tua, Jesu, dilectio,
    Grata mentis reflectio,
    Replens sine fastidio,
    Dans famem desiderio.

20. Qui te gustant esuriunt;
    Qui bibunt, adhuc sitiunt:
    Desiderare nesciunt
    Nisi Jesum, quem diligunt.

21. Quem tuus amor ebriat,
    Novit quid Jesus sapiat:
    Quam felix est, quem satiat!
    Non est ultra quod cupiat.

22. Jesu, decus angelicum,
    In aure dulce canticum,
    In ore mel, mirificum,
    In corde nectar cœlicum.

23. Desidero te millies,
    Mi Jesu; quando venies?
    Me lætum quando facies?
    Me de te quando saties?

24. Amor tuus continuus
    Mihi languor assiduus,
    Mihi fructus mellifluus
    Est et vitæ perpetuus.

25. Jesu summa benignitas,
    Mira cordis jucunditas
    Incomprehensa bonitas,
    Qua me stringat charitas.

26. Bonum mihi diligere
    Jesum, nil ultra quærere,
    Mihi prorsus deficere,
    Ut illi queam vivere.

27. O Jesu mi dulcissime,
    Spes suspirantis animæ,
    Te quærunt piæ lacrymæ,
    Te clamor mentis intimæ.

28. Quocunque loco fuero,
    Mecum Jesum desidero;
    Quam lætus, cum invenero!
    Quam felix, cum tenuero!

29. Tunc amplexus, tunc oscula,
    Quæ vincunt mellis pocula,
    Tunc felix Christi copula;
    Sed in his parva morula.

30. Jam quod quæsivi, video:
    Quod concupivi, teneo;
    Amore Jesu langueo,
    Et toto corde ardeo.

31. Jesus cum sic diligitur,
    Hic amor non exstinguitur;
    Non tepescit, nec moritur;
    Plus crescit, et accenditur.

32. Hic amor ardet jugiter,
    Dulcescit mirabiliter,
    Sapit delectabiliter,
    Delectat et feliciter.

33. Hic amor missus cœlitus
    Hæret mihi medullitus,
    Mentem incendit penitus,
    Hoc delectatur spiritus.

34. O beatum incendium,
    Et ardens desiderium!
    O dulce refrigerium,
    Amare Dei Filium!

35. Jesu, flos matris virginis
    Amor nostræ dulcedinis,
    Tibi laus, honor numinis
    Regnum beatitudinis.

36. Veni, veni, rex optime,
    Pater immensæ gloriæ,
    Affulge menti clarius,
    Jam exspectatus sæpius.

37. Jesu, sole serenior,
    Et balsamo suavior,
    Omni dulcore dulcior,
    Cæteris amabilior.

38. Cujus gustus sic afficit
    Cujus odor sic reficit,
    In quo mens mea deficit,
    Solus amanti sufficit.

39. Tu mentis delectatio,
    Amoris consummatio;
    Tu mea gloriatio,
    Jesu, mundi salvatio.

40. Mi delecte, revertere,
    Consors paternæ dexteræ;
    Hostem vicisti prospere,
    Jam cœli regno fruere.

41. Sequar te quoquo ieris,
    Mihi tolli non poteris,
    Cum meum cor abstuleris,
    Jesu laus nostri generis.

42. Cœli cives, occurrite,
    Portas vestras attollite
    Triumphatori dicite,
    Ave, Jesu, rex inclyte.

43. Rex virtutum, rex gloriæ,
    Rex insignis victoriæ,
    Jesu largitor veniæ,
    Honor cœlestis patriæ.

44. Tu fons misericordiæ,
    Tu veræ lumen patriæ;
    Pelle nubem tristitiæ,
    Dans nobis lucem gloriæ.

45. Te cœli chorus prædicat,
    Et tuas laudes replicat;
    Jesus orbem lætificat,
    Et nos Deo pacificat.

46. Jesus in pace imperat,
    Quæ omnem sensum superat:
    Hanc mea mens desiderat,
    Et ea frui properat.

47. Jesus ad Patrem rediit,
    Cœleste regnum subiit;
    Cor meum a me transiit
    Post Jesum simul abiit.

48. Quem prosequamur[1] laudibus,
    Votis, hymnis, et precibus:
    Ut nos donet cœlestibus,
    Secum perfrui sedibus.
        Amen.[2]

[1] Or: "*Jesum sequamur.*"

[2] Wackernagel adds as the last quatrain:

"*Sis, Jesu, meum gaudium,
Qui est futurum præmium,
In te sit mea gloria
Per cuncta semper sæcula.*"

From a Frankfort MS. of the 14th century, in Mone's *Lateinische Hymnen des Mittelalters*, 1853, vol. 1, 329 sq., under the title *Cursus de æterna sapientia*.

Ad Matutinos.

1. Jesu dulcis memoria
   Dans vera cordis gaudia,
   Sed super mel et omnia
   Dulcis ejus præsentia.

2. Nil canitur suavius,
   Auditur nil jocundius,
   Nil cogitatur dulcius
   Quam Jesus, Dei filius.

3. Jesu, spes pœnitentibus,
   Quam pius es petentibus,
   Quam bonus es quærentibus,
   Sed quid invenientibus?

4. Æterna sapientia,
   Tibi Patrique gloria
   Cum Spirito paraclito
   Per infinita sæcula.

In Laudibus.

1. Jesu, rex admirabilis
   Et triumphator nobilis,
   Dulcedo ineffabilis,
   Totus desiderabilis.

2. Nec lingua potest dicere,
   Nec littera exprimere,
   Experto potes credere,
   Quid sit Jesum diligere.

3. Amor Jesu continuus
   Mihi languor assiduus,
   Mihi Jesus mellifluus
   Fructus vitæ perpetuus.

4. Æterna sapientia,
   Tibi Patrique gloria
   Cum Spirito paraclito
   Per infinita sæcula.

Ad Primam.

1. Amor Jesu dulcissimus
   Et vere suavissimus,
   Plus millies gratissimus,
   Quam dicere sufficimus.

2. Jesus decus angelicum,
   In aure dulce canticum,
   In ore mel mirificum,
   In corde nectar cœlicum.

3. Jesu mi bone, sentiam
   Amoris tui copiam,
   Da mihi per pœnitentiam
   Tuam videre gloriam.

4. Æterna sapientia,
   Tibi Patrique gloria
   Cum Spirito paraclito
   Per infinita sæcula.

Ad Tertiam.

1. Tua, Jesu, dilectio,
   Grata mentis affectio,
   Replens sine fastidio,
   Dans famem desiderio.

2. Qui te gustant, esuriunt,
   Qui bibunt, adhuc sitiunt,
   Desiderare nesciunt
   Nisi Jesum, quem diligunt.

3. Desidero te millies,
   Mi Jesus, quando venies,
   Quando me lætum facies,
   Me de te quando saties?

4. Æterna sapientia,
   Tibi Patrique gloria
   Cum Spirito paraclito
   Per infinita sæcula.

Ad Sextam.

1. Jesu, summa benignitas,
   Mira cordis jocunditas,
   Incomprehensa bonitas,
   Tua me stringit caritas.

2. Bonum mihi diligere
   Jesum, nil ultra quærere,
   Mihi prorsus deficere,
   Ut illi queam vivere.

3. Jesu mi dilectissime,
   Spes suspirantis animæ,
   Te quærunt piæ lacrimæ
   Et clamor mentis intimæ.

4. Æterna sapientia,
   Tibi Patrique gloria
   Cum Spirito paraclito
   Per infinita sæcula.

Ad Nonam.

1. Quocunque loco fuero,
   Mecum Jesum desidero,
   Quam felix, cum invenero,
   Quam lætus, quum tenuero!

2. Tunc amplexus, tunc oscula,
   Quæ vincunt mellis pocula,
   Tunc felix Christi copula,
   Sed in his brevis morula.

3. Jam, quod quæsivi, video,
   Quod concupivi, teneo,
   Amore Christi langueo
   Et corde totus ardeo.

4. Æterna sapientia,
   Tibi Patrique gloria
   Cum Spirito paraclito
   Per infinita sæcula.

Ad Vesperas.

1. Jesus sole præclarior
   Et balsamo suavior,
   Omni dulcore dulcior,
   Præ cunctis amabilior.

2. Tu mentis delectatio,
   Amoris consummatio,
   Tu mea gloriatio,
   Jesu, mundi salvatio.

3. Jesus, auctor clementiæ,
   Totius spes lætitiæ,
   Dulcoris fons et gratiæ,
   Veræ cordis deliciæ.

4. Æterna sapientia,
   Tibi Patrique gloria
   Cum Spirito paraclito
   Per infinita sæcula.

Ad Completorium.

1. Jesus in pace imperat,
   Quæ omnem sensum superat,
   Hanc mea mens desiderat
   Et illa frui properat.

2. Te cœli chorus prædicat,
   Et tuas laudes replicat,
   Jesus orbem lætificat
   Et nos Deo pacificat.

3. Jesus at patrem rediit,
   Cœleste regnum subiit,
   Cor meum a me transiit,
   Post Jesum simul abiit.

4. Æterna sapientia,
   Tibi Patrique gloria
   Cum Spirito paraclito
   Per infinita sæcula.

English Translations of Jesu Dulcis Memoria.
Rev. Edward Caswall, Roman Catholic (1814-1878).
From "*Lyra Catholica, containing all the Breviary and Missal Hymns,*"
London, 1849 (pp. 56-59).

VESPERS.
(*Jesu dulcis memoria.* Verse 1-4, Bened. ed.)

1. Jesu! the very thought of Thee
   With sweetness fills my breast;
   But sweeter far Thy face to see,
   And in Thy presence rest.

2. Nor voice can sing, nor heart can frame,
   Nor can the memory find,
   A sweeter sound than Thy blest name,
   O Saviour of mankind!

3. O hope of every contrite heart,
   O joy of all the meek,
   To those who fall, how kind Thou art!
   How good to those who seek!

4. But what to those who find? ah! this
   Nor tongue nor pen can show:
   The love of Jesus, what it is,
   None but His lov'd ones know.

5. Jesu! our only joy be Thou,
   As Thou our prize wilt be:
   Jesu! be Thou our glory now,
   And through eternity.

MATINS.
(*Jesu, Rex admirabilis.* Ver. 9 sqq.)

1. O Jesu! King most wonderful!
   Thou Conqueror renown'd!
   Thou Sweetness most ineffable!
   In whom all joys are found!

2. When once Thou visitest the heart,
   Then truth begins to shine;
   Then earthly vanities depart;
   Then kindles love divine.

3. O Jesu! Light of all below!
　　Thou Fount of life and fire!
　Surpassing all the joys we know,
　　All that we can desire:

4. May every heart confess thy name,
　　And ever Thee adore;
　And seeking Thee, itself inflame
　　To seek Thee more and more.

5. Thee may our tongues forever bless;
　　Thee may we love alone;
　And ever in our lives express
　　The image of Thine own.

LAUDS.

(Jesu, decus angelicum.　Ver. 21 sqq.)

1. O Jesu! Thou the beauty art
　　Of angel worlds above;
　Thy Name is music to the heart,
　　Enchanting it with love.

2. Celestial sweetness unalloy'd,
　　Who eat Thee hunger still;
　Who drink of Thee still feel a void,
　　Which nought but Thou can fill.

3. O my sweet Jesu! hear the sighs
　　Which unto Thee I send;
　To Thee mine inmost spirit cries,
　　My being's hope and end.

4. Stay with us, Lord, and with Thy light
　　Illume the soul's abyss;
　Scatter the darkness of our night,
　　And fill the world with bliss.

5. O Jesu! spotless Virgin flower!
　　Our life and joy! to Thee
　Be praise, beatitude and power,
　　Through all eternity.

Rev. James Waddell Alexander, d.d., Presbyterian (1804–1859).

First published in the "Mercersburg Review" for April, 1859 (p. 304, with the Latin text and an introductory note by Philip Schaff).

JESUS, HOW SWEET THY MEMORY IS.

(*Jesu dulcis memoria.* Ver. 1 sqq.)

1. Jesus, how sweet Thy memory is!
   Thinking of Thee is truest bliss;
   Beyond all honeyed sweets below
   Thy presence is it here to know.

2. Tongue cannot speak a lovelier word,
   Nought more melodious can be heard,
   Nought sweeter can be thought upon,
   Than Jesus Christ, God's only Son.

3. Jesus, Thou hope of those who turn,
   Gentle to those who pray and mourn,
   Ever to those who seek Thee, kind,—
   What must Thou be to those who find!

4. Jesus, Thou dost true pleasures bring,
   Light of the heart, and living spring;
   Higher than highest pleasures roll,
   Or warmest wishes of the soul.

5. Lord, in our bosoms ever dwell,
   And of our souls the night dispel;
   Pour on our inmost mind the ray,
   And fill our earth with blissful day.

6. If Thou dost enter to the heart,
   Then shines the truth in every part;
   All worldly vanities grow vile,
   And charity burns bright the while.

7. This love of Jesus is most sweet,
   This laud of Jesus is most meet;
   Thousand and thousand times more dear
   Than tongue of man can utter here.

8. Praise Jesus, all with one accord,
   Crave Jesus, all, your love and Lord,
   Seek Jesus, warmly, all below,
   And seeking into rapture glow!

9. Thou art of heavenly grace the fount,
   Thou art the true Sun of God's mount;
   Scatter the saddening cloud of night,
   And pour upon us glorious light!

Rev. Ray Palmer, d.d., Congregationalist (1808–1887).   Written, 1858, at Albany, N. Y.

A free reproduction of five stanzas.

JESUS, THOU JOY OF LOVING HEARTS.

("*Jesu, dulcedo cordium.*"   Ver. 4 sqq.)

1. Jesus, Thou Joy of loving hearts,
   Thou Fount of life, Thou Light of men,
   From the best bliss that earth imparts,
   We turn unfilled to Thee again.

2. Thy truth unchanged hath ever stood;
   Thou savest those that on Thee call;
   To them that seek Thee, Thou art good,
   To them that find Thee, All in all.

3. We taste Thee, O thou living Bread,
   And long to feast upon Thee still;
   We drink of Thee, the Fountain Head,
   And thirst, our souls from Thee to fill.

4. Our restless spirits yearn for Thee,
   Where'er our changeful lot is cast;
   Glad, when Thy gracious smile we see,
   Blest, when our faith can hold Thee fast.

5. O Jesus, ever with us stay;
   Make all our moments calm and bright;
   Chase the dark night of sin away;
   Shed o'er the world Thy holy light.

Dr. Abraham Coles, 1889.

Verses 1, 2, 3, 5.

1a. The memory of Jesus' Name
    Is past expression sweet:
    At each dear mention, hearts aflame
    With quicker pulses beat.

1b. But sweet above all sweetest things
    Creation can afford,
That sweetness which His presence brings,
    The vision of the Lord.

2. Sweeter than His dear Name is nought;
    None worthier of laud
Was ever sung or heard or thought
    Than Jesus, Son of God.

3. Thou hope to those of contrite heart!
    To those who ask, how kind!
To those who seek, how good Thou art
    But what to them who find?

4. No heart is able to conceive;
    Nor tongue nor pen express:
Who tries it only can believe
    How choice that blessedness.

A GERMAN TRANSLATION BY COUNT ZINZENDORF.

Originally 31 stanzas. See Albert Knapp's edition of *Geistliche Lieder des Grafen von Zinzendorf*, Stuttgart, 1845, pp. 94, 95, and Schaff's *Deutsches Gesangbuch*, Philadelphia, 1859, etc., No. 160.

1. Jesu! Deiner zu gedenken,
Kann dem Herzen Freude schenken;
Doch mit süssen Himmelstränken
    Labt uns Deine Gegenwart!

2. Lieblicher hat nichts geklungen,
Holder ist noch nichts gesungen,
Sanfter nichts in's Herz gedrungen,
    Als mein Jesus, Gottes Sohn.

3. Tröstlich, wenn man reuig stehet;
Herzlich, wenn man vor Dir flehet;
Lieblich, wenn man zu Dir gehet;
    Unaussprechlich, wenn Du da!

4. Du erquickst das Herz von innen,
Lebensquell und Licht der Sinnen!
Freude muss vor Dir zerrinnen;
    Niemand sehnt sich g'nug nach Dir.

5. Schweigt, ihr ungeübten Zungen!
   Welches Lied hat Ihn besungen?
   Niemand weiss, als der's errungen,
   　Was die Liebe Christi sei.

6. Jesu, wunderbarer König,
   Dem die Völker unterthänig,
   Alles ist vor Dir zu wenig,
   　Du allein bist liebenswerth.

7. Wenn Du uns trittst vor's Gesichte,
   Wird es in dem Herzen lichte,
   Alles Eitle wird zunichte,
   　Und die Liebe glühet auf.

8. Ach, Du hast für uns gelitten,
   Wolltest all Dein Blut ausschütten,
   Hast vom Tod uns losgestritten,
   　Und zur Gottesschau gebracht!

9. König, würdig aller Kränze,
   Quell der Klarheit ohne Grenze,
   Komm der Seele näher, glänze!
   　Komm, Du längst Erwarteter!

10. Dich erhöhn des Himmels Heere,
    Dich besingen unsre Chöre:
    Du bist unsre Macht und Ehre,
    　Du hast uns mit Gott versöhnt!

11. Jesus herrscht in grossem Frieden;
    Er bewahrt Sein Volk hienieden,
    Dass es, von Ihm ungeschieden,
    　Fröhlich Ihn erwarten kann.

12. Himmelsbürger, kommt gezogen,
    Oeffnet eurer Thore Bogen,
    Sagt dem Sieger wohlgewogen:
    　"Holder König, sei gegrüsst!"

13. Jesus, Den wir jetzt mit Loben
    Und mit Psalmen hoch erhoben,
    Jesus hat aus Gnaden droben
    　Friedenshütten uns bestellt!

ST. BERNARD'S PASSION HYMNS.[1]

St. Bernard wrote seven passion hymns addressed to the wounded members of Christ's body suspended on the Cross (the feet, the knees, the hands, the side, the breast, the heart, and the face), as follows:—

Ad Pedes:
"Salve, mundi salutare."

Ad Genua:
"Salve, Jesu, rex sanctorum."

Ad Manus:
"Salve, Jesu pastor bone."

Ad Latus:
"Salve, Jesu, summe bonus."

Ad Pectus:
"Salve, salus mea Deus."

Ad Cor:
"Summi regis cor, aveto."

Ad Faciem:
"Salve, caput cruentatum."

The last two hymns are the best and have been well translated.

AD COR CHRISTI.
Summi regis cor, aveto.

1. Summi regis cor, aveto,
   Te saluto corde læto,
   Te complecti me delectat,
   Et hoc meum cor affectat,
     Ut ad te loquar, animes.
   Quo amore vincebaris,
   Quo dolore torquebaris,
   Cum te totum exhaurires,
   Ut te nobis impartires,
     Et nos a morte tolleres!

2. O mors illa quam amara,
   Quam immitis, quam avara;
   Quæ per cellam introivit,
   In qua mundi vita vivit,
     Te mordens, cor dulcissimum.
   Propter mortem quam tulisti
   Quando pro me defecisti,
   Cordis mei cor delectum,
   In te meum fer affectum,
     Hoc est quod opto plurimum.

---

[1] *Rhythmica Oratio ad unum quodlibet membrum Christi patientis et a cruce pendentis.* Königsfeld has abridged and combined the seven hymns into one, in his German translation. *Lat. Hymnen und Gesänge,* Second selection, Bonn, 1865, pp. 191–200.

3. O cor dulce prædilectum,
　Munda cor meum illectum,
　Et in vanis induratum ;
　Pium fac et timoratum
　　Repulso tetro frigore.
　Per medullam cordis mei,
　Peccatoris atque rei,
　Tuus amor transferatur,
　Quo cor totum rapiatur
　　Languens amoris vulnere.

4. Dilatare, aperire,
　Tanquam rosa fragrans mire,
　Cordi meo te conjunge,
　Unge illud et compunge ;
　　Qui amat te, quid patitur ?
　Quidnam agat nescit vere,
　Nec se valet cohibere,
　Nullum modum dat amori,
　Multa morte vellet mori,
　　Amore quisquis vincitur.

5. Viva cordis voce clamo,
　Dulce cor ; te namque amo :
　Ad cor meum inclinare,
　Ut se possit applicare,
　　Devoto tibi pectore.
　Tuo vivat in amore
　Ne dormitet in torpore,
　Ad te oret, ad te ploret
　Te adoret, te honoret,
　　Te fruens omni tempore.

6. Rosa cordis, aperire,
　Cujus odor fragrat mire,
　Te dignare dilatare,
　Fac cor meum anhelare
　　Flamma desiderii.
　Da cor cordi sociari,
　Tecum, Jesu, vulnerari.
　Nam cor cordi similatur
　Si cor meum perforatur
　　Sagittis improperii.

7. Infer tuum intra sinum
　Cor ut tibi sit vicinum,
　In dolore gaudioso
　Cum deformi specioso,
　　Quod vix se ipsum capiat.
　Hic repauset, hic moretur,
　Ecce jam post te movetur,
　Te ardenter vult sitire.
　Jesu, noli contraire,
　　Ut bene de te sentiat.

"HEART OF CHRIST MY KING."

(*Summi regis cor, arcto.*)

Translated by the REV. E. A. WASHBURN, D.D., New York, late Rector of Calvary Church and member of the American Bible Revision Committee (d. 1881). First published in Schaff's *Christ in Song*, 1868.

1. Heart of Christ my King ! I greet Thee :
　Gladly goes my heart to meet Thee ;
　To embrace Thee now it burneth,
　And with eager thirst it yearneth,
　　Spirit blest, to talk with Thee.
　Oh ! what love divine compelling !
　With what grief Thy breast was swelling !
　All Thy soul for us o'erflowing,
　All Thy life on us bestowing,
　　Sinful men from death to free !

2. Oh, that death! in bitter anguish,
   Cruel, pitiless to languish!
   To the inmost cell it entered,
   Where the life of man was centred,
       Gnawing Thy sweet heart-strings there.
   For that death which Thou hast tasted,
   For that form by sorrow wasted,
   Heart to my heart ever nearest,
   Kindle in me love the dearest;
       This, O Lord, is all my prayer.

3. O sweet Heart! my choicest blessing,
   Cleanse my heart, its sin confessing;
   Hardened in its worldly folly,
   Make it soft again, and holy,
       Melting all its icy ground.
   To my heart's core come, and quicken
   Me a sinner, conscience-stricken;
   By Thy grace my soul renewing,
   All its powers to Thee subduing,
       Languishing with love's sweet wound.

4. Open flower, with blossom fairest,
   As a rose of fragrance rarest;
   Knit to Thee mine inmost feeling;
   Pierce, then pour the oil of healing;
       What to love of Thee is pain?
   Naught he fears, whom Thy love calleth,
   No self-sacrifice appalleth;
   Love divine can have no measure,
   Every death to him is pleasure,
       Where such holy love doth reign.

5. Cries my heart with living voices;
   In Thee, heart of Christ, rejoices;
   Draw Thou nigh with gracious motion,
   Knit it, till in full devotion
       Thou its every power employ.
   Love be all my life; no slumber
   E'er my drowsy thought incumber;
   To Thee praying, Thee imploring,
   Thee aye praising, Thee adoring,
       Thee my sempiternal joy!

6. Heart Rose, in thy fulness blossom,
   Shed Thy perfume o'er my bosom;
   Be Thy beauty in me growing;
   Light the fires for ever glowing
       On the altar of my heart.
   Aid me, Thy dear image wearing,
   E'en Thy wounds, my Jesu, sharing,
   Till Thy very form I borrow,
   When my bosom feels Thy sorrow,
       Piercing with its keenest dart.

7. To Thy holy heart, oh, take me!
   Thy companion, Jesu, make me,
   In that sorrow joy exceeding,
   In that beauty scarred and bleeding,
       Till my heart be wholly Thine.
   Rest, my soul! now naught shall sever;
   After Thee it follows ever;
   Here its thirst finds glad fulfilling;
   Jesu! be Thou not unwilling,
       Take this loving heart of mine!

AD FACIEM CHRISTI.

Salve, caput cruentatum.

1. Salve, caput cruentatum,
   Totum spinis coronatum,
   Conquassatum, vulneratum,
   Arundine sic verberatum,
     Facie sputis illita.
   Salve, cujus dulcis vultus,
   Immutatus et incultus,
   Immutavit suum florem,
   Totus versus in pallorem,
     Quem cœli tremit curia.

2. Omnis vigor atque viror
   Hinc recessit, non admiror,
   Mors apparet in adspectu
   Totus pendens in defectu,
     Attritus ægra macie.
   Sic affectus, sic despectus,
   Propter me sic interfectus,
   Peccatori tam indigno
   Cum amoris in te signo
     Appare clara facie.

3. In hac tua passione,
   Me agnosce, Pastor bone,
   Cujus sumpsi mel ex ore,
   Haustum lactis cum dulcore,
     Præ omnibus deliciis.
   Non me reum asperneris,
   Nec indignum dedigneris,
   Morte tibi jam vicina,
   Tuum caput hic inclina,
     In meis pausa brachiis.

4. Tuæ sanctæ passioni,
   Me gauderem interponi,
   In hac cruce tecum mori;
   Præsta crucis amatori
     Sub cruce tua moriar.
   Morti tuæ tam amaræ
   Grates ago, Jesu care;
   Qui es clemens, pie Deus,
   Fac quod petit tuus reus,
     Ut absque te non finiar.

5. Dum me mori est necesse,
   Noli mihi tunc deesse;
   In tremenda mortis hora
   Veni, Jesu, absque mora,
     Quere me et libera.
   Cum me jubes emigrare,
   Jesu care, tunc appare:
   O amator amplectende,
   Temet ipsum tunc ostende
     In cruce salutifera.

HAIL, THOU HEAD! SO BRUISED AND WOUNDED.

(Salve, caput cruentatum.)

English Translation by Mrs. ELIZABETH RUNDLE CHARLES, authoress of the *Chronicles of the Schönberg-Cotta Family* (1863). From *Christian Life in Song*, p. 159 (Am. ed.)

1. Hail, Thou Head! so bruised and wounded,
   With the crown of thorns surrounded;
   Smitten with the mocking reed,
   Wounds which may not cease to bleed,
     Trickling faint and slow.
   Hail! from whose most blessed brow
   None can wipe the blood-drops now;
   All the flower of life has fled,
   Mortal paleness there instead;
   Thou, before whose presence dread
     Angels trembling bow.

2. All Thy vigor and Thy life
   Fading in this bitter strife;
   Death his stamp on Thee has set,
   Hollow and emaciate,
     Faint and drooping there.
   Thou this agony and scorn
   Hast for me, a sinner, borne,
   Me, unworthy, all for me!
   With those signs of love on Thee,
     Glorious Face, appear!

3. Yet, in this Thine agony,
   Faithful Shepherd, think of me;
   From whose lips of love divine
   Sweetest draughts of life are mine,
     Purest honey flows.

All unworthy of Thy thought,
Guilty, yet reject me not;
Unto me Thy head incline,
Let that dying head of Thine,
    In mine arms repose!

4. Let me true communion know
With Thee in Thy sacred woe,
Counting all beside but dross,
Dying with Thee on Thy cross:
    'Neath it will I die!
Thanks to Thee with every breath,
Jesus, for thy bitter death;
Grant Thy guilty one this prayer,
When my dying hour is near,
    Gracious God, be nigh!

5. When my dying hour must be,
Be not absent then from me;
In that dreadful hour, I pray,
Jesus, come without delay:
    See and set me free!
When Thou biddest me depart,
Whom I cleave to with my heart,
Lover of my soul, be near;
With Thy saving cross appear,
    Show Thyself to me.

DR. ABRAHAM COLES, 1889.

DR. COLES, of Scotch Plains, New Jersey, the successful translator of *Dies Iræ*, and *Stabat Mater*, has reproduced, but has not yet published, all the passion hymns of St. Bernard, and kindly placed this last at my disposal.

1. Hail, O bleeding Head and wounded,
With a crown of thorns surrounded,
Buffeted, and bruised and battered,
Smote with reed by striking shattered,
    Face with spittle vilely smeared!
Hail, whose visage sweet and comely,
Marred by fouling stains and homely,
Changed as to its blooming color,
All now turned to deathly pallor,
    Making heavenly hosts affeared!

2. Back the life-blood hath retreated,
   Of all vital force depleted,
   In Thy looks death plainly painting—
   There Thou hangest pale and fainting,
     Wasted, haggard, worn and lean :
   Thus affected, disrespected,
   For me thus to death subjected,
   Be to me a sinner gracious,
   Of Thy love let token precious
     In Thy shining Face be seen !

3. O Good Shepherd, favor show me,
   In Thy passion deign to know me !
   From Thy mouth I've honey eaten,
   Milk have drunk, with power to sweeten
     More than aught the senses charms.
   Spurn not me, a culprit pleading,
   Me disdain not, mercy needing !
   Now Thy life about resigning,
   Hitherward Thy Head inclining,
     Breathe Thy life out in my arms !

4. That Thy passion be not single
   I would like therein to mingle ;
   I would wish to share Thine anguish,
   On the cross with Thee to languish,
     Of Thy cross enamored be :
   For Thy bitter death, I render
   Thanks to Thee, O Jesu tender !
   God of mercy, I beseech Thee,
   May the prayer I offer reach Thee,—
     Let me die not without Thee.

5. While to die is necessary,
   Fail me not then, be not very
   Far from me in that dread season,
   Quickly come, for urgent reason
     Guard, defend, and set me free.
   When, dear Jesu, Thou dost call me,
   Then appear lest ill befall me :
   O divine and gracious Lover,
   In Thy saving Cross discover
     Thyself able to save me !

MODERN REPRODUCTIONS OF ANCIENT HYMNS.

Some hymns, like the Hebrew Psalms, have had the good fortune to be renewed in countries and languages of which the authors never dreamed. The oldest Christian poem, written by Clement of Alexandria (c. 200), in praise of the Divine Logos, remained for sixteen centuries unknown, except to students of church history, until it was popularized in our age by a felicitous transfusion of Dr. Dexter, an American clergyman.[1] Dr. John Mason Neale has brought to light the hidden treasures of Greek hymnody, and enriched English and American hymn books with some of the choicest lyrics of Anatolius, John of Damascus, Cosmas of Jerusalem, St. Theophanes, Andrew of Crete, Theodore of the Studium, Theoctistus of the Studium, and Stephen of St. Sabas (author of "Art thou weary, art thou languid").[2] He has also popularized by abridgment and free reproduction the heavenly Jerusalem hymn, *Hora novissima*, of Bernard of Cluny (a contemporary of St. Bernard of Clairvaux).[3]

The last of the seven passion hymns of St. Bernard has passed through two transformations which are fully equal to the original and have made it familiar to a much larger number of readers in Europe and America. The first is the famous passion hymn of Paul Gerhardt, "*O Haupt voll Blut und Wunden*," which appeared first in 1656, and may be found in every good German hymn book. The second is Dr. Alexander's "*O Sacred Head*

---

[1] See both in Schaff's *Church History*, II. 230 sq. (revised fifth ed.)

[2] See Neale's *Hymns of the Eastern Church*, London 1862, third ed. 1866, and an account of Greek Hymnody in Schaff's *Church History*, vol. IV. 402–415.

[3] Neale's *Mediæval Hymns and Sequences*, London, 1851, third ed. 1867. Comp. Schaff's *Christ in Song*, pp. 511–516, London ed. I have a copy of the original poem (perhaps the only one in this country), published by Matthias Flacius, and printed at Basel with a preface dated Magdeburg, May 1, 1556, under the title: *Varia Doctorum piorumque Virorum de corrupto Ecclesiæ statu Poëmata*, pp. 494. Bernard's poem *De Contemptu Mundi, ad Petrum abbatem suum*, pp. 247–349, begins: "*Hora novissima, tempora pessima sunt, vigilemus*," and contains nearly three thousand lines of dactylic hexameters with the leonine and tailed rhyme, each line being broken up in three equal parts. Neale has selected the incidental description of the heavenly Jerusalem, which is contrasted with the misery of this corrupt world.

now wounded," which was first published in Schaff's "*Deutsche Kirchenfreund*," for March, 1849, and has passed into several American hymn books, though in some of them with arbitrary abridgments and mis-improvements.[1]

I present them both in parallel columns:—

PAUL GERHARDT. 1656.

1. O Haupt voll Blut und Wunden,
   Voll Schmerz und voller Hohn!
   O Haupt, zum Spott gebunden
   Mit einer Dornenkron!
   O Haupt, sonst schön gezieret
   Mit höchster Ehr und Zier,
   Jetzt aber höchst schimpfiret,
   Gegrüsset seist Du mir!

2. Du edles Angesichte,
   Davor sonst schrickt und scheut
   Das grosse Weltgewichte,
   Wie bist Du so bespeit,
   Wie bist Du so erbleichet,
   Wer hat Dein Augenlicht,
   Dem sonst kein Licht nicht gleichet,
   So schändlich zugericht't?

3. Die Farbe Deiner Wangen,
   Der rothen Lippen Pracht
   Ist hin und ganz vergangen:
   Des blassen Todes Macht

JAMES W. ALEXANDER. 1849.

1. O sacred Head, now wounded,
   With grief and shame weighed down;
   Now scornfully surrounded
   With thorns, Thy only crown;
   O sacred Head, what glory,
   What bliss, till now was Thine!
   Yet, though despised and gory,
   I joy to call Thee mine.

2. O noblest brow, and dearest,
   In other days the world
   All feared, when Thou appearedst;
   What shame on Thee is hurl'd!
   How art Thou pale with anguish,
   With sore abuse and scorn;
   How does that visage languish
   Which once was bright as morn!

3. The blushes late residing
   Upon that holy cheek,
   The roses once abiding
   Upon those lips so meek;

---

[1] Dr. James W. Alexander sent me the hymn from New York, where he was then pastor, with the remark that some stanzas of his version had been previously "so mutilated and butchered by editors of papers that I cannot own as my offspring any but the text which I annex." He added: "Though very Anglican in my origin, education and tenets, I have a deep interest in German Christianity, and, as one of its richest manifestations, in German hymns. You will guess as much when I add that I have around me not only Wackernagel's Paul Gerhardt, but his larger work, as well as the hymns of the *Unitas Fratrum*, the whole of Zinzendorf, and two collections of Latin hymnology. In my humble judgment, he who has produced one such hymn as that of the Electress (of Brandenburg) '*Jesus, meine Zuversicht*,' or (Paul Gerhardt's) '*Wie soll ich Dich empfangen*,' has not lived in vain; even though he has done nothing else." (*Der Deutsche Kirchenfreund*, Mercersburg, Penna., vol. II. 1849, p. 90 sq.) Dr. Alexander is beyond a doubt one of the best translators of German hymns into idiomatic English, and for this, if for no other reason, "has not lived in vain."

Hat alles hingenommen,
Hat alles hingerafft,
Und daher bist Du kommen
Von Deines Leibes Kraft.

Alas! they have departed;
Wan Death has rifled all!
For weak, and broken-hearted,
I see Thy body fall.

4. Nun, was Du, Herr, erduldet,
Ist alles meine Last,
Ich hab es selbst verschuldet,
Was Du getragen hast.
Schau her, hier steh' ich Armer,
Der Zorn verdienet hat:
Gib mir, O mein Erbarmer,
Den Anblick Deiner Gnad'!

4. What Thou, my Lord, hast suffered
Was all for sinners' gain;
Mine, mine was the transgression,
But Thine the deadly pain.
Lo! here I fall, my Saviour!
'Tis I deserve Thy place;
Look on me with Thy favor,
Vouchsafe to me Thy grace.

5. Erkenne mich, mein Hüter,
Mein Hirte, nimm mich an!
Von Dir, Quell aller Güter,
Ist mir viel Guts gethan,
Dein Mund hat mich gelabet
Mit Milch und süsser Kost,
Dein Geist hat mich begabet
Mit mancher Himmelslust.

5. Receive me, my Redeemer,
My Shepherd, make me Thine;
Of every good the fountain,
Thou art the spring of mine.
Thy lips with love distilling,
And milk of truth sincere,
With heaven's bliss are filling
The soul that trembles here.

6. Ich will hier bei Dir stehen,
Verachte mich doch nicht!
Von Dir will ich nicht gehen,
Wann Dir Dein Herze bricht;
Wann Dein Haupt wird erblassen
Im letzten Todesstoss,
Alsdann will ich Dich fassen,
In meinen Arm und Schoss.

6. Beside Thee, Lord, I've taken
My place—forbid me not!
Hence will I ne'er be shaken,
Though Thou to death be brought.
If pain's last paleness hold Thee
In agony opprest,
Then, then will I enfold Thee
Within this arm and breast!

7. Es dient zu meinen Freuden
Und kommt mir herzlich wohl,
Wenn ich in Deinem Leiden,
Mein Heil, mich finden soll.
Ach! möcht ich, o mein Leben,
An Deinem Kreuze hier
Mein Leben von mir geben,
Wie wohl geschähe mir!

7. The joy can ne'er be spoken,
Above all joys beside,
When in Thy body broken
I thus with safety hide.
My Lord of life, desiring
Thy glory now to see,
Beside the Cross expiring,
I'd breathe my soul to Thee.

8. Ich danke Dir von Herzen,
O Jesu, liebster Freund,
Für Deines Todes Schmerzen,
Da Du's so gut gemeint.
Ach! gib, dass ich mich halte
Zu Dir und Deiner Treu,
Und wann ich nun erkalte,
In Dir mein Ende sei.

8. What language shall I borrow
To thank Thee, dearest Friend,
For this, Thy dying sorrow,
Thy pity without end?
O make me Thine forever,
And should I fainting be,
Lord, let me never, never,
Outlive my love to Thee.

9. Wann ich einmal soll scheiden,
   So scheide nicht von mir;
  Wann ich den Tod soll leiden,
   So tritt Du dann herfür.
  Wann mir am allerbängsten
   Wird um das Herze sein,
  So reiss mich aus den Aengsten
   Kraft Deiner Angst und Pein.

10. Erscheine mir zum Schilde,
   Zum Trost in meinem Tod,
  Und lass mich seh'n Dein Bilde
   In Deiner Kreuzesnoth.
  Da will ich nach Dir blicken,
   Da will ich glaubensvoll
  Dich fest an mein Herz drücken;
   Wer so stirbt, der stirbt wohl.

9. And when I am departing,
   O part not Thou from me;
  When mortal pangs are darting,
   Come, Lord, and set me free!
  And when my heart must languish
   Amidst the final throe,
  Release me from my anguish
   By Thine own pain and woe![1]

10. Be near when I am dying,
   O show Thy Cross to me!
  And for my succor flying,
   Come, Lord, to set me free.
  These eyes new faith receiving
   From Jesus shall not move;
  For he who dies believing,
   Dies safe'y through Thy love.

[1] This stanza was substituted by the translator in Schaff's *Kirchenfreund* for 1849, p. 421, as an improvement on his earlier translation (*Ibid.*, p. 92), which reads as follows:—

    9. If I, a wretch, should leave Thee,
      O Jesus, leave not me;
     In faith may I receive Thee,
      When death shall set me free.
    When strength and comfort languish,
     And I must hence depart,
    Release me then from anguish,
     By Thine own wounded heart.

THE UNIVERSITY: PAST, PRESENT, AND FUTURE.

Including an account of the Eighth Centenary of the University of Bologna, June, 1888.—An Address delivered before the University of the City of New York at the Celebration of Founders' Day, April 18th, 1889.

I.—THE MEDIEVAL UNIVERSITY.

Universities are institutions for the cultivation of every branch of knowledge, human and divine, to the highest attainable degree of perfection. They are the centres of the intellectual and literary life of nations, the workshops of learning and research, the nurseries of the men of power and influence in the various professions. They receive the best minds from all ranks of society, and mould them for public usefulness.

These institutions originated in the Middle Ages. They were partly an expansion of monastic and cathedral schools, partly independent foundations. A vague tradition traces the University of Paris back to Charlemagne in the eighth, and the University of Oxford to King Alfred in the ninth, century. These noble rulers were indeed lights shining in the darkness, the legislators, educators, and benefactors of Europe in that chaotic period of transition from ancient to modern civilization. But universities, in any proper sense of the term, do not appear before the close of the eleventh or the beginning of the twelfth century. They are intimately connected with that remarkable revival of Western Christendom which reformed the papacy, roused the crusades, built the cathedrals, founded the monastic orders, and produced the scholastic and mystic theology. They owe their origin to the enthusiasm of scholars. Emperors, kings, popes, and cities granted them charters and various privileges, but some of them were in vigorous existence before they received governmental recognition and authority. They gradually grew from humble rudiments to their present state of completeness, and they are still expanding with the progress of knowledge.

The original idea of a university differs from that which obtains at the present time. It was not a university of letters (*universitas literarum*), but a university of teachers and students (*universitas magistrorum et scholarium*). The usual designation in the thirteenth century for such a literary community was "Study," or "General Study" (*studium generale* or *studium universale*). The University of Bologna was called "*Studium Bononiæ*," or "*Bononiense;*"[1] that of Paris, "*Studium Parisiense;*" that of Oxford, "*Studium Oxoniense.*" The addition "*generale*" had reference likewise to scholars, not to different branches of knowledge. It meant a centre of study for all.[2] Some "Studies" were only for medicine, or law, or theology. But the tendency and aim of a mediæval university was to provide for all branches of learning then attainable, and thus the name naturally passed from the personal sense of a body of teachers and learners to the literary sense of a body of studies.[3] The designation of the University as "*alma*" or "*alma mater*" dates from the thirteenth century. The term "*faculty*" meant both the body of teachers of a particular branch of knowledge, and the science taught.

A full university requires four faculties—theology, philosophy (arts), law, and medicine—corresponding to the four learned professions. But some of the best universities were incomplete for a long time. Nearly one-half of them excluded theology, because this was provided for in the monastic and episcopal schools. On the other hand, Paris, where theology and the canon law were taught from the beginning, had no provision for teaching civil law from 1219 to the seventeenth century.[4]

The philosophical faculty embraced originally the seven liberal arts of the *Tricium* (grammar, logic, and rhetoric) and *Quadrivium* (music, arithmetic, geometry, and astronomy); but in its modern

---

[1] The Italians still call it *Lo Studio Bolognese*.

[2] Comp. Denifle: *Die Universitäten des Mittelalters bis 1400* (Berlin, 1885), Vol. I. 5 *sqq.* A "general" study might be founded for each separate faculty. Hence the phrase: "*Vigeat studium generale in theologica facultate.*"

[3] The German emperor, Frederick II., in 1224, expressed the desire that the University of Naples should have "doctors and masters in every faculty," and that "the studies of every profession should flourish." Denifle, I. 28.

[4] Denifle, I. 703.

expansion it includes all branches of metaphysical, linguistic, mathematical, historical, scientific, and other studies, which may claim the dignity of independent departments.

Besides the literary division into faculties there was a national division, with provincial subdivisions. The students of Paris were divided into the four nations of France, Picardy (including the Netherlands), Normandy, and England (which in 1430 gave place to Germany). They had distinct suffrages in the affairs of the university. In Bologna, Padua, and Vercelli there were four "*universitates*," composed of different nationalities—Italians, English, Provençals, and Germans. The provincial division is still kept up in the Swedish universities of Upsala and Lund.

A university formed a republic of letters, a state within the state, a church within the church. It had an independent government and jurisdiction, large endowments and privileges, granted by popes, kings, cities, and individuals. An elective rector or chancellor stood at the head of the whole corporation, a dean at the head of each faculty, and each nation had its procurator; these officers constituted the governing and executive body. The academic senate embraced the ordinary professors of all the faculties and was the legislative body.

Each faculty granted the license to teach, and conferred the academic degrees of bachelor, licentiate (master), and doctor. These degrees looked originally to public teaching, and marked as many steps in the promotion to this office. In law, there were doctors of civil law, and doctors of canon law. The doctorate of divinity required nine years of preparation, but is now usually bestowed *honoris causa* for actual services rendered to sacred learning. The academic degrees conveyed important rights and privileges, and were carefully guarded and highly esteemed. This is still the case in all the leading universities of Europe.

In our country the lavish bestowal of diplomas by several hundred colleges, the feeblest as well as the strongest, has made those dignities as numerous and as cheap as leaves in Vallombrosa. There are more doctors of divinity in the State, if not in the city of New York alone, than in the whole German Empire, which is emphatically the land of learning. The only present remedy for this abuse is the indication of the source from which the degree is derived. The stronger an institution, the greater should be the discrimination and care in the distribution of these honors.

Italy, France, and England took the lead in the history of the universities. Germany was behind them till the period of the Reformation; but the Hohenstaufen emperors—Frederick Barbarossa, and Frederick II.—began the university legislation and granted the first charters to Italian universities, which took the lead, especially in law and medicine. They were followed by Paris and Oxford. In modern times the German universities are the chief nurseries of progressive learning, and attract students from all parts of the world.

The attendance of students in the Middle Ages was larger than in modern times, because there were fewer universities and libraries. This scarcity made oral instruction all the more valuable. If one desired to be taught by Abelard or Thomas Aquinas, he must go to Paris. We read that Bologna had at one time as many as 10,000, Paris 25,000, and Oxford 30,000 scholars. Abelard lectured before 3,000 hearers. In like manner the scarcity of preaching and good preachers increased the number of hearers. Berthold of Regensburg, a Franciscan monk and revival preacher in the middle of the thirteenth century, is reported to have preached at times to an audience of 60,000.[1]

These figures are probably exaggerated, but not impossible. The time for study was more extended. Men in mature age, even priests, canons, and professors, often turned students for a season. The line between teachers and learners was not closely drawn, and both were included in the name of scholar or student (*scholaris* or *scholasticus*).

The professors were called *Doctor, Magister, Dominus*. They

---

[1] The largest number of students for 1887 was 5,357 in Berlin, 4,893 in Vienna, 3,234 in Leipzig, 3,176 in Munich. The number of professors (ordinary, extraordinary, and Privatdocenten) for the same year was 296 in Berlin, 301 in Vienna, 180 in Leipzig, 165 in Munich, 131 in Breslau, 121 in Göttingen, 110 in Prague. The largest number of Italian students in 1887 was in the University of Naples and reached 4,083.

had no regular salary, and lived on lecture fees or private means or charitable funds. Some were supported from the royal purse or private endowments. Most of them were monks or ecclesiastics, and had no families to support. They had no common building, and taught wherever it was most convenient, in colleges, in convents, in public halls or private rooms. University buildings, libraries, antiquarian and artistic collections were of slow growth, and the effects of successful teaching. With us colleges often begin with brick and mortar, and have to wait for teachers and students. Brain produces brick, but brick will not produce brain.

A papal bull was usually required for a university.[1] Every doctor and public teacher of theology was sworn to defend the Scriptures and the faith of the holy Roman Catholic Church. Luther took that oath. Paris, Louvain, and Cologne condemned him as a heretic.

Yet from the universities proceeded, in spite of papal prohibitions and excommunications, the intellectual and ecclesiastical revolutions of modern times. The last mediæval university—Wittenberg—became the first Protestant university. Heidelberg, Leipzig, Tübingen, Oxford, and Cambridge, once among the chief nurseries of scholastic theology and Roman orthodoxy, have long since transferred their loyalty and zeal to a different creed. The oldest Scotch university—St. Andrews—founded for the defence of the Roman Catholic faith, became a bulwark of the Reformation, so that the phrase "to drink from St. Leonard's well" (one of the colleges of St. Andrews) was equivalent to imbibing the doctrines of Calvin. Almost every new school of theological thought, and every great ecclesiastical movement were born or nursed in some university.

Salerno is the oldest university so called; it dates from the ninth century, but never acquired general influence, and was confined to the study of medicine. In 1231 it was constituted by the Emperor Frederick II. as the only school of medicine in the kingdom of Naples, but was subsequently overshadowed by

---

[1] This mediæval custom has long since ceased in Europe, but has been renewed in our country by Pope Leo XIII., in chartering the Catholic university in the city of Washington, which was dedicated November 13, 1889.

the University of Naples, which had likewise a medical faculty. It has long since ceased to exist.

The oldest surviving, and at the same time most important, universities of the Middle Ages are those of Bologna, Paris, and Oxford.

The total number of mediæval universities, founded before A.D. 1500, amounts to about sixty. They were Roman Catholic in religion. Most of them still survive, but have undergone many changes. The universities which date from the last three centuries are chiefly Protestant, or purely scientific and literary. Germany heads the list with twenty-two universities, which include all the four or five faculties; France has probably as many, but some are incomplete as to the number of faculties; Italy has twenty-one; Spain, ten; Austria-Hungary, seven; Switzerland, six; Holland, five; Belgium, four; England, three; Scotland, four; Ireland, two; Sweden, two; Norway, one; Denmark, one; Portugal, one; Greece, one. The nine Russian universities are all of modern date, and profess the Greek religion; but Dorpat has a Lutheran faculty of theology, which is taught in the German language.

Colleges are not to be confounded with universities, as is often the case in our country. They were originally charitable institutions for poor students, called "bursars" (*bursier*, hence the German *Burschen*), who lived together under the supervision of masters. Canon Robert de Sorbon, chaplain and confessor of Louis IX., endowed such a monastic, beneficiary college in Paris (1274), which was called after him the Sorbonne (Sorbona)—a name often incorrectly given to the theological faculty or even to the whole University of Paris.

On the Continent, colleges or gymnasia are subordinate and preparatory to the university, and cannot confer degrees. In England, on the contrary, the colleges have absorbed the university, and constitute the university. In Oxford, Cambridge, and Durham the several colleges and halls have separate endowments, buildings, libraries, and corps of teachers, retain the dormitory system and instruction by masters and tutors or fellows, and enforce attendance upon the daily devotions in the chapel. The American college and university system is built on the English rather than the Continental model, but boldly ventures on all sorts of new experiments, some of which will fail, while others will succeed.

II.—THE UNIVERSITY OF BOLOGNA.[1]

Bologna (Bononia), a beautiful old city on the northern slope of the Apennines, which formerly belonged to the Papal States (from 1513 to 1860), but now to the United Kingdom of Italy, derives her fame chiefly from the university, which is the oldest in existence. Tradition traces its origin back to the reign of Theodosius II., in 425; but there is no evidence of its existence before the close of the eleventh or the beginning of the twelfth century, when Irnerius, a native of Bologna, discovered and expounded in that city the Civil Code of Justinian. He is called the Restorer and Expounder of Roman jurisprudence.[2] He was in the service of the Emperor Henry V., as counsellor, between 1116 and 1118, and died before 1130.[3]

Shortly after him, Gratian, a Camalduensian monk, taught the canon law in the Convent of St. Felix in Bologna, and published in 1150 the famous *Decretum Gratiani*, which was adopted as a text-book in all universities. The *Decretum*—or, as he called it, "the Concordance of Discordant Canons," is a systematic and harmonistic collection of canons of ancient councils and papal decretals, based upon older collections, and explained by glosses. It forms the first part of the *Corpus juris canonici*, or catholic church law, which was gradually enlarged by synodical decrees and papal bulls to its present dimensions.

Thus we find in Bologna before the middle of the twelfth cen-

---

[1] The best accounts of the University of Bologna during the Middle Ages, with special reference to the study of the Roman law, are given by Professor Fr. Carl von Savigny in the third volume of his great German work on the *History of the Roman Law*, pp. 159–272 (2d ed., 1834-1851, 7 vols.), and by Giacomo Cassani (formerly Professor of Canon Law in Bologna), in *Dell'antico studio di Bologna e sua origine*, Bologna, 1888. Much information may also be obtained from works on the canon law, and from the publications issued in commemoration of the eighth centenary of the university, which are mentioned in the appendix to this address.

[2] "*Scientiæ legalis illuminator*"

[3] Von Savigny treats very fully of Irnerius in his *Geschichte des römischen Rechts*, Vol. IV. 9–67 (2d ed., 1850).

tury two law schools. The teachers of the Roman, or civil, law were called Legalists; the teachers of the canon law, Canonists or Decretists.

The Emperor Frederick I., called Barbarossa, on a visit to Bologna, on Whitsunday, 1155, took these schools under his protection and gave them the first university charter.[1]

In 1158 he extended the privileges at the Diet of Roncaglia, at which four professors of law from Bologna were present, to other schools of Italy, and secured imperial protection to scholars on their journeys.[2]

From this time Bologna was the greatest law school, the nurse of jurisprudence (*legum nutrix*), and could proudly adopt the device: "*Bononia docet.*"

Students flocked to her from all countries and nationalities of Europe by hundreds and thousands. In the fourteenth century she had four faculties—two for law (civil and ecclesiastical), one for medicine, one for theology. The liberal arts were also taught. The double faculty of law continued to be the most important. Six years were required for a full course in canon law, eight years in civil law.

The influence which the Roman law and the canon law have exerted on the civilization of Europe down to the present time is simply incalculable. It surpasses the influence of the arms of pagan Rome. The power of law is silent, but deep, constant, pervasive. It touches society at every point and accompanies human life from the cradle to the grave. Conquered by the barbarians, Rome in turn conquered their descendants, and by substituting the law for the sword she once more ruled the world for centuries, mindful of the prophetic line of Virgil:—

"*Tu, regere imperio populos, Romane, memento.*"

But the Roman and the canon law, like heathen Rome and the Roman papacy, became in course of time an intolerable yoke which independent nations would no longer bear, and gradually

---

[1] See a historical poem on Frederick I., discovered and first published by Giesebrecht in 1879, and the remarks of Denifle, *l. c.*, I. 49 *sqq.*

[2] "*Omnibus qui causa studiorum peregrinantur, scolaribus et maxime divinarum atque sacrarum legum professoribus.*"

shook off. When Luther threw the papal bull of excommunication into the flames, answering fire by fire, he also burnt the canon law with its cruel enactments against heretics. Abuses were abolished, what is good will remain.

Bologna is still one of the best law schools, but since the last century she has chiefly cultivated physical, medical, and mathematical sciences. She has chairs for almost every department of knowledge, except theology. She has rich antiquarian and scientific collections, and one of the finest libraries, over which once the famous Cardinal Mezzofanti presided, who could familiarly converse with every visitor in his own language and dialect. As to attendance, Bologna stands third among the twenty-one universities of the kingdom of Italy; the number of her students from 1887–'88 was 1,338, that of Turin 2,102 and that of Naples 4,083.[1]

An original and romantic feature of the University of Bologna, is the admission of learned ladies to the corps of teachers. Properzia de Rossi, of Bologna (d. 1530), was a skilful sculptor and musician, and acquired fame by her cameos of peach-stones, and her masterpiece, "Joseph rejecting the Overtures of Potiphar's Wife." Laura Bassi was doctor and professor of philosophy and mathematics in her native city (d. 1778). Madame Manzolina lectured on anatomy. Maria Gaetana Agnesi was a prodigy of linguistic and mathematical learning, and filled the chair of her father, who was professor in Bologna; after his death she retired to a nunnery (d. 1799). Clotilda Tambroni, a Bolognese by birth, expounded the Greek classics from 1794 to 1817. Miss Giuseppina Cattani is at this time a popular lecturer on pathology and a noted contributor to medical journals.

[1] The University Calendar for 1887–'88 (*Annuario della regia Università di Bologna*) mentions the departments of the University in the following order: *facoltà di lettere e filosofia; f. di scienze matematiche, fisiche e naturali; f. di giurisprudenza* (without a professorship for canon law); *f. medico-chirurgica; scuola di farmacia; scuola superiore di medicina veterinaria; scuola d'applicazione per gli ingegneri; scuola di magistero*. The Calendar (pp. 211–255) gives a chronological list of rectors and vice-rectors from Joannes de Varanis, 1244, to Giovanni Capellini, 1888. The theological faculty and the professorship of canon law seem to have been abolished when Bologna ceased to be a papal city. Giacomo Cassani was the last professor of canon law, and is now professor emeritus.

One of the earliest of these learned lady professors, Novella d'Andrea (d. 1366), was distinguished for beauty as well as learning, and used to lecture from behind a curtain,

> "Lest the students
> Should let their young eyes wander o'er her
> And quite forget their jurisprudence."

III.—THE BOLOGNA FESTIVAL.

In the summer of 1888, the University of Bologna celebrated its eight hundredth anniversary. It was the literary event of that year, and marks an epoch in the history of that institution.

I had the honor to represent your University as a delegate. The dignity of that position might have been more befittingly assigned to a scholar eminent in jurisprudence or natural science, than to a theologian. But the duties were light, and I discharged them to the best of my ability. Two years before I had attended the celebration of the fifth centenary of the University of Heidelberg, the oldest in Germany (for the older Universities of Prague and Vienna are in Austria), and I shall ever remember these two visits as among the most pleasant and interesting episodes in my life.

The Bologna celebration occupied three days, June 11th, 12th, and 13th. It was supplemented, on the 14th, by a commemoration of Luigi Galvani, the discoverer of animal magnetism, who was born at Bologna and professor of anatomy in its university.

The festival was honored by an imposing galaxy of about three hundred and fifty academic dignitaries, and by the presence of their Majesties, King Umberto and Queen Margherita, and their only son, the Crown Prince of Italy. Nearly every university of Europe sent its Rector Magnificus, or a distinguished professor of law or of science. Several American institutions besides your own University—Harvard, Yale, Princeton, Hartford, Johns Hopkins, Cornell, Columbia, the Universities of Pennsylvania, Virginia, Michigan, Iowa, and Wisconsin, the Smithsonian Institute, the American Academy of Sciences,—were directly or indirectly (some, however, only nominally or collectively) represented. Even Buenos Ayres, and Santiago of South

America, Bombay of Asia, Adelaide and Sydney of Australia, took part by delegates. The students' societies of several universities sent large deputations, recognizable by their different colors and badges, and contributed much to the joy and cheer of the feast. The European delegates appeared, as is customary on such occasions, in their academic gowns with hoods, golden chains, and decorations, and presented a picturesque mediæval spectacle. The American delegates (with the exception of two distinguished gentlemen who wore Oxford gowns) were conspicuous by the absence of ornaments, and found compensation in the modest charm of republican simplicity. I doubt whether there ever has been such a numerous and brilliant gathering of professors and students, except at the fifth centennial celebration of the University of Heidelberg in 1886, which lasted a whole week, and had the special attractions of an illumination of the celebrated castle, and of a historic procession enacting the manners and customs of past generations.

On the morning of the first day the King and Queen arrived from Rome and were received with the heartiest demonstrations of joy. They gave to the eighth centenary a national and patriotic character. It was a celebration of united and free Italy fully as much as a literary festival. Every patriotic allusion met with enthusiastic response. The whole population was in sympathy, and manifested it again and again with dramatic demonstrativeness. It was made very manifest that the citizens of Bologna, who took a prominent part in the liberation of Italy, are not willing to take their politics from the pope of Rome, whatever they may think of his religion. The attempt at the restoration of the temporal power of the papacy will nowhere find stronger resistance than in Roman Catholic Italy. The clergy of Bologna showed their indifference or hostility by their absence from the festivities and by preventing the use of the historic Church of San Petronio, where academic promotions formerly took place, and where Charles V. was crowned emperor by Pope Clement VII., the only German emperor crowned outside of Rome, and the last German emperor crowned by a pope.

On the morning of Monday, the 11th, the deputies were

received by the Sindaco of Bologna, in the magnificent library hall of the old university, the Archiginnasio.

The first public act of the festival took place in the afternoon, and accorded with its patriotic character. The equestrian statue of Victor Emmanuel II., the first king of united Italy and the model Italian gentleman, was unveiled by his son amidst the unbounded enthusiasm of the spectators, who occupied every inch of ground. The statue stands in the centre of the large place of the Church of San Petronio, and presents the King in military posture, giving command to the army.

In the evening the Queen gave a brilliant reception in the palace. She is a highly accomplished lady, full of grace and beauty, and had a pleasant word to say to every delegate presented to her, in his own language. The King also made a happy impression by his courtesy, affability, and kindly manner. He is an enlightened and liberal monarch, has the welfare of his people at heart, and well deserves his popularity.

Tuesday, the 12th, was the great day of the feast. The representatives of Italian, German, French, Spanish, Dutch, Portuguese, English, Scotch, Irish, Austrian, Hungarian, Scandinavian, Russian, Swiss, and American universities, together with the professors and directors of Bologna University, the dignitaries of the city, and a very large train of students in every variety of costume and color, marched in procession from the new university building to the old. The streets were lined and the windows crowded with people, cheering the strangers, and covering them with laurels and flowers. Prominent among the cheers was "Evviva Germania!"—in view of the political alliance of the two nations, and the personal friendship of their rulers.

In the crowd of spectators I saw, for the last time, Father Gavazzi, a Bolognese, who in 1848—with Bassi, his friend and fellow-Barnabite friar—so fired the heart of his fellow-townsmen by his dramatic eloquence, on the square before the Church of San Petronio, that men and women in large numbers were seen emptying their purses, and laying their watches, chains, and earrings at his feet as an offering to the cause of Italian unity and liberty. The venerable octogenarian lived to see the triumph of the cause to which he had devoted his life, and his face was beaming with joy and gratitude.[1]

Arrived in the cortile of the Archiginnasio, the guests were seated according to their nationality. The ladies occupied the galleries, and shone in all the ornaments of personal beauty, flowers, and precious stones.

After a while, King Humbert, the Queen, and the youthful prince and heir to the throne arrived amidst deafening acclamations and took their seats, on an elevated tribune in the centre of the back wall, under a baldachin. They followed the festivities with unwearied attention to the close.

The picture of the whole assembly beggars description. The cortile of the Archiginnasio is a magnificent square court, surrounded by four rows of columns. It was now decorated with artistic taste, and filled as never before with living representatives of the highest institutions of learning from every clime under the sun, forming a literary cosmos in festal array. I was reminded of Goethe's minstrel, who, "*im Saal voll Pracht und Herrlichkeit,*" exclaimed:—

> "*Gegrüsset seid mir, edle Herrn,
> Gegrüsst ihr, schöne Damen!
> Welch reicher Himmel! Stern bei Stern!
> Wer kennet ihre Namen?*"

The ceremonies were introduced by the musical performance of an ode of Enrico Panzacchi, set to tune by Baron Alberto Franchetti. It begins with this verse:—

> "*Entra. Da qual tu vengа
> Viaggio lungíaqua e strana,
> Sotto la salata insegna,
> Della scienza umana,
> Entra, o cultor del Vero,
> Qui tu non sei straniero.*"

Mrs. Professor Vincenzo Botta—a name as well known in Italy as in America—has kindly favored me with a free and happy reproduction of this Ode of Welcome:—

---

[1] Gavazzi died since, January 9th, 1889, at Rome,—with the wish to be called on his tomb what he truly was, "*Patriotta Cristiano.*"

"Stranger from far off lands,
 Who dost to Science bow,
A worshiper of Truth,
 No stranger here art thou.

"Truth, Science, wondrous power,
 Who can thy limits stay,
Or dim the lustrous beams
 Of thy new risen day?

"Speed on thy wingéd thought,
 Thy war with darkness wage,
Till all the sorrowing race
 Shall hail a happier age.

"Speak, O eternal Word,
 And rend blind Error's chain,
Till, over earth redeemed,
 Love, Truth, and Justice reign."

Signor Paolo Boselli, the Minister of Public Instruction, read, in behalf of the King and the Government, an eloquent Address of Welcome, in which he sketched the history of the university, not forgetting the learned lady professors, and closed with a glance at the recent regeneration of Italy.

Next followed an Address by Professor Giovanni Capellini, a distinguished geologist, who had the good fortune to be Rector in that memorable year. He read an Italian translation of a letter of congratulation from the death-bed of Emperor Frederick III.,—probably his last public document. As crown prince he had attended the semi-millennial celebration of the Heidelberg University in the name of his venerable father, the first Emperor of United Germany. I well remember how intelligently he advocated, in his opening address, the progress of every branch of liberal learning, and with what ease and grace he conversed, in the illuminated castle, with the academic delegates in their own language. He was then in blooming health and the very type of manly beauty and strength, without a symptom of that terrible disease which was to terminate his life a few weeks after ascending the throne of Prussia and the German empire.[1]

[1] I may be permitted here to make public two incidental private remarks which are highly favorable to his character. He inquired, during the festival of August 1886, at the castle of Heidelberg, very kindly after his former tutor,

His letter to Bologna University is singularly appropriate, and will be engraved on a marble table in the University:—

"With lively sympathy I accompany the celebration of the University of Bologna and the inspiring reminiscences which its eighth centenary awakens for Germany. I gladly recall the ancient relations which bound Germany to your University. They began seven hundred years ago with the charter of the Emperor Frederick Barbarossa, and were continued by a stream of innumerable sons of Germany, who crossed the Alps to be illuminated in the newly revived science of jurisprudence, and to bring home to their fatherland the creations of classical antiquity. In Bologna the seeds were sown from which the legal culture of Germany has derived nourishment to this day, and the institutions of your University served as a model for the academic freedom of the German Universities.

Mindful of the debt which Germany owes to the renowned University of Bologna, I send to her, for the memorable festival, blessing and greeting: May she in united Italy ever remain true to her honorable title in science and culture, *Bononia docens!* (Signed) FRIEDRICH IMP. REX.
Schloss Friedrichskron, June 6th, 1888."

The great festive Oration was intrusted to Giosuè Carducci, ordinary Professor in the Faculty of Letters and Philosophy, the first living poet of Italy, and since 1861 the founder of a flourishing school of Italian literary history. It was a most eloquent composition in the purest Italian, pervaded by the glow of patriotism, and delivered with an animation and earnestness that kept the audience spell-bound to the close. It was largely historical, and dwelt upon the influence which Bologna, by teaching the civil and the canon law, exercised in civilizing and Romanizing the barbarians of Europe,—an influence greater and more beneficent than the conquests of the Roman eagles. From Rome, the fountain of law, he said, Italy derived her best gifts. New Italy, as Giuseppe Mazzini saw, requires as its centre a

my friend and fellow-student, Dr. Frédéric Godet of Neuchatel, the well known divine and biblical commentator, and gave free expression to his grateful attachment and regard for him. He carried on a familiar correspondence with him to the last, and Godet showed me several of his letters. A year before, in August 1885, I saw the emperor, then crown prince, at Andermatt in Switzerland, where he spent the summer with his family. He attended the worship of the Church of England in a little room opposite the hotel, and followed the service very devoutly. The sermon was rather dull and empty; but he listened attentively and said to me afterwards: "Never mind the sermon; the *prayers* are always beautiful; I like the Episcopal service."

third Rome, which is not aristocratic, not imperial, not papal, but democratic and Italian. This third Rome we owe to the sacrifices, the prisons, the battle-fields, the parliaments of the last and present generation. He wound up with a eulogy of Victor Emmanuel II., who lies buried in the Pantheon of Rome, and left to his son the task of guarding the Eternal City as an inalienable conquest. The conclusion elicited an uproarious applause. The royal majesties pressed the hand of the orator with grateful emotion.

Then followed the interesting ceremony of presentations and congratulations. The academic deputations, divided into groups according to their nationalities in alphabetical order, approached one after another the royal tribune,—the Europeans in their academic ornaments, the Americans in their dress-coats and white cravats. They were presented by the Rector to the King and Queen, deposited their credentials and memorial gifts, and received in return a royal smile of thanks. Each nation was allowed one speaker, and each speaker three minutes. The Americans selected the Hon. James Russell Lowell, who could have so well represented American literature and statesmanship in elegant Italian; but, as he was sick on that day, Professor W. W. Story, the famous sculptor, and for many years a resident of Rome, was requested to express the compliments of young America to venerable Bologna, which he did in a few well-chosen Italian sentences. As the son and biographer of Judge Joseph Story, of the Supreme Court of the United States, who was also professor of law in Harvard College, he represented at the same time American jurisprudence. All the speeches were in Italian, except one in French, and one in Greek.

Professor Gandino concluded the ceremony by an Address of Thanks in Ciceronian Latin.

At six o'clock the Government of the Province of Bologna gave a banquet, and at nine o'clock the delegates were invited to listen to Wagner's music ("Tristan and Isolde") in the theatre. Bologna is at present the seat of Italian enthusiasm for Wagner.

On the 13th of June the literary honors were distributed to a number of the most celebrated jurists and scientists of the age, in the same locality and before the same audience. Those present received the diplomas in person from the hands of the Rector.

The festivities were concluded by a learned and able Address of Giuseppe Ceneri, Professor of the Roman Law, which once was the great title of the glory of Bologna. He looked forward to a universal reign of liberty, justice and peace (*libertà, giustizia, pace*). The address was delivered with consummate oratorical art, and elicited as much applause as the oration of Carducci on the previous day.

Thus ended the *Ottavo Centenario dello Studio Bolognese sotto l'alto patronato di S. M. Umberto I., Rè d'Italia.*

One dark cloud was cast over the assembly as it was about to disperse. Telegrams were received announcing that the Emperor of Germany, after unspeakable sufferings borne without a murmur, was dying. The King of Italy, his personal friend and political ally, was moved to tears, and departed without delay in a special train. The German professors hurried home to learn on the way that their beloved Emperor, from whom so much was expected for the liberal progress of the Fatherland, had ended his short, sad reign of three months, leaving a nation to mourn his loss, and a world to drop a tear on his grave. The newspapers were dressed in mourning. The expressions of sorrow were sincere and universal; even the leading papers of France, forgetting Weissenburg and Sedan, spoke generously of the personal qualities and liberal views of the departed monarch. In Italy, Frederick III. had spent, as crown-prince, the early months of his fatal sickness, and received a visit from the King. To Bologna he had sent his last public greeting and blessing.

Much as the Germans and Italians differ in their national traits, their political fortunes have been closely interwoven, for good and for evil, from the time when Pope Leo III. crowned Charlemagne in St. Peter's in Rome, to the time when Clement VII. conferred the same crown upon Charles V. in the Church of San Petronio in Bologna. But, while the mediæval history of Germany and Italy was a history of conflict between the Papacy and the Empire, each despotic and each aspiring after supremacy, their modern history is a successful struggle for national unity and liberty. They were closely allied for this purpose. At the head of both nations in this momentous crisis stood the greatest statesmen, the greatest soldiers, and the greatest monarchs of the age. Germany had her Bismarck, her Moltke, and her William I.; Italy had her Cavour, her Garibaldi, and her Victor Emmanuel. Such two trios history has never seen before, and may never see again. When the German army returned to Berlin to celebrate the unification of twenty-eight sovereignties under the crown of Prussia, the Italian army entered Rome, henceforth the national capital of Italy—no longer separated into petty, despotic, rival states, but Italy regenerated, united, and free.

The literary and patriotic festival we have described, celebrated this great fact and sealed it with all the authority of *Bononia docens*. This is its historic significance.

IV.—THE AMERICAN UNIVERSITY.

The academic feast of Bologna has carried us back to the dawn of modern civilization in the beginning of the twelfth century. Let us now cast a glance into the future.

America has the unspeakable advantage of starting with the capital of Europe. The labors of two thousand years have accumulated immense treasures of knowledge and wisdom which are at our disposal. We have no right to live unless we are willing to profit by the lessons of the past, and to add our share to the wealth of the future. America should advance as much beyond Europe as Europe has improved upon Asia. Every nation of the Old World sends her sons and daughters as well as her literature to help us in this magnificent task.

"Time's noblest offspring is the last."

The chief instruments in shaping and perfecting American civilization are the public schools, colleges, and universities. Considering the youth of our nation, the progress of education has been marvelous. In two hundred years the United States have advanced as much in this direction as Europe in two thousand years, although, of course, with the benefit of European experience. The past is a sure pledge of a still brighter future. We are only in the beginning of the development of our resources. We are charged with national vanity and boastfulness, not without reason. But it is impossible to live a year in this country with one's eyes open, without becoming an optimist. Literary and charitable institutions, churches, and schools are multiplying in every direction, and follow the settler across the prairies and primitive forests, where buffaloes and wild Indians were in undisputed possession not many years ago. The donations for these institutions exceed in amount all previous precedents in the history of Europe, and are increasing and multiplying by the irresistible power of example. One citizen of California, prompted by religious and literary motives, has recently consecrated twenty millions for a university in that Pacific State, which has not yet celebrated its semi-centennial. Where is the Government under the sun that has done so much for such an object as this single individual? Of course, money will not build up an institution; but the race of scholars keeps pace with the growth of the country.

The University of the City of New York is to-day only fifty-eight years of age, and has already a corps of eighty teachers and lecturers in the faculty of arts and science (dating from 1832), the faculty of medicine (dating from 1841), and the faculty of law (dating from 1858). It was founded neither by pope nor king, but, in truly democratic American style, by the people and for the people. Among those who originated the idea of a university in this metropolis, who endowed it with their means, and who carried it on to its present degree of prosperity, we find the honored names of clergymen, lawyers, physicians, bankers, merchants, and useful citizens of every rank in society. Its facilities and opportunities are expanding with the growth of this city, whose future no one can predict. The first centenary of the University of the City of New York will outshine the eighth centenary of the University of Bologna, as the twentieth century will be in advance of the nineteenth. Your University has already furnished invaluable contributions to the civilization of the world by two inventions made in this your building by two of your professors—the invention of the Recording Telegraph, and the invention of the application of Photography to the representation of the human countenance. Your Professor Morse and your Professor Draper have immortalized themselves and immortalized your University as much as Irnerius and Galvani have immortalized Bologna. Nor should Dr. Draper the son, at first student, then professor here, be unmentioned to-day, for his unexampled application of photography to the heavenly bodies.

If your University is so far incomplete as to exclude a theological department, it has its precedent in Bologna, which had no theological faculty for the first two hundred years of its existence, and has none now. But exclusion with you means no hostility or indifference; on the contrary, it is based on respect for religious freedom, and reflects the relation which the State holds to the Church in our country, that is, a relation of friendly independence. The separation of Church and State means a free Church in a free State, each sovereign in its own sphere, both mutually recognizing and aiding each other, the State protecting the Church by its laws, the Church promoting the welfare of the State by training good Christians, who are the best citizens. Separation of Church and State is quite compatible with the religious character of the nation. Christianity, general, unsectarian Christianity, with freedom of conscience for all; Christianity, as taught by its Founder in the New Testament, is embodied in our laws, institutions and customs, and can never be eradicated. It prospers all the more because it is free. No government in Europe, no matter how closely united to the Church, does so much for the promotion of Christianity at home and abroad as the people of these United States do by their voluntary efforts and gifts.

We shall witness in a few days one of the grandest spectacles a nation can present: the first centenary of the Inauguration of our Government, when—in imitation of the example set by the Father of our Country and the Founders of our National Government, and at the invitation of President Harrison—the people of all denominations will assemble in their respective houses of divine worship, "to implore" (in the language of the Presidential proclamation) "the favor of God that the blessings of liberty, prosperity and peace may abide with us as a people, and that His hand may lead us into the paths of righteousness and good deeds." [1]

The founders of this University, from the very start, in a printed appeal to the community, dated January 27th, 1830, have clearly defined its relation to religion, in these words :—

"In our general statement it is declared that no faculty of theology shall be created in the University. We deemed this exclusion to be necessary in order the more effectually to secure the institution from the introduction of sectarian influence. But are we therefore to be accounted as proclaiming ourselves indifferent to our religion, and as expecting to build up an institution which *proscribes* what should be the primary and all-important object of education? We trust that the names of the gentlemen already engaged in this enterprise would alone be sufficient to secure us from such an injurious imputation. Were we so weak and so wicked as to project a seminary of learning from which religion was to be banished, or by which its holy influences were to be weakened, we should anticipate neither the favor nor the support of men, nor—what is of infinitely greater consequence—the blessing of God upon our endeavors. In all systems of instruction and seminaries for training youth, we consider religion to be of paramount importance.

"And while we esteem the *rights of conscience* and the great principle of *religious liberty* to be of inestimable value, and would most sacredly preserve them from present or remote danger, we still believe that it will be perfectly competent to the supreme government of the university, and that it will be their duty to provide for the religious instruction of those youths who may be entrusted to their care."

To meet this view, the statement proposes that the University be authorized to provide for general instruction in the evidences of Christianity, and to designate religious teachers of different Christian denominations when represented by a sufficient number of students; but not to compel attendance upon this special instruction without the will of the parent or guardian.

The University has lived up to this programme. Its chancellors, from the first to the last, have consistently and successfully maintained a friendly attitude to evangelical Christianity without in the least interfering with religious liberty. They were, with one exception, themselves honored ministers of the gospel

---

[1] The centennial celebration of Washington's Inauguration has since taken place, from April 29th to May 1st, 1889, and has itself become a historic event of great significance for the second century of the United States of America.

and doctors of divinity, and yet none the less zealous and effective as promoters of all the scientific and literary branches of education. And the one layman who served as chancellor from 1838–1850, Theodore Freylinghuysen, was not only a distinguished statesman, but an influential leader in many religious and charitable movements of his day.

The future of our country depends largely upon a voluntary friendly alliance of education with the Christian Church with equal justice to all its branches. The ultimate aim of education is to build up character. This cannot be done without morality and religion, which are inseparably bound together. Morality and religion are the crowning features of individual character, and the pillars of society and government. No liberty without education, no education without virtue, no virtue without piety, no piety without love to God and man.

This was the conviction of Washington, exemplified in his pure private and public life, and proclaimed in his first inaugural, and in his last farewell address to the people who revere him as their father. It is an unspeakable blessing that the Almighty Ruler of nations placed at the head of our history a man who feared God and loved righteousness, who appreciated education in connection with virtue and religion, and who, as a gentleman, a citizen, and a patriot, set a bright example for imitation; a man whose greatness was his goodness—the best, because the most solid, the most beneficent, and the most enduring kind of greatness. Let his counsel of wisdom, confirmed by the experience of a century, go forth with double force as the motto of the second century of our nation.

APPENDIX.

CENTENNIAL PUBLICATIONS OF THE UNIVERSITY OF BOLOGNA.

The following interesting works in commemoration of the *Ottavo Centenario dello Studio Bolognese* were sent by the University of Bologna to Dr. Schaff, and deposited by him in the library of the University of the City of New York:—

Statuti della Università e dei Collegi dello Studio Bolognese. Pubblicati da CARLO MALAGOLA: dottore collegiato onorario della facoltà giuridica della R. Università e direttore dell' archivio di stato di Bologna. Bologna, Nicola Zanichelli, MDCCCLXXXVIII. (524 pp. fol.)

Annuario della Regia Università di Bologna. Anno scolastico, 1887-'88. Bologna, premiato stab. tip. successori Monti, 1887. (pp. 349.)

Stabilimenti Scientifici della R. Università di Bologna in rapporto col Piano Regolatore della città secondo il progetto del Rettore G. CAPELLINI. Bologna, stab. tip. succ. Monti, 1888.

Orazione di LUIGI GALVANI, *prof. di Anatomia nella Università di Bologna letta nel 25 Novembre, 1782, per la laurea del nipote* GIOVANNI ALDINI *edita per solennizzare il 1° centenario della scoperta fatta dal Galvani nel 26 Settembre, 1786.* Bologna, premiato stab. tip. succ. Monti, 1888.

Bologna al tempo di LUIGI GALVANI *nel suo governo civile ed ecclesiastico, nelle sue istituzioni di scienze, di arti e di pubblica beneficenza con miscellanea di notizie biografiche, artistiche, aneddotiche e di costumanze patrie particolari. Compilazione sopra autentici documenti raccolti ed ordinati dal* DOTT. ALESSANDRO BACCHI. Bologna, tipografia gamberini e parmeggiani, 1887.

Conosci Te Stesso e L'Ambiente della tua Attività. Dialoghi per l'istruzione popolare di ANGELO MARESCOTTI, *senatore del regno.* Bologna, Nicola Zanichelli, 1888.

Guida del R. Istituto Geologico di Bologna. Bologna, tipografia Fava e Garagnani, 1888.

Universitati Litterarum et Artium Bononiensi ferias saeculares octavas pridie idus Iunias anno P. N. C. MDCCCLXXXVIII celebranti Cantabrigia, typis academicis). A Greek Poem of Salutation, by Professor R. O. JEBB, of the University of Glasgow, beginning: "Μάκαρ ἄρχα α οσίας, ἰαχε Ἑλλάδα πᾶσαν."

An Italian Translation, by G. PELLICCIONI, of Jebb's Poem of Salutation, entitled: *Allo Studio Di Bologna festeggiante l'ottavo suo centenario il XII. Giugno MDCCCLXXXVIII.*

FACCIOLI. *Archiginnasio di Bologna.* Bologna, 1888.

A Bronze Medal of HUMBERTUS I. REX ITALIAE, UNIVERSITATIS LITTERARUM ET ARTIUM BONONIENSIS PATRONUS.

DANTE ALIGHIERI.

DANTE, SHAKESPEARE, GOETHE.

Dante, Shakespeare, and Goethe are the greatest poets of the Christian era; as the author of the Book of Job, Homer, and Virgil are the greatest of the era before Christ. They rise like pyramids in the history of literature. Their works have a universal and perennial interest.

Their theme is man as man. They sympathize with all that is human. They reproduce with the intuition of genius, in classical style, our common nature in all its phases from the lowest to the highest, from the worst to the best. Hence they interest all classes of men.

But while they agree in this general characteristic, they differ as widely as the nations and ages to which they belong, and as the languages in which they wrote. They are intensely human, and yet intensely national. Dante (1265–1321) could only have arisen in Italy, and in the thirteenth century; Shakespeare (1564–1616) only in England, and in the sixteenth; Goethe (1749–1832) only in Germany, and in the eighteenth century. Dante is the poet of the Middle Ages; Shakespeare is the poet of the transition period of the Renaissance and Reformation; Goethe is the poet of modern cosmopolitan culture.

It is impossible to say who is the greatest and the most universal of the three. Shakespeare is an unexplained literary miracle as to creative fertility of genius which "gives to airy nothing a local habitation and a name," and as to intuitive knowledge of human nature—English, old Roman, Italian, French, Scandinavian, Christian, Jewish, heathen, noble and wicked, angelic and Satanic. Goethe presents greater variety of poetic and literary composition, and excels equally in drama, epos, and song, in narrative prose and literary criticism. Dante is the most exalted and sublime of the three, as he follows men into the eternal world of bliss and woe.

Viewed in their relation to religion, Dante is the most religious of the three. He is the Homer of mediæval Christianity, and reflects the theology of St. Thomas Aquinas. The divine inspiration and authority of the Scriptures, the Holy Trinity, the divinity of Christ and the Holy Spirit, the necessity of the atonement, conversion and sanctification, future rewards and punishments, were to him as certain truths as mathematical propositions, and heaven and hell as real facts as happiness and misery in this life. In this respect he resembles the singer of Paradise Lost and Paradise Regained, and the singer of the Messiad much more than Shakespeare and Goethe; but the English Milton and the German Klopstock, with a purer and simpler faith, do not reach the height of the genius of the Tuscan poet.

Dante and Milton have several points in common: both are intensely religious, one as a Catholic, the other as a Puritan; both stood at the height of learning and culture, the one of the thirteenth, the other of the seventeenth century; both were champions of freedom against despotism; both engaged in party politics, and failed; both ended their life in unhappy isolation; but both rose in sublime heroism above personal misfortune, and produced in sorrow and disappointment their greatest works, full of inspiring thoughts for future generations.

Shakespeare is a secular poet, and professes no religion at all, whether Catholic or Protestant; he is hid behind his characters. But he always speaks respectfully of religion; he makes virtue lovely and vice hateful; he punishes sin and crime, and his tragedies have the moral effect of powerful sermons. He is full of reminiscences of, and allusions to, the Bible.[1] He passed through the great convulsion of the Reformation without losing his faith. There can be no doubt that he reverently bowed before Him whose

> "Blessed feet were nailed
> For our advantage on the bitter cross." [2]

---

[1] Bishop Charles Wordsworth, of St. Andrews, has written a book of 420 pages on *Shakespeare's Knowledge and Use of the Bible* (London, third ed., 1880), in which he traces over 400 passages of the Bible quoted or referred to by Shakespeare. As he wrote most of his works before 1611, when the Authorized Version appeared, he used earlier translations. Wordsworth asserts (p. 9) that King James' translators owed more to Shakespeare than he to them.

[2] Henry IV., P. I., Act I., Sc. 1.

And we look in vain in all literature, outside of the New Testament, for a more eloquent and truly Christian description of mercy than that given by "gentle William": [1]

> "The quality of mercy is not strain'd,
> It droppeth as the gentle rain from heaven
> Upon the place beneath. It is twice bless'd;
> It blesseth him that gives, and him that takes:
> 'Tis mightiest in the mightiest; it becomes
> The throned monarch better than his crown:
> His sceptre shows the force of temporal power,
> The attribute to awe and majesty,
> Wherein doth sit the fear and dread of kings;
> But mercy is above this sceptred sway:
> It is enthroned in the hearts of kings,
> It is an attribute to God himself,
> And earthly power doth then show likest God's,
> When mercy seasons justice."

Goethe is likewise a worldly poet, and touches religion only incidentally and casually as one of the essential elements of human life; as for instance in the confessions of a beautiful soul (Fräulein von Klettenberg, a pious Moravian lady and friend of his mother), inserted among the mixed theatrical company of Wilhelm Meister. He characterized himself as a liberal and impartial outsider,[2] and as a child of the world between two prophets.[3] He had a Pelagian or Unitarian view of the way of salvation, and expressed it in the Second Part of *Faust*, which has been called the tragedy of the modern age of the eighteenth and nineteenth centuries. Faust is saved, not in the evangelical way by free grace through repentance and faith in Christ, but by his own constant endeavor and self-culture, aided by divine love, and by Mary and Gretchen drawing him heavenward. Angels bear Faust's immortal part and sing—

---

[1] Merchant of Venice, Act IV., Sc. 1.

[2] "*Ich bin kein Unchrist, kein Widerchrist, doch ein decidirter Nichtchrist.*" Letter to the pious Lavater, the friend of his youth, 1782.

[3] "*Prophete rechts, Prophete links,
Das Weltkind in der Mitten.*"

> "*Gerettet ist das edle Glied*
> *Der Geisterwelt vom Bösen:*
> *Wer immer strebend sich bemüht,*
> *Den können wir erlösen.*
>
> "*Und hat an ihm die Liebe gar*
> *Von oben teilgenommen,*
> *Begegnet ihm die sel'ge Schaar*
> *Mit herzlichem Willkommen.*"[1]

We need not wonder that Goethe had the highest admiration for Shakespeare, but disliked Dante, and called his *Inferno* "abominable;" his *Purgatorio* "ambiguous" and his *Paradiso* "tiresome" (May, 1787). In showing a bust of Dante to Eckermann, he said: "He looks as if he came out of hell." The contrast between the two men is almost as great as the contrast between Gretchen and Beatrice. And yet the First Part of the tragedy of *Faust* furnishes a striking parallel to the *Inferno* of the *Divine Comedy*, and contains some of the profoundest Christian ideas, expressed in the purest language. Think of the prelude in heaven, imitated from the Book of Job, the sublime songs of the three archangels, the triumphant Easter hymn, which prevents Faust from committing suicide, the solemn cathedral scene, the judgment trumpet of the *Dies Iræ*, the terrors of a guilty conscience, and the downward progress of sin begetting new sin and leading step by step to insanity, prison and death. The description of Mephistopheles is far more true to the character of the sneering, scoffing, hideous arch-fiend of the human race than Dante's horrid monster at the bottom of the *Inferno*. The concluding act before the day of execution, the salvation of the innocently guilty and penitent Gretchen,

---

[1] The emphasis lies on the third and fourth lines, the earnest and constant endeavor of man, as the chief condition of salvation, to which is added divine love as a help from above. Goethe himself declared to Eckermann (June 6, 1831) that in these verses lies the key for the redemption of Faust. "*In Faust selber eine immer höhere und reinere Thätigkeit bis an's Ende, und von oben die ihm zu Hülfe kommende ewige Liebe. Es steht dies mit unserer religiösen Vorstellung durchaus in Harmonie, nach welcher wir nicht bloss durch eigene Kraft selig werden, sondern durch die hinzukommende göttliche Gnade.*" This reverses the evangelical order, which puts Divine grace first and human endeavor second, and puts both in the relation of cause and effect.

and the perdition of her guilty seducer, followed by the cry of pity: "Henry, Henry!" is the very perfection of tragical art, and overpowering in its moral effect. The Second Part, which occupied the trembling hand of the aged poet during the last seven years of his life, is full of unexplained allegorical mysteries, and ends with the attraction of "the eternal womanly." So far, but no further, it resembles the Paradise of Dante and the attraction of Beatrice. The Purgatory is missing in *Faust*, or hid in silence between the First and Second Part.

Of the life of Dante and Shakespeare we know very little, and that little is uncertain and disputed. Goethe left a charming record of his early life, and his later years are equally well known. Dante and Shakespeare died in the vigor of manhood, the former at the age of fifty-six, the latter at the age of fifty-three, both in the Christian faith and the hope of immortality. Goethe lived to a serene old age of eighty-two, praying for "more light," and left, ten days before his departure from this world of mystery to the world of light, as his last wise utterance, a testimony to the Christ of the Gospel which is well worth pondering by every thinking skeptic, saying: "Let mental culture go on advancing, let mental sciences go on gaining in depth and breadth, and the human mind expand as it may, it will never surpass the elevation and moral culture of Christianity as it glistens and shines forth in the Gospels." Add to this his emphatic declaration: "I consider the Gospels to be thoroughly genuine; for there is reflected in them a majesty and sublimity which emanated from the person of Christ, and which is as truly divine as anything ever seen on earth."

The great poet of Weimar pointed in these testimonies to the strongest and most convincing internal evidence of Christianity: the perfect teaching and perfect example of its Founder. If this once takes hold of the heart as well as the mind of a man, he is impregnable against the attacks of infidelity. This was the confession of one of the profoundest thinkers of the nineteenth century. "The foundation of all my thinking," says Richard Rothe,[1] "I may honestly declare, is the simple faith in Christ,

[1] Preface to the first edition of his *Theologische Ethik*, reprinted in the second edition (Wittenberg, 1-67, sqq.), vol. I., p. xvi.

as it (not this or that dogma or this or that theology) has for eighteen centuries overcome the world. It is to me the ultimate certainty, in view of which I am ready, unhesitatingly and joyfully, to cast overboard every other assumption of knowledge which should be found to contradict it. I know no other fixed point into which I could cast out the anchor for my thought except the historical manifestation, which is designated by the sacred name, Jesus Christ. It is to me the unassailable Holy of Holies of mankind, the most exalted thing that has ever come into a human consciousness, and a sunrise in history, from which alone light diffuses itself over the collective circle of the objects which fall within our view. With this one absolutely undiscoverable datum, the knowledge of which moreover bears direct testimony to its reality, as the light to itself, and in which lie involved consequences beyond the reach of anticipation, stands and falls for me, in the ultimate ground, every certainty of the spiritual and therefore eternal nobility of the human race."

Will America ever produce a poet equal in genius to Dante, Shakespeare, Goethe, but free from their errors; a poet who shall identify his life and work with the cause of Christianity pure and undefiled, and show forth the blissful harmony of beauty, truth, and goodness? Or must we wait for the millennium, or for Paradise?

THE LIFE OF DANTE.

"Behold the man who has been in Hell,"[1] exclaimed the women of Verona when they looked on Dante, as an exile, walking lonely, thoughtful, sad and solemn through the streets. They might have added, "and in Purgatory and in Paradise." But the *Paradiso* was at that time not yet finished, and the women were naturally struck with the most prominent feature; they expressed the popular preference for the *Inferno*, which is most read and best known. Few have the patience to climb up the mountain of the *Purgatorio*, and to follow him into the *Paradiso*, though this is the purest and sublimest part of the *Divina Commedia*. Eternity in all its phases seems impressed upon that countenance, painted by his friend Giotto, which once

---

[1] "*Eccovi l'uom ch'è stato all' inferno.*"

seen can never be forgotten. We behold there combined the solemn sadness, the discipline of sorrow, and the repose of faith.

Dante's life is a tragedy. It opens with the sweet spring of pure love, passes into the summer heat of severe study and political strife, and ends in an autumn of poverty and exile; but the outcome of all was the *Divina Commedia*, by which he continues to live.

> "Nurtured into poverty by wrong
> He learnt in suffering what he taught in song."

His inner life is written in his works; but of his outward life we know only a few facts with any degree of certainty; others are doubtful or differently interpreted; hence we must be guarded in our assertions.

Dante—an abridgment of Durante, the Enduring—was descended from the ancient and noble family of the Aligeri or Alighieri (Allighieri), and born at Florence in the month of May or June, 1265, during the pontificate of Clement IV. (1265–1268), in the age of the Crusades, the cathedrals, the scholastic philosophy, the monastic orders, the papal theocracy in conflict with the empire, and of the gigantic contrast between monkish world-renunciation (*Weltentsagung*) and popish world-dominion (*Weltbeherrschung*).

He was a boy of thirteen when Conradin, the last scion of the illustrious imperial house of Hohenstaufen, was beheaded at Naples (1268); he was fifteen at the death of St. Louis, of France, the last of the Crusaders (1270); nineteen, when St. Thomas Aquinas and St. Bonaventura, his masters in theology, ascended to the beatific vision in Paradise (1274). He was yet a youth when Giotto was born (1276), when Albertus Magnus died (1280), when the Sicilian Vespers took place (1282). In the year 1289, Francesca da Rimini was murdered, whom he immortalized in the fifth Canto of the *Inferno*. The death and glorification of Beatrice occurred in 1290, when he had reached his twenty-fifth year.

Some important events fell in the period of his exile: the first papal jubilee at Rome (1300), the conflict of Boniface VIII. with Philip the Fair; the beginning of the Babylonian exile of the papacy (1309–1370); the suppression of the Templars

(1312); the birth of Petrarca (1304), and of Boccaccio (1313); and from these two poets may be dated the Italian Renaissance, and that Revival of Letters which, in turn, prepared the way for modern civilization.

Dante's father was a lawyer. His mother, Donna Bella, is once mentioned by Virgil in the words addressed to Dante:—

"Blessed is she that bore thee."[1]

DANTE AND BEATRICE.

In his ninth year Dante saw for the first time, on a festive May-day, under a laurel tree, a Florentine maiden of angelic beauty and loveliness, with fair hair, bright blue eyes and pearl-white complexion, only a few months younger than himself. She was the daughter of Falco Portinari, a noble Florentine, and bore the Christian name of Bice or Beatrice, which recalls the idea of beatitude or blessedness.

He touchingly describes the interview in his *New Life* (*Vita Nuova*). "She appeared to me," he says, "clothed in a most noble color, a modest and becoming crimson, garlanded and adorned in such wise as befitted her very youthful age. At that instant the spirit of life which dwells in the most secret chamber of the heart, began to tremble, and said: 'Behold a god, stronger than I, who, coming, shall rule me' (*Ecce deus fortior me, qui veniens dominabitur mihi*)."

"This most gentle lady reached such favor among the people, that when she passed along the way persons ran to see her, which gave me wonderful delight. And when she was near any one, such modesty took possession of his heart, that he did not dare to raise his eyes or to return her salutation; and to this, should any one doubt it, many, as having experienced it, could bear witness for me. She, crowned and clothed with humility, took her way, displaying no pride in that which she saw and heard. Many, when she had passed, said: 'This is not a woman, rather is she one of the most beautiful angels of heaven.' Others said: 'She is a miracle. Blessed be the Lord who can perform such a marvel.' I say that she showed herself so gentle and so full of

---

[1] *Inferno*, VIII., 45: "*Benedetta colei che in te s'incinse.*"

all beauties, that those who looked on her felt within themselves a pure and sweet delight, such as they could not tell in words."[1] At the end of that book he calls this Florentine maiden "the blessed Beatrice who in glory looks upon the face of Him *qui est per omnia secula benedictus.*"

The meeting of Dante with Beatrice was to him a revelation and an inspiration, the beginning of a new life, the turning point of his career, the germ of his great poem. It opened to him the fountain of love and poetry. Beatrice was not destined to be the companion of his life, but they continued to be united by the bands of Platonic love.

Nine years after the first interview, when they were eighteen, he saw her again, clothed in pure white, and received her smiling salutation, which filled him with such an ecstacy of delight, that on returning home he fell into a sweet slumber and had a marvelous vision. He described this vision in a sonnet, his first poetic composition, and sent it, according to the custom of the age, to several eminent persons, among others to Guido Cavalcanti, who became his faithful friend till his death (1300).

From this time dates his fame as a poet. He continued to dream and to love, and to gaze at Beatrice from a distance and to write poems in her praise, yet without naming her, lest he should offend her modesty or compromise her honor.

In a canzone he describes a dream in which he beheld the lifeless form of Beatrice in sorrowful procession carried to the grave, while angels in a white cloud took up her spirit to God.

Soon after this dream Beatrice died, in her twenty-fifth year, June 9th, 1290.

But Beatrice rose again in his imagination under a higher character, as the symbol of divine wisdom, and accompanied him as guide and interpreter in the *Divina Commedia* through the regions of the Blessed in Paradise up to the dazzling vision of the Triune God. Earthly love was thus transformed into heavenly love and wisdom.

Beatrice is the golden thread which runs through the *Divina Commedia.* She is, so to say, the heroine of the poem. She appeared as a "fair, saintly lady," with eyes shining brighter

---

[1] *The New Life*, translated by C. E. Norton, pp. 51, 52.

than the stars, to the poet Virgil of imperial Rome, and commanded him, with the angelic voice of love, to extricate Dante from the dangers of the dark forest and to lead him through Hell and Purgatory to the gates of Paradise. She meets him on the top of the mountain of Purgatory, "smiling and happy." She rebukes him for his sins, and then leads him to Paradise. He sees her—

> "Gazing at the sun;
> Never did eagle fasten so upon it."

> "And she such lightnings flashed into mine eyes,
> That at the first my sight endured it not."

> "Beatrice gazed upon me with her eyes
> Full of the sparks of love, and so divine,
> That, overcome my power, I turned my back
> And almost lost myself with eyes cast down."

> "And Beatrice, she who is seen to pass
> From good to better, and so suddenly
> That not by time her action is expressed,
> How lucent in herself must she have been!"

> "While the eternal pleasure, which direct
> Rayed upon Beatrice, from her fair face
> Contented me with its reflected aspect,
> Conquering me with the radiance of a smile,
> She said to me, 'Turn thee about and listen;
> Not in mine eyes alone is Paradise.'"

> "And so translucent I beheld her eyes,
> So full of pleasure, that her countenance
> Surpassed its other and its latest wont."—

> "O Beatrice, thou gentle guide and dear!"

> "And around Beatrice three several times
> It whirled itself with so divine a song,
> My fantasy repeats it not to me."—

> "So from before mine eyes did Beatrice
> Chase every mote with radiance of her own,
> That cast its light a thousand miles and more."—

> "She smiled so joyously
> That God seemed in her countenance to rejoice."—[1]

As Dante approached the Empyrean or the highest heaven, he again turns to Beatrice with intense admiration and love.

> "If what has hitherto been said of her
>   Were all concluded in a single praise,
>   Scant would it be to serve the present turn.
>
> Not only does the beauty I beheld
>   Transcend ourselves, but truly I believe
>   Its Maker only may enjoy it all.
>
> Vanquished do I confess me by this passage
>   More than by problem of his theme was ever
>   O'ercome the comic or the tragic poet.
>
> For as the sun the sight that trembles most,
>   Even so the memory of that sweet smile
>   My mind depriveth of its very self.
>
> From the first day that I beheld her face
>   In this life, to the moment of this look,
>   The sequence of my song has ne'er been severed;
>
> But now perforce this sequence must desist
>   From following her beauty with my verse,
>   As every artist at his uttermost.
>
> Such as I leave her to a greater fame
>   Than any of my trumpet, which is bringing
>   Its arduous matter to a final close,
>
> With voice and gesture of a perfect leader
>   She recommenced: 'We from the greatest body
>   Have issued to the heaven that is pure light;

---

[1] See references to Beatrice in *Inferno*, II. 53 sqq., 70, 103; X. 131; XII. 88; XV. 90. *Purgatorio*, I. 53; VI. 47; XV. 77; XVIII. 48, 73; XXIII. 128; XXVII. 36, 53, 136; XXX. 73; XXXI. 80, 107, 114, 133; XXXII. 36, 85, 106. *Paradiso*, I. 46; III. 127; IV. 139-142; X. 37-40; XVIII. 16-21; 55-58; XXIII. 34; XXIV. 22-25; XXVI. 76-79; XXVII. 104, 105; XXIX. 8; XXX. 14, 128; XXXI. 59, 66, 76; XXXII. 9; XXXIII. 38. The passages quoted are from Longfellow's translation.

> Light intellectual replete with love,
>   Love of true good replete with ecstasy,
>   Ecstasy that transcendeth every sweetness.
>
> Here shalt thou see the one host and the other
>   Of Paradise, and one in the same aspects
>   Which at the final judgment thou shalt see.'"[1]

So far all is pure and lovely. Dante and Beatrice are an ideal and inspiring pair of beauty, and exert a perennial charm upon the imagination. They represent a love that is kindled by an earthly and by a heavenly flame, and blends in harmony the natural and spiritual. As Uhland sings:—

> "Ja! mit Fug wird dieser Sänger
>   Als der göttliche verehret,
>   Dante, welchem irdsche Liebe
>   Sich zu himmlischer verkläret."

The relation of Dante to Beatrice is altogether unique. It is the last and highest stage of chivalric sentiment, but transformed into a mystic devotion to an ideal. Beatrice was a woman of flesh and blood, and at the same time the impersonation of Divine wisdom; the lovely daughter of Folco Portinari and the symbol of theology, that queen of sciences which comes from God and leads to God. She was both real and ideal, terrestrial and celestial, human and divine. She was to him all that is pure, lovely and attractive in innocent womanhood, and all that is sacred and sublime in Divine wisdom. She was while on earth the guardian angel of his youth, and after her death the guardian angel of his lonely exile. She was to him the golden ladder from earth to heaven, the bridge from Paradise Lost to Paradise

---

[1] *Parad.* XXX. 16-45, Longfellow's translation. If Beatrice represents true theology, or the knowledge of God, then God only can fully know and fully enjoy it, ver. 21. The artist fails in his highest aim, which is the perfect revelation of his ideal, ver. 32. The heaven of pure light, ver. 39, is the tenth and last heaven, above all space. Dante says (*Convito*, II. 15): "The Empyrean Heaven, by its peace, resembles the Divine Science, which is full of all peace; and which suffers no strife of opinions or sophistical arguments, because of the exceeding certitude of its subject, which is God." In ver. 45 we must distinguish the host of angels who have the same aspect after the last judgment as before, and the host of saints who will wear "the twofold garment," the spiritual body and the glorified earthly body (Canto XXV. 92).

Regained. She symbolizes that "love which moves the sun and the stars," that "eternal womanly," which in its deepest Christian sense is the ever watchful love of God irresistibly drawing us onward and upward.

> "Mortal that perishes
> Types the ideal;
> All that faith cherishes
> Thus becomes real;
> Wrought superhumanly
> Here it is done;
> The ever-womanly
> Draweth us on."[1]

The double character of Beatrice agrees with the double sense, the literal and spiritual, which Dante gives to his poem. He accepted the exegetical canon of mediæval theology which distinguished in the Bible four senses—the literal, the allegorical, the moral, and the anagogic (corresponding to history, and to the three cardinal virtues, faith, love and hope).

There are some distinguished Dante scholars who deny the historic character of Beatrice and regard her as a pure symbol, as a creature of the poet's imagination.[2] But this is inconsistent with a natural interpretation of the *Vita Nuova*, and of the sonnets to Beatrice which are addressed to a living being. Dante might in his ninth year have fallen in love with a pretty girl, but not with an abstract symbol of which he knew nothing.

---

[1] The mystic conclusion of the Second Part of Goethe's *Faust:*—

> "Alles Vergängliche
> Ist nur ein Gleichniss;
> Das Unzulängliche
> Hier wird's Ereigniss;
> Das Unbeschreibliche
> Hier ist's gethan;
> Das Ewig-Weibliche
> Zieht uns hinan."

[2] Canon Biscioni (1723) understood Beatrice to mean simply wisdom or theology; Rossetti, the imperial monarchy; Prof. Bartoli, woman in her ideal character. According to other Italian commentators, she is *la teologia; la grazia cooperante; la grazia sdeificante; la scienza divina*. Katharine Hillard, in the introduction to her translation of *The Banquet* (London, 1889, pp. XXXIX, sqq.), favors the purely allegorical conception of Beatrice and the Donna gentile. She discredits "the untrustworthy romancer, Boccaccio." Gietmann (*Beatrice*, 1889) makes Beatrice the symbol of the ideal church.

This was an after-thought of later years, when she was in heaven. Her death and his deep grief over it have no meaning if she was a mere allegory.[1]

There is one spot on this bright picture. Judging from the standpoint of Christian ethics, we should think that such an ideal relationship must end either in legitimate marriage, or in perpetual virginity. But neither was the case. Beatrice did not return the love of Dante, except by a smile from a distance. She married—if we are to credit Boccaccio—a rich banker of Florence, Simone de' Bardi, and became the mother of several children. Dante, after two years of grief for Beatrice, married Gemma Donati, who bore him four or seven children. He never mentions the husband of Beatrice, nor his own wife, and remained true to the love of his youth.

These facts mar both the poetry and the reality of that relationship. But the chivalry of the Middle Ages and the custom of Italy allowed a division of affection which is inconsistent with modern ideas. The troubadours ignored their own wives, and idolized other women, married or single.

THE DONNA PIETOSA.

Dante mourned the death of Beatrice, "the first delight of his soul," till he had no more tears to give ease to his sorrow.

> "The eyes that weep for pity of my heart
> Have wept so long that their grief languisheth,
> And they have no more tears to weep withal."

He gave utterance to his grief in sonnets to

> "That lady of all gentle memories."

He thus celebrated the first anniversary of her departure (June 9th, 1291).

About that time he saw the "gentle and compassionate lady,"

---

[1] Giov. da Serravalle, who wrote a Latin translation and commentary (as quoted by Dean Plumptre, I, p. LII, from the MS. in the British Museum), sums up the case with the words: "*Dante dilexit hanc puellam Beatricem historice et literaliter, sed allegorice, sacram Theologiam.*" But theology is too narrow a conception; Beatrice in her ideal nature combines Divine revelation, Divine wisdom, and Divine love.

whom he does not name, but who captivated his eyes and his heart. She has given great trouble to his biographers and commentators, who are divided between a literal and an allegorical conception, or combine the two.

"I lifted up mine eyes"—so he tells the story towards the end of the *Vita Nuova*—"and perceived a gentle (noble) lady, young and very beautiful, who was gazing upon me from a window with a gaze full of pity, so that the very sum of pity appeared gathered around her.[1] And seeing, that unhappy persons, when they beget compassion in others, are then most moved into weeping, as though they also felt pity for themselves, it came to pass that mine eyes began to be inclined unto tears. Wherefore, becoming fearful lest I should make manifest mine abject condition, I rose up, and went where I could not be seen by that lady; saying afterward within myself: 'Certainly with her also must abide most noble love.' And with that I resolved upon writing a sonnet, wherein, speaking unto her, I should say all that I have just said."

Then follows this sonnet, after which he continues: "It happened after this, that whensoever I was seen by this lady, she became pale and of a piteous countenance, as though it had been with love; whereby *she reminded me many times of my own most noble lady, who was wont to be of a like paleness*. And I know that often, when I could not weep nor in any way give ease to mine anguish, I went to look upon this lady, who seemed to bring the tears into mine eyes by the mere sight of her. . . . At length, by the constant sight of this lady, mine eyes began to be gladdened overmuch with her company; through which thing many times I had much unrest and rebuked myself as a base person; also many times I cursed the unsteadfastness of mine eyes. . . . The sight of this lady brought me into so unwonted a condition that I often thought of her as of one too dear unto me; and I began to consider her thus: 'This lady is young, beautiful, gentle, and wise: perchance it was Love himself who

---

[1] "*Vidi una gentil donna, giovane e bella molto, la quale da una finestra mi riguardava molto pietosamente quant' alla vista; sicchè tutta la pietade pareva in lei accolta.*" Dante uses *gentile* in the old English sense of *noble*, and *gentilezza* and *nobiltà* as synonymous.

set her in my path, that so my life might find peace.' And there were times when I thought yet more fondly, until my heart consented unto this reasoning."

He then describes in a sonnet the battle between reason and appetite, and a vision of "the most gracious Beatrice," which led him painfully to repent of his evil desire. From this time on his thoughts turned again to Beatrice with his whole humbled and ashamed heart. He concludes the *Vita Nuova* with a wonderful vision, which determined him "to say nothing further of this most blessed lady until such time when he could discourse more worthily of her who now gazes continually on the countenance of God, blessed for ever. *Laus Deo.*"

In the *Banquet*, which was written several years later, he refers to the same gentle lady, and remarks that she appeared to him a year after the death of Beatrice, who "lives in heaven with the angels, and on earth with his soul," and that she was accompanied by *Amor* and took possession of his mind.[1]

This is a clear hint at the sensual character of his new love.

In the same *Banquet* he tells us that after the death of Beatrice he read for his comfort the famous book of Boëthius on the *Consolation of Philosophy*, and Cicero's treatise on *Friendship*, and speaks of the philosophy of these authors as "a gentle lady." And he describes her as "the daughter of God, the queen of all, the most noble and most beautiful philosophy."[2]

Connecting these passages, it is very evident that the gentle and piteous lady has a double character, like Beatrice, but is in some respects her counterpart. Dante himself says at the close of the first sonnet addressed to the compassionate lady:—

> "Lo! with this lady dwells the counterpart
> Of the same Love who holds me weeping now."

The fair lady of the window was an actual being, a Florentine

---

[1] *Convito*, Trattato Secondo, cap. 2 (ed. Fraticelli, p. 111): "*quella gentil donna, di cui feci menzione nella fine della 'Vita Nuova,' apparve primamente accompagnata d'Amore agli occhi miei, e prese alcuno luogo nella mia mente.*" This reference sets aside the supposition of two distinct ladies.

[2] ll. 13: "*E immaginava lei fatta come una donna gentile: e non la potea immaginare in atto alcuno, se non misericordioso . . . Questa donna fu figlia d' Iddio, regina di tutto, nobilissima e bellissima filosofia.*"

beauty of flesh and blood, and at the same time a symbol of philosophy as represented by Cicero and Boëthius. She symbolizes sensual love and worldly wisdom; while Beatrice symbolizes ideal love and heavenly wisdom. We have again here a combination of the literal or historical with the spiritual or allegorical sense which runs through Dante's whole poem and the events of his life.

We reject therefore the notion that the Donna Pietosa was merely an abstract symbol of philosophy[1], or skepticism[2], or something higher.[3] Nor can we identify her with Gemma Donati;[4] for how could he reproach himself for loving his legitimate wife and the mother of his children? She must have been a different lady who captivated him between the death of Beatrice and his marriage. She was probably that "little girl" (*pargoletta*), or other transient vanity (*altra vanità con sì breve uso*), for which he was reproved by Beatrice.[5]

It is useless to deny that Dante went astray for a period from the path of purity and the love of Beatrice. Boccaccio, his first biographer and commentator, who lived in Florence, reports that

---

[1] George B. Carpenter, the most recent investigator of this subject, comes to the conclusion that she is simply "a symbol of Dante's love for and study of philosophy, which began in September, 1291, and came to a sudden close in 1298." See his *Episode of the Donna Pietosa*, in the "Eighth Annual Report of the Dante Society," Cambridge, Mass., 1889, p. 75. But Dante's study of philosophy did not come to a close in 1298; it runs through the whole *Divina Commedia*.

[2] So Scartazzini, who, however, distinguishes two "gentle ladies."

[3] Some Italian theological commentators have identified her with *la grazia preveniente*, *la pietosa orazione*, *la clemenza divina*, and even with *Maria Virgine!*

[4] So Rossetti in *Dante and his Circle*, p. 101, note.

[5] *Purg.* XXXI, 58-60:—
"Thou oughtest not to have stooped thy pinions downward
 To wait for further blows, or little girl,
 Or other vanity of such brief use."

"There is," says Longfellow (II., 365), "a good deal of gossiping among commentators about this little girl or *pargoletta*." He takes it as a collective term (with Ottimo), and includes in it the lady of Bologna, of whom Dante sings in one of his sonnets:
"And I may say
 That in an evil hour I saw Bologna,
 And that fair lady whom I looked upon."

he was much given to sensuality.¹ This testimony is confirmed by Dante's own son, Jacopo², and by a sonnet of his friend Guido Cavalcanti, who reproaches him with falling from his "many virtues" into an "abject life."³ But the strongest proof we have in the *Divina Commedia*, which is autobiographic and implies his own need of purification and Divine pardon. He puts into the mouth of Beatrice, when she meets him on the mountain of *Purgatory*, the following severe reproof:—

> "Some time did I sustain him with my look;
> Revealing unto him my youthful eyes,
> I led him with me turned in the right way.
> As soon as ever of my second age
> I was upon the threshold and changed life,
> Himself from me he took and gave to others.
> When from the flesh to spirit I ascended,
> And beauty and virtue were in me increased,
> I was to him less dear and less delightful;
> And into ways untrue he turned his steps,
> Pursuing the false images of good,
> That never any promises fulfil;
> Nor prayer for inspiration me availed,
> By means of which in dreams and otherwise
> I called him back, so little did he heed them.
> So low he fell, that all appliances
> For his salvation were already short,
> Save showing him the people of perdition.
> For this I visited the gates of death,
> And unto him, who so far up hath led him,
> My intercessions were with weeping borne.
> God's lofty fiat would be violated,
> If Lethe should be passed, and if such viands
> Should tasted be, withouten any scot
> Of penitence, that gushes forth in tears."⁴

---

¹ "*molto dedito alla lussuria.*"

² In an unpublished commentary on the *Inferno* in the National Library of Paris, as quoted by Ozanam, in *Les Poëtes Franciscains*, p. 356 sq., third edition, Jacopo says that when Dante began the *Commedia* he was "*peccatore e vizioso, e era quasi in una selva di vizi e d'ignoranza,*" and a man who lived carnally (*carnalmente vivo*), but that after his ascent to the mountain of true knowledge and true love he left "*questa calle e vita di miseria.*"

³ The sonnet is translated in Rossetti's *Early Italian Poets*, p. 358, and in Longfellow's *Dante*, II., 364.

⁴ *Purg.*, XXX., 121–145. Longfellow's translation. Compare Canto XXXI., 37–63, where Beatrice continues her censure of Dante.

"Pricked by the thorn of penitence," and "stung at the heart by self-conviction,"[1] Dante makes his confession, falls to the ground, and is drawn neck-deep by Matilda through the river Lethe to be cleansed. On the other shore he is presented first to the four nymphs, who symbolize the four natural virtues; these in turn lead him to the Gryphon, a symbol of the Divine-human Saviour, where Beatrice is standing; and three virgins, who represent the evangelical virtues of faith, hope and love, intercede for him with Beatrice that she would display to him her second beauty.[2]

Most of the Dante scholars refer these reproaches and confessions to practical transgressions.[3]

Dante's aberrations were probably confined to the transition period from Beatrice's death and the early part of his political life to his exile, and are not inconsistent with the testimonies in favor of his many virtues.[4]

The self-accusations and repentance of Dante, like the confessions of St. Augustin, impart a personal interest to his *Commedia*, bring him nearer to our sympathy and lessen his guilt.[5]

---

[1] *Purg.*, XXXI., 35, 38 *sqq.* [2] *Ibid.*, XXXI., 130 *sqq.*

[3] Cary, Longfellow, Lowell, Plumptre, Ozanam, D'Ancona, Carducci, Rossetti, Philalethes, Witte, Wegele, Döllinger, Scheffer-Boichorst, and others. Witte takes a comprehensive view and combines philosophical, political and erotic aberrations. "*Es wäre ein Irrthum*," he says (*D. A. Göttl. Kom.*, p. 20), "*wenn man die Entfremdung von dem Andenken an Beatrice, deren Dante sich selber anklagt, ausschliesslich in philosophisch-theoretischen Untersuchungen finden wollte. Gewiss haben wir dabei zugleich an ein weltliches Treiben von mancherlei Art (Fegefeuer, XXIII., 115), an leidenschaftliche Betheiligung bei den Parteikämpfen und mehr dergleichen zu denken; auch ist kein Grund vorhanden, neuentkeimende Neigungen zu anderen Frauen (Fegefeuer, XXXI., 58) auszuschliessen.*" Compare the notes of Longfellow on *Purgat.* XXX.

[4] Melchiore Stefano Coppi says that Dante led a moral life (*moralmente visse*), and Sebastiano Engubinus, that he excelled by gifts of nature and every virtue (*inter humana ingenia naturæ dotibus coruscantem et omnium morum habitibus rutilantem*).

[5] He alludes to St. Augustin in the *Convito* I. 2: "The other case [in which speaking of oneself is allowable] is when the greatest good may come to others by the teaching conveyed; and this reason moved Augustin in his *Confessions* to speak of himself; since in the course of his life, which was from bad to good, and from good to better, and from better to best, he set forth an example and instruction, to which we could have no such true testimony." St. Augustin is mentioned in *Par.* X., 120, and XXXII., 35.

> "O noble conscience and without a stain,
> How sharp a sting is trivial fault to thee." [1]

DANTE'S EDUCATION.

Dante received a good education, and was a profound student. He passed through the usual course of the *Trivium* and *Quadrivium*. He studied grammar, rhetoric, music, chronology, astronomy (or astrology rather), medicine, and the old Roman classics, especially Virgil and Cicero. He learned a few Greek and Hebrew words, but depended for his knowledge of the Bible, with nearly all the Christian scholars of the Middle Ages, on the Vulgate of Jerome. He mastered the philosophy of Aristotle (in Latin translations), and the theology of Thomas Aquinas. He had an encyclopædic knowledge of the learning of his age, and worked it up into an independent organic view of the universe. The best proof he gives in his *Convito*. But his knowledge of history was very limited and inaccurate. He believed with his whole age in the false donation of Constantine, and made no distinction between facts, legends and myths.

He attended the schools of his native city, which was the centre of intellectual life in Italy, and probably also the Universities of Bologna, Padua, and Paris, although the date is uncertain. His visit to Oxford is more than doubtful.

His principal teacher in Florence was Brunetto Latini (d. 1294), to whom he addressed a sonnet, accompanied by a copy of the *Vita Nuova*.[2] He is described by Villani (in his *Cronica*) as a worthy citizen, a great philosopher and perfect master of rhetoric both in speaking and writing, also as the first master in refining the Florentines, and teaching them to speak correctly and to govern the Republic on political principles. He wrote several books, among them a poem in a jingling metre, the *Tesoretto*, which describes a vision, with the customary allegorical personages of the Virtues and Vices. He is supposed by some to have suggested to Dante the first idea of the *Commedia*.

---

[1] *Purgat.*, III., 8, 9 (Witte's text):—
> "O dignitosa coscienza e netta,
> Come t'è picciol fallo amaro morso!"

[2] Translated by Rossetti, in *Dante and his Circle*, p. 110, beginning
> "Master Brunetto, this my little maid."

But—strange to say—Dante placed him in Hell for a sin against nature, and forever branded him with the mark of infamy.[1] We may admire the stern impartiality of justice, but it would have been far better if he had covered the name of his teacher and friend with the charity of silence.

Dante passed through a period of skepticism, which tempted independent thinkers even in those ages of faith. He substituted, as he informs us in the *Convito*, philosophy for faith, classical literature for the Bible and the Fathers, Athens for Jerusalem. The study of natural science and of medicine emancipates from superstition, but often tends towards materialism and pantheism; hence the proverb which originated in the period of the *Renaissance*, if not earlier: "Where are three physicians, there are two atheists."[2]

But Dante, like all truly profound intellects, returned to faith, and verified Bacon's maxim, that philosophy superficially tasted leads away from God, thoroughly studied, leads back to God.[3] He subordinated philosophy to theology, regarding it as the handmaid of religion, and retained a profound regard for Aristotle and Virgil.

HIS MARRIAGE.

In 1292, two years after the death of Beatrice, in the 27th year of his life, according to others in 1294, he married Gemma Donati, who bore him at least four children (some reports say six, others seven). Two sons, Pietro and Jacopo, and two daughters, Imperia and Beatrice, survived him. Beatrice became a Franciscan nun at Ravenna, and received some aid from the city of Florence through Boccacio.

Dante never mentions his wife, nor did he see her after his exile. This silence has given rise to the suspicion, supported by Boccaccio, that she was a Xanthippe, or at all events that he was unfortunate in his domestic relations, like Socrates, Milton, Goethe, Byron, Dickens, Carlyle, and other men of genius, who are apt to move in an ideal world above the prosy realities and

---

[1] *Inferno* XV., 30 sqq.; 101 sqq.

[2] "*Ubi tres medici, duo athei.*"

[3] "*Philosophia, obiter libata, abducit a Deo, penitus hausta, reducit ad eundem.*"

homely duties of ordinary life. It is quite likely that she could not appreciate him, or she would have followed him into exile. But in this case, silence on his part was kinder than speech, and his poverty would go far to explain, if not to excuse, the permanent separation from his family, which it was his duty to support.

A highly gifted German lady, who translated the *Divina Commedia* within the brief space of sixteen months,[1] has taken up the cause of Dante's wife in a remarkable poem, of which I give the first and last stanzas :—

> " On every tongue is Beatrice's name :
> Of thee, much sorrowing one, no song doth tell ;
> The pang of parting like a keen dart came,
> And pierced thee with a wound invisible :
> Art brings her incense to the fair,
> Virtue must wait her crown in heaven to wear.
>
> . . . .
>
> Yes, thou brave woman, mother of his sons,
> 'Twas thine to know the weight of daily care ;
> 'Twas thine to understand those piteous tones,
> Thine much to suffer, all in silence bear ;
> How great thy grief, thy woes how manifold,
> God only knows—of them no song hath told."

DANTE IN PUBLIC LIFE.

The public life of Dante was a disastrous failure. He plunged himself into the whirlpool of party politics. Poetry and politics rarely agree ; the one or the other must suffer by the contact. The one is soaring to the skies, the other cleaves to the earth. Dante was a man of much uncommon sense, but of little common sense which, in practical life, is far more important than the former.

Dante joined the guild of Physicians and Apothecaries, being familiar with their arts, and his name was entered in 1295 as

---

[1] Josepha von Hoffinger, born at Vienna, 1820, died in 1866, in consequence of her over-exertions in nursing the sick and wounded during the war between Austria and Prussia. She studied theology with Döllinger. Her translation of Dante appeared as a contribution to the sixth centenary of Dante, at Vienna (Braumüller), 1865, in 3 small vols. with brief notes. See Plumptre's *Dante*, II., 492, where her poem on Dante's wife is translated.

"the poet of Florence" (*poeta Fiorentino*). It was one of the seven guilds which controlled the city. In 1299 he was sent as ambassador to the Commune of S. Gemignano to settle a dispute. This is the only embassy before that to Rome, of which we have documentary evidence; other embassies to Siena, Genoa, Perugia, Ferrara, Venice, Naples, and to foreign kings, reported by some writers (Filelfo, Balbo), are mere myths, or at least very doubtful. He was not long enough in political life to fulfill so many missions, and during the seven years from 1294 to 1301 he seems to have been in Florence.

In 1300 he was elected one of the six *Priori delle Arti*, who ruled the city for two months at a time. The Signory of Florence was composed of seven persons, namely, six Priors of professions, and one Gonfaloniere of justice. They were subject to the popular will and an assembly of nobles called the Council of the Hundred. Dante was to hold office from June 15th to August 15th. His colleagues were insignificant persons, scarcely known by name. From that appointment to the priorship, he dated the beginning of his misfortunes.

The little aristocratic Republic of Florence was involved in the great contest between the Guelfs (*Guelfi, Welfen,* from Wolf, a family name) and the Ghibellines (*Ghibellini, Ghibellinen,* from Waiblingen, the patrimonial castle of Conrad of Hohenstaufen, in Swabia), or between the Papists and the Imperialists. This contest may be dated from the time of Pope Gregory VII. and Emperor Henry IV. and the humiliating scene at Canossa, and continued for three or four hundred years. It caused 7200 revolutions and more than 700 wholesale murders in Italy.[1] Every city of Italy was torn by factions headed by petty tyrants. Every Italian was born to an inheritance of hatred and revenge, and could not avoid sharing in the fight. The war between the Guelfs and Ghibellines, under its general and most comprehensive aspect, was a war for the supremacy of Church or State in temporal matters. Boniface VIII., who ascended the chair of St. Peter in 1294, and celebrated the first papal Jubilee in 1300,

---

[1] This calculation has been made by Ferrari, *Histoire des révolutions d' Italie, ou Guelfes et Ghibelins,* Paris, 1858, 4 vols. (quoted by Döllinger, *Akad. Vorträge,* I., 117.)

claimed the two swords of the Apostles (Luke xxii. 38), the spiritual and the temporal; the spiritual sword to be wielded by the pope directly, the temporal to be wielded by the emperor, but under the pope's authority. The Imperialists maintained the divine origin and independent authority of the State in all things temporal. They anticipated the modern theory which has come to prevail since the sixteenth century.

Besides this, there was in Florence a local family quarrel between the party of Corso Donati, called the Neri or Blacks, and the party of Bianco, called the Bianchi (also Cerchi) or Whites. Florence was predominantly Guelf. Dante himself belonged originally to that party, and fought for it in 1289, at the battle of Campaldino, and at the siege of the castle of Caprona; but when the Bianchi families united with the Ghibellines, he joined them, with the reservation of a certain independence.[1] Pope Boniface VIII. interfered with the government of Florence, and threw all his influence in favor of the Neri and Guelfs.

Dante and his five obscure colleagues acted with strict impartiality, and banished the leaders of both factions. This is the only memorable act in his political career, and it proved fatal to him. Both parties plotted against him. The banished Corso Donati, the *gran barone* of Florence, was determined on revenge, and appealed to Pope Boniface, who eagerly accepted the opportunity of dividing and governing the cities of Tuscany.

Dante was sent with three others to Rome by the Priors who held office from Aug. 15th to Oct. 15th, 1301. He was to oppose the coming of Charles of Valois, brother of King Philip of France, or to induce him to wait for the consent of the ruling party. On that occasion he uttered the proud word of contempt: "If I go, who is to remain; if I remain, who is to go?" This saying was treasured up and promoted his ruin.

He went to Rome without dreaming that he was never to return to his native city, never to see his family, never to sit again on the *Sasso di Dante* in the Piazza of the magnificent

---

[1] Boccaccio represents him as a most violent Ghibelline, from his exile until his death (see Longfellow, I., 222); but this is inconsistent with his friendship for Guido da Polenta, who was a Guelf, and with his impartial distribution of members of both parties to the places of punishment or reward.

cathedral of Santa Maria del Fiore, whose foundations had been laid a few years before (1298).

THE BANISHMENT. DANTE AND BONIFACE VIII.

On Nov. 1st, 1301, Charles of Valois entered Florence by authority of the Pope, under the title of "Pacifier of Tuscany." With his aid the Guelf or Donati party triumphed.

Dante and three of his colleagues in office as Priori were banished from Tuscany for two years, and declared incapable of holding any public office, on the charge of extortion, embezzlement, and corruption, and of having resisted the Pope and expelled the Neri, the faithful servants of the Pope. Having been cited for trial and not appearing, they were also fined 5000 florins each for contumacy. The sentence is dated January 27th, 1302. It was repeated March 10th, with the threat that they would be burnt alive if they ever returned to the territory of Florence. Their property was confiscated.

The charges were never proved, and were no doubt invented or exaggerated by the party fanaticism of his enemies. Dante treated the charges with the contempt of silence. His innocence is asserted by all his biographers, including Giovanni Villani, who was a Guelf.

Dante spent several months in Rome. The Pope summoned him and his fellow-ambassadors, and scolded them for their obstinacy, but promised them his benediction on condition of obedience to his authority. This is all we know about this embassy, and even this is very uncertain.[1]

Dante assigned to Boniface, for his grasping ambition, avarice and simony, a place in hell.[2] He calls him "the

---

[1] Quite recently the fact of Dante's embassy to Boniface VIII., which rests on the authority of Boccaccio and Bruni, has been denied by Scartazzini (*Handbook to Dante*, transl. by Th. Davidson, p. 82), on the ground chiefly of the silence of Giovanni Villani, the contemporary chronicler of Florence. If Dante was in Florence at the time of the catastrophe, he must have fled with his political partisans after the first sentence of banishment.

[2] *Inferno*, XIX., 53 sqq. The *Divina Commedia* was commenced in 1300, but not completed before 1321; Boniface died 1303.

prince of modern Pharisees,"[1] and a usurper, who turned the cemetery of St. Peter (that is, the Vatican hill) into a common sewer.[2]

This was the pope who asserted, but could no longer maintain, the most extravagant claims of divine authority over the church and the world, and marks the beginning of the decline of the papacy from such a giddy height. He frightened Celestine into a resignation, and was inaugurated with extraordinary pomp, riding on a white horse instead of an humble ass, two kings holding the bridle, but amidst a furious hurricane which extinguished every lamp and torch in St. Peter's. A similar storm interrupted the crowning ceremony of the Vatican Council in 1870, when Pope Pius IX. read the decree of his own infallibility by candle-light in midnight darkness.

Yet Dante did not spare his righteous wrath against Philip the Fair of France, that "modern Pilate," who with sacrilegious violence seized the aged Boniface at Anagni,

"And Christ in his own Vicar captive made."[3]

DANTE IN EXILE.

Dante learned the sentence of his banishment at Siena, on his return from Rome, probably in April, 1302. The other exiles joined him and engaged with the Ghibellines in vain plots for a recovery of power. "Florence," he said, "we must recover: Florence for Italy, and Italy for the world." They established a provisional government, raised an army and made

---

[1] *Inferno*, XXVII., 85.

[2] *Parad.*, XXVII., 22–27, where St. Peter says:

"He who usurps upon the earth my place,
My place, my place, which vacant has become
Before the presence of the Son of God,
Has of my cemetery made a sewer
Of blood and stench, whereby the Perverse One,
Who fell from hence, below there is appeased!"

["*Fatto ha del cimiterio mio cloaca
Del sangue e della puzza; onde il perverso,
Che cadde di quassù, laggiù (i. e., nell' inferno) si placa.*"]

[3] *Purg.*, XX., 87 sqq.

two attacks upon Florence, but were defeated, and the prisoners were slaughtered without mercy.

Dante became discouraged, and finally withdrew from all parties. He always was a patriot rather than a partisan, and tried to reconcile parties for the good of the country. He esteemed patriotism as the highest natural virtue, and abhorred treason as the most hideous crime, worthy of a place with Judas in the lowest depth of hell.

The confiscation of his property left him and his family destitute; but his wife, being of the wealthy Donati family, may have recovered a portion under the plea of a settlement for dowry.

From the time of his banishment to his death, a period of nearly twenty years, Dante wandered through Upper and Middle Italy from city to city, from court to court, from convent to convent, a poor, homeless and homesick exile, with the sentence of death by fire hanging over him; everywhere meeting friends and admirers among Ghibellines and those who could appreciate poetry and virtue, but also enemies and detractors, finding rest and happiness nowhere except in the study of truth and the contemplation of eternity. "Florence," he says in his *Convito* (I. 3), "the beautiful city, the famous daughter of Rome, has rejected me from her sweet bosom, where I was born, where I grew to middle life, and where, if it may please her, I wish from my heart to end my life and then to rest my weary soul. Through almost all parts where our language is spoken, I have gone, a wanderer, well-nigh a beggar, showing against my will the wounds of fortune. Truly I have been a vessel without sail or rudder, driven to divers ports and shores by that hot blast, the breath of dolorous poverty." It must have been hard, very hard indeed, for such a proud spirit to eat the salty bread of others, and to go up and down the stairs of strangers.[1] He fully experienced the bitter truth of the words of Ecclesias-

---

[1] *Parad.*, XVII., 58–60:

> "Thou shalt have proof how savoreth of salt (*sa di sale*)
> The bread of others, and how hard a road
> The going down and up another's stairs."

ticus: "It is a miserable thing to go from house to house; for where thou art a stranger, thou darest not open thy mouth. . . . My son, lead not a beggar's life, for better is it to die than to beg."

When stopping at the convent of Santa Croce del Corvo and asked by the prior what he wanted, he replied: "Peace."[1]

And yet it was during this sad period of exile that he wrote his *Divina Commedia*. It brought him no earthly reward (for authorship was unprofitable in the Middle Ages), but immortal fame. It was truly a child of sorrow and grief, like many of the greatest and most enduring works of man. For—

> "Poesie ist tiefes Schmerzen,
> Und es kommt das schönste Lied
> Nur aus einem Menschenherzen,
> Das ein schweres Leid durchglüht."[2]

He seems to have spent most of the years of his banishment in Bologna, Padua, and Verona, studying everywhere and gathering local and historical information for his great poem. He probably visited Paris also about the year 1309, and buried himself in theological study. Other reports place this visit before his exile. Perhaps he was there twice. The chronicler Villani simply says: "Dante was expelled and banished from Florence, and went to study at Bologna, and then to Paris, and into several parts of the world." Boccaccio's account is vague and confused.

The expedition of Emperor Henry VII., of Luxemburg, to Italy in 1310, excited in him the hope of the overthrow of the Guelfs and the realization of his theory on the Monarchy, that is, the temporal supremacy of the holy Roman Empire in independent connection with the Catholic Church. He hailed him as a "Second Moses," who was called to heal Italy, which had been without an emperor since the extinction of the house of

---

[2] Justinus Kerner, the Swabian poet and friend of Uhland and Schwab. Remember also Goethe's—

> "Wer nie sein Brot mit Thränen ass,
> Wer nie die kummervollen Nächte
> Auf seinem Bette weinend sass,
> Der kennt euch nicht, ihr himmlischen Mächte."

Hohenstaufen, and torn by feuds, civil wars and anarchy.[1] He would not recognize Rudolph of Habsburg (1273–1292), nor Albert I. ("*Alberto tedesco*", 1298–1308), as emperors, because they never came to Italy and were not crowned by the pope. He regarded Frederick II. (1220–1250) as the last emperor, but placed him in Hell among the heretics.[2] He exhorted Henry in a letter to pursue energetic measures for the restoration of peace. He addressed a letter to all the rulers of Italy, urging them to yield obedience to the new Cæsar consecrated by the successor of Peter. But the emperor could accomplish nothing. He died—it was said of poison—Aug. 24th, 1313, after a short reign of five years, near Siena and was buried in the Campo Santo of Pisa.[3]

With his death the cause of the Ghibellines and the political aspirations of Dante were well-nigh crushed.

In the year 1316 or 1317, the government of Florence, in the feeling of security, offered amnesty to political exiles, but on condition of a fine and penance in the church, thus degrading them to a level with criminals. A nephew of Dante and his friends urged him to accept, but he proudly refused pardon at the expense of honor.

---

[1] Schiller calls the interregnum, from 1254 to 1273, "*die kaiserlose, die schreckliche Zeit.*"

[2] *Inf.*, x., 118–20:
"Within here is the second Frederick,
And the Cardinal; and of the rest I speak not."
Frederick II., the most brilliant of the Hohenstaufen emperors, successively the pupil, the enemy and the victim of the papacy, was called by Pope Gregory IX. "a beast, full of the words of blasphemy," and accused of being the author of the sentence "*De Tribus Impostoribus*" (Moses, Jesus, Mohammed), which haunted the Middle Ages like a ghost. "The Cardinal" is Ottaviano degli Ubaldini, of Florence, who doubted the immortality of the soul. On the skepticism of Frederick II., see H. Reuter's *Geschichte der Aufklärung im Mittelalter* (Berlin, 1877), Vol. II., 251–304, especially 275 sqq. He thinks that the word about "the three impostors" is probably authentic, but cannot be proven.

[3] See Robert Pöhlmann, *Der Römerzug Kaiser Heinrichs VII. und die Politik der Curie, des Hauses Anjou und der Welfenliga*, Nürnberg, 1875; and Georg Irmer, *Die Romfahrt Kaiser Heinrichs VII.*, 1881. They shed light on many obscure passages in the *Purgatorio* and *Paradiso*. See Plumptre, I., p. cxxviii. sq.

"Has my innocence," he wrote to a priest, "which is manifest to all, after nearly fifteen years of banishment, deserved such a recall? Have my incessant labors and studies deserved it? Far be it from a man familiar with philosophy to submit to such indignity. Far be it from a man who is a preacher of righteousness and suffered injustice, to pay those who did him injustice, as if they were his benefactors? This is not the way to return to my native city. I will rather never enter Florence. And what then? Can I not everywhere behold the mirrors of the sun and the stars? Can I not everywhere study the sweetest truths rather than render myself inglorious, yea, most ignominious to the people and commonwealth of Florence? Nor will bread fail me."[1]

CAN GRANDE, THE VELTRO, AND THE DUX.

In the year 1317, Dante went to Can Grande, of the family della Scala (Scaligeri) of Verona, who was the leader of the Ghibelline party in Lombardy, and appointed Vicar of Henry VII. in 1311. He was much younger than the poet and survived him eight years (b. 1291, d. 1329). Many exiled Ghibellines and other unfortunate persons of distinction found refuge at his hospitable court, which displayed a barbaric magnificence similar to the court of Frederick II. in Sicily. He kept, we are told, actors, buffoons, musicians and parasites, who were more caressed by the courtiers than poets and scholars. "Various apartments in the palace were assigned to them, designated by various symbols; a Triumph for the warriors, Groves of the Muses for the poets; Mercury for the artists; Paradise for the preachers; and for all inconstant Fortune. . . . . All had their private attendants, and a table equally well served. At times Can Grande invited some of them to his own table, particularly Dante and Guido di Castel di Reggio, exiled from his country with the friends of liberty."[2]

Dante fixed his political hopes, after the death of Henry VII. (1313), upon Can Grande, and gave him an undeserved celebrity.

---

[1] An extract from *Ep.* x., 500–503 (ed. of Fraticelli).

[2] Quoted by Longfellow, III., 308. A lively picture of Can Grande's court and Dante's life there is given by Ferrari in his comedy, *Dante a Verona*.

He made him the subject of predictions in the *Commedia*, none of which were fulfilled.

He mentions him first in the introductory canto of the *Inferno* under the allegorical name of *Veltro*, which means *greyhound*, and was suggested by the name *cane*, *hound*, and the boundary of his territory, "*tra Feltro e Feltro*," *i. e.*, between Feltro in Friuli and Montefeltro in Romagna. He describes him as the coming saviour of Italy, who sets his heart not on land and money, but on wisdom, love and virtue, and who will slay the wolf of avarice, the root of many evils (1 Tim. 6: 8, 9).[1]

> "Many the animals with whom she [the she-wolf, *lupa*] weds,
> And more they shall be still, until the greyhound [*il veltro*]
> Comes, who shall make her perish in her pain.
>
> He shall not feed on either earth or pelf,
> But upon wisdom, and on love and virtue ;
> 'Twixt Feltro and Feltro shall his nation be ;
>
> Of that low Italy shall he be the saviour,
> On whose account the maid Camilla died,
> Euryalus, Turnus, Nisus, of their wounds ;
>
> Through every city he shall hunt her down,
> Until he shall have driven her back to Hell,
> There from whence envy first did let her loose."

In the *Paradiso* he praises his benefactor in similar terms.[2]

> "But ere the Gascon cheat the noble Henry,
> Some sparkles of his virtue shall appear
> In caring not for silver nor for toil.
>
> So recognized shall his magnificence
> Become hereafter, that his enemies
> Will not have power to keep mute tongues about it.
>
> On him rely, and on his benefits ;
> By him shall many people be transformed,
> Changing condition rich and mendicant."[3]

---

[1] *Inferno*, I., 100 sqq.

[2] *Parad.*, XVII., 82-90, sqq.

[3] The Gascon is Clement V., who was elected Pope in 1305. The "noble Henry" is the Emperor Henry VII., who came to Italy in 1310, when Can Grande was about 19 years of age. Clement publicly professed to be Henry's friend, but secretly he was his enemy, and is said to have instigated or connived at his death by poison.

He dedicated to him the first cantos of the *Paradiso*, and wrote him a letter which furnishes the key to the allegorical understanding of the *Commedia*.

In all probability Can Grande is also meant in that passage of the *Purgatorio*—the obscurest in the whole poem—where Beatrice predicts the coming of a mighty captain and messenger of God who would restore the Roman empire and slay the Roman harlot, (*i. e.*, the corrupt, rapacious papacy), together with her giant paramour (*i. e.*, the King of France who transferred the papacy to Avignon).[1]

"Without an heir shall not forever be
The Eagle that left his plumes upon the car,
Whence it became a monster, then a prey;

For verily I see, and hence narrate it,
The stars already near to bring the time,
From every hindrance safe, and every bar,

Within which a *Five-hundred, Ten, and Five*,
One sent from God, shall slay the thievish woman,
And that same giant who is sinning with her."[2]

The mystic number 515, in Roman numerals DXV, or with a slight transposition DVX, means not a period (as between Charlemagne and Louis the Bavarian, 799–1314), but a person, a *Dux*, a captain, a prince. Some eminent commentators refer it to Emperor Henry VII.;[3] but he was more than a *Dux*, and died (1313) before the *Purgatorio* was completed (about 1318). We must, therefore, either think of some unknown future Roman emperor,[4] or of Can Grande whom

---

[1] *Purg.*, XXXIII., 37–45.

[2] "Nel quale un cinquecento diece e cinque,
Messo da Dio, anciderà la fuia,
Con quel gigante che con lei delinque."

[3] Longfellow, Plumptre, and others who understand the *Veltro* of Can Grande.

[4] So Witte (p. 649): "*Der Dichter wird in der Zeit die vergangen war, seit er die Prophezeiung zu Anfang der Hölle geschrieben hatte, erkannt haben, dass Can Grande der Aufgabe, die er ihm damals gestellt hatte, nicht genügte, und so überweist er uns deren Erfüllung entfernteren unbestimmteren Hoffnungen. Ob Dante dabei an eine schon lebende, bestimmte Persönlichkeit gedacht habe, und an welche, ist zweifelhaft. Möglich wäre es, dass er um diese Zeit noch von dem mehr als zwanzigjährigen Sohne Heinrichs VII., dem König Johann von Böhmen, solche Erwartungen gehegt hätte.*"

Dante praised both before in the *Inferno*, and afterward in the *Paradiso*.[1] The initials of his name and title have been found in the number 515.[2]

Dante was sadly disappointed in his expectations. Henry VII. died before he could accomplish any reform. Can Grande, though a liberal patron of the poet, was a tyrant, and in no way qualified for such a high task. Dante overestimated his character. Men of genius are often lacking in knowledge of human nature, or understand it better in general than in particular. It is always dangerous to prophesy.

But if we apply Dante's hermeneutical canon of a double sense to this case, we may find in the *Veltro* and the *Dux* some future restorer and reformer for whom Can Grande was merely to pave the way.

NOTE.—The name *Veltro* and the mystic number DXV have given as much trouble to Dante scholars, as the apocalyptic number 666 (Rev. 13: 18) to biblical commentators. Scartazzini, in a special excursus (*Com. on Purgat.*, II., 802, sqq.), enumerates a list of no less than 65 separate monographs and essays on the subject. The majority understand both terms, or at least *Veltro*, of Can Grande. Other interpretations are:—

1. Uguccione della Faggiola, a brave Ghibelline captain, who, with the remaining soldiers of Henry VII. and other Ghibellines subdued Lucca, and defeated the Guelfs, in 1315, but afterwards met reverses and retired to Can della Scala. (Troya, *Del Veltro allegorico di Dante*, Firenze, 1826; and *Del Veltro allegorico dei Ghibellini*, Napoli, 1856).

2. Emperor Henry VII. Very plausible, but impossible, for chronological reasons.

[1] So Blanc, Philalethes, Wegele, Scartazzini, and many others.

[2] According to the following computation of the numerical value of letters:—

$$k = 10 \quad s = 90$$
$$g = 7 \quad d = 4$$
$$d = 4 \quad e = 5$$
$$e = 5 \quad v = 300$$
$$s = 90$$
$$\overline{}$$
$$515$$

Kan [for Can] Grande DE Scala Signore DE Verona. Scartazzini (in his *Com.* II., 779) remarks: "*Tutto s' accorda adunque a rendere assai verisimile l' opinione che il DXV sia Cangrande della Scala, opinione che, come vedremo nella digressione, fu adottata dal maggior numero dei commentatori antichi e moderni.*" The computation, however, is very artificial, more so than the reference of the apocalyptic number 666 to Nero [n] Cæsar (קסר נרון = 50, 200, 6, 50, 100, 60, 200, in all 666).

3. Emperor Louis the Bavarian, who was chosen Henry's successor in October, 1314, crowned in Milan, and in Rome by two bishops. He quarreled with Pope John XXII., declared him a heretic, was excommunicated, deposed the pope and elected an anti-pope, but could not maintain the opposition, and died in 1347 while preparing for another expedition to Italy.

4. An undefined future emperor and reformer.

5. Jesus Christ coming to judgment. DXV is interpreted *Dominus Xristus Victor*, or *Vindex*.

6. The archangel Michael.

7. A Roman Pontiff: DXV = **D**omini **X**risti **V**icarius. But Dante had a poor opinion of popes and saw none of them in heaven. Still less can he mean a particular pope of his own time, as Benedict XI, who was elected 1303 and died 1304, or Clement V. (1305-1314), or John XXII. (1316-1334), who resided in Avignon.

The most absurd interpretations are: Dante himself; Luther (*Veltro = Lutero*); Garibaldi; Victor Immanuel II.; William I. of Prussia, first Protestant Emperor of Germany!!!

DANTE IN RAVENNA.

Dante spent two or three years at the court of Can Grande. Even there he was not happy. He lost more and more the hope of the regeneration of Italy during his lifetime, and put it off to the indefinite future.[1] He felt the salt savor of the bread of poverty, and the want of appreciation among his surroundings. His patron once asked him why a buffoon won greater favor with the courtiers by his wit than he by his genius. Dante replied: "Because like loves like.[2] The friendship was seriously disturbed, though not entirely broken.

Dante repaired to the ruined city of Ravenna on the Adriatic, famous for its pine woods, basilicas and baptisteries from the post-Nicene age. It is the last outpost of Byzantine rule in the West, and to the historian and antiquarian one of the most remarkable spots in Italy.

In this city the weary pilgrim spent the rest of his life under the protection of Guido Novello da Polenta, the lord of Ravenna, who, being himself well educated, knew how to appreciate scholars. Although he was a Guelf, he treated the Ghibelline poet with all due honor.

[1] *Purg.* XXXIII., 40; *Parad.* XXVII., 42.

[2] "*Perchè ciascuno ama il suo simile.*" "*Similis simili gaudet.*" "*Gleich und gleich gesellt sich gern.*"

Here he finished the *Paradiso.* Here, it seems, his sons Pietro and Jacopo, and his daughter Beatrice joined him. Long after his death we find her, whose very name reminded him of the love of his youth and the solace of his manhood, as a nun in a Franciscan convent at Ravenna. The city of Florence sent her, through Boccaccio, some aid, which was the first sign of regret for the injustice done to her father.

DEATH AND BURIAL.

Once more Dante's rest was disturbed by a mission to Venice to settle a quarrel between that city and the lord of Ravenna. This mission, like all his political life, was a failure. The senate of Venice refused him permission to return in one of her ships, and passing in midsummer through that unhealthy region which lies between the two cities, he caught a fever which proved fatal.

He died under the roof of Guido da Polenta, after having devoutly partaken of the last sacrament, at the age of fifty-six years and four months, on September 14th, 1321, the day of the elevation of the cross. "He was no doubt" says Boccaccio, "received into the arms of his most noble Beatrice, and now enjoys with her, after the miseries of this earthly life, that bliss which has no end."

Dante lost his early love, but found it again in Paradise. His labors for Florence were rewarded with exile from his native city. But he always held fast to his principles and ideals. What his age refused him, posterity has abundantly granted, and will continue to grant, to the sublimest of poets. "The homeless exile found a home in thousands of grateful hearts." *E venne dall' esilio a questa pace.*

Dante was honorably buried in the Franciscan chapel of St. Mary with a wreath of laurel on his head and a lyre at his feet, perhaps, also, according to an uncertain tradition, in the garb of a Franciscan friar. A plain monument repeatedly restored[1] is erected over his remains, with a Latin inscription of six

---

[1] Lowell describes it as "a little shrine covered with a dome, not unlike the tomb of a Mohammedan saint," and as "the chief magnet which draws foreigners and their gold to Ravenna." I visited the shrine and the old Basilicas and the Baptistery of St. John in June, 1888.

hexameters, said to have been written by himself, and ending with the words :—

> "*Hic claudor Dantes, patriis extorris ab oris,*
> *Quem genuit parvi Florentia mater amoris.*"
>
> "Here am I, Dante, shut, exiled from the ancestral shore,
> Whom Florence, the of all least loving mother, bore." [1]

POSTHUMOUS FAME.

Florence asked in vain for the ashes of her greatest son, but she created a chair for the explanation of his *Divina Commedia*, in 1373,[2] and erected a costly monument to his memory in the church of Santa Croce, the pantheon of Italian geniuses, between those of Michael Angelo and the poet Alfieri, with the inscription :—

> "*Onorate l'altissimo poeta!*"
> "Honor the loftiest of poets." [3]

The example of Florence was followed by other cities, and before the end of the fourteenth century Dante chairs were erected in Bologna, Pisa, Piacenza, and Milan. Quite recently such a chair was established also in the University of Rome, and offered to the distinguished liberal poet Carducci, of Bologna, who, however, declined the call (1888). In Germany, England and America special Dante societies have been organized for the same purpose.

During the seventeenth and eighteenth centuries Dante was

---

[1] A close translation of J. Russell Lowell in his essay on Dante. Plumptre (I., p. CXXVII.), translates the two hexameters more freely thus :—

> "Here am I laid, I, Dante, far from home,
> Exiled from that fair city, doomed to roam,
> To whom I owed my birth, who yet did prove
> To me, her child, without a mother's love."

There is reason to doubt that Dante thus took revenge in his last word on his native city. The first inscription, according to Villani and Boccaccio, was that of his scholarly friend, Giovanni di Virgilio, who praises his merits and likewise reproaches Florence for her ingratitude. It is given by Plumptre, with a translation I., CXXVII., sq.

[2] The Dante chair was first occupied by Boccaccio, who explained the first 17 cantos of the *Inferno*, when he was interrupted by a fatal sickness (d. Dec. 21st, 1375), and then by Villani, and Filelfo.

[3] Words which Dante applies to Virgil. *Inf.* IV., 80.

neglected even in Italy, and between 1629 and 1726 no edition of his works appeared.

But in the present century, especially during the last fifty years, Italian, German, French, English and American scholars have vied with each other in editing and expounding the works and reproducing the ideas of the great poet for the benefit of the present generation. Between 1800 and 1865, the sixth centenary of his birth, no less than 238 editions of the *Divina Commedia* have been published; while the total sum of editions to date reaches about 350 or more.[1]

THE SIXTH CENTENARY OF DANTE'S BIRTH.

The veneration for Dante culminated in the celebration of the sixth centenary of his birth in Florence, Ravenna, and other Italian cities. It was at the same time a patriotic festival of united and free Italy, toward which his name and genius had richly contributed. For more than a year the *Giornale del Centenario*, devoted to Dantesque subjects, had prepared the public mind. A hundred thousand people, including representatives of poetry, literature, science and politics, gathered in Florence— then the national capital—to do honor to his memory. Three days were given up to public rejoicings, eloquent speaking, processions, tournaments, illuminations, banquets, musical and theatrical entertainments. The great feature was the unveiling of Piazzi's statue of Dante in the Piazza of Santa Croce, by Victor Emanuel II., the first king of united Italy. The multitude shouted:

"Honor to the loftiest of poets."

Five years afterward Rome was made the capital of Italy, and thus Dante's political aspirations, as far as Italy is concerned, were fulfilled.

[1] Hettinger, *Die Göttliche Kömodie*, etc. (1880), p. 55. Scartazzini (*Handbook to Dante*, p. 159) counts 15 editions from 1472-1500, 30 editions from 1501-1600, 3 editions from 1601-1700, 257 editions from 1801-1882; in all he counts 336 editions including his own (1882). Several new editions from stereotype plates have appeared since. Botta (p. 142) estimates the total number of editions at about four hundred (in 1886). Catalogues of the editions are given by Lord Vernon in his *édition de luxe*, in Ferrazi's *Manuale Dantesco*, and other bibliographical works on Dante.

CHARACTER AND HABITS OF DANTE.

The personal appearance and habits of Dante are described by Boccaccio, his first biographer, who knew his nephew, and delivered lectures on the *Divina Commedia* in 1373.

According to him, Dante was of middle height, slightly bent in later years, dignified and courteous, always decently dressed; his face long, his nose aquiline, his eyes large, his cheeks full, his lower lip somewhat protruding beyond the upper; his complexion dark, his hair and beard black, thick and crisp; his countenance always sad and thoughtful; his manner calm and polished. He was most temperate in eating and drinking, fond of music and singing, most zealous in study, of marvellous capacity of memory; much inclined to solitude, and familiar with few; grave and taciturn, but fervent and eloquent when occasion required. The author of the *Decamerone* charges him with incontinence, which, in his eyes and that of his age and nation, was an excusable weakness; but, whatever view we may take of his unfaithfulness to Beatrice, for which he was severely rebuked in Purgatory, he deeply repented of it.[1]

Dante was no saint, any more than Milton or Goethe, but profoundly religious and serious to austerity. He charges himself with pride and envy. He had a violent temper, and indulged in the language of scorn and contempt. He was deficient in the crowning graces of humility and charity. But his principles were pure, and his ideas rose to the highest peak of grandeur and sublimity. He was capable of the sweetest love and the bitterest hatred. His relation to Beatrice reveals an unfathomable depth of soul. He was a man of intense belief, and thought himself invested with a divine mission, like the Hebrew Prophets. He loved truth and righteousness, and hated falsehood and iniquity. He loved his native Florence and Italy, in spite of ill treatment. He was the most ardent patriot—the Italian of Italians—and yet a cosmopolitan. He was true to his convictions, and uttered them without fear or favor of men, and without regard to his own comfort and happiness.

[1] See above, pp. 295 sqq.

In his immortal work he wrote his own biography, his passage through the knowledge of sin and the struggle of repentance to the holiness and bliss of heaven.

PORTRAITS OF DANTE.[1]

There are two contemporaneous and equally characteristic pictures of Dante: the portrait painted by Giotto on wood and copied al fresco on the altar-wall of the chapel of the Palace of the Podestà in Florence (now the Bargello, a police-station and prison), and a plaster cast of his face taken after his death and preserved in the Museum in Florence. They substantially agree with the description of Boccaccio (except the absence of the beard), but differ as youth differs from mature age. Giotto represents the poet in the beauty and vigor of youth or early manhood with a pomegranate in his hand and a cap gracefully covering his head. Professor Charles E. Norton, of Harvard College, places "this likeness of the supreme poet by the supreme artist of mediæval Europe at the head of all the portraits of the revival of art." After centuries of neglect it was recovered in 1848 and chromo-lithographed by the Arundel Society from the tracing of the fresco, which Seymour Kirkup, an English artist, made previously to its restoration or *rifacimento*.[2] The mask represents the poet in the repose of death at the age of fifty-six years, grave, stern, melancholy, with the marks of the conflict of an iron will with misfortune. It furnished the outlines to Raphael's pictures, which have made Dante's mortal frame so familiar to the world.[3] "The face of the youth," says

---

[1] Much has been written on the portraits of Dante by Italians, in the *Giornale del Centenario di Dante* (Florence 1864-65); by Witte, Weleker, Savi and Paur, in the "Transactions of the German Dante Society" (1869, 1871, etc.); by Charles E. Norton (*On the Original Portraits of Dante*, Cambridge, Mass., 1865, reprinted in Longfellow's *Dante* I., 363 sqq.), S. F. Clarke (1884), and Dean Plumptre (vol. II., 529-532). *See* note on p. 325.

[2] The original of the tracing is in possession of Lord Vernon, the liberal patron of Dante scholarship. A facsimile in the first volume of Plumptre's *Dante* (1887), in Fraticelli's and other editions of the *Commedia*.

[3] Norton gives three photographs of the plaster cast; and Plumptre puts a copy in front of his second volume.

Norton, "is grave, as with the shadow of distant sorrow; the face of the man is solemn, as of one who had gone

"*Per tutti i cerchj del dolente regno.*"[1]

"All the portraits of Dante," says Lord Macaulay, in his essay on Milton, "are singularly characteristic. No person can look on the features, noble even to ruggedness, the dark furrows of the cheek, the haggard and woful stare of the eye, the sullen and contemptuous curl of the lip, and doubt that they belonged to a man too proud and too sensitive to be happy."

Thomas Carlyle, a poet in prose and a painter in words, calls Dante's portrait "the mournfullest face that ever was painted from reality; an altogether tragic, heart-affecting face. There is in it, as foundation of it, the softness, tenderness, gentle affection as of a child; but all this is as if congealed into sharp contradiction, into abnegation, isolation, proud, hopeless pain. A soft, ethereal soul looking out so stern, implacable, grim, trenchant, as from imprisonment of thick-ribbed ice! Withal it is a silent pain too, a silent, sorrowful one; the lip is curled in a kind of god-like disdain of the thing that is eating out his heart,—as if it were withal a mean, insignificant thing, as if he whom it had power to torture and strangle were greater than it. The face of one wholly in protest, and life-long, unsurrendering battle against the world. Affection all converted into indignation—an implacable indignation; slow, equable, silent, like that of a god! The eye too, it looks out as in a kind of surprise, a kind of inquiry, why the world was of such a sort? This is Dante: so he looks, this 'voice of ten silent centuries,' and sings us 'his mystic, unfathomable song.'"

What Giotto painted from life, Raphael, with equal genius, reproduced from the mask. In his "Disputa" on the mystical presence, he places Dante between Thomas Aquinas and Duns Scotus, the heads of the two rival schools of scholastic theology; in his "Parnassus," he places Dante between Virgil and Homer, the two master poets of classical antiquity.

[1] The famous descriptions of Dante's picture by Macaulay (1825), and Carlyle (1840), apply to the copies made from the mask rather than the picture of Giotto, which was recovered afterward, and they must be judged accordingly.

This was Dante: the poet, philosopher, theologian, prophet. He made love and poetry, learning and art subservient to faith, which lifts man from the abyss of hell to the beatific vision of saints in heaven.

THE WORKS OF DANTE.

The writings of Dante (with the exception of that on Vulgar Eloquence), are autobiographic and turn around his personal experience.

The *Vita Nuova*, the *Convito*, and the *De Monarchia* form a trilogy: the first represents youth, poetry and love; the second manhood, philosophy and learning; the third statesmanship and an ideal commonwealth.

THE NEW LIFE.

The *Vita Nuova*[1] is the charming story of his love for Beatrice, and the transfiguration of an earthly into a heavenly beauty and of human into divine wisdom. It is the autobiography of his youth, the rising and the setting of the morning star of his life. The narrative is interspersed with sonetti, ballate and canzoni. It was written in Florence, shortly after the death of Beatrice, in his 26th or 27th year (1290 or 1291), while his tears for her were still flowing.[2] It is dedicated to his friend Guido Cavalcanti, who died in 1300.[3]

THE BANQUET.

The *Convito* (*Convivio*),[4] or *Banquet* (*Feast*), so called probably

---

[1] Some explain the title literally: *The Early* or *Youthful Life*; others mystically: *The New Life*, or Palingenesia. Regeneration, caused by Beatrice.

[2] As Boccaccio says: "*duranti ancora le lagrime della sua morta Beatrice.*"

[3] Best Italian editions by Alessandro d'Ancona (2d ed., Pisa), 1884, with commentary and a discourse on Beatrice, pp. lxxxviii., and 257; by Pietro Fraticelli (in the second vol. of *Opere Minori di Dante*, Firenze, 1835, etc.); by Giambattista Giuliani (*Vita Nuova e il Canzoniere di D. A.*, Firenze, 1863, with a list of editions, pp. 155-168; and by Karl Witte (Leipzig, 1876, with an account of all earlier editions). Best English translations by Charles Eliot Norton (Prof. of Fine Arts in Harvard College, Cambridge): *The New Life of Dante Al.*, Boston, 1876 (pp. 149), and by Dante Gabriel Rossetti, in his *Dante and His Circle* (pp. 29-110, Boston ed., 1876). Comp. also Rod. Renier, *La Vita Nuova e la Fiammetta*, Turin and Rome, 1879; and Gietmann, *Beatrice*, Freiburg, i. B., 1889.   [4] Witte prefers *Convivio*.

in reminiscence of Plato's Symposion, is an encyclopædic compend of the theological, philosophical and scientific knowledge of his age for the unlearned in their own language. It is likewise composed of prose and poetry, but unfinished. It was to embrace fifteen books or *trattati* (including the introduction), and fourteen canzoni, but only four books and three canzoni were completed. It is esteemed as the first masterpiece of Italian prose, and contains passages of great eloquence and pathos. It is, however, very hard reading, and the text is exceedingly corrupt.

The *Banquet* contains, as far as it goes, the raw material of the *Comedy*. In it theology and philosophy are for the first time addressed to the laity in the vernacular language.

The *Convito* was begun perhaps as early as 1298, but enlarged during his exile, to which it alludes.[1]

ON THE EMPIRE.

The book *De Monarchia* is a political treatise in which Dante unfolds in the Latin language, for scholars, his views on government and the relation of the papacy and the empire. It contains the programme of the Ghibellines or the imperial party, but it is rather an ideal Ghibellinism which rose above the narrowness of party spirit. He proves, in three parts, first, that there must be a universal monarchy or empire; secondly, that this monarchy belongs of right and by tradition to the Roman people; and thirdly, that the monarchy depends immediately upon God, and not upon the pope.

The conflicting interests of society in his judgment require an impartial arbiter, and only a universal monarch can be an impartial arbiter, since kings of limited territories are always liable to be influenced by selfish motives and aims. A universal monarch alone can insure universal peace. The right of Rome is based upon the facts that Christ was born under the reign of Augustus and died under Tiberius. The universal rule of God is divided

---

[1] The Italian text with notes in Fraticelli's ed. of *Dante's Opere Minori* (Firenze, ed. II., 1862, pp. 399); Giuliani's ed. (1875); English translation by Elizabeth Price Sayer, London, 1887, with an introduction by Henry Morley, and another by Katharine Hillard, London, 1889, with an introduction. The chronology of the *Convito* is much disputed; the estimates vary from 1295 to 1314. Witte assigns it to the period from 1300 to 1308.

between the emperor and the pope; the emperor is supreme by divine right in temporal things, and is to guide the human race to temporal felicity in accordance with the teaching of philosophy; the pope also by divine right is supreme in spiritual or ecclesiastical things, and is to guide men to eternal life in accordance with the truth of Revelation.

This theory is in direct opposition to the ultramontane doctrine of the two swords as proclaimed in the same age by Boniface VIII., in his famous bull *Unam Sanctam* (Nov. 24, 1302), which teaches an absolute papacy with supreme control over temporal sovereigns. Dante placed this pope in hell; no wonder that after his death the book *De Monarchia* (as Boccaccio reports) was condemned and burnt as heretical, in 1329, by the papal legate, Cardinal del Pogetto, with the authority of Pope John XXII., of Avignon. He intended also to burn the bones of the poet, but was restrained by powerful friends. The Council of Trent put the book on the Index.

The political theory of Dante has never been realized, except in part and on a limited national scale. Some have compared it with the constitution of the Netherlands, others with that of the United States; but neither comparison will hold. Dante was thoroughly aristocratic, monarchical and imperial. He had no proper conception of liberty and popular rights, no idea of "a government of the people, by the people, and for the people," but he approached modern ideas by laying down the important principle, that the government is for the people, and not the people for the government.[1] He strove for the political unity of Italy through the legitimate Roman empire; that empire is gone, but a new German empire arose in 1870, and stands in friendly alliance with united Italy. If Dante lived in the present age, he would no doubt sympathize with the United Kingdom of Italy and its independent relation to the papacy. He would accept Cavour's programme of a Free Church in a Free State, but probably look forward to a universal empire.

The book on the Monarchy, according to Boccaccio, was occasioned by the expedition of Emperor Henry VII. to Rome, in 1310, as a programme for the restoration of the empire. But

---

[1] "*Non enim gens propter regem, sed e converso rex propter gentem.*"

Witte, a very high authority, puts the composition before 1300, as there is no allusion in it to his exile.[1]

THE CANZONIERE.

The lyric poems of Dante embrace the sonnets, ballads and canzoni scattered through his *Vita Nuova* and *Convito*, and other pieces, some of doubtful origin.

The theme of these lyrics is love to Beatrice, and devotion to natural and spiritual beauty. He infused into the chivalrous love-poetry of the troubadours a mystic afflatus, and directed it to philosophy and theology. His love wandered away for a while to the "gentle lady" of this world, but returned to Beatrice in Paradise.

In the editions of the Canzoniere are also included an Italian version of the seven Penitential Psalms in terza rima, and the Latin eclogues addressed to Giovanni del Virgilio, a teacher of Latin literature in Bologna (1318–1325). Giovanni praised Dante while at Ravenna, in a Latin ode, for his *Comedy*, but blamed him for writing it in a vulgar tongue, and invited him to come to Bologna, and to surpass his Italian *Comedy* by Latin poetry. Dante proved in his replies that he was master of Latin as well, and could resuscitate the bucolic poetry of the age of Virgil.[2]

---

[1] *Opere Minori*, ed. Fraticelli, vol. II. English translation by F. C. Church, pub., with his father's Essay on Dante. 1878. Scartazzini says (*Handbook to Dante*, p. 250): "The first edition of *De Monarchia* was issued at Bâle in 1559, by John Oporinus. Between that date and 1618 it was reprinted in Germany five times. It was first printed in Italy in 1740, at Venice, with the date Geneva. At the present day some twenty editions can be counted, the latest being that of Giuliani, with many textual emendations and a prolix commentary." Hettinger fully discusses Dante's politics, from the Roman Catholic point of view, in his *Die Göttl. Komödie des D. A.* (1880). pp. 510–554.

[2] Fraticelli (*Il Canzoniere di Dante A.*, Firenze, 1856, and later editions) includes *le rime sacre e le poesie latine*, i.e., the Penitential Psalms, the versified creed, and the eclogues. He vindicates to Dante 41 sonnets, 10 ballads, 20 odes or canzoni, 3 sextains; Giuliani, in his edition, gives the number of genuine sonnets as 37, ballads 5, odes 20, sextain 1. All the rest are doubtful or spurious. Comp. Giosuè Carducci, *Delle Rime di Dante*, in "Studi Letterari," 1874, pp. 139–237. English translation of the *canzoniere* and the *eclogues* by Plumptre, *Dante*, II., 199–344.

ON POPULAR ELOQUENCE.

De Vulgari Eloquio,[1] is a defense of the literary use of the vernacular language, but written in Latin to influence the learned despisers of the language of the people. It was to embrace ten books, but only two have come down to us. It treats of language in general, and the different dialects of Italy, and is important for the development of a national Italian literature which Dante founded as the first and unsurpassed classic.

The treatise was written in the latter part of his exile, to which he touchingly alludes when he writes: "I have most pity for those, whosoever they are, that languish in exile, and revisit their country only in dreams."

ON WATER AND EARTH.

A Latin essay on the two elements of water and earth (*Quæstio de Aqua et Terra*) contains the substance of a disputation which Dante held January 20th, 1320, before the assembled clergy at Verona, in the chapel of St. Helena. It concludes with an honest confession of humble agnosticism, asking men to cease troubling their brains about subtle questions which transcend their capacity, and reminding them of Paul's words: "O the depth of the riches of both the wisdom and knowledge of God: how unsearchable are his judgments, and his ways past tracing out" (Rom. xi. 33).

In this treatise Dante maintains that the sea-level is uniform, that the earth is spherical, that the moon is the chief cause of the tides. Some zealous admirers claim for him an anticipation of Newton's theory of gravitation and other important discoveries of truths of modern science.[2] But this is about as preposterous as to assert that Shakespeare discovered the circulation of the blood before Harvey, or that St. James anticipated the Copernican system when speaking of the "Father of lights," with whom there can be "no shadow of turning" (i. 17). Dante was original as a poet, but as a philosopher he was a pupil of Aristotle, and as a theologian a pupil of Thomas Aquinas.

---

[1] Or better, *De vulgari Eloquentia*. See Scartazzini, p. 243.
[2] He was, however, aware of universal attraction. *Inf.* XXXIV., 106-114.

LETTERS.

Fourteen letters, two of them recently discovered by Professor Witte. They illustrate the prophetic character with which Dante believed himself to be endowed.

The longest and most important is addressed to his patron and friend, Can Grande della Scala, of Verona, and furnishes the key for the understanding of the *Divina Commedia*. The letters to Emperor Henry VII., and to the princes of Italy and the people of Florence cast light on his politics.

THE CREED.

The *Credo* of Dante, so called, is a series of didactic poems or poetic paraphrases of the Apostles' Creed, the seven Sacraments, the Ten Commandments, the seven Penitential Psalms, the seven deadly sins, the Lord's Prayer, and the Ave Maria. It is a sort of manual of faith and devotion and written in the same metre as the *Commedia*.[1] But it is so much inferior to his genuine poetry that it betrays either great haste, or premature decline of power, or, more probably, the hand of an admirer who wished to clear him of the suspicion of heresy.[2] This was a very unnecessary task. His *Comedy* is sufficiently orthodox for every intelligent Catholic, if we judge it from the mediæval, and not from the modern Vatican or ultramontane standard. His genuine prayer to the Virgin Mary in the thirty-third Canto of the *Paradiso* is far superior to the questionable Ave Maria of the *Credo*, both in ardor of devotion and poetic beauty.

---

[1] Plumptre (II., 318–325) gives a rhymed translation of the *Credo*, but confesses that he cannot find in it the traces of the master's hand. It is not mentioned by Boccaccio and the earliest commentators, and comes to us through an anonymous MS. in the Bibliotheca Riccardiana of Florence, but is received by Fraticelli and included in his edition of the *Canzoniere*, and by Witte and Krafft in their German translations of Dante's Minor Poems.

[2] According to an uncertain tradition, the Franciscans took offense at the lamentations of St. Francis over the degeneracy of his order in *Paradiso*, XI., 120–139, and brought Dante before the Inquisitor, but Dante asked for a short respite to prepare his defense, and produced over-night this *Credo*; whereupon he was acquitted.

THE COMEDY.

The *Divina Commedia*, which requires a separate essay, is Dante's last and greatest work, to which all others are preparatory and contributory. He calls it a "sacred poem"—

"To which both heaven and earth have set their hand."[1]

[1] *Par.*, XXV., 1:—

"*Il poema sacro,
Al quale ha posto, mano e cielo e terra.*"

NOTE TO p. 317, THE PORTRAITS OF DANTE.—Since the preceding pages were stereotyped, Prof. Thomas Davidson directed my attention to *Le Opere di Giorgio Vasari con nuove annotazioni e commenti di* GAETANO MILANESI (Firenze, 1878), which contains (p. 413 sqq.) a lengthy discussion on Giotto's portrait of Dante. Milanesi shows that Giotto was not the author, as is generally supposed, of the fresco picture of Dante in the capella del Palazzo del Poestà in Florence, but of a portrait on wood which stood on the altar, and was lost about the beginning of the fifteenth century, having, however, been previously copied on the wall of said palazzo and also on that of the Church of Santa Croce.

DANTE CHRONICLE.

- A. D., 1265. May or June. Dante born at Florence.
- 1268. Conradin, grandson of Frederick II., and the last of the Hohenstaufen, defeated at Tagliacozzo by Charles of Anjou, and beheaded at Naples. (Cf. *Inf.* XXVIII. 17 *sqq.*; *Purg.* XX. 67 *sqq.*)
- 1274. May. Dante's first meeting with Beatrice (see *Vita Nuova*). Death of Thomas Aquinas, "the angelic doctor," and Bonaventura, "the seraphic doctor." (*Purg.* XX. 67-69; *Par.* X. 96 : XII. 110, 127.)
- 1276. Birth of Giotto, the painter. (*Purg.* XI. 95.)
- 1280. Death of Albertus Magnus. (*Par.* X. 95.)
- 1281. Dante's second meeting with Beatrice. Death of Pope Nicholas III. (*Inf.* XIX. 71.)
- 1282. The Sicilian Vespers, and revolt of Palermo. (*Par.* VIII. 73 *sqq.*)
- 1289. June 11. Dante fights as a Guelf in the battle of Campaldino and the siege of Caprona. (*Inf.* XXI. 95.) Murder of Francesca da Rimini. (*Inf.* V. 71 *sqq.*) Death of Count Ugolino. (*Inf.* XXXII. 124, XXXIII. 78.)
- 1290. December 31. Death of Beatrice. (*Purg.* XXXII. 2, "decennial thirst.")
- 1290 or 1291. Dante wrote the *Vita Nuova*, the story of Beatrice.
- 1290-'92. Episode of the Donna Pietosa. Study of philosophy and secular pursuits. (See end of *Vita Nuova*, and beginning of *Convito*.)
- 1292. Dante marries Gemma Donati, of the noble family of Corso Donati, the leader of the Guelfs. (*Purg.* XXIV. 82 : "he whose guilt is most.")
- 1294. Pope Celestine V. makes, through cowardice, "the great refusal." (*Inf.* IV. 59 *sqq.*, XXVII. 104 *sqq.*) But the reference to this sainted pope is doubtful. Election of Boniface VIII.
- 1295. Dante joins the guild of Physicians and Apothecaries, and is entered as Poeta Fiorentino.
- 1296. Dante exercises his civil rights as a citizen of Florence.
- 1299. May. Dante is sent as an ambassador of the republic of Florence to S. Gemignano.
- 1300. June 15th to Aug. 15th. Dante is one of the six Priors of the Republic of Florence. Joins the Ghibellines; opposes the interference of Boniface VIII.; expels the leaders of the Blacks and Whites. The Papal jubilee in Rome. (Alluded to in *Inf.* XVIII. 29 *sqq.*; *Purg.* II. 98.)
- 1301. September or October. Dante sent as ambassador to Rome.
- 1301. November. Charles of Valois, by authority of Pope Boniface VIII., enters Florence as "Pacificator of Tuscany." Triumph of the Guelfs.

1302. January 27th. Dante banished from Florence for two years and punished by a fine of 5000 florins.
1302. March 10th. Dante banished for life, on pain of being burnt alive in case of his return.
1303. Capture and death of Boniface VIII., at Anagni. (*Inf.* XIX. 53; XXVII. 70, 85; *Purg.* XVII. 50; XX. 85 *sqq.*; XXVII. 22; XXX. 148; XXXII. 148 *sqq.*; XXXIII. 44 *sqq. Par.* IX. 132; XII. 19; XXVII. 20 *sqq.*)
1305. Election of Pope Clement V. Transfer of the papal see to Avignon. (*Inf.* XIX. 83; *Par.* XVII. 82; XXX. 143.)
1308. Murder of Emperor Albert I. (*Purg.* VI. 98; *Par.* XIX. 115.) Death of Corso Donati, Dante's political enemy. (*Purg.* XXIV. 82.)
1309. Henry VII., Duke of Luxemburg, elected Emperor.
1310. Henry VII. arrives in Italy and is crowned at Milan, with the iron crown of Lombardy. Dante meets him at Susa, or Turin, or Milan, greets him as a second Moses, exhorts him to subdue Florence, and calls upon all the rulers of Italy to submit to the authority of the new Emperor, who was again crowned with the golden crown at Rome, 1312, but died in 1313. (*Par.* XVII. 82, "the noble Henry;" XXX. 135, 138.)
1311. September 6th. The sentence of banishment renewed against Dante.
1313. Death of Henry VII. Dante's political hopes transferred to Can Grande, of Verona, or some future deliverer and reformer.
1314. Uguccione della Faggiola conquers Lucca. Death of Clement V. and of Philip the Fair, of France. (*Inf.* XIX. 83 *sqq.*; *Purg.* VII. 109; *Par.* XIX. 118.)
1315. November 6th. Florence again renews the sentence of banishment, and extends it to the sons of Dante.
1316. John XXII. elected Pope. (*Par.* XXVII. 58.) Dante refuses to be pardoned on condition of admitting his guilt.
1317–1319 or 20. Dante resides at Verona with Can Grande. (*Inf.* I. 100 *sqq.*; *Par.* XVII. 75 *sqq.*; *Purg.* XXXIII. 39 *sqq.*)
1320–21. Dante at Ravenna, under the protection of Guido Novello da Polenta. Completes the *Divina Commedia*.
1321. September 14th. Death of Dante at Ravenna.
1865. Celebration of the sixth centenary of Dante's birth.

DANTE LITERATURE,

Selected, classified and arranged according to nationality and language.

The Dante literature is very extensive, and constantly increasing. It was most fruitful in 1865 (the sixth centenary of Dante's birth) and in the last few years (to 1890). It is very fully noticed in the following books:—

COLOMB DE BENTINES: *Bibliografia Dantesca.* Prato, 1846; with the supplements of GUIDO BIAGI, Firenze, 1888.

FERRAZI: *Manuale Dantesco.* Bassano, 1865–'77, vols. IV. and V.

J. PETZHOLDT: *Catalogus Bibliothecæ Danteæ. Nova editio,* Dresdæ, 1855.

U. HOEPLI: *Biblioteca Dantesca; opere di Dante e commenti.* Milano, 1888, pp. 41.

Jahrbücher der Deutschen Dante Gesellschaft. Leipzig, 1877, vol. IV., 594–672.

Bollettino delle publicazioni italiane of the National Library of Florence.

Catalogue of the British Museum, London, 1887 (Dandagnan–Daventrys, col. 3–58).

Harvard University Bulletin, Cambridge, Mass., vol. IV., Nos. 2–6 (1885–'87); and vol. V., Nos. 2–6 (1888–'89).

W. C. LANE: *Dante Bibliography for the Year 1888,* in the "Eighth Annual Report of the Dante Society," Cambridge (University Press), 1889, pp. 83–98.

The richest Dante library in America belongs to Harvard College, Cambridge, Mass., and consists (as Mr. Justin Winsor, the librarian, informed me) of 1164 volumes of Dante and on Dante. The three most eminent Dante scholars in America—Longfellow, Lowell, and Norton—were connected with that college. The American Dante Society has its centre in Cambridge, and adds annually to the literature. Next to Harvard College, the Public Library of Boston has, perhaps, the largest Dante collection in America. I examined them both in July, 1889, without profit. The Astor Library of New York and Cornell University have also a considerable number of works of Dante and on Dante.

I. STANDARD EDITIONS OF THE DIVINA COMMEDIA AND MINOR WORKS OF DANTE.

There are in all about 350 printed editions of the *Commedia* since 1472. (to 1890). Most of them appeared in the 19th century. Scartazzini counts 257 editions from 1801–1882. Lord Vernon gives a list of 394 complete and incomplete editions, translations, comments and illustrations of Dante, from 1472–1850. The best and most useful editions are those of LOMBARDI, FRATICELLI, BIANCHI, WITTE, and SCARTAZZINI, all with comments (except Witte's). HOEPLI's edition (Milan, 1878) is the smallest.

Le Prime Quattro Edizione della Divina Commedia litteralmente ristampate per cura di G. G. WARREN, LORD VERNON. Londra (Boone), 1858, pp. 748 fol. Reprints of the four earliest and very rare editions of Foligno, Jesi, Mantua, and Naples. (Only 100 copies printed. A copy in the Astor Library.)

DANTE ALIGHIERI.

L' Inferno di Dante Alighieri . . . . da G. G. WARREN, LORD VERNON (1803–'66). Londra (Boone), 1858–'65; 3 vols. fol. In Vol. I. fol. 487–529 there is a chronological list of 394 printed editions and translations of Dante's *Inferno*, and other parts of the *Commedia*, from 1472–1850. Vol. I. contains the Italian text with brief notes; Vol. II. documents; Vol. III. magnificent illustrations. An *édition de luxe*. A copy presented to the Astor Library by the son of Lord Vernon.

La Commedia di Dante Alighieri col Commento inedito di Stefano Talice da Ricaldone, pubblicato p. c. cura di VINCENZO PROMIS *e di* CARLO NEGRONI. Torino, 1886, pp. XIX. and 593 fol. The Italian text with a Latin commentary from the year 1474. An ed. gotten up by King Umberto I. of Italy and dedicated to his son Vittorio Emanuele. Few copies printed and presented by the King—one to the Astor Library, one to Prof. Botta, in New York. The same text and commentary in 3 vols. 8°. published by Ulrico Hoepli, Milano, 1888.

La Divina Commedia di Dante Alighieri col commento del P. BALDASSARRE LOMBARDI. Roma, 1815, 3 vols.; Padua, 1822; Firenze, 1830, in 4 vols. 8°. The 4th Vol. contains the minor works of Dante. Also other edd.

L' Inferno di Dante Alighieri colle figure di G. DORÉ. Parigi, 1861, pp. 184 fol. *Le Purgatoire et Paradis avec les dessins de* G. DORÉ. *Traduction française de Pier-Angelo Fiorentino, accompagnée du text italien.* Paris, 1868, pp. 407. A French prose translation with the Italian text below and the magnificent illustrations of Doré interspersed.

CARLO (KARL) WITTE: *La Divina Commedia di Dante Alighieri ricorretta sopra quattro die più autorevoli testi a penna.* Berlino (Ridolfo Decker), 1862, with critical prolegomena and notes, 725 pp. fol. Dedicated to King John of Saxony (Philalethes). The best critical text, which may be called the textus receptus. A small ed. without Prolegomena, Berlin, 1862, reprinted at Milan, 1864. I have followed Witte in the Italian quotations, but have also compared Scartazzini and Fraticelli.

GIOVANNI A. SCARTAZZINI: *La Divina Commedia di Dante Alighieri riveduta nel testo e commentata.* Leipzig (F. A. Brockhaus), 1874–'82, 3 vols. 12° (vol. I. pp. 444; vol. II, pp. 817; vol. III. p. 905). The text with an exhaustive commentary in very small type. In the Preface to vol. I., dated Coira (or Coire in Switzerland), July, 1873, the editor says that he has collected and studied all the commentaries, Italian, German and French, and promises a fourth volume containing *Prolegomeni storico-letterari*. Comp. the favorable notice of Witte in his *Dante-Forschungen*, II, 455, which I have not seen.

BRUNONE BIANCHI: *La Commedia di D. A.*, Firenze, 7th ed., 1868. Text and commentary (pp. 762), with rimario (pp. 112).

P. FRATICELLI's ed. in one volume, with rimario. Firenze, 1873, 1877; nova ed., 1887 (pp. 723 and 112).

RAFFAELE ANDREOLI: *La Divina Commedia di Dante Alighieri col commento.* Napoli, 1856, etc., Firenze (editione stereotipa), 1887 (pp. 351).

TOMMASO CASINI: *La Divina Commedia* col commento. Firenze, 1889.

Contributions to the Textual Criticisms of the Divina Commedia, including a complete Collation throughout the 'Inferno' of all the MSS. at Oxford and Cambridge. By the Rev. EDWARD MOORE, D.D., Principal of St. Edmund Hall, Oxford, and Barlow Lecturer on Dante in the University of London. Cambridge (University Press) and N. York, (Macmillan), 1889, pages 723, and Prolegg. LVI. Dedicated to the memory of Dr. Karl Witte. The most important contribution since Witte's edition, to the settlement of the true text. Moore reprints Witte's text of the 'Inferno' with a complete collation of 17 MSS., and a partial examination of the 500 to 600 known MSS. in regard to the most important test passages of the whole poem. He regards the *Commedia* as "perhaps the greatest work of human genius in any language."

Opere Minori di Dante (the *Vita Nuova*, the *Convito*, the *Canzoniere*, *De Monarchia*, *De Vulgari Eloqio*, *Credo*, and *Epistolæ*), by PIETRO FRATICELLI and others, with notes. Firenze, 1834–'40. 3 vols. 12mo.; new ed. 1861, and 1873, several times reprinted; and by G. R. GIULIANI, Firenze, 1868–'82, 4 vols., 12mo.

II. ITALIAN WORKS ON DANTE.

GIOVANNI BOCCACCIO (1313–1375): *La Vita di Dante*. Venice, 1477, etc., last ed. Firenze, 1888, pp. 100. *Il Commento sopra la Commedia di Dante*. Roma, 1544, often republished (*e. g.*, Firenze, 1831 and 1844, 3 vols., 1863, 2 vols.). Boccaccio's comments reach only to the 17th canto of the *Inferno*.

BENVENUTO RAMBALDI DA IMOLA: *Commentum*, etc., *Sumptibus Guil. Warren Vernon, curante Philippo Lacaita*. Florence, 1887, 5 vols. Benvenuto da Imola was a friend of Boccaccio and the oldest lecturer on Dante at Bologna (1375).

L'OTTIMO COMMENTO *della Divina Com. Testo inedito d'un contemporaneo di Dante* (1334) *pubblicato per cura di Aless. Torri*. Pisa, 1827–'29, 3 vols. 8°. Usually quoted *Ottimo*. Comp. Witte, *Dante-Forsch.* I., 358.

CESARE BALBO: *Vita di Dante*. Firenze, 1853. Translated by F. J. BUNBURY, in *The Life and Times of Dante*. London, 1852, 2 vols.

PIETRO FRATICELLI: *Storia della Vita di Dante Alighieri*. With documents partly unpublished. Firenze, 1861.

GUISEPPE JAC. FERRAZZI: *Manuale Dantesco*. Bassano, 1865–'77, 5 vols. The last two vols. contain the bibliography.

Giornale de Centenario di Dante Allighieri. Firenze, 1864–'65.

Dante e il suo secolo. Firenze, 1865. By various Dante scholars, in honor of the 600th anniversary of his birth.

A. G. DE MURZO: *Studi filosofici, morali, storici, politici, filologici su la Divina Commedia di Dante Alighieri*. Firenze, 1864–'81, 3 large fol. vols.

GIOVANNI A. SCARTAZZINI (a Swiss pastor and eminent Dante scholar, who writes German and Italian): *Dante Alighieri, seine Zeit, sein Leben und seine Werke*. Biel, 1869; 2d ed., 1879. *Dante in Germania, storia letteraria e bibliografia Dantesca Alemanna*. Milano, 1881, 2 vols. *Abhandlungen über Dante*, 1880. *Dante* Milano, 1883; and other works. His edition of the *Com.* and commentary mentioned above. Thomas Davidson has translated his *Handbook to Dante*. See below.

ADOLFO BARTOLI: *Della Vita di Dante Alighieri*. Firenze, 1884 (pp. 365). This is the fifth volume of his *Storia della letteratura Italiana*.

G. GIORDANO: *Studi sulla Divina Commedia di Dante Alighieri*. Napoli, 1884–'86, 2 vols.

G. POLETTO: *Dizinario Dantesco*. Siena, 1885–'87. 7 vols.

D. FRANSONI: *Studi vari sulla Divina Commedia di Dante*. Firenze, 1887.

G. STIAVELLI: *Gli amori di Dante raccontati da lui medesimo (Vita Nuova e Canzoniere) con prefazione e note*. Roma, 1888.

GIOSUÈ CARDUCCI: *Della varia Fortuna di Dante*, in his "Studi letterari." Leghorn, 1874, pp. 239–370; and *L'opera di Dante* (a discourse delivered in Rome, Jan. 8th, 1888), Bologna, 2d ed., 1888 (pp. 62).

GUISEPPE FINZI: *Saggi Danteschi*. Torino, 1888 (pp. 148).

F. SCARAMUZZA: *Illustrazioni della Divina Commedia*. Milano, 1874–'76, 3 vols. fol. with 243 photographs.

III. FRENCH WORKS.

B. GRANGIER: *La comédie di Dante . . . mise en rime françoise et commentée*. Paris, 1596–'97, 3 vols.

VOLTAIRE, the keenest and sharpest wit of the 18th century, regarded Dante and Shakespeare as semi-barbarian monsters. In a sketch of Dante in the "Dictionnaire Philosophique," he says: "*Les Italiens l'appellent divin; mais c'est une divinité cachée; peu de gens entendent ses oracles; il a des commentateurs: c'est peut-être encore une raison de plus pour n'être pas compris. Sa réputation s'affermira toujours, parce qu'on ne le lit guère.*" Renan remarks, "Voltaire understood neither the Bible, nor Homer, nor Greek art, nor the ancient religions, nor Christianity, nor the Middle Ages."

A. F. OZANAM: *Dante et la philosophie catholique au 13me siècle*. Paris, 1840; new ed. 1845; third ed. 1855; 4th ed. 1859. Also translated into Italian, German and English. He translated the *Purgatoire*, 1862. He happily calls Dante "the Homer of Catholicism."

ARTAUD DE MONTOR: *Histoire de Dante Al.* Paris, 1841; *La divine comédie, traduite en français*; 3d ed. Paris, 1849. A prose translation first publ. 1811–13.

EDGAR QUINET: *Dante*, in his *Les révolutions d'Italie*. Paris, 1848. He calls the Commedia "*l'Odyssée du chrétien; un voyage dans l'infini, mêlé d'angoisses et de chants de sirènes, un itinéraire de l'homme vers Dieu*."

M. FAURIEL: *Dante et les origines de la littérature Italienne.* Paris, 1854, 2 vols.

M. DE SAINT-MAURIS: *La Div. comédie, trad., avec un résumé historique et une notice sur Dante.* Paris, 1853, 2 vols.

SÉB. RHÉAL: *La Divine comédie, traduction nouvelle, avec des notes d'après les meilleurs commentaires, par L. Barré.* Paris, 1854.

E. AROUX: *La comédie de Dante, traduite en vers selon la lettre, et commentée selon l'esprit.* Paris, 1856. *Dante hérétique, révolutionnaire et socialiste. Révélations d'un catholique sur le moyen-âge.* Paris, 1854 (pp. 472). This book is dedicated to Pope Pius IX., and the author is as good a Catholic as Ozanam, but he views Dante in an altogether different light, as a conceited heretic and enemy of the papacy.

F. BOISSARD: *Dante révolutionnaire et socialiste, mais non hérétique; révélation sur les révélations de M. Aroux et défense d'Ozanam.* Paris, 1854.

LOUIS RATISBONNE: *L'enfer, traduit en verse.* Paris, 1853; 3ᵉ ed. 1860; *Le purgatoire*, 1856; *Le paradis*, 1860.

M. MESNARD: *La D. comédie de Dante A., trad. nouvelle. Notes per M. Léonce Mesnard.* Paris, 1854–'57, 3 vols.

LAMENAIS: *La D. comédie de Dante A., précédée d'une introduction sur la vie, la doctrine et les œuvres de Dante.* Paris, 1855, 3 vols.

J. A. DE MONGIS: *La D. comédie de D. A., traduite en vers français.* Dijon et Paris, 1857.

E. MAGNIER: *Dante et le moyen-âge.* Paris, 1860.

F. BERGMANN: *Dante, sa vie et ses œuvres.* Paris, 1866.

FRANCISQUE REYNARD: *La Divine Comédie. Traduction nouvelle.* Paris, 1877, 2 vols. (prose translation with a life of Dante).

MARC-MONNIER: *La renaissance de Dante à Luther.* Paris, 1884 (528 pp.).

H. VISON: *L'enfer, traduit.* Paris (Hachette), 1888 (232 pp.).

GUST. DORÉ's 125 large illustrations, Paris (Hachette), 2 vols. fol., often reproduced in many editions.

IV. GERMAN WORKS.

JOS. VON SCHELLING: *Ueber Dante in philosophischer Beziehung.* An essay in the "Kritisches Journal der Philosophie," ed. by Schelling und Hegel, vol. II., No. 3, pp. 35–50, Tübingen, 1803. Reprinted in his *Works*, vol. v. 152 *sqq.* A masterpiece of philosophical criticism. An English translation in Longfellow's Dante, II. 435–446. Schelling has translated also some parts of the *Commedia*, viz.: the inscription on the gate of Hell (unrhymed) and the second canto of the Paradise (in terza rima). He fully appreciated Dante. So did also Hegel, who calls the D. Comedy "the purest and richest work, the proper epos of the Christian Catholic Middle Ages," and "the greatest poem in the department of religious heroic poetry." (*Lectures on Æsthetics*, III. 408.)

B. K. ABEKEN: *Beiträge für das Studium der Göttlichen Komödie Dante Alighieri's.* Berlin, 1826.

L. G. BLANC: *Dante Alighieri.* Leipzig, 1832. Article in Ersch and Gruber's "Encycl." Sect. 1. Part XXIII., 34-79. Very elaborate and accurate. Blanc was one of the first Dante scholars, who wrote also a *Vocabolario Dantesco*, Leipzig, 1852, and a translation of the *Commedia* with commentary, 1864.

J. K. BÄHR: *Dante's Göttl. Komödie in ihrer Anordnung nach Raum und Zeit*, etc. Dresden, 1852.

EMIL RUTH: *Studien über Dante Alighieri, ein Beitrag zum Verständniss der göttl. Komödie.* Tübingen, 1853.

F. CHR. SCHLOSSER: *Dante-Studien.* Leipzig, 1855.

H. FLOTO: *Dante A., sein Leben und seine Werke.* Stuttgart, 1858.

TH. PAUR: *Ueber die Quellen zur Lebensgeschichte Dante's.* Görlitz, 1862. A careful collocation of all the older reports of Dante's life.

F. PIPER: *Dante und seine Theologie.* In his "Evangel. Kalender." Berlin, 1865.

K. F. GOSCHEL: *Vorträge und Studien über Dante* (posthumous), Berlin, 1863. His article *Dante*, in Herzog's "Encycl." III. 286-296; revised by K. WITTE, in the second ed. vol. III. 485-495.

KARL WITTE (Prof. in Halle): *Dante-Forschungen. Altes und Neues.* Halle and Heilbronn, 1869-'79. 2 vols. Witte was the greatest German Dante scholar. He and Scartazzini have made Dante a life-long study, and are his best interpreters. Witte wrote about 48 books and essays on Dante, and published one of the best editions of the Italian text (see above, p. 329,) and an excellent German version, *Dante Alighieri's Göttliche Komödie, im sechsten Säcularjahr nach des Dichters Geburt*, with introduction and notes, Berlin, 1865, pp. 728; 3d ed. 1876. Most of his minor Dante publications are collected in his *Dante-Forschungen*. Dean Plumptre (II., 487) pays him a just tribute of praise.

FRANZ X. WEGELE (Prof. of History in Würzburg): *Dante Alighieri's Leben und Werke.* Jena, 1852; 2d ed. 1865 (pp. 604); 3d. ed., 1879 (pp. 629). A critical account of Dante's life, his politics, and *Divina Commedia*, with documents.

DEUTSCHE DANTE-GESELLSCHAFT: *Jahrbücher*, Leipzig, 1867-'77, 4 vols. Contributions from Witte, Scartazzini, Giuliani, Paur, Huber, etc.

F. HETTINGER (R. Cath. Professor of Theol. in Würzburg): *Die göttliche Komödie des Dante Alighieri nach ihrem wesentlichen Inhalt und Charakter dargestellt.* Freiburg im Breisgau, 1880 (586 pages). Abridged English translation by *H. S. Bowden*, London, 1887. French transl. by *P. Mansion*. Gand, 1888. Hettinger also wrote *Dante and Beatrice*. Frankfurt-a-M., 1883. He gives the best exposition of Dante's theology from the Roman Catholic point of view, as Ozanam does in French.

PAUL SCHEFFER-BOICHORST: *Aus Dante's Verbannung.* Strassburg, 1882 (254 pp.).

LUDW. GEIGER: *Renaissance und Humanismus in Italien und Deutschland.* Berlin, 1882, pp. 7–23.

IG. VON DÖLLINGER (Old Cath.): *Dante als Prophet.* An address delivered before the Munich Academy of Sciences, Nov. 15, 1887. Publ. in his *Akadem. Vorträge,* Nördlingen, 1888, pp. 78–117.

G. GIETMANN, (S. J.): *Beatrice. Geist und Kern der Deutschesten Dichtungen.* Freiburg i. B., 1889 (pp. 198). By the same: *Die Göttliche Komödie,* in "Klassische Dichter und Dichtungen." First Part (pp. 426).

German translations of the *D. Com.* with comments by CHR. JOS. JAGEMANN (the *Inferno,* unrhymed, 1781–'82); A. W. SCHLEGEL (portions only, but very well done, 1795); K. L. KANNEGIESSER (1809, '14, '25, 4th ed. 1843, in ternary rhyme); KARL STRECKFUSS (1824, third ed. 1853, in triple rhyme; new ed. by Rud. Pfleiderer, 1876); AUG. KOPISCH (1837–'42, 3d ed. 1882); PHILALETHES (King John of Saxony —one of the very best translations, unrhymed, 1828, 1839, '65, '71); KARL GRAUL (*Hölle,* Leipzig, 1843; in triple rhyme); L. G. BLANC (1864, in blank verse); KARL WITTE (1865, 3d ed. 1876, in blank verse); KARL EITNER (1865); JOSEFA VON HOFFINGER (Wien, 1865, 3 vols., in triple rhyme); FR. NOTTER (Stuttgart, 1872); KARL BARTSCH (Leipzig, 1877); JUL. FRANCKE (1885); OTTO GILDEMEISTER (Berlin, 1888, pp. 551; with a general introduction of 23 pp., and brief introductions to each canto).

There are also fragmentary translations, especially of the fifth canto of the *Inferno* (Francesca da Rimini) of which Reinhold Köhler has published twenty-two in his *Der fünfte Gesang der Hölle in zwei und zwanzig Uebersetzungen seit 1763 bis 1865.* Weimar, 1865 (pp. 176).

Plumptre says (*Dante,* II. 486): "It is no exaggeration to say that the Germans have taught Italians to understand and appreciate their own poet, just as they have at least helped Englishmen to understand Shakespeare."

Prof. Botta (*Introd. to the Study of Dante,* p. 145), gives a list of Dante lectures delivered in German Universities, and says: "It is in Germany that Dantephilism has made most rapid progress. The writings of Schlosser, Kopisch, Ruth, Wegele, Paur, Blanc, Karl Witte, and Philalethes furnish a vast amount of valuable criticism and research in the various branches of history, theology, philosophy and æsthetics, as connected with the great poem."

V. ENGLISH AND AMERICAN WORKS.

(Lord) T. B. MACAULAY: *Criticisms on the Principal Italian Writers. No. I. Dante.* In "Knight's Quarterly Magazine," January, 1824; comp. also his essay on *Petrarch* (1824), and on *Milton* (1825); all these reprinted in the first volume of his *Essays.* In his essay on *Milton* is his brilliant comparison of the two poets. See Longfellow II. 395 sqq.

THOMAS CARLYLE: *The Hero as Poet,* in his *Heroes and Hero Worship.* London, 1840, etc. Reprinted in Longfellow II. 381–395.

JAMES HENRY LEIGH HUNT (d. 1859): *Stories from the Italian Poets,* with *Lives of the Writers*. London, 1846, 2 vols. (Vol. I.) Reprinted in part by Longfellow, II. 409, *sqq.* Hunt calls the Comedy "the saddest poem in the world," "an infernal tragedy," "a series of imaginative pictures altogether forming an account of the author's times, his friends, his enemies, and himself, written to vent the spleen of his exile and the rest of his feelings, good and bad, and reform church and state by a spirit of resentment and obloquy, which highly needed reform itself." Hunt would have him send nobody to Hell. But, he adds, "when Dante is great, nobody surpasses him. . . . He was a gratuitous logician, a preposterous politician, a cruel theologian; but his wonderful imagination, and (considering the bitterness that was in him) still more wonderful sweetness, have gone into the hearts of his fellow-creatures, and will remain there in spite of the moral and religious absurdities with which they are mingled."

PHILIP SCHAFF: *Dante. An Address on the Divina Commedia, delivered before the Goethean Literary Society of Marshall* [now Franklin and Marshall] *College, at its Anniversary, Aug. 28, 1846.* Translated by Jeremiah H. Good, A.M. Chambersburg, Penn., 1846, pp. 47. [Written at a time when the author knew more Italian but less English than afterwards. His articles on Dante in this volume are entirely new, but the estimate of Dante is the same as that in his youthful address.]

R. W. CHURCH (Dean of St. Paul's): *Dante: an Essay.* First publ. in the "Christian Remembrancer" of Jan. 1850; then separately, London, 1854, and 1878, with a translation of Dante's *De Monarchia*, by F. C. Church (a son of the Dean). The Essay was published again under the title: *Dante and other Essays*, London, 1888.

H. H. MILMAN: *History of Latin Christianity.* Book XIV., chs. 2, 5.

H. C. BARLOW: *Contributions to the Study of the D. Commedia.* London, 1864.

VINCENZO BOTTA: *Dante as Philosopher, Patriot, and Poet. With an Analysis of the Divina Commedia, its Plot and Episodes.* New York, 1865, '67. A new ed. under the title: *Introduction to the Study of Dante.* New York, 1886 (413 pages).

DANTE GABRIEL ROSSETTI (1828–'82, poet and painter, son of Gabriele Rossetti, an Italian poet and patriot who settled in London, 1824, and wrote books on Dante in an anti-papal spirit): *Dante and his Circle: With the Italian poets preceding him (1100–1200–1300). A collection of Lyrics*, ed. and transl. in the original metres. London, 1861; revised, London, 1874; Boston (Roberts Brothers) 1876 (pp. 468). The first part contains a translation of the *Vita Nuova* (pp. 29–110), and 13 contemporary poets (Guido Cavalcanti, Cino da Pistoia, Guido Orlandi, etc.), the second part, 44 poets before Dante (St. Francis of Assisi, Frederick II., King Enzo, Guido Guinicelli, etc.).

MARIA FRANCESCA ROSSETTI (1827–1876, sister of the former): *A Shadow of Dante: being an Essay towards studying himself, his world and his pilgrimage.* London (Rivingtons), 1871; 2d ed. 1872 (pp. 296); 4th ed. 1884. With illustrations. The same illustrations are found in many editions, *e. g.* that of Fraticelli. Dante's portrait, his universe, the hell, purgatory, and the rose of the blessed.

REPORTS OF THE DANTE SOCIETY. Cambridge, Mass., 1882–'89. James Russell Lowell is President.

S. F. CLARKE: *The Portraits of Dante.* New York, 1884. (The head from Raphael's *Disputa* in the Vatican, Giotto's portrait, and the profile on the mausoleum in Ravenna.) "The article reproduces a large part of Professor Norton's paper on the portraits of Dante," Harvard University Bulletin, Vol. IV., No. 7. p. 379.

THOMAS DAVIDSON: *A Handbook to Dante. By Giovanni A. Scartazzini. Translated from the Italian, with notes and additions.* Boston (Ginn & Comp.), 1887, (pp. 315.)

E. ALLEN FAY: *Concordance of the Divina Commedia.* Published by the Cambridge (American) Dante Society, Boston and London, 1888 (pp. 819). 500 copies printed.

GEORGE RICE CARPENTER: *The Episode of the Donna Pietosa, being an attempt to reconcile the statements in the Vita Nuova and the Convito concerning Dante's life in the years after the death of Beatrice and before the beginning of the Divina Commedia. Dante Prize Essay,* 1888. Published in Cambridge, Mass., 1889, pp. 23–79 of the Eighth Annual Report of the Dante Society.

MAY ALDEN WARD: *Dante: A Sketch of his Life and Works.* Boston 1887 (pp. 303).

HON. WM. WARREN VERNON: *Readings, of the Purgatorio of Dante chiefly based upon the commentary of Benvenuto da Imola. With an Introduction by the Dean of St. Paul's.* London, 1889, 2 vols. Similar *Readings* on the *Inferno* by the same author are in course of preparation.

Good articles on *Dante* in the "Encyclopædia Britannica, vol. II., and in Schaff-Herzog's "Rel. Encycl." I. 607 sqq. **(by DR. MARVIN B. VINCENT).**

English Translations of the *Commedia,* with notes and comments, by REV. HENRY FRANCIS CARY (1805, '14, '31, '44, '88, etc., in iambic verse of easy elegance, but more Miltonic than Dantesque, still the most readable and popular translation, highly praised by Macaulay both for its intimacy with the language of Dante, and its extraordinary mastery over the English); J. C. WRIGHT (London, 1843; 4th ed. 1861); J. A. CARLYLE (brother of Thomas C., only the *Inferno,* in literal prose with the Italian text and brief notes, 1849, '67, '82); H. W. LONGFELLOW (Boston, 1867, 3 vols., in many American and English editions; the most faithful of all English translations, in the metre of the original, but unrhymed); Th. W. PARSONS (*The Inferno,* in rhyme, Boston, Mass. the first ten cantos in 1843; completed, 1867); JAMES FORD (1870); WILLIAM STRAT-

FORD DUGDALE (the *Purgatorio*, the Italian text with a prose translation, similar to Carlyle's *Inferno*, London, 1883); JAMES ROMANES SIBBALD (1884, the *Inferno*, in single rhyme); ARTHUR JOHN BUTLER (The *Purgatory*, London, 1880; the *Paradiso*, 1885; the Italian text with prose translation, after the manner of Carlyle and Dugdale, useful for comparison); FRED. K. H. HASELFOOT (1887, in terza rima of the original); E. H. PLUMPTRE, Dean of Wells, 1887, '88, 2 vols., in monosyllabic terza rima, with a learned biographical introduction, and studies on important topics, and including a translation of the *Canzoniere*); JOHN AUGUSTINE WILSTACH (Boston and N. York, Houghton, Mifflin & Co., 1888, 2 vols.).

22

POETIC TRIBUTES TO DANTE.

TWO SONNETS ON DANTE.

BY MICHAEL ANGELO BUONAROTTI.

Translated from the Italian by DEAN PLUMPTRE (*Dante*, II. 420).

I.

Into the dark abyss he made his way;
   Both nether worlds he saw, and in the might
   Of his great soul beheld God's splendor bright,
And gave to us on earth true light of day;

Star of supremest worth with his clear ray,
   Heaven's secrets he revealed to our dim sight,
   And had for guerdon what the base world's spite
Oft gives to souls that noblest grace display.

Full ill was Dante's life-work understood,
   His purpose high, by that ungrateful state,
That welcomed all with kindness but the good.
   Would I were such, to bear like evil fate,
To taste his exile, share his lofty mood!
   For this I'd gladly give all earth calls great.

II.

What should be said of him speech may not tell;
   His splendor is too great for men's dim sight;
   And easier 'twere to blame his foes aright
Than for his poorest gifts to praise him well.

He tracked the path that leads to depth of Hell,
   To teach us wisdom, scaled the eternal height,
   And Heaven with open gates did him invite,
Who in his own loved city might not dwell.

Ungrateful country, step-dame of his fate,
   To her own loss; full proof we have in this
   That souls must perfect bear the greatest woe.
Of thousand things suffice it this to state:
   No exile ever was unjust as his,
   Nor did the world his equal ever know.[1]

---

[1] Comp. Witte's German translation of these sonnets in *Dante-Forschungen*, I., 20.

DANTE.
By Ludwig Uhland.

War's ein Thor der Stadt Florenz,
    Oder war's ein Thor der Himmel,
Draus am klarsten Frühlingmorgen
    Zog ein festliches Gewimmel?

Kinder, hold wie Engelschaaren,
    Reich geschmückt mit Blumenkränzen,
Zogen in das Rosenthal
    Zu den frohen Festestänzen.

Unter einem Lorbeerbaume
    Stand, damals neunjährig, Dante,
Der im lieblichsten der Mädchen,
    Seinen Engel gleich erkannte.

Rauschten nicht des Lorbeers Zweige,
    Von der Frühlingsluft erschüttert?
Klang nicht Dante's junge Seele,
    Von der Liebe Hauch durchzittert?

Ja! ihm ist in jener Stunde
    Des Gesanges Quell entsprungen,
In Sonetten, in Kanzonen
    Ist die Lieb' ihm früh erklungen.

Als, zur Jungfrau hold erwachsen,
    Jene wieder ihm begegnet,
Steht auch seine Dichtung schon
    Wie ein Baum, der Blüthen regnet.

Aus dem Thore von Florenz
    Zogen dichte Schaaren wieder,
Aber langsam, trauervoll,
    Bei dem Klange dumpfer Lieder.

Unter jenem schwarzen Tuch,
    Mit dem weissen Kreuz geschmücket,
Trägt man Beatricen hin,
    Die der Tod so früh gepflücket.

Dante sass in seiner Kammer,
    Einsam, still, im Abendlichte,
Hörte fern die Glocken tönen
    Und verhüllte sein Gesichte.

In der Wälder tiefste Schatten
    Stieg der edle Sänger nieder,
Gleich den fernen Todtenglocken
    Tönten fortan seine Lieder.

Aber in der wildsten Oede,
    Wo er ging mit bangem Stöhnen;
Kam zu ihm ein Abgesandter
    Von der hingeschiednen Schönen;

Der ihn führt' an treuer Hand
    Durch der Hölle tiefste Schluchten,
Wo sein ird'scher Schmerz verstummte
    Bei dem Anblick der Verfluchten.

Bald zum sel'gen Licht empor
    Kam er auf den dunkeln Wegen;
Aus des Paradieses Pforte
    Trat die Freundin ihm entgegen.

Hoch und höher schwebten Beide
    Durch des Himmels Glanz und Wonnen,
Sie, aufblickend, ungeblendet,
    Zu der Sonne aller Sonnen;

Er, die Augen hingewendet
    Nach der Freundin Angesichte,
Das, verklärt, ihn schauen liess
    Abglanz von dem ew'gen Lichte.

Einem göttlichen Gedicht
    Hat er alles einverleibet,
Mit so ew'gen Feuerzügen,
    Wie der Blitz in Felsen schreibet.

Ja! mit Fug wird dieser Sänger
    Als der Göttliche verehret,
Dante, welchem ird'sche Liebe
    Sich zu himmlischer verkläret.

UHLAND'S DANTE.
TRANSLATED BY REV. W. W. SKEAT, M.A. (1864).

Was it but the gate of Florence,
    Was't the gate of Paradise,
Whence, upon a fair May morning,
    Poured a troop in festal guise?

Children, fair as troops of angels,
    Richly dight with garlands gay,
Hastened tow'rd the vale of roses,
    There to join in dance and play.

Dante, who nine years had numbered,
    Stood beneath a laurel's shade;
Straight his glance discerned an angel
    In the loveliest youthful maid.

Rustled not the laurel's branches
    When the zephyr caught the grove?
Trembled not young Dante's spirit,
    Breathed on by the breath of love?

Yes! within his heart that instant
    Forth the fount of music brake;
Soon in canzonets and sonnets
    Tenderly his love outspake.

When once more she met the poet
    In her prime of maidenhood,
Like a tree that raineth blossoms,
    Firm and fair his glory stood.

See! from out the gates of Florence
    Pours once more a num'rous train;
Slowly, mournfully, it issues
    To a sad and plaintive strain.

'Neath a pall of sable velvet
    Which a silver cross doth wear,
Plucked by Death in bloom of beauty,
    Beatricé forth they bear.

Dante in his chamber rested
    Lonely, still, till sunlight failed,
Heard afar the death-bell booming;
    Silently his face he veiled.

Through the forest's deepest shadow
    Paced the noble bard alone;
Like the death-bell's distant booming,
    Sounded then his music's tone.

But within that dreary desert
    Full to him of grief and fear,
From the band of souls departed
    Came a God-sent messenger,

Who his steps securely guided
    Far through Hell's remotest gloom;
Where his earthly grief was silenced,
    Seeing souls fulfil their doom. [1]

Soon, his gloomy path pursuing,
    Came he to the blessèd light;
Then, from Heav'n's wide-opened portals
    Came his love, to greet his sight.

Far through Heav'n's delightful regions
    Soared on high the favored ones;
She, with eyes intent, unblinded,
    Gazing on the Sun of Suns; [2]

He, with eyes aside directed
    Tow'rds his loved one's countenance,
Which, all-glorious, like a mirror,
    Shewed him the Eternal's glance.

Shrined in an immortal poem
    Is the splendid vision shown,
Written with such fiery traces
    As the lightning writes on stone.

Rightly was this poet honored
    With the title—"the Divine"—
Dante, who could earthly passion
    To celestial love refine.

---

[1] In the first Canto of the "Inferno," Dante describes himself as lost in a dreary forest; where, as he wandered about in terror, he was met by Virgil, the "God-sent messenger," who guided him safely through the realms of Hell. [Note of the translator.]

[2] "*Beatrice tutta nell' eterne ruote* [the heavens]
    Fissa con gli' occhi stava; ed io in lei
    Le luci fisse, di lassù remote."—*Paradiso*, i. 64–670.

"Her eyes fast fixed upon th' eternal wheels,
    Beatrice stood unmoved; and I with ken
    Fixed upon her, from upward gaze removed."—
                      Cary's translation.

DANTE.
By Henry Wadsworth Longfellow.

Tuscan, that wanderest through the realms of gloom,
  With thoughtful face, and sad, majestic eyes,
  Stern thoughts and awful from thy soul arise,
Like Farinata from his fiery tomb.[1]

Thy sacred song is like the trump of doom;
  Yet in thy heart what human sympathies,
  What soft compassion glows, as in the skies
The tender stars their clouded lamps relume!

Methinks I see thee stand, with pallid cheeks,
  By Fra Hilario in his diocese,
  As up the convent-walls, in golden streaks,
The ascending sunbeams mark the day's decrease;
And, as he asks what there the stranger seeks,
  Thy voice along the cloister whispers, "Peace!"

Alfred Tennyson.

Tennyson probably alludes to Dante in the first two stanzas of his "The Poet:"—

"The poet in a golden clime was born,
  With golden stars above;
Dower'd with the hate of hate, the scorn of scorn,
  The love of love.

He saw thro' life and death, thro' good and ill,
  He saw through his own soul.
The marvel of the everlasting will,
  An open scroll,
Before him lay" . . .

At the sixth centenary of Dante's birth (1865) Tennyson sent, at the request of the Florentines, the following lines:—

"King, that hast reign'd six hundred years, and grown
In power, and ever growest! Since thine own
Fair Florence, honoring thy nativity—
Thy Florence, now the crown of Italy,
Hath sought the tribute of a verse from me,
I, wearing but the garland of a day,
Cast at thy feet one flower that fades away."

---

[1] Comp. *Inf.* vi. 79; x. 32 sqq. Farinata degli Uberti was the most valiant leader of the Ghibellines in Florence, and routed the Guelfs at the battle of Monte Aperto in 1260, but denied the immortality of the soul and hence was damned as a heretic.

DANTE IN VERONA.
By Emanuel Geibel.

Gedichte, Erste Periode. Stuttgart, 1888, 111th ed., p. 291. Geibel wrote also a sonnet on Dante: "Sobald die Nacht mit dunklem Flügelpaar." *Neue Gedichte, Dritte Periode* (21st ed., 1886, p. 192).

Einsam durch Verona's Gassen wandelt' einst der grosse Dante,
Jener Florentiner Dichter, den sein Vaterland verbannte.

Da vernahm er, wie ein Mädchen, das ihn sah vorüberschreiten,
Also sprach zur jüngern Schwester, welche sass an ihrer Seiten:

"Siehe, das ist jener Dante, der zur Höll' hinabgestiegen,
Merke nur, wie Zorn und Schwermut auf der düstern Stirn ihm liegen!

Denn in jener Stadt der Qualen musst' er solche Dinge schauen,
Dass zu lächeln nimmer wieder er vermag vor innerm Grauen."

Aber Dante, der es hörte, wandte sich und brach sein Schweigen:
"Um das Lächeln zu verlernen, braucht's nicht, dort hinabzusteigen.

Allen Schmerz, den ich gesungen, all die Qualen, Greu'l und Wunden
Hab' ich schon auf dieser Erden, hab' ich in Florenz gefunden."

THE DIVINA COMMEDIA.
GENERAL ESTIMATE.

Dante's *Divina Commedia* is one of those rare works of human genius which will command study and admiration to the end of time. There are many poems which interest and charm a much larger number of readers, but there is none which combines so many attractions for the man of letters, the philosopher, the theologian, and the historian. It is a poetic encyclopædia of mediæval civilization, learning and religion, a moral universe in song by the loftiest genius of that age. Hence few books have been so often edited, commented upon by scholars, and illustrated by artists; and few books have been like this, made the subject of serious and long continued study in all civilized countries.

The *Commedia*, it is true, can never be popular. It is no easy task to read it through. It requires the closest attention and the aid of a commentary. Lord Macaulay says, the great majority of young gentlemen and ladies who profess to know Italian, "could as soon read a Babylonion brick as a canto of Dante." Of those who make the attempt, few get through the *Inferno*, or even from this they select only the cantos on Francesca da Rimini and the Count Ugolino.[1] The reason lies partly in the severe solemnity, partly in the obscurity of the poem, its allegorical imagery, and its many allusions to contemporary characters and events. It presupposes a considerable knowledge of classical mythology, scholastic philosophy and theology, and mediæval history. It can only be understood in connection with the condition of Florence and Italy during the thirteenth and fourteenth centuries, and with the great conflict between the Guelfs and Ghibellines, the popes and emperors.

But the more the poem is mastered and comprehended in the

[1] Alfieri affirmed, at the beginning of the nineteenth century, that there were then not thirty persons in Italy who had really read the *Commedia*; but the number of readers, editions and commentaries has since been steadily increasing.

light of its age, the more it becomes an object of admiration. "What a fullness of intellectual treasures," says Witte, who himself devoted almost a lifetime to the study of Dante, "must that poet have to dispense who excited the same enthusiastic love in the youthful Schelling and the octogenarian Schlosser."[1] The German philosopher, here alluded to, who was gifted with poetic imagination and taste as well as speculative genius, calls Dante the high priest in the Holy of holies where religion and poetry are united.[2]

As a work of art, the *Commedia* is the first and the greatest classic of Italian literature, and has very few rivals in any language. Longfellow calls it "the mediæval miracle of song"; Tieck, "the mystic, unfathomable song." King John of Saxony, who, under the name of 'Philalethes,' published one of the best translations and commentaries of the *Commedia*, aptly compares it to "a Gothic cathedral where the exaggerations of ornament may sometimes offend our more refined taste; while the sublime and austere impression of the whole, and the exquisite finish and variety of details, fill our mind with wonder." And Thomas Carlyle describes it as "a great supernatural world-cathedral piled up there, stern, solemn, awful; Dante's world of souls!"

The *Commedia* is not simply a poem of the highest order, but a philosophy and theology as well; it reflects the social, intellectual, moral and political conditions of the Middle Ages; it embraces the present and future state of mankind; it has even a prophetic character, as a voice of warning and comfort for all time. Dante wrote in the assurance of a prophetic mission similar to that of Isaiah, Jeremiah, and Daniel. He felt it his imperative duty, without fear or favor of men, at the risk of exile and poverty, to tell the truth and nothing but the truth, to popes

---

[1] "*Welche Fülle von geistigen Schätzen muss der Dichter zu bieten haben, in dessen Lied mit gleicher Vorliebe, wie der achtundzwanzigjährige Schelling, so der achtzigjährige Schlosser sich versenkt!*"—Witte, *Dante-Forschungen* (*Halle*, 1869), I. p. 221.

[2] In the essay on Dante (1803) quoted in the Literature, p. 332: "*Im Allerheiligsten, von Religion und Poesie verbunden, steht Dante als Hoherpriester und weiht die ganze moderne Kunst für ihre Bestimmung ein; es ist die Durchdringung der Begebenheiten der ganzen Zeit des Dichters mit den Ideen der Religion, Wissenschaft und Poesie in dem überlegensten Geiste jenes Jahrhunderts.*"

and emperors, to kings and nobles, to the rich and the poor. He rebukes the evil-doers, he cheers the righteous, he paints in the strongest colors the eternal consequences of our conduct in this life of probation and trial, and holds up the prospects of an ideal commonwealth of justice, liberty and peace. He is a prophet of evil to the wicked, and a prophet of glad tidings to the righteous. He kindles from time to time the flame of patriotism among his countrymen, and keeps alive the hope and desire of a regeneration of the State and a reformation of the Church.

The attempt to describe the regions of the unseen world and to assume the office of the all-knowing judge of the living and the dead in the distribution of eternal rewards and eternal punishments, could originate only either in the brain of a fool or a madman, or in the bold imagination of a poetic genius, under the influence of a secondary inspiration. Dante has shown by the execution of this design that he was a genius of the highest order, though regarded by many of his countrymen as fit for a lunatic asylum rather than an office of public trust or any ordinary business of life.

Milton, who of all poets comes nearest to Dante, ventured on a poetic description of Paradise Lost and Paradise Regained, but abstained from peopling it with other than Scriptural characters. Emanuel Swedenborg, the Seer of the North, who claimed the supernatural gift of spiritual vision and intercourse with the departed, reports his conversations with men of different ages and religions in Heaven and Hell, but these conversations, though far superior to the twaddle and gossip of modern Spiritualism, are prosy, monotonous and tedious. Dante, without claiming a revelation, fixed the eternal destiny of eminent men and women of his age and country as well as of past generations, in the name of impartial justice to friend and foe: condemning the impenitent sinner to hopeless misery, comforting the penitent believer with the prospect of ultimate deliverance, and crowning the saints with the reward of celestial bliss.

THE SOURCES OF THE COMMEDIA.[1]

Nothing falls abruptly from heaven. Dante had many predecessors in the attempt to describe the invisible world, but he surpassed them all.

Homer and Virgil furnished illustrious precedents among classical authors and suggested to Dante the outlines of his *Inferno*. They divide Hades or the realm of the departed into Tartarus, the dark abode of the bad, and Elysium, the sunny fields of the good, but know no intervening Purgatory. They represent the dead as shadowy phantoms fluttering about in the air under an empty form.

Homer, in the eleventh book of the Odyssey, describes the visit of Ulysses to the joyless land of Hades, where he conversed with the Theban seer Tiresias, and with his own mother, and saw the shades of Agamemnon, Achilles and many heroes and heroines slain in battle and clad in bloody armor.[2]

Virgil, the favorite poet and guide of Dante, to whom he was much more indebted for material than to Homer, minutely describes, in the sixth book of the *Æneid*, the descent of Æneas, accompanied by the Sibyl of Cumæ, to the infernal regions where he learns from his father Anchises his fate and the future of the world-conquering Romans.

Nor should Cicero's Vision of Scipio be forgotten among the pre-Christian antecedents of the *Commedia*.

The *Inferno* of Dante is a strange commingling of heathen and Christian mythology. He invokes Apollo and the Muses

---

[1] Comp. Ozanam on the poetic sources of the *Div. Com.* appended to his *Les Poètes Franciscains en Italie* (Paris, third ed. 1859, pp. 351-469; tom v. of his *Œuvres complètes*); Rossetti, *Dante and His Circle* (London, 1874); Aless. d'Ancona, *I precursori di Dante* (Florence, 1874); Labitte, *La D. Comédie avant Dante* (Paris, 1842); Th. Wright, *St. Patrick's Purgatory, an essay on the Legends of Purgatory, Hell and Paradise current during the Middle Ages* (London, 1844). Longfellow, in his Illustrations to the *Inferno* (I. 384 sqq.), gives several visions of the unseen world, beginning with the 11th book of the Odyssey and ending with the Anglo-Saxon description of Paradise.

[2] Dante had a very limited knowledge of Greek and of Homer. He says (*Convito* I. 7), that Homer was not yet turned, or could not be turned, from Greek into Latin (*non si mutò di greco in latino*), like other Greek writers, because translation would destroy all his "sweetness and harmony."

to aid him in his Christian poem.[1] He gives room to heathen gods and demi-gods, but transforms them into demons (as they are represented by sculpture in the Gothic cathedrals). He retains Minos as judge at the door, and Charon as boatman over the Stygian lake, and associates Centaurs and Furies with the agents of diabolical torture. But he puts even the best of the heathen, including his own honored Virgil and Aristotle, into Hell, with two singular exceptions,—Cato of Utica, who keeps watch at Purgatory, and the Emperor Trajan, who was believed to have been saved by the prayers of Pope Gregory I. nearly five hundred years after his death.[2]

The Christian religion purified and intensified the belief in the immortality of the soul, gave realness to the future life by teaching the resurrection of the body, and created a new idea of Heaven as an abode of holiness and bliss in communion with God and the saints. After the fourth century the Christian eschatology was enriched and obscured by the semi-heathenish conception of Purgatory as an intervening state of purification and preparation for Heaven. It was suggested as a probability by St. Augustin, and taught as a certainty by Pope Gregory I., and gave rise to many crude superstitions which haunted the Middle Ages, and which to this day disturb the peace of pious Roman Catholics in the hour of death. This good but credulous pope, in the fourth book of his "Dialogues" (593), tells incredible tales of visions of departed souls, which greatly

---

[1] *Inf.* II. 7; *Purg.* I. 8, 9; *Par.* I. 13; II. 8, 9.

[2] Dante refers twice to these prayers: *Purg.*, X. 75; and (without naming Gregory) *Par.*, XX. 109–111. He followed a curious legend current in the Middle Ages, as told by Paulus Diaconus in his *Life of Gregory*, by Brunetto Latini, in the *Fiore di Filosofi* attributed to him, and also in the famous *Legenda Aurea*, and other books. It is this: Trajan, though he persecuted the Christians, was reputed a just emperor. About five hundred years after his death, Pope Gregory, on hearing of his justice and seeing his statue, had him disinterred, and prayed God with tears to take the soul of this man out of Hell and put him into Heaven. The prayer was heard, and Trajan relieved; but an angel told Gregory never to make such a prayer again: and God laid upon him a penance, either to spend two days in Purgatory, or to be always ill with fever and side-ache (*male di fianco*). St. Gregory chose the latter as the lesser punishment.

strengthened the mediæval belief in Purgatory.[1] Dante mentions Gregory in Paradise, but only as differing from St. Dionysius in the arrangement of the celestial hierarchy.[2] He ought to have placed him in the fourth Heaven, among the great doctors of the Church.[3]

The Acts of the female (probably Montanist) martyrs Perpetua and Felicitas (quoted by Tertullian and Augustin), and still more the monastic literature of the Middle Ages and the Lives of Saints, abound in marvelous legends, visions and revelations of the future world. Such visions are reported by the venerable Bede (d. 735), St. Boniface (d. 755), Wettin of Reichenau (824), Prudentius of Troyes (839), Charles the Bald (875), in the Life of St. Brandan (eleventh century), in St. Patrick's Purgatory (twelfth century, by a monk, Owen), by Elizabeth of Schönau (d. 1162), St. Hildegardis (d. 1197), Joachim of Fiore (d. 1202), St. Matilda or Mechtildis (d. 1310). The Vision of Frate Alberico of Monte Cassino in the twelfth century contains a description of Hell, Purgatory and Paradise with Seven Heavens. "It is," says Longfellow, "for the most part a tedious tale, and bears evident marks of having been written by a friar of some monastery, when the afternoon sun was shining into his sleepy eyes." Dante's own teacher, Brunetto Latini, describes, in his *Tesoretto*, how he was lost in a forest and then led by Ptolemy the astronomer to the vision of the unseen world, and the punishments of the wicked. The *Golden Legend* of Jacopo da Voragine, archbishop of Genoa (d. about 1298), teems with supernatural marvels of saints; it was the most popular book in the Middle Ages, and passed through innumerable editions.[4]

The whole poetry of the Middle Ages, and the arts of painting

---

[1] *Dialogorum libri* IV. *de vita et miraculis patrum Italicorum, et de æternitate animæ.* King Alfred ordered an Anglo-Saxon translation. Gregory acknowledged that he knew these ghost stories only from hearsay, and defends his recording them by the example of Mark and Luke, who reported the Gospel second-hand on the authority of eye-witnesses.

[2] *Par.*, XVIII. 133.   [3] *Par.*, X.

[4] See an interesting article on the literary history of the *Aurea Legenda*, by Professor E. C. Richardson, in the first volume of the "Papers of the American Society of Church History," N. York, 1889, pp. 237-248.

and sculpture delighted in spectacles of the future world. Labitte states, as the result of his investigations, that the architecture of France alone—the frescoes, windows and porches of the cathedrals of Notre Dame, Chartres, Auxerre, etc.—supplies more than fifty illustrations of the *Commedia* by way of anticipation. The most popular plays in Europe were the miracle plays or mysteries, which enacted the descent into Hell and the scenes of the last Judgment. The theatres represented by three stories the three regions of the invisible world.

One of the grandest, but most disastrous, of these spectacles took place in Florence during Dante's lifetime, May, 1304, and is described by Villani in his Chronicle. The infernal regions were represented on one of the Arno bridges by misshapen men, hideous demons, divers torments, groans and cries, and other horrible scenes to satisfy the morbid curiosity of the multitude who crowded the banks of the river and the boats and wooden rafts, when suddenly the bridge fell with its weight, and many people were drowned.

The only survival of these mediæval miracle plays is the Passion Play of Oberammergau in the highlands of Bavaria, which is enacted once in every ten years, but is singularly free from superstitious admixtures and preternatural horrors, and confined within the limits of the biblical narrative.

The mediæval faith in a future life was strong, and lively, but sensuous, materialistic and superstitious. Everybody held the Ptolemaic and geocentric system of the universe, and believed in a material hell beneath the earth, a material heaven above the sky, and an intervening material purgatory or transition place and state for the discipline of those who by faith in Christ have escaped hell, but are not yet good enough for heaven. The reality of these subterrestrial and celestial regions was as little doubted as the reality of our terrestrial existence. There were, of course, skeptics who denied or doubted even the immortality of the soul, but they were rare, and abhorred or pitied as madmen. Dante says in his *Convito*[1]—"of all idiocies, that is the most stupid, most vile, and most damnable[2] which holds that

---

[1] Bk. II. ch. 9 (Fraticelli, p. 139, Miss Hillard's translation, p. 90).

[2] "*Intra tutte le bestialitadi quella è stoltissima, vilissima e dannosissima,*" etc

after this life there is none other; because if we look through all the writings of the philosophers, as well as of the other wise authors, they all agree in this, that there is some part of us which is immortal." He then refers for proof to Aristotle, Cicero, the Gentile poets, the Jews, the Saracens, or any others who live at all according to law, to our aspiration after immortality, to the experience in the divinations of our dreams, and to "the most veracious teaching of Christ, who is the Way, the Truth, and the Light (Life). This teaching gives us more certainty than all other reasons. . . . This should be the most potent of arguments; and thus I believe, assert and am certain, that after this I shall pass to another, better life where that glorious lady [Beatrice] lives, of whom my soul was enamored."

Thus Dante found and shared the general belief in the three regions and states of the future world. But he mastered the crude material of tradition for his supernatural journey with the independence of genius, and reduced the legendary chaos to order and beauty. He threw all his predecessors into the shade, and has not been surpassed or equaled by any of his successors.

NAME OF THE POEM.

Dante called his poem a *Comedy* in distinction from a *Tragedy*, for two reasons: because it begins horribly with Hell and ends happily in Paradise, and because it is written in vulgar or popular language.[1] An admiring posterity long after his death added

---

[1] In the Letter to Can Grande, ch. 10, in which he dedicates to him the Paradiso, he says: "*Libri titulus est: Incipit Comœdia Dantis Alagherii, Florentini natione, non moribus.*" He derives comedy from κώμη, *villa*, and ᾠδή, *cantus*, so as to mean *villanus cantus, a village poem*, and tragedy from τράγος and ᾠδή, *cantus hircinus, a goat song*, and distinguishes comedy from tragedy in matter and style. "*Comœdia inchoat asperitatem alicujus rei, sed ejus materia prospere terminatur, ut patet per Terentium in suis Comœdiis . . . Similiter differunt in modo loquendi: elate et sublime tragœdia, comœdia vero remisse et humiliter, sicut vult Horatius in sua Poëtica . . . Et per hoc patet, quod Comœdia dicitur præsens opus. Nam si ad materiam respiciamus, a principio horribilis et fœtida est, quia Infernus; in fine prospera, desiderabilis et grata, quia Paradisus. Si ad modum loquendi, remissus est modus et humilis, quia loquutio vulgaris, in qua et mulierculæ communicant.*" He calls his poem a "Comedy" in *Inf.* XVI. 128; XXXI. 2 (*la mia commedia*). He does not seem to know the other derivation of comedy, from κῶμος, *merry-making, revelry* (a word which occurs several times in the Greek Testament).

the epithet *divine*, and bestowed it also upon the poet.[1] He himself calls it a *sacred* poem that made both heaven and earth co-partners in its toil.[2]

The ordinary meaning of *Comedy* does not apply at all to such a solemn and serious poem.[3] The *Inferno* is rather an awful tragedy; the *Purgatory* is filled with penitential sorrow, irradiated by the hope of final deliverance; the *Paradiso* is joyful indeed, but far above earthly felicity. The whole poem has lyric episodes, epic and dramatic features, and a didactic aim. It may be called an allegorico-didactic epos of the religious history of the world. But it cannot be strictly ranked with lyric, or epic, or dramatic, or didactic poetry, any more than the Book of Job. It stands by itself without a parallel. In the judgment of Schelling, it is an "organic mixture" of all forms of poetry, "an absolute individuality, comparable with itself alone, and with nothing else. . . . It is not plastic, not picturesque, not musical, but all of these at once and in accordant harmony. It is not dramatic, not epic, not lyric, but a peculiar, unique, and unexampled mingling of all these."[4]

---

[1] Scartazzini says that the epithet occurs first in Dolce's edition, Venice, 1555, but that Landino had previously called the poet *divine* in the edition of 1481.

[2] *Parad.*, XXV. 1 sq.
"*Se mai continga che il poema sacro,
Al quale ha posto mano e cielo e terra.*"

[3] Macaulay (in his essay on Milton): "In every line of the Divine Comedy we discern the asperity which is produced by pride struggling with misery. There is perhaps no work in the world so deeply and uniformly sorrowful. The melancholy of Dante was no fantastic caprice. . . . It was from within. . . . His mind was, in the noble language of the Hebrew poet, 'a land of darkness, as darkness itself, and where the light was as darkness.' The gloom of his character discolors all the passions of men, and all the face of nature, and tinges with its own livid hue the flowers of Paradise, and the glories of the eternal throne."

[4] "*Ein absolutes Individuum, nichts anderem und nur sich selbst vergleichbar.*" Schelling's essay on *Dante in philosophischer Beziehung*, first published in 1803, and in his collected *Works*, vol. v. 152 sqq.

TIME OF COMPOSITION.

The *Commedia* is the life-work of Dante, conceived in his early love for Beatrice, composed during the twenty years of his exile, and completed shortly before his death. It was begun in the year 1300, when he had reached the meridian of life,[1] or finished the first half of the course of seventy years which the Psalmist of old sets as the normal limit to our mortal life.

> "The days of our years are three score years and ten,
> Or even by reason of strength four score years;
> Yet is their pride but labor and sorrow;
> For it is soon gone, and we fly away."

The year 1300 is memorable in church history for the first papal jubilee, when two millions of Christian pilgrims visited Rome to offer their countless oblations to St. Peter, and to receive in return absolution from his successor, Boniface VIII.[2] It was a gigantic scheme for the increase of the papal power and wealth, to be repeated each hundredth year thereafter, and led in its ultimate consequences to the Protestant Reformation which began with Luther's Theses against the shameful traffic in indulgences for the rebuilding of St. Peter's. Dante may himself have been one of the pilgrims.[3] He alludes twice to the jubilee, but without approval.[4] He abhorred Boniface VIII. for his avarice and simony, and puts into the mouth of St. Peter a protest against being made

---

[1] *Inf.* I. 1. "*Nel mezzo del cammin di nostra vita*," etc. He was born in 1265.

[2] Giovanni Villani, one of the Florentine pilgrims, says (*Chronica*, VIII. 36) that throughout the year there were in Rome, besides the Roman population, 200,000 pilgrims, not counting those who were on the way going and returning. G. Ventura, the chronicler of Asti, reports the total number of pilgrims as no less than two millions. The oblations exceed all calculation. Two priests stood with rakes in their hands, sweeping the gold from the altar of St. Peter's; and this immense treasure was at the irresponsible disposal of the pope.

[3] As Ozanam conjectures (*l. c.*, p. 360), though without evidence.

[4] *Inf.*, XVIII. 29 sqq.; *Purg.*, II. 98.

> "The figure of a seal
> To privileges venal and mendacious,
> Whereat I often redden and flash with fire." [1]

The *Inferno* was probably completed in substance about 1308,[2] the *Purgatorio* about 1318, the *Paradiso* in 1321. But the chronology is not certain. He may have worked at different parts, revised the manuscript, and inserted allusions to facts which had occurred in the meantime.[3]

Boccaccio tells the story that the first seven cantos of the *Inferno* were written at Florence before the banishment, then lost and recovered, and that the last thirteen cantos of the *Paradiso* were found eight months after Dante's death, in a hiding-place in his bed-room, thanks to a marvelous dream, in which Dante appeared to his son Jacopo and revealed to him the place. This implies that those cantos were not published before his death.

Goethe's *Faust* furnishes a modern parallel of a poem on which the author labored for many years. He conceived the idea of *Faust* in his youth, 1769, composed at different times portions which interested him most, and published them from 1790 to 1808, when the First Part appeared complete under the title *Faust, eine Tragödie*. The Second Part he took in hand in August, 1824, at the age of seventy-five and completed it in August, 1831, when he sealed it up and directed that it should not be published till after his death. This "tragedy of the modern age," then, covers the youth, manhood, and extreme old age of the poet.

---

[1] *Par.*, XXVII. 52-55. In Plumptre's translation:
> "Not that I should, engraved on seal, give right
> To venal and corrupt monopolies,
> Which make me blush and kindle at the sight."

The whole indignant invective of St. Peter against the corruption of his successors (ver. 19 *sqq.* and 66 *sqq.*) applies primarily to Boniface VIII., or to Rome in 1300, but as well also to John XXII., or the Papal court at Avignon in 1320.

[2] Scartazzini thinks that the composition of the *Inferno* was not begun till after the death of Henry VII. (1313), but this is contradicted by Dante's own statement (*Inf.* I. 1), and by Boccacio's account of the composition of the first seven cantos in Florence before the banishment.

[3] For illustration I may refer to his translator Cary, who informs us in his preface that he began the translation of the *Purgatorio* and the *Paradiso* long before the translation of the *Inferno*.

DURATION OF THE VISION.[1]

Dante presents his poem in the form of a spiritual journey or vision. He began it in the year 1300, on Good Friday, which commemorates the Crucifixion of our Lord.[2] He spent two days (Friday and Saturday) in Hell, as long as Christ remained in the spirit world to redeem the waiting saints of the old dispensation, and to transfer them to Paradise.[3] On Easter morning (giorno di Pasqua) he again rises to the light. He needs one whole day and night for his subterranean journey from Hell to the foot of Purgatory, on the other hemisphere. In four days of toiling, from Monday till Thursday of the Easter week, he ascends to the top of the mountain of Purgatory. Then he flies through Purgatory in a day,[4] or, according to another view, in three days; namely, Friday, Saturday and Sunday, so that the whole action would occupy ten days.[5]

---

[1] On the dates of the *Commedia*, see Kannegiesser's translation, and E. Moore, *the Time-References in the Div. Com. and their bearing on the assumed date and duration of the Vision*. London, 1887. Unfortunately, I could not procure this book.

[2] Inf. XXI., 112-114, where Virgil says to Dante :—

"Yesterday, five hours later than this hour,
One thousand and two hundred sixty-six
Years were complete, that here the way was broken."

At the close of Canto XX., the time is indicated as being an hour after sunrise. Five hours later would be noon, or the sixth hour of the Crucifixion (Luke 23 : 44). Add to the 1266 years the 34 years of Christ's life on earth, and we get the year 1300, when Dante began his pilgrimage. The break or rent in the work alluded to was caused by the earthquake at the time of the Crucifixion.

[3] He combines for this purpose, with Thomas Aquinas, the two passages Luke 23 : 43 and 1 Pet. 3 : 19.

[4] According to Blanc, and Butler, who says (*The Paradise of Dante*, p. XIV.) : "The time occupied in the journey through the different Heavens is twenty-four hours."

[5] So Fraticelli (*La Divina Com.*, p. 723) : "*Il giorno di venerdì e quello di sabato (sicome rilevasi dal canto XXVII., 79-87) gl' impiega nel trapassare i nove cieli mobili ; e nel giorno di domenica, ottava di Pasqua, sale all' empireo. E così in tutto l'azione del Poema dura dieci giorni.*" Davidson (in his translation of Scartazzini's *Handbook to D.*, p. 312) adopts the same view on the basis of

THE UNIVERSE.

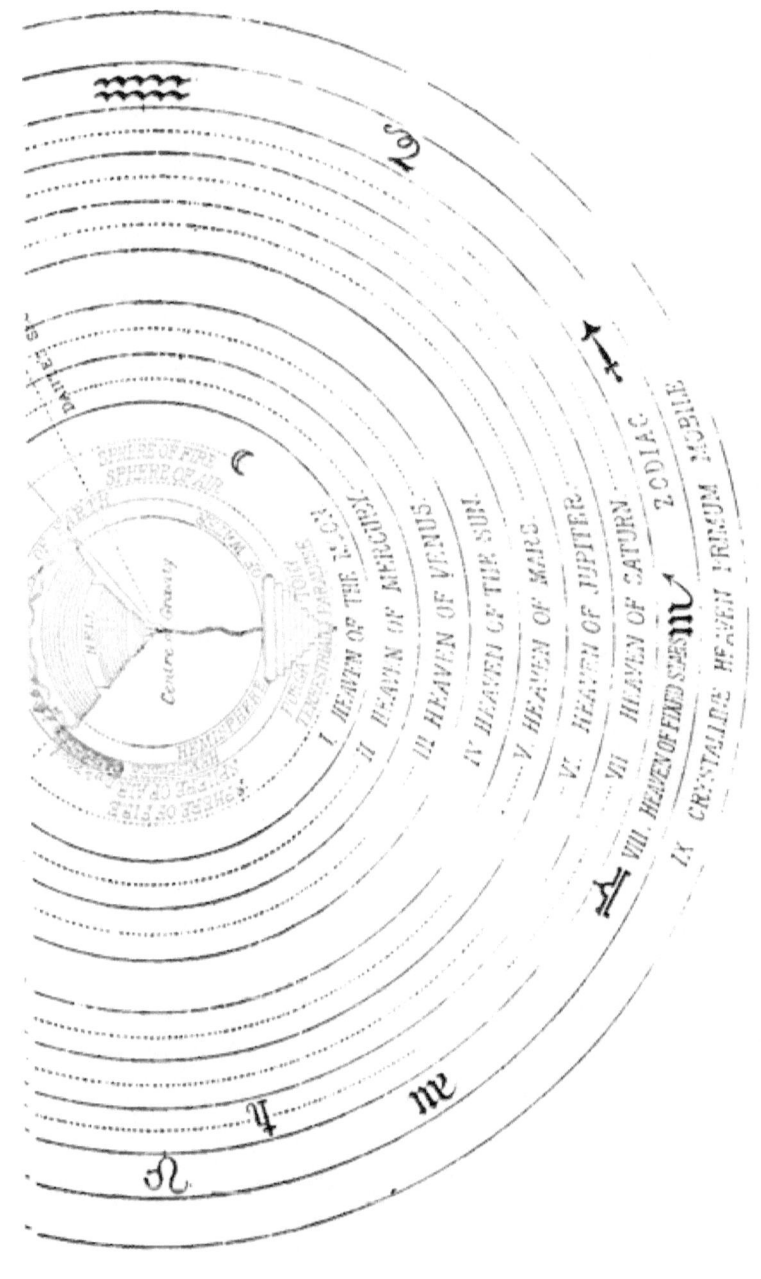

DANTE'S COSMOLOGY.[1]

Dante did not rise above the geography and astronomy of his age, but took poetic liberties in detail. His *Commedia* is based upon the Ptolemaic system, which prevailed till the middle of the sixteenth century, when it was gradually supplanted by the Copernican system.

The geography of the church in the Middle Ages did not extend much beyond the old *Orbis Romanus*, that is, those portions of three continents which are washed by the waters of the Mediterranean. Eastern Asia (except East India), Southern Africa and Northern Europe were *terræ incognitæ*, lying beyond the boundaries of civilization. America and Australia were not yet discovered. The earth was divided into two hemispheres, the eastern hemisphere of the inhabited land with Jerusalem as its centre, and the western hemisphere of water. Columbus undertook his voyage across the Atlantic in the hope of finding a western passage to East India, and died in the belief that he had found it when he discovered the "West Indies" in 1492.

The mediæval cosmology was geocentric. It regarded the earth as the immovable centre of the universe. It maximized our little globe, and made sun, moon and stars revolve around it as obedient servants, to give it light by day and by night. It was moreover, mixed up with astrology and the superstitious belief of the mysterious influence of the celestial bodies upon the birth and fate of men. Dante was full of it.

Par., XXVII., 79-87, but I confess I cannot find there no more than that Dante had been then six hours (*dal mezzo al fine*) in the Heaven of the Fixed Stars. Butler (p. 349) suggests the conjectural reading: "*Che va* (for *fa*) *dal mezzo al fin del* (for *il*) *primo clima.*"

[1] See especially Witte, *Dante's Weltgebäude* in "Jahrbuch der deutschen Dante-Gesellschaft" (1867), vol. I., 73-93; his *Dante-Forschungen* (1879), vol. II., 161-182; and the introduction to his German translation of the *Commedia* (1865 and 1876). Also Philalethes, *Ueber Kosmologie und Kosmogonie nach den Ansichten der Scholastiker in Dante's Zeit*, a dissertation in his translation of the first Canto of Paradise (pp. 11-19). Maria Francesca Rossetti, *A Shadow of Dante* (1871), pp. 9-13. Several editions of the *Commedia*, and the work of M. F. Rossetti give illustrations of Dante's Universe, which are very helpful.

The Ptolemaic system has lost all scientific value, but it retains its historical interest, and a certain practical necessity for our daily vision of sunrise and sunset. It is less grand, but more definite, phenomenal, and, we may say, more poetic than the Copernican system.

Dante locates Hell beneath the surface of the land hemisphere and extends it down to the centre of the earth at the opposite end of Jerusalem. He gives it the shape of a funnel or inverted cone, which ends in a narrow pit for the traitors, where Satan is stuck in ice. According to the data given by the poet, the dimensions of Hell would be four thousand miles in depth, and as many in breadth at its upper circumference. It is preceded by a vestibule. The entrance is beneath the forest at the "Fauces Averni," near Cumæ, on the coast of Campania, where Virgil places the entrance to Hades. Dante divides the infernal amphitheatre into three divisions, separated from each other by great spaces. Each division is subdivided into three concentric circles, corresponding to the several classes of sinners and the degrees of guilt. As they become narrower, the punishment increases.

Purgatory is located in the water hemisphere opposite Mount Sion and distant from it by the whole diameter of the globe, that is, somewhere near the South Sea Islands. Dante represents it as a vast conical mountain rising steep and high from the waters of the Southern ocean.[1] He surrounds the mountain with seven terraces for the punishment and expiation of the seven deadly sins. As sin and punishment increase in a descending line in Hell, so, on the contrary, sin and punishment decrease in an ascending line in Purgatory. Rough stairways, cut into the rock, lead from terrace to terrace. On the summit is the table land of the garden of Eden or the terrestrial Paradise, which must not be confounded with the celestial Paradise. Human history began in the innocence of the terrestrial Paradise; to it man is led back by penitence and purification till he is fit for the holiness and bliss of the celestial Paradise.

The fall of Lucifer, the archrebel, from heaven convulsed and perverted the original world which God had made. He

[1] "The mount that rises highest o'er the wave." (*Par.* XXVI., 139.)

struck the earth with such violence as to open a chasm clear through the centre and to throw up the Mount of Purgatory on the opposite side of the earth.[1] The Inferno is the eternal prison for the impenitent and lost; Purgatory is the temporary prison or penitentiary for penitent sinners and will be empty on the day of judgment. Paradise is the eternal home of holy angels and men. Dante reaches it, under the guidance of Beatrice, by flight from the top of Mount Purgatory, where the law of gravity has an end.

Paradise consists of nine heavens and the Empyrean. The nine heavens correspond to the nine circles of Hell and of Purgatory. The first seven heavens revolve around the earth as the immovable centre of the universe and are called after the then known planets: Moon, Mercury, Venus, Sun (which was likewise regarded as a planet), Mars, Jupiter, Saturn. Each is supposed to be inhabited. Above them is the eighth heaven or the heaven of the Fixed Stars. The ninth heaven is the crystalline heaven or the Primum Mobile, which is the most rapid in motion, keeps the eight lower heavens in perpetual motion and is the root of time and change throughout creation. Without and beyond the Primum Mobile is the tenth heaven or the Empyrean, which contains the universe, is timeless, spaceless and motionless, the special abode of God and the eternal home of his saints. It is arranged in the form of a rose around a sea of light. All the blessed dwell in the Empyrean, but they appear to the poet in the different heavens according to the degrees of their merit and happiness.

The cosmology of Dante is complicated with astrology inherited from heathen times, and with the theory of a celestial hierarchy which was developed in the mystical writings of pseudo-Dionysius, the Areopagite, and excited great influence on the scholastic theology of the Middle Ages;[2] nine angelic orders are divided into three hierarchies: the Seraphim, Cherubim and Thrones; the Dominions, Virtues and Powers; the Principalities, Archangels and Angels. They move the nine Heavens and

---

[1] *Inf.*, XXXIV., 121 sqq.

[2] On the pseudo-Dionysian writings, see Schaff, *Church History*, vol. IV., 589-600.

are themselves unmoved. They receive power from the Empyrean above and stamp it like a seal upon the spheres below.

Dante, in accordance with Thomas Aquinas, placed the creation of the Angels on the first day, and the fall of Lucifer and the rebel Angels within the twenty minutes succeeding. The fall of man must have taken place after the upheaval of Paradise which was caused by the fall of Lucifer.

The localities and sceneries of the future world are measured by Dante with mathematical precision, and described with the genius of an architect and painter. Everything is definite and visible. He furnishes the richest material for painters. In this respect the *Comedy* strikingly contrasts with the vagueness and indefiniteness of Milton's *Paradise Lost*, which Ruskin has admirably described.[1]

Even the departed souls assume a clear, definite shape. They are not nebulous shades, but clothed with a refined corporality resembling their earthly tabernacle. They can roll stones, lift burdens and feel the punishments of Hell and the penal sufferings of Purgatory. The blessed in the lower regions of Paradise retain human lineaments, but in the higher regions they appear only as flames, and in the Empyrean each regains his own body in glorified shape.

EXPLANATION OF THE COMMEDIA.

To understand the *Divina Commedia*, we must keep in mind that Dante accepted the mediæval hermeneutical canon of a fourfold sense of the Scriptures and applied it to his poem: a literal or historical sense, and three spiritual senses—the allegorical proper, the moral, and the anagogical, corresponding to the three cardinal graces: faith (*credenda*), love (*agenda*), and hope (*speranda*), as expressed in the couplet:—

> "*Litera gesta docet; quid credas, allegoria;
> Moralis, quid agas; quo tendas, anagogia.*"

Thus, Jerusalem means literally or historically the city in Palestine; allegorically, the church; morally, the believing soul;

---

[1] In *Modern Painters*, vol. III., ch. 14, copied in Longfellow's *Dante*, II., 422 sqq.

anagogically, the heavenly home of saints. Babylon may mean the city on the Euphrates, or the world, or heathen and anti-Christian Rome, or the enemies of the church. The three spiritual senses may be united in one sense, called allegorical or mystical.

The allegorical interpretation was first systematized by Origen in the third century, who followed in the steps of Philo, the Jewish Platonist, and distinguished three senses in the Bible, a somatic or literal, a psychic or moral, and a pneumatic or mystical sense, which correspond to the body, soul, and spirit of man (according to the Platonic trichotomy). The theory of a fourfold sense was developed in the fifth century by Eucherius (d. 450) and Cassian (d. 450), and more fully by Rabanus Maurus (d. 856). All the patristic, scholastic, and many of the older Protestant commentators indulged more or less in allegorical exposition and imposition. The grammatico-historical exegesis of modern times assumes that the biblical, like all other writers, intend to convey one and only one definite meaning, according to the use of words familiar to the readers. This sound principle is not inconsistent with the hidden depth and manifold applicability of the Scripture truths to all ages and conditions. But explication is one thing, and application is another thing. The business of the exegete is not to put his own fancies into the Bible, but to take out God's facts and truths from the Bible and to furnish a solid basis to the preacher for his practical application. An exception may be made with allegories, parables and fables, where the author, at the outset, contemplated a double meaning; and this was the case with the *Commedia*.

Dante expounds his theory in the *Convito* as follows:[1]—

"We should know that books can be understood, and ought to be explained, in four principal senses. One is called *literal*, and this it is which goes no farther than the letter, such as the simple narration of the thing of which you treat [of which a perfect and appropriate example is to be found in the third canzone treating of nobility]. The second is called *allegorical*, and this is the meaning hidden under the cloak of fables, and is a truth concealed beneath a fair fiction; as when Ovid says that Orpheus with his lute tamed wild beasts and moved trees and rocks; which means that the wise man, with the instrument of his voice, softens and humbles

---

[1] Book II., ch. I., p. 51 sqq. in K. Hillard's translation.

cruel hearts, and moves at his will those who live neither for science nor for art, and those who, having no rational life whatever, are almost like stones. And how this hidden thing [the allegorical meaning] may be found by the wise, will be explained in the last book but one. The theologians, however, take this meaning differently from the poets; but because I intend to follow here the method of the poets, I shall take the allegorical meaning according to their usage.

"The third sense is called *moral*; and this readers should carefully gather from all writings for the benefit of themselves and their descendants; it is such as we may gather from the gospel when Christ went up into the mountain to be transfigured, and of the twelve apostles took with him but three; which, in the moral sense, may be understood thus, that in most secret things we should have few companions.

"The fourth sense is called *anagogical* [or mystical], that is, beyond sense; and this is when a book is spiritually expounded, which, although [a narration] in its literal sense, by the things signified refers to the supernal things of the eternal glory; as we may see in that psalm of the Prophet (Ps. 114:2), when he says that when Israel went out of Egypt Judæa became holy and free. Which, although manifestly true according to the letter, is nevertheless true also in its spiritual meaning—that the soul, in forsaking its sins, becomes holy and free in its powers [functions].

"And in such demonstration the literal sense should always come first, as that whose meaning includes all the rest, and without which it would be impossible and irrational to understand the others; and, above all, would it be impossible with the allegorical. Because in everything which has an inside and an outside, it is impossible to get at the inside if we have not first got at the outside. Therefore, as in books the literal sense is always outside, it is impossible to get at the other [senses], especially the allegorical, without first getting at the literal."

In a long letter to Can Grande della Scala,[1] in which Dante dedicates to him the opening cantos of the *Paradiso*, he makes the same distinction and illustrates it more fully by the same example of the Exodus from Egypt (Ps. 114:1), which, he says, means literally, the historical fact; allegorically, our redemption by Christ; morally, the conversion of the soul from the misery of sin to a state of grace; and anagogically, the exodus of the sanctified soul from the servitude of this corrupt state to the liberty of eternal glory. Then he makes the appli-

---

[1] *Magnifico atque victorioso domino, Kani Grandi de la Scala . . . devotissimus suus Dantes Alagherii, florentinus natione, non moribus*, etc., in Fraticelli's ed. of *Il Convito e le Epistole*, p. 508 sqq. Fraticelli assigns the letter to 1316 or 1317, others to 1320. The genuineness has been disputed, but without good reason.

cation of this exegetical canon to his own *Comedy* in this important passage:—

"The subject of the whole work, taken literally, is the condition of souls after death, simply considered. For on this and around this the whole action of the work turns. But if the work be taken allegorically, the subject is man, how by actions of merit or demerit, through freedom of the will, he justly deserves reward or punishment."[1]

Plumptre (II. 358) directs attention to an interesting parallelism, the double sense of Spenser's *Faerie Queene*, as explained in his Epistle to Sir Walter Raleigh, where he describes his book as "a continued Allegory or Dark Conceit." The story of King Arthur is the outward framework; the Fairy Queen (resembling Beatrice) is both Queen Elizabeth and Glory; Duessa is Queen Mary of Scots [?] and the Church of Rome.

The hermeneutical canon of Dante does not require us to seek four senses in every word or character of the *Commedia*. This would be sheer pedantry and lead to endless confusion. It is enough to find a literal and a spiritual meaning in the work as a whole, and in its leading actors. Thus Dante is an individual and at the same time a representative of man in his pilgrimage to Heaven. Virgil is the old Roman poet, who wrote the Æneid and taught Dante his beautiful style, but represents at the same time human reason or the light of nature. Beatrice is the angelic maiden of Florence, and a symbol of divine revelation, wisdom and love. Lucia is the saintly virgin and martyr of Syracuse, the patroness of the blind, and signifies the illumination of prevenient grace. The mysterious DUX is Can Grande of Verona, and some future reformer of church and

---

[1] *Est ergo subjectum totius operis, literaliter tantum accepti, status animarum post mortem simpliciter sumptus. Nam de illa et circa illam totius operis versatur processus. Si vero accipiatur opus allegorice, subjectum est homo, prout merendo et demerendo per arbitrii libertatem Justitiæ præmianti aut punienti obnoxius est.*" In *Par.*, V., 19 sqq., Beatrice thus instructs him on the high importance of the freedom of the will:—

"The greatest gift that in his largess God
 Creating made, and unto his own goodness
 Nearest conformed, and which he doth prize
Most highly, is the freedom of the will,
 Wherewith the creatures of intelligence
 Both all and only were and are endowed."

state. The dark forest in which the poet finds himself at the beginning is the labyrinth of sin and error. The three beasts which prevent him from climbing up the illuminated mountain are the human passions (lust, pride, and greed of gain) and at the same time Florence, France, and the corrupt papacy.

It is inconsistent with Dante's rule to deny either the allegorical meaning, or the historical reality of the persons introduced, and to resolve them into mere abstractions. The last has been done frequently in the case of Beatrice and the Donna Pietosa. The most recent writer on Beatrice makes her simply an allegory of the ideal church, as the spouse of Christ, the Shulamite of the Song of Solomon, and explains her death to mean the transfer of the papacy to Avignon and the Babylonian exile.[1] But Dante does not identify the church with the papacy, and attacks the papacy at Rome in the person of Boniface VIII., as well as the papacy at Avignon in the persons of Clement V. and John XXII. The severest rebuke of the Roman Church is put into the mouth of Beatrice and of St. Peter.[2] Beatrice distinguishes herself from the church triumphant when she, with flaming face and eyes full of ecstasy, points Dante to "the hosts of Christ's triumphal march."[3] She is only one among the most exalted saints, and occupies in Paradise the same seat with Rachel, the emblem of contemplation, below Eve and the Virgin Mary.[4]

In calling one of his daughters *Beatrice*, Dante wished her to be a reflection of his saintly patron in heaven. His other

---

[1] G. Gietmann (of the Society of Jesus); *Beatrice, Geist und Kern der Dante'schen Dichtung*, Freiburg i. B. 1889. This book came to hand while writing the essay. My views of Beatrice are given in the article on Dante, p. 290 sq.

[2] Comp. *Inf.*, XIX., 53; XXVII., 70, 85; *Purg.*, XX., 87; XXXII., 149; XXXIII., 44; *Par.*, IX., 132; XII., 90; XVII., 50, sq. ("Where every day the Christ is bought and sold"); XXVII., 18 sqq. (Peter's fearful censure of the Church of Rome); XXX., 145 sqq. (where Beatrice predicts that Clement V. shall soon be thrust down to keep company with Simon Magus). The death of Boniface and the removal to Avignon is prophesied as a deliverance of the Vatican "from the adulterer" (Boniface VIII.). *Par.* IX., 139–142.

[3] *Par.* XXIII., 19–21.

[4] *Par.*, XXXII., 7; comp. *Inf.*, II., 102: "Where I was sitting with the ancient Rachel."

daughter he named *Imperia*, probably with reference to his political ideal, the *imperium Romanum*, which he set forth in his work on the Monarchy.

DESIGN OF THE COMMEDIA.

To the double sense of the *Commedia* corresponds a double design; one is individual, the other is general. Dante says, in the same letter to Can Grande, that the poem aims to remove the living from the state of misery and to lead them to the state of felicity.[1]

The *Commedia* is Dante's own spiritual biography, his pilgrimage from the dark forest of temptation and sin through suffering and purification to the purity and peace of heaven. He is an interested spectator and participant in the awful sufferings of Hell,[2] and a penitent in Purgatory, from whose heart the seven mortal sins, like the seven P's upon his forehead, are gradually purged away.[3] Then only he obtains a foretaste of that happiness which he hoped and longed to inherit.[4] And this longing increased as he advanced in life and grew weary of the corruptions of this evil world.[5]

---

[1] "*Finis totius et partis esse potest multiplex, scilicet propinquus et remotus. Sed omissa subtili investigatione, dicendum est breviter quod finis totius et partis est, removere viventes in hac vita de statu miseriæ, et perducere ad statum felicitatis.*"

[2] *Inf.*, V., 140 sqq :—
"The other one did weep so, that, for pity,
    I swooned away as if I had been dying,
    And fell, even as a dead body falls."

[3] *Purg.*, IX., 112–114 :—
"Seven P's upon my forehead he described
    With the sword's point, and 'Take heed that thou wash
    These wounds, when thou shalt be within,' he said."

[4] *Par.*, V., 105; XXX., 135 :—
"Before thou suppest at this wedding feast."

[5] *Purg.*, XXIV., 76–81 :—
"How long," I answered, "I may live, I know not;
    Yet my return will not so speedy be,
    But I shall sooner in desire arrive;
    Because the place where I was set to live
    From day to day of good is more depleted,
    And unto dismal ruin seems ordained."

But the *Commedia* has a much wider meaning. It is the spiritual biography of man as man; it is the sinner's pilgrimage from earth to heaven. Ruskin calls Dante "the central man of all the world." Dante's conceptions of the universe and the locality of the future world have passed away with the Ptolemaic system; but the moral ideas of his poem remain. He knew no more than we do, and we know no more than he did about

"The undiscovered country, from whose bourn
No traveler returns."

The supernatural geography is a subject of uncertain opinion and speculation, but not of revelation and of faith. We know nothing of the future world beyond that which God has chosen to reveal, and this is very little. There are more things in heaven and hell than "are dreamed of in our philosophy," or are taught us in the Bible. One thing is certain, however, that there is somewhere within or without the created universe a heaven and a hell, or a future state of reward and punishment. Without this final solution the present life has no meaning. Sin and misery is hell; repentance and godly sorrow is purgatory; holiness and bliss is heaven—already here on earth, and more fully hereafter. The way to heaven leads through knowledge of sin and through repentance.

In Dante's *Inferno* all is darkness and despair; in the *Purgatorio*, sunlight and hope; in the *Paradiso*, pure light and bliss. In the first we are repelled, shocked and disgusted by the pictures of moral deformity and hopeless misery; in the second we are moved to tears by the struggles of penitent souls, their prayers, their psalms, their aspirations for purity and longings for peace; in the third we are lost in the raptures of the beatific vision.

Purgatory, as a third or distinct place and state in the future world, is a mediæval fiction and has lost its significance in the Protestant creeds; but as a poetic description of the transition state from sin to holiness, it comes home to our daily experience and appeals to our sympathies. For this life is a school of moral discipline and a constant battle between the flesh and the spirit. The *Inferno* is diabolic, the *Purgatorio* is human, the *Paradiso* is angelic.

THE WAY TO PARADISE.

On this pilgrimage from earth to heaven man needs the guidance of reason and revelation. The former is embodied in Virgil, the latter in Beatrice.

The Scholastic theology regarded Aristotle as the representative of reason and philosophy, who, like another John the Baptist, prepared the way for Christ. Dante himself calls him the "master of those who know," who presides over the philosophic family in the border land of the *Inferno*.[1] Nevertheless, he chose Virgil as his guide, for several reasons: Virgil was a poet and Dante's master and favorite author;[2] he had described the descent to the spirit world and thereby anticipated the *Commedia*;[3] he was the prophet of imperial Rome and its successor, the holy Roman empire. Virgil and Aristotle combined represent the highest wisdom—poetry and philosophy—of which human reason is capable without the aid of divine grace.

Virgil came to Dante, not of his own accord, but at the request of Beatrice, who had been urged by St. Lucia at the desire of the Virgin Mary.[4] Sympathetic, intercessory, and prevenient grace made use of human wisdom in the preparatory process of salvation. Reason is under higher influence and subservient to revelation.

Virgil leads Dante through the *Inferno* and *Purgatorio*, but is most at home in the former, where he takes sure steps and well knows the way.[5] Only in that region where Hell has changed its form by reason of the earthquake at the death of

---

[1] *Inf.*, IV., 131 sq :—
"*Vidi il Maestro di color che sanno,
Seder tra filosofica famiglia.*"

[2] *Inf.*, I., 85 sqq :—
"Thou art my master, and my author thou,
Thou art alone the one from whom I took
The beautiful style that hath done honor to me."

In *Inf.*, VIII., 110, and *Purg.*, XXVII., 52, he calls him his "father sweet," *lo dolce padre*.

[3] In the sixth book of the *Æneid*.

[4] *Inf.*, II., 52 sqq. ; 94 sqq.

[5] *Inf.*, IX. 30 : "*Ben so il cammin.*"

Christ is he forced to enquire the way.[1] In Purgatory he calls himself a stranger and takes uncertain and timid steps.[2] Hence, he himself needs the guidance of angels from terrace to terrace. He represents here that prophetic anticipation which goes beyond ordinary paganism. Human reason knows much of sin and misery, but very little of repentance unto life.

Having reached the summit of the Mount of Purgatory or the terrestrial Paradise, Virgil is compelled to return to the infernal region of darkness. Philosophy can only lead to the threshold of revelation.[3] A higher guide is now needed. Beatrice conducts the poet from the terrestrial to the celestial Paradise in the name of revealed wisdom and the three Christian graces—faith, hope, love—which dance around her.[4]

God is love, and love only can know God. Hence St. Bernard of Clairvaux is given a prominent place in Paradise.[5] His motto was: "God is known as far as he is loved."[6] He is the champion of orthodox mysticism which approaches divine truth by devout contemplation and prayer; while scholasticism tries to reach it by a process of reasoning. He leads Dante to gaze upon the mystery of the Holy Trinity after preparing himself for it by prayer to the Holy Virgin.[7]

The Virgin Mary, St. Bernard, St. Lucia, Beatrice and all

---

[1] *Inf.*, XII., 91–94; XXIII., 127–132 (comp. ver. 37 sqq.).

[2] *Purg.*, II., 61–63:—

"And answer made Virgilius:—'Ye believe,
Perchance that we have knowledge of this place,
But we are strangers (*peregrin*), even as yourselves.'"

[3] *Purg.*, XVIII., 46–49:—

"And he to me: 'What reason seeth here,
Myself can tell thee; beyond that await
For Beatrice, since 'tis a work of faith.'"

[4] *Purg.*, XXXI., 130–135.

[5] *Par.*, XXXI., 94 sqq.; 139 sqq.; XXXII., 1 sqq.

[6] "*Tantum Deus cognoscitur quantum diligitur.*"

[7] *Par.*, XXXIII., 1 sqq.:—

"Thou Virgin Mother, daughter of thy Son,
Humble and high beyond all other creatures."

other saints are only agents of the one only Mediator Christ, without whom there is no salvation.

> "Unto this Kingdom never
> Ascended one who had not faith in Christ
> Before or since He to the tree was nailed."[1]

Many, however, here cry, "Christ, Christ," who at the judgment shall be far less near Him than "some shall be who knew not Christ."[2] In the Rose of Paradise are seated on one side the saints of the Old Dispensation,

> "Who believed in Christ who was to come;"

on the other side the saints of the New Dispensation,

> "Who looked to Christ already come."[3]

Under the Christian Dispensation baptism is necessary to salvation, so that even unbaptized innocence is detained in hell.[4]

Christ is often alluded to in the *Purgatorio* and *Paradiso* as our Lord and Saviour, as "the exalted Son of God and Mary," as "God of very God," as "the Lamb of God who taketh sins away," who "suffered death that we may live."[5]

In the *Inferno* the name of Christ is never mentioned, for the damned cannot endure it, but he is twice alluded to by Virgil as "the Mighty One" whom he saw descending into Hell "with the sign of victory crowned," and in the closing Canto, when passing from the *Inferno* to the *Purgatorio*, as

> "The Man who without sin was born and lived."[6]

It is also significant that the Name, which is above every name and in which alone we can be saved, is made to rhyme only with itself. Hence he repeats the word *Cristo* three times whenever it closes a line.[7]

---

[1] *Par.*, XIX., 103-105.   [2] *Par.*, XIX., 106-108.   [3] *Par.*, XXXII., 22-24.

[4] *Par.*, XXXII., 76-84. This fearful doctrine of the damnation of unbaptized infants dying in infancy was first clearly stated by St. Augustin and is still held by the Roman Church.

[5] *Purg.*, XVI., 18; XXIII., 75; XXXII., 113 sq.; *Par.*, XVI., 18; XXIII., 136; XXVI., 59; XXXI., 107; XXXII., 115, sq.

[6] *Inf.*, IV., 53, 54; XXXIV., 115.

[7] See the passages ending with *Cristo*, e.g. *Par.*, XIV., 104, 106, 108; XIX., 104, 106, 108; XXXII., 83, 85 and 87. The reason for this repetition is not a defect of the Italian language, which has many rhymes to *Cristo*, as *visto*, *misto*, *acquisto*, *tristo*.

THE POETIC FORM OF THE COMMEDIA.

The *Commedia* consists of three parts, Hell, Purgatory, and Paradise. Each part includes nine sub-divisions, and thirty-three songs or cantos. Hell, however, has an additional canto, which serves as a general introduction to the whole, so that the poem numbers altogether one hundred cantos, and fourteen thousand two hundred and thirty verses.

The system of versification chosen by Dante for the expression of his thoughts, is the terza rima, borrowed from the Provençal Troubadours, which combines the character of earnestness and solemnity with that of gracefulness and melody, and is admirably adapted to the contents of the poem. Each stanza consists of three lines, each line of eleven syllables, making thirty-three syllables for each stanza. One line rhymes with two in the following stanzas; but the last four rhymes of each canto are couplets instead of triplets. The accent falls regularly according to the law of poetic harmony. Thomas a Celano, who died several years before Dante was born, had used the triple rhyme in Latin (but in unbroken succession) most effectively and inimitably in his *Dies Irae*.

Everywhere in the *Commedia* we meet with the number three. It is the symbolic number of the Deity. The *Paradiso* is full of the praise of the Triune God. The superscription of the *Inferno*, consisting of three stanzas, reminds us already of Him with fearful earnestness, and the thirty-third canto of the *Paradiso* closes with the vision of the Trinity. According to Aristotle, everything consists of beginning, middle, and end. According to Thomas Aquinas, this fundamental idea of Christianity pervades the whole constitution of the world. The name of the Holy Trinity is written upon creation, and stamped upon eternity. Our poet represents even Satan with three faces, as the terrible antitype of the Triune God. The fact that the *Commedia* embraces one hundred songs, symbolizes the perfection of the poem which is complete in itself, a true picture of the harmonious universe. The number ten is the symbol of perfection,[1] and its square, one hundred, designates absolute perfection or completion.[2]

---

[1] "*Numero perfetto*," as Dante designates it in the *Vita Nuora*.
[2] "*Numero perfettissimo*."

To show how strictly Dante made it his object to reach an even measure, or to make use of a certain economy in the form, we may mention the circumstance that each of the three parts closes with the word "*stelle*," or stars; for these are, according to him, the blessed abodes of peace, whither his view is ever directed, and to which he would also gladly draw with him his readers. "Can I not everywhere look up to the stars?" he wrote to the government of Florence when he proudly refused the offer of pardon.

As already remarked, he always rhymes the peerless name of Christ three times with itself, and with itself only.

The rhyme came to him most naturally as the expression of the idea. Both were born together as body and soul. A contemporary of Dante (the unknown author of the *Ottimo commento*) heard him say "that a rhyme had never led him to change his thought, but that often he had made words express for him new meanings."

The language of the poem is everywhere made to correspond with the character of the thought: in Hell, it is awfully earnest; in Purgatory, affectingly pensive; in Paradise, transportingly charming; in all parts simple and noble, solemn and elevated. It abounds in symbols and images, and sounds like cathedral music.

A striking feature is Dante's terseness and conciseness, which reminds one of Tacitus and Tertullian. He says no more than enough, and condenses *multum in parvo*, even at the expense of clearness. He writes as the lightning writes on rocks. "One smiting word, and then there is silence, nothing more said. His silence is more eloquent than words." (Th. Carlyle.)[1]

Altogether, the form of the poem as much as the contents reveals the highest order of creative genius.

Dante intended to write the *Commedia* in Latin, but wisely abandoned the idea and chose the vernacular. He thus became the creator of Italian poetry, as Boccaccio, of Italian prose.

[2] Prof. Botta (*Introd. to Dante*, p. 137) thus describes Dante's style: "It combines sublimity with simplicity, strength with ardor, and intellectual speculation with glowing imagination. Vigorous and concise, it may be said of Dante as has been said of Homer, that it is easier to wrench the club from the hand of Hercules than to take a word from his verses without endangering their harmony and significance."

THE DARK FOREST.

"Midway upon the journey of our life
  I found myself within a forest dark,
  For the straightforward pathway had been lost.

Ah, me! how hard a thing it is to say
  What was this forest savage, rough and stern,
  Which in the very thought renews the fear."

The gloomy and savage forest to which the poet transports us in these first lines, represents the condition of the human heart lying in sin and error, and also the condition of the world at the time of Dante.

With the dawn of day he reaches the end of the forest, and seeks to ascend a delectable mountain illuminated by the sun, the symbol of virtue and of the empire. His efforts are in vain, for he is confronted and driven back by a spotted, deceitful and light-footed leopard, a haughty and terrible lion, and a meagre and ravenous she-wolf.[1] This allegory has a moral as well as a political and historical meaning. The three animals reflect the ruling passions of the human heart in youth, manhood, and old age, and symbolize at the same time the principal powers of the times: the leopard stands for cunning, and the republic of Florence; the lion for violence, and the kingdom of France; the she-wolf for avarice, and the papal court at Rome.

Just as the poet rushes down the mountain and back again into the dark forest, he beholds the shade of the old singer of the Æneid and prophet of the Roman empire, who represents secular wisdom and statesmanship, and had taught him the poetic art.[2] Virgil was sent to his rescue by Beatrice, the impersonation of divine love and wisdom, who herself was moved by the prayers of St. Lucia and the sympathy of the Virgin Mary. He comforts Dante by predicting, under the

---

[1] Doubtless he had in mind here the passage in Jeremiah v., 6: "Wherefore a lion out of the forest shall slay them, a wolf of the evenings [or, deserts] shall spoil them, a leopard shall watch over their cities; every one that goeth out thence shall be torn in pieces; because their transgressions are many, and their backslidings are increased." The three sins may have been suggested by "the lust of the flesh, and the lust of the eyes, and the vainglory of life." 1 John ii., 16.

[2] "Lo bello stile che m' ha fatto onore." Inf., 1., 89.

form of a Greyhound, a reformer of church and state, and offers to lead him on a journey through Hell and Purgatory that he might witness the terrible punishments of the wicked, and the purifying sufferings of the penitent. Through Paradise he would be conducted by a worthier spirit, Beatrice herself.

And thus the two brother poets enter upon their visionary pilgrimage.

THE INSCRIPTION ON THE GATE OF THE INFERNO.

> Per me si va nella città dolente ;
> Per me si va nell' eterno dolore ;
> Per me si va tra la perduta gente.
>
> Giustizia mosse il mio alto Fattore :
> Fecemi la divina Potestate,
> La somma Sapienza, e il primo Amore.
>
> Dinanzi a me non fur cose create,
> Se non eterne, ed io eterna duro :
> Lasciate ogni speranza, voi, ch' entrate![1]

This inscription written in dark colors on the gate to the abode of the lost has, for terrific grandeur, no parallel in poetic literature. It is as trying to translators as the *Dies Iræ*. Let us compare some of the best versions, unrhymed and rhymed.

H. F. CARY. 1805.	HENRY W. LONGFELLOW. 1867.
Through me you pass into the city of woe :	Through me the way is to the city dolent ;
Through me you pass into eternal pain :	Through me the way is to eternal dole ;[2]
Through me among the people lost for aye.	Through me the way among the people lost.
Justice the founder of my fabric moved :	Justice incited my sublime Creator ;
To rear me was the task of power divine,	Created me divine Omnipotence,
Supremest wisdom, and primeval love.	The highest Wisdom, and the primal Love.
Before me things create were none, save things	Before me there were no created things,
Eternal, and eternal I endure.	Only eterne, and I eternal last.
All hope abandon, ye who enter here.	All hope abandon, ye who enter in !

[1] *Inf.*, III., 1-9. Witte's text, but I have capitalized the three nouns which refer to the Persons of the Holy Trinity. Fraticelli and Scartazzini read : *eterno (eternamente)* for *eterna* (which refers to *porta*, vers. 11).

[2] Longfellow (as he told me himself in his study, where I saw him once, not long after the publication of his translation) wished to imitate the repetition of sounds like the tolling of a funeral bell : *dolente, dolore*. But it is too literal for easy idiomatic English, as is, in fact, his whole otherwise admirable translation.

ICHABOD CHARLES WRIGHT. 1833.

Through me ye enter the abode of woe:
  Through me to endless sorrow are conveyed:
  Through me amid the souls accurst ye go.

Justice did first my lofty Maker move:
  By Power Almighty was my fabric made,
  By highest Wisdom, and by primal Love.

Ere I was form'd, no things created were,
  Save those eternal—I eternal last:
  All hope abandon—ye who enter here.

DEAN E. H. PLUMPTRE. 1887.

Through me men pass to city of great woe;
  Through me men pass to endless misery;
  Through me men pass where all the lost ones go.

Justice it was that moved my Maker high,
  The Power of God it was that fashioned me,
  Wisdom supreme, and primal Charity.

Before me nothing was of things that be,
  Save the eterne, and I eterne endure:
  Ye that pass in, all hope abandon ye.

KARL STRECKFUSS. 1824.

Ich führe dich[1] zur Stadt der Qualerkornen,
  Ich führe dich zum unbegrenzten Leid,
  Ich führe dich zum Volke der Verlornen.

Mich schuf mein Meister aus Gerechtigkeit,
  Die erste Liebe wirkte mich zu gründen,
  Die höchste Weisheit und Allmächtigkeit.

Vor mir war nichts Erschaffenes zu finden,
  Als Ewiges, und ewig daur' auch ich.
  Lasst, die ihr eingeht, jede Hoffnung schwinden!

OTTO GILDEMEISTER. 1888.

Ich führe zu der Stadt voll Schmerz und Grausen,
  Ich führe zu dem wandellosen Leid,
  Ich führe hin, wo die Verlornen hausen.

Ihn, der mich schuf, bewog Gerechtigkeit,
  Mich gründete die Macht des Unsichtbaren,
  Die erste Lieb und die Allwissenheit.

Geschöpfe giebt es nicht, die vor mir waren,
  Als ewige, die selbst ich ewig bin.
  Lasst, die ihr eingeht, alle Hoffnung fahren!

Hell was founded after the fall of Adam by the Holy Trinity, the Almighty power of the Father (*la divina Potestate*), the Wisdom of the Son (*la somma Sapienza*), and the Love of the Holy Spirit (*il primo Amore*). Love is called the "first" because it is the motive of the creation and of all the works of God. According to Thomas Aquinas, all the works of the Holy Trinity are common to the three Persons.

[1] *Durch mich geht man*, would be more literal and just as good. A door cannot be said to *lead*.

ENDLESS PUNISHMENT.

Dante agrees with the orthodox Catholic faith as to endless punishment, and peoples hell not only with all impenitent sinners who rejected the gospel, but also with all unbaptized adults and children who never heard the name of Christ. This would include all the heathen, Jews and Mohammedans who, before and after Christ, constitute the overwhelming majority of the human race. He exempts only the Hebrew saints who were redeemed by Christ from their subterranean prison at his descent into the nether world.

It is true, he moderates, in accordance with Catholic doctrine, the sufferings of unbaptized children and the nobler heathen. The Scholastic divines make a distinction between the negative penalty of loss (*pœna damni*), and the positive penalty of sense (*pœna sensus*), and usually exempted infants from the latter. According to Dante, they utter "no lamentations but only sighs" from "sorrow without pain."[1] The reason of their exclusion from heaven is not that they sinned, but that they "had not baptism, which is the portal of the faith."[2]

The heathen are lost, as Virgil says, who includes himself in the number, because

> "In the right manner they adored not God, ...
> For such defects, and not for other guilt,
> Lost are we, and are only so far punished,
> That without hope we live on in desire."[3]

Dante is "seized with grief in his heart" when he hears this, because "some people of much worthiness" he knew "were suspended in that Limbo." Virgil informs him that at one time Adam, Abel, Noah, Moses, Abraham, David, Rachel and many others were confined there, but were released and transferred to Paradise by "a Mighty One (Christ) at his triumphant entrance."

Virgil has no hope that he and his heathen brethren will be released in a similar manner at some future day. Their lot, however, is tolerable, and virtually a continuation of their life on earth. The poets and philosophers sit in the dim twilight of

---

[1] *Inf.*, IV., 25–30.   [2] *Inf.*, IV., 36.   [3] *Inf.*, IV., 37–42.

reason, continue their occupation, and are very courteous and polite to each other.

Dante sees first on a summit enlightened by a fire the shades of Homer, the poet sovereign, Horace, the satirist, Ovid and Lucan. They respectfully salute Virgil as he reappears among them, and then after proper introduction they salute Dante also, and receive him as the sixth in the distinguished band of master poets.[1]

Then coming into "a meadow of fresh verdure," he beholds in a place open, luminous and high, a company of the mighty spirits of ancient Greece and Rome, walking on "the green enamel." Electra, Hector and Æneas, Cæsar "in armor, with falcon eyes," King Latinus with his daughter Lavinia, Brutus "who drove Tarquin forth," Lucretia, Julia, Marcia, and Cornelia; and associated with them, but in a separate spot, the noble Saracen knight Saladin; and higher up Aristotle, "the master of those who know," surrounded by his philosophic family, "all gazing upon him and doing him honor;" nearest to him Socrates and Plato; and after them Democritus, "who puts the world on chance," Diogenes, the cynic, Empedocles, Thales, Heraclitus, the weeping philosopher, Dioscorides, Orpheus, Cicero and Livy, and "moral Seneca," Euclid, the geometrician, Ptolemy, the astronomer, Galen, the physician, Hippocrates, Avicenna, and Averrhoës, the Arabian translator and commentator of Aristotle, and many others whom he "cannot all portray in full."[2]

As for the bad heathen and bad Christians, they are doomed to fearful, never ending torments, which Dante describes in picturesque, but horrible forms.

The doctrine of eternal punishment is the most awful that can be conceived of. The more we think of it, the more we shrink from it, and the more we desire to escape from it. The Roman Catholic doctrine of Purgatory applies only to imperfect Catholic Christians, and leaves the entire heathen world to outer darkness and despair. The theory of an ultimate restoration of all human beings to holiness and happiness would give absolute relief, and completely restore the harmony of the universe and the concord of all the discords of history, but it is not sustained by the

[1] *Inf.*, IV., 67 sqq.   [2] *Inf.*, IV., 121-145.

Bible or any orthodox Church. The theory of the annihilation of rational beings made in the image of God and redeemed by the blood of Christ is hard enough, but not nearly as revolting to every sentiment of sympathy and compassion, as the doctrine of never-ending punishment. It is difficult to conceive that an infinitely wise and merciful God should have created so many beings in full foreknowledge of such a terrible fate. But we humbly bow before the highest authority of Him who came into this world for the express purpose to save it from sin and perdition.

There is, however, good scriptural ground for a very serious modification of the orthodox doctrine as far as the *number* of the lost and the *mode* of their punishment are concerned. There is no Scripture warrant for excluding from heaven the overwhelming majority of mankind, *i.e.*, not only all bad Christians, but also all the heathen, Jews, Mohammedans, together with their unbaptized (or, in Calvinistic phraseology, non-elect) children dying in infancy. St. Augustin, who exerted more influence upon the Creeds of Christendom than any other divine, first clearly taught the "terrible dogma" of the damnation of all unbaptized infants, though he reduces their sufferings to a minimum. He inferred it from the doctrine of the absolute necessity of water baptism for salvation, which he based upon a one-sided interpretation of John 3 : 5 and Mark 16 : 16. But these passages can only refer to those who come within the reach of the visible church and the ordinary means of grace. We are bound to these means, but God is free and his Spirit can work where, when, and how he pleases (John 3 : 8). As regards children dying in infancy before they have committed any actual transgression, we have the word and act of our Saviour who invited them to his arms, blessed them, and declared, without any reference to circumcision or baptism, and before Christian baptism was instituted or could be exercised: "Of such is the Kingdom of God" (Mark 10 : 13–16). Here is a firm and immovable ground of hope for all bereaved parents. Surely there is nothing in the Bible rightly interpreted to prevent, and much, very much to encourage the charitable hope that the overwhelming mass of God's creatures made in his own image and redeemed by the blood of his Son, will ultimately be saved and join "the great multitude which no man can number, of all nations, and kindreds, and people, and tongues" (Rev. vii : 9), in the praise of his infinite wisdom and love.

THE VESTIBULE.

As the poets enter through the gate of despair they are overwhelmed with the horrid lamentations of the lost.

> "There sighs, complaints, and ululations loud
>   Resounded through the air without a star,
>   Whence I, at the beginning, wept thereat.
> Languages diverse, horrible dialects,
>   Accents of anger, words of agony,
>   And voices high and hoarse, with sound of hands
> Made up a tumult that goes whirling on
>   Forever in that air forever black,
>   Even as the sand doth, when the whirlwind breathes."[1]

The description reminds one of the fearful words of the ghost of Hamlet's father who, however, was not in Hell but only in Purgatory.

> "I am thy father's spirit ;
> Doom'd for a certain term to walk the night,
> And for the day confin'd to lasting fires,
> Till the foul crimes, done in my days of nature,
> Are burnt and purg'd away. But that I am forbid
> To tell the secrets of my prison-house,
> I could a tale unfold, whose lightest word
> Would harrow up thy soul, freeze thy young blood,
> Make thy two eyes like stars start from their spheres,
> Thy knotted and combined locks to part,
> And each particular hair to stand on end,
> Like quills upon the fretful porcupine ;
> But this eternal blazon must not be
> To ears of flesh and blood."

The vestibule or outer court of Hell is the abode of the melancholy crowd of cowards and indifferentists, who are too bad for Heaven and too good for Hell, and hence spit out by both in disgust. Dante pours upon them the vial of his scorching sarcasm, of which he was a perfect master. He had in his mind the lukewarm Laodiceans who were neither hot nor cold, and

---

[1] *Inf.*, III., 22-30.

whom the Lord threatened to spew out of his mouth (Rev. iii.:
15, 16). The inhabitants of the Ante-Hell lived in selfish
indifference, without fame or infamy, unconcerned about the
great moral struggle going on in the world. Mercy and justice
alike disdain them. Hell would be too proud to receive such
guests who had not courage enough to be bad. Their names
are unknown, lost and forgotten.[1] They are mingled with that
caitiff choir of angels who remained neutral in the great rebellion
of Satan against God. This miserable rabble is driven by an
unceasingly whirling flag; while wasps and flies sting their
naked bodies. Dante is surprised at their large number. Virgil
tells him:

> "Let us not speak of them, but look and pass."[2]

Yet Dante recognizes the shade of him,

> "Who made through cowardice the great refusal."[3]

This is usually referred to Pope Cœlestine V. (elected July 5,
1294), and "the great refusal," to his abdication of the papacy
(December 13, 1294)—an event which had never occurred
before. He was a saintly monk, but ignorant of the world and
human nature. Cardinal Benedetto Gaetano, afterwards Boniface VIII., persuaded him, a few months after his election, to
resign the highest dignity on earth, and imprisoned him, to prevent a schism, in a castle near Anagni, where he died (May 19,
1296). The resignation of Cœlestine was regarded as a sublime
act of self-denial and sacrifice, for which he was canonized by
Clement V., in 1313.

It is strange that the first person whom Dante met in Hell
should be a pope; and stranger still, that it should be such an
humble and innocent pope whom he exposes to contempt, in
direct opposition to the judgment of the Church. He may have
looked upon the resignation as an act of cowardly escape from
solemn duty, prompted by the unholy ambition of Pope Boniface

---

[1] Like that tyrant in Uhland's *Minstrel's Curse*:

> "Versunken und vergessen! das ist des Sängers Fluch."

[2] *Inf.*, III. 51:

> "Non ragioniam di lor, ma guarda e passa."

[3] *Ibid.*, III., 60:

> "Che fece per viltate il gran rifiuto."

VIII., whom above all popes he hated as a bad man and a disgrace to the papacy.[1] But resignation is not "refusal."

Some have conjectured that Dante meant Esau who sold his birthright, or the rich youth who was invited by Christ to follow him, but "went away sorrowful" (Matt. xix.: 22). But "the great refusal" points to a historic person and act well known in the time of the poet under that name.

I deem it most probable that the poet had in mind Pontius Pilate, who was perfectly convinced of the innocence of Christ, but from cowardice and fear of losing his place refused to do him justice and surrendered him to the bloodthirsty design of the Jewish hierarchy.[2] The basest act a judge could commit. Of all men in biblical or ecclesiastical history, Pilate was the fittest representative of cowardly and selfish neutrality. He was also best known to the readers of the *Commedia*, as his name is embedded in the Apostles' Creed to designate the historic connection of Christ's death with the Roman empire. Dante does not mention Pontius Pilate elsewhere, except figuratively by calling Philip the Fair of France "the modern Pilate," for his cowardly cruelty to a defenceless old pope.[3]

THE STRUCTURE OF THE INFERNO.

From the Vestibule the poets are in sleep as by a divine miracle transported across the cheerless Acheron to the *Inferno* proper. I shall confine myself to an outline of the pilgrimage.

The structure of the *Inferno*, as already observed, is that of a huge subterranean amphitheatre in the shape of a funnel, becoming narrower and narrower in the descent till it reaches the abode of Satan in the centre of the earth. This form corresponds to the nature and progress of sin, which consists in ever narrowing and contracting selfishness. As the number of slight and ordinary sinners is larger than that of great trans-

---

[1] In *Inf.*, XXVII., 104, 105, he makes Boniface say of his predecessor, that he despised the two keys of the papal power.

[2] This interpretation as far as I know is new, and was suggested to me recently by a friend in a conversation on Dante, as a plausible conjecture. I wonder that it has not occurred to any of the numerous commentators on Dante.

[3] *Purg.* XX., 91.

SECTION OF THE HELL.

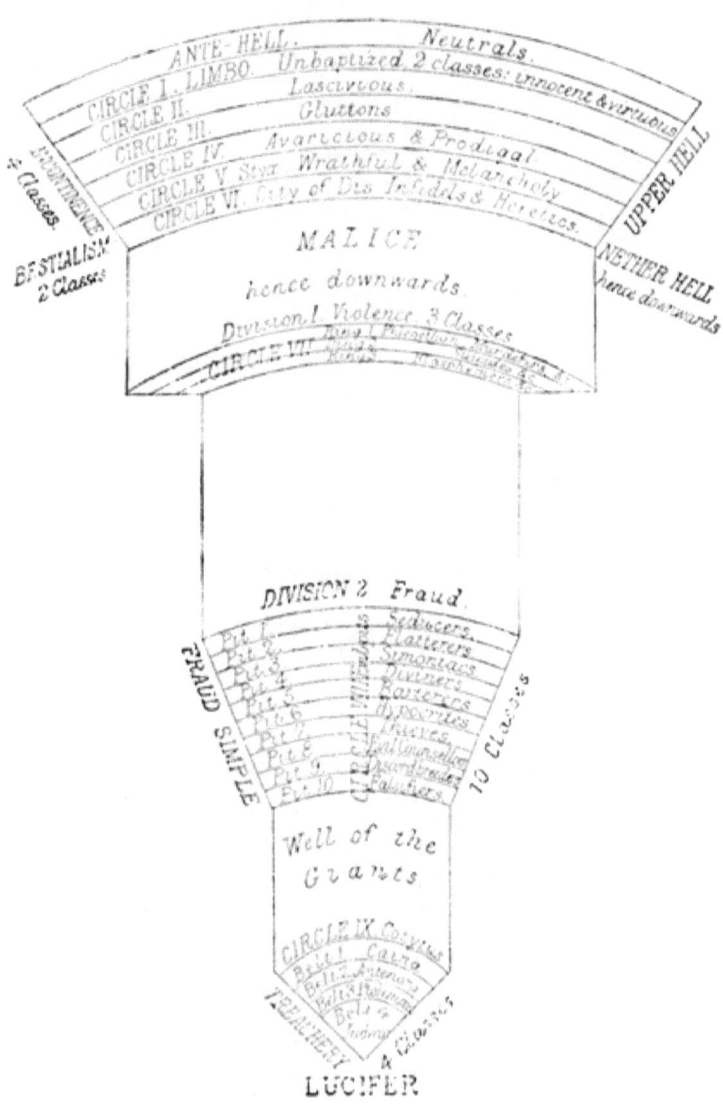

gressors, the upper circles are broader and more densely crowded.

It is also very expressive, that over these regions there reigns a constant darkness[1] growing denser with the depth. Still, a faint gleam of light overspreads the gloomy terraces; and the lower portions are illumined by the unquenchable fire,[2] but only to increase the horror of the damned by rendering their misery visible to them. Thomas Aquinas teaches that the inhabitants of Hell see their misery "*sub quadem umbrositate.*"

Milton describes Hell as

> "A dungeon horrible, on all sides around,
> As one great furnace, flam'd; yet from those flames
> No light, but rather darkness visible,
> Serv'd only to discover sights of woe,
> Regions of sorrow, doleful shades, where peace
> And rest can never dwell, hope never comes
> That comes to all, but torture without end
> Still urges, and a fiery deluge, fed
> With ever burning sulphur unconsumed."[3]

In consequence of the meaning of the number three, reaching as it does even to the lower world, Dante divides Hell into three regions, each one comprising three terraces, so that it on the whole consists of nine circles. To them must be added a preliminary circle, the vestibule of Hell.

The regions are separated from one another by the windings of a large stream, which flows in circles through Hell. Of these circular windings there are four. The first, separating the fore-court from Hell properly so called, is the joyless Acheron; the second, the marshy Styx; the third, the burning Phlegethon; and the fourth, the cold Cocytus. The stream ends at last in an icy lake, in the centre of which sits the Devil. This is probably intended to represent the stream of Belial, mentioned in 2 Samuel xxii.: 5, as encompassing the dead in Hell. It rises, according to Dante, in the island of Crete, from the confluence of all the tears which the human race has ever wept in

---

[1] Matt. viii.: 12, "Cast into outer darkness."

[2] Compare Mark ix.: 44; Matt. iii.: 12 ("unquenchable fire").

[3] *Par. Lost*, Book I., 61 sqq.

consequence of sin, and will yet weep during the different ages of its existence, which increase in wickedness, and find their representatives in these four streams.

SIN AND PUNISHMENT.

In the division of sins our poet follows Aristotle, who divides the sins into three classes; namely, incontinence (ἀκρασία), wickedness (κακία), and violence, or beastliness (θηριότης).[1] But, in accordance with his Christian standpoint, Dante differs from Aristotle in that he places wickedness, or as he terms it cunning (*froda*), lowest in the scale. The first kind of sin, that of incontinence, is human; the second, violence, is bestial; the third, cunning, is demoniacal. Each of these genera comprises again a number of distinct species. Under incontinence, for example, he ranks licentiousness, avarice, prodigality, wrath, etc.; under violence he includes murder, blasphemy, etc.; under cunning, the different forms of treachery.

The punishments of the damned are, according to Dante, both spiritual and bodily. The spiritual punishments consist chiefly in an impotent hatred towards God, in envying the happy condition of the blessed, in dissensions among themselves, and in a continual lust for sin without the power or prospect of satisfying it. This everlasting torment expresses itself also externally, and Dante exhausts ingenuity in describing the bodily punishments.

In doing this he follows the general principle laid down in the Book of Wisdom, xi., 17: "Wherewithal a man sinneth, by the same also shall he be punished." A similar thought was supposed to be implied in the assertion of our Lord: "With what measure ye mete, it shall be measured to you again" (Mark iv.: 24; Luke vi.: 38). Sin itself, in the other world, is the punishment of sin. Sinners flee from punishment, but desire the sin; the desire is present, but its satisfaction is unattainable; the desire itself has become a tormenting sting.

This general idea of a close connection between sin and the form of its punishment is, however, carried out, not in a pedantic and literal, but in a very free and manifold way. The lazy, for

---

[1] *Ethics*, vii., 1.

example, roll themselves about in the mire; the licentious are driven to and fro by a whirlwind; the irascible smite each other in the muddy Styx; the Archbishop Ruggieri, who upon earth had denied food to Count Ugolino, is doomed to have his head chewed by him in Hell.

IMPARTIALITY OF DANTE.

Dante brings together a variegated mass of pictures from all ages and ranks. Poets, scholars, philosophers, heroes, princes, emperors, monks, priests, cardinals, and popes, in short, all that Truth and History, Poetry and Mythology, have been able to afford of distinguished sins and vices, he causes to pass before us, living, speaking, and suffering, until overcome with horror we feel compelled to bow before the terrible justice of God, to whom every sin is an abomination. There is opened here to the careful reader, a wide field of the most interesting, historical, psychological, metaphysical, theological and edifying observations. No poet has ever so forcibly and graphically described the sinfulness of sin and the well deserved terror of its guilt.

In his stern impartiality Dante spares neither friends nor foes, neither Ghibellines nor Guelfs, neither popes nor emperors, and restrains the claims of mercy. He assigns to everlasting woe Farinata degli Uberti, the most valiant and renowned leader of the Ghibellines in Florence who died 1264;[1] Cavalcante de' Cavalcanti, the father of his most intimate friend, Guido Cavalcanti;[2] even Brunetto Latini, his own beloved teacher;[3] and the unfortunate Francesca da Rimini, a near relative of his last patron, Guido da Polenta, under whose roof he died.[4] She is said to have been deceived by her father into marrying the deformed and repulsive Gianciotto Malatesta, son of the Lord of Rimini, while she loved his handsome brother Paolo, and was

---

[1] *Inf.*, x., 32 sqq.

[2] *Ibid.* x., 52 sqq. He was a Guelf and doomed to the same torment with the Ghibelline.

[3] *Ibid.* xv., 30 sqq.

[4] *Ibid.* v., 80 sqq. She was either an aunt, or niece of Guido. See Nota A., in Scartazzini's *La Div. Com.* I., 45, who gives the reports of Boccaccio and the anonymous Florentine edited by Fanfani.

murdered with him by her husband during the lifetime of Dante (1289). When he saw her he was moved to tears, and when he heard her delicate and touching tale of her temptation by reading a romantic love story, he "for pity swooned away as if he had been dying, and fell, even as a dead body falls."[1] He would have sent the guilty couple to Purgatory if they had had time to repent of their illicit love. But it was too late, too late! And so they have to feel that "there is no greater sorrow than to be mindful of the happy time in misery." Poor Francesca is the only Christian woman whom he branded; the other females whom he locates in the same region of despair, are all heathen—Semiramis, Dido, Helen, and "the voluptuous Cleopatra;"[2] and so are the women located in the eighth circle of Hell.[3] It would have been far more consistent with justice if he had substituted for the relation of his patron those infamous Roman amazons—Marozia and Theodora—who during the period of the papal "pornocracy" placed their paramours and bastards on the throne of St. Peter and dragged the papacy down to the lowest depth of depravity. But they are ignored.

THE NINE CIRCLES OF HELL.

Let us briefly survey the nine circles of Dante's *Inferno*.[4]

1. The first circle is the moderate hell for the least guilty class of sinners who were ignorant of Christianity and deprived of the benefit of baptism, yet are included among the lost in consequence of Adam's fall.[5] It is the border region or *Limbo*, which was formerly divided into the *Limbus Infantum* for unbaptized infants whose sighs cause the air to tremble, and the *Limbus Patrum*, the temporary prison of the pious souls from Adam to John the Baptist, who died in the hope of the coming Saviour, but were transferred to Paradise when Christ descended

---

[1] *Ibid.* v., 140-142. [2] *Ibid.* v., 58 sqq.

[3] Thais, the famous courtesan of Athens, *Inf.*, XVIII., 130 sqq.; Hecuba, Polyxena, and "the nefarious Myrrha who became, beyond all rightful love, her father's lover," *ibid.* XXX., 16 sqq.; 38 sqq.

[4] A minute description with suitable illustrations would require a volume. I may refer to the works of Professor Botta, Francesca Rossetti, and Dr. Hettinger, who give large extracts from the poem itself. See Lit., p. 333, 335.

[5] See p. 375 sq.

and proclaimed to them the accomplished redemption. Their place is occupied by the great poets, sages, statesmen, and heroes of ancient Greece and Rome who lived up to the dim light of natural reason and conscience. The wicked heathen are distributed among the impenitent Christians.

The Limbo is not a place of actual suffering, but rather corresponds to the Pagan Elysium. The distinguished heathen lead there a dreamy life of longing and desire, without hope, vainly groping in the dark after the unknown God. They still move in the element of worldly ambition, according to the maxim of Cicero: "*Optimus quisque maxime gloria ducitur.*" They seek honor and take honor, and constantly compliment each other. They look grave with an air of great authority, but speak seldom and with gentle voices. Dante was seized with grief to see among them persons of great worth; but the orthodox theology did not allow him to entertain any hope of their ultimate deliverance. "*Lasciate ogni speranza!*"

2. The Second Circle is the proper commencement of Hell; and Minos, the infernal Judge, watches at the entrance. It contains the souls of carnal sinners who are driven by fierce winds in total darkness. Here are the adulterous and voluptuous women, from Semiramis and Cleopatra to Francesca da Rimini among the poet's contemporaries. Canto V.[1]

3. The Third Circle is inhabited by epicures and gluttons, whose god is their belly. They are lying on the ground exposed to a constant shower of hail, foul water or snow, and to the barking of the three-headed monster Cerberus. Canto VI.

On the brink of the next Circle the poets find Plutus, the god of riches, who swells with rage when he sees strangers invade his realm, but is sharply reproved by Virgil.

4. The Fourth Circle is intended for the prodigal and avaricious doomed to roll large dead weights forwards and backwards. Among them are many popes and tonsured clergymen. Canto VII.

---

[1] This canto is the most popular in the whole poem and has often been separately translated. R. Köhler published twenty-two German translations from 1763–1863. See Lit., p. 334, and p. 383 sq.

5. The Fifth Circle is approached by a broad marsh and contains the filthy spirits of brutal arrogance and wrath. Dante recognizes among them Filippo Argenti, a worthless man of irascible temper, Herculean strength and immense wealth, whose riding horse was shod with silver (*argento*). He was of the Neri faction in Florence, and seems to have provoked the animosity of Dante, who belonged to the Bianchi. Canto VIII.

The first five Circles constitute the Upper Hell of Incontinence. We descend now to the Lower Hell of Malice.

6. The Sixth Circle is the dreary City of Dis or Lucifer, full of burning sepulchres open on the top. Here heretics and infidels are punished. Cantos VIII, 76 sqq.–XI. Among them are very distinguished persons, the valiant Ghibelline chief, Farinata of Florence, Cavalcante de' Cavalcanti (Farinata's son-in-law, and father of Dante's most intimate friend, Guido Cavalcanti), the Ghibelline Cardinal Ottaviano degli Ubaldini, of Florence, who said, "if there be any soul, I have lost mine for the Ghibellines," and the liberal and accomplished Hohenstaufen Emperor Frederick II., to whom was ascribed the fabulous book on The Three Impostors (Moses, Jesus, Mohammed).[1] It is strange that Dante omits the far more notorious arch-heretics of the ancient church, as Marcion, Manichæus, Arius, Nestorius, Pelagius, etc. But he wished to strike with his lightning the summits of Italian history still within the memory of his generation.

To them he adds a supreme pontiff. On the edge of a rocky precipice between the Sixth and Seventh Circle he found a large monument with an inscription: "Anastasius I hold whom Photinus drew from the straight way."[2] He means Anastasius II., an obscure pope, who ruled only two years (496–498), and is reported to have received the monophysitic deacon, Photinus of Thessalonica, into church communion. For this he was himself branded as a heretic in the famous *Decretum Gratiani*, and so

---

[1] Comp. above p. 307. In his book *De Vulg. Eloquio*, I., 12, Dante speaks highly of Frederick's literary merits.

[2] *Inf.*, XI., 8, 9:

"Anastasio papa guardo,
Lo qual trasse Fotin della via dritta."

considered in the Church down to the sixteenth century.[1] He died suddenly, and this was construed as a divine judgment.

Dante no doubt followed the authority of Gratian, the great teacher of the canon law at Bologna. He might have selected clearer and stronger examples of heretical popes, as Liberius (352–366), who was charged with Arianism, and Honorius I (625–638), who was condemned by œcumenical councils and by his own successors as a Monothelite. The case of Honorius figured most prominently in the Vatican Council of 1870, and was the chief argument of the anti-infallibilists.[2]

7. *The Seventh Circle* (Cantos XII.–XIV.), in three divisions, is the abode of murderers, suicides and blasphemers, and is surrounded by a river of blood. The way to it leads through a wild chasm of shattered rocks. It is guarded by the Minotaur, the horror of Crete and emblem of bloodthirsty violence and brutality. Among the murderers are mentioned Alexander the Great, the tyrant Dionysius of Sicily, Guy de Montfort, who during mass stabbed Prince Henry from revenge, and Attila, the King of the Huns, who called himself the Scourge of God.

Among the suicides, naked and torn, is Pietro delle Vigne (de Vineis), the famous secretary and chancellor of the Emperor Frederick II., otherwise a noble-hearted man, who was charged with treason and was unwilling to outlive his honor.

The small class of blasphemers against God are lying supine upon a plain of burning sand. They are more severely punished than their neighbors, by a slow and constant shower of flakes of fire, which fall upon them like flakes of snow in the Alps; yet they continue to blaspheme with their old fury. (Canto XIV.) Their representative is Capeneus, one of the seven kings who besieged Thebes. He was struck by Jupiter with his thunder.

> "Not any torment, saving thine own rage,
> Would be unto thy fury pain complete." [3]

Cantos XV. and XVI. describe the punishment of violence against nature. Here Dante does not spare his own teacher and

---

[1] See a full account of this case in Döllinger's *Papstfabeln des Mittelalters*, p. 124 sqq.; Eng. transl. 210 sqq.

[2] Schaff, *Creeds of Christendom*, I., 178 sqq ; *Church History*, IV., 500 sqq.

[3] *Inf.*, XIV., 65, 66.

friend, Brunetto Latini (xv., 30 sqq.), but he speaks to his baked and withered figure with great respect and affection.

Canto XVII. describes the punishment of usurers who do violence to nature and to art.

We now descend to the sins of bestiality.

8. The Eighth Circle, called the Malebolge[1] or Evil-budgets, consists of ten concentric ditches or pits for the following sinners: (1) Seducers, (2) Flatterers, (3) Simoniacs, (4) Soothsayers, (5) Barrators, (6) Hypocrites, (7) Thieves, (8) Evil Counselors, (9) Schismatics, (10) Falsifiers. Cantos XVIII.–XXXI.

Dante is especially severe, in Canto XIX., against the Simoniacs or Simonists, that is, the wretched followers of the arch-heretic and arch-hypocrite, Simon Magus, who prostitute for gold and silver the things of God, and turn his temple into a den of thieves. They are fixed one by one in narrow round holes along the sides of the rock, with the head downwards, with the feet and part of the legs standing out and tormented with flames.

At the bottom of the chasm are three popes, Nicholas III. (d. 1281), who enriched all his nephews by open simony; Boniface VIII., who "seized the comely Lady (the Church) and then made havoc of her" (d. 1303), and Clement V. (d. 1314), "the lawless shepherd from the west" (who was made pope under shameful conditions by the influence of Philip the Fair, of France). The last two Dante condemns by prophetic anticipation before their death (as the *Inferno* was begun in 1300). Such false shepherds St. John had in view when he saw the Roman harlot committing fornication with the kings. (Rev. xvii: 1–15.)

> "Ye have made yourselves a god of gold and silver;
> And from the idolater wherein do ye differ,
> Save that he worships one, and ye a hundred?"[2]

Then follows the famous passage of Constantine and his reputed donation of the temporal power to the pope.

This fearful severity does not make Dante an enemy of the papacy. On the contrary, he says that his reverence for the lofty keys prevented him from using still greater severity.[3]

---

[1] *Bolgia* (Lat. *bulga*, Fr. *bouge*) means a bag, budget, and in a wider sense any dark hole or gulf.

[2] *Inf.*, XIX., 112–114.   [3] *Ibid.* XIX., 100 sq.

Even Thomas Aquinas, his theological master, says that the pope, like any other mortal, may fall into the vice of simony, and his guilt is all the greater, the higher his position as the supreme disposer, not possessor, of the property of the Church.[1]

Among the sowers of scandal and schism are Mohammed and Ali, fearfully mutilated, and

"Cleft in the face from forelock unto chin."[2]

9. The Ninth and last Circle is the abode of traitors, furthest removed from the source of all light and heat, the frozen lake of Cocytus. Cantos XXXII.–XXXIV. Cold is expressive of the heartless selfishness of treason, and to a southern imagination, like Dante's, as severe a punishment as a burning furnace would be to a Scandinavian poet. He divides the circle into four concentric rings or belts, corresponding to four classes of traitors: (1) Caina for traitors to blood relations, called after Cain who murdered his brother. (2) Antenora for the traitors to their country, from Antenor who betrayed his native Troy. (3) Ptolemæa for the traitors to confidants, either from Ptolemy the Egyptian king who betrayed Pompey when he fled to him for protection, or, more probably, from Ptolemy who treacherously slew Simon, the high priest, and his two sons at a feast, 1 Macc., xvi.: 15–17. (4) Judecca for traitors to their benefactors, called after Judas Iscariot.

Dante finds many Florentines in the first two rings, both Guelfs and Ghibellines. He especially detests Bocca degli Abati, who by his treachery caused the slaughter of the Guelfs at the battle of Monte Aperto, in 1260, and threw every family of Florence into mourning.

But the most horrible scene in the Antenora, and the whole poem, is the punishment of Count Ugolino, Podestà of Pisa and chief of the Guelfs, and Archbishop Ruggieri, chief of the Ghibellines.[3] The count betrayed the Ghibellines in 1284, and united with the archbishop in 1288 in betraying Judge Nino, his own grandson, but was betrayed in turn by the archbishop, thrown into prison with two innocent sons and two

---

[1] *Summa*, II., II., q. 100. a. 1 a. 2, quoted by Hettinger. p. 166, 191.

[2] *Ibid.* XXVIII., 33.   [3] *Inf.*, XXXII., 124; XXXIII., 75.

grandsons and starved to death in a tower at Pisa, called ever since "the Tower of Famine." The two traitors "are frozen together in one hole so closely that one head was a cap to the other; and as bread is chewed for hunger, so the uppermost put his teeth into the other where the brain joins with the nape." Dante saw Ugolino as he raised " his mouth from the fell repast and wiped it on the hair of the head he had laid waste behind." The count tells the poet his last sufferings in the prison when he bit both his hands for grief, and his sons, thinking that he did it from hunger, said to him :

> "Father, much less pain 't will give us
> If thou do eat of us; thyself didst clothe us
> With this poor flesh, and do thou strip it off."

This tragedy, immortalized by Dante and Chaucer, gives a frightful picture of the ambition, treachery, cruelty and ferocity of the Middle Ages, and illustrates the law, that sin is its own worst punishment.

The thirty-fourth and last Canto of the *Inferno* opens with

> "*Vexilla Regis prodeunt Inferni!*"
> "The banners of the King of Hell come forth."

A parody of the hymn of triumph on the mystery of the cross by Fortunatus.[1] It is a startling introduction into the Judecca, the circle of the arch-traitor to God, the traitor to our Saviour, and the traitors to Cæsar.

Lucifer, "the Emperor of the dolorous Realm,"[2] is described as a hideous monster, immersed in the icy lake up to his breast. He had three faces, the counterpart of the Holy Trinity, the one fiery red in front, the others pale and black on the side. The three colors may symbolize the three continents then known over which his dominion extends. Under each face issued forth two mighty wings broader than sea-sails, in form and texture like a bat's; and he was flapping them so that three winds went forth

---

[1] "*Vexilla Regis prodeunt,
Fulget crucis mysterium,
Quo carne carnis conditor,
Suspensus est patibulo.*"

[2] "*Lo Imperador del doloroso regno.*" XXXIV., 28.

from him. With six eyes he wept, and down three chins gushed tears and bloody foam. In every mouth he champed a sinner with his teeth, like a brake, so that he thus kept three of them in torment. The worst of these three sinners, who suffers greatest punishment, is Judas Iscariot. He is suspended from the front mouth of Satan and has his head within, his feet outside. The other two, with their heads beneath, are Brutus, who "utters not a word," and Cassius, " who seems so stark of limb."

Shakespeare differs with Dante in the judgment of Brutus, "the noblest Roman of them all," who loved his country and the freedom of the Republic more than his benefactor. But Dante saw in the murder of Cæsar an assault upon the divinely constituted Roman empire, which was the type of the holy Roman empire, and the words of the dying Cæsar to Brutus: " Even thou, my child" (καὶ σὺ, τέκνον), may have reminded him of our Saviour's word to Judas: " Friend, do that for which thou art come" (ἑταῖρε, ἐφ᾽ ὃ πάρει, Matt. 26 : 50). Here is the culmination of Dante's view of Church and State as developed in his book *De Monarchia*. Judas sinned against the Divine Head of the Church, Brutus and Cassius sinned against the temporal head of the Imperial State, all sinned against God and humanity.

The triple-headed Satan with three sinners in his mouth corresponds to the grotesque demons in mediæval art. He is absolutely hideous, without one noble feature remaining. He thus differs widely from Milton's "archangel ruined," "in shape and gesture proudly eminent," whose "form had not yet lost all his original brightness."[1] Goethe abstains from a description of the outward form of Mephistopheles, but describes his character in words and actions more philosophically than Dante or Milton:

> " Ich bin ein Theil von jener Kraft,
> Die stets das Böse will und stets das Gute schafft;
> Ich bin der Geist der stets verneint."

Having reached the lowest depth of Hell, Virgil, bearing Dante, slides down the shaggy sides of Beelzebub between the tangled hair and frozen crusts, and passing through a cavern, the poets ascend to the opposite side of the earth, in the South Pacific Ocean.

> "Thence we came forth to rebehold the stars."

[1] Comp. *Parad. Lost*, 1., 192, 589; 11., 636; IV., 9-5.

THE PURGATORIO.

What a change from the region of eternal darkness to the sight of the sun and starry firmament, and from the despair of the lost to the hope of the saved! Purgatory is the temporary abode of the penitent who died in the grace of God, and look for that perfect peace which awaits them after completing the process of sanctification.[1] Still it is a place of suffering, and so far of dread. All pious Catholics expect to go there, with mingled fears and hopes, and none considers himself fit for the company of saints in light. Even popes are not exempt; their title "Holiness" applies only to their official character; personally they may be very unholy. Pope Pius IX., by an inscription on his coffin, requested the faithful to pray for his soul (*Orate pro me*). The suffering church in Purgatory is in constant contact with the militant church on earth by prayers and masses for the dead.

In Purgatory all is human, and appeals to our sympathy: a mingling of weakness and sorrow with virtue and hope, of the tears of repentance with the joys of forgiveness, of prayers and supplications with hymns of praise, of constant effort with the brightening prospect of ultimate purity and deliverance.

Dante's Purgatory is a steep, spherical mountain in the Western Hemisphere, which, according to the original plan of Providence was to have been the abode of the human race. It is the highest mountain in the world. Its summit is crowned with the terrestrial Paradise, out of which Adam was thrust on account of his transgression. It is the direct antipode of Sion, the mountain of salvation, on the inhabited hemisphere, and at the same time the threshold of Heaven. Both mountains rise, in a direct line, above the middle point of Hell. Christ, the second Adam, has again recovered, by his death upon Golgotha, the Paradise which was lost by the sin of the first Adam. But the way now leads through Purgatory, *i. e.*, through the deep knowledge of sin, and the purifying pains of penitence.

At the foot of the mountain of purification Dante meets Cato of Utica, the Stoic friend of liberty, who committed

[1] *Purg.*, III., 73 sqq.

suicide that he might not survive the Roman Republic. He is
described as a solitary old man with a venerable aspect, long
gray beard and double lock. He is the guardian of Purgatory,
and the only heathen who escaped the eternal prison, except the
Emperor Trajan.[1] He wonders at the appearance of Virgil,
who assures him that he came not of his own accord, but at the
behest of Beatrice. By his direction, Virgil must first wash
from Dante's face the filth of Hell, and gird him with a smooth
rush (the symbol of humility). Then an angel, the direct re-
verse of the dreadful Charon, who conducted the dead across
Acheron, brings them in a light bark to the opposite shore.

Purgatory has, like Hell, a vestibule where all those are required to tarry, who have postponed repentance while upon earth
to the last moment. An angel escorts the wanderers over three
stairs, which represent the three stages of penitence (*contritio*,
confessio, and *satisfactio*), through the gate of absolution, and, in
order that he may think upon the seven mortal sins, cuts the
letter P (*peccata*) seven times upon his forehead with his sword.[2]

The mountain itself has seven broad terraces cut into its
sides, and on these dwell the penitent. The different penances
correspond with the punishments of Hell, in inverted order. In
Hell Dante descended from the lesser to the greater transgressions; in Purgatory he leads us from the greater sins and
penances upward to those of less enormity. The sins for which
penance is done here, are the same which are punished there;
but with this difference, that there we have to do with obdurate
and impenitent sinners, here with contrite souls. As in Hell,
sin and punishment, so in Purgatory, sin and penance, stand in a
causal relation toward one another; but the relation here is one
of opposition, sin being destroyed, since the will is brought to
break and yield, in direct contrariety to what it was before.

The proud, who fill the first and lowest terrace, are compelled
to totter under huge weights, in order that they may learn humility. The indolent in the fourth terrace are constantly and rapidly walking. In the fifth, the avaricious and prodigal, their
hands and feet tied together, lie with their faces in the dust, weeping and wailing. In the sixth, the gluttons must, like Tantalus,

---

[1] See above, p. 349.   [2] *Purg.*, IX., 93 sqq.; 102 sqq.

suffer hunger and thirst, in sight of a tree richly laden with fruits, and of a fresh flowing fountain, until they have learned moderation. In the seventh, the licentious wander about in flames, that their sensual passions may be purged from them by fire.

At the entrance into every circle the angel who conducts them obliterates one of the P's upon the forehead of the poet. In the same measure also his ascent becomes easier at every terrace. In place of the fearful darkness of the *Inferno* he is here lighted on his way by the three stars of the theological virtues, Faith, Hope, and Love. In place of the heart-rending lamentations of the damned, he hears the Lord's Prayer, the prayers to the saints and the ever sweeter sounding hymns of Salvation, as sung by the souls which are longingly gazing toward Paradise, and step by step approach nearer to its confines. At the beginning of the eleventh Canto we hear a most beautiful paraphrase of the Pater Noster from the mouth of the proud who have to become as little children of the Father in heaven before they can enter the kingdom of heaven (Matt. xviii., 3).[1] Whenever a soul has completed its purification a trembling of the whole mountain announces its entrance into heaven.[2]

Having reached the Terrestrial Paradise on the summit of the mountain, Dante sees in a great vision the Church triumphant, under the image of a triumphal car drawn by a griffin, a fabulous animal, half eagle, half lion, which symbolizes the double nature of Christ, the Head of the Church. The mystery of the incarnation and the cross had been explained to him previously by Beatrice (in Canto VII., 19 sqq.).

Beatrice now descends from Heaven and appears to Dante in the triumphal car. She takes the place of Virgil, who is not permitted to tread the Courts of Heaven. She rebukes Dante in strong language for his sins, and exhorts him to bathe in the

---

[1] " *O Padre nostro, che ne' cieli stai,*
Non circonscritto, ma per più amore,
Che ai primi effetti di lassù tu hai," etc.

[2] *Purg.*, XXI., 58 sqq.
" It trembles here, whenever any soul
Feels itself pure, so that it soars, or moves
To mount aloft, and such a cry attends it." (Luke xv., 10.)

brook Lethe, that he may forget all evil and all past afflictions. A second vision displays to him the corruption of the Church. Beatrice prophesies its restoration, and causes him to drink conversion from the brook Eunoe, whereby he becomes capable of rising upward to Heaven.

THE PARADISO.

Lightly now, as upon the wings of light, Dante flies upward through the different spheres of the Celestial Paradise, and marks his progress only by the higher glory of his exalted companion.[1]

Since very few Christians, according to Catholic theology, die in a state sufficiently mature for the company of the saints in light, Dante could not people Paradise with contemporaries or persons recently deceased, and confined himself to canonized saints and the great lights of the Church, who are the common property of mankind. He stretched, however, a point in favor of his ancestor Cacciaguida, who in the heaven of Mars praises the virtues of the great Florentines of former times, and prophesies Dante's banishment,[2] and in favor of two of his personal acquaintances, namely Piccarda (a sister of Forese and Corso Donati and of his wife Gemma Donati), who was a saintly nun of Santa Clara,[3] and Charles Martel of Hungary, his friend and benefactor, who married the beautiful daughter of Emperor Rudolph of Habsburg and died at the age of twenty-three (1295).[4] In the cases of those eminent schoolmen, Thomas Aquinas, Bonaventura, and Albert the Great, who died during Dante's youth, he anticipated the judgment of the Church which canonized them.

High up in Dante's Paradise are the Apostles and Evangelists, and the redeemed of the Old Dispensation from Adam down to John the Baptist. Then we meet in different stars, according to merit and station, Christian emperors and kings, as Constantine the Great, Justinian, Charlemagne, William the Good (King of Apulia and Sicily), and the Roman emperor Trajan (whom he believed to have been saved by the intercession of

[1] *Par.*, XXI., 7 sqq.
[2] *Ibid.*, Cantos XV.-XVII.
[3] *Par.*, III., 49 sqq.
[4] *Par.*, VIII., 49 sqq.

Pope Gregory I.),[1] the great doctors of the Church, as Augustin, Chrysostom, Anselm, Thomas Aquinas, Albertus Magnus, Bonaventura; holy monks, as St. Bernard, St. Dominic, Joachim de Flore, and St. Francis of Assisi. Dante mentions also a few pious popes, as Gregory I., and Agapetus, but only casually in a word, and ignores the great missionaries who converted the northern and western barbarians. But who can make even a limited selection of the cloud of witnesses from all nations and kindreds and tongues? No mortal man, not even the saints in heaven know the number of God's elect.

> "O thou predestination, how remote
> Thy root is from the aspect of all those
> Who the First Cause do not behold entire!
> And you, O mortals! hold yourselves restrained
> In judging; for ourselves, who look on God,
> We do not know as yet all the elect:
> And sweet to us is such a deprivation,
> Because our good in this good is made perfect,
> That whatsoe'er God wills, we also will."[2]

The spirits of the saints show themselves to Dante in different planets to indicate the different stages of perfection and glory which they enjoy, and the planetary influences under which they were while living on earth. But their proper common abode is the Empyrean, as explained in the fourth Canto:[3]

> "He of the Seraphim most absorbed in God,
> Moses, and Samuel, and whichever John
> Thou mayst select, I say, and even Mary,
> Have not in any other heaven their seats,
> Than have those spirits that just appeared to thee,
> Nor of existence more or fewer years;
> But all make beautiful the primal circle,
> And have sweet life in different degrees,
> By feeling more or less the eternal breath.
> They showed themselves here, not because allotted
> This sphere has been to them, but to give sign
> Of the celestial which is least exalted.
> To speak thus is adapted to your mind,
> Since only through the sense it apprehendeth
> What then it worthy makes of intellect."

---

[1] See above, p. 349.   [2] Par., XX., 130-134.   [3] Par., IV., 28-42.

Paradise is a region of pure light, and offers no such variety of definite localities and physical sensations as Hell and Purgatory. Hence it is less picturesque, but all the more spiritual and musical.

It is located according to the Ptolemaic system, in and beyond the heavenly bodies known at that time, and viewed as transparent spheres that roll around the stationary earth with different degrees of velocity, so that those which are nearest move slowest, while the most distant revolve with greatest rapidity. Dante gives us his astronomical theory in the second Book of the *Convivio* as follows [1]:

"The order of position [of the heavens] is this, that the first one enumerated is that where the Moon is; the second that where Mercury is; the third that where Venus is; the fourth that where the Sun is; the fifth that where Mars is; the sixth that where Jupiter is; the seventh that where Saturn is; the eighth that where the Fixed Stars are; the ninth is that which is not perceptible to sense (except by the motion spoken of above), and which is called by many the Crystalline, that is, the diaphanous, or wholly transparent. However, beyond all these, the Catholics place the Empyrean Heaven, which is as much as to say the Heaven of *Flame* or *Luminous* Heaven; and they hold it to be immovable, because it has within itself, in every part, that which its matter demands. And this is the reason that the *Primum Mobile* moves with immense velocity; because the fervent longing of all its parts to be united to those of this [tenth and] most divine and quiet heaven, makes it revolve with so much desire that its velocity is almost incomprehensible. And this quiet and peaceful heaven is the abode of that Supreme Deity who alone doth perfectly behold Himself. This is the abode of the beatified spirits, according to the holy Church, who cannot lie; and Aristotle also seems to think so, if rightly understood, in the first of The Heavens and Earth. This is the supreme edifice of the universe, in which all the world is included, and beyond which is nothing; and it is not in space, but was formed solely in the Primal Mind, which the Greeks call *Protonoe*. This is that magnificence of which the Psalmist spake, when he says to God, 'Thy magnificence is exalted above the heavens.' And thus, summing up what has here been discussed, it seems that there are ten heavens, of which that of Venus is the third; and this will be spoken of in the place where I intend to explain it."

In the same work he gives the symbolic significance of these heavenly bodies.[2]

[1] Bk. II., Ch. 4. In K. Hillard's translation, p. 64 sqq.
[2] Bk. II., Ch. 14, pp. 104–107, K. Hillard's translation.

1. "To see what is meant by the third heaven, we must first see what I mean by the single word 'heaven;' and then we shall see how and why this third heaven was necessary to us. I say that by *heaven* I mean science, and by *heavens* the sciences, because of three resemblances which the heavens bear to the sciences, above all in order and number, which seem to correspond in them; as will be seen in treating of this word 'third.'

2. "The first resemblance is the revolution of each around its immovable [centre]. Because each movable heaven revolves around its centre, which, however forcible that motion may be, remains immovable; and so each science revolves around its subject, which is not moved by it, because science demonstrates its own subject, but presupposes it.

3. "The second resemblance is in their power of illumination. For as each heaven illuminates visible things, so each science illuminates those that are intelligible.

4. "And the third resemblance is in their [the heavens] conducting towards perfection of things disposed thereto. Of which influence, in so far as it concerns the primal perfection, that is, material generation, all philosophers are agreed that the heavens are the cause, although they state it in different ways; some that it comes from the motive Powers, like Plato, Avicenna, and Algazel; some, from the stars (especially in the case of human souls), like Socrates, and also Plato, and Dionysius the Academician; and some from the celestial virtue which is in the natural heat of the seed, like Aristotle and the other Peripatetics.

5. "And thus the sciences are the causes that bring about our second perfection; for through their means we can speculate on truth, which is our ultimate perfection, as the Philosopher has said in the sixth of the *Ethics*, when he says that the true is the good of the intellect. For these, as well as for many other resemblances, we may call science *heaven*.

6. "Now we must see why we say *third* heaven. Here we must reflect upon a comparison between the order of the heavens and that of the sciences. For, as has been said above, the seven heavens nearest to us are those of the planets; then there are two heavens above these, movable, and one over all the rest, motionless. To the first seven correspond the seven sciences of the *Trivium* and *Quadrivium*, that is, Grammar, Dialectics, Rhetoric, Arithmetic, Music, Geometry, and Astrology. To the eighth sphere, that is, to the Starry Heaven, correspond Natural Science, called *Physics*, and the first of sciences, called *Metaphysics;* to the ninth sphere corresponds *Moral Science;* and to the Quiet Heaven corresponds Divine Science, which is called *Theology*. And the reason of all this may be briefly seen."

He then goes on to explain the reasons of these symbolic references, which are very fanciful.

Between the different spheres and their inhabitants, and the grades of their felicity, there is an intimate correspondence.

Paradise consists of three chief regions, the Star Heaven, the Crystal Heaven, and the Empyrean. With the seven subdivisions of the first, it comprehends ten places of abode for the blessed, whereby is indicated the fullness and perfection of Paradise.

All Paradise resounds with the praise of the Triune God.

> "'Glory be to the Father, to the Son,
> And Holy Ghost!' all Paradise began,
> So that the melody inebriate made me.
> What I beheld seemed unto me a smile
> Of the universe; for my inebriation
> Found entrance through the hearing and the sight.
> O joy! O gladness inexpressible!
> O perfect life of love and peacefulness!
> O riches, without hankering secure!"[1]

Let us now briefly survey the different spheres of the celestial world of Dante.

1. The Moon. It was reached by Dante, after passing through the region of air and fire. Here are the souls of those who did not quite fulfill their spiritual vows or were forced to violate them. (Canto II.–IV.)

2. Mercury. Here dwell the souls of those who, although virtuous, yet strove in their bodily life after earthly fame. (V.–VII.)

3. Venus contains those spirits that in their pious strivings were not sufficiently free from earthly love. (VIII.–IX.)

4. The Sun holds a middle position among the stars, sending forth his rays equally in all directions, and is the clearest

---

[1] *Par.*, XXVII., 1–9. Here, as in the inscription on the gate of Hell, no translation comes up to the beauty and melody of the original.

> "Al Padre, al Figlio, allo Spirito Santo
> Cominciò Gloria tutto il Paradiso,
> Sì che m'inebbriava il dolce canto.
> Ciò ch'io vedeva, mi sembiava un riso
> Dell' universo; perchè mia ebbrezza
> Entrava per l' udire e per lo viso.
> O gioja! O ineffabile allegrezza!
> O vita intera d' amore e di pace!
> O senza brama sicura ricchezza!"

mirror of God for the inhabitants of the earth. Here reside the most worthy theologians and doctors of the Church; for "the wise shall shine as the brightness of the firmament; and they that turn many to righteousness, as the stars for ever and ever."[1] Here we meet Albertus Magnus, the Universal Doctor; Thomas Aquinas, the Angelic Doctor; Bonaventura, the Seraphic Doctor; Peter the Lombard, the Master of Sentences; Gratian, the great authority on canon law; King Solomon; Dionysius the Areopagite, the mystic philosopher; Boethius, the senator and philosopher in the days of Theodoric the Goth; St. Isidore of Seville; the venerable Bede of the Anglo-Saxon Church; Richard of St. Victor of Paris, and "Master Sigier," who lectured on Logic in Paris, but is known only in the verse of Dante and his commentators. Hugo of St. Victor, John Chrysostom, Anselm of Canterbury, Rabanus Maurus, the Calabrian Abbot Joachim are also mentioned in irregular order. Thomas Aquinas, Bonaventura, and Francis of Assisi instruct the poet in the mysteries of salvation, and the depths of Divinity. (X.–XIII.)

5. Mars is the abode of the blessed martyrs, crusaders and other heroes who have fought for the true faith. These shine as stars, and are arranged in the form of a bright cross, from the midst of which beams forth the form of Christ. (XIV.–XVII.)

6. Jupiter is the star of Justice ("*a Jore justitia*"), and holds the souls of just and righteous princes. These are arranged first in letters so as to express the words "*Diligite justitiam, qui judicatis terram,*" afterwards in the form of an eagle as the symbol of the German Roman empire, in which Dante saw the concentration of secular power according to divine institution. (XVIII.–XX.)

7. Saturn. Here reside the pious hermits and contemplative mystics who, like flames, are constantly ascending and descending a ladder. St. Benedict laments over the corruptions of the monks. (XXI. and XXII.)

8. Dante reaches now the Fixed-Star Heaven. Here, in a vision, he sees the triumph of Christ and the Virgin Mary, and

---

[1] Comp. Dan. xii., 3; Matt. xiii., 43.

is instructed in the nature of Faith by the Apostle Peter, in the nature of Hope by James, and in the nature of Love by John. Love is that which gives Heaven its peace—the Alpha and Omega of the Holy Scriptures. It arises from a knowledge of God, who is Love itself. It is with transport that Dante becomes aware of being in possession of the true Apostolic Faith, over which Heaven exults, and the blessed spirits shout for joy. The Apostle Paul, who is emphatically the Apostle of Faith, is not mentioned here, but elsewhere called "the mighty Vessel of the Holy Spirit."[1] I find in the whole *Commedia* 25 references to Peter, 8 to John, 7 to Paul, 4 to James. Peter reproves the bad popes. (XXIII.–XXVI.)

9. In the ninth sphere, the Crystal Heaven or *Primum Mobile*, Dante sees the eternal hierarchy of angels who rule the nine heavenly spheres, and move in nine concentric circles around a bright, light-giving, central point—the Deity. Beatrice instructs him on the creation of Angels, the fall of Lucifer, and reproves the ignorance and avarice of preachers and the sale of indulgences. (XXVII.–XXIX.)

10. Now Dante nears the pinnacle of Glory and Blessedness, the Empyrean, to which the last four cantos are devoted.[2] It is in itself immovable, and yet the original cause of all movement. For God is without longing for anything that is out of him, but yet gives forth all life out of himself. The poet here sees all those blessed spirits, which, like innumerable leaves, form a boundless snow-white rose that spreads and multiplies and breathes an odor of praise throughout the heavens, and whose cup is a lake of light.

---

[1] *Par.*, XXI., 127 sq.; also XXIV., 62–65; XXVIII., 138, and other places.

[2] Empyrean or Empyreal (from πῦρ, *fire*, ἔμπυρος, *in* or *by the fire*) is the highest heaven formed of pure fire or light, the seat of the Deity. Milton, *Par. Lost*, III., 56:

> "Now had the Almighty Father from above,
> From the pure Empyrean where he sits
> High throned above all height, bent down his eye,
> His own works and their works at once to view.
> About Him all the sanctities of heaven
> Stood thick as stars, and from His sight received
> Beatitude past utterance."

> "In fashion then of a snow-white rose
> Displayed itself to me the saintly host
> Whom Christ in his own blood had made his bride."[1]

This beautiful imagery was probably an original creation of Dante's genius, or suggested by the rose windows of Gothic cathedrals. Others connect it with the golden rose which the popes present from time to time to royal personages as a mark of special favor.[2]

Here Beatrice leaves her friend, as Virgil had left him in Purgatory, and resumes her place among the blessed in the third circle at the side of the contemplative Rachel, just below the seat of Eve and the throne of the Blessed Virgin. The last words of Beatrice, strange to say, were words of condemnation of the corrupt papacy and the prediction that God would cast the pope (Clement V.) down to the place of Simon Magus and his followers, in the eighth circle of the *Inferno*.[3] We should rather expect from the guardian angel of his youth and manhood some sweet parting words of love and wisdom. Dante is at first not aware of her departure, and looking for her, he sees a fatherly old man, clothed in light, with a look of mild benignity, who informed him that he was sent by Beatrice. It was St. Bernard of Clairvaux, the godly mystic, "the honey-flowing doctor," the singer of the sweetest hymn of the Middle Ages. He is the master of hearts, as Thomas Aquinas is the master of

---

[1] *Par.*, XXXI., 1–3:

> "*In forma dunque di candida rosa
> Mi si mostrava la milizia santa,
> Che nel suo sanguine Cristo fece sposa.*"

[2] Pope Innocent III. in blessing a rose (1206): "*Hæc tria designantur in tribus proprietatibus hujus floris, quem vobis visibiliter præsentamus: caritas, in colore; jucunditas, in odore; satietas, in sapore; rosa quippe præ cæteris floribus colore delectat, odore recreat, sapore comfortat; delectat in visu, recreat in olfactu, comfortat in gustu.*" Then follow Scripture quotations. See the whole passage in Scartazzini's *Com.*, III., 821.

[3] Canto XXX., 145–148. Beatrice must mean either Clement V., who ruled at Avignon, 1305–'14, or John XXII., 1316–'34, but more probably the former, since the prediction of the fate of the pope follows immediately after the prophecy concerning the Emperor Henry VII., whose failure was caused by the double dealing of that pope. Boniface VIII. and Clement V. died before the *Paradiso* was finished, but Dante always prophesies from 1300.

THE ROSE OF THE BLESSED.

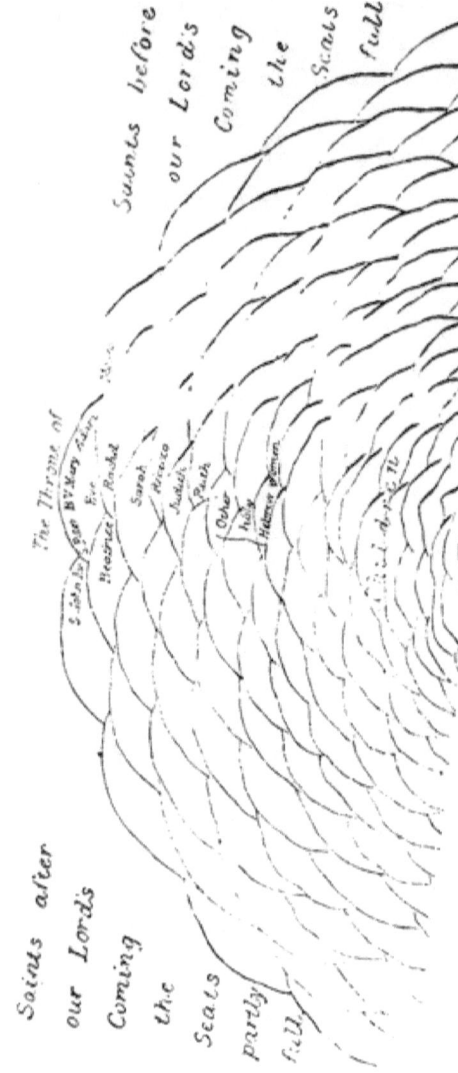

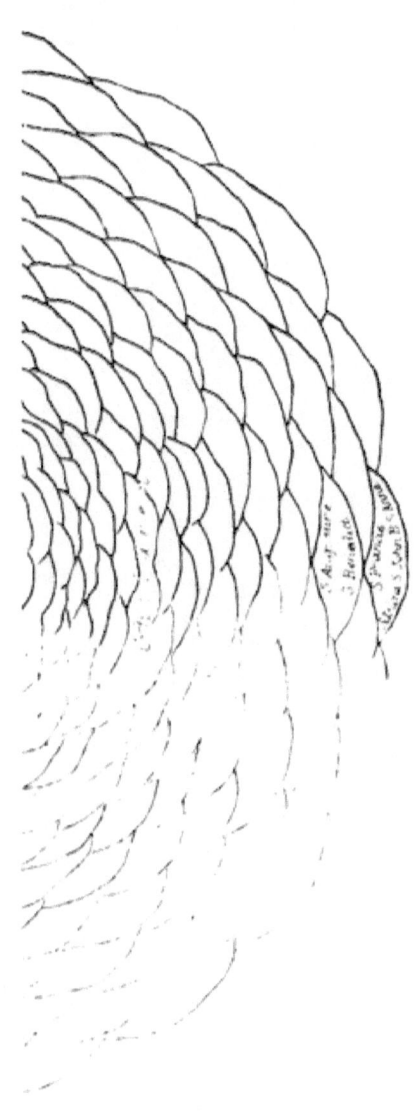

intellects; he represents the theology of love, as the latter represents the theology of faith. The intuition of mysticism rises higher than the reflexion and speculation of scholasticism, and attains to the beatific vision.

Dante looked up once more thankfully to Beatrice crowned with glory, and thanked her for delivering him from the slavery of sin unto the freedom of the sons of God. She cast on him a loving smile from her distant height, and then turned again to the eternal fountain of light and love.[1]

St. Bernard now takes charge of Dante on this last stage of his pilgrimage. He explains to him (in Canto XXXII.) the Rose of the Blessed, and points out the seats of the saints. Around the cup of the Rose or the lake of light are the innocent children, with their childlike faces and voices. The saints in heaven retain their ages in which they died; while according to Thomas Aquinas they all shall rise in the unfading bloom of youth. The Rose is divided into two semicircles, the left for the saints who were saved before Christ's coming, the right for the saints after Christ's coming. The seats of the former are filled; in the latter there are still vacant seats for the elect of the church militant below. In the middle of the top tier of the Rose is enthroned the Blessed Virgin Mother, surrounded by an army of angels. She looks most like Christ, and sends from her smiling countenance joy and peace to all the saints who delight in gazing at her. To her left is Adam, the first of sinners and the first of the redeemed, and Moses, the lawgiver; to her right St. Peter, the prince of the Apostles, and St. John the beloved disciple. Opposite the Virgin and on the same level is John the Baptist, with St. Anna on the left and St. Lucia on the right, and next to him St. Francis, St. Benedict, and St. Augustin, the three teachers who, next to the Apostles, exerted the greatest influence on the Church.

The poet now approaches the highest bliss of saints and angels—the beatific vision. St. Bernard prepares him for

---

[1] XXXI., 92, 93:

" *ed ella si lontana,*
Come parea, sorrise e riguardommi;
Poi si tornò all' eterna fontana."

it by a prayer of unrivaled fervor and beauty to the Virgin Mother.[1]

Beatrice and many a saint join with the venerable Bernard in this prayer for the vision of glory and its ennobling and sanctifying effect upon the after-life of the pilgrim. It is granted. Dante is permitted to gaze upon the Holy Trinity. It is but one moment of intuition, but eternity is condensed in that moment. He beholds three circles of equal circumference, but of threefold color; one of them exhibiting the divine-human countenance of the incarnate Son of God and Saviour of the world.

"O Light Eterne, sole in Thyself that dwellest,
Sole knowest Thyself, and, known unto Thyself,
And knowing, lovest and smilest on Thyself."

The pen refuses its office; the mind of the poet is, as it were, electrified by a sudden shock; power fails to his lofty fancy, and he is inexpressibly happy in the surrender of his will to the love of God, which illumines the Sun and all the Stars, gives Heaven and Earth their motions, fills time and eternity, and draws from the choir of the Blessed an endless song of praise.

Thus ends this "deep unfathomable song."

If we cast a glance once more at the mutual relation of the separate parts, we shall be struck with the profound truth of the hint given by Schelling, that the first is sculptural, the second picturesque, and the third musical, in accordance with the subjects therein treated. The *Inferno* is an immense group of sharply-defined statues, of dusky shadow-forms, fearful monuments of Divine justice, illumined by the touch of poetry. The *Purga-*

---

[1] Canto XXXIII., 1-39:

"*Vergine Madre, figlia del tuo Figlio.
Umile ed alta più che creatura.
Termine fisso d'eterno consiglio,*" etc.

Dante must have been very familiar with St. Bernard's Homilies on the Song of Solomon, and *De Laudibus Virginis Matris*. St. Bernard was a devout worshiper of the Virgin, and contributed very much to the spread of that worship; but he opposed the dogma of her immaculate conception as being contrary to Catholic tradition and derogatory to the dignity of Christ, the only sinless being. We may infer, therefore, that Dante did not share this belief. The immaculate conception remained an open and disputed question till 1854, when Pope Pius IX. proclaimed it an article of the Catholic faith. On the history of this dogma, see Schaff, *Creeds of Christendom*, Vol. I., 108-128.

torio is a gallery of variegated pictures, opening, in an endless perspective, into Heaven. The *Paradiso* is a harmonious unison of the music of spheres with the praises of the blessed rational creation; here all swims in light; here all is feeling, sound, Hallelujah. The poem opens with the cry of despair; it flows through the sadness of longing; it closes with the jubilee of bliss.

Beyond Dante's description of the beatific vision there can be nothing more beautiful, sublime and enrapturing, than the beatific vision itself.[1]

THE THEOLOGY OF DANTE.

Dante is the theologian among poets, and the poet among theologians. As he stands between Homer and Virgil on the Parnassus, so also between St. Thomas Aquinas and St. Bonaventura before the altar of the holy mystery. His theology and his relation to modern Christianity and civilization have been the subject of considerable dispute. Three views may be distinguished.

1. He was an orthodox Catholic. This is held by the great majority of Dante-scholars, especially Giuliani, Ozanam, Artaud de Montor, Boissard, Philalethes, Wegele, Gietmann, Hettinger.[2] But the most orthodox Catholics cannot deny Dante's fearless opposition to the popes of his age, nor can they accept his politics.

2. He was a forerunner of Protestantism. Matthias Flacius, the first Lutheran church historian,[3] numbers him among his

---

[1] "*Post Paradisum Dantis nihil est nisi visio Dei.*" With these words Cardinal Manning recommends Father Bowden's translation of Hettinger, *Dante's Göttlich Komödie*, to English readers.

[2] See their works quoted in Literature, pp. 331 and 333. Hettinger gives, as far as I know, the fullest exposition of Dante's theology, from scholastic sources and the Catholic standpoint. In his *Die göttl. Komödie*, etc., pp. 331–510, and of his politics (in which he differs from Dante), pp. 511–578. He approvingly quotes (p. 578) a passage from Scartazzini, that burning coffins would be ready in the sixth circle of Dante's poetic Hell for Luther, Melancthon, Zwingli, Calvin and the other Reformers; but this is not the personal view of Scartazzini, who is a Protestant minister at Soglio in the Grisons, Switzerland. Ozanam puts Luther on a par with Fra Dolcino, who was burned alive at Vercelli in 1307, and is assigned to the eighth circle of the *Inferno* (xxviii., 55) among the schismatics and disturbers of the peace.

[3] Originator and chief editor of the "Magdeburg Centuries," so called, an anti-papal Church History of the first thirteen centuries, Basle, 1560–'74, 13 vols. fol. He was a fierce Lutheran polemic who outluthered Luther in his

420 "Witnesses of the Evangelical Truth" in the Dark Ages, *i. e.*, among the Lutherans before Luther, as he regarded them, and quotes in proof some passages in the *Commedia* and *De Monarchia* which bear on the corruptions of the Roman Church.[1] Thirty years afterwards a French nobleman, François Perot de Mezières, endeavored to gain the Italians for the Reformation by means of the *Commedia*.[2] Another Frenchman, Philippe de Mornay du Plessy Marly, the most accomplished and influential controversialist and diplomat among the Huguenots of his age, led Dante into the field against popery.[3] The controversy has been renewed in our century by Goeschel and Karl Graul, who claim Dante as a Reformer before the Reformation.[4]

3. He was a heretic in disguise, and even a revolutionist and socialist, in league with wide-spread anti-papal and anti-catholic societies for the overthrow of Church and State. He was a master of the symbolic language of the Templars, used for their destructive aims, a friend of the Albigenses, a Provençal

zeal for orthodoxy, but a remarkable man of vast learning and indomitable perseverance and industry. See W. Preger, *Matthias Flacius Illyricus und seine Zeit*, Erlangen, 1859–'61, 2 vols.

[1] *Catalogus Testium Veritatis Evangelicæ*, Basle, 1556. In the same Protestant city appeared a German translation of Dante's *De Monarchia* by Heroldt in 1559, before any edition of it had been published in Italy. Some have gone so far as to attribute to Dante a direct prophecy of Luther, by discovering his very name, anagrammatically, in *Veltro*, *i. e.*, *Lutero* (see above p. 312), and the approximate date of his birth (Nov. 10, 1483), in the calculation of Landino, the Florentine commentator of the *Commedia* (1481), that Dante's reformer would be born Nov. 15, 1484, according to *Purg.* XXX., 31. This is the opposite extreme to Ozanam's view of Fra Dolcino as a forerunner of Luther.

[2] *Avviso piacevole dato alla bella Italia da un nobile giovane Francese*, 1586. Bellarmin, the great Roman controversialist, takes great pains to refute this anonymous book, in his *Appendix ad Libros de Summo Pontifice* (in *Disputat. de controversiis Christ. Fidei*, etc., Roman ed. 1832, Tom. I., 851 sqq.).

[3] *Mysterium iniquitatis s. Historia papatus*, or *Le Mystère d'iniquité ou Histoire de la papauté*, 1611. He finds in the name of the reigning pope (Paul V) the apocalyptic number of the beast (666)! See the article of Gaufrès in Lichtenberger's "Encyclopédie," Tom. IX. 440.

[4] Goeschel, in his Dante writings, quoted p. 333; Graul, in the Introduction to his translation of the *Inferno*, 1843 (LV sqq.). Giambattista Giuliani, a distinguished Dante scholar, wrote a discourse against Graul in 1844, to silence the attempts of the followers of the "insolent Luther" (*insolente Lutero*) to claim the first Christian poet for their heretical opinions.

mocker, a worshiper of classical heathenism, a pantheist, an infidel. This strange theory was first proposed by Gabriele Rossetti, an Italian patriot, in an anti-catholic spirit, 1832,[1] and afterwards (1854) in a modified form by Aroux, an orthodox Catholic, and a translator of the *Commedia*.[2]

The third theory must be dismissed as a radical misunderstanding and ingenious absurdity. The first is essentially correct, but there is also an element of truth in the second theory. Dante was a sincere and earnest Catholic of the mediæval, but not of the modern ultramontane type. He belonged to the party of progress which demanded a reformation of the Church, especially of the papacy; and in this respect we may regard him as a prophet of a purer form of Christianity.

We can, of course, only judge from what he actually believed and taught, not from what he might have believed in another age and under other conditions. But judging him from the spirit of his works he would have advocated the cause of truth and righteousness, of progress and moral reform in any subsequent age.

He would have thoroughly sympathized with Savonarola, the stern monk, prophet and reform preacher, in opposition to the frivolity of Florence and the wickedness of Pope Alexander VI., who demanded his execution at the stake. He would have gone half way with Luther, in his war against the shameful traffic in indulgences, and the corruptions of the papacy, but no further. In the year 1870 he would have opposed, with the Old Catholics, the two Vatican dogmas of papal infallibility and papal absolutism. In politics he, the Italian of Italians, and the

---

[1] Gabriele Rossetti (1783–1854) wrote *Commento analitico sulla Divina Commedia* (1826–'27); *Sullo spirito antipapale che produsse la Riforma* (1832); *Il mistero dell' amor Platonico del medio evo, derivato da' misteri antichi* (1840), and *La Beatrice del Dante* (1842). He tries to show that Dante and his contemporaries adopted a peculiar idiom to veil their aversion to the papacy, and introduced a woman as the special object of their adoration, to symbolize true Christianity. He was a political exile from his native Italy and settled in England, 1824. He is the father of a distinguished family of artists, poets, and Dante-scholars. See p. 335. For a critical examination of his theory compare K. Witte, *Rossetti's Dante-Erklärung*, in his *Dante-Forschungen*, I., 96–139.

[2] Quoted in Literature on p. 332. Add to it his work *L'hérésie de Dante démontrée par Francesca da Rimini, devenue un moyen de propagande Vaudoise*, 1857. Aroux was refuted by Boissard, also by Witte, *l. c.*, pp. 109 sqq., 131 sqq.

idol of Italian patriots, would have hailed the union and independence of Italy, the destruction of the temporal power of the papacy, and the separation of Church and State.

But we must not identify him with Protestantism in any of its systems of doctrine or church polity. He probably even to-day would look forward to an ideal Catholicism of the future and prophesy the coming of another *Veltro* and *Dux*, who would restore a universal church and a universal empire in friendly independence and confederation for the spiritual and temporal welfare of mankind.

We cannot find in his writings any distinctively Protestant principles, either the supremacy of the Scriptures over traditions, or justification by faith alone, or the general priesthood of the laity. He is full of Scripture facts and Scripture doctrines, but throughout assumes that the teaching of the Church is in harmony with them; he believes in salvation by the grace of God and the atoning sacrifice of Christ, but demands good works and crowns them with reward; he teaches the divine origin and independence of the State, but expects the German emperor to be in communion with the Roman Church. In all essential doctrines which distinguish the Protestant from the Roman Catholic system he stands on the Roman Catholic side.[1]

---

[1] The eminent Dante-scholar, Karl Witte, expresses substantially the same view, in his revision of Goeschel's article in the second ed. of Herzog, III., 491 sqq., and at the close of the Introduction to his German version of the *Commedia*, p. 39 sq., where he says:

"Er ist Katholik im schönsten Sinne, welcher das allgemein Christliche bezeichnet; denn auch den frommen Protestanten werden Dante's Verse tief ergreifen, ja sicherlich mehr erbauen, als die beiden christlichen Epopöen des englischen und des deutschen protestantischen Dichters der beiden letzten Jahrhunderte. Aber auch in dem Sinne ist er katholisch, dass wo einmal Unterscheidungslehren zur Sprache kommen, wie z. B. Paradies XXV., 69, sein Bekenntniss allerdings nicht auf Seiten der evangelischen Kirche steht. Mit gerechtem Bewusstsyn ist es also, dass der Dichter, nachdem er seinen Glauben bekannt hat, vom Apostel Petrus, als dem Felsen, auf den die katholische Kirche sich gründet, zum Zeichen seiner Rechtgläubigkeit sich segnen und umkränzen lässt. Führet ihn doch lehrend und ausdeutend die verklärte Beatrice, dies Sinnbild der vollen Erkenntniss rechtgläubig religiöser Wahrheit, von einer Himmelsphäre zur andern. Und so hält aller Zorn gegen das Papstthum seiner Zeit den Dichter nicht ab, dem Nachfolger Petri als solchem, ja selbst seinem bittern Feinde Bonifaz VIII., die Ehrerbietung eines gläubigen Katholiken zu beweisen. (*Hölle* XIX., 100; *Fegefeuer* XIX., 127; XX., 87)."

The same may be said of Savonarola, who has so often been misrepresented as a forerunner of Luther.

Dante is the poet of mediæval Catholicism. His poetry reflects the theology of St. Thomas Aquinas and St. Bernard, that is, orthodox scholasticism and orthodox mysticism combined. The *Commedia* is a poetic transfiguration of mediæval theology and piety. He worked into it all the subtleties of scholastic speculation and all the warmth of mystic devotion to the very height of the beatific vision. He is a strong believer in the fundamental doctrines of the Trinity and Incarnation and all the articles of the œcumenical faith from creation to life everlasting. He clothes these truths in the shining garb of poetic beauty, and impresses them all the more deeply on the mind and heart. To a devout student the *Divina Commedia* is a powerful sermon accompanied by solemn organ music. Neither Milton, nor Klopstock, nor any other poet, Catholic or Protestant, can equal him in the poetic vindication and glorification of our common Christian faith.

In connection with this faith Dante held also those mediæval doctrines which the Protestant Reformers, wisely or unwisely, rejected on account of their abuse, as the doctrines of Purgatory, the worship of saints, and the divine foundation of the papacy. Purgatory with its expiatory penances is one of the three divisions of his poem. The intercession of the saints in behalf of the living and the petitions of the living for that intercession run through the whole, and culminate in that wonderful prayer of St. Bernard to the holy Virgin Mother who is enthroned in Paradise as the Queen of Saints. He assumes throughout the closest communion between the militant and triumphant church. Beatrice, Lucia, and Matilda are interested in his salvation and act under the inspiration of Mary. But as a follower of St. Bernard, he must have disapproved of the belief in her immaculate conception which then began to be advocated in the form of a special festival in France. He peoples heaven with orthodox saints, and excludes from it all impurity and heresy, and even all the unbaptized. He puts heretics in the sixth circle of the *Inferno*. He believes in the supremacy of Peter as the prince of the Apostles and founder of the Roman Church, who "keeps the keys," and examines and instructs him in the faith. He regards the pope as Peter's successor and as the vicar of Christ. He knows only one Church, and condemns schism even more than heresy.

But here his connection with the Roman Catholic Church stops. It remains for us to consider his reformatory or Protestant element, if we may so call it.

DANTE'S RELATION TO THE PAPACY AND THE REFORMATION.

Dante is a most earnest and consistent advocate of a moral (not doctrinal) reformation in Church and State, especially of the papacy. He urges and predicts such a reformation in the head and the members again and again, in all parts of his poem and in a variety of images.[1] The very last words of his beloved Beatrice in Paradise are a condemnation of the popes Boniface VIII. and Clement V., who shall be thrust down

"Where Simon Magus is for his deserts."

The key to his position is his prediction of the Greyhound (*Veltro*) and Leader (*Dux*), who should bring about such a reformation, and the political theory of his book on the Empire (*De Monarchia*), which was condemned by the Council of Trent.[2]

He treats the popes with the same stern impartiality as emperors, kings and private persons, according to their moral merits. He respects the office, but condemns those who disgraced it, in such a fearless manner as would not be tolerated in the Roman Church of the present day. He mentions indeed several popes and cardinals among the blessed in heaven, as Gregory I. and Agapetus, but none of them is assigned so high a position as the great doctors of the church and founders of monastic orders. He ignores Gregory VII., the greatest of the

---

[1] Comp. *Inf.* I., 101–111; *Purg.* VI., 97–125; XX., 10–15; 91–96; XXXIII., 31–60; *Par.* XVII., 76–99; XXI., 118–120; XXII., 11–18; 90–96; XXVII., 40–66; 142–148.

[2] Comp. the previous discussion on pp. 308–312; 320–322.

popes, probably because of his quarrel with the emperor.[1] Innocent III. is barely mentioned.[2] He met two popes among the penitents in Purgatory, namely, Adrian V. who sits among the avaricious in the fifth circle, but was pope only thirty-nine days (d. 1276), and Martin IV., who suffers among the gluttons, because his fondness for eels from the lake of Bolsena in the Papal States, and the vernaccia wine brought his life to a sudden close (1285).[3] He saw a multitude of avaricious popes and cardinals in the fourth circle of Hell, which is guarded by Plutus as their jailer.[4] He condemns a heretical pope, Anastasius II. (496).[5] He is most severe on the simoniacal popes who are already, or will soon be tormented in the eighth circle, notably Nicholas III. (d. 1281), Boniface VIII. (d. 1303), and Clement V. (d. 1314). The last two were still living when the *Commedia* was begun (1300), but Nicholas, with the foresight of disembodied spirits, knew that they were coming, and wondered only that they should come so soon and not tarry longer with their golden idols on earth.[6]

---

[1] For this reason I cannot identify the Matilda of the Purgatory who carries Dante over the river Lethe to Beatrice (XXVIII., 40 sqq.; XXXI., 92; XXXII., 28, 82; XXXIII., 119, 121), with the Countess Matilda of Tuscany who protected Gregory at Canossa and bequeathed to the papal see a large amount of her possessions, thus increasing the evil of the fatal gift of Constantine. Nearly all the older commentators, as also Ruskin and Longfellow, identify the two Matildas; others think of Matilda, wife of Emperor Henry the Fowler, distinguished for goodness and beauty, or Matilda of Hackenborn, a saintly Benedictine nun, or Matilda of Magdeburg, or a friend of Beatrice whose death is mentioned in the *Vita Nuova*. See the notes of Scartazzini and Plumptre (I., 337 sq.); Witte's *Dante-Forschungen*, II., 311 sqq., and Preger, *Dante's Matelda*, München, 1873.

[2] *Par.* XI., 92.   [3] *Purg.* XIX., 99; XXIV., 22.
[4] *Inf.* VII., 44–48.   [5] *Inf.* XI., 8, 9. See above p. 386.

[6] Nicholas III., of the Orsini (Bear) family of Rome, "the son of the she-bear (*orsa*), so eager to advance the cubs (*orsatti*)" (*Inf.* XIX., 70 sq.), first mistook Dante for Boniface VIII. (XIX., 52 sqq.):

"And he cried out: Dost thou stand there already,
  Dost thou stand there already, Boniface?
  By many years the record lied to me.
Art thou so early satiate with that wealth
  For which thou didst not fear to take by fraud
  The beautiful Lady [the Church] and then work her woe?"

In *Par.* XXX., 145 sqq., Boniface is supposed to be already with Simon Magus, and to be followed soon by Clement.

The pope whom he most severely condemns and pursues a dozen times in all parts of his poem with fiery indignation and almost personal animosity, is Pope Boniface VIII. He regarded him as the chief author of his exile and all his misfortune, and as the worst of Simoniacs.

Boniface was a man of great learning, ability and energy, but violent, cruel, ambitious, avaricious and utterly unscrupulous. He scared the humble Cœlestin V. into a resignation, which was never before heard of in the history of the papacy, shut him up in a castle, bought the papal crown, created two of his very young nephews cardinals, appointed twenty bishops and archbishops from among his relatives and friends, and left them enormous sums of money. He made war upon the powerful family of the Colonnas and confiscated their vast possessions. He introduced the first papal jubilee with its abuses, in the very year in which Dante began the *Commedia*. He carried the system of papal absolutism to the utmost extreme of audacity and pretension, and claimed in the bulla *Unam Sanctam* (1302) the highest temporal as well as ecclesiastical power on earth. A commission of investigation after his death, composed of Italians and Frenchmen well acquainted with him, charged him with the worst of crimes and even with infidelity. His haughty reign ended in humiliation, insult and grief—the very opposite of the scene at Canossa. The public opinion of his contemporaries is expressed in the sentence: "He entered like a fox, he reigned like a lion, he died like a dog."

Dante and Boniface were political, ecclesiastical and moral antipodes, but the poor exile triumphed over the mighty pope in the judgment of posterity. Dante called his antagonist the prince of modern Pharisees, a usurper of the papal chair, who bought and then abused the church, and turned the cemetery of St. Peter, the Vatican hill, into a common sewer of corruption.[1]

Nevertheless he justly condemns with the same impartiality Philip the Fair, of France, that "modern Pilate," for his cruel treatment of the aged pope at Anagni.[2] He distinguished

---

[1] See the passages quoted on p. 364, note 2.
[2] *Purg.* XX., 87 sqq.

between the chair of Peter and "him who sits there and degenerates."[1]

Dante was an ideal imperialist in direct opposition to the papal absolutism of Boniface. He believed in the unity of empire with two independent heads in amicable relation: the Roman pope as the spiritual ruler, the German Roman emperor as the secular ruler. Church and State are both divine institutions, the one for the eternal, the other for the temporal welfare of mankind. He borrowed his theory from the ante-Nicene period, but substituted a Christian for a heathen emperor. We may say, that he anticipated the American theory of a friendly separation of Church and State; yet with this important difference that he had in mind one Catholic Church instead of a number of denominations, and one Roman Empire instead of a federal Republic. The two powers should remain separate and distinct. A mixture of the two and a supremacy of one over the other (either in the form of the papal theocracy, or in the form of Cæsaropapacy) is a source of evil, of friction and war. There are two suns which give light to the world, the pope and the emperor. The State must not be degraded to a mere moon that borrows her light from the one sun, as is done in the Hildebrandian system.

> "Rome, that reformed the world, accustomed was
> Two suns to have, which one road and the other,
> Of God and of the world, made manifest.
> One has the other quenched, and to the crosier
> The sword is joined, and ill beseemeth it
> That by main force one with the other go,
> Because, being joined, one feareth not the other."[2]

Dante derived, with the common opinion of the Middle Ages, the temporal power of the pope from the fictitious donation of Constantine to Sylvester I., and repeatedly alludes to this fatal gift which was well meant but "bore bad fruit."[3]

---

[1] *Par.* XII., 89, 90.   [2] *Purg.* XVI., 106–112.

[3] *Purg.* XXXII., 125; *Par.* XX., 55, and in the third book of his treatise *De Monarchia*. Constantine, on account of his good intention and ignorance of the ill effects of his donation, is pardoned and placed in the sixth heaven among the righteous kings.

> "Ah, Constantine! of how much woe was mother,
> Not thy conversion, but that marriage-dower
> Which the first wealthy Father took from thee!"[1]

He believed that the gift, if ever made, was unlawful, although it is incorporated in the canon law (the *Decretum Gratiani*). How would he have rejoiced if he could have seen the book of the Roman critic and humanist Laurentius Valla (Lorenzo della Valle, d. 1457) who proved beyond contradiction that the donation of Constantine was nothing but a hierarchical fable.[2]

The principal evil which resulted from the temporal power of the pope and his connection with all the political quarrels and intrigues of the age, was Simony, or the sin of Simon Magus, who wished to buy the Holy Ghost for lucrative purposes and incurred the fearful rebuke of St. Peter. "Thy silver perish with thee, because thou hast thought to obtain the gift of God with money. Thou hast neither part nor lot in this matter: for thy heart is not right before God. Repent therefore of this thy wickedness, and pray the Lord, if perhaps the thought of thy heart shall be forgiven thee. For I see that thou art in the gall of bitterness and in the bond of iniquity" (Acts viii: 20-23). This passage is the text of Dante's invectives against the popes who

---

[1] *Inf.* XIX., 115-118:

> "*Ahi, Constantin, di quanto mal fu matre,
> Non la tua conversion, ma quella dote
> Che da te prese il primo ricco patre!*"

In Milton's translation:

> "Ah Constantine! of how much ill was cause,
> Not thy conversion, but those rich domains
> That the first wealthy pope received of thee!"

[2] *Declamatio de falso credita et ementita Constantini donatione.* It was written about 1440, while the author was in the service of the liberal-minded Alfonso V., King of Arragon, and republished by Ulrich von Hutten, with an ironical dedication to Pope Leo X., in 1517. It had a great influence upon Luther, who received a copy through a friend in February, 1520. See Strauss, *Ulrich von Hutten*, p. 211 sqq. (4th ed. 1878); Köstlin, *M. Luther*, I., 324 sq. Constantine's donation is admitted to be a forgery, as well as the pseudo-Isidorian Decretals, by all historical scholars of repute. See e. g. Streber in the new ed. of Wetzer and Welte's *Kirchenlexikon*, vol. III., 979-985, and J. Friedrich, *Die Konstantinische Schenkung*, München, 1889.

made themselves guilty of the same sin and incurred double guilt on account of their exalted position as successors of St. Peter, and the incalculable influence of their bad example upon clergy, monks and laity. It is notorious that many popes made merchandise of holy things, bought the papal crown, sold cardinals' hats and bishops' mitres, and perverted the property of the church for the enrichment of their nephews and other members of their families. Nearly all the rich palaces of Roman nobles with their picture galleries and treasures of art owe their origin to papal nepotism. The worst period of the papacy was that of the so-called pornocracy in the tenth and eleventh centuries, which cannot be mentioned without humiliation and shame. It was then that the German emperors had to interfere and to depose those wicked popes, the paramours and bastards of some bold, bad Roman women. Henry VII., at the synod of Sutri (1046), deposed three rival popes, all Simonists, and elected the worthy bishop Bruno of Toul in their place (1048), as Leo IX., the first reforming pope under the direction of Hildebrand, who himself succeeded to the papal chair as Gregory VII. (1073) and made war upon simony, but as well also upon sacerdotal marriage, and the power of the emperor. With all his zeal against Simony, Gregory could not prevent his successors from relapsing into the same sin.

Dante condemns the Simonists to the eighth circle of Hell, where they are turned upside down with their heads in a narrow hole and their feet and legs standing out and burning—a fit punishment for perverting the proper order of things by putting the material above the spiritual, and money above religion. The greatest sufferers in this pit are the simoniacal popes. The corruption of the Roman court contaminated the higher and lower clergy and the whole church.

Dante looked to Germany for a reformation of the Church and a restoration of the Empire, but he was doomed to disappointment in the hope he set on Henry VII., and his vicar in Lombardy. In the meantime after the death of Boniface, the papacy had been transferred to Avignon, and became subservient to the French monarchs. Then followed the scandalous papal schism, the reformatory councils, the restoration and renewed corruption of the papal power. At last the reformation came from Germany, but not from an emperor, and in a much more radical form than the poet dreamed of.

In another sense, however, he proved a true prophet; for it was by the aid of Germany, in the wars of 1866 and 1870, that Italy achieved her political unity and independence.

DANTE AND THE JOACHIMITES.

Dante stood not alone in his attitude to the papacy. There runs through all the Middle Ages a protest against the abuses in the Church and a desire for a reformation which grew stronger and stronger and ultimately culminated in the mighty religious revolution of the sixteenth century.

Before him and during his lifetime there was a considerable commotion in the Franciscan order with which he was in sympathy. Tradition connects him with this order.[1] He was buried in the Franciscan church at Ravenna. His daughter Beatrice was a nun in a Franciscan convent of that city. He fully appreciated the monastic principle of apostolic poverty, and considered wealth and temporal power a curse to the clergy. He puts into the mouth of Thomas Aquinas, who was a Dominican, a high eulogy of St. Francis of Assisi; while Bonaventura, a Franciscan, in the spirit of true brotherhood, without envy and jealousy, celebrates the life and deeds of St. Dominic.[2] He assigns one of the uppermost places in the Rose of the Blessed to St. Francis, the most childlike, the most amiable, and the most poetic monk of the Middle Ages, the sympathizing friend of all God's creatures, whose highest aim and crowning glory was transformation into the image of the Saviour, who married Christ's poverty and dying left the care of this his "lady-love" (*la sua donna più cara*) to every one of his disciples. Dante, who was probably familiar with Bonaventura's life of the saint, thus tersely describes his character:

---

[1] He joined the lay brethren of the Franciscan Order, according to the testimony of Francesco da Buti, one of his earliest commentators, who wrote about 1385. [2] *Par.* XI., 40 sqq.; XII., 31 sqq.

> "On the rough rock 'twixt Tiber's and Arno's plain,
> From Christ received he the last seal's impress,
> Which he two years did in his limbs sustain.
>
> When it pleased Him, who chose him thus to bless,
> To lead him up the high reward to share
> Which he had merited by lowliness,
>
> Then to his brothers, each as rightful heir,
> He gave in charge his lady-love most dear,
> And bade them love her with a steadfast care." [1]

At the same time he complains of the departure of the Franciscans from the apostolic simplicity of their founder, and makes like complaint of the degeneracy of the Dominican order. He was in sympathy with the puritanical or spiritual party of the Joachimites, and the reform movement which agitated the Franciscan order from the middle of the thirteenth century. He esteemed Joachim of Flore, who gave the first impulse to the movement, as a true prophet and assigned him a high place in Paradise with Rabanus Maurus, Dominic, Bonaventura, Chrysostom, and Anselm.

> "Here is Rabanus, and beside me here
> Shines the Calabrian Abbot Joachim,
> He with the spirit of prophecy endowed."

Joachim was a prophet in the same sense as Dante was a

---

[1] *Par.* XI., 106–114. Plumptre's translation. The final seal (*l' ultimo sigillo*, line 107) of Francis and his Order is the miracle of stigmatization or the impression of the five wounds of the crucifixion. It was reported by his biographers that St. Francis after long and intense meditation on the sufferings of the Saviour, received in 1224, on the rocky Mount Alvernia, in the Apennines, while absorbed in prayer, on his hands and feet and side the wounds of the nails and the spear, and bore them two years till his death (1226). The place is still shown near the monastery which the saint founded. Thomas a Celano, the author of the *Dies Iræ*, was his intimate friend and first biographer. On St. Francis, see above p. 146 and 193 sqq.

[2] *Par.* XII., 139–141:

> "*Il Calavrese* [*Calabrese*] *abate Gioacchino*
> *Di spirito profetico dotato.*"

His Latin name was *Johannes Joachimus de Flore* (or *de Floris, de Floribus*); his Italian name was *Giovanni Gioacchino di Fiore* (or *del Fiore, Santa Fiora*). His convent was called *monasterium Florense* (*de Flore, de Floribus*). See Scartazzini, Tom. III., 333.

prophet. He roused the conscience, he reproved wickedness, he predicted a better future, like the Hebrew prophets. A brief notice of this remarkable man and his school may not be out of place here.[1]

Joachim was abbot of a Cistercian convent at Flore or Fiore in Calabria, an older contemporary of St. Francis (Renan calls him his Baptist), and like him an enthusiast for entire conformity to Christ in spirit and outward condition. He made a pilgrimage to the Holy Land, fasted forty days on Mount Sinai, led a life of self-denial and devotion to his fellow-men, studied with special zeal the prophetic portions of the Scriptures, opposed the worldliness and earthly possessions, the simony, nepotism and avarice of the clergy, and predicted a reformation. He died about 1202. He was revered by the people as a wonder-working prophet and saint. Neander says of him: "Grief over the corruption of the Church, longing desire for better times, profound Christian feeling, a meditative mind, and a glowing

---

[1] The Literature on this chapter of mediæval church history is quite extensive, although several points need to be cleared up. The *Acta Sanctorum* for May 29th give many documents. Wadding, the historian of the Franciscan Order, treats the history of the Spiritual party with sympathy, *Annales Ordinis Min.* IV., 6 sqq. Maurique, *Annales Cistercienses*, Regensburg, 1741. Gervaise, *Histoire de l'Abbé Joachim*, Paris, 1745, v. vol. * Engelhardt, in his "Kirchengeschichtliche Abhandlungen," Erlangen, 1832 pp. 1-150; 265-291. * Hahn, *Geschichte des Ketzer im Mittelalter* (Stuttgart, 1850), vol. II. 69-175. * Neander, *Church History*, IV. 220-232 (Torrey's translation). * Döllinger, *Pope Fables and Prophecies of the Middle Ages*, Eng. transl. by Plummer, Am. ed. by H. B. Smith, N. York, 1872, pp. 364-391; and his *Akad. Vorträge*, 1888, I., 95 sqq. Rousselot, *Histoire de l'évangile éternel*, Paris, 1861, I. Renan, *Joachim de Flore et l'évangile éternel*, in the "Revue des deux mondes," July, 1866 (the same somewhat enlarged in his "Nouvelles études d'histoire religieuse," Paris, 1884). Preger, *Das Evangelium æternum und Joachim von Floris*, in the "Abhandlungen der Königl. Bayerischen Akademie der Wiss.," München 1874. * Reuter, *Gesch. der Aufklärung im Mittelalter* (Berlin, 1875), vol. II., 194-218. Möller in Schaff-Herzog, sub "Joachim von Floris." Tocco, *L'eresia nel medio evo*, Firenze, 1884. P. Heinrich Denifle, *Das Evangelium æternum und die Commission zu Anagni*, with the *Protocoll der Commission zu Anagni*, in the "Archiv für Literatur-- und Kirchengeschichte des Mittelalters "ed. by Denifle and Ehrle, vol. I. (1885), pp. 49-142. Franz Ehrle, *Die Spiritualen, im Verhältniss zum Franciscaner Orden und zu den Fraticellen*, ibid. pp. 509-570. The last two treatises publish important documents.

imagination, such are the peculiar characteristics of his spirit and of his writings."[1]

Joachim wrote three works: The Harmony of the Old and New Testament; Exposition of the Apocalypse; Psalter of Ten Chords. To the last are attached two hymns of Paradise, the second of which was, as Renan conjectures, one of the sources of Dante's *Commedia*. Several other works of uncertain authorship, especially commentaries on Isaiah and Jeremiah, were also ascribed to him.[2]

He wished to be orthodox and remained in the communion of the Catholic Church, but his apocalyptic opinions could easily lead astray and be utilized for heretical purposes. After his death he was condemned by the fourth Lateran Council (1215) for tritheism.[3] He gave great offence by his attacks on the papacy and his prediction of the Eternal Gospel.

An older contemporary, St. Hildegard, abbess of the Rupert convent near Bingen on the Rhine (b. 1098, d. 1197), took a similar position on the church question, and was generally revered as a prophetess. Pope Eugene III. and St. Bernard of Clairvaux, while preaching the second crusade in Germany, recognized her divine mission, and persons of all ranks flocked to her for advice, intercession, consolation, and light on the future.[4]

Joachim attacked as severely as Dante the corruption of the papacy, although it was better represented in the early than in the latter part of the thirteenth century. He, too, traced the decay of morals and discipline to the temporal power and the love of money, which is "a root of all kinds of evil." (1 Tim. vi. 10.) He complains of the exactions of the Roman curia.

---

[1] *Church History*, IV., 220 (Am. ed.).

[2] On his works, see Engelhardt, *l. c.*; Hahn, *l. c.* III., 84; Neander, IV., 221; Reuter, II., 356; and Denifle, 91.

[3] He wished to escape the inference, from the unity of essence, that the incarnation of the Son would imply an incarnation of the Father and Spirit as well. It is uncertain whether he wrote a special book against Peter the Lombard, or whether his views on the Trinity were simply gathered from his *Psalterium decem chordarum*. See Hahn, *l. c.* p. 87 sqq., and Hefele, *Conciliengesch.* V., 180 (second ed. by Knöpfler). The Synod of Arles, 1260, condemned the *doctrina Joachimitica* of the three ages.

[4] See Neander, IV., 217 sqq.

"The whole world is polluted with this evil. There is no city nor village where the church does not push her benefices, collect her revenues. Everywhere she will have prebends, endless incomes. O God, how long doest thou delay to avenge the blood of the innocent which cries to thee from beneath the altar of the (Roman) capitol!"[1] He condemns indulgences dispensed from Rome, and rebukes the proud and carnal cardinals and bishops who seek their own instead of the things of Christ. He often compares the Roman Church with the Babylon and the harlot of the Apocalypse, who commits fornication with the kings of the earth, and he predicts that the last and worst Antichrist will sit in the temple of God and the chair of Peter, and exalt himself above all that is called God. He agreed with Hildegard in announcing a terrible judgment and consequent purification and transformation of the Church and the papacy.

He divided the history of the world into three periods, which correspond to the persons of the Holy Trinity, the three leading Apostles—Peter, Paul, and John, and the three Christian graces—faith, hope, love. The period of the Father extends from the creation to the incarnation; the period of the Son to the year 1260; the period of the Holy Spirit to the end of the world. The first period is the period of the laity, the second that of the clergy, the third that of the spiritual monks under a *papa angelicus*. The first was ruled by the letter of the Old Testament; the second by the letter of the New Testament; the third will be ruled by the spirit of the New Testament, *i. e.*, the spiritual understanding of the Gospel of Christ (*spirituale evangelium Christi, spiritualis intelligentia Novi Testamenti*). This is "the Everlasting Gospel," to be proclaimed by the angel in the Apocalypse (Rev. xiv. 6). It is not a written book, but a *donum Spiritus Sancti*, a *donum contemplationis*, and the order which is to proclaim it, is an *ecclesia contemplativa*, a *populus spiritualis*.[2]

The last period is the period of love represented by the be-

---

[1] See Neander, IV., 222.

[2] A distinction should be made between the unwritten Gospel of Joachim and the written Gospel of the Joachimites. He was too modest to identify the Everlasting Gospel with his own writings. Comp. Hahn, *l. c.* p. 158, sqq.; Denifle, *l. c.* p. 56.

loved disciple, the period of peace, the Sabbath which remains for the people of God. It will be preceded by a terrible conflict with the concentrated power of Antichrist in its last and most powerful form. Then will be fulfilled the prophecy of Isaiah (xiii., 9 sqq.), " when the day of Jehovah cometh with wrath and fierce anger to make the land a desolation and to destroy the sinners thereof, when the sun shall be darkened, and the moon shall not shine."

The three periods are also subdivided into seven sub-periods, corresponding to the days of creation and the Sabbath of rest.

These prophecies are more fully developed in the doubtful, than in the three genuine, writings of Joachim, and are involved in mystical fog.

The views of Joachim were adopted, enlarged and exaggerated after his death by the Joachimites, a branch of the Franciscans who opposed the prevailing laxity which had crept into the order, and who insisted on the severe rule of the founder. They were called Spirituals (*Spirituales, Zelatores, Fraticelli*). They indulged in ascetic extravagances and apocalyptic fancies, vehemently opposed the worldliness of the clergy and monks, and became more and more antipapal and antichurchly. Their war cry was *"the Everlasting Gospel,"* which created a great sensation about the middle of the thirteenth century.[1]

---

[1] Franz Ehrle (a Jesuit scholar and co-editor of the *Archiv für Literatur- und Kirchengesch. des Mittelalters*) thus estimates the importance of this movement (*l. c.* p. 509):—

"*Sowohl für die kirchliche als für die politische Geschichte des 13. und 14. Jhs. hatte die im Franciscanerorden erstandene Bewegung, welche wir gewöhnlich an die Namen der Spiritualen und Fraticellen zu knüpfen pflegen, eine nicht zu unterschätzende Bedeutung. Dieselbe war zunächst im 13 Jh. von grösster Tragweite für die Entwicklung des auf das kirchliche, ja auch auf das bürgerliche und politische Leben mächtig einwirkenden Ordens. Sodann ist die Geschichte der Spiritualen eng verbunden mit dem bedeutungsvollen Wechsel, welcher sich auf dem Stuhle Petri durch die Abdankung Cölestins, die Erwählung und kirchlich-politische Richtung Bonifaz VIII. vollzog; sie spielt in die gewaltigen Kämpfe hinein, welche dieser letztere Papst mit den Colonnas und noch unvergleichlich mehr mit deren Beschützer Philipp dem Schönen zu bestehen hatte. Ohne ein genaues Verständniss dieser Streitigkeiten sind mehrere der wichtigsten Decrete des Vienner Concils unverständlich. Allbekannt ist ferner die massgebende Rolle, welche die Fraticellen in dem so hartnäckigen, für Kirche und Reich gleich verderblichen Zwiste zwischen Johann XXII. und Ludwig dem Bayern spielten.*

Gerard, or Gherardino, of Borgo-San-Donnino, a Franciscan monk, published at Paris, in 1254, a popular epitome of Joachim's prophetic and apocalyptic writings, with an Introduction (*Introductorius*), under the title, "The Everlasting Gospel," and announced the near advent of the Era of the Holy Spirit, which would abrogate the economy of the Son or the New Testament, as the economy of the Son had abrogated the economy of the Father or the Old Testament. By the Everlasting Gospel he meant the three chief works of Joachim, which were to take the place of the New Testament, and to be the canon of the dispensation of the Holy Spirit.[1]

The publication excited a great commotion in the University of Paris and throughout the Church. Pope Alexander IV. appointed a Commission of investigation at Anagni, where he then resided. The result was the condemnation of "The Everlasting Gospel" in 1255.[2] Gherardino refused to recant, and was condemned to prison for life. He died there after eighteen years. The failure of the prophecy destroyed its effect after 1260 more effectually than the papal anathema. The expectations of the people were raised to the highest pitch in November of that year by a procession of the Flagellants of Perugia through Italy, but the year passed without ushering in the new era.

But the spirit of Joachim and Gerard revived in the party of the Spirituals and their successors, the Fraticelli. Their prophecies were renewed in modified forms, especially by Peter John de Oliva, who was styled Dr. Columbinus (the *columba*, or dove, being the symbol of the party, and of the Holy Spirit), and were published in a mystic commentary on the mysteries of the Apocalypse about 1290. History was now divided into seven periods. The sixth period was dated from St. Francis of Assisi

---

Wer endlich ein Gegenstück zu dem Ideenkreis und der Litteratur unserer deutschen Mystiker und der sogenannten 'Gottesfreunde' sucht, wird in der Geschichte, den Schriften und Anschauungen der Spiritualen manche frappante Vergleichspunkte finden."

[1] The *Introductorius in Evangelium Æternum* is lost, with the exception of some extracts preserved by Eymerich from the Roman Acts. See Hahn, *l. c.* p. 164-174.

[2] The report of the Commission was published from MSS., by Denifle, in 1885, *l. c.* p. 97-145.

(b. 1182), and extended to the time when the temporal power of the papacy, and with it the general corruption of the world, would reach its height and hasten the Divine judgment on the carnal Church. Then would appear the true spiritual Church of the Holy Spirit, free from the poison of earthly possessions, and would convert the Jews and Gentiles.

From year to year the Spirituals waited for the advent of the seventh period, but waited in vain. They led a pure and austere life, according to the strict rule of their founder. They declined to recognize any pope since John XXII. (1316–1324), and were fearfully persecuted for more than a hundred years. The bones of de Oliva were dug up and burnt, and his writings were prohibited until Sixtus IV. (1471–1484), himself a Minorite, ordered a new investigation, which declared them orthodox.

The persecutions heightened the anti-papal spirit of the party and matured the opinion that the papal chair was or might become for a season the very seat of Antichrist in the temple of God. This opinion was confirmed under Boniface VIII. by his audacious claim of supremacy over the whole world, his tyranny and immorality. It found expression in the writings of Giacopone da Todi, of the order of the Minorites, the author of the *Stabat Mater*, and in the *Commedia* of Dante, his younger contemporary. Giacopone was excommunicated and imprisoned by Boniface, but pronounced blessed by posterity.[1] Dante was exiled by the Guelf government of Florence under the influence of the same pope, but his exile gave the world the *Divina Commedia*.

Dante kept aloof from the ascetic extravagancies and apocalyptic fancies of the Joachimites and Spirituals. He had too much respect for Thomas Aquinas and Bonaventura, too much knowledge of theology, and too much taste for art to fall into such extremes. Besides, he had political aspirations which

[1] See p. 197. Hase thus admirably characterizes him (*Kirchengesch.*, p. 309 sq., 11th ed.): "*Giacopone da Todi* († 1306) hat das höchste Glück und tiefste Leid der jungfräulichen Mutter besungen, die Wonneschau chinaulischer Liebe und das Vergehn des Menschenherzens in Gott; er war aus glänzender Weltstellung durch Schmerz und Wahnsinn hindurchgegangen, ist vom Papste gebannt und wie ein wildes Thier gefangen gehalten, aber vom Volke, in dessen Mund- und Denkart er auch gedichtet hat, selig gesprochen worden."

looked towards the restoration of the German Roman empire. But he agreed with the Joachimites in their warfare against the corrupt papacy of Boniface VIII., which he calls "a shameless whore firm as a rock seated on a mountain high,"[1] and in their zeal for a reformation of the church in the head and members.

DANTE AND SCHELLING. THE THREE AGES OF CHURCH HISTORY.

In the confused rubbish of the prophetic and pseudo-prophetic writings of Joachim of Flore, there are not a few grains of gold and fruitful germs of truth. His division of three ages of history corresponding to the three persons of the Trinity, and the three leading Apostles, is one of these fruitful germs.

A modern German philosopher, who was a profound student of Dante,[2] has independently arrived at a somewhat similar, though far superior construction of the history of Christianity.

Schelling starts from the fact that Christ elected three favorite disciples—Peter, James, and John—to whom he gave new names (Rock, and Sons of Thunder), and whom he made sole witnesses of some of the most important events in his life. They correspond to Moses, the lawgiver, Elijah, the fiery prophet, and John the Baptist, who concluded the Jewish dispensation by pointing to Christ.

Peter is the fundamental Apostle, the rock on which the Church was built, the Apostle of the Father, the Apostle of authority, the Apostle of law and stability, the type of Catholicism.

But the foundation of a building is only the beginning, and is followed by a succession, by a middle and end. These are represented by James and John, or rather by Paul and John. James died early, before he could fully develop his mission, and his place was filled by Paul, whom the Lord had called before

---

[1] *Purg.* XXXII., 148-150:—

"*Sicura, quasi rocca in alto monte,
Seder sopr' essa una puttana sciolta
M'apparve, con le ciglia intorno pronte.*"

[2] See above, p. 353, 403.

the martyrdom of James, and who is in the earliest seals of the popes associated with Peter as joint founders of the Roman Church.

Paul is the Elijah of the Church,[1] who burst forth like a fire, and whose word burns like a torch. He is the Apostle of God the Son. He built on the foundation of Peter, yet independently, and even in opposition to him; for it is by contrasts (ἐξ ἐναντίων), not by uniformity, that the Spirit of God brings about the greatest things. He insists (in the Galatians) on his direct call by Christ, not by or through men, and at Antioch he openly withstood Peter and the Jewish pillar-apostles (οἱ δοκοῦντες στῦλοι εἶναι) when they demanded the circumcision of the Gentile Christians, and their subjection to the bondage of the law.[2] Paul represents the principle of independence, motion, development and freedom; he is the type of the Protestant Reformation, that revolt long prepared against the exclusive and tyrannical authority of Peter.[3]

Whatever may be said against the Roman Church is foreshadowed in Peter, and is not concealed in the Gospels, least in that of Mark (which is Peter's Gospel). He, and he alone among the Apostles, took the sword, which is inseparable from an earthly kingdom, and the Roman Church wielded the sword, especially in the thirteenth century, against the heretics so-called, not only the New-Manichæans and Albigenses, but also against the

---

[1] Melanchthon called Luther an Elijah and the true successor of St. Paul.

[2] Peter may have had especially in mind the Epistle to the Galatians when he says that in the Epistles of Paul there "are some things hard to be understood" (δυσνόητά τινα, 2 Pet. iii. 16). The Papal Encyclical of May 8th, 1844, against the Bible Societies, makes use of this passage to prove the danger of an indiscriminate reading of the Scriptures : "Sed vos quidem minime latet, Venerabiles Fratres, quorsum haec societatum biblicarum molimina pertineant. Proba enim nostis consignatam in sacris ipsis literis monitum Petri, Apostolorum Principis, qui post laudatas Pauli epistolas esse, ait, in illis quaedam difficilia intellectu, quae indocti et instabiles depravant, sicut et ceteras Scripturas ad suam ipsorum perditionem, statimque adjicit : Vos igitur fratres praescientes custodite, ne insipientium errore traducti excidatis a propria firmitate."

[3] "Ist derjenige ein Protestant," says Schelling (l. c. p. 310), "der ausser der auf die Auktorität Petri gegründeten Kirche, unabhängig von ihr sich hält, so ist der Apostel Paulus der erste Protestant, und die älteste Urkunde, die der Protestantismus für sich aufzuweisen hat, die Magna Charta desselben, ist das zweite Kapitel des Briefs an die Galater."

Spirituals among the Franciscans, who perished in the flames of the stake by the thousands, and could find refuge only with the German emperor, Louis the Bavarian. It was among these sects that the opinion first arose that the pope was the veritable Antichrist and the beast of the Apocalypse. The same Peter who was called the Rock of the Church, was soon afterwards called a Satan by our Saviour when he presumed to turn his Master away from the path of the cross. In the former character he was to be guided by Divine wisdom and power, in the latter he followed the instinct of worldly prudence. But Christ says: "If any man would come after me, let him deny himself, and take up his cross daily, and follow me." (Luke ix., 23.) The threefold denial of Peter has likewise a typical significance. The Roman Church has denied Christ in three ways: first, by striving after political power; then by using the political power as executioner of her bloody decrees, and last by yielding herself as an instrument to the secular arm. But as Christ intrusted the same Peter who had thrice denied him, thrice with the feeding of his flock, so the Roman Church, in whose bosom so many holy members have uttered sighs and complaints over her corruptions, has not ceased to be a Church of Christ, and to hold fast to the foundation of the faith. Perhaps the time is not far distant when she will, with Peter, weep bitterly over her denial.

John is the Apostle of the Holy Spirit, the Apostle of the future, the Apostle of love, and represents the New Jerusalem from heaven, the truly catholic, ideal Church of the union of Catholicism and Protestantism. He alone speaks of the Spirit whom the Son will send from the Father, who proceeds from the Father, and who will guide the Church into the whole and perfect truth. His position is indicated in the mysterious prediction of Christ to Peter concerning John: "If I will that he tarry till I come, what is that to thee?" (John xxi., 22.) This was at an early time misunderstood to indicate that John was not to die, but the real meaning is that his mission would begin with the second advent, that is, in the last age of the Church. It has no reference to the existence of John, but to his work, which can only be accomplished after the exclusiveness of Peter is done away with, and the Church arrives at the unity of the one flock and one Shepherd. (John x., 16.)

The Church of St. Lateran in Rome has the first rank in the Catholic world, as the Latin inscription says: "*Sacrosancta Lateranensis ecclesia, omnium urbis et orbis ecclesiarum mater et caput.*" The splendid temple of St. Peter, which was the next occasion for the Reformation, stands in the centre of the city of Rome. The Church of St. Paul, which burned down under Pius VII., and is not yet quite rebuilt, is outside of the walls. At some future time a church will be built for all three Apostles— a true pantheon of Church History.[1]

This is a summary of Schelling's philosophy of Church History. It is, like all philosophical constructions which anticipate the future-known only to God, more or less fanciful; but it is certainly grand and ingenious and involves a truth, which illuminates the past and casts light on the future. It impresses itself indelibly upon the mind. I have it from the lips of such historians as the evangelical Neander and the catholic Döllinger, that they were in sympathy with it.[2] The three chief Apostles

---

[1] See the two concluding lectures of Schelling's *Philosophie der Offenbarung* in *Sämmtliche Werke, Zweite Abtheilung,* vol. IV (1858), pp. 294-332. He claims originality for his view, but says expressly (p. 298) that he found it confirmed, even in most of the details, by the writings of Joachim of Floris as presented in the fifth volume of Neander's *Church History,* which appeared in 1841 (in the American edition it is vol. IV). I heard Schelling's lectures in 1842 at the University of Berlin and reported his views of the three ages of Church History in 1844 (14 years before their publication) at the close of my Inaugural Address, *The Principle of Protestantism,* pp. 171-176. I saw Schelling for the last time at Ragatz, in Switzerland (where he is buried), a few days before his death (Aug. 20, 1854), when he told me that he still held fast to this idea and derived much comfort from it, but would supplement it by making room for James, as the typical Apostle of the Greek Church.

[2] Neander expressed a similar view at the close of the third edition of his *History of the Planting and Training of the Christian Church.* He dedicated the first volume of the revised edition of his *Church History* to Schelling in the same year in which the latter delivered his lectures on the Philosophy of Revelation (1842). He says in the dedication: "In what you publicly expressed respecting the *studia* in the development of the Christian Church, how much there was which struck in harmony with my own views!" I might also refer for similar statements to Steffens, Schmieder, Lange, Ullmann.

and their work, the Jewish Christianity of Peter, the Gentile Christianity of Paul, the temporary collision of the two, and the final consolidation of both branches by John—anticipate and foreshadow the past and future development of Christ's kingdom on earth.

Dante likewise recognizes three typical Apostles who represent the three Christian graces, but he adheres to the original trio of Christ's first selection, and omits the Apostle Paul. He regards Peter as the Apostle of Faith, James the Elder (John's brother) as the Apostle of Hope,[1] and John as the Apostle of Love. In Paradise he places Peter, as the keeper of the keys of the glorified Church, and John, as the seer of "the beautiful bride who with the spear and with the nails was won," next to the Queen of Paradise in the mystic Rose of the Blessed.[2] He sees John (with an allusion to the legend of his sleep till the second advent) in the chariot of the Church triumphant as

"An aged man alone
Walking in sleep with countenance acute."

The difference as well as the harmony in the Catholic and Protestant estimate of the Apostles is characteristic. A Protestant would subordinate James to Paul, and coördinate Peter and Paul as Apostles of Faith, and joint Founders of the Church, the one among the Jews, the other among the Gentiles. Paul was not one of the Twelve, and does not fit into the regular succession, but he is of equal power and authority with them, and as to the abundance of labors he surpassed them all. He was soon thrown into the background in the early Church, as a sort of holy outsider and dangerous innovator, and was never thoroughly appreciated till the time of the Reformation. Even such fathers as Origen, Chrysostom and Jerome could not conceive it possible that he should have so boldly and sharply rebuked the older Apostle Peter at Antioch, and hence they perverted the scene into a theatrical farce or substituted an imaginary Peter for the historical Peter. Nor does

---

[1] Dante seems to have confounded him with the writer of the Epistle of James, which emphasizes good works. He believed in the impossible Spanish legend of Campostello. *Par.* XXV., 17, 18.

[2] *Par.* XXXII., 124–129. *Purg.* XXIX., 143 sq.; comp. *Par.* XXV., 112–126.

the papal Church, in her official denunciations of Bible Societies, forget to quote Peter's words about the difficult matters in Paul's Epistles, and about the danger of "private interpretation" of the Scriptures.

But Joachim, Dante, and Schelling, agree in the hopeful outlook toward a higher and purer age of the Church, and connect it with the name of the beloved Disciple, the bosom friend of Jesus, the seer of the new heavens and the new earth, the apostolic forerunner of an age of love, concord and peace.

INDEX.

Abelard, 232.
Abrahall, J. H., 170.
Ad Cor Christi, 245; translation into English, 247.
Ad Faciem Christi, 248; translation into English, 250.
Adam, 375.
Albertus Magnus, 285, 399.
Albizzi, B., 146.
Adoration, 192.
Agapetus, 410.
Alfieri, 343, 345.
Alexander the Great, 387.
Alexander, J. A., 46, 108.
Alexander, J. W., 241, 252.
Alfred, King, 256.
Alford, Henry, 154, 156.
Alma mater, 257.
American civilization, 273.
Amos, 107.
Anastasius II., 386.
d'Andrea, Novella, 265.
Angus, Joseph, 73, 115.
Annihilation, 377.
Anonymous translations, 167, 171, 178, 180, 208, 209, 215, 229.
Anselm, St., 139, 396, 417.
Antenora, 389.
Aquinas, *see* Thomas Aquinas.
Archiginnasio, of Bologna, 267, 268.
Argenti, 386.
Aristotle, 367, 376, 382, 396.
Arius, 386.
Asaph, 73.
Astrology, 359.
Attila, 387.
Augustin, St., 137, 207, 377, 395, 402.
Avicenna, 397.
Aylward, J. D., 171.

Bacon, Francis, 299.
Banquet (Convivio), the, 294, 298, 305, 319, 396, 397, 398.
Bartoli, 291.
Bassi, Laura, 264.
Beatific vision, the, 403.
Beatrice, 286, 288, 290, 310, 364, 367, 393, 402.
Bede, 299.
Beethoven, 64.
Belial, stream of, 381.

Benedict XIV., 198.
Benedict, St., 399.
Benedict, E. C., 169, 203.
Bernard, St., of Clairvaux, 139, 142, 198, 234, 245, 368, 401.
Bernard, of Cluny, 252.
Bickell, G., 124.
Blacks (Neri), 302.
Blew, W. J., 164.
Boccaccio, 295, 355.
Boëthius, 294, 399.
Bologna, 298.
Bologna University, 262; size, 263; attendance, 264; octo-centennial, 265; visitors, 265; encomium from the German Emperor, 270; literature, 278.
Bonaventura, St., 147.
Boniface VIII., 197, 302, 305, 321, 379, 388, 412, 423.
Boselli, 269.
Botta, A. C., Mrs., 268.
Botta, V., 371, 384.
Breviary, the Roman, 150, 234.
Briggs, Chas. A., 124.
Brown, Goold, 2.
Brown, J. M., 172.
Brunet, 229.
Brunetto Latini, 298, 388.
Brutus, 390.
Bülow, von, 213.
Bull, Papal, 260, 412.
Bunsen, Chev., 177.
"Bursars," 261.
Buti, F. da, 416.
Buxtorf, 124.
Byron, Lord, 38, 47.

Caedmon, 10.
Caesar, 376.
Can Grande, 308, 311.
Canon, 262.
Canzoniere, 322.
Capellini, 269.
Capeneus, 387.
Carducci, G., 270.
Carlyle, Thomas, 78, 318, 346, 371.
Carlyle, John A., 336.
Carpenter, G. B., 295.
Cary, H. F., 336, 373.
Caswall, E., 164, 199, 234, 239.
Catholic Hymn Book, Erfurt, 213.

Catholic Hymn Book, Munich, 173.
Cat of Utica, 394.
Cattani, Guiseppina, 264.
Cavalcanti, C, de, 383.
Cavalcanti, G., 287, 296.
Cecilia, St., 64.
Ceneri, G., 272.
Charge of the Light Brigade, 49.
Charlemagne, 256, 395.
Charles, Eliz. B., Mrs., 143, 164, 249.
Charles of Valois, 302.
Chaucer, 22, 390.
Christ, 284, 369, 375.
Chronicle of Dante, 325.
Church, corruptions of, 364, 394, 400, 412, 419, 424.
Church and education, 277.
Church and state, 275, 390, 410, 413.
Chrysostom, 395.
Cicero, 17, 99, 264, 385.
City of New York, University, 274; its religious basis, 276.
Clement V., 364, 388, 401, 411.
Clement of Alexandria, 252.
Cleopatra, 384.
Cœlestin V., 379.
Coles, Abraham, 138, 143, 154, 155, 165, 191, 201, 202, 225, 242, 250.
Colleges, 261.
Common Prayer Book, 53.
Constantine the Great, 394, 413, 414.
Conviria (Convito), see Banquet.
Copeland, W. J., 171.
Coppi, M. S., 297.
Correggio, 223.
Conard, C. L., 178.
Cousin, Victor, 143.
Crashaw, Richard, 153, 163.
Creed of Dante, 324.

Daniel, the prophet, 107.
Daniel, H. A., 141, 148, 150, 153, 179, 180, 189, 211.
Dante, 95, 140, 279, 293, 306, 308, 312, 321, 323, 351, 371, 409, 423, 427. See Table of Contents.
Dante—Chronicle, 325.
Dante—Literature, in Italian, 328-331 French, 331; German, 332-334; English, 334-337.
David, King, 72, 137, 379.
Davidson, R., 167.
Deborah, song of, 87.
De Contempto Mundi, 252.
Decretist, 263.
Degrees, 258.
Delitzsch, Fr., 101, 103, 122, 129.
Democritus, 376.
Denifle, 257, 418, 420.
De Vere, Schele, 22.
De Wette, 124, 129.
Dexter, H. M., 252.
Didactic poetry, 98.
Dido, 384.

Diepenbrock, M., 221.
Dies Iræ, 134, 149. See Table of Contents.
Dillmann, 82, 90.
Dionysius, the Areopagite, 359.
Dix, J. A., 168, 204.
Dix, W. G., 166.
Divina Commedia, 315. See Table of Contents.
Dobl, C. M., 170.
Dolce, Carlo, 190.
Dominic, 416
Donati, Gemma, 292, 299, 305; encomium on, 300.
Donation of Constantine, 413.
Döring, A. C., 176.
Dramatic poetry, 112.
Draper, H., 272.
Draper, J. W., 275.
Dreves, L., 179.
Dryden, 65.
Duffield, S. W., 158.
Dux, 308, 310, 311, 363.
Dwight, B. W., 11.

Ebeling, C. D., 173.
Ecclesiastes, 104.
Ecker, J., 124.
Ehrle, F., 418, 421.
Elijah, 421.
Emolument to professors, 260.
Empire, on the, 320, 365, 410.
Empyrean, the, 395, 400.
English Language. See Table of Contents.
Erasmus, 68.
Erhard, H. A., 177.
"Eternal womanly," 283, 291.
Eucherius, 361.
Eusebius, 123.
Ewald, H., 67, 72, 78, 81, 82, 106, 108, 112.

Faber, F. W., 62.
Fable, 105.
Fabricius, 233.
Fahnestock, A. H., 172.
Faust, Goethe's, 281.
Ferrari, 304.
Fichte, J. G., 175.
Flagellants, 192, 422.
Florence, 314.
Follen, Ad. L., 175, 214.
Förster, 221.
Fortlage, K., 179,
Fortunatus, 390.
Fouqué, de L. M., 214.
Fox, 25.
Francis of Assisi, 146, 191, 193, 196, 416.
Franke, 177.
Fraticelli, 322.
Frederick I., 263.
Frederick II., 257, 307, 386.

INDEX. 433

Frederick III., Emperor, 270, 272.
Friedrich, F., 414.
Friends, the, 196.

Galvani, Luigi, 265.
Gavazzi, Father, 267.
Geibel, E., 344.
Gerard (Gherardino), 422.
Gerhardt, Paul, 146, 252.
Ghibellines, 305, 320.
Giacopóne, 148, 193, 196, 220, 423.
Gietmann, G., 364.
Gildemeister, O., 374.
God, 280, 400.
Godet, F., 270.
Goethe, 65, 78, 139, 144, 192, 268, 279, 281, 283, 306, 315, 355, 390.
Gratian, 262, 387, 399.
Grau, C., 215.
Green, W. H., 114.
Gregory of Nazianzen, 113.
Gregory, the Great, 147, 395.
Gregory VII., 410.
"Greyhound" (*Veltro*), 309, 373.
Grimm, Jacob, 5.
Gryphius, A., 173.
Guelf, 301.
Gymnasia, 261.

Habakkuk, 107.
Hager, J. S., 172.
Hagiographa, 67.
Hämmerlin, Felix, 147, 150.
Händel, 64.
Hahn, 418, 420.
Harms, C., 177.
Harrison, B. H., 272.
Hase, 423.
Haydn, 193.
Hayes, J. L., 172, 205.
Heathen, the, 375.
Hebrew poetry, 122. *See* Table of Contents.
Hebrews, arts among, 66.
Henry IV., 301.
Henry VII., 306, 321, 415.
Hengstenberg, 90.
Herder, 67, 77, 124, 153, 173.
Hettinger, 315, 322, 406.
Hildegard, St., 419
Hillard, Katherine, 291, 396.
History, 383.
Hitchcock, R. D., 208.
Hoflinger, Josefa von, 300.
Homer, 73, 279, 348, 376.
Honorius I., 387.
Hood, 48.
Horace, 376.
Hosea, 107.
Humboldt, Alex. von, 78.
Husenbeth, F. C., 164.

28

Indifferentists, 379.
Infant salvation, 377.
Inferno, 358, 366, 369, 393, 403; writing on gate, 373, vestibule of, 378; configuration, 380; rivers in, 381; persons and vices, 384.
Innocent II., 232.
Innocent III., 401.
Irnerius, 262.
Irons, W. J., 155.
Isaiah, 108, 109, 110.
Italy, 266, 273, 301, 304.

Jacapone, Jacobus de Benedictis, *see* Giacopóne.
Jäck, M. F., 165.
Jahn, 124
James, the Apostle, 400, 424, 428.
James II., 152.
Jasher, Book of, 69, 86.
Jeremiah, 94, 107.
Jerome, 89, 122, 428.
Jesu dulcis memoria, 223.
Joachim de Flore, Abbot, 396, 418.
Joachimites, 417.
Job, Book of, 116.
John, the apostle, 400, 402, 420, 424, 426, 428.
John XXII., 321.
John de Oliva, 422
Johnson, F., 171, 205, 226.
Johnson, Samuel, 145.
Jonah, 107.
Jones, William, 77, 114.
Josephus, 123.
Jubilee, papal, 354.
Judas Iscariot, 390.
Judecca, 389.
Justinian, 394.

Kerner, Julius, 144, 306.
Kind, Fr., 175.
Klopstock, 280.
Knapp, Albert, 142, 153, 179, 211, 243.
Königsfeld, G. A., 179, 212, 230, 245.
Kosmeli, M., 214.

Labitte, 351.
Lament of David, 88.
Lamentations, The, 93.
Language, its uses and origin, 1; its dignity and diversity, 3; primary, character, 3.
Languages, Anglo-Saxon, 10, 12; King Alfred's, 10; Aryan, 9; French, 55, 88; German, 41; Gothic, 11; Greek, 4, 55; Hebrew, 4; Latin, 4; Norman, 23; Platt-Deutsch, 10; Romanic, 4; Sanscrit, 11; Saxon, 23.
Latham, R. G., 7, 18.
Latini, B., 298, 358.
Latinisms, 16, 32.

434 INDEX.

Lavater, J. C., 213.
Law, 263.
Leeke, R., 178, 215.
Letters, of Dante, 323.
Lewis, Tayler, 83, 104.
Ley, Julius, 83, 124.
Liberius, Pope, 387.
Limbo, 384.
Lindsay, A. W. C., 164, 210.
Lisco, 151, 175, 178, 210, 215.
Lives of Saints, 350.
Logan, 113.
Longfellow, H. W., 40, 343, 346, 373.
Louis, St., 285.
Louis XIV., 152.
Lowell, J. R., 271.
Lowth, Robert, 66, 67, 89, 124, 125.
Lucia, St., 363, 367, 402.
Lucifer, city of, 386, 390.
Luther, 74, 264, 414.
Lyrics in New Testament, 83.
Lyrics in Old Testament, 95.

Macaulay, T. B., 154, 163, 318, 353.
McKenzie, W. S., 161, 206, 227, 228.
"Malebolge," 388.
Maltitz, Fr. von, 214.
Manzolina, Mme., 264.
Marcion, 386.
Mariolatry, 191.
Marozia, 384.
Marsh, G. P., 8.
Mary, the Virgin, 223, 369, 372, 402, 409.
Maurus, Rabanus, 361.
Matilda, 297, 409, 411.
Mazzini, G., 240.
Meier, E., 124.
Mephistopheles, 282, 391.
Merget, A., 215.
Merx, 124.
Messiah's empire, from Isaiah, 109–111.
Metaphysics, 397.
Meusch, C., 176.
Meyer, J. F. von, 141, 174, 214.
Mezzofanti, Cardinal, 264.
Michael Angelo, 137, 338.
Middle Ages, 292, 351, 416.
Mills, Henry, 15, 160, 169, 208.
Milman, H. H., 142.
Milton, 26, 77, 280, 381, 390, 409.
Minos, 385.
Miracle-plays, 351.
Mohammed, 307, 389.
Mohnike, 146, 147, 149, 153, 177, 214.
Mone, 118, 189, 198, 233, 237.
Monosyllables, 45.
Monsell, J. S. B., 200.
Moore, E., 356.
Morison, J. C., 233.
Morse, S. F. B., 275.
Moses, 83, 86, 307, 375, 424.
Mozart, 64.
Müller, John von, 77.
Müller, Max, 2, 37.

Murillo, 223.
Music, origin of, 64.
Myrrha, 384.
Mythology, 383.

Neale, J. M., 221, 222, 223, 252.
Neander, 233, 418, 427.
New Life of Dante, the, 286, 291, 293, 319.
Newman, J. H., 64.
Nicholas III., 388, 411.
Niemeyer, J. C. W., 177.
Norton, C. E., 287, 317.

O Haupt voll Blut und Wunden, 253.
"O sacred Head, now wounded," 253.
O'Hagan, John, 171.
Origen, 361, 428.
Ozanam, 194, 218, 220, 222, 296, 348.

Ps., 365, 393.
Palestrina, 193.
Palmer, Ray, 212.
Panzacchi, E., 268.
Papacy, 364, 410, 412, 415.
Parable, 105.
Paradiso, 359, 366; residents, 394; perfections, 396.
Parallelism, 101; synonymous, 126; antithetic, 128; synthetic, 128.
Passion hymns, 190, 245.
Passions, the, 372.
Patriotism, 114.
Paul, the apostle, 400, 420, 424.
Pechlin, F. von, 177, 215.
Pelagius, 386.
Penitential Psalms, 322.
Périès, Adolphe, 169.
Perowne, J. J. S., 72, 79, 80.
Peter, the apostle, 400, 402, 409, 420, 424, 425, 428.
Petrarcha, 95, 286.
Philalethes, 346.
Philip the Fair, 304, 412.
Philo, 361.
Pick, B., 186.
Pilate, Pontius, 380.
Pius IX., 304, 391, 403.
Plato, 320, 397.
Plumptre, 363, 374, 411, 417.
Plutus, 385.
Poet, defined, 64.
Poetry, origin of, 64; and inspiration, 65; and religion, 66; of the Bible, 66, see Table of Contents; Old Testament, 67; New Testament, 68; antiquity of, 69; biblical, 73; lyric, 80; didactic, 97; prophetic, 106; dramatic, 112.
Polenta, G. N. da, 312.
Pompey, 389.
Popes, condemned, 411.
Popular Eloquence, 323.
Porter, T. C., 159.

Predestination, 395.
Prophecy, allied to poetry, 106.
Prophetic poetry, 107.
Protestant transfusion of *Stabat M. Dolorosa*, 209.
Prout, Father, 40.
Proverbs, The, 99.
Psalms, classified, 93.
Psalter, The, 81.
Ptolemæa, 389.
Punishment, future, 375.
Purgatorio, 358, 365; grades in, 392; characters in, 392.

Quadrivium, 257, 397.

Rabanus Maurus, 361, 417.
Raphael, 64, 66, 318.
Reason, relation to speech, 1.
Renan, 95, 112, 418.
Repentance of Job, 119.
Requiem, Mozart's, 135, 145, 175.
Revision of the English Bible, 61.
Rhyme, 75; in Hebrew, 122.
Riedel, F. X., 173.
Rimini, F. da, 383.
Ringwalt, B., 180.
Rockwell, C., 167.
Rölker, K., 180, 216.
Rome, 271, 427.
Rome, Church of, its denial, 426.
Roscommon, Earl of, 145, 163.
Rose of the Blessed, 401, 402.
Rossetti, D. G., 295, 335.
Rossetti, G., 407.
Rossetti, Francesca, 335.
Rossi, P. de, 264.
Rossini, 193.
Rothe, R., 283.
Ruggieri, Archbishop, 383.
Ruskin, 360, 366.

Sandford, D. K., 77.
Sargent, E., 107.
Savigny, Fr. C. von, 262.
Savonarola, 409.
Scaliger, Joseph, 124.
Scartazzini, 303, 315, 355, 383, 411, 417.
Schaff, Philip, 138, 159, 191, 243, 252, 359, 387, 403, 427.
Schelling, 346, 353, 403, 424, 427.
Schlegel, A. W. von, 153, 174.
Schlosser, F. H., 179.
Schmedding, 175.
Scholtz, J. A., 176.
Scott, Walter, 145, 154, 163.
Scotus, Duns, 18.
Scriptures, the, 280, 291, 420.
Seld, von, 179, 215.
Selden, 12.
Semiramis, 385.

Seneca, 376.
Serravalle, G. de, 292.
Shakespeare, 65, 279, 280, 378, 390.
Sibyl, 137.
Silbert, J. P., 175.
Simon Magus, 386, 388.
Simon, Richard, 124.
Simrock, 177, 214.
Skeat, W. W., 3, 6, 11, 340.
Slosson, E., 169.
Socrates, 299, 376.
Solomon, 98, 399.
Song of Deborah, 87.
Song of Lamech, 82.
Song of Moses, 83.
Song of Moses, farewell, 86.
Song of Songs, 113.
Song of the creatures, 194.
Song of the Sun, 195.
Spelling, 37.
Spirituales, 421, 426.
Stabat Mater Dolorosa, 187. See Table of Contents.
Stabat Mater Speciosa, 218. See Table of Contents.
Stanley, A. P., 66, 72, 78, 100, 106, 108, 112, 170.
Steckling, L., 178.
Stella, G., 189, 198.
Stephen of St. Sabas, 252.
Stephens, Henry, 77.
Story, W. W., 271.
Streckfuss, K., 374.
"Study," 257.
Sylvester, Joshua, 153.
Swedenborg, E., 347.
Swobeda, W. A., 176.
Synonyms, 51.

Tacitus, 371.
Tambroni, Clotilda, 264.
Tantalus, 392.
Tauler, 139.
Taylor, Isaac, 68, 78, 95.
Tennyson, 48, 342.
Tersteegen, 114.
Tertullian, 371.
Terza rima, 370.
Thais, 384.
Theodora, 384.
Theodosius II., 262.
Theology, 292, 359, 361, 375, 377, 397.
Tholuck, 144, 146.
Thomas Aquinas, 280, 389.
Thomas à Kempis, 139.
Thomas of Celano, 145, 146, 370, 417.
Thought and language, 1.
Thurston, Archbishop, 147.
Tieck, L., 192.
Trajan, 349, 395.
Trench, R. C., 7, 142, 154, 156, 234.
Trivium, 257, 397.
Trinity, The, 370, 374, 398, 403, 420.

436 INDEX.

Ubaldini, Cardinal O. d, 386.
Uberti, F. d, 383.
Ugolino, Count, 389.
Uhland, 290, 339.
Umberto, King, 265.
University, The, its scope, 256.
University of Middle Ages, foundation, 256; intent, 257; faculties in, 257; government, 258; where fostered, 259, 261; attendance on, 259, 264; lodging of students, 260.
University, The American, 273; heritage, 273; prospects, 274; of Prague, 265; of St. Andrew's, 260; of Wittenberg, 260; of Heidelberg, 260; of Oxford, 260; of Salerno, 260; Paris, 261; Roman Catholic at Washington, 260; of Naples, 264; of Turin, 264.

Vallo, Laurentius, 414.
Van Buren, J. D., 171, 210.
Veith, J. E., 177.
Veltro, 309, 311.
Veneration, 192.
Versification, 122.
Victor Emmanuel II., 267.
Vigne, P. de, 387.
Villani, G., 303, 354.
Virgil, 73, 137, 279, 367.
Vita Nuova, see New Life.
Voragine, J. de, 350.
Vossius, G., 124.
Vowel sounds, 38.

Wackernagel, Ph., 148, 189, 198, 233.
Wackernagel, W., 11.

Wadding, L., 147, 197, 198, 418.
Wagner, Richard, 271.
Washburn, E. A., 246.
Washington, George. 277.
Water and Earth, 323.
Webster, D., 26.
Webster, N., 3, 54.
Weiser, C. Z., 167.
Welsh, A. H., 8.
Wessenberg, J. H. von, 176, 214.
Westcott and Hort, 97.
Wetzer and Welte, 414.
Whately, 25.
Whites, 302.
Whitney, W. D., 37, 58.
Wienzierl, Fr. J., 213.
Williams, W. R., 142, 158.
Winer, G. B., 73.
Witte, 310, 357.
Worcester's Dictionary, 37.
Words, and intelligence, 2; in English Bible, 14, 60; Americanisms, 34; Arabic, 33; Celtic, 29; Dutch, 32; Greek, 31; Hebrew, 31; Hybrid, 35; Indian, 34; Italian, 33; Johnson's, 8; Milton's, 8, 25; Norse, 30; Persian, 33; Saxon, 12; Shakespeare's, 8, 15, 46; Slavonic, 34; Spanish, 33; Turkish, 34.
Wordsworth, 47.
Wordsworth, Charles, 280.
Worship as defined by Roman Catholics, 192.
Wright, I. C., 374.
Wright, W. A., 116.
Wulfila, 11.
Wyckliffe, 22.

Zinzendorf, Count, 243.